_T_

Southern India

by George Michell

A&C Black • London
WW Norton • New York

BLUE GUIDE

First edition, October 1997

Published by A&C Black (Publishers) Limited
35 Bedford Row, London WC1R 4JH

© George Michell 1997

ISBN 0–7136–4158–4

Maps and plans © A&C Black (Publishers) Ltd; those on pages 62, 63, 65, 93, 120, 142, 162, 173, 177, 202, 203, 213, 215, 233, 236, 249, 253, 270, 277, 281, 290, 299, 310, 311, 313, 321, 329, 388, 389, 403, 409, 423, 437, 443, 455, 469, 473, 501, 509 drawn by Robert Smith
Line drawings © Jaideep Chakrabarti

A CIP catalogue record for this book
is available from the British Library.

Published in the United States of America by
WW Norton & Company, Incorporated
500 Fifth Avenue, New York, NY 10110 USA

Published simultaneously in Canada by
Penguin Books Limited
10 Alcorn Avenue, Toronto, Ontario M4V 3BE

ISBN 0–393–31748–X   USA

The author and the publishers have done their best to ensure the accuracy of all the information in Blue Guide Southern India; however, they can accept no responsibility for any loss, injury or inconvenience sustained by any reader as a result of information or advice contained in this guide.

'Blue Guides' is a registered trademark.

The **cover picture** shows the Gommateshvara at Sravana Belgola. The photograph is by Clare Arni.
The illustration on the title page is of the Char Minar in Old Hyderabad

Dr George Michell trained as an architect in Melbourne and then studied Indian archaeology in London where he still lives. Much of his research has been concentrated at Hindu and Muslim sites in Southern India, especially the ruined city of Vijayanagara in Karnataka.

Printed and bound in Great Britain by Butler & Tanner, Frome and London.

Contents

Introduction

Travel Information 11

Background Information

The Guide

Maharashtra

Goa

Karnataka

Andhra Pradesh

Maps and Plans

Town plans

Site plans

Architectural plans

Key to location maps

major centre

places of interest (solid dot) and places not described (open dot)

highway with number

minor roads

railways

coast with river

open water

state boundary

Preface

In writing this volume in the *Blue Guide* series I have imagined an enthusiastic but not necessarily experienced traveller, eager to take an interest in one or other aspects of Southern Indian history, religion, archaeology, architecture and art. My aim has been to furnish such a traveller with a comprehensive survey of historical cities, towns and sites in the region. Of course, such a person may incline towards familiar destinations such as Bombay, Ajanta and Madurai, now fairly well developed for tourists; but he or she may also be attracted to some of the relatively unknown places that I have included here. The hope is that both the inexperienced and the more knowledgeable traveller will be adequately catered for.

Though almost 400 separate localities are described in this *Blue Guide*, there is no claim to completeness. Southern India is a vast area approximately half the size of Western Europe, richly endowed with historical buildings and monuments. No single work could possibly encompass them all, nor could even the most indefatigable traveller find enough time to reach them all. Nevertheless, I would like to think that there is sufficient here to engage the interests of any tourist and to introduce him or her to unusual but worthwhile destinations. Securing reliable information about places to visit can be more difficult than reserving train tickets, finding adequate hotels or eating safely and well.

I have conceived the first part of this *Blue Guide* as a general introduction, with short sections on essential travel information, as well as Southern Indian history, religion, architecture and art. A suggested reading list is included to encourage the visitor to pursue his or her interests. The second and much larger part of the volume is devoted to travel itineraries, each of which is conceived as a separate chapter, complete with notes on transport, accommodation and tourist information. The itineraries may be regarded as travel hubs, suitable places to stay, from where various excursions may be made. A map is given for each chapter, showing the distribution of historical sites in the vicinity. The itineraries are arranged according to state, beginning with capital cities. A cross reference system permits the visitor to move freely from one itinerary to another, without having to follow the sequence presented here. The itineraries are followed by a glossary of Indian names and a gazetteer.

Though this *Blue Guide* was written over three years, the volume actually embodies more than 20 years of wandering all over Southern India. Even so, it has not been possible for me to visit every site in order to confirm the information. Users of the volume are encouraged to send in corrections and suggestions to be incorporated in later editions.

Assistance with travel and accommodation did much to facilitate my 1995–96 tour of Southern India. The Government of India Tourist Office kindly made air tickets available within the country. Mahesh Lakhanpal in London, and Chiranjiv Singh and Raj Mittal in New Delhi were particularly helpful. The Taj Group of Hotels graciously offered hospitality in Bombay, Bangalore, Hyderabad and Madras, thanks largely to the personal interest of Pankaj M. Baliga and Sunita Nair.

Throughout my research I have benefitted enormously from scholarly friends and colleagues, who have been generous with their information, advice and encouragement. In the UK, Bob Alderman, Raymond Allchin, Richard Blurton, Henry Brownrigg, Ilay Cooper, Anna Dallapiccola, Phillip Davies, Simon Digby, Adam Hardy, Christopher London, Louise Nicholson, Mehrdad and Natasha Shokoohy, Robert Skelton and Mark Zebrowski have been especially supportive.

Archaeological directors, monument attendants, and local experts in Southern India have over the years provided specialised information and general assistance without which I would have been unable to locate many of the monuments. Among such people are Shaikh Ansar Ahmed (Ahmadnagar), S.K. Aruni (Pune), K.M. Balasubramaniam (Thanjavur), Balasubramanya (Kamalapuram), R.R. Borkar (Nagpur), N.K. Chandrashekhara (Mysore), Khandu Deokar (Karla), Vikas Dilawari (Bombay), P.K. Ghanekar (Pune), Françoise L'Hernault (Pondicherry), A.P. Jamkhedkar (Bombay), P. Joseph (Hyderabad), Suresh Joshi (Ahmadnagar), Raju Kalidos (Thanjavur), Jagdish Mittal (Hyderabad), K.K. Muhammed (Panaji), M.S. Nagaraja Rao (Mysore), S. Nagaraju (Hyderabad), R. Nagaswamy (Madras), Sunithi Narayan (Madras), Foy Nissen (Bombay), C.S. Patil (Mysore), Balasaheeb and Jaywant Patil (Paithan), Jayaram Poduval (Payyanur), S. Rajasekhara (Dharwad), B. Rajendran (Tiruchirapalli), R.S. Ramakrishnan (Karaikkudi), K.V. Raman (Madras), Ranga Reddy (Hyderabad), Klaus Rötzer (Pondicherry), N. Sethu Raman (Kumbakonam), Shaikh Ramzan (Aurangabad), Shivapriyananda (Mysore), Vijayanath Shenoy (Udupi), Michael J. Stephen (Madras), Deborah Thiagarajan (Madras) and R. Vasanth (Anantapur).

The production of this volume with minimal delays was only possible thanks to the editorial enthusiasm and expert direction of Gemma Davies, the painstaking editing and checking of facts by Ian Kearey, and the graphic skills of Jaideep Chakrabarti, Graham Reed and Robert Smith. Anne Engel and John Fritz provided much-needed personal reassurance that the project could ultimately be fulfilled.

I give profound thanks to all these individuals but take full responsibility for the inaccuracies and mistakes that are unavoidable in a work of this ambition.

George Michell

INTRODUCTION

Travel Information

Planning a journey

The itineraries in this guide are conceived as travel hubs with tourist facilities where visitors may base themselves for one or more days and from where they can make different excursions. Each itinerary or travel hub is numbered; each city, town or site of interest in the vicinity is given a letter: thus, Ajanta [5F] or Srirangam [41B]. This pattern is broken for Bombay, Hyderabad and Madras, each of which is treated in two chapters, for example Bombay [1] and Around Bombay [2]: the first tackles the sights within the city, the second the sights beyond the city limits accessible as day trips.

Probably the most difficult decision for travellers is to select destinations that reflect their individual interests and to arrange these into a feasible journey, allowing sufficient time for travel and sightseeing. Full- and half-day excursions are indicated wherever possible, giving tourists an opportunity to organise their time to best advantage. But difficulties in road and rail travel over long distances cannot always be anticipated.

When to visit

By far the best months for travelling in Southern India are those in the cooler season from October to March. But November and the first half of December can be wet in parts of Tamil Nadu and Kerala, with occasional storms on the east coast of Andhra Pradesh and Tamil Nadu. March warms up suddenly and can be uncomfortably hot (up to 39°C), in interior Maharashtra, Karnataka and Andhra Pradesh. The debilitating heat of April and May should be avoided unless the journey consists mostly of higher-altitude touring. The monsoon rains from June to August are severe on the west coast of Maharashtra, Goa and Kerala, but are usually light and intermittent elsewhere, and need not interfere with travelling.

Passports and formalities

Visitors to India require a valid passport and a tourist visa, available from the embassies and consulates listed below. There are 15-day visas for single or double-entry transit, which are valid from the day of issue; three-month multiple-entry visas, which are valid from the date of first entry into India, within 30 days of the date of issue of the visa; and six-month multiple-entry visas. Unlike the others, these latter are extendable, but they are valid only from the date of issue of the visa. For travellers intending to stay for up to six months, it is worth obtaining a visa as near to the date of entering India as possible. An

All India Liquor Permit can be obtained at the same time as a visa; this allows visitors to buy alcoholic drinks at permitted times in 'dry' states such as Andhra Pradesh and Gujarat.

The Indian Embassy in the **UK** is at India House, Aldwych, London WC2B 4NA (☎ 0171 836 8484; fax 0171 836 4331), and the Consulate at 8219 Augusta Street, Birmingham B18 6DS (☎ 0121 212 2782; fax 0121 212 2786).

The Embassy in the **USA** is at 2107 Massachusetts Ave NW, Washington, DC 20008 (☎ 202 939 7000; fax 202 939 7027), and the Consulates at 3 East 64th Street, Manhattan, New York, NY 10021-7097 (☎ 212 879 7800; fax 212 988 6423) and 540 Arguello Blvd, San Francisco, CA 94118 (☎ 415 668 0662; fax 415 668 2073).

The Embassy in **Canada** is at 10 Springfield Road, Ottawa, K1M 1C9 (☎ 613 744 3751; fax 613 744 0913).

Separate permits are required for visits to the Andaman and Nicobar Islands, and Bangaram and Suheli in the Lakshadweep Islands. A permit of up to 30 days for the Andamans can be obtained on arrival at the airport in Port Blair, or one can be issued at the same time as a visa. A permit to visit Bangaram and Suheli can be obtained from the Lakshadweep Administration office on Harbour Road, Willingdon Island, Kochi.

Tourist information

Information may be obtained in the **UK** from the Government of India Department of Tourism office at 7 Cork Street, London W1X 2AB (☎ 0171 437 3677; fax 0171 494 1048).

In the **USA** the offices are at 30 Rockefeller Plaza, 15 North Mezzanine, New York, NY 10112 (☎ 212 586 4901; fax 212 582 3274) and 3550 Wilshire Blvd, Suite 204, Los Angeles, CA 90010 (☎ 213 380 8855; fax 213 380 6111).

In **Canada** the office is at 60 Bloor Street West, Suite #1003, Toronto, Ontario M4W 3B8 (☎ 416 962 3787; fax 416 962 6279).

Tour operators

A good travel agent is invaluable. In addition to help with airline and train tickets, car hire and hotel bookings, agents are able to assist in the planning stages of any trip, though of course they will be more familiar with popular tourist spots than little-frequented sites. Visitors should be encouraged to make their own choice of places they wish to see and then ask an agent to advise on timetables and make necessary bookings. *Abercrombie & Kent* (☎ 0171 730 9600), *Cox & Kings Travel Ltd* (☎ 0171 873 5000), *Sita World Travel* (☎ 0171 437 4337), *Butterfields Indian Railway Tours* (☎ 01262 470230), *Greaves Travels Ltd* (☎ 0171 487 5687), *British Airways Holidays* (☎ 01293 723180), *Hayes & Jarvis Travel Ltd* (☎ 0181 748 5050), *Steppes East Ltd* (☎ 01285 810267) and *Travel Corporation of India* are among a host of experienced companies who can offer such services. Some of these companies (eg Sita and Cox & Kings) are represented in the larger Indian cities, and some companies maintain offices in the USA and Australia. Among the many tour operators that offer inclusive packages are *Kuoni Travel Ltd* (☎ 01396 740500), and *Bales Worldwide* (☎ 01306 885 923).

Getting to Southern India

Direct airline services operate through the year between London and Bombay and Madras, and from several other British cities to Delhi, from where internal flights may be made to Bombay, Madras, Hyderabad, Aurangabad, Bhubaneswar, Goa, Bangalore, Tiruchirapalli, Kochi, Madurai and Thiruvanathapuram. The direct services between Britain and Southern India are *British Airways* (☎ 0181 897 4000), *Air India* (☎ 0171 491 7979) and *Singapore Airlines* (☎ 0181 747 0007). Services requiring a connection in Europe are offered by Egyptair, KLM, Air France, Aeroflot, Air Lanka and Emirates. Charter flights are also run to Goa; see your travel agent for details of these. Most flights from North America require connections at, among others, Europe, Moscow, Hong Kong and Britain, but *Air India* (☎ 1 800 223 7776) offers services from New York and Toronto direct to Bombay and Madras, and from New York to Goa; airlines offering connecting flights include Aeroflot, Air France, KLM, Lufthansa, Gulf Air, Cathay Pacific, PIA and Air Canada.

Note that when leaving India by air, a departure tax of Rs 300 must be paid for international flights. A tax of Rs 150 is levied for internal domestic flights and for flights to Sri Lanka, Bangladesh, Pakistan, Nepal, Burma, Afghanistan and the Maldives.

At the time of writing, there is only one entry into India by rail, from Lahore in Pakistan to Amritsar, from where connections to Delhi and then to the south can be made. Check with travel agents for details and bookings.

Although there are a number of border crossings between India and Pakistan, Nepal, Bhutan and Bangladesh, they are not always open, depending on the political situation. Visitors intending to enter India by road should check beforehand with the relevant embassy or high commission. Among the companies offering bus or truck journeys from Europe are Encounter Overland (☎ 0171 370 6951), Exodus (☎ 0181 675 5550) and Top Deck Travel (☎ 0171 244 8641).

The only way to reach or leave Southern India by sea is on one of the round-the-world passenger cruise ships that stop at Bombay, Madras or Kochi. Note that a departure tax of Rs 300 is levied for international departures by sea.

Money

The Indian currency is the **rupee**, abbreviated to **R**, which is divided into 100 **paise**. There are coins of 5, 10, 20, 25 and 50 paise and Rs 1, 2 and 5, and new banknotes of Rs 2, 5, 10, 20, 50, 100 and 200; Rs 1 banknotes are still in circulation, but are no longer printed. Because banknotes tend to stay in circulation for longer than Western ones, many may be torn or very worn. The visitor should refuse these, as they will not be accepted in most outlets, although a very few banks will change them for newer ones. It is worth carrying low-denomination notes, particularly for local travel or tipping.

With identification such as a passport, **travellers' cheques** can be cashed at banks and hotels. Not all brands are accepted everywhere, and the most reliable are American Express, Thomas Cook (both of whom have offices in large cities), Visa and Citibank. Although it is possible to change most currencies in major cities, US dollars and sterling are the best choice for further afield.

Outside the major cities, **credit cards** are not universally accepted, but an increasing number of hotels, restaurants and shops will take them. The most accepted brands are Visa, Diners Club, MasterCard and American Express, the last of which has offices in Ahmadabad, Coimbatore, Goa, Hyderabad, Pune and Thiruvanathapuram, from which rupees can be cashed by cheque. American Express cards can also be used to buy sterling or dollar travellers' cheques.

Unlimited amounts of foreign currency or travellers' cheques may be brought into India, but anything with a value over US $10,000 should be declared on arrival. It is illegal to bring rupees into India or to take them out of the country.

Customs and duty-free

Travellers to India may bring with them 0.95 litres of alcohol and 200 cigarettes or 50 cigars, a camera or a pair of binoculars without declaring them at customs. Other items, such as video cameras, sound recorders, jewellery and lap-top computers, and their serial numbers, must be declared on a Tourist Baggage Re-export form on entry. This form must also be shown at customs when departing from the country.

It is illegal to export any item containing animal or snake skins or ivory from India, and the export of antiques is restricted. Gold jewellery bought in India can be exported, as long as its value is under Rs 2000, and other jewellery and precious stones under a value of Rs 10,000.

Arriving in Southern India

Buses and taxi services operate from international and domestic airports into city and town centres. It is advisable to take a pre-paid taxi rather than use an independent company or operator.

Maps

The route maps given for each itinerary locate all the destinations; maps of the major cities and the larger historical and archaeological sites position the important features. Visitors may be surprised to learn that many places of historical significance in Southern India still lack published surveys. This volume may be supplemented with maps from the Nelles Verlag series, in particular *India 4 South*. Lonely Planet Publications has recently issued a travel atlas for the region which is unsurpassed for accuracy and graphic quality. Locally printed maps of Southern Indian states and cities are now available at local bookshops.

Southern Indian place names

Travellers should be aware that many places in Southern India have more than one spelling. The confusion derives from the governmental decision to replace Anglo-Indian spellings with Romanisations of the vernacular: for instance, Pune instead of Poona, and Thanjavur instead of Tanjore. The current versions of place names are used here, with a few exceptions where the older names are more familiar, particularly to visitors, and still widely in use, such as Bombay and Madras. The older names are included in the relevant text.

Transport

National and private **airline companies** provide an ever-expanding network linking the cities of Southern India with Delhi, Bombay and Calcutta, the principal arrival points for international visitors. The air connections relevant to each itinerary are given, but timetables are not attempted, since these often change.

Although plane is the obvious choice for long hops, overnight **trains** can also be convenient. Travel agents can advise on express rail connections, and computer bookings are now available at the larger stations. Train services in Southern India range from the comfortable (First class) to the basic (Second class passenger), and reservations can be made up to six months in advance. The city and larger town stations are likely to have computerised booking systems.

Public and private **bus companies** operate an astonishingly comprehensive system throughout Southern India. With very few exceptions, all the destinations described here can be reached by bus. Local transport makes journeys to even the most remote villages and sites once or twice a day. Enquire at bus stands for timings.

The ideal way to move around the country, especially for small groups, is with a **car and driver**, generally beginning and ending in one of the larger centres. Note that it is necessary to pay for a car to return to the point of departure; the cost is usually related to distance. Drivers are invariably courteous and helpful, though their English may be limited. With their own car and driver, tourists can explore city sights, plan daily excursions, embark upon journeys involving one or more itineraries and then be delivered at airports, railways stations or the next travel hub. Cars also permit a certain degree of improvisation, which is a luxury on any journey.

Motorcycles and bicycles can also be hired relatively inexpensively, or even bought, although this can involve a large amount of paperwork. Neither an International Driving Licence or a helmet is compulsory for motorcyclists in India, but these are both strongly recommended.

Tourist information

The addresses of governmental tourist agencies are given for each itinerary, wherever available. These offices provide maps and information about local sights, but are sometimes uninformed about far-off and less frequented destinations. The bigger tourist offices in the state capitals offer daily sightseeing tours and longer trips, sometimes with overnight stays at their own chains of hotels. Bookings for these hotels, sometimes the best available in more remote regions, can be made at the offices.

Accommodation

Southern India's boom in hotel building reflects the growing needs of professional businessmen, families attending social functions, pilgrims and tourists. Only the best hotels for each travel hub are listed here, though these are not necessarily luxurious. Visitors may expect international standards in the grand hotels of the big cities. A range of lesser accommodations is available at most centres, but a complete listing is not attempted. In any case, new hotels are opening every year, and it is worth checking with the relevant local Tourist Information office for up-to-date listings.

Food and drink

The best places to eat in any Southern Indian city or town are in the hotels. In fact, the word 'hotel' generally refers to a restaurant rather than a place of lodging. It is possible to eat well at just about all the accommodations noted in the travel hubs. Most Southern Indians are vegetarians, but non-vegetarian needs are invariably catered for, sometimes in separate restaurants within the same building. Southern Indian cuisine specialises in freshly prepared snacks, the most famous of which are *idlis* (rice dumplings), *wadas* (lentil rings), *dosas* (lentil and rice pancakes) and *uttapams* (similar to *dosas*), served with various accompaniments, which make ideal breakfast fare or later refreshments. Many restaurants switch over to 'meals' in the middle of the day, at which time metal dishes, known as *thalis*, or washed banana leaves are filled with *puris* (fried puffed flour) and rice and accompanied by an assortment of spicy preparations, such as curries, *chapatis* and poppadums; these are generally eaten with the fingers, but visitors are often offered spoons. Such fare, available with variations everywhere in Southern India, is mostly delicious and safe, even in smaller centres.

Indian desserts are mostly made from milk and rice or flour, and are very sweet to Western tastes; *rasgullas* and *jalebis* are fried and served in syrup. *Kulfi* is the Indian version of ice cream, usually with almonds or pistachios. Fruits can be purchased in local markets.

Coffee is the most popular drink in Southern India, and is usually sweetened and served with milk, as is tea. Fruit juices, particularly coconut milk straight from the coconut, and soft drinks, both domestically and internationally produced, are popular. Kingfisher is the best-known brand of the many Indian beers, and Indian wine and whisky are also available.

Health

Although there is no legal requirement for vaccinations before entering India, the traveller should take steps to ensure that the risk of infectious diseases is as low as possible. Jabs for typhoid, hepatitis A and B, rabies and meningitis are recommended, and boosters, such as those for polio and tetanus, should be regularly maintained. A course of malaria tablets is essential, but this will not work unless the tablets are taken for the period before and after the visit. Make sure that children have had treatment against, mumps, measles, diptheria, HIB and whooping cough. Travellers who need to inject themselves regularly, such as diabetics, should ensure that they take more than enough sterilised needles with them. Should it be necessary to purchase medicine while in India, whether on prescription or over the counter, make sure that the sell-by date has not been passed.

Apart from the dangers of too much sun, the most common health problems encountered by Western visitors to India are intestinal; although there is no way of avoiding these completely, some basic precautions can be taken to minimise the possibility of them occurring. The golden rule is not to drink any water or soft drinks that are not bottled, and then only if the seal on the bottle is intact. For this reason, ice in drinks should also be avoided. If there is no access to 'safe' water, tap water can be treated best by purification or sterilisation, or by being boiled for at least five minutes, even for cleaning one's teeth.

Opening hours

The following times should be taken as a general guide to opening hours, as there are sometimes variations to these in different regions. **Banks** are open from 10.30 to 14.30 Mondays to Fridays, and from 10.30 to 12.30 on Saturdays; some top hotels offer 24-hour banking facilities. Most **shop** opening hours are from 9.30 to 18.00 Mondays to Saturdays; local bazaars are often open for longer. **Post Offices** are open from 10.00 to 17.00 Mondays to Fridays and on Saturday mornings. **Government offices** open from 9.30 to 17.00 Mondays to Fridays and from 9.30 to 13.00 on Saturdays. *

Consulates

In **Bombay**, the *British Consulate* is at Maker Chambers IV (1st floor), 222 Jamnalal Bajaj Marg, Nariman Point (☎ 283 3602; fax 202 7940); the *American Consulate* is at Lincoln House, 78 Bhulabai Desai Marg, Cumballa Hill (☎ 363 3611); the *Canadian Consulate* is at 41/42 Maker Chambers IV, 222 Jamnalal Bajaj Marg, Nariman Point (☎ 287 6028).

In **Madras**, the *British Consulate* is at 24 Anderson Road, Nungabakkam (☎ 827 3136); the *American Consulate* is at Gemini Circle, 220 Anna Salai (☎ 827 3040).

Crime and personal security

The visitor to India is unlikely to be subjected to violent or personal attacks, although this type of crime has increased in Goa over the last few years. Theft of personal belongings is a danger, however, so it is strongly recommended to carry passports, money, travellers' cheques and other valuables in a money belt or close-fitting pouch at all times; hotel rooms should not be regarded as safe places to store such belongings. Keeping copies and records of travellers' cheque serial numbers is also advised. When transporting baggage, do not put valuables in it and keep it within sight at all times if possible, particularly in crowded areas; if not, make sure that it is securely fastened or even chained to its location. Should anything be stolen, this should be reported to the police promptly, otherwise there will be no chance of making a successful insurance claim.

Two other forms of crime are not uncommon in India. Confidence tricksters often target tourists with money-making or hard-luck stories, and should be discouraged from the start. If paying with a credit card, insist that the form is run off where this operation can be seen, to prevent more than one form being run off.

Women travellers

For Western women, serious sexual assault is very rare in Southern India, but physical harrassment, obscenities and uninvited verbal advances are quite common in the cities and large towns. These can usually be dealt with by firmness, and by not wearing clothes that might be seen as provocative, such as sleeveless tops and short skirts; dark glasses can be used to avoid appearing to return the ubiquitous staring by men. At the same time, there are women-only queues and waiting rooms at train and bus stations, and compartments on trains and seats on buses are reserved exclusively for women.

Disabled travellers

For the disabled visitor travelling alone, there is almost nothing in the way of purpose-built help in Southern India, although baggage ramps in airports and hotels may be utilised for wheelchairs. Outside this, the visitor will be reliant on help, which is usually forthcoming, from guides, drivers and local people.

Telephone and postal services

Local, interstate and international telephone calls are best made through the private STD/ISN call booths, usually located in shops and businesses, which allow you to call direct and display the time and cost of the call on a computer screen. Many of the booths are fitted with fax-sending facilities. The international code for the UK from India is 00 44, and that for the USA and Canada 00 1; from these countries, the code for India is 00 91. Another service available is Home Country Direct, which enables you to phone the international operator in the UK, USA and Canada and then make collect or credit-card calls; this can, however, be more expensive than going through STD/ISN; the code for the UK with this service is 000 44 17, that for the USA is 000 1 17, and for Canada 000 1 67.

Recent improvements in telecommunications within India mean that it is now feasible to telephone and/or fax ahead to make hotel reservations and travel arrangements. Local STD codes and relevant hotel and agency telephone numbers are given wherever available. However, it is important to remember that these numbers keep changing, so it is wise to check with local operators.

Letters sent to and from India can take up to three weeks to arrive, but the service is generally accurate and good. Stamps, aerogrammes and airmail letters are inexpensive, but sending parcels can be a long and complicated procedure, involving having the parcel stitched inside linen and then having customs declaration forms glued and stitched onto it. Books and printed matter must be wrapped so that the contents are either visible, or the packet must be able to be opened for inspection. When collecting letters sent Poste Restante to a Post Office, make sure that both the surname and forename are checked, as letters are often filed under the latter.

Newspapers, magazines and media

India has a large number of English-language daily newspapers, among which are the *Times of India*, the *Indian Express*, the *Independent*, the *Economic Times* and the *Hindu*, all of which tend to concentrate on Indian issues. There are also magazines published weekly or fortnightly, such as *India Today*, *Sunday* and the *Illustrated Weekly*, which have more of an international slant. International newspapers are available at many of the better hotels and in all large cities, though these may be days or weeks old. The BBC World Service radio is the main source of news for English speakers, and satellite TV broadcasts of UK and USA channels have become quite widespread.

Local customs and etiquette

The following is not a complete list of etiquette in Southern India, but an awareness of the most sensitive issues will help to prevent embarrassment. Because the left hand is regarded as unclean, only the right hand should be used for eating, shaking hands, pointing, and giving and receiving items. Women should not shake hands with men, and permission should be asked when wishing to photograph women. Women's dress should be modest and men should not appear bare-chested in public, except on beaches; nudity is banned on all Indian beaches. Public displays of affection, such as holding hands, embracing or kissing, are seen as unacceptable, and swearing is extremely bad etiquette. If invited into someone's home, it is the usual custom to remove one's shoes.

Visiting monuments and museums

A strict etiquette is observed when visiting Hindu and Jain places of worship. Shoes are always removed at the entrance and left with an attendant, sometimes at a special counter. Photography is usually not allowed inside temples, and certainly never of images under worship. There are also prohibitions on admitting non-Hindus in some Tamil Nadu temples, and unfortunately in almost every temple in Kerala. The points at which access is restricted have been indicated in the descriptions. Temples in Tamil Nadu and Kerala tend to close in the afternoons, but the custom varies and visitors should check local timings. Temples elsewhere in Southern India are open throughout the day, or keys will be found on request. Visitors should be prepared to salute the god, goddess or saviour enshrined in the sanctuary; indeed, they may be encouraged to do so by attendant priests. Male worshippers in Kerala have to remove their shirts and wear a white *mundi* instead of trousers.

Mosques and shrines of Muslim saints generally admit all visitors, though women are sometimes excluded. Shoes are invariably removed, and photography is discouraged at prayer times. Christian places of worship are accessible to all, and shoes are generally worn.

Most museums are closed one day a week, as indicated in the descriptions, but the timings are not standardised and should be confirmed, especially lunchtime closing, which is optional. The rules for photography vary: some museums sell tickets for still cameras and videos; other museums prohibit all photography. Adequately illustrated catalogues are rarely available.

Ancient monuments managed by governmental archaeological agencies are generally open from dawn to dusk, seven days a week. There may be a small charge. Photography is generally allowed, but permission may be required to use flash and stand. Since this can only be issued in Delhi or at state capitals, this procedure is unworkable for most tourists.

Certain public and private buildings which are not generally open to the public are included here. Entry is sometimes possible with a special permit from the appropriate authority. Enquiries should be made at the local tourist office or with a travel agent.

Public holidays and festivals

The official Indian national calendar corresponds with the Gregorian calendar, but the Indian New Year begins on 22 March. The dates in this section are those of the Western calendar.

India has four official public holidays, which fall on the same day each year:

26 Jan	Republic Day
15 Aug	Independence Day
2 Oct	Mahatma Gandhi's birthday
25 Dec	Christmas Day

The list below contains the major religious festivals celebrated in Southern India and some of the better-known secular ones. In such a huge region, there are many other local holidays and festivals, and it is worth checking with State and regional Tourist Offices to find out where and when these take place.

Key: AP=Andhra Pradesh, Ke=Kerala, Ka=Karnataka, Ma=Maharashtra

1 Jan	*Ugadi* (AP): New Year
	Vishu (Ka): New Year
Feb	*Vasant Pachami*: Hindu, spring festival
	Ramadan: Muslim, month of fasting
	Id-ul-Fitr: Muslim, end of *Ramadan*
	Makar Sakranti: Harvest festival, end of winter
	Elephanta Festival (Ma)
Feb/Mar	*Shivaratri*: Hindu, Siva's creation dance
	Holi: Hindu, water and colour festival
Mar	Ellora Festival (Ma)
Mar/Apr	*Mahavir Jayanti*: Jain, birth of Mahavira
	Ramanavami: Hindu, birth of Rama
	Good Friday
Apr	Carnival (Goa)
Apr/May	Kochi Spice Festival (Ke)
	Basakhi: Hindu, solar new year
Jun/Jul	*Rath Yatra:* Hindu, Krishna's journey to Mathura
	Id-ul-Zuha: Muslim, Ibrahim's sacrifice of his son
Jul	*Milad-un-Nabi*: muslim, birth of Muhammed
Jul/Aug	*Narial Purnima*: Hindu, offering coconuts to Varuna
	Naag Panchami (Ma): Hindu, *naga* snake festival
Aug	*Muharram*: Muslim, martyrdom of the Prophet Hussain
Aug/Sep	*Ganesh Chaturthi* (Ma): Hindu, festival of Ganesha
	Janamashtami: Hindu, birth of Krishna
Sep/Oct	*Dasara*: Hindu, Rama's victory over Ravana (Mysore)
Oct/Nov	*Diwali (Deepavali)*: Hindu, festival of lights
	Nayak Jayanti: Sikh, birth of Guru Nayak
Dec	Hampi-Vijayanagar Festival (Ka)

Background Information

The Land

The region. Southern India, as defined in this volume, encompasses all of the Subcontinental peninsula south of the Narmada and Godavari Rivers. This triangle of land protruding into the Indian Ocean measures about 1600km from north to south and 1200km to 600km from east to west. The region encompasses almost 950,000 sq km, an area greater than France and Germany combined. Like these European countries, it is dotted with cities, towns and sites reflecting over 2000 years of history.

Southern India's 275 million people (1991 estimate) live in five major states, each a linguistically demarcated zone. Maharashtra is home to speakers of Marathi, the only language in Southern India to belong to the Indo-Aryan group. The other four states, Karnataka, Andhra Pradesh, Tamil Nadu and Kerala, make use of Kannada, Telugu, Tamil and Malayalam respectively, all languages of the Dravidian group. The inhabitants of Goa, the smallest Southern Indian state, speak Konkani, a language restricted to the west coast, as well as Marathi.

Physical features. The heart of the Southern Indian peninsula, constituting much of Maharashtra, Karnataka and Andhra Pradesh, is an elevated plateau known as the Deccan, bounded on the north by the Narmada range, the traditional frontier between Northern and Southern India, and on the south by rugged hills, where it rises to more than 1000m. The plateau is traversed by the west-flowing Narmada and Tapti Rivers at its northern perimeter, and by the east-flowing Godavari, Bhima, Krishna and Tungabhadra Rivers further south. The Deccan is hemmed in by two lines of forested hills known as Ghats. The Western Ghats, the higher of the two spines, run down the west side of Southern India, defining a narrow strip of land on the Arabian Sea coast. In Maharashtra and Goa these Ghats are referred to as the Sahyadris and are characterised by steep escarpments. The coast here, known as the Konkan, is indented with river estuaries, some with rocky islands. Coastal Karnataka incorporates the Kanara district, similarly constricted by forested ranges. The Malabar Coast further south is a well-watered strip of land with inland lagoons that constitute the heart of Kerala. The Western Ghats rise here to their highest point of more than 2000m. The Eastern Ghats, which serve as the eastern margin of the Deccan plateau, have deep gorges through which the Godavari and Krishna Rivers run before terminating in fertile deltas that fan outwards into the Bay of Bengal.

The strip of land flanking the Bay of Bengal, familiar to Europeans as the Coromandel Coast, continues south into Tamil Nadu at the bottom of Southern India. This state is divided between wooded uplands and fertile plains crossed by east-flowing rivers such as the Palar, Kaveri and Tambraparni. Rugged granite outcrops occur abruptly throughout the landscape.

Except for Kerala and the southern extremity of Tamil Nadu, two zones which benefit from heavy and frequent rainfalls, the remainder of Southern India is relatively dry for most of the year. The southwest monsoon lashes the Western Ghats in June, July and August, feeding the rivers which rise here. The Eastern Ghats tend to be wettest between October and early December, when the retreating monsoon hits the Coromandel Coast. Cyclonic storms with flooding are common at this time. The Deccan lies in the rain shadows of both lines of Ghats. Habitation here relies on artificial reservoirs, known as tanks, with great earthen dams, a traditional form of trapping rainwater. Southern India's great rivers are now mostly harnessed to feed irrigation channels and to supply the region with hydroelectric power.

Agriculture and industry. Long-established seaborne contacts between Southern India and the Middle East and Europe are reflected in the mixed peoples and religions of the Konkan and Malabar coasts. Bombay [1], the capital of Maharashtra, the undisputed commercial and financial centre of the region, is located here; so, too, are the historical ports of Panaji [11A], the capital of Goa, and Kozhikode [48A] and Kochi [47A], the main ports of Kerala. This coastal tract has been famous through the centuries for its rich supplies of rice, pepper, cardamom and other spices much prized by Arabs and Europeans. Today's exports also include fruits, coconuts, cashew nuts and minerals such as manganese and iron ore. Shipbuilding is a major industry, the main centres being at Bombay, Mormugao in Goa, and Kochi. The wooded hills of the Western Ghats offer a perfect habitat for tea, coffee and rubber estates, as well as for plantations of teak and other valuable hardwoods.

The industrial triangle of Bombay, Pune [3A] and Nasik [4A] in Maharashtra is the most developed in Southern India. Textile manufacturing, engineering, petrochemicals, electronics, pharmaceuticals and sugar refining are the primary activities. Bangalore [14B], the capital of Karnataka, is the centre of the nation's aerospace and hi-tech electronics industry. Agriculture in the arid Deccan uplands of Maharashtra, Karnataka and Andhra Pradesh is mostly restricted to wheat, cotton, tobacco, oilseeds and groundnuts. Irrigation permits the cultivation of sugar cane and fruits. Steel and iron mills are fuelled by rich reserves of coal, iron ore and manganese. The diamond mines for which Hyderabad [26], the capital of Andhra Pradesh, was once famous have been revived recently.

The Coromandel Coast of Andhra Pradesh and Tamil Nadu, including the fertile deltas of the Godavari, Krishna and Kaveri Rivers, has been familiar to Europeans for centuries as a source of finely woven cotton fabrics. Brightly printed and dyed textiles are still produced here. Rice, grains, tobacco and sugar cane are the most important crops in this zone. Heavy engineering and shipbuilding are located at the port of Visakhapatnam [31A], while Madras [36], the capital of Tamil Nadu, is home to production of automobiles, motorcycles, fertilisers, chemicals and paper.

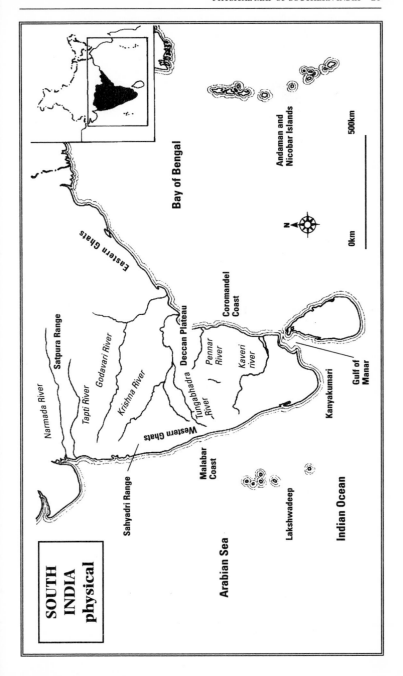

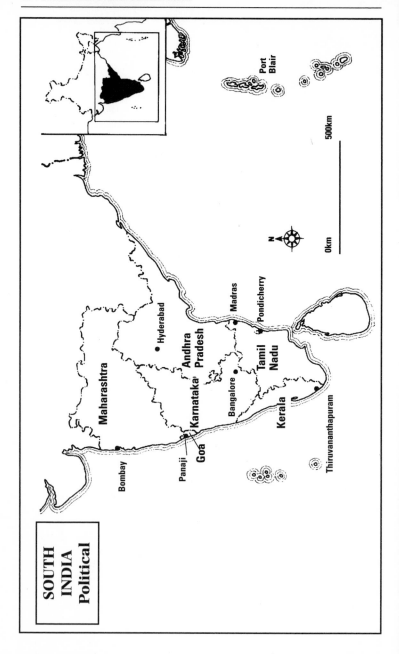

History

The first kingdoms. While the presence of Ashokan edicts at sites such as Brahmagiri [20L] and Maski [20M] in Karnataka suggest contacts with the Maurya empire of Northern India in the 3C BC, it is not until the 2C BC that Southern India emerges as a historical entity. The **Satavahanas**, known also as the **Andhras**, rose to power in Maharashtra, Paithan [5L] serving as their main centre. From here they fanned out into northern Maharashtra, Andhra Pradesh and even beyond into Madhya Pradesh, conquering a vast territory that encompassed much of the central peninsula. The Satavahanas were responsible for inaugurating Buddhist architecture in Southern India: the rock-cut sanctuaries at Ajanta [5F] and Pandu Lena [4B] and free-standing complexes at Amaravati [29K] and Guntupalle [30B] are among the many monuments assigned to their reign. Some sites, like Ter [9D], are rich in coins, terracottas and ivories.

Though the Satavahanas were challenged on their western flank by the **Shakas** of Middle-Eastern origin in the 1C AD, they retained their independence until the end of the 2C, when they were supplanted by the **Ikshvakus**. This line of rulers was not so long-lived as its predecessors. Even so, they controlled much of Andhra Pradesh in the 3C–4C, selecting Nagarjunakonda [27H] on the Krishna River as their headquarters. At about the same time the Tamil country came under the sway of the **Pallavas** of Kanchipuram [37F], but only fragmentary information is available for the first kings of this dynasty.

The **Vakatakas** of Madhya Pradesh held an importance place in politics and culture in the 4C–5C, and their influence extended into Maharashtra. Nandavardhan served as one of their capitals, and vestiges of their presence are still seen on nearby Ramtek Hill [10B]. It is, however, for the excavated Buddhist shrines and monasteries at Ajanta and Aurangabad [5B] that these rulers and their subordinates are best known. Harishena (460–78) is the outstanding personality of the era, and the painted depiction of a king receiving gifts from foreigners in Cave 1 at Ajanta may be his portrait.

Early Hindu dynasties. The next phase of Southern Indian history witnesses the simultaneous growth of several lines of kings who sponsored Hindu monuments. The **Kalachuris** were active in Maharashtra in the 6C, deriving their wealth from the trade routes that led from the Konkan coast up into the interior plateau. Their cave-temples at Elephanta [2A] and Ellora (Caves 21 and 29) [5E] are the most elaborate of the era. These rulers were to some extent displaced by the **Chalukyas** of Badami [22A] who controlled most of Karnataka as well as parts of Andhra Pradesh. It was under the Early Chalukyas that structural architecture made its first advances, as can be seen at Badami and at nearby Pattadakal [22D] and Aihole [22E]. As they expanded south the Early Chalukyas came into conflict with their rivals, the **Pallavas**. Pulakeshin II (609–54) was one of the prominent figures of this line. He attained renown by defeating Harsha of Kanauj, the most powerful king of Northern India, and carrying out raids on Kanchipuram. The Pallavas retaliated, and in 654 occupied Badami. Struggles with the Pallavas continued into the 8C, but the career of the Early Chalukyas was terminated in 753 with the invasion of the **Rashtrakutas**. These kings brought a large part of Maharashtra, Karnataka and Andhra

Pradesh under their sway. An idea of their ambitions may be had from the colossal Kailasa monolith (Cave 16) at Ellora, initiated by Krishna I (756–73).

The Pallavas established themselves as the leading power in the north part of the Tamil zone in the 7C–9C. Their earliest monuments are rock-cut or mono-lithic, as at Mamallapuram [37A] and Mandagapattu [39E], but later develop-ments at their capital, Kanchipuram, and at Panamalai [39G] show a preference for structural techniques. The Pallavas were constrained on their south flank by their contemporaries, the **Pandyas** of Madurai [44A]. These rulers were masters of the southern part of Tamil Nadu, and even extended their influence into neighbouring Kerala.

In the 10C–13C Central Karnataka and southern Andhra Pradesh came under the sway of the **Nolambas** and **Gangas**, who ruled from Hemavati [33H] and Talkad [15E] respectively. The latter kings were the first sponsors of Sravana Belgola [18F], the most important Jain site in Southern India. At this time northern Karnataka and the adjacent Andhra Pradesh zone were ruled by the **Late Chalukyas** of Basavakalyan [25D], so-called to distinguish them from their predecessors. Their temples at Ittagi [20G] and Dambal [21D] are among the finest of the era. Meanwhile, the remainder of Andhra Pradesh was domi-nated by another line of the Badami family, known for convenience as the **Eastern Chalukyas**. These kings built extensively throughout the Bay of Bengal provinces, as at Bikkavolu [30E] and Samalkot [30H].

The rise of the **Cholas** signifies a new period in the history of Southern India. These kings first established their supremacy in the Tamil zone in the 9C–10C before invading parts of Karnataka and Andhra Pradesh, absorbing the Nolamba and Ganga territories and progressing up the east coast as far as Orissa. Chola naval campaigns even reached Sri Lanka and Southeast Asia. Under forceful personalities like Rajaraja (985–1016) and Rajendra I (1012–44), the Chola state took on the dimensions and apparatus of a grand empire. Thanjavur [40A] served as the principal capital, temporarily supplanted by Gangaikondacholapuram [40J]. Magnificent temples at both sites testify to the unparalleled resources available to the Cholas in the 11C, a situation that continued into the 12C, judging from large-scale projects at Chidambaram [39H] and Tribhuvanam [40H].

Chola expansion was resisted towards the end of the 12C by the **Hoysalas**, who ruled from Halebid [18B] in southern Karnataka. These kings set about to conquer the Tamil zone, but were checked in this endeavour by the resurgent Pandyas in the extreme south. Even so, the Hoysalas managed to bring all of Karnataka under their control, subduing the Late Chalukyas. They also spon-sored a uniquely ornate style of religious architecture, as can be seen in the temples at Halebid and at nearby Belur [18A]. As the Hoysalas were consoli-dating their hegemony, the **Kakatiyas** of Warangal [28A] emerged as the domi-nant power in the Andhra Pradesh country. Their domains encroached on those of the Eastern Chalukyas, which were steadily absorbed into the Warangal kingdom.

The dissolution of Rashtrakuta power in the course of the 10C was hastened by the rise of their successors, the **Yadavas**. Basing themselves at the great rock citadel of Devagiri [5C], the Yadavas consolidated their gains in the 11C–12C, bringing peace and prosperity to much of Maharashtra. Though they built extensively, only a few of their temples survive intact. The example at Sinnar

[4D] shows stylistic influences from Northern and Western India, regions with which the Yadavas had commercial contact. Like the Hoysalas and Kakatiyas, the Yadavas continued to rule until the invasion of the Delhi army at the end of the 13C.

The Delhi conquest and its aftermath. The first intrusion into Southern India by the forces of the **Muslim** kings of Delhi occurred in 1296. This was followed by a series of campaigns that eventually dislodged all the previous ruling houses of the region, bringing to an end the Yadava, Kakatiya, Hoysala and Pandya lines. By 1323 the commanders of the **Tughluq** army were firmly established at Madurai. In an effort to control this newly won part of the country, the Delhi ruler Muhammad Tughluq shifted the capital to Devagiri in 1327, rebuilding the fortifications and renaming it Daulatabad. Soon after, in 1334, Muhammad Tughluq recalled the army to Delhi to assist in wars elsewhere. The results were twofold: the Muslim governors of Madurai and Daulatabad proclaimed their independence, and an obscure line of Hindu chiefs known as the **Sangamas**, based at Hampi [20B] on the Tungabhadra River in Karnataka, set about reclaiming the lands lost to the Tughluqs. These events led to the creation of the **Bahmani** and **Sangama** kingdoms, the latter known as Vijayanagara after the newly founded capital near Hampi.

After securing their autonomy in 1347, the Bahmanis shifted from Daulatabad to Gulbarga [24A], remaining there until the early 15C, when they relocated to Bidar [25A]. The Bahmanis ruled over a vast domain incorporating all of Maharashtra and large tracts of northern Karnataka and Andhra Pradesh. The influx of Persians, Arabs and Turks to Southern India introduced a new language, culture and religion. This was accompanied by an equally novel architecture which rapidly reconciled Persian forms and decorative devices with indigenous techniques. Among the greatest patrons were Tajuddin Firuz (1397–1422), Ahmad I (1422–36) and Mahmud Gawan, Prime Minister under Muhammad III (1463–82). The Bahmanis protected their capitals with great circular citadels, inside which they erected mosques and palaces. Royal tombs were situated on the outskirts, as were the graves of the saintly personalities who did much to bolster the prestige of these kings. That the Bahmanis maintained a series of outposts to guard their realm is indicated by the forts that they founded at Purandhar [3J], Sholapur [9A] and Raichur [20N].

The first task of the Sangamas was to liberate the lands lost to the Delhi forces; this they achieved with astonishing swiftness. By 1371 the Sangamas had reached the southern tip of Tamil Nadu, extinguishing the line of Madurai rulers, thereby earning the allegiance of lesser chiefs and governors in the whole region. At the turn of the 15C the Sangamas were in command of almost all the peninsula south of the Tungabhadra and Krishna Rivers. Only parts of the Malabar Coast lay beyond their grasp. The centralised government of the Sangamas rapidly assumed the authority of an empire, with all of the finances being siphoned to the capital. Under Bukka I (1354–77) and Devaraya II (1423–46), two influential Sangama kings, Vijayanagara was built up as a showpiece of imperial magnificence and furnished with imposing military, ceremonial and religious structures [20C].

Bahmani-Vijayanagara conflict in the 14C–15C mainly concentrated on control of the richly irrigated triangle of land lying between the Tungabhadra

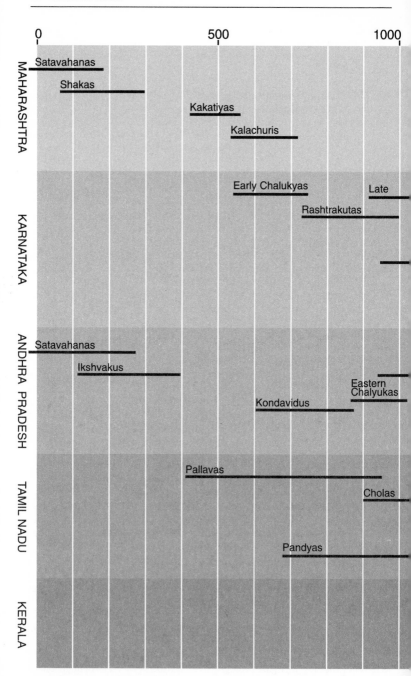

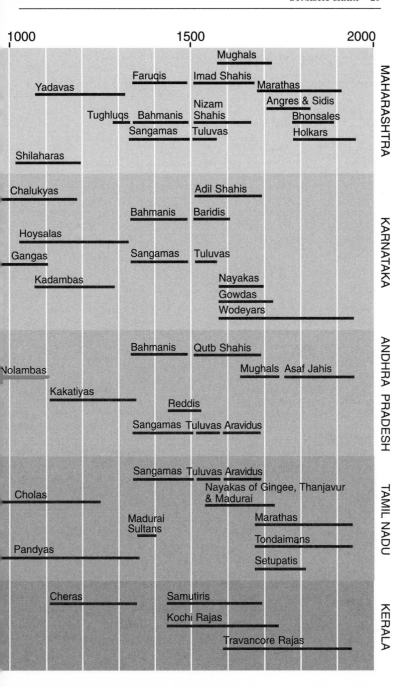

and Krishna Rivers. In spite of repeated wars, sieges and raids, the two kingdoms coexisted uneasily until the end of the 15C, when both were subjected to internal forces of disintegration.

The rise of successor states. Rivalry between immigrants from the Middle East and local inhabitants contributed to the break-up of the Bahmani kingdom. By the beginning of the 16C this had fragmented into smaller states, each founded by a former provincial governor. The three most significant figures of the era were Yusuf Adil Khan (1490–1510), who established the **Adil Shahi** dynasty, which ruled from Bijapur [23A] in Karnataka, Ahmad Nizam Shah, who performed a similar role for the **Nizam Shahis** at Ahmadnagar [6A] in Maharashtra, and Quli Qutb al-Mulk (d. 1543), originator of the **Qutb Shahi** line at Golconda [26E] in Andhra Pradesh. Lesser personalities were Qasim Barid (1488–1504), first of the **Baridi** rulers of Bidar, the capital of a much reduced dominion, and Fathullah Imad Shah (d. 1510) of Achalpur [10E]. A review of the simultaneous careers of these kingdoms reveals a history of shifting alliances that effectively prevented any single kingdom from attaining supremacy. Only when these rulers perceived Vijayanagara, on their southern flank, as a common enemy was a consortium formed that led to the battle of January 1565, in which the Vijayanagara forces were vanquished.

With the removal of the immediate threat of Vijayanagara, Bijapur and Golconda emerged as the two most prosperous kingdoms, the former eventually engulfing the territories of the Baridis. The Nizam Shahi kingdom was the first to bear the impact of the **Mughals**, who began to intrude into Southern India in the last years of the 16C. Ahmadnagar was lost to the Mughals in 1636, but it took another 50 years of constant warring before Bijapur and Golconda capitulated. In the meantime, both states were able to achieve a high degree of affluence and cultural sophistication. This is clear from the grand building programmes initiated by Ibrahim II (1580–1627) and Muhammad (1627–56), both of whom erected imposing mausoleums at Bijapur. No less impressive was Muhammad Quli (1580–1611), the ruler responsible for shifting the Qutb Shahi capital to the newly planned city of Hyderabad [26A].

The **Tuluva** emperors of Vijayanagara ruled with unprecedented splendour in the first half of the 16C. Investment in large-scale religious complexes was sustained at the capital and at newly popular religious sites like Ahobilam [32F] and Tirumala [35B]. Local governors also acted as sponsors of temple projects, as at Tadpatri [33B] and Lepakshi [33G]. Krishnadevaraya (1510–29) made extensive tours of his dominions, as well as embarking upon warring campaigns against his neighbours to the north. His expedition to Orissa in 1516 was marked by the capture of Udayagiri [34D], guarding the east coast of Andhra Pradesh. Achyutadevaraya (1529–42) sustained this aggressive policy, but courtly intrigue under his successor, Sadashiva, gave Ramaraya, the commander of the imperial forces, an excuse to seize control. However, he antagonised the kings of Bijapur, Golconda and Ahmadnagar.

After the abandonment of the Vijayanagara capital in 1565, the new line of rulers, known as **Aravidus**, who were descended from Ramaraya, retreated to Penukonda [33D] before settling permanently at Chandragiri [35C]. In consequence of losing much of their lands in Karnataka and Andhra, the Vijayanagara emperors were greatly reduced in prestige and influence. This situation encouraged the governors in Tamil Nadu to assert their independence in the second half of the 16C. Known as **Nayakas**, these figures gradually emerge as independent rulers, especially those based at Gingee [39F], Thanjavur and Madurai. Conflicts between the Nayakas and the Aravidus led to the civil war in which the emperor Venkatapatideva (1586–1614) lost his life. The later Aravidus were of minor significance.

The 17C marks the supremacy of the Nayakas in the Tamil zone. Raghunatha (1614–34) and Vijayaraghava (1634–73) were among the greatest of the Thanjavur Nayakas; the latter was killed in battle against the Madurai forces. Tirumala Nayaka (1623–59) was the outstanding statesman and warrior of the era. His grandiose building programmes are evident at Madurai, Srirangam [41B] and Alagarkoil [44C].

This pattern of provincial figures emerging as autonomous rulers in the wake of Vijayanagara's decline also occurred in Karnataka. The **Nayakas** of Keladi [19B] and Ikkeri [19C] were the first to stake their claim to sovereignty, governing freely over the forested tracts in the western part of the state. The **Wodeyars** of Mysore [15A] and **Gowdas** of Bangalore [14A] came into competition over the territories further south, with the former eventually triumphing over the latter.

The 16C–17C also marks the period of the first European settlements in Southern India. Vasco da Gama landed on the Malabar Coast in 1498, and by 1510 the Portuguese had made Goa [11B] the headquarters of their seaborne Asian empire. They made contacts with the rulers of Kerala and became much involved in local affairs at Kochi [47A] and Kozhikode [48A]. The Portuguese were followed in the 17C by the Dutch, who managed to take several ports from them, including Kochi. The English arrived not long after, and by the end of the 17C the newly formed East India Company had established lucrative trading posts at Bombay [1C] and Madras [36A].

The Mughals and the Marathas. The **Mughal** conquest of Southern India occupied all of the later years of the emperor Aurangzeb's reign (1658–1707). After absorbing the Bijapur and Golconda kingdoms into the Deccan provinces of the Mughal empire, Aurangzeb's forces swept south into Tamil Nadu. They were, however, impeded in their progress by daring raids executed by the **Maratha** forces under Shivaji (1674–80) and his successors. Mughal-Maratha skirmishes became a constant feature of warfare, continuing into the 18C. By this time large portions of Southern India were firmly in Maratha hands, including Thanjavur, the seat of an independent line of rulers that survived into the 19C. Aurangabad and Hyderabad, on the other hand, remained with the Mughals. Under the command of Nizamul Mulk (1723–48) the Mughal Deccan provinces were separated from Delhi to become the independent state of Hyderabad. The **Asaf Jahis**, known also by their title of **Nizams**, lived on beyond Independence.

The 18C witnessed the remarkable expansion of Maratha power beyond Southern India. This rapidly growing empire was directed by the **Peshwas**, prime ministers of Shivaji's descendants, based in Pune [3A]. Wars between the Asaf Jahis and the Marathas continued throughout the era, with the British and French contributing troops to Hyderabad in return for trading rights on the Coromandel Coast. The outstanding event of the second half of the 18C was the growing influence of Haidar Ali, former Mughal governor in Karnataka. After usurping the Wodeyar throne of Mysore, Haidar pursued a series of aggressive campaigns throughout Southern India, a policy continued by his son, Tipu Sultan. Only in 1799, after the Maratha, Asaf Jahi and British armies joined forces, was Tipu finally vanquished in the siege of Srirangapattana [15C]. The Maratha state thereafter disintegrated into civil war, prompting the British to intervene. By 1818 the Maratha factions were defeated, and the British were in charge of all their former territories in Southern India.

The 18C also witnessed struggles between different European powers for control of the coastal trade. The Portuguese maintained their hold on Goa, while the British and French came into conflict over commercial supremacy of the Bay of Bengal ports. The French raided Madras on several occasions, but in the end retired to a minor position from their headquarters at Pondicherry [39E].

From empire to independence. Peace and prosperity returned to Southern India in the 19C. More than half the region was absorbed into the Bombay and Madras Presidencies, the two major British provinces, while the remainder was divided among princely realms such as Hyderabad, Mysore and Travancore, the last based at Thiruvananthapuram [46A]. The rulers of these, and lesser states at Kolhapur [8A] and Pudukkottai [41G], were under the control of British Residents. Revenues previously used to support private armies were redirected towards building programmes, and all of these princely capitals came to be furnished with handsome palatial and civic edifices. Meanwhile, Bombay and Madras developed into manufacturing and shipping centres of global significance. Grandiose public monuments in both cities express the wealth and confidence attained by the end of the 19C.

The Indian Mutiny of 1857, though only a minor disturbance in Southern India, led inexorably to demands for self-rule. The Indian National Congress was founded in Bombay in 1885, and was followed by other parties. From 1915 Mahatma Gandhi was the major focus for the independence movement, and many decisions of national importance were taken from his retreat near Wardha [10C] in rural Maharashtra. Independence was finally achieved in 1947, two years after the end of the Second World War. The former British Presidencies and princely dominions of Southern India were thereupon dismantled and reorganised along linguistic lines into the modern states of the Indian Union.

After Independence. Southern India since 1947 presents an impressive picture of development and increased prosperity. The most lasting achievement of the era was the creation of the modern Southern Indian states out of portions of the old British Presidencies of Bombay and Madras, the former Portuguese and French colonies of Goa and Pondicherry, and the older princely kingdoms of Hyderabad, Mysore and Travancore. The insistence on linguistic unity in these newly formed states has not always been possible, and borders have been adjusted from time to time in accordance with the languages spoken by local peoples. In spite of such efforts, many zones of Southern India and many of its major cities, remain multi-linguistic. Education has made advances in most areas, especially in Kerala which claims the highest literacy of any Indian state.

Dramatic improvements in transport and communications over the last 50 years mean that the middle classes of major urban centres of Bombay, Bangalore, Hyderabad and Madras now enjoy a comfortable and cosmopolitan lifestyle. While rapid progress in manufacturing and industry have brought wealth to a limited sector of the urban populous, the problems of poverty, over-crowding and environmental pollution have not been avoided. Extensive irriga-tion projects, including the cosntruction of major dams on the Tungachadra and Krishna Rivers, have brought benefits to the africultural hinterland of Southern India. Famines are a thing of the past; so, too, cultural isolation. Most villagers today enjoy improved economic conditions, as well as the conveniences of telephones and television sets. Improved rail connections and road conditions mean that more and more people are on the move. Attendance figures at reli-gious festivals have grown dramatically since Independence, over 3.5 millions visiting the hill temple at Tirumala in Andhra Pradesh each year, for instance. An indicator of the increased wealth of worshippers at Hindu, Jain and Muslim shrines can be seen in the profusion of improvements and structural additions to ancient structures.

The growing influence of Southern India in the political life of the whole country is reflected in the fact that two of India's recent Prime Ministers, P.V. Narasimha Rao and H.D. Deve Gowda, came from Andhra Pradesh and Karnataka respectively.

Religion

Buddhism and Jainism. These two religions were introduced into Southern India as early as the 3C–2C BC. Buddhism disappeared after about 1000 years, but not before profoundly affecting religious architecture and art. Monasteries and shrines dating from the 2C BC to the 5C AD testify to the widespread influ-ence of Buddhist communities in Maharashtra and Andhra Pradesh under the Satavahana, Ikshvaku and Vakataka dynasties. A modern revival led by the social reformer Dr Babasahib Ambedkar resulted in large numbers of the lower classes in central Maharashtra being converted to Buddhism in the middle of the 20C.

Buddhism derives its inspiration from the teachings of Buddha, an historical figure known as Gautama or Siddhartha, who lived in Northern India in the 6C–5C BC. Buddha's philosophy, which was more concerned with practical instruction than with mystical speculation, grew out of a quest for a rationally enlightened experience. Buddha preached penance and meditation as a means of achieving insight into the causes of human suffering and the way to remove them. He propounded an Eightfold Path of right conduct to eliminate the burden of suffering.

Later scriptures illuminate the career of Gautama, focusing on his mysterious birth, life as a young prince, renunciation, penance, enlightenment under the *bodhi* tree, first sermon and final extinction, or Parinirvana. Buddhist art visu-alises all these episodes, with a preference for dramatic events: the temptations of Mara, an evil spirit, to distract the Master from meditation; Buddha's taming of the wild elephant sent to trample him by Devadatta, his jealous cousin; the miracle at Sravasti, when Buddha levitated to meet the challenge of rival teachers. Folk tales known as *Jatakas* relate the stories of Buddha in his previous births as a prince, animal, or even bird. These delightful narratives form the principal topic of early Buddhist sculpture and painting, as can be seen in the 5C murals at Ajanta [5F]. Buddha's teachings are symbolised by the hemispherical funerary mound, or *stupa*, a solid mass enshrining relics of the Master or his followers. Such monuments became the focal feature of Buddhist complexes erected at various sites overlooking the Krishna River, as at Amaravati [29K].

While Buddha never considered the idea of a supreme god, he came to be venerated as a sacred being after his death. The doctrine of the Mayahana, the Great Vehicle, as developed in the early centuries AD, propounded a series of Buddhas and compassionate saviours known as Bodhisattvas. These were especially popular, since they delayed their own extinction into *nirvana* so as to aid ordinary men and women in their quest for enlightenment. While several past appearances of Buddha in Bodhisattva form were imagined, such as Avalokiteshvara, the Merciful Lord, there was also the future incarnation of Maitreya.

Jainism was promoted by the Ganga and Hoysala rulers of Karnataka in the 9C–13C, and small Jain communities survive to this day in coastal Karnataka, as at Mudabidri [17C]. Recent efforts to revive Jain traditions reached a climax in 1981, with the celebrations to commemorate the 1000th anniversary of the great monolithic statue of Gommateshvara at Sravana Belgola [18F].

Like Mahayana Buddhism, Jainism also posits a series of saviours, but these are known as Ford Makers, or Tirthankaras. The religion founded by Mahavira, a contemporary of Buddha in Northern India, propagates a doctrine intended for ascetics. Mahavira was the last of a line of 24 spiritual leaders referred to as Conquerors, or Jinas, all of whom achieved *moksha*, or liberation. With the dispersal of Jainism throughout the country, a schism arose based on conflicting accounts of the founder's teachings. The sect which flourished in Southern India insisted on nudity among its followers and was known accordingly as Digambara, or Space-Clad.

Parshvanatha and Mahavira, the only two Tirthankaras for whom any historicity is claimed, are believed to be the last two of a line of 24 Jain saviours. Their lives and those of the other Jinas are described in considerable detail in sacred literature and painting. One of the most complete narratives is that painted on the ceiling of the Jain shrine at Tiruparuttikunram [37F]. A popular legend in Southern India is that of the penance of Gommateshvara, known also as Bahubali, son of the first Tirthankara.

Major Hindu cults. The major divinities of Hinduism enjoy a huge following among a large proportion of Southern India's population. Some cults appear to derive from ancient traditions dating back to prehistory, such as the worship of the phallus, or *linga*; others evolved at different stages in Southern Indian history. It is important to distinguish local legends and traditions from those common to all parts of the country. Only the barest outline of the immensely complicated mythological system that forms the basis of Hinduism can be given here. (The Glossary on pp 539–556 identifies the most important names under which gods and goddesses receive worship in Southern India.)

Hinduism concentrates on three principal divinities, Shiva, Vishnu and the Goddess. These deities are regarded as multiple personalities and are endowed with a large variety of appellations and epithets. As the Great Lord, Maheshvara or Mahadeva, **Shiva** is the supreme principle of the universe. He is venerated for the essential characteristic of energy which dominates his diverse mythological appearances. This energy is manifested in the guise of fertility as the *linga*, or as the force of destruction in which the god annihilates demons. Shiva's energy is sometimes directed inwardly to achieve the powerful meditation that characterises the god in his role as the supreme teacher, Dakshinamurti. One famous aspect of Shiva is as Lord of the Dance, Nataraja, pacing out the steps of cosmic creation. This form of the god is particularly associated with the temple at Chidambaram [39H]. Shiva is invariably accompanied by the bull, Nandi, on which he rides.

Vishnu embodies the qualities of mercy and goodness, and is accorded the role of preserving the balance between ordered and disruptive forces. He is also responsible for the creation of the universe. As Ranganatha, Vishnu sleeps upon the serpent Shesha in the primeval ocean, dreaming the scheme of the cosmos yet to be born. It is in this form that Vishnu is worshipped in the famous temple at Srirangam [41B]. The doctrine of incarnations, or *avataras*, literally 'descents', forms an important part of the cult of Vishnu. The first three *avataras* of fish, tortoise and boar present Vishnu as the hero of different creation myths. As the terrifying man-lion, Narasimha, Vishnu appears in a vengeful form to disembowel his enemy Hiranyakashipu. In the Vamana or dwarf incarnation, the god transforms himself into the giant Trivikrama, who paces out the universe in three gigantic strides. In the next three appearances, Parashurama, Rama and Krishna, Vishnu comes to live among men as a warrior prince. Rama is the hero of the *Ramayana*, one of the most popular Hindu epics. Krishna, around whom a vast mass of legends have been gathered, is the charioteer of Arjuna, one of the five Pandava brothers in the *Mahabharata*, the other well-known Hindu epic. Krishna also appears as the child god and as the flute-playing lover of the *gopis* who tend the cows.

According to the third great cult of Hinduism, the **Goddess** is considered the embodiment of female strength, and is accordingly known as Energy, or **Shakti**. She is the mother of all, embracing the maternal and nourishing principles connected with life-giving waters and lotus flowers. The idea of Shakti causes the Goddess to be associated with Shiva, with whom she develops her most characteristic features. The eternal couple Shiva-Shakti is represented as the conjunction of the male and female sexual emblems, the *linga* and the *yoni*. According to legend, Shakti was created by all the gods, who equipped her with weapons so that she might destroy Mahishasura, the buffalo demon who had threatened the heavens. In her forceful and destructive role she is Durga, pursuing evil throughout the universe. She also becomes Kali, the symbol of death.

In her peaceful aspect as Parvati, Shakti is worshipped as the consort of Shiva, personifying the benevolent and philosophical nature of her lord. As Lakshmi, the companion of Vishnu, she is the goddess of prosperity. Marriage ceremonies binding these and similar goddesses with their male partners are universally celebrated in Southern India. Marriage halls, or *kalyana mandapas*, are an important part of most temple complexes. Goddesses derive much of their significance from the fact that they represent the power of specific sites or cities. They are for this reason adopted as protective deities by ruling dynasties: thus Chamundeshvari of Mysore [15A] became the tutelary goddess of the

Wodeyars, and Minakshi of Madurai [44A] fulfilled a similar role for the Pandyas and, later, the Nayakas. Such goddesses were of crucial importance for Hindu kings, since it was their cosmic energy that empowered royal regalia, weapons and animals, ensuring rulers of success in battle. Exactly this rite was celebrated at Vijayanagara [20C] in the great Mahanavami festival, known in later times as Dasara.

In Southern India, gods are identified with particular holy spots, where local legends explain the miraculous appearance of the deity or his decision to move there. Thus, for example, Mallikarjuna, an aspect of Shiva, is worshipped at Srisailam [32C] in the remote forests of the Eastern Ghats, where the Lord manifested himself in order to marry a local tribal girl. Venkateshvara, a form of Vishnu, takes his name from the Seven Hills (Venkatachala) at Tirumala [35B], where he chose to reside. Sacred sites in Southern India are connected by interlocking networks of related divinities; thus the five elemental *lingas* of Shiva, fire at Tiruvannamalai [38E], earth at Kanchipuram, water at the Jambukeshvara temple on Srirangam Island, air at Sri Kalahasti [35F] and ether at Chidambaram, or the seven sanctuaries of Murugan at Tiruttani [37H], Tirupparankunram [44B], Palani [44E] and other centres in Tamil Nadu.

Hindu religious life. Brahmin priests are indispensable for most rites of worship, known as *puja*. They attend on the images of gods and goddesses housed within temple sanctuaries, treating them as if they were actual royal figures. The deities are awakened, washed, dressed, fed, honoured, entertained and finally put back to sleep at fixed times throughout the day. In some temples, gods and goddesses even spend nights together in special mirrored chambers. No congregation is required at these times, though some devotees choose to be present. Priests also convey offerings to divine figures on behalf of worshippers, reciting appropriate prayers and hymns. Visual contact is crucial to all these rites, the moment of looking directly at sacred icons being known as *darshana*. No interaction between humans and deities can be achieved without this auspicious gaze. These visual alignments are reflected in architectural axes, with gates, colonnades and aisles all leading up to the focal sanctuary.

Ceremonies which take place at greater intervals of time, like the annual celebration of the marriage of the god and goddess, assume the dimensions of major festivals. On these occasions, metal images of the deities are brought out of the innermost sanctuaries and paraded publicly in front of huge crowds. The richly dressed and jewelled images are carried on palanquins or ride in huge chariots covered with wooden carvings and topped by brightly coloured cloth towers. They may be conveyed to lesser shrines in the vicinity, to pay respect to subordinate deities, or placed in boats and floated around temple tanks. Fairs, theatrical performances and recitations of sacred scriptures accompany these events.

Pilgrimage in Southern India is determined by ritual calendars, with devotees travelling all over the region to visit their favourite shrines on suitable auspicious occasions. The Tirumala Temple benefits from enormous revenues contributed by the 10,000 and more daily visitors who come to honour Venkateshvara and to ask him favours. Sabarimalai [47O], in the wooded hills of Kerala, is a newly popular destination, where pilgrims climb a forested path to reach the far-off shrine of Ayyappa.

Education is another feature of religious life, and many temples are associated with a *matha*, or college, where Hindu scriptures such as the ancient Vedas are taught. One of the oldest such institutions, that located at Sringeri [19H] in western Karnataka, was founded in the 9C by the great philosopher Shankara. Not all teachers, or *gurus*, are affiliated to temples; some have established their own retreats, or *ashrams*. Sai Baba, perhaps the most internationally known of Southern India's living gurus, has his headquarters in the obscure village of Puttaparthi [33E] in Andhra Pradesh, to which devotees make a special journey. He calls himself after an earlier spiritual figure who lived quietly at Shirdi [6C] in interior Maharashtra. Tamil Nadu has several celebrated *ashrams*, including those of Ramana Maharishi at Tiruvannamalai and of Aurobindo at Pondicherry [39A].

Saints are another feature of Hindu religious life. The stories of their lives and the miracles that they performed are vital manifestations of their devotion, or *bhakti*, to Shiva and Vishnu. The emotional intensity of their poems and songs is still appreciated today. 63 saints, known as Nayanmars, are celebrated in the Shaiva canon. They include historical personalities such as Sambandar, Sundarar and Manikkavachakar. Saintly followers of Vishnu are referred to as Alvars. Such figures are invariably associated with particular holy spots. Kannappa, the hunter who offered his eyes to Shiva, for example, worshipped the god at Sri Kalahasti. Ammaiyar, a female worshipper who performed austerities in honour of Shiva, lived at Karaikal [40P].

Islam. Though Islam arrived with Arab traders who settled on the coasts of Kerala and Karnataka from the 7C onwards, it was not until the invasion of the Delhi army at the beginning of the 14C that this religion was forcibly introduced into Southern India. Islam was the creed of the Bahmani kings and their successors; the faith was sustained under the Mughals and the Asaf Jahis, and was even promoted by Haidar Ali and Tipu Sultan.

More than 10 per cent of Southern India's population is Muslim, and this figure is higher in Kerala and certain districts of Karnataka and Andhra Pradesh. Most of these Muslims are orthodox **Sunnis**; that is, they regard the Caliph as the head of the community, responsible for the administration of justice through the *sharia*, or law. Islam posits a single unseen God, Allah, who is all-powerful but compassionate. His messenger, Muhammad, was the author of the Koran, the faithful and unalterable transcript of God's words. Reciting the Koran and proclaiming submission to God are the principal rites observed in any mosque. The niche in the middle of the rear wall of the prayer hall, known as a *mihrab*, indicates the direction of Mecca towards which all worshippers must face.

Jami mosques with spacious courtyards are intended as central places of assembly for the male population of a town or city. Kings or governors would publicly pray here on Fridays, and then listen to the sermon of the *imam*, the spiritual head of the community. Larger mosques were often associated with *madrasas*, or theological colleges, where Arabic language and Koranic studies were taught. Such colleges were also a means of promoting the **Shia** doctrine, which was adopted for a time by rulers at Ahmadnagar [6A] and Bijapur [23A]. Shia Muslims differ from Sunnis in their belief in the need for intermediaries between God and man. The *imams* served as suitable leaders, explaining the powers of such figures in Shia religion.

The mystical tradition in Islam is represented by **Sufism**, a popular development in Southern India. Sufi philosophy concentrates on individual communion with God, rather than on received wisdom and strict laws. In its emphasis on emotional personal experience, Sufism provides a striking parallel to the Hindu devotional movement, with which it interacted. The Sufi tradition in Southern India focuses on the careers of gifted holy men who settled in the region, often at the encouragement of local rulers who wished to bolster their newly established kingdoms with religious authority. Hazrat Gesu Daraz, a celebrated Sufi saint of the Chishti order, who lived in Gulbarga [24A] in 1401–22, was an influential figure in the politics of the Bahmani court.

Dargahs, or tombs of saintly personalities, play an important role in Muslim religious life. Devotees visit tombs in order to benefit from the spiritual influence, or *baraka*, believed to emanate directly from the graves. *Dargahs* such as that of Gesu Daraz at Gulbarga, or of Hamir Qadir Wali at Nagore [40O], are popular places of pilgrimage, even for Hindus, especially on the occasion of the *urs*, or death anniversary of the saint. Kings, too, made a habit of visiting *dargahs* and even of having themselves buried in the vicinity of the holy personalities that they chose as spiritual preceptors. Aurangzeb gave instructions to be buried in the simplest manner next to the tomb of a Sufi saint at Khuldabad [5D].

Christianity. Some 70 per cent of the country's 16 million Christians live in Southern India, about half of these in Kerala. Many of these Christians trace their origins to the Apostle St Thomas, who is believed to have landed near Kodungallur [47T] on the Malabar Coast in AD 52. A more historically certain tradition is that the merchant Thomas Cana emigrated from Syria to Kerala in the 4C with a group of 400 families, to found a branch of what was to became the Nestorian Church. This sect, which recites its liturgy in Armenian and which has some 30,000 members in and around Thrissur [47W], still acknowledges the authority of the Patriarch of Baghdad. Other Eastern Orthodox sects in Kerala, including Jacobites and Canaanites, also maintain formal relations with patriarchs in the Middle East. The head of the Malankara Orthodox Syrian church, based at Kottayam [47I], is styled as the spiritual successor to the Apostle Thomas.

With the arrival of Vasco da Gama and the subsequent establishment of Portuguese trading posts on the Arabian Sea coast, the Roman Catholic church gained a foothold in Southern India. Old Goa [11B], the principal headquarters of Portuguese power, and lesser settlements like Vasai [2E] and Chaul [2H] served as bases for various religious orders. The Franciscans were the first to arrive, followed soon after by the Dominicans, Augustinians and Jesuits. All these groups pursued vigorous programmes of preaching and conversion, and for these purposes erected churches, monasteries and schools. The most famous missionary of the era, the Spanish Jesuit St Francis Xavier, was active in Southern India in 1542–52. His tomb in Old Goa remains the most popular Catholic sanctuary in Southern India. The Portuguese also extended their commercial and missionary activities to the Coromandel Coast. They were responsible for rebuilding the chapel at San Thomé near Mylapore [36G], the legendary burial place of the Apostle in AD 68.

Protestant forms of Christianity in Southern India date from the period of the Dutch, Danish and English. These powers also supported missionary activities, and Lutheran and Anglican converts grew steadily in the 18C–19C. The present-day Church of South India incorporates most of these former Protestant movements.

The Parsis and Jews. Parsis are followers of Zorastrianism as practiced in Iran before the Arab invasion. Fleeing persecution, the first Zoroastrians arrived on the west coast of India in the 10C, where they were called Persians (Parsis). Although they remained a tiny minority, wealthy Europeanised Parsi families, such as the Wadias and Tatas, attained prominence as industrialists and philanthropists in 19C Bombay [1]. They continue to dominate business and social life.

Zoroastrians trace their beliefs to the prophet Zarathustra, who lived in Iran in the 7C–6C BC. Fire plays a central and symbolic role in the religion of the Parsis, and their places of worship are known as *atash barams*, or fire temples.

The Jews of Southern India, though now reduced to only a handful of families in Bombay and Kerala, also trace their origins to the Middle East. Kodungallur in Kerala is claimed as one of the earliest Jewish settlements in the 1C–2C. The Jews later moved to Kochi [47A] to benefit from lucrative business opportunities. The 19C witnessed another wave of Jewish migration, mainly from Baghdad. The Sassoon family attained particular renown in Bombay and Pune [3B].

Architecture

Wooden traditions. Early evidence for a lost wooden tradition in Southern India is seen in stone imitations of timber-and-thatch structures. 2C–1C BC Buddhist *chaitya* halls have horseshoe-shaped openings derived from flexible bamboo construction. 2C–4C AD masonry *stupas* are surrounded by stone posts and railings that imitate wooden originals. Timber-and-thatch buildings are also the source for roof forms in Hindu temple architecture, but only the hut-like shrine at Chidambaram [39H] actually preserves its wooden structure, renewed through the centuries. Hut-like roofs were reproduced for the first time in stone in the 7C Pallava period monoliths at Mamallapuram [37A], and remain a constant feature of Southern Indian architecture thereafter.

Stone temples in Karnataka and Andhra Pradesh display open halls with intricately worked circular columns reproducing lathe-turned wooden originals. Peripheral supports are sheltered by eaves that angle or curve outwards in the semblance of thatch, supported by timber-like rafters and ribs. The sloping stone roofs of 8C Early Chalukya temples at Aihole [22E] have their joints covered with log-like strips, a feature common in temples on the west coast of Karnataka, as at Mudabidri [17C].

Kerala never gave up its reliance on sloping roofs to shed the heavy rains. Timber beams and rafters support pyramidal and conical roofs, often in multiple tiers, clad in copper or terracotta tiles. Finely worked wooden screens, beams and ceilings are typical of this style, as can be seen in temples at Ettumanur [47G] and Kaviyur [47K]. Mosques in Kerala employ the same multi-tiered wooden roof systems; with the exception of those at KozikHode [48A], these have now mostly disappeared. Palaces display a similar fascination with timber techniques. The 17C–18C complex at Padmanabhapuram [45O] is assembled almost entirely from wooden columns and slatted screens sheltered by sloping tiled roofs with decorated gables.

Royal structures in other parts of Southern India must also have employed timber columns and tiled roofs, but these have vanished, leaving only stone foundations and footing blocks, as in the 14C–16C royal enclosures at Vijayanagara [20C]. An exception is the 16C Rangin Mahal in the palace at Bidar [25A], which preserves ornately carved wooden columns, brackets and beams. Similar timber elements may be seen in the 19C–20C mansions of the Chettinad area of Tamil Nadu [44K].

Cutting into rock. Monumental stone architecture in Southern India begins with excavation rather than construction. The basaltic plateau of Maharashtra is punctuated by escarpments and deep river gorges, ideal sites for cutting into rock. *Chaitya* halls and monasteries were created for Buddhist communities as early as the 2C–1C BC, as can be seen at Karla [3C] and Bhaja [3D]. The apsidal-ended halls are divided into three aisles by two rows of columns which support rounded vaults, creating horseshoe-shaped arches on the outer façades. The interiors are dominated by monolithic *stupas* raised on cylindrical drums. *Chaitya* halls of the 5C–8C Vakataka and Early Chalukya eras, as at Ajanta (Caves 19 and 26) [5F] and Ellora (Cave 10) [5E], add screen walls with doorways and arched windows. *Viharas*, or monasteries, at these sites follow a standard pattern, with small sleeping cells opening off central halls. The end shrine rooms accommodate Buddha images. The 2C BC monasteries at Pandu Lena [4B] have octagonal columns standing in pot bases imitating the brass vessels in which actual timbers would have been placed. The balcony seating is adorned with relief representations of wooden railings. (That these halls and monasteries had structural equivalents is indicated by salvaged structures at Nagarjunakonda [27H] and by brick shrines at Ter [9D] and Cherzala [29N], all assigned to the 3C–4C Ikshvaku period.)

Cutting into rock was also the preferred technique for early Hindu sanctuaries. The 6C Early Chalukya cave-temples at Badami [22A], excavated into red sandstone cliffs, consist simply of verandahs and columned halls, with small shrines protruding beyond the rear walls. Such schemes are amplified at Ellora in the 7C–8C (Caves 11 and 15). The 6C cave-temple at Elephanta [2A] has a sanctuary standing freely in the middle of the columned hall. Granite outcrops in Tamil Nadu were exploited under the Pallavas and Pandyas in the 7C–8C, as can be seen at Mamallapuram and Tirupparankunram [44B]. The excavated monuments here have verandahs overhung by curving eaves, with small arch-shaped windows in relief.

The habit of fashioning monolithic temples in the semblance of actual structures was also popular at this time. The five *rathas* at Mamallapuram present contrasting roof typologies. This tradition reaches a climax in the 8C–9C under the Rashtrakutas. The greatest monolith of all, the stupendous Kailasa (Cave 16) at Ellora, reproduces the features of an actual built complex. The Indra Sabha (Cave 32), a Jain excavation at the same site, brings this monolithic phase to an end.

Temple styles 7C–8C. It was not until the 7C–8C that structural techniques in Southern India were sufficiently developed for temple architecture to advance. Experiments of the Early Chalukyas at Badami show simple tripartite arrangements of porch, columned hall and sanctuary. Such schemes are developed at nearby Pattadakal [22D] and at Kanchipuram [37F], the Pallava capital. The outer walls of temples here are divided into pilastered projections framing sculpture niches, above which are parapets of miniature roof forms. These features are repeated at diminishing scales to create multi-storeyed superstructures. Influences from Madhya Pradesh and Gujarat also had their impact: temples at Alampur [32B] show towers with curving surfaces covered with miniature arch-shaped motifs and topped by circular ribbed elements.

The Late Chalukya temples at Ittagi [20G] and Dambal [21D] show slender pilasters and split-arched motifs on walls and towers. Lathe-turned and multi-faceted columns enliven the interiors of porches and halls. These elements became the hallmark of later architecture in Karnataka and Andhra Pradesh. The Hoysala temples at Halebid [18B] and Somnathpur [15D] have multiple shrines laid out on complicated plans, with multiple angles taken up into the towers. The attached halls have projecting porches with balcony seating, exactly like those in Kakatiya temples at Hanamkonda [28B] and Palampet [28C].

A quite different style was developed at this time under the Yadavas in Maharashtra. The temples at Amarnath [2J] and Sinnar [4D] demonstrate the sustained influence of Madhya Pradesh and Gujarat. The curving towers show complex designs, with tiers of miniature towered elements on the central shafts. Bands of tapering ornament in the middle of each side lead to crowning circular elements, surrounded by deeply cut ribs.

Beginning in the 9C with modest shrines like the Nageshvara at Kumbakonam [40G], the Cholas went on to complete great projects at Thanjavur [40A] and Gangaikondacholapuram [40J] in the early 11C. The sanctuaries of these temples are crowned with imposing pyramidal towers that rise to unprecedented heights. As in earlier practice, the ascending storeys are defined by pilastered wall projections and parapets of ornamental roof forms. That Chola architecture was able to sustain this achievement in the 12C is demonstrated at Darasuram [40F], but the emphasis soon shifted from sanctuaries to towered entrance gates known as *gopuras*. The quartet of *gopuras* at Chidambaram, the finest of the Chola era, are two-storeyed granite structures complete with pilastered walls and sculpted niches. Brick-and-plaster pyramidal towers, divided into multiple storeys, are capped by vaulted roofs with arched ends.

Temple styles 15C–18C. The next phase of temple architecture coincides with the revival of previous styles after the disruption caused by the conquest of Southern India by the Delhi forces. The 15C Hazara Rama Temple at Vijayanagara [20C], for example, shows a dependence on Chola models in its pilastered wall surfaces and storeyed brick-and-plaster tower. The 16C temples at the same site are developed into large complexes, with rectangular walled compounds entered through *gopuras* on one or more sides. The open halls attached to shrines have columns transformed into complex piers with cut-out colonettes. Other halls have platforms for ritual ceremonies or performances of sacred dance. The Garuda subshrine in the Vitthala Temple [20B] is treated like a chariot, complete with wheels. The Anantashayana Temple at nearby Hospet [20A] is roofed with a remarkable brick vault.

The architecture of Vijayanagara inspired developments throughout Southern India in the 16C–17C. The temples at Tadpatri [33B] are densely orna-mented, with the carvings almost obscuring the basement and wall mouldings. The detached *gopuras* at Sri Kalahasti [35F] and Tirupati [35A] demonstrate the monumental possibilities of the Vijayanagara idiom. Their steeply pyramidal brick towers are divided in usual fashion into ascending and diminishing storeys. The free-standing halls at Vellore [38A] and in the Varadaraja complex at Kanchipuram have their outer supports transformed into virtuoso sculpted compositions. Similarly treated columns line the interior aisles, which lead to elevated podiums.

Variant temple forms are simultaneously developed in the forested zone of western Karnataka. The 16C shrine at Sringeri [19H] blends earlier Hoysala features with current Vijayanagara elements. The temple at Ikkeri [19C] fuses Hoysala-styled porch seating and column forms with arch profiles and parapet details derived from contemporary Adil Shahi mosques and tombs (see below).

17C Nayaka architecture in Tamil Nadu demonstrates the climax of the Southern Indian temple style. The outstanding feature of this period is the outward expansion of the religious complex, made by multiplying the quadran-gular walled compounds containing the focal shrine. *Gopuras* are axially aligned with the largest and highest gates at the peripheries, dwarfing the shrines in the middle. There is no standard arrangement. The Ranganatha Temple at Srirangam [41B] has seven concentric compounds, while that at Tiruvannamalai [38E] has only four, though these are extended towards the east to create a sequence of spacious open courts. The outermost quartet of *gopuras* are aligned with the central *linga* shrine in four directions. The temple at Tirukkalukkundram [37B] is framed by four perfectly matched *gopuras*. The great religious monument at Madurai [44A] has twin shrines with colonnades and corridors disposed along double axes. The single *gopuras* in the outer walls have slender towers with slightly concave profiles. These are exceeded only by the *gopura* at Srivilliputtur [44G], reputedly the highest in Southern India.

18C religious architecture in Maharashtra draws on diverse traditions to create novel forms. The temples sponsored by the Peshwas of Pune and their subordinates at Sasvad [3I] and Wai [7F], for instance, have domed interiors imitating mosques and tombs; the 12-sided towers incorporate Mughal-styled niches. The larger projects at Trimbak [4C] and Ellora revive earlier Yadava traditions, complete with curved towers displaying clustered elements on the shafts and spacious porches with balcony seating.

Temples in Goa adapt Christian Baroque architecture to Hindu ritual needs. The examples at Mangeshi [11G], Mardol [11H] and Quelem [11K] have octag-onal towers crowned with domes. Multi-storeyed lamp towers, enlivened by Neo-Classical pilasters and round-headed windows, stand freely in temple court-yards.

Mosques and tombs. 14C Muslim religious buildings in Southern India show a dependence on Tughluq architecture in Delhi, with an emphasis on sloping walls, battlemented parapets, arched openings and flattish domes. The Jami Mosque at Daulatabad [5C], the first and largest mosque in the region, has a vast square court overlooked by a colonnaded prayer hall fronted by a trio of arched portals. In contrast, the Jami Mosque at Gulbarga [24A] dispenses with any court, its interior being entirely roofed with vaults and domes carried on broad arches with angled profiles. The royal mausoleums at Gulbarga tend to be modest domed chambers, sometimes joined together as double tombs and decorated with fine plasterwork. The 15C Bahmani architecture at Bidar [25A] demonstrates direct contacts with the Persian world, the *madrasa* here being an actual architectural transplant from Central Asia. Its arcaded façade is decorated with the finest coloured tile mosaic of the period. The court within has Iranian-styled arched portals in the middle of each side. The royal tombs at Ashtur [25B] show a preference for arcaded façades topped with ornate parapets. The Chaukhandi is a modest domed chamber contained within an unusual octagonal screen wall.

Mosques and tombs developed variant forms in the 16C–17C. The Nizam Shahis were responsible for a distinctive style that concentrated on carved decoration and perforated stone screens. The finest examples are the small but exquisite Damri Mosque at Ahmadnagar [6A] and the Tomb of Malik Ambar at Khuldabad [5D]. The Adil Shahis built on a grander scale, as is obvious from the Jami Mosque at Bijapur [23A], the first to have a dome raised on intersecting arches. This device was perfected in the colossal Gol Gumbad, the largest domed chamber to be erected in Southern India, where the austere design is relieved by corner octagonal staircase towers.

That the Adil Shahis were capable of a more ornate manner is demonstrated in the Ibrahim Rauza, a paired tomb and mosque on the outskirts of Bijapur. Both structures present pyramidal arrangements of minarets and domical pinnacles surmounted by three-quarter spherical domes on leafy bases. Intricately worked relief and cut-out designs in stone adorn the walls of the tomb chamber. A similar fascination with carved detail is seen in the multistoreyed gateway to the Mihtar Mahal and in the Mosque of Malika Jahan Begum, also at Bijapur.

Plaster was the primary medium of decoration for the Qutb Shahis, as can be seen in the ornate Mushirabad and Toli Mosques on the outskirts of Hyderabad [26C, F]. The emphasis here is on richly treated cornices, arcaded galleries and parapets; the flanking minarets have shafts covered with boldly incised patterns. The royal tombs outside Golconda [26F] present pyramidal arrangements of arcaded storeys topped with imposing bulbous domes. Such schemes were the inspiration for later funerary architecture in Southern India, as in the 18C Mausoleum of Haidar Ali and Tipu Sultan at Srirangapattana [15C].

Mughal religious architecture in Southern India is mostly concentrated in and around Aurangabad [5A–B]. Lobed arches and rooftop pavilions are characteristic features of the many mosques and tombs erected here by the emperors and their governors. The grandest Mughal monument is also one of the earliest. The mid-17C Bibi-ka Maqbara is obviously modelled on the Taj Mahal at Agra, but incorporates fresh features, such as the raised gallery that looks down onto the grave. Like its predecessor, the Maqbara stands in the middle of a formal garden.

The final phase of Muslim religious architecture is represented by the austere Wallajah Mosque in Madras [36F] and the *dargah* at Nagore [40O], the latter with five unusual square minarets.

Forts. The earliest example of defensive architecture in Southern India is the remarkable circular city of Warangal [28A], the capital of the 13C Kakatiya rulers. This is surrounded by triple rings of fortifications, the innermost walls being of finely jointed granite slabs reinforced with square or rectangular bastions and protected by a broad moat. The gateways, shielded by barbicans with massive ramparts, have entrances requiring two changes of direction. Vestiges of Kakatiya fortifications at other sites include the inner circuit of walls at Raichur [20N].

The fortified core of Vijayanagara was first laid out in the 14C. Though irregular in configuration, the city employs walls and gates comparable to those at Warangal. That this system was widespread in Southern India is revealed by the 15C–16C outposts of the Vijayanagara domains at Chitradurga [20K] and Penukonda [35C]. These formidable citadels have granite walls climbing up and over the rugged hills against which they are built. Gingee [39F], the greatest stronghold in the Tamil country, encompasses three separate mountain citadels, each encircled by ramparts, with a vast triangular zone in between. The fort at Vellore displays round bastions with curved battlements interspersed with projecting guardrooms, attributes derived from Bahmani architecture.

The Delhi army developed Daulatabad into the greatest stronghold of the Deccan. Double lines of sloping ramparts strengthened with round and polygonal bastions, crenellated parapets and projecting guardrooms fan outwards in part-circular formation from the focal rock citadel. The preference for circular configurations was maintained in the 15C–16C by the Bahmanis at Gulbarga and Bidar, as well as by their successors at Ahmadnagar, Bijapur and Golconda. Quadrangular forts were also known, as at Sholapur [9A] and Parenda [9F], where the gateways have arched openings capped with bold parapets and shielded by barbicans. Massive outworks defining passageways with multiple changes of direction are standard devices for deflecting cavalry attacks. Nor are these entrances devoid of ornamentation: heraldic animals in stone or plaster adorn the entrances to the forts at Bidar and Golconda. The triple west gate to the Adil Shahi hill fort of Panhala [8B] is unsurpassed for its carved decoration. A significant aspect of all these citadels is the elaborate hydraulic works with which they were furnished: the aqueducts, channels and ventilation towers to regulate water flow are still in operation at Bijapur, as are the large storage tanks.

A new phase of military architecture was inaugurated by the Marathas in the second half of the 17C. Shivaji was responsible for establishing an impregnable line of hill forts that exploited the rugged terrain of the Sahyadri ranges of western Maharashtra. The ramparts of Rajgad [3M] and Pratapgad [7B] follow the edges of the cliffs in continuous undulations, reinforced by round bastions. The same system was employed in the coastal and island forts of the Konkan, as can be seen at Sindhudurg [8D]. Gates shielded by curving massive outworks are a particular feature of Maratha military architecture, as in the mountain stronghold at Raigad [7C].

Fort building was sustained in the 18C. Janjira [2I], the finest island citadel on the Arabian Sea coast, is the work of the Sidi admirals. The walls, which rise sheerly from the water, have curving battlements alternating with arched openings for cannons. Forts with more regular layouts were preferred for cities. The Peshwa citadel at Pune [3A] is a simple rectangle of high walls with corner round bastions, the main entrance being flanked by an additional pair of polygonal outworks.

A completely different tradition of military architecture was introduced into Southern India by the Europeans. The Portuguese were the first to build forts on any scale in the 16C–17C. The stronghold at Aguada [12A] consists of a quadrangle of sloping walls with sharply attenuated corners, guarded by a moat and an earthen embankment. The corner towers at Chapora [12D] have circular chambers with domical tops. The French and Dutch were also active fort builders, but little has survived. Of the Danish enterprise, there is only the oceanside enclosure at Tarangambadi [40Q]. The British were also concerned with providing adequate protection for their commercial outposts. Fort St George at Madras [36A] is the most elaborate to be preserved. Laid out as an irregular pentagon facing the Bay of Bengal, its sloping walls are reinforced by triangular bastions that protrude into the moat.

Palaces. The reception halls, pleasure pavilions, bath-houses, stores and stables in the royal compounds at Vijayanagara have pointed and lobed arches carrying domes and vaults, often of fanciful designs, decorated with geometric and arabesque patterns in finely worked plaster. These features, which derive from Bahmani architecture, contrast with the curving eaves and multi-storeyed towers drawn from temple architecture. This syncretic idiom appears to have been invented specially for the Vijayanagara court. Its royal associations were maintained throughout the 16C–17C, as is apparent from the Raja Mahal at Chandragiri [35C].

The syncretic idiom continued to evolve under the Nayakas, as can be seen in the courtly pavilions at Gingee. The granaries, with their lofty curved vaults, are the most remarkable structures at this site. This royal style reaches its climax in the spacious audience hall and dance chamber at Madurai, where massive circular columns support broad arches with pointed and lobed profiles, and lofty domes and vaults, elevated on clerestories, rise above.

Courtly architecture at the capitals of the Bahmani kingdom and its successor states reflects the influence of Persian and Central Asian models, as illustrated by the formal arrangements of residential apartments, audience halls and ceremonial portals. The Bahmani remains at Firuzabad [24D] indicate a residential palace zone as well as a vaulted ceremonial reception hall. Firuzabad is of interest for its vaulted *hammams*, the earliest in Southern India. The complex at Bidar consists of a formally planned ensemble of audience halls and residential suites. The apartments face into courtyards surrounded by high walls. The imposing arched gateways include one example with royal lions and sunburst emblems in coloured tiles.

The impact of Iranian architecture is clearly evident in the Farh Bagh, on the outskirts of Ahmadnagar [6B]. This large pavilion has monumental portals in the middle of four sides, framing half domes plastered with multiple facets. The double-height chamber in the middle is roofed with a flat dome. Audience halls with lofty central arches facing onto places of public assembly are a particular feature of the walled citadel that stands at the core of Bijapur. Such halls probably formed part of the extensive royal complex at Golconda, but are no longer extant. Even so, the progression from public to private zones is clearly indicated by a succession of vaulted chambers and open courts. Individual structures, such as the royal bath, armoury and barracks, are identified. Of the original Qutb Shahi residence at Hyderabad, only the quartet of free-standing arches that marked the central square in front of the parade grounds still stand. The adjacent Char Minar, erected as a ceremonial urban marker at the intersection of two main streets, continues to dominate the city.

Overgrown ruins are all that can now be seen of Shah Jahan's Palace at Daulatabad; the *hammam* outside the walls is better preserved. Residences of the Asaf Jahis and their nobles in Hyderabad combine revived Qutb Shahi forms with Neo-Classicism, with the latter predominating from the end of the 19C. The Falaknuma Palace is an imposing Palladian composition that rivals any British project. Other palaces present imaginative stylistic hybrids, often devised by British architects for princely patrons, such as Mant's New Palace in Kolhapur [8A] and Irwin's Amba Vilas in Mysore [15A].

Churches and civic building. The appearance of European styles in Southern India coincided with the arrival of the Portuguese. The 16C–17C Baroque churches of Old Goa [11B] make extensive use of Neo-Classical columns framing doorways and windows. Façades with pedimented tops and voluted sides are framed by pairs of towers, and naves are roofed with coffered vaults that frame ornate carved and gilded wooden altars. An Italianate influence is obvious in the Church of St Cajetan, which has a dome rising over the interior crossing. The majestic church at Santan [11D] and the ruined cathedrals at Vasai [2E] and Chaul [2H] testify to the spread of the Baroque idiom to lesser sites. 18C churches in Goa tend to be smaller, and have altarpieces decorated in an intricate Rococo manner, as at Calangute [12C] and Moira [12E]. Baroque architecture was by no means restricted to Portuguese possessions, as is demonstrated by churches at Kaduthuruthi [47F] and Palai [47H] in Kerala. Churches in Pondicherry [39A] confirm the popularity of the Baroque style under the French.

A more severe Neo-Classical mode was preferred by the British for their religious and civic buildings in the 18C–19C. Innumerable churches were erected with colonnaded porticos, steepled towers and vaulted interiors. The Madras examples are among the finest, especially St Andrew's Kirk, which has an unusual circular nave roofed with a dome [36C]. The Neo-Palladian style was adopted for ceremonial projects such as the Banqueting Hall (Rajaji Hall) in Madras [36E] and the British Residency (University College for Women) in Hyderabad [26C], the latter with a dignified Corinthian colonnade topped by a pediment containing the arms of the East India Company. A Neo-Greek manner was preferred for the Town Hall in Bombay [1C] and Paichaiyappa's College in Madras [36B].

By the middle of the 19C the Neo-Gothic manner had asserted itself as an alternative to Neo-Classicism. The Afghan Memorial Church in Bombay [1F], the first such stone building in Southern India, makes use of a single attenuated steepled tower as well as pointed arched windows filled with stained glass. Its richly appointed interior was not to be matched in later churches, such as the starkly unadorned St Thomé Cathedral Basilica in Madras [36G]. This ecclesiastical style continued into the present century, as can be seen at Mysore [15A] and Medak [27C]. An unusual adaptation of this style for Jewish liturgical purposes is seen in the synagogue at Pune [3B].

The application of the Neo-Gothic mode to public buildings inspired consider-

Principal British Architects in Southern India

Few major towns and cities in Southern India are without some vestiges of the British presence. Although the architects of many of the remaining buildings are unknown, some of the most famous and prolific architects are listed here, with examples of their work in India.

Robert Fellowes Chisholm (1840–1915) University Senate House, Egmore railway station and Board of Revenue Offices, Madras

Thomas Cowper, Lieutenant-Colonel, Bombay Engineers (1781–1825) Town Hall, Bombay

Thomas de Havilland, Colonel, Royal Engineers (1775–1866) St George's Cathedral and St Andrew's Kirk, Madras

Vincent Esch (1876–1950) High Court, High School and railway station, Hyderabad

John Goldingham (1765–1849) Government House, Banqueting Hall and Observatory, Madras

Henry Irwin (1841–1922) Amba Vilas, Mysore; High Court, Madras

Charles Mant, Major, Royal Engineers (1840–81) New Palace, Kolhapur; Mayo College, Ajmer; Lakshmi Vilas, Vadodara (Baroda)

Henry Medd (1892–1977) Cathedral and churches, New Delhi; High Court, Nagpur

George Gilbert Scott (1811–78) Bombay University

Frederick William Stevens (1847–1900) Victoria Terminus station, New Municipal Buildings and Royal Alfred Sailors Home, Bombay

Henry St Clair Wilkins, General, Royal Engineers (1828–96) Secretariat and Public Works Office, Bombay

George Wittet (1880–1926) Post Office, Gateway of India and Prince of Wales Museum, Bombay

able creativity on the part of local architects, as well as those like Scott, who sent out designs from London. Bombay preserves a unique series of imposing High Victorian monuments built in a striking mixture of revived Gothic, Venetian and Mughal modes. Stevens's Victoria Terminus [1E], the masterpiece of the series, is unsurpassed for its immense scale, symmetrical and dramatic arrangement of arcades, turrets and domes, and richly carved and inlaid surfaces. Scott's Bombay University, including the Rajabai Tower that rises over the library, is another fine Neo-Gothic scheme.

Architects at this time also took their inspiration from indigenous traditions, which were beginning to be better appreciated by the end of the 19C. Wittet's Prince of Wales Museum and Post Office in Bombay are based on careful studies of mosques and tombs at Bijapur; his Gateway of India was inspired by ceremonial portals in Ahmedabad in Gujarat. The High Court and Art Gallery in Madras [36B, D], works of Irwin, are closer to the Mughal traditions of Northern India, though with much improvisation. Neo-Mughal schemes were also adopted by Esch for public buildings sponsored by the Nizam of Hyderabad. Chisholm represented a more original approach: the Senate House of Madras University blends Middle-Eastern Islamic forms with Neo-Mughal detailing [36F], and his Art Museum in Thiruvananthapuram presents an equally inventive synthesis [46A].

That this revivalist mode survived into the Independence era is illustrated by the grandly conceived Vidhana Soudha at Bangalore [14B]. This has now been supplanted by the international Modernist and Post-Modernist styles preferred by most architects.

Art

Early sculptural traditions. Sculptural art in Southern India can be traced back to the 2C–1C BC Satavahana period, the earliest examples being the carved reliefs in the Buddhist rock-cut sanctuaries of western Maharashtra. The wall panels at Bhaja [3D] show celestial deities riding majestically through the heavens; stately donor couples in affectionate embrace and riders on animals appear at Karla [3C]. The figures are modelled in robust relief, with finely etched jewellery and costumes.

A contrasting school of sculpture flourished under the Ikshvakus of Andhra Pradesh. Limestone posts, railings and curved drum pieces from 2C–4C AD *stupas* at Amaravati and Nagarjunakonda, now on display in the Archaeological Museum, Vijayapuri [27H], and the Government Museum, Madras [36D], are enlivened with friezes showing scenes from the life of Buddha and episodes from *Jataka* stories. Other panels depict the *stupa* being worshipped by celestials, as well as fully open lotus flowers. Certain compositions and individual figures recall Roman art, suggesting that artistic influences must have accompanied commercial contacts between Southern India and the Mediterranean at this time. Classical traits are especially evident in fully sculpted three-dimensional Buddhas clad in elegant fluted costumes, such as those in the Salar Jung Museum, Hyderabad [26B] and the Archaeological Museum, Amaravati [29K]. That Hindu cults also occasionally resorted to stone carving in these early centuries is illustrated by the emblem under veneration at Gudimallam [35E]. Dated to the 1C BC, this unique *linga* incorporates a fully modelled figure of Shiva, the earliest in Southern Indian art.

Rock-cut sculpture. Buddhist sculpture was much developed under the Vakatakas in the 4C–5C. The rock-cut monasteries and *chaitya* halls at Ajanta [5F] are embellished with fully modelled figures of Buddha seated in teaching posture accompanied by Bodhisattva attendants. Cave 26 is of outstanding interest for its expressive rendition of the Parinirvana, with the recumbent Buddha being mourned by his disciples. Accessory motifs such as flying couples, serpent deities, musicians and amorous maidens decorate the column shafts, brackets and doorways. These themes are fulfilled in Cave 10 (Vishvakarma) at Ellora [5E].

Under the Kalachuris and Early Chalukyas in the 6C–7C, Hindu mythological themes found graphic expression in fully evolved sculptural compositions. The deeply cut panels at Elephanta [2A] are conceived as large tableaux illustrating diverse aspects of Shiva. They are dominated by the colossal triple-headed bust in the middle of the rear wall. This masterpiece contrasts the central introspective face of the god with side female and fierce male faces. A contemporary but contrasting tradition of rock-cut art is found at Badami [22A]. Cave 3, the largest at this site, has bracket figures fashioned as amorous couples embracing

embracing beneath trees. The imposing panels at the ends of the verandah show Vishnu in his boar incarnation and as Trivikrama kicking one leg high. The vitality of the figures is matched by the solidity of the modelling in vivid red sandstone.

This tradition reaches a climax in the 8C Rashtrakuta art of Ellora. Wall panels in Cave 15 (Dashavatara) illustrate Shiva and Vishnu in various mythological appearances, characterised by figures in energetic postures. Cave 21 (Rameshvara) is of outstanding interest for the sensuous beauty of the female figures on the brackets and the images of the river goddesses on the end panels. These sculptural tendencies are fully realised in Cave 16 (Kailasa), where large-scale visualisations of the major deities contrast with relief friezes illustrating *Ramayana* and *Mahabharata* scenes. One celebrated panel shows Shiva, seated with Parvati on Kailasa, being disturbed by multi-headed Ravana.

A quite separate tradition was evolved in the Tamil zone, where Hindu topics achieved a gentle plastic expression in smoothly rounded granite. Nowhere is this better conveyed than in the 7C Pallava period cave-temples and external reliefs at Mamallapuram [37A]. Two large-scale compositions, Krishna lifting up Govardhana to shield the herd of cows, and Arjuna's penance, in which the hero is rewarded with the magic axe from Shiva, are characterised by an unmistakable naturalism and vitality. The same vigour is expressed in Pandyan carvings, such as the savage depiction of Narasimha disembowelling Hiranyakashipu in the 8C cave-temple at Namakkal [42D].

Monolithic granite sculpture is the only aspect of rock-cut art to continue into later centuries. The 10C colossus at Sravana Belgola [18F], which is 17.7m high, shows naked Gommateshvara, the Jain saviour, with his legs and arms overgrown by vines. Later copies are seen at Karkala [17D] and Venoor [17E]. The 16C monoliths of Narasimha, the man-lion incarnation of Vishnu, and of Ganesha are sculpted out of boulders near Hampi [20B]. The finest of several richly decked ceremonial Nandis of the same period is that at Lepakshi [33G].

Stone temple sculpture. Temple exteriors are encrusted with carvings that cover basements, walls, cornices and towers. Sculpted monsters, such as *makaras* and *yalis*, are common motifs on basements, sometimes combined with miniature panels illustrating narrative scenes, as at Darasuram [40F] where the stories of all the Nayanmars are depicted. The basement here is distinguished by leaping horses and spoked wheels suggesting a chariot. The grey-green schist basements of 11C–13C Hoysala temples are even more ornate. The example at Halebid [18B] displays superimposed friezes of precisely rendered elephants, lions, horses, scrollwork, narrative epic scenes, *makaras* and geese with foliated tails.

Sculpted panels set into walls illustrate the full range of Hindu divinities and attendant figures. The 8C Virupaksha Temple at Pattadakal [22D] has major icons of Shiva and Vishnu set into niches on either side of the main entrance; the contemporary Durga Temple at Aihole [22E] presents images of both gods, as well as of Durga in the curving passageway that runs around the sanctuary. Panels in Tamil Nadu temples generally focus on a more restricted range of icons. Shiva as Dakshinamurti, Ardhanarishvara and Brahma appear on three sides of the sanctuary walls of the 9C Nageshvara Temple at Kumbakonam [40G]. The gods are accompanied by sages and maidens. The refinement of the carving, with the figures turned slightly to the wall plane, is unsurpassed. The emphasis on wall sculptures reaches a climax at Thanjavur [40A] and Gangaikondacholapuram [40J] in the 11C, with double tiers of wall panels representing all the important aspects of Shiva, including Natesha, Bhikshatanamurti and Dakshinamurti. The emphasis in 12C temple sculpture shifted to entrance *gopuras*, as at Chidambaram [39H], where female dancers in different poses and river goddesses clutching creepers adorn the jambs within the passageway.

Somewhat different traditions were developed in Karnataka and Andhra Pradesh at this time. The walls of the Halebid Temple consist entirely of carved panels set at angles to each other. Hindu divinities with richly decorated costumes and headdresses stand beneath luxuriant scrollwork or foliage. A similar sculptural density is seen in the (mostly) 16C Chennakeshava temple at Pushpagiri [34B] and the contemporary *gopuras* at Tadpatri [33B]. The 15C Hazara Rama Temple at Vijayanagara [20C] is covered with *Ramayana* reliefs, repeated with variations on the compound walls of the complex. The outer faces of these walls present a unique array of royal topics: processions of elephants and horses, parades of militia, lines of dancing girls and female musicians. Enclosure walls of the contemporary Srisailam Temple [32C] display another series of carved panels showing scenes from Shaiva mythology.

The stone towers of shrines are often enlivened with fine carvings of divinities. Dancing Shiva is a popular icon in 8C–9C monuments, as can be seen on the frontal panels of the towers rising over the temples at Alampur [32B] and the splendid image set into the tower above the main sanctuary at Kodumbalur [41D]. Temple towers from the 13C onwards tended to be fashioned out of brick and plaster, thereby initiating the art of polychromed stucco. The superstructures of sanctuaries and *gopuras* are provided with a profuse imagery, all brightly painted. Nowhere is this better illustrated than at Madurai [44A], where the 17C quartet of outer *gopuras* presents a dazzling assemblage of vividly coloured plaster divinities, guardians, attendants and animals. The horseshoe-shaped arched ends of the capping roofs are transformed into monster masks surrounded by flaming tufts, all rendered in deeply modelled plaster.

Temple interiors are no less sculptural. Columns in Pallava architecture generally have seated or rearing lions at the bases, as in the 8C Kailasanatha Temple at Kanchipuram [37F]. This theme is only fully developed in Vijayanagara times, as is obvious in the 16C hall addition to the Virupaksha Temple at Hampi, which has rearing *yalis* with riders. A similar use of animals and warriors, together with female attendants bearing offerings, is seen in the temples at Tadpatri. The columns in the outer halls at Vellore [38A] and at Srirangam [41B] are fashioned into leaping *yalis* and horses ridden by armed warriors; lesser warriors beneath battle with wild panthers and other animals. Various deities, including Manmatha and Rati riding on parrots, carved almost in the round, animate the hall in the outermost enclosure of the Varadaraja complex at Kanchipuram.

This theme continued to evolve in Tamil Nadu under the Nayakas in the 17C, as can be seen at Madurai and Alagarkoil [44C], where divinities and epic heroes project outwards from the columns lining the central aisles of halls and corridors. The Pudu Mandapa at Madurai serves as a royal gallery, portraying all the Madurai Nayakas up to Tirumala, the patron of the monument. The figures are shown with swelling limbs, richly adorned with jewelled costumes, crowns and daggers. A comparable gallery is seen at Srimushnam [39I] where the Gingee Nayakas are depicted on the central columns of the hall in front of the main shrine. A later example is the outer corridor of the Rameswaram [44J] Temple, where the piers are enlivened with effigies of the Setupati rulers. Meanwhile, the emphasis on corridors lined with *yali* columns continued, as at Srivilliputtur [44G]. Columns with divinities and heroes carved almost in three dimensions are also found in temples at Suchindram [45N] and Thiruvananthapuram [46A].

Other parts of temple interiors also received elaborate treatment. The angled brackets in the porches and halls of Hoysala and Kakatiya monuments are fashioned as maidens and embracing couples beneath trees. Elegant females adjusting their hair, admiring themselves in a mirror and playing with a parrot adorn brackets in temples at Belur [18A] and Palampet [28C]. The maidens at Palampet have distinctive elongated bodies and sinuous postures.

Ceilings are equally ornate compositions, generally with deeply cut lotuses surrounded by flying figures or sets of Dikpalas. The Aihole temples show trios of divinities, one set now removed to the Prince of Wales Museum, Bombay [1B]. The refinement of the Natesha image on the ceiling of the remotely located Temple at Aralaguppe [18E] is unique. So, too, are the textile patterns incised on the ceiling of the Temple at Keladi [19B].

Bronzes. The larger temples in Southern India are repositories of fine bronzes. Elaborately dressed and jewelled bronzes receive worship in sanctuaries and serve as processional images on festival occasions. Many fine examples have now been removed from temples and are on display in the Government Museum, Madras, and the Art Gallery, Thanjavur, the largest and most impressive collections in Southern India.

Bronzes from the 10C–12C Chola period are admired for the elegant postures and gentle facial expressions. The smoothly modelled bodies of the figures and finely detailed jewellery and costumes which they wear represent the highest achievement of the bronze casters. Representations of Shiva include the celebrated Nataraja icon, which shows the god with one foot upraised, his hair flying outwards, surrounded by a fiery halo. The example from Tiruvengadu in Madras is unsurpassed for its poised majesty. The image of Ardhanarishvara in the same collection perfectly balances the male and female bodies of Shiva and Devi, here combined in a single figure. The god also appears with Parvati, sometimes with the infant Subrahmanya in Somaskanda family groups. Vishnu is usually accompanied by consorts, and Rama is often shown together with Sita and Lakshmana. Saints such as Sundarar and Manikkavachakar appear as youthful devotees of Shiva, their hands brought together in adoration.

That Chola art was not confined to Hindu icons is demonstrated by the Buddhist bronzes from Nagapattinam [40M], now in Madras, which show the Master standing within an ornate frame or seated beneath a tree. The remarkable bronzes under veneration in the Manjunatha Temple on the outskirts of Mangalore [17A] depict Buddha as Manjushri and Lokeshvara.

The 16C–17C bronzes produced in Vijayanagara and Nayaka times rival their Chola predecessors in quality, such as the seated icon of Kali with flame-like hair in Thanjavur, and the image of Krishna dancing on the serpent, now in the

Prince of Wales Museum, Bombay. Effigies of Krishnadevaraya and his two queens in the Temple at Tirumala [35B] testify to the development of portraiture during this period. Another fine portrait is that of Vijayaraghava Nayaka, in the Thanjavur Gallery.

Images produced for Jain worship illustrate a further aspect of bronze art. The Jain Matha at Sravana Belgola houses a large collection of Tirthankara icons, some going back to the 9C. Later images are distinguished by their ornate frames. Other fine pieces are displayed in the Chandranatha Basti at Mudabidri [17C].

Wood and ivory carving. Wood carving was evidently widespread in Southern India, but only a fraction of this tradition survives. In Tamil Nadu and parts of Karnataka and Andhra Pradesh, great wheeled chariots are parked outside temple gateways, waiting for the festival occasions when they are pulled through the streets. Only then are they decked with bamboo and cloth to shelter the metal images of gods and goddesses brought out of the temple. The chariots are entirely wooden in construction. Protruding beams carved with beasts and monster masks provide a framework for tiers of panels that cantilever outwards. These are sculpted with a full range of divinities and accessory figures, as can be seen in the trio of chariots parked in the main street at Chidambaram. The small example in front of the Ramaswami Temple at Kumbakonam is carved entirely with *Ramayana* subjects.

Kerala preserves the most extensive evidence of wood carving in Southern India. The temples at Ettumanur [47G], Kaviyur [47K] and Chengannur [47L], for instance, have sanctuaries surrounded by timber screens framed by relief panels illustrating mythological subjects. Wooden struts, angled beneath roof overhangs, are fashioned as three-dimensional figures, generally female musicians and dancers, as well as *yalis*. Struts on shrines at Peruvanam [47V] and Taliparamba [48H] show figures in twisting postures holding bows and arrows, in illustration of the story of Arjuna fighting Shiva as the hunter. The entrance porches and open halls have miniature wooden brackets fashioned as characters from the *Ramayana* or the Arjuna story; beams show friezes of narrative episodes. The ceilings above are divided into compartments filled with divinities and lotus flowers, a common scheme combining Brahma with the Dikpalas, as in the temple at Thiruvanchikulam in Kodungallur [47T].

Church art also exploited the skills of Southern Indian wood carvers. The richly carved and gilded altarpieces in the cathedrals and chapels of Old Goa [11B] show polychromed figures of Christ and saints accompanied by winged angels. The swaying figure of St Francis Xavier in the Cathedral of Bom Jesus is a typical example of the exuberant manner developed by Goan artists. Pulpits have their sides and canopies covered with saints in the company of angels; the same is found on the panels that sometimes line chancel walls, as at Rachol [13D]. That this exuberant figural style was not confined to Goa is demonstrated at Kaduthuruthi [47F] in Kerala, which preserves one of the most elaborate altarpieces in Southern India.

Ivories often imitate wooden figures. Goan work is celebrated for delicate images of the Christ Child, the Crucifixion and Christ as the Good Shepherd, fine examples of which are displayed in the Prince of Wales Museum, Bombay, and the Museum of Christian Art, Rachol. Ivory carving in Southern India was by no means confined to Christian subjects; figurines produced under the Nayakas of Tamil Nadu show divinities, embracing courtly couples and even Europeans with dogs, as can be seen in the Art Museums at Srirangam and Madurai.

Mural painting. Pictorial traditions in Southern India date back to the 2C–1C BC, as indicated by fragmentary compositions in the rock-cut halls at Ajanta; more complete cycles from the 5C survive at the same site. The Ajanta murals are unparalleled for the wide range of subjects illustrated and the assured mastery of the medium. Buddhist divinities and incidents from the life of the Master appear repeatedly. Vibrant episodes from the *Jataka* legends show crowded compositions depicting life in the court, town, hermitage or forest, with princes, consorts, attendants, musicians and servants. Never again did Southern Indian mural painting exhibit such virtuosity and freedom, nor such perspective-like effects. The colours are harmoniously blended, with ochres, browns and greens predominating; the linework is sinuous and sensitive.

Except for tantalising fragments at Badami (Cave 3), Ellora (Cave 16) and Kanchipuram (Kailasanatha temple) [37F], dating from the 6C–8C, there is an almost total lack of mural art in Southern India until the Vijayanagara and Nayaka periods. The first great cycle of paintings to be preserved from this era is that at Lepakshi [33G]. The frescos on the ceiling of this 16C temple show the donors of the monument in the company of male and female retinues, dressed in vivid costumes. Narrative compositions include one panel showing the boar hunt of Arjuna and another of Virabhadra, the fierce form of Shiva to whom the temple is dedicated.

17C paintings on the ceilings of temples in Tamil Nadu are generally supplied with identifying labels. One of the most complete cycles is that in the Shivakamasundari shrine at Chidambaram. The compositions here are characterised by a fluid linework and bright red, ochre and green tones, mostly on white backgrounds. The panels, arranged in narrow registers, depict the story of Bhikashatanamurti and Mohini seducing the wives of the sages. The long and eventful life of the saint Manikkavachakar is related in some 40 panels. Animated scenes on red backgrounds, depicting temple festivities, appear on the ceiling of an accessory hall within the complex at Tiruvarur [40L]. The story of Muchukunda, another Shaiva saint, here forms the subject of a series of animated episodes.

Painted Jain narratives cover the ceiling of the Temple at Tiruparuttikunram [37F], on the outskirts of Kanchipuram. The stories of Rishabhadeva and Vardhamana, two popular Jain saviours, follow a standard pattern, with courtly scenes crowded with processions alternating with forest episodes. A fascinating cycle of murals is seen in the upper chambers of the entrance *gopura* at Tiruppudaimarudur [45K], where varied mythological subjects alternate with scenes of boats transporting merchants and soldiers, all executed in a bold linear style.

The Ramalinga Vilasa at Ramanathapuram [44H], the residence of the Setupati rulers, is of outstanding interest for its extensive murals executed in vivid reds, ochres and blues. As well as stories from the Hindu epics and depictions of shrines within the Setupati territories, these 18C paintings show reception scenes, hunting expeditions and battle episodes.

18C–19C paintings in Karnataka belong to a different tradition, partly revived by Tipu Sultan, and for this reason influenced by provincial Mughal art. The Daria Daulat Bagh at Srirangapattana [15C] has murals depicting military victories over the British. Royal pastimes are shown on the walls of the upper chambers of the Chamarajendra Art Gallery in Mysore [15A]. An engaging but little-known cycle of paintings is preserved on the ceilings of the temple at Sibi [14D]. Here, mythological topics contrast with courtly scenes and parades of troops in European dress. One large composition places flute-playing Krishna in a remarkable rocky landscape. A comparable array of ceiling panels is seen at Hampi [20B].

A contrasting, but equally spirited, mural tradition is preserved in Kerala, with most examples dating from the 17C–19C. The Kerala style is distinguished by compositions that extend continuously across the walls of temples and palaces. The crowded panels are dominated by figures with exaggerated expressions dressed in elaborately jewelled costumes and crowns; the vigorous linework contrasts with deep red, green, ochre and yellow tones. Murals at Vaikom [47E] show Vishnu riding on Garuda and Rama battling with Ravana. Large-scale panels at Ettumanur juxtapose Vishnu reclining on the serpent with dancing Shiva surrounded by celestials. The compositions at Tripráyar [47U] concentrate on *Ramayana* combat scenes and the story of Narasimha.

These and other mythological themes appear in the murals of the royal complexes at Padmanabhapuram [45O] and at Mattancheri in Kochi [47A]. Representations of Vishnu as Padmanabha reclining on the multi-headed serpent cover the walls of the shrine room in the tower that rises in middle of the Padmanabhapuram Palace. *Ramayana* scenes decorate the king's bedchamber in the Mattancheri Palace.

Fine Arts. Southern India is celebrated for its **decorative arts**, examples of which are on show in museum collections in Bombay, Hyderabad and Madras. **Miniature painting** was much favoured by courts at Ahmadnagar [6A], Bijapur [23A] and Golconda [26E] in the 16C–17C. Brilliantly coloured pages portray royal, noble and saintly personalities in formal postures, animated hunting expeditions and animal fights, and languishing maidens and youths. In the 18C, miniature painting came under the sway of provincial Mughal art, as practiced in Hyderabad, Shorapur [24G] and Kurnool [32A]. New schools appeared in the 19C at the Maratha and Wodeyar courts of Thanjavur and Mysore. **Paintings on wood and glass** illustrate traditional South Indian mythological and courtly subjects; Thanjavur paintings are recognised by their encrusted textures and mirrored surfaces.

Southern Indian *metalwork* attained technical perfection at Bidar [25A], after which an inlaid technique known as *bidri* became widely known. 17C–18C ewers, basins, bowls and *huqqa* bases have delicately worked silver designs employing stylised petals, leaves and arabesque motifs. Ornate weapons express another aspect of Southern Indian metalwork. The largest assemblage, which comes from the Thanjavur armoury and is now in Madras, includes *pattar* swords, *katar* daggers and ceremonial *ankushas*, or elephant goads, many with pierced metal hilts and handles.

Brightly printed and dyed cotton **textiles**, known as *kalamkaris*, produced at workshops on the Coromandel Coast, were exported in bulk to Europe and Southeast Asia in the 16C–18C. (Some of the best-preserved examples are now in London, Paris and New York.) Temple cloths and canopies used for display on festival occasions are divided into strips crowded with mythological figures with labels in the framing bands, sometimes surrounding enlarged panels, exactly as in ceiling paintings.

Further Reading

Few general studies focus exclusively on Southern Indian culture, history, religious traditions and monuments. The following should be consulted for their relevant chapters or sections. Most works offer comprehensive bibliographies.

The Land. Gordon Johnson, *Cultural Atlas of India* (Time-Life Books, Amsterdam, 1995) provides a well-illustrated introduction to India's geography, history and culture. For more detailed information, see Joseph E. Schwartzberg (ed.), *A Historical Atlas of South Asia* (2nd edn, Oxford University Press, New York, 1992). A useful reference work is Francis Robinson (ed.), *The Cambridge Encylopedia of India, etc.* (Cambridge University Press, Cambridge, 1989).

History. A comprehensive survey is offered by Hermann Kulke and Dietmar Rothermund, *A History of India* (Croom Helm, Beckenham, 1986). K. A. Nilakanta Sastri, *A History of South India from Prehistoric Times to the Fall of Vijayanagara* (3rd edn, Oxford University Press, Madras, 1966) remains the best introduction to the region. A more general work is Francis Watson, *India, A Concise History* (Thames & Hudson, London, 1993). For more specialised topics, see John F. Richards, 'The Mughal Empire', Burton Stein, 'Vijayanagara', Richard Eaton, 'Social History of the Deccan', and Stewart Gordon, 'The Marathas', in *The New Cambridge History of India* (Vols I.2, I.5, I.7 and II.4, Cambridge University Press, Cambridge, 1982–98). For a perceptive survey of India since Independence, see Sunil Khilnani, *The Idea of India* (Hamish Hamilton, London, 1997).

Religion. Diana L. Eck, *Darshan: Seeing the Divine Image in India*, (2nd edn, Anima Books, Chambersburg, 1985), Madeleine Biardeau, *Hinduism: Anthropology of a Civilisation* (Oxford University Press, Delhi, 1989) and C. J. Fuller, *The Camphor Flame: Popular Hinduism and Society in India* (Penguin Books, New Delhi, 1992) provide approachable and insightful introductions to Hinduism. Margaret and James Stutley, *A Dictionary of Hinduism: Its Mythology, Folklore and Development 1500 BC–AD 1500* (Heritage Publishers, New Delhi, 1986) is a helpful reference work.

Edward Conze, *Buddhism, Its Essence and Development* (Harper & Row, New York, 1975) may be consulted for the general background on Buddhism, as may Peter Harvey, *An Introduction to Buddhism: Teachings, History and Practices* (Cambridge University Press, Cambridge, 1990). For Jainism, see Peter Dunday, *The Jains* (Routledge, London, 1992). Christianity and Islam are covered by Susan Bayly, *Saints, Goddesses and Kings: Muslims and Christians in South Indian Society 1700–1900* (Cambridge University Press, Cambridge, 1989).

Architecture. Christopher Tadgell, *The History of Architecture in India: From the Dawn of Civilization to the End of the Raj* (Architecture Design and Technology Press, London, 1990) offers a broad and generously illustrated survey. This may be supplemented by Susan L. Huntington, *The Art of Ancient India, Buddhist, Hindu, Jain* (Weatherhill, New York and Tokyo, 1985) and J. C. Harle, *The Art and Architecture of the Indian Subcontinent* (Penguin Books, London, 1986). For the later centuries not covered in these last two works, see George Michell, *Architecture and Art of Southern India: Vijayanagara and the Successor States* (Cambridge University Press, Cambridge, 1995), George Michell and Mark Zebrowski, *Architecture and Art of the Deccan: 14th to 18th centuries* (Cambridge University Press, Cambridge, 1998) and Philip Davies, *Splendours of the Raj, British Architecture in India, 1660 to 1947* (John Murray, London, 1985).

Art. In addition to the works mentioned above, T. Richard Blurton, *Hindu Art* (British Museum Press, London, 1992) places sculpture and painting objects with an appropriate religious context. For wooden sculpture, see George Michell, *Living Wood: Sculptural Traditions of Southern India* (Marg Publications, Bombay, 1992). Southern Indian paintings are illustrated in Madanjeet Singh, *Ajanta: Painting of the Sacred and the Secular* (Macmillan, New York, 1965), Amancharla Gopala Rao, *Lepakshi* (Andhra Pradesh Lalit Kala Akademi, Hyderabad, 1969) and Mark Zebrowski, *Deccan Painting* (Sotheby Publications, London, 1983). Metalwork and textiles are covered in S. Stronge, 'The Sultanates of the Deccan' in John Guy and Deborah Swallow (eds), *Arts of India: 1550–1900* (Victoria & Albert Museum, London, 1990).

Literature. Bruce Palling, *India, a Literary Companion* (John Murray, London, 1992) offers a stimulating selection of extracts. Southern India is a constant presence in modern Indian writing in English. Malgudi, an imagined town located vaguely in Karnataka or Tamil Nadu, appears repeatedly in the amusing novellas of R.K. Narayan. Rohin Mistry's, *Such a Long Journey* and *A Fine Balance* (Faber & Faber, London, 1991 and 1995) are both situated in Bombay. The first two parts of Salman Rushdie's *The Moor's Last Sigh* (Vintage Books, London, 1996) are set in Kochi and Bombay. Kerala serves as the background for Arundhati Roy's *The God of Small Things* (Flamingo, London, 1997).

Ornithology. Readers interested in finding out more about the birds of Southern India may wish to consult, R. Grimmett, C. Inskipp and T. Inskipp, *Birds of the Indian Sub-Continent* (Helm, London, 1998).

THE GUIDE

Maharashtra

Any tour of the largest and most populous state in Southern India begins at
Bombay [1], a city noted for its distinguished heritage of 19C Neo-Gothic
monuments.

Day trips from Bombay can include visits to the 16C Portuguese fort at **Vasai**
[2E] and the island citadel of **Janjira** [2I], headquarters of the Sidi admirals in
the 18C.

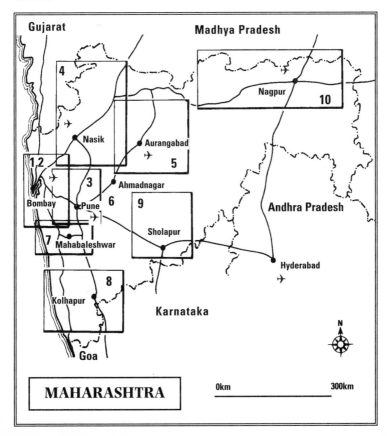

MAHARASHTRA

A picturesque route through the rugged bluffs of the Sahyadri ranges links Bombay to **Pune** [3], capital of the 18C Peshwa rulers. Excursions from here can be made to **Nasik** [4], one of the holiest cities of Southern India, or to **Ahmadnagar** [5], with its palaces, mosques and tombs associated with the 16C Nizam Shahi kings.

South of Pune lies the hill station of **Mahabaleshwar** [7], a fashionable resort since British days, surrounded by remote mountain strongholds such as **Raigad** [7C]. The highway running south passes through **Kolhapur** [8], once a small princely state, on the way to **Mapusa** [12] in Goa or to **Hubli** [21] in northern Karnataka.

Southeast of Pune lies **Sholapur** [9], with its important fort and nearby pilgrimage shrine of **Pandharpur** [9G]. **Bijapur** [23] in northern Karnataka and **Hyderabad** [26] in Andhra Pradesh are easily accessible from here.

Plane is the preferred mode of transport from Bombay to **Aurangabad** [5], the residence of the Mughal conquerors of Maharashtra in the 18C. The city makes a convenient base from which to visit the rock-cut sites of **Ellora** [5E] and **Ajanta** [5F], and the majestic citadel of **Daulatabad** [5C], Maharashtra's principal historical attractions. **Nagpur** [10], in the extreme eastern end of the state, is the nearest stopping-off point for the wildlife park at **Navegaon** [10D].

1 · Bombay

Officially renamed Mumbai in 1995 but still referred to by its old name, Bombay is the capital of Maharashtra and Southern India's largest and most cosmopolitan city. Though Bombay suffers from overcrowding, traffic jams and air pollution, these ever-worsening problems have not obscured the beauty of its natural setting. The city occupies a long thin piece of land, originally a string of seven islands separated by lagoons and creeks, jutting out into the Arabian Sea. The ocean frontage on the west is marked by tree-lined hills interspersed with sandy stretches, such as Back Bay, which sweeps in a broad curve south from Malabar Hill. Bombay Harbour separates the city from the mainland to the east, beyond which rise the rugged ridges of the Western Ghats.

Bombay preserves a splendid architectural heritage, its noble ensemble of Victorian monuments being the finest in the country. The principal examples are located in the busy downtown area, near the **Gateway of India** [A], the **Fort Area** [C], **Maidan** [D] and **Victoria Terminus** [E]. At least one full day will be required to cover the buildings described here. Other notable historical buildings are located in **Colaba** [F] to the south and in the residential districts of **Malabar Hill** [G], **Byculla**, **Parel** and **Mahim** [H] to the north. These zones may be combined variously into one or more half-day tours. Full-day excursions to sites beyond the metropolitan limits are described in the following itinerary.

■ **Transport**. Bombay (STD code 022) is served by international airlines offering direct flights from Europe and Southeast Asia. International flights arrive and depart at Sahar International Airport (☎ 6329090), and domestic ones at Santa Cruz Airport (☎ 6144433). Internal flights link Bombay with Delhi and Calcutta, as well as with Bangalore [14], Hyderabad [26], Madras

[36], Thiruvananthapuram [46] and Kochi [47]. Flights within Maharashtra are available to Pune [3], Aurangabad [5], Nasik [4] and Nagpur [10]. Several companies serve Panaji [11] in Goa, now also accessible by a daily hydrofoil service.

Trains connect Bombay to all these destinations. The Konkan Railway, currently under construction, will link Bombay with Panaji and points in between. The Central Railway is at Victoria Terminus (☎ 2623535) and the Western Railway at Churchgate (☎ 2031952). Local trains arrive and depart from Bombay Central Station (☎ 4933535).

Buses travel from Bombay to all major towns in Maharashtra, as well as to Hyderabad, Bangalore, Mangalore and Goa (☎ 2660253). There is also a comprehensive network of local bus services. Yellow-topped taxis operate throughout Bombay, and horse-drawn carriages and auto-rickshaws are available in central areas.

Cars can be hired Budget and Hertz (☎ 4942644), Auto Comforts (☎ 4936581) and Blaze (☎ 2020073).

■ **Accommodation**. Downtown Bombay is the setting for luxurious hotels, the most famous being the *Taj Mahal* (☎ 2023366), overlooking Bombay Harbour, and the *Oberoi* (☎ 2025757), facing Back Bay. First-class standards are also offered at the *Ambassador* (☎ 2041131), *Hotel Nataraj* (☎ 2044161) and *Hotel President* (☎ 21500808). More modestly priced hotels are found throughout the city, particularly in the streets behind the *Taj Mahal*.

Because the airport is at Santa Cruz, 22km north of downtown Bombay, many visitors with overnight or early morning connections chose to stay at **Juhu**, 10km northwest of the airport. This formerly quiet seaside resort is now crowded with hotels, the most comfortable being the *Ramada Inn Palm Grove* (☎ 6112323), *Hotel Sea Princess* (☎ 6117600) and *Holiday Inn* (☎ 6204444). The *Centaur Airport* (☎ 6116660) is conveniently located within walking distance of the domestic terminal.

■ **Tourist Information**. The Government of India tourist office is at 123 Maharshi Karve Road, opposite Churchgate Station (☎ 2032932); tourist office counters are also maintained at both the international and domestic airport terminals. The Maharashtra Tourist Development Corporation (MTDC) has its head office at Express Towers, Nariman Point (☎ 2024482). Their booking offices are located on Madame Cama Road (☎ 2026713), also at Victoria Terminus and the domestic and international airport terminals.

■ **Travel agents and tour companies**. Among the many companies offering services for hotel bookings and travel arrangements are *American Express*, Majithia Chamber, 276 Dr D. N. Road (☎ 2048949), *Cox & Kings*, Grindlays Bank Building, Dr D. N. Road (☎ 2043065), *Sita*, 8 Atlanta, Nariman Point (☎ 233155) and *Thomas Cook*, Cooks Building, Dr D. N. Road (☎ 258556).

■ **Consulates**. The **British** Consulate is at Maker Chambers IV, Nariman Point (☎ 2832330); the **USA** Consulate is at Lincoln House, Bhulabhai Desai Road (formerly Warden Road) (☎ 3633611); the **Canadian** Consulate is at Maker Chambers VI, Nariman Point (☎ 2876028).

■ **Banks**. The main *State Bank of India* offices are at Samachar Marg, Vir Nariman Road (formerly Churchgate Street) and the Centaur Airport Hotel. The *Bank of India* and *Bank of America* are at Express Towers, Nariman Point. *American Express* and *Citibank* are on Dr D.N. Road; *Barclays Bank* at Maker Tower F, Prakash Pethe Marg (formerly Cuffe Parade); *Grindlays Bank* on Mahatma Gandhi Road. Money can also be changed at the airport and at the Bureau de Change at the Air India Building on Nariman Point.

■ **Post Offices**. The main Post Office is on Nagar Chowk; there are smaller Post Offices around the city.

■ **Hospitals and Chemists**. The *Bombay Hospital* is on Thackersay Marg (formerly New Marine Lines Road) (☎ 2863343), *Prince Aly Khan Hospital* is on Nesbit Road (☎ 3754343), and *St George's Hospital* is on P. D'Mello Road (formerly Frere Road) (☎ 2620301). The emergency ambulance telephone number is 102. Most hospitals have day-and-night chemists nearby, and some top hotels have pharmacies on the premises.

History

Bombay's strategic location explains its remarkable commercial history, profiting from seaborne links with Gujarat to the north and Kerala to the south, as well as with ports on the the Persian Gulf, the Red Sea and the Swahili coast of East Africa. The arrival of the Portuguese at the beginning of the 16C marked the beginning of European domination of the Arabian Sea traffic. In 1535 the Portuguese concluded a treaty with Bahadur Shah of Gujarat, granting them trading rights at Bombay and nearby Vasai [2E] and Chaul [2G]. Even so, Bombay was little developed at first. The most celebrated European to live there in the later 16C was Garcia Orta, a physician and botanist. His Manor House, at the time the largest at Bombay, later became the residence of the Portuguese Governors. Meanwhile, Parel and Mahim, two of the northern islands of Bombay, were taken over by the Franciscans.

By the turn of the 17C Bombay had emerged as a lively port. Its growing wealth attracted the English, who landed in 1626, burning down the Manor House, but this raid did little to curb Portuguese activities. Competition with newly arrived Dutch merchants in the area persuaded the Directors of the newly formed East India Company in London to establish trading stations on the Arabian Sea coast. Diplomatic negotiations with Portugal culminated in the marriage agreement of 1668 between Charles II and the Infanta Donna Catherina, by which the islands of Bombay passed into the possession of the English crown.

Under the English, Bombay developed steadily into a lucrative port. Gerald Aungier, Governor in 1669–77, did much to improve the settlement, remodelling the Manor House, thereafter known as the Castle, establishing the first church and building forts on rocky promontories. Bombay became a haven for oppressed minorities, most notably the Parsis, who arrived after 1670, and later the Jews. In 1708 Bombay displaced Surat in Gujarat as the principal headquarters of the East India Company on the Arabian Sea coast. The area around the Castle, known as the Fort, was strengthened with earthen ramparts to shield British fleets from attacks by the Marathas, the leading power on the mainland in the 18C. Under William Hornby, Governor in 1771–84, the ramparts were replaced by stone walls and gates.

Bombay grew rapidly in the 19C, mainly due to private enterprise which was much stimulated by the abolition of the Company's trade monopoly. This era witnessed the rise in the fortunes of Parsi and Jewish families such as the Wadias, Jeejeebhoys, Tatas, 'Readymoneys' and Sassoons. The first railway in India was completed in 1854, connecting Bombay with Thana on the mainland; other lines followed. With the disruption of cotton deliveries from the United States to Europe due to the American Civil War of 1861–65, Bombay boomed as an alternative source of supply, textile mills springing up all over the city. The opening of the Suez Canal in 1868 brought Bombay closer to Europe. The increased volume of shipping necessitated a new dockyard with extensive shipbuilding facilities, which was laid out on the Harbour side of the city.

Bombay's expansion was led by dynamic figures like Governors Mountstuart Elphinstone (1819–27) and Bartle Frere (1862–67). These Governors were responsible for ambitious reclamation schemes which transformed Bombay into a continuous peninsula by draining the lagoons and joining together the islands. Additional land was gained by demolishing the walls and gates surrounding the Fort. This provided a setting for a new and imposing series of municipal, educational and commercial monuments designed in an exotic variation of the Victorian Neo-Gothic style. Many of these survive to give the city its distinctive architectural personality.

Bombay's development has been sustained throughout the 20C, with new residential and commercial complexes crowding the reclaimed land fringing Back Bay. Though much of the city's heavy industry has now moved beyond the metropolitan limits, the port continues to benefit from the largest and busiest dockyard in the country. A thriving film industry lends the city a certain glamour and notoriety, to the extent that the 'Bollywood' stars enjoy what seems like phenomenal adulation. The enormous, garish posters and hoardings advertising new films are to be seen everywhere in Bombay.

A. Gateway of India

The tour of downtown Bombay described here begins at the **Gateway of India**, a prominent landmark overlooking the Harbour. Erected in 1927 on Apollo Bunder (a corruption of local words meaning 'fish quay'), the Gateway was designed by George Wittet to commemorate the visit of George V and Queen Mary on their way to the Delhi Darbar of 1911. It was the point of departure for the last British regiment to leave India in 1948. In spite of these British associations, the Gateway is clearly modelled on Indian prototypes, being inspired by the ceremonial portals of mosques in Ahmedabad, capital of Gujarat. Its triple arches lead to a central hall with side chambers, all domed. The wider and higher arches in the middle are flanked by part-octagonal buttresses capped with tiered domical finials. The narrower, lower side arches contain doorways framed by pierced stone screens with varied geometric patterns. The bold eaves carried on curved brackets unify the whole scheme. The small garden in front forms part of a civic improvement scheme and is now a favourite picnic spot. An equestrian **Statue of Shivaji**, was placed here in 1961. Launches leave for

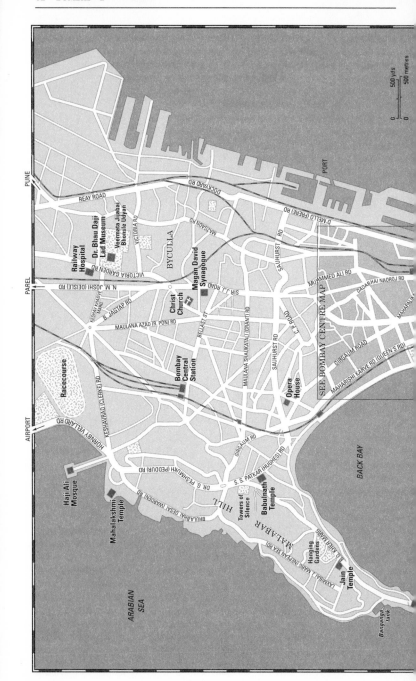

500 yds
500 metres

PUNE

REAY ROAD

DOCKYARD RD

D'MELLO (FRERE) RD

PORT

Railway Hospital

Dr. Bhau Daji Lad Museum

Veermata Jijabai Bhonsle Udyan

VICTORIA RD

BYCULLA

MAZAGON RD

PAREL

N. M. JOSHI (DEISLE) RD

KESHAV KHADE MARG

B. JAGTAP RD

MAULANA AZAD (R. PON) RD

Magan David Synagogue

Christ Church

SIR J.J. ROAD

BELAST ST

MAULANA SHAUKATALI (GRANT) RD

SAUHURST RD

C. ROAD

SAUHURST RD

MUHMMED ALI RD

DADABHAI NAOROJ RD

GIRGAUM ROAD

MAHARSHI KARVE RD (QUEEN'S RD)

SEE BOMBAY CENTRE MAP

AIRPORT

HORNBY VELARD RD

KESHAVRAO (CLERKE) RD

Racecourse

Bombay Central Station

Opera House

DR. G. PESHMUKH (PEDDUR) RD

GIRGAUM RD

BACK BAY

Haji Ali Mosque

Mahalakshmi Temple

BHULABHAI DESAI (WARDEN) RD

S. S. PATKAR (HUGHES) RD

Towers of Silence

Babulnath Temple

HILL

MALABAR

Hanging Gardens

LAXMIBAI J. MARG (NEPEAN SEA RD)

B. G. KHER MARG

Jain Temple

ARABIAN SEA

Banganga tank

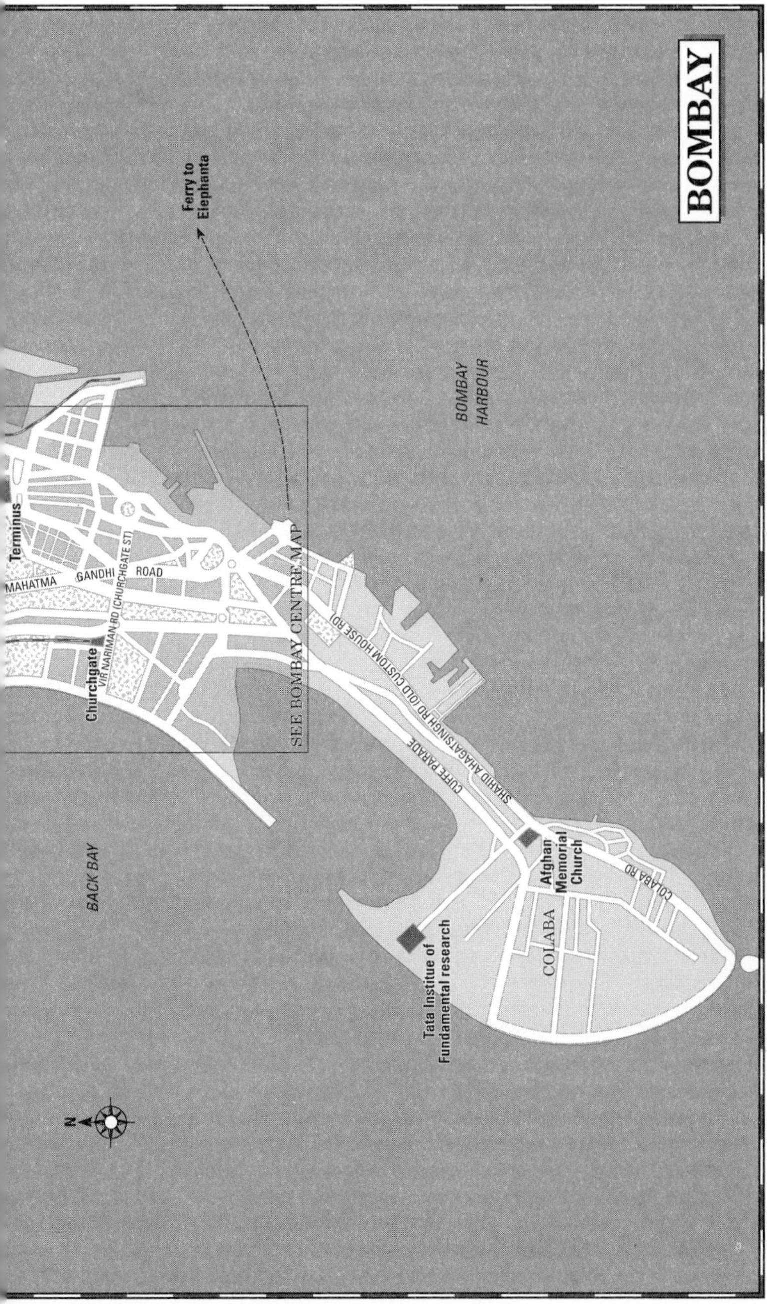

BOMBAY

Ferry to Elephanta

BOMBAY HARBOUR

Terminus

MAHATMA

GANDHI ROAD

VIR NARIMAN RD (CHURCHGATE ST)

Churchgate

SEE BOMBAY CENTRE MAP

SHAHID BHAGATSINGH RD (OLD CUSTOM HOUSE RD)

CUFFE PARADE

BACK BAY

Tata institue of
Fundamental research

COLABA

Afghan
Memorial
Church

COLABA RD

N

Elephanta [2A] and Alibag [2G] from the jetty behind the Gateway.

The Statue of Shivaji is overshadowed by the tower of the **Taj Mahal Hotel** annex. This adjoins the original building built by Jamsetji Nusserwanji Tata, a prominent Parsi businessman who is supposed to have suffered the humiliation of being asked to leave Watson's Hotel, then the best in Bombay, on the grounds that he was a native. He swore that he would one day build a more luxurious hotel of his own. Completed in 1904 at a cost of half a million pounds, the Hotel faces east towards Bombay Harbour. Its façade presents a busy but symmetrical assemblage of arcades, balcony projections, gabled turrets and domical towers. The composition is dominated by a central octagonal dome capped with an open pavilion and flanked by a quartet of smaller domes that roof an interior staircase decorated with cast-iron balconies. The residential wings on either side have corridors originally open to the sky for natural ventilation.

Just behind the Statue of Shivaji is the **Yacht Club** of 1880–83. Its pleasant clutter of arcades and gables is offset by a rounded corner tower. A short street passing to one side of the Club arrives at the spacious S. P. Mukharji Chowk (formerly Wellington Circle) with **Wellington Fountain** in the middle. This was erected in 1865 in honour of the Duke of Wellington, who visited Bombay in 1801 and 1804.

A varied ensemble of buildings surveys the traffic. On the east side of the Chowk is the **Maharashtra State Police Headquarters** (permission required to visit), built as the Royal Alfred Sailors' Home and then used by the legislature of the Bombay Presidency, later the State of Maharashtra. Prior to its construction in 1872, this was the site of a European cemetery. The Home marks the beginning of the career of Frederick William Stevens, one of Bombay's chief architects. Conceived in the Neo-Gothic manner, with arcades headed by polychrome stonework, the building has a central four-storeyed wing. The relief compositions in the upper gable depict Neptune with nymphs and dolphins, an obvious salute to Bombay's seaborne trade.

The commercial and residential buildings on the south side of the Chowk echo the Neo-Gothic style of the Sailor's Home, though with the addition of Mughal-derived portals and turrets. They contrast with the **Royal Institute of Science**, a vast Neo-Classical pile occupying the west side of the Chowk at the beginning of Mahatma Gandhi Road. The Institute owes its foundation to Parsi and Jewish benefactors, who commissioned Wittet for a new building in 1910. The yellow basalt façade is dominated by a corner portico with solid Ionic columns and a domed hall beyond. The newly opened **National Gallery of Modern Art** occupies part of the premises.

On the north side of Mukharji Chowk is the **Prince of Wales Museum**, the largest in Bombay. (The art collection is described below in [B].) The Museum stands in a well-maintained garden in the middle of which, partly hidden by trees, is a bronze portrait by Leonard Jennings of George V as Prince of Wales. The Museum, designed by Wittet in 1908, shows the same knowledge of Indian traditions that characterises his Gateway of India. Here, the model is that of Bijapur [23A] rather than Ahmedabad, as is clear from the large central tower and smaller end towers surrounded by corner finials with petalled domical tops. The entrance porch has a balcony with an unusual curving vault framed by slender minarets. The portal rising above contains an imposing arch flanked by balconied windows filled with pierced stone screens. Arcaded wings open off to

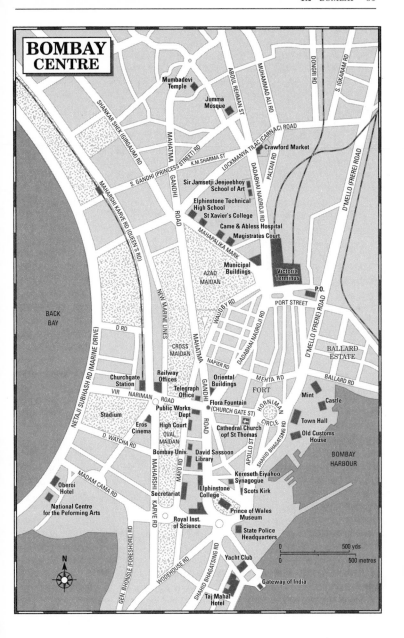

BOMBAY
CENTRE

Mumbadevi
Temple

Jumma
Mosque

ABDUL REHMAN ST

MUHAMMAD ALI RD

DONGRI RD

S. (KARAM RD

SHANKAR SHEK (GIRGAUM) RD

MAHATMA

GANDHI

S. GANDHI (PRINCESS STREET) RD

K.M. SHARMA ST

LOKMANYA TILAC (CARNAC) ROAD

DADABHAI NAOROJI RD

PALTAN RD

Crawford Market

D'MELLO (FRERE) ROAD

Sir Jamsetji Jeejeebhoy
School of Art

Elphinstone Technical
High School

St Xavier's College

Came & Abless Hospital

Magistrates Court

MAHAPALIKA MARK

ROAD

MAHARISHI KARVE RD (QUEEN'S RD)

Municipal
Buildings

AZAD
MAIDAN

Victoria
Terminus

P.O.

PORT STREET

BACK
BAY

D RD

NEW MARINE LINES

CROSS
MAIDAN

MAHATMA

WAUD-B Y RD

NAPIER RD

DADABHAI NAOROJI RD

D'MELLO (FRERE) ROAD

BALLARD
ESTATE

BALLARD RD

NETAJI SUBHASH RD (MARINE DRIVE)

Churchgate
Station

VIR   NARIMAN   ROAD

Railway
Offices

Telegraph
Office

GANDHI

Oriental
Buildings

MEHTA RD

FORT

Mint

Castle

Stadium

Eros
Cinema

D. WATCHA RD

High Court

OVAL
MAIDAN

Public Works
Dept

Flora Fountain
(CHURCH GATE ST)

Cathedral Church
opf St Thomas

HORNIMAN

CIRCLE

SHAHID BHAGATSING RD

Town Hall

Old Customs
House

ROAD

APOLLO ST

BOMBAY
HARBOUR

MADAM CAMA RD

MAHARISHI

Bombay Univ.

David Sassoon
Library

Kereseth Eiyahoo
Synagogue

Scots Kirk

Oberoi
Hotel

National Centre
for the Peforming Arts

KARVE RD

MAYO RD

Secretariat

Elphinstone
College

Royal Inst.
of Science

Prince of Wales
Museum

State Police
Headquarters

GEN. BHONSLE (FORESHORE) RD

WODEHOUSE RD

SHAHID BHAGATSING RD

Yacht Club

Gateway of India

Taj Mahal
Hotel

N

500 yds

0

0

500 metres

the sides. The large dome over the central chamber rises on a petalled frieze; internally, it is carried on intersecting arches.

St Andrew's Kirk stands just behind the Museum within what was once the Fort area. This simple Neo-Classical building with a severe Doric portico dates from 1818; the current steeple was added in 1827. A circular structure on a site next door, now demolished, served as a store for blocks of ice shipped from Massachussetts.

From Wellington Fountain visitors have a choice of three walks: Mahatma Gandhi Road to the north will take them into the Fort Area, with Victoria Terminus beyond; Madame Cama Road runs west to the Maidan; Shahid Bhagat Singh Road, traversing Mukharji Chowk, proceeds south to Colaba.

B. Prince of Wales Museum

This art collection (closed Mondays) is the most important in Bombay. A **Domed Gallery** occupies the ground floor of the triple-height space in the middle of the Museum. Among the items shown here are 16C–17C miniature paintings, jade cups and weapons from the Mughal period, and wooden and ivory figures, including those of the infant Christ, made in Goa [11B] at about the same time. Archaeological fragments from 5C–6C sites, now in Pakistan, include stucco heads and figurines from Gandhara and terracotta Buddhist figures from Mirpur Khas. A gracefully posed 12C nymph from Karnataka is placed in the middle.

The **Sculpture Gallery** to the right is crowded with fine Buddhist, Jain and Hindu images. A set of delicately modelled 7C ceiling panels from Aihole [22E] depicts a trio of Hindu divinities. The plaster cast of a gigantic Shiva figure at Parel and a fragmentary Durga and an image of Brahma from Elephanta give an idea of artistic traditions in the Konkan in the 6C–9C. Among the other carvings are a remarkable 6C panel from Samalaji in Gujarat, showing Shiva with trident and snakes against a background of rocks, and a 5C seated dwarf attendant with curly hair, from Koh in Madhya Pradesh.

A staircase ascends through a **Mezzanine Gallery** with showcases crammed with prehistoric pots, beads, tools and toys. The **Octagonal Gallery**, on the first floor beneath the dome, is surrounded by a wooden arcade. The glass showcases here contain inlaid metalwork and beaten silver trays, mostly 19C work, as well as ivory items. Miniature paintings adorn the walls. The **Himalayan Gallery** to the rear specialises in inlaid brass objects and gilded figures, such as a superb 12C Maitreya. The painted cloth compositions include a *mandala* and a set of Buddhist scenes, both from Nepal.

The **Painting Gallery** represents all of the major schools, ranging from 14C–15C Jain manuscripts to 16C–17C Mughal and Rajput miniatures. The Deccan paintings include a large composition showing a procession of Abdullah Qutb Shah of Golconda [26E], hung at the end of the Gallery. Among the finest paintings are an elephant scene from Bundi in Rajasthan, a depiction of Rama with Sita from Aurangabad [5A] and a portrayal of Krishna dallying with *gopis*, from Shorapur [24G].

The adjacent **Fine Arts Gallery** presents Mughal glass, especially *huqqa* bowls, gold jewellery, enamelwork, embossed silver and ivory figurines. The items are overlooked by an ornate wooden façade removed from a house in Gujarat. The **Bronze Gallery**, though small, has a variety of items spanning the 9C–17C. Krishna dancing on Kaliya, and Vishnu standing in an ornate frame are notable, as is the small, delicately modelled icon of the Jain saviour Bahubali.

Stairs ascend to the second floor, mostly reserved for non-Indian art. The **Octagonal Gallery** beneath the dome houses Chinese and Japanese porcelain, jade and ivory, as well as European crystal and porcelain. Other East Asian works are crowded together in a chamber to the rear. The **Painting Galleries** on both sides are hung with European oils from the collection of Sir Ratan Tata, whose statue is also on display. The landscapes and figurative compositions are of indifferent quality, with the exception of two seascapes by Eugène Boudin. The nearby **Textile Gallery** has a dazzling selection of shawls from Kashmir, ikat cloths from Gujarat, and saris from Thanjavur [40A] and Kanchipuram [37F]. Swords with animal hilts and daggers with ornate blades may be viewed in the adjacent **Weapons Gallery**.

C. Fort Area

Though the defensive walls and gates of the original British settlement were demolished after 1862, this area is still known as the Fort. The original outline of the ramparts on the west can still be made out by following Mahatma Gandhi Road and Dadabhai Naoroji Road, which create an arc, some 1.5km from north to south, facing east towards Bombay Harbour. The crowded commercial streets of this zone still constitute Bombay's business heart. Here stand many old buildings with cantilevering upper storeys on angled wooden brackets.

The route followed described here proceeds north along Mahatma Gandhi Road from Mukharji Chowk. Passing beside the Prince of Wales Museum, the visitor arrives at the **Jehangir Art Gallery** (closed Mondays), one of Bombay's principal venues for contemporary painting and sculpture. In Forbes Street nearby, just off Mahatma Gandhi Road, stands the **Kereseth Eliyahoo Synagogue**, the finest in Bombay, erected in 1884 by David Sassoon, a prominent Jewish benefactor. The building is distinguished by its brightly painted blue-and-white Neo-Classical façade. The prayer hall at the upper level is reached by a flight of steps from a side entrance. The cast-iron columns that support galleries on three sides have Star of David motifs incorporated into the brackets. Stained-glass windows are positioned over the ark in the rear wall.

Elphinstone College stands on Mahatma Gandhi Road, diagonally opposite the Jehangir Art Gallery. The impressive Neo-Gothic College has triple-storeyed arcades on either side of a central rectangular tower crowned by a pyramidal tiled roof and framed by turrets at two levels. The porch at ground level, also with turrets, incorporates a sculpted bust of Sir Cowasji Jehangir, nicknamed 'Readymoney', the patron of the College. The **David Sassoon Library** next door displays a gabled portico, repeated in the pediment that caps the façade. The basalt columns on the upper level carry polychromed arcades. A marble portrait of Sassoon dominates the stairwell.

Mahatmi Gandhi Road arrives at Hutatma Chowk, a broad circle with the **Flora Fountain** in the middle. This coincides with the site of Church Gate, the original west entrance to the Fort, after which the station beyond the Maidan is named. The much-loved Fountain shows the figure of Flora standing upon a quartet of dolphins, with shells beneath. The monument is the work of James Forsyth in 1869, in honour of Governor Frere.

On the north side of Hutatma Chowk are the **Oriental Buildings**, completed by Stevens. These occupy the triangular plot at the junction of Mahatma Gandhi and Dadabhai Naoroji Roads. The angled Neo-Gothic ranges of the Buildings culminate in a five-storeyed corner tower framed by slender circular turrets and crowned by a pyramidal tiled roof. A shorter tower at the north end of the building has an octagonal steeple.

Other Neo-Gothic monuments face each other across Vir Nariman Road (formerly Churchgate Street), immediately west of Hutatma Chowk. The **Public Works Department** on the south was erected in 1869, according to a design by Wilkins. The central rectangular tower has a pyramidal roof with twin turrets. The side wings are terminated by end bays with arcaded storeys enriched by polychrome stonework. The **Telegraph Office** opposite, originally the General Post Office, dates from the same year. Its handsome façade is punctuated by twin towers with steeply pitched roofs rising over arcaded galleries in finely worked decoration. A two-storeyed porch marks the entrance in the middle.

Vir Nariman Road continues west across the Maidan towards Churchgate Station, but the tour described here returns to Hutatma Chowk before proceeding east along the same route into the middle of the Fort area. The first building of importance to be seen is **Readymoney Mansion**, the home of the Parsi philanthropist. Its superimposed arcaded balconies in carved wood echo local architectural traditions.

Further east along Vir Nariman Road stands the **Cathedral Church of St Thomas**. Begun in 1672 by Governor Aungier, but not completed until 1718, this is the oldest structure still in use in Bombay. The two-storeyed battlemented tower replaced the original belfry in 1839. The interior is spacious but simple, with double rows of plain Doric columns carrying shallow vaults. The stained glass in the chancel dates from the reconstruction of 1869. A rich assortment of carved memorials is seen here. One of the earliest commemorates Jonathan Duncan, Governor of Bombay in 1795–1811; another shows Lieutenant Colonel Charles Burr surrounded by Indian officers. The most remarkable tomb is the full marble reclining figure of Thomas Carr, the first Bishop of Bombay. The delicately sculpted Neo-Gothic fountain outside the west entrance to the Cathedral is the work of Sir George Gilbert Scott, the famous Victorian architect, who never visited Bombay.

Immediately east of the Cathedral is **Horniman Circle**, laid out in 1860 as Elphinstone Circle on the site of Bombay Green, the original open space within the Fort. The garden in the middle is ringed by cast-iron railings with four ornate gates flanked by lanterns. The Circle is overlooked by Italianate styled buildings with deep arcades at street level. At the corner of Vir Nariman Road on the west fringe of the Circle stands **Elphinstone Building**, a splendid Neo-Gothic mansion of 1870. Its triple-arcaded storeys in golden sandstone are enlivened with basalt and granite inlays. The top level has intersecting arches in the Venetian manner.

The east side of Horniman Circle is dominated by the **Town Hall**, an accomplished Neo-Greek scheme designed in 1821 by Thomas Cowper and finished by others after his death in 1833. The central portico with eight Doric fluted columns is approached by a broad flight of steps. The side and end porticos employ similar columns, all shipped in pieces from England. The windows with wooden shuttered doors and curving sun-shades are original features. Corinthian and Ionic columns adorn the interior chambers. Marble statues of Elphinstone and other Governors, executed by Francis Chantrey, are displayed in

Flora Fountain, Bombay

the lobby and stairwell. The Asiatic Society of Bombay occupies one end of the Town Hall. Founded in 1804, its library stocks more than 100,000 volumes.

The vestiges of Bombay's earliest structures are engulfed by the Dockyards behind the Town Hall (permission required to visit). The only portion that survives of the **Castle**, the original Manor House, is an entrance gate in the bastion wall. This is surmounted by a coat of arms flanked by reliefs of Portuguese soldiers. The **Old Customs House**, south of the Town Hall, incorporates a Portuguese barracks block of 1665. The **Mint** to the north dates partly from 1824.

D. The Maidan

Bombay is justly famous for the magnificent group of Victorian buildings that overlooks the great open space in the middle of the downtown area. Partly created by dismantling the walls of the Fort, the **Maidan** was originally intended for civic ceremonies and military parades; it is now mostly used for recreation. The panorama of Back Bay, once enjoyed by the Neo-Gothic monuments that face onto the Maidan, is now blocked by apartments and offices built on reclaimed land.

The tour of this zone begins at the south end of Karmavip Bhaurao Patel Marg, the road that flanks the east side of the Maidan. The **Secretariat** of the Government of Bombay, built in 1867–74 by Wilkins, has a 140m long Neo-Gothic façade. The wings with verandahs are enriched with polychromed arches on four levels. The 52m high square tower in the middle is dominated by an arched recess framing a circular window. The roof above is crowned with a tiled pyramid.

Next comes the **Bombay University Complex** of 1869–74, Scott's most important contribution to Bombay. The **Senate Hall** was financed by 'Readymoney', to whom there is a statue by Thomas Woolner in front. The south end of the Hall is apsidal, in the manner of a church; the rose window above the arcaded north porch is flanked by square towers with slender colonettes and octagonal steeples. Open spiral staircases set in octagonal towers provide external access to the side verandahs. A carved timber gallery carried on cast-iron brackets encloses the interior on three sides. The adjacent **University Library** comprises a two-storeyed structure with arcaded galleries, stained-glass windows, pierced parapets and delicately carved stonework. The circular corner towers, with tapering spires on the west, contain spiral staircases.

The vaulted porch in the middle serves as the base for the magnificent 79m high **Rajabai Tower**, the loftiest Neo-Gothic edifice in the city. Added in 1878, the Tower is named after the mother of the benefactor, Premchand Raichand. The lowest stage exhibits large pointed arches containing windows filled with stained glass. Sculpted figures set in corner niches and part-octagonal buttresses also appear at this point. The topmost stage is marked by clock faces framed by steep gables. The Tower is capped by an intricately worked octagonal lantern with figures at the corners and on top of the turrets.

The **High Court**, the next monument on this side of the Maidan, was begun in 1869 under the direction of John Augustus Fuller. Its immense bulk is lightened through extravagant use of Neo-Gothic detail. The central tower is topped by a steeply pyramidal tiled roof with side gables, attaining a height of 53m. The corners are enlivened by octagonal steeples, repeated at a lower level on the front, where they are capped by figures of Justice and Mercy. The tower contains a staircase reserved for judges. The northern and southern extremities of the building are emphasised by octagonal towers.

Crossing the Maidan by proceeding west along Vir Nariman Road, the visitor will arrive at the **Railway Offices**, designed by Stevens in 1894 for the Bombay, Baroda and Central India Railway. The Offices have an almost Byzantine appearance due to the bands of red sandstone and white plaster set into basalt and the clusters of domes at different levels. Each façade has a gabled centrepiece flanked by projecting wings and topped by pairs of domes. A female statue on the west gable, representing the Spirit of Progress, grasps a locomotive body and wheel.

The central domed tower crowning the whole composition rises in diminishing square and octagonal stages.

The Railway Offices face the ugly block of **Churchgate Station**. Opposite, on the south side of Vir Nariman Road, is the former **Eros Cinema**, one of the city's most striking Art Deco schemes. Its painted concrete façade, culminating in a circular tower, punctuates this corner of the Maidan. The Cinema blends with the nearby **Apartments** that line the streets running from the Maidan to Back Bay. Many of these projects were executed by European architects who settled in Bombay in the years between the World Wars. The Apartments have curving balconies and cast-iron grilles in the fashionable Art Deco manner. Similar residences line the great curve of **Marine Drive** completed in 1940, now renamed Netaji Subhash Road. The Drive terminates at Nariman Point, created out of landfill over the last 20 years, where stand the lofty towers of the Air India Offices and the Oberoi Hotel. Beyond is the **National Centre for the Performing Arts**, Bombay's largest auditorium, designed in 1975 by the American architect Phillip Johnson in an International Modernist style, which opened in 1981.

E. Victoria Terminus

The tour continues north from Flora Fountain or the Maidan to a traffic Circle on Dadabhai Naoroji Road, the site of the original north gate to the Fort. The Circle is overshadowed by **Victoria Terminus**, previously known simply as VT, but now increasingly referred to by its new name Chhatrapati Shivaji Terminus. This, the chief landmark of the downtown area, was constructed by Stevens in 1878–88. Arguably the masterpiece of the Neo-Gothic Bombay style, the Terminus was apparently inspired by Scott's St Pancras Station in London. Even so, it surpasses its British predecessor in grandeur of conception and wealth of detail.

The imposing but symmetrically organised arcades of Victoria Terminus are animated by polychromed stonework, intricate ironwork, marble and ceramic inlays, and vigorous relief carving. The west frontage displays side wings with gabled ends and corner towers topped with squat octagonal spires. The central wing is marked by a massive octagonal tower with tall decorated windows. The dome above, lined with eight ornamented ribs, is crowned by a 4m high figure of Progress by Thomas Earp. Other carved motifs fill the rounded and triangular tympanums over the porches and windows. Busts in medallions portray civic worthies of the era, and coats of arms represent the railway company. The interior of the booking hall in the left wing is conceived as a church nave, complete with tiled floor and painted ribbed vault. A majestic staircase is placed beneath the central dome.

The **General Post Office** stands a sort distance east of Victoria Terminus. Like the Prince of Wales Museum, it is influenced by the architecture of Bijapur. Wittet was also involved and, together with John Begg, supervised its construction in 1904–10. The long façade of the Post Office has a central portal distinguished by an ornate parapet running between octagonal finials. The framing towers, including those at the ends of the side wings, are topped with domes on petalled fringes. The intermediate bays are defined by part-octagonal buttresses rising above the roof as domical finials. The central booking office is roofed with a flattish dome carried on pointed intersecting arches. Beyond the Post Office lie the regular blocks of **Ballard Estate**, a commercial development dating from the first decades of the 20C.

Returning to the west front of Victoria Terminus, the visitor will notice opposite the **Municipal Buildings** of 1893, also by Stevens. This confident Neo-Gothic edifice dramatically exploits its corner location at the junction of Mahapalika Marg and Dadabhai Naoroji Road. The building is dominated by an impressive 71m high corner tower capped with a bulbous dome. The gabled façade beneath the dome is crowned with a winged figure labelled *Urbs Prima in Indis*. Flanking towers repeat the domed theme. The porch is animated by winged griffins at the corners of the roof, and similar beasts crown the gables and porches of the wings extending along the side streets.

A further series of fine buildings lines Mahapalika Marg. The first is the **Magistrates Court** of 1884–89, designed by John Adams. Its central porch is punctuated by an unusual part-circular balcony with decorated corbels. A slender spire is placed to one side. The adjacent **Cama and Abless Hospital** has a central square tower enlivened by circular corner buttresses with smoothly tapering spires. Next come **St Xavier's College** and the **Elphinstone Technical High School** of 1872–79, the latter at the corner of Lokmanya Tilak Road. The triple-arcaded entrance to the School, filled with cast-iron gates, is approached by a broad flight of steps. The towers flanking the central wing and punctuating the corners have octagonal pavilions crowned with tiered pyramidal roofs.

The tour returns to Victoria Terminus before proceeding north along Dadabhai Naoroji Road. Just after the *Times of India* offices on the left is the **Tyebji High School**, built in a revivalist Islamic manner with a prominent domed tower. Next comes the **Sir Jamsetji Jeejeebhoy School of Art**, Bombay's oldest institution of this type, which was founded in 1854. John Lockwood Kipling was Principal here when his son Rudyard was born in 1865. Carvings by students of the School adorn many buildings in the city, notably Victoria Terminus. The Art School, built in the Neo-Gothic style by Wittet in 1874–78, has an entrance porch with local craftsmen carved on the brackets. The later Architecture School has unusual semicircular windows interrupted by Ionic colonettes.

The corner of Dadabhai Naoroji and Lokmanya Tilak Roads, a short distance north, is commanded by **Crawford Market**, now renamed Phule Market, designed by William Honour in honour of Arthur Crawford, Commissioner of Bombay in 1865–71. Its triple-arched entrance has reliefs in the tympanums by Kipling, which depict local occupations. The octagonal clock tower above is capped with a small lantern. A small Neo-Gothic fountain inside the Market is surrounded by stalls selling meat, poultry, fruits and vegetables.

The area north of Crawford Market is characterised by narrow lanes crowded with shops, the location of Bombay's busiest markets, including the celebrated **Chor Bazaar**; this area is also home to the notorious 'Cages', the red-light district of Bombay. Javeri Bazaar, just off Muhammad Ali Road, is overlooked by the **Jumma Mosque**. Its prayer hall and minarets, raised high above the surrounding streets, are executed in a Neo-Mughal manner, with lobed arches and domed pavilions picked out in bright green and white. The nearby **Minar** and **Baydari Mosques** are built in a similar idiom.

Shaikh Menon Street, west of the Jumma Mosque, leads directly to the **Mumbadevi Temple**, recognised by its curved tower, which soars above the rooftops. The Temple is dedicated to the goddess worshipped by the original inhabitants of the islands and lagoons of Bombay; the city's new name was chosen in response to the growing popularity of Mumbadevi. The present building is a 19C replacement of an earlier shrine that occupied a site near Victoria Terminus. The Temple is entered through a hall with Neo-Classical pilasters and shutters. The tower over the main shrine, built in the Gujarat manner, displays clustered elements and superimposed balconies on the sides and a gleaming brass finial at the summit.

F. Colaba

The southern extremity of Bombay was once a separate island joined to the Fort by a causeway. Known as Colaba, this part of the city preserves a peaceful atmosphere, with spacious houses and apartment blocks standing in tree-lined streets. The principal historical feature is the **Afghan Memorial Church**, consecrated to St John the Baptist, commemorating those who fell in the First Afghan War of 1838–43. The Church was built by Henry Conybeare in 1858 in a sombre Neo-Gothic manner, the earliest stone example of this style in Southern India. Its steeply gabled façade is dominated by a square corner tower with a tapering octagonal spire rising a total of 58m, completed in 1865. The interior is divided into triple aisles by pointed arches. Stained-glass windows in the chancel show the Crucifixion and seated Christ; mosaic patterns adorn arched recesses in the walls beneath. The tiled pavement and ironwork screen in the choir partly follow drawings sent out to Bombay by William Butterfield.

G. Malabar Hill

The peninsula formed by Malabar Hill provides a spectacular backdrop to Back Bay. Surrounded on three sides by the Arabian Sea, this part of the city was once the setting for extravagant villas, with imposing Neo-Classical façades and grand staircases set in gardens furnished with European statuary. One of the few such residences to survive the onslaught of recent development is **Mount Nepean** (permission required to visit) on the road of the same name. This imposing pile is raised high on a balustraded terrace reached by curving flights of steps. The corner tower is capped with a Mughal-styled dome; similar half-domes top the curving balconies. Today's business barons and film personalities prefer the high-rise apartments that cluster closely together on the steeply rising ground of the Hill, benefiting from fine ocean views and refreshing sea breezes. At night the apartments present a brightly lit mass.

The **Hanging Gardens**, built on the tanks that supply Bombay with water, skirt the south flank of Malabar Hill and offer sweeping panoramas of down-town Bombay. The **Towers of Silence** (access restricted to visitors) nearby are where Parsis, who do not practise burial or cremation, expose their dead to vultures and other birds of prey. The Towers are secluded in a garden intended to foster contemplation and spiritual repose. The **Babulnath Temple**, east of the Tower, dates from 1900. A mechanical lift transports worshippers from S.S. Patkar Road beneath. **Mani Bhavan**, at 19 Labernam Road a short distance away, is where Gandhi stayed on his visits to Bombay. The house is converted into a museum and library (closed Mondays) dedicated to the life of the Mahatma.

A small **Jain Temple** is located on B.G. Kher Marg that runs along the south flank of Malabar Hill. Dating from 1904 and dedicated to Adinatha, the ornate white marble structure is built in the Gujarat style. Its walls are covered with paintings of the lives of the Jain saviours.

Raj Bhavan (permission required to visit), the official residence of Bombay's Governors since 1884, occupies beautifully maintained grounds at the extreme point of Malabar Hill. The house has a pitched roof and pleasant verandahs with tiled roofs. A short distance north is the sacred tank of **Banganga**, overlooked by shrines and traditional wooden houses. Stray stone blocks from the 10C–11C suggest an early history for Banganga, the name of which refers to Rama's magical bow. The **Walkeshwar Temple**, facing the tank near its southwestern corner, dates from about 1715, when it was built to replace a temple destroyed by the Portuguese. Its curving plastered tower is divided into clustered elements, with carved images of sages and musicians beneath. A stone tortoise and Nandi are placed in front of the *linga* sanctuary. The southeastern corner of the tank is marked by a pair of stone lamp towers.

A popular place of worship in Bombay is the **Mahalakshmi Temple**, near the northern tip of Malabar Hill. This stands with its back to the ocean on a promontory just off Bhulabhai Desai Road (formerly Warden Road). The Temple has been completely renovated in recent years, and is now cloaked in marble and topped with a massive but plain curving spire. Images of Lakshmi, Sarasvati and Kali receive worship in the same sanctuary.

The **Haji Ali Mosque** nearby occupies an islet in the watery shallows of the bay separating Malabar Hill from Worli, reached by a causeway at low tide. The prayer hall and slender minaret commemorate a local saint who was drowned here. Lala Lajpatrai Marg, the road which skirts the bay, follows the course of **Hornby Vellard**, the sea wall erected by Governor Hornby as one of Bombay's first great reclamation projects. The **Racecourse** opposite is the largest in Southern India.

An unusual edifice in the Malabar Hill area is the **Opera House** on Vithalbhai Patel Road. The setting of lavish productions after its inauguration in 1924, the Opera House is now mostly used as a cinema. Its Neo-Classical façade has tapering Corinthian pilasters alternating with shuttered windows. The pediment above is filled with statuary.

H. Byculla, Parel and Mahim

Further historical features are located in Byculla and Parel in central Bombay. These densely populated districts are dotted with textile mills with high circular chimneys. The **Magan David Synagogue** on Sir Jamsetji Jeejeebhoy Road was erected by David Sassoon in 1861 and renovated by his son Jacob in 1910. The church-like east façade has a lofty Neo-Classical portico topped by a four-stage clock tower. The cream-and-white interior has a raised women's gallery on three sides. The ark is accommodated in an apsidal recess. **Christ Church** of 1834 stands a short distance away on Mirza Ghalib Street (formerly Clare Road). The quartet of Doric columns in its west porch belongs to the batch imported for use in the Town Hall. The triple-stage tower above has Greek-styled palmettes at the corners. The interior is enhanced by by well-formed Corinthian columns.

Memorials line the walls, the earliest being the grave of Robert Grant, the Governor of Bombay in 1835–38.

Further north, beyond Byculla railway station on Dr Babasaheb Ambedkar Road, is the **Dr Bhau Daji Lad Museum** (closed Wednesdays), founded as the Victoria and Albert Museum by Sir George Birdwood in 1857. The present building, which dates from 1871, has pedimented windows set between fully formed Corinthian columns. This heavy Neo-Classical scheme contrasts with the light-weight cast-iron columns and brackets of the interior, which carry the balustraded gallery and painted wooden ceiling. The lower level is home to an exhibition of local crafts. The display is dominated by a marble portrait of Albert, the Prince Consort, executed by Mathew Noble in 1869. The upper level, with its fine array of floor tiles, has a selection of maps, watercolours, models and coins illustrating the history of Bombay. Among the displaced statuary deposited in the garden at the rear of the Museum is a worn sculpture of an elephant shipped from Elephanta, as well as a large but defaced portrait of Queen Victoria of 1872. An ornate metal fountain nearby is dated 1867.

The Museum stands next to the beautifully planted Victoria Gardens of 1861, now a popular zoological park known as **Veermata Jijabai Bhonsle Udyan**. This is entered through an ornate Italianate gate with triple arches. The tropical planthouse has an attractive curvilinear cast-iron frame; the Oriental Garden is a recent donation by the Japanese Government.

The curious **Clocktower** in front of the Museum on Dr Babasaheb Ambedkar Road was a gift of David Sassoon in 1865. The arched openings at the base are decorated with polychrome tiles and allegorical terracotta heads portraying Morning, Noon, Evening and Night. The **Railway Hospital** opposite was built in 1871 as a college by 'Readymoney'. Its arcaded range has a lofty central tower topped with a pyramidal metal roof.

Parel lies north of Byculla. The **Haffkine Institute**, within the medical complex on Acharya Dhonde Road, is one of the city's most ancient structures. The site was first occupied by a Franciscan chapel in 1673. In 1719 it was taken over by the British, who converted it into a government residence, using it as an alternative to the Castle in the Fort. The banqueting hall and ballroom built within the shell of the original chapel survive, though much altered. The accompanying park and lake are, however, lost. The building was transformed into a medical institution at the end of the 19C, a role it continues to fulfill.

The **Baladeva Temple**, located in a side lane about 350m east of the Institute, is of interest for its remarkable 6C stone sculpture. Discovered only in 1931 and now under veneration, this 3.5m high image represents Shiva in cosmic form, expanding through multiple figures that extend upward and outward. Squatting dwarfs with musical instruments are seen beneath.

Mahim, one of Bombay's northern suburbs, is best known for the **Shrine of Makhtum Faikh Ali Paru**, a saint who was active in the Konkan in the early 15C. The brightly painted green-and-white Shrine is a recent construction, no doubt a replacement of a structure dating from the earliest years of the European occupation. The domed chamber is surrounded by an arcaded verandah, with corners marked by slender minarets. The *Urs* anniversary of the saint in November–December is the occasion for a lively fair that attracts huge crowds.

The nearby **Fort** built on a rocky point overlooking Mahim Creek is a vestige from the early period of British occupation. Little is preserved other than battlemented walls rising directly out of the water.

2 · Around Bombay

Bombay's situation on a long narrow peninsula, joined to the mainland at its northern end, means that road or rail trips beyond the metropolitan area are unavoidably tedious. The exception is the pleasurable one-hour launch ride from the Gateway of India across Bombay Harbour to **Elephanta** [A]. Allow half a day to reach the island and to view the impressive carvings in its Cave Temple. (Note that Elephanta is now closed on Mondays.) Elephanta may be compared to rock-cut monuments at **Kondivte** [B], **Jogeshwari** [C] and **Kanheri** [D], all located on Salsette Island, north of Bombay's airport at Santa Cruz. The ruins of the Portuguese sea fort at **Vasai** [E] and the Buddhist *stupa* at **Sopara** [F] lie yet further north. These sites all may be reached by suburban rail.

The ports on the coast south of the city reveal the varied history of the Konkan. **Alibag** [G] is accessible by boat from Bombay via Mandve, and can also be approached by road. From here it is possible to reach **Chaul** [H], with its Portuguese ruins, and the island fort of **Janjira** [I], the headquarters of the Sidi admirals. A visit to these three spots will occupy a full day and more.

Places of interest on the mainland east of Bombay include the ruined temple at **Amarnath** [J] and the hill resort of **Matheran** [K] in the Western Ghats. Amarnath and Matheran are situated on the rail and road routes to **Pune** [3].

■ **Accommodation**. For tourists taking the coastal route south of Bombay, it is possible to stay at the *MTDC Holiday Resort* at **Murad**, 5km from Janjira, or to continue on to **Mahabaleshwar** [7], where ample accommodation is available. An overnight stop at **Matheran** (STD code 02148) is another option; its many hotels, such as the *Rugby* (☎ 30291), *Lord's* (☎ 30228) and *Usha Ascot* (☎ 30360), are popular with Bombayites.

A. Elephanta

This wooded island in Bombay Harbour, 11km from the Gateway of India [1A], is famous for the majestic carvings of its 6C **Cave Temple**. This monument lacks historical records, but is usually associated with the Kalachuri rulers. The island is traditionally known as Gharapuri, its European name deriving from the stone elephant found here in Portuguese times. (The damaged piece has been removed to the garden of the Dr Bhau Daji Lad Museum in Bombay [1H].)

The Cave Temple is excavated into a basalt cliff, approached from the old jetty (no longer used for sightseeing boats) by a long flight of steps. The principal shrine, flanked by rock-cut courts on the east and west, is entered through openings scooped out on three sides. The ingenious layout combines two axial progressions: from east to west towards the sanctuary, and from north to south towards the impressive triple-headed bust of Shiva that dominates the interior. The columns have squat tapering shafts and fluted cushion-shaped capitals; the

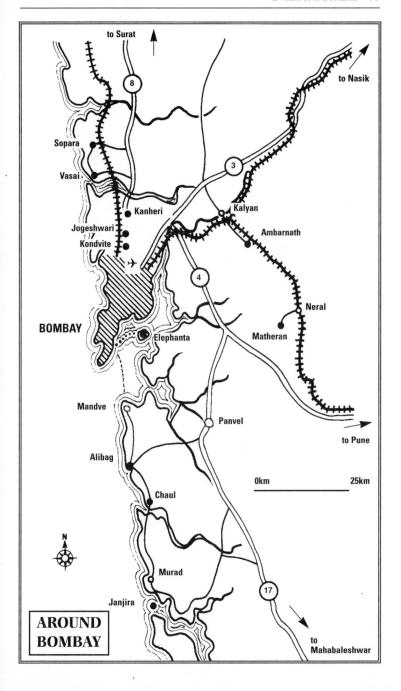

to Surat

to Nasik

8

Sopara

Vasai

3

Kanheri

Kalyan

Jogeshwari

Ambarnath

Kondvite

4

BOMBAY

Elephanta

Neral

Matheran

Mandve

Panvel

Alibag

to Pune

0km   25km

Chaul

N

Murad

17

Janjira

AROUND
BOMBAY

to
Mahabaleshwar

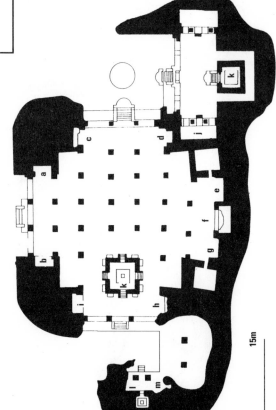

ELEPHANTA, Cave temple

N

a   Lakulisha
b   Nataraja
c   Shiva and Paravati on Kailasa
d   Shiva and Paravati playing dice
e   Ardhanarishvara
f   Triple-headed Shiva
g   Shiva receiving Ganga
h   Marriage of Shiva and Parvati
i   Shiva spearing Andhaka
j   Matrikas with Karttikeya and Ganesha
k   Linga Shrine
l   Shiva as Yogi
m   Nataraja

0   15m

beams articulate the east-west aisles. A square *linga* sanctuary detached from the walls is entered through four doorways, each framed by a pair of gigantic guardian figures in symmetrical swaying poses.

Large-scale scenes are deeply recessed into the walls of the Cave Temple. The damage to the figures, partly inflicted by the Portuguese, does not diminish the artistic impact of the carvings which are among the greatest masterpieces of Hindu art. The compositions depict different aspects of Shiva. The **North Entrance**, which serves today as the principal doorway, is flanked by images of the god seated in yogic posture as Lakulisha (left) and vigorously dancing as Nataraja (right). Coupled images of Shiva and Parvati seated on Kailasa are seen either side of the **East Entrance**. The god and his consort gamble at dice (left), or sit unperturbed by multi-headed Ravana, who attempts to shake their mountain home (right). Panels showing Shiva spearing the demon Andhaka (left) and the marriage of Shiva and Parvati (right) are positioned at the **West Entrance**. This last pair of compositions contrasts violence with peace.

Three panels are set into the rear wall. To the left, Shiva and Parvati are joined in a composite and androgynous figure; to the right, Shiva assists in the descent of the goddess Ganga, observed somewhat warily by Parvati. These complex male-female, husband-wife relationships are embodied in the immense triple-headed bust of Shiva in the middle. The god emerges only partly from the mountain, his fourth head turned unseen into the rock. The two side profiles contrast a feminine aspect (left) with a fierce masculine aspect (right); the central head is introspective and serene.

Other carvings are found in the small side courts. On the south side of the east court is a porch with side chambers adorned with images of Karttikeya, Ganesha and the Matrikas, now damaged. The porch leads to a small *linga* shrine. Another smaller sanctuary opens off the west court. Its porch has unfinished images of Shiva as the yogi and the dancer. The adjacent cistern is rock-cut.

This Cave Temple was not the only one to be excavated on Elephanta Island. 1.5km southeast is a **Second Cave Temple** with a 36m long façade supported by a row of columns, now partly collapsed. This monument is devoid of sculpture, except for the decoration of the shrine doorway.

B. Kondivte

This little-visited Buddhist site is located 6km east of Andheri station on the main suburban line, 22km north of downtown Bombay. Some 18 cave-temples are arranged on the sides of a small rocky hill. Two excavations are of particular interest.

Cave 9 is a plain *chaitya* hall dating from the 2C. It has an unusual circular sanctuary cut into the rock at the rear. This is fashioned in imitation of a thatched hut, with a door placed between trellis windows and overhung by curving eaves. The domical interior of the sanctuary is almost entirely filled with a monolithic hemispherical *stupa* elevated on a circular drum. A dedicatory inscription is seen beside one of the windows. The reliefs of Buddha on the right wall of the hall are later additions.

Cave 13, fashioned as a monastery, is assigned to the 5C–6C. This comprises a columned verandah, a hall with four central pillars, off which open eight small cells, some with rock-cut beds, and a central shrine with a vacant pedestal.

C. Jogeshwari

The large **Cave Temple** at this site is located 24km north of Bombay's centre, about 1.5km east of Jogeshwari railway station. Though this 6C monument is now badly eroded and encroached by slum dwellings, it is worth visiting by enthusiasts for its unusual layout. The Cave Temple is approached by long flights of steps deeply cut into the rock on the east and west. The east doorway is flanked by guardians; the lintel above shows a figure of Nataraja and a scene of Shiva and Parvati playing dice. The columned hall within has a sanctuary in the middle entered through four doorways. The verandah on the north has windows and doorways in the rear walls.

D. Kanheri

More than 100 Buddhist rock-cut monuments may be discovered deep within the **Krishnagiri Upavan National Park**. This attractive site lies about 10km by bus or taxi from Borivili, a station on the main suburban line 35km north of downtown Bombay. The Park is notable for its tree-lined reservoirs, including Tulsi Lake, 3km south.

Kanheri was occupied for about a millennium from the 1C AD onwards by a large Buddhist community, supported by local merchants. Most of the features are modest excavations with frontal verandahs and adjacent cisterns. Some are adorned with carvings of Buddhas, Bodhisattvas and *naga* deities. The caves are numbered haphazardly, not all the labels being visible.

Cave 3 is easily found by following the trail leading to the main group. This 2C monument, the most impressive at Kanheri, takes the form of a *chaitya* hall in imitation of that at Karla [3C]. The exterior is concealed by a rock-cut wall, partly restored, flanked by columns with sculpted bases and capitals. The façade has three doors with carvings of donor couples in between. The semicircular window above lacks carved ornamentation, but the side walls of the verandah are covered with 5C–6C reliefs of standing Buddhas. The apsidal-ended hall is divided into three aisles by octagonal columns, several with pot bases and bell-shaped capitals. Carved brackets show animal riders and Buddhist motifs such as worship of the *stupa* and footprints beneath the bodhi tree. The vaulted roof was once provided with wooded ribs, now lost. The hemispherical *stupa* at the rear is unadorned. Structural *stupas* stand outside the hall. When excavated, they yielded urns with relics and an inscription dated 495.

Caves 1 and **2** are located south of Cave 3, but are of no particular interest. Further along the same path is **Cave 41**. This has an unusual image of Avalokiteshvara displaying four arms and eleven heads.

A circuitous path following the south side of a forested ravine leads to **Cave 11**. This 5C–6C monastic excavation is approached through a verandah with eight octagonal columns. Three doorways lead into a hall with columned aisles and small cells on three sides. A central shrine housing Buddha images is located to the rear. Two low benches on the floor were probably for eating or reading.

Other important rock-cut monuments are located on the opposite side of the ravine. **Cave 90** has a carving of Avalokiteshvara between female deities. The surrounding miniature scenes show the Bodhisattva delivering his devotees from the eight Great Perils. The **Terrace** beyond is occupied by commemorative *stupas*, both rock-cut and brick-built.

E. Vasai

The ruined Portuguese fort at Vasai overlooks the confluence of the Ulhas Creek with the ocean 8km west of Vasai Road, a station on the suburban network, 52km north of downtown Bombay. (Take a taxi from Vasai station.) A visit is recommended for the massive ramparts and grandiose churches and convents, dating from the 16C and 17C. The decayed laterite buildings, attractively cloaked in vines and bushes, are shaded by plantations of mango trees and palms. The site is partly inhabited by local fishermen whose boats are moored in the Creek.

Originally known as Bassein, the port has a similar origin to Bombay, having been granted to the Portuguese in 1535 by Bahadur Shah of Gujarat. The Portuguese developed Bassein into a flourishing city, renowned for its wide streets, luxurious mansions and impressive churches, monasteries and public offices. Apparently, only Christians were permitted to live inside the walls. Francis Xavier visited Bassein four times and after his death was adopted as patron saint of the city. Bassein survived an attack of plague in 1695 which decimated a third of its population, but its fortunes declined after 1738 when it was besieged by the Marathas, who took the city in the following year. The Marathas were expelled in 1780 by the British, who heavily bombarded the ramparts and buildings. The settlement was virtually abandoned in 1818, when it was absorbed into the Bombay Presidency.

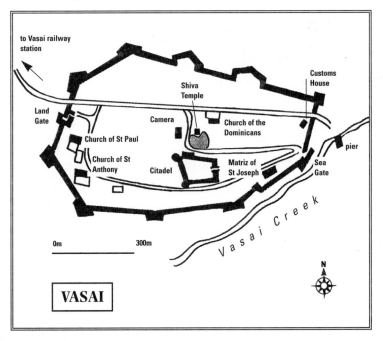

Vasai is contained by comparatively well-preserved angled **Walls** defining an irregular elliptical zone almost 1km along its greater east–west axis, extending up to the water on the east and south. Nine massive bastions of triangular shape, originally named after saints, protrude outwards from the Walls. The round-headed openings in the Walls are for cannon; angled bastions line the walkway at the top. Visitors coming from Vasai Road arrive at the **Land Gate** on the west, shielded by a bastion wall. The inner portal has an upper arched opening flanked by pairs of colonettes with crudely fashioned leaf-like capitals.

South of the Land Gate are the remains of the **Church of St Paul**, a Franciscan foundation. The Church is entered through an unusual triple-arched portal framed by Doric columns. The doorway leads to the imposing nave, roofless except for the coffered vault in the chancel and the broad arch of the gallery.

Land Gate, Vasai

Tombstones are set into the floor. Several columns in the adjacent cloister still stand.

A short distance further south is the **Church of St Anthony**, associated with the Jesuit order, founded in 1548 by Francis Xavier on his third visit to Bassein. The façade, the finest at Bassein, has pairs of Corinthian columns on either side of an arched doorway. A rectangular pedimented window flanked by volutes and pinnacles and a smaller circular window are seen above. The composition is topped with a rounded pediment. The panels set into the façade are carved with IHS, a typical Jesuit motto. Nothing remains of the interior decoration except for the coffered vault in the chancel. The dilapidated cloister next door frames a spreading mango tree.

The **Citadel** to the east, standing roughly in the middle of the fort, is a quadrangular walled zone with prominent corner bastions. Access is from the east through a gate with the Portuguese coat of arms over the arched door. No structures are preserved inside.

The **Matriz of St Joseph**, founded in 1546 as Bassein's cathedral, lies a short distance further east, beside the Walls. The entrance is marked by a triple-staged tower with pot finials at the summit, dating from the rebuilding of 1601. The interior is reduced to a mere shell. The **Sea Gate** to the rear of the Matriz, at the eastern extremity of the city, consists of two arched doorways. The outer one preserves its iron-clad doors, framed by massive round buttresses. The Gate leads directly to the port, with its small fleet of fishing vessels.

The tour of Bassein continues by returning through the Sea Gate to the fortified zone and proceeding northwest towards a small 19C **Shiva Temple** on the edge of a pond, recognised by its fluted dome. North of the Temple stands the **Church of the Dominicans**, the largest at Bassein. The interior is mostly ruined, but the decorated door leading to the side cloister is worth noting. A four-staged tower rises over the southeast corner of the Church. The south door of the nave has side volutes framing dogs, an unusual motif. A short distance in front (west) of the Church are the remains of civic buildings. They include the **Camera**, or Town Hall, with an arcaded porch. A carved panel over one of the interior doorways shows a royal coat of arms and an armillary sphere.

F. Sopara

This peaceful town is most conveniently reached from Nola Sopara station on the main line, 8km north of Vasai Road. Sopara is identified with the ancient emporium of Shurparaka, which traces its history back to the 3C–2C BC. This early date is confirmed by the discovery of stone fragments inscribed with edicts of the emperor Ashoka, the Maurya emperor of Northern India. Sopara seems also to have been known in the 2C AD to Ptolemy, who refers to it as Supara.

The most important feature that can be seen at Sopara today is the ***Stupa* Mound**, which stands in a pleasant mango grove 500m west of the railway station. The Mound is almost 90m in circumference, with steep earthen sides on a brick base rising more than 5m. The *Stupa* is surrounded by brick and stone foundations which define a rectangular enclosure entered on the east and south. Small mounds indicate votive *stupas*. A pile of 11C–12C temple carvings is seen on the east. Excavations here in the 1880s revealed a brick chamber set into the base of the Mound. A circular stone coffer within the chamber disclosed a remarkable sequence of caskets of different materials, one placed inside the other. The outermost casket, of copper, contained almost 300 tiny gold flowers, as well as semiprecious stones, stone beads, a small gold plaque showing Buddha preaching and an unworn silver coin of a 2C Satavahana king. Eight bronze Buddha images of about the 8C–9C were arranged around the casket. The innermost casket, of gold, contained pottery fragments believed to be pieces of the begging bowl of Buddha. These finds are now in the collection of the Asiatic Society of Bombay.

A path from the *Stupa* Mound leads for about 750m to a small lake overlooked by the **Chakreshvara Temple**, a recent construction. Among the 11C–12C carvings strewn about is an extraordinary 2m high image of Brahma and a charming panel showing a maiden holding a parrot.

G. Alibag

This port lies about 90km south of Bombay, via Panvel on NH17. It is also accessible by catamaran from the Gateway of India in Bombay, which brings visitors to Mandve, from where there are buses to Alibag. It is difficult now to imagine that this small town, nestling peacefully in palm groves overlooking the estuary of the Sakhar Creek, was once a busy naval station.

In 1662 Shivaji made Alibag the headquarters of the Maratha fleet, and in the following years it became the headquarters of the Angres. These skilled admirals had a reputation for piracy, challenging European shipping until the town was taken by the British in 1840.

The principal feature of Alibag is the **Hirakot**, the Diamond Fort, a short distance northwest of the town, erected by Kanhoji Angre in 1820. The Hirakot is built of massive basalt blocks and is entered on the south by a steep flight of steps. A small shrine dedicated to Maruti is built into the gate. Cells for prisoners and a small treasury stand within the enclosure.

Kanhoji is also associated with the more impressive **Kolaba Fort**, which occupies a narrow rocky island in the middle of Alibag harbour. Kolaba consists of a quadrangular arrangement of basalt walls with 17 round towers. The main entrance, at the northeast corner, is shielded by an outwork with a long causeway. The pointed arched doorway is flanked by towers; the teak doors within preserve iron spikes. Immediately inside the Fort are two domed storerooms and a dilapidated shrine consecrated to Padmavati and Bhavani. The ruined lines of buildings to the south have been identified as granaries and stables. The remains of the residence built by the younger Raghoji Angre in 1816 are seen further south, in the vicinity of a large reservoir. The Ganapati Panchayatana Temple opposite is the work of the elder Raghoji before 1793. The jail and guardrooms lie beyond.

H. Chaul

The remains of this Portuguese settlement overlook the mouth of the Roha River, 18km south of Alibag from where taxis are available.

The history of Chaul, known also as Revdanda, goes back to pre-European times. Under the Bahmanis of Gulbarga [24A] in the 15C, this was one of the pre-eminent ports of the Konkan. It was the Portuguese, however, who were responsible for developing Chaul into an international emporium; their first factory here was established as early as 1516. In spite of repeated raids on Chaul by the forces of Ahmadnagar [6] and Bijapur [23A], commerce flourished, especially with Gujarat and the ports of the Persian Gulf and Red Sea. Merchants from different parts of India settled in Chaul, where they traded in rice, precious stones and locally manufactured cotton and silk textiles. In 1592 Burhan Nizam II established a fort at Korle on the opposite side of the harbour, but was expelled soon after by the Portuguese. Trade declined after the establishment of Bombay. The port passed into the hands of the Marathas in 1740, but was virtually abandoned by the time it was occupied by the British in the early 19C. Chaul is today a verdant quiet spot, with little indication of the vigorous activities of former times.

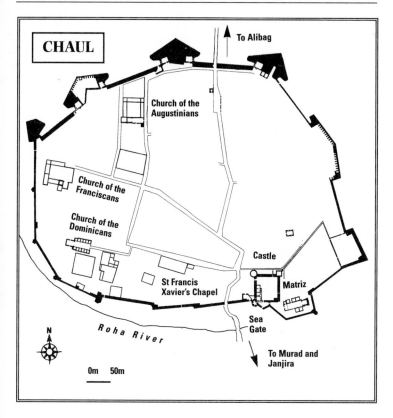

The overgrown **Fortifications**, containing dense palm groves, are picturesquely bordered by the Roha River on the south and west. The basalt **Walls** defining an approximately circular zone, more than 500m across, have massive triangular bastions on the landward sides. Their sloping flanks can still be seen, though the moat which protected them is now filled in. The road from Alibag passes through a small gate in the northern arc of the Walls. Instead of continuing south, however, visitors should take the path immediately to the right. This leads to the **Church of the Augustinians** of 1587, now a collapsing pile of masonry.

The **Church of the Franciscans**, a short distance southwest, was begun in 1535 and dedicated to St Barbara. It preserves a 30m high six-storeyed tower, the loftiest in the city. The **West Gate** of Chaul, which lies beyond, has an arched entrance surmounted by a royal coat of arms and two crosses flanked by saints. The **Church of the Dominicans** to the south retains a portion of its coffered vault over the chancel. Fragments of other vaulting with fanciful designs roof the side chapels. The ruins of **St Francis Xavier's Chapel** lie to the east.

The path continues until it joins the main road from Alibag. Here can be seen the collapsing enclosure of the **Castle**, the fortified residence of the Governor and the site of the original Portuguese factory. The entrance has an arched door surmounted by royal arms and a cross. A path passing by the wall of the Castle arrives at the **Matriz**, now much overgrown. The arched portals and decaying walls of this large cathedral date from 1534. The only other building of interest is the **Church of the Jesuits**, situated on the main road running through the middle of the the fort. This is represented by a single façade with an arched doorway. The **Sea Gate**, south of the Castle, is protected by a small outwork. A slab carved with a figure of a warrior wearing the insignia of the Order of Christ is set into the walls. An inscribed panel to the right records that the Walls along the water were completed in 1577.

The Sea Gate gives onto a modern bridge that crosses the Roha River, beyond which lies **Korle Fort**. This citadel consists of a fortified ridge, almost 100m high, shielding the estuary from the ocean. On the river side of the ridge is the village of Korle, with a well-kept **Church** partly dating from Portuguese times.

Upper Chaul is reached by returning to the Alibag road, and proceeding 2.5km north. This small settlement has a quite different history, since it was under the Marathas for a longer time. Thickly wooded and well watered, the village is built beside a row of ponds at the foot of a hilly ridge. A domed 18C **Tomb** is built on the rise overlooking Bhavle Pond to the west. The **Dancing Girls' House**, consisting of a domed hall and a mosque within a walled enclosure, occupies a pass in the hills 500m north of the village. Simple excavations dating back to the 1C–4C AD dot the southeast face of the ridge. The **Temple of Hinglaj** at the summit is reached by a flight of steps.

I. Janjira

The town of **Murad** lies 33km south of Chaul; 5km further south is the fishing village of **Rajpuri**, from where boats can be hired to transport visitors to Janjira. This remarkable island citadel commands the mouth of a tidal creek that gives access to the Konkan hinterland.

> Janjira was founded in 1511 by the Sidis, Abyssinian admirals in the service of the Adil Shahis. The Sidis gradually affirmed their autonomy from Bijapur, and by 1618 were relatively independent. They derived their revenues from the armed escort that they provided for pilgrims bound for Mecca. Shivaji attacked the fort in 1659, followed some years later by his son, Sambhaji. But neither they nor the European powers that operated in the Arabian Sea were able to capture Janjira. The Sidis even raided Bombay on several occasions betrween 1672 and 1690. The rulers of this virtual island kingdom survived into modern times, but abandoned their citadel after it was burnt in 1860. A fanciful mansion with domical turrets erected on the hill above Murad in the early years of the 20C is the residence of the modern descendants of the Sidis.

Janjira presents a formidable appearance, due to the carbuncled basalt blocks of the **Fortifications**, which rise sheerly 15m out of the water. Begun in 1694, the walls were completed in 1707 by Sirul Khan. They have battlements with angled tops separated by arched openings for cannon, some still in place. Circular bastions punctuate the walls at regular intervals. The lead used in the joints between the lower blocks helped to avoid the corroding effects of salt water.

Janira is entered through a single **Gate** on the north side of the island. The arched opening is surmounted by a frieze of battlements flanked by lions with curling tails. The guardroom on top has a balcony carried on lotus brackets. Steps lead up to a domed chamber, the walls of which have carved panels showing lions clutching captive elephants.

The interior of the island is crowded with overgrown ruins attractively grouped around two **Tanks**, one elliptical and other circular, partly scooped out of the rock. A **Mosque** with plain arches and a *mihrab* with faintly Neo-Classical detailing face toward the elliptical reservoir. On the south side of the circular reservoir stands the **Darbar Hall**. This four-storeyed mansion has bold cornices running between square corner towers. The central doorways display lobed arches, lotus medallions in the spandrels, motifs which are repeated in the round-headed windows above. The **Magazine** is situated on the highest point of the island, more than 60m above the sea.

The tour continues by returning by boat to **Rajpuri**. The **Jami Mosque** here has an arcaded prayer chamber flanked by corner buttresses with cut-out curving brackets. Windows are placed in both the side and rear walls. The **Sidi Tombs** are reached by following a road upstream for about 1.5km. They are dominated by an arcaded mausoleum elevated on a double terrace and surrounded by a ditch. The large but flattish dome has boldly moulded petals at its base. This Tomb was completed by Sirul Khan before his death in 1733. Two smaller Tombs, which stand together on a common plinth, are associated with earlier rulers.

J. Amarnath

Amarnath lies on the main line to Pune, 6km southeast of Kalyan, an important railway junction. The town derives its name from the **Ambaranatha Temple** 1km to the east. Together with the example at Sinnar [4D], this is the finest religious monument of the Yadava era. The Temple, which is dedicated to Shiva, preserves an inscription referring to its repair in 1016. The sanctuary and hall, the latter with three porches, expand rhythmically outwards in multiple projections. The walls have moulded basements, carved panels and prominent cornices; the axial niches are sheltered by angled eaves. The curved tower rising over the sanctuary displays a cluster of miniature elements that repeat the form of the central shaft while continuing the wall projections beneath; a band of meshed arch-like motifs adorns the middle of each side. The hall is roofed with a pyramid of recessed capping elements. Most of the wall carvings are damaged, but graceful female figures are preserved in the recesses. Niches on the south wall of the sanctuary house images of Nataraja, Harihara, Brahma and Bhairava.

K. Matheran

The nearest hill station to Bombay, Matheran occupies an even-topped spur of the Sahyadris ranges of the Western Ghats, some 50km directly east of Bombay. Matheran is most comfortably reached by narrow-gauge train from **Neral**, the journey of 20km taking about two hours. Neral is a station on the main line, 86km from Bombay and 120km from Pune. Road access from Neral ends at a car park 4km from the centre, with no motor transport being permitted on top.

Matheran is popular because of the climatic relief it offers to Bombayites, the hill rising more than 750m above sea level; this popularity means that the town can become very crowded at weekends, and it is advisable to book accommodation in advance.

Sensational views may be had on all sides of the bluffs of the Sahyadris, dropping more than 500m to the misty plains beneath. The metropolis can only sometimes be sighted, generally after the monsoon rains. The topmost scarp consists of a central block and two small side ridges. Lookouts are dotted along the main headland, such as **Panorama Point**, 5km northwest of the post office, and **Hart Point** and **Monkey Point** to the south. **Porcupine Point** is a popular sunset spot. **Louisa Point**, 3km away, is a plateau with views of the ruined hill forts of **Prabal** and **Vishlagarh**. **Chowk Point** lies at the extreme southwest flank of the hill, 4km distant.

The **Hill Station** itself dates from the middle of the 19C, when its dams were first built. The first European house was built in 1851 by Hugh Poyntz Malet, Collector of Thana District. Lord Elphinstone, Governor of Bombay, had a road leading to a private lodge constructed in 1858. Thereafter, Matheran became fashionable for Bombay's elite. A church, consecrated in 1865, was soon surrounded by civic buildings and private bungalows. The first hotels opened at beginning of the present century.

3 · Pune

Pune is a thriving industrial, commercial and educational centre, second in Maharashtra only to Bombay [1]. The city is situated on the Deccan plateau at an altitude of 580m, within sight of the Sahyadri ranges of the Western Ghats. The military and religious monuments in **Old Pune** [A] are linked with the Peshwas, the Prime Ministers of the Maratha kings. Vestiges of the British period are mostly confined to **New Pune** [B]. One day should be sufficient to tour both parts of the city.

The Pune region is rich in historical localities on or beneath the rugged crests of the Sahyadris. The sites are described here according to four full-day excursions. The rock-cut Buddhist shrines at **Karla** [C], **Bhaja** [D] and **Bedsa** [E] may be combined in a tour to the west. Similar exacavations surrounding Junnar, and the adjacent hill fort of **Shivneri** [H] to the north can be visited together with the mosque and tomb at **Rajgurunagar** [F] and the pilgrimage shrine at **Bhimashankar** [G].

A trip southeast of Pune can take in the charming town of **Sasvad** [I], the hill fort of **Purandhar** [J] and the temple at **Jejuri** [K], one of the most popular in Maharashtra. A full day will be required to reach the remoter hill forts of **Sinhagad** [L] and **Rajgad** [M], southwest of the city.

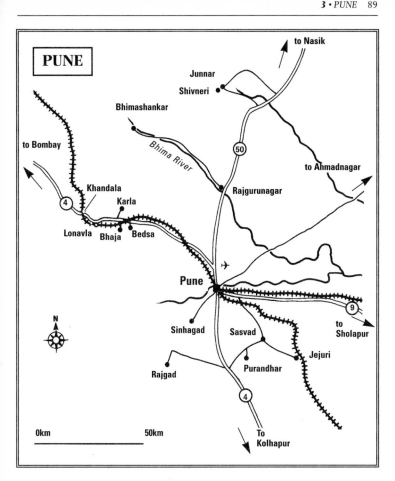

The monuments at Ahmadnagar, 116km northeast of Pune, may be covered briefly in a full-day excursion from Pune, but are described here in a separate itinerary [6].

■ **Transport**. Pune is easily reached from Bombay, 190km away, to which it is connected by highway (NH4) and rail, as well as by a 20-minute flight. The rail trip is spectacular, particularly in the monsoon season, ascending 650m through the rugged bluffs of the Western Ghats. Pune makes a convenient stopping-off point on any journey linking Nasik [4], Aurangabad [5], Ahmadnagar [6], Mahabaleshwar [7] or Sholapur [9], all of which are easily reached by road, the last also by rail. Bus services are available to all the places described here. Note that the ascents of Purandhar and Rajgad forts demand strenuous climbing.

■ **Accommodation**. There is an abundance of hotels in Pune (STD code 0212). The best are the *Holiday Inn, Blue Diamond* (☎ 625555), *Aurora Towers* (☎ 631818) and *Executive Ashoka* (☎ 3324567). A newly developed commercial quarter to the north, near the Mutha River, includes the *Regency* (☎ 629411). A comfortable stopover between Bombay and Pune may be had at either **Lonavla** or **Khandala** (STD code for both 02104) on NH4. These attractive hill stations offer a full range of accommodation, including the *Span Hill Resort* (☎ 73685) and *Fariyas Holiday Resort* (☎ 73852) at Lonavla, and the *Duke's Retreat* (☎ 73817) and *Mount View* (☎ 72335) at Khandala.

■ **Tourist Information**. The MTDC maintains offices in the Central Building, I Block, on Mankaji Mehta Road (☎ 626867) and at the Saras Hotel, Nehru Stadium (☎ 430499).

History

The Pune region is linked with the rise of the Marathas in the second half of the 17C, this being the main arena of Shivaji's raids on the Mughals, who were established at Aurangabad. Shivaji never actually occupied Pune, preferring the security of the nearby hill forts of Rajgad and Purandar. His successors, Sambhaji and Shahu, were similarly disinclined to settle in the Deccan plains, even though they captured Pune from the Mughals. It was the Peshwas who made Pune one of the main centres of Maratha power, shifting their capital here from Satara [7G] in 1750. The city was subsequently contested by the Nizams of Hyderabad [26], who raided it in 1763, and then disputed by rival Maratha factions, such as the Holkar and Shinde chiefs. Stability was restored by Nana Phadnavis, the capable Minister of the last Peshwas. In October 1802 the Holkar forces defeated the combined armies of the Peshwa and the Shindes, and British troops were called in for assistance. In 1803 Pune was occupied by Arthur Wellesley, the future Duke of Wellington. But it was not until the battle of 1818, fought at Khadki (Kirkee to the British), a site now within the city limits, that Pune was finally taken by the British. Thereafter it became an important military station, the Cantonment there being one of the largest in Southern India. Commerce flourished once peace was restored, and Pune attracted industrialists from Bombay, including Parsis and Jews. Benefactions of the Sassoon family dot the city.

A. Old Pune

The 18C Peshwa capital is situated on the south bank of the Mutha River, near to its confluence with the Mula River. The heart of Old Pune consists of crowded streets and lanes overlooked by traditional brick houses with timber frames and sloping tiled roofs, punctuated by Hindu shrines with brightly painted spires.

The core of Old Pune is marked by the great fort of **Shanwar Wada**, immediately south of Shivaji Bridge. This was the chief residence of the Peshwas from 1727 until 1808, when the Palace inside was destroyed by fire. The agreement between the East India Company and the Peshwas to combat Tipu Sultan was signed here in 1790. Shanwar Wada is contained by a rectangle of high walls of stone (beneath) and brick (above), 170m by 150m. Prominent round bastions occur at the corners and in the middle of three sides; polygonal bastions flank the **Delhi Gate** on the north, its arched stone entrance being surmounted by a timber balcony with a wooden roof. The **Palace** that stood inside has completely vanished, except for masonry foundations of the various halls and courts. The present landscaping draws attention to the formal arrangement of water channels and differently shaped ponds. The open space in front of Shanwar Wada, now mostly used for recreation, has an equestrian statue serving as a **Memorial** to soldiers who fell in the First World War. A short distance south is the **Vishram Bagh**, a Peshwa mansion with an ornate wooden façade, for a time used as a Post Office.

Only a selection of Old Pune's numerous shrines is described here. The **Omkareshvara Temple**, built by the second Peshwa, Bajirao I, in 1736, stands in the middle of a compound beside Shinde Bridge over the Mutha River. The compound is entered through an arched gate on the east, outside which is a stone lamp column. The Temple within has nine arcaded bays roofed with alternating flat domes and pyramidal vaults. The *linga* shrine in the central bay is topped with a square tower displaying double tiers of lobed arches that shelter plaster figural reliefs. A small lotus dome marks the summit.

Other shrines are tucked away behind the crowded shops in the commercial heart of Old Pune. **Tulsi Bagh** is the name given to a tree-filled court surrounded by traditional timber dwellings. The **Rama Temple** in the middle, dating from 1761, was a favourite of Nana Phadnavis. It consists of an unadorned cube topped with a lofty decorated spire some 45m high. This has a lower square storey adorned with Mughal-styled niches filled with plaster figures; turrets mark the corners. The tower rises in five diminishing stages, each with twelve niches, and is crowned with double lotus domes on petals. The front of the temple is partly obscured by a wooden arcaded hall with a decorated ceiling.

The nearby **Bel Bagh Temple**, begun in 1765 by Nana Phadnavis, presents a similar scheme. The shrine, which is dedicated to Krishna, is approached through a triple stone arcade with Mughal-styled columns. Paintings of divinities cover the flat ceiling of the antechamber. An open wooden hall stands in front. The 12-sided polychrome tower is devoid of plaster sculpture.

The **Mahatma Phule Market** opposite, the busiest in Pune and the most distinguished architecturally, dates from 1886. It is named after a 19C social reformer. The central octagonal tower has Neo-Gothic windows and a pointed tiled spire. Eight wings with gabled ends fan outwards in regular formation.

The **Raja Dinakar Kelkar Museum** (no closed days), south of the Phule Market, occupies a Peshwa-period mansion. The Museum houses a vast collection of items from all parts of India, including architectural fragments, sculptures, paintings and innumerable small objects associated with everyday life, such as ivory and wooden combs, *kumkum* boxes and even ornamental footscrubbers. The **First Floor Galleries** display brass and ceramic pots and dishes, papier-mâché utensils and wooden kitchen wares, such as decorated noodlemakers. A large variety of textiles is presented in the **Second Floor Galleries**. The embroidered children's clothing is particularly delightful. There is also a remarkable range of brass lamps, figurines, ink pots, ritual spoons and betel-nut crackers. Musical instruments and painted textiles are seen in the extension of the Galleries in the other half of the Museum. The **Ground Floor Galleries**, which are visited only at the end of the tour, show ivory games, pen boxes, chess sets and carved wooden doors, many dating from Peshwa times.

Further religious monuments are to be found in the northeast sector of Old Pune, not far from the Mula River. Here stands the **Trishund Ganapati Temple**, completed in 1770, the only Peshwa shrine to be built entirely in stone. The Temple is entered through a elaborate doorway with an ornate frame incorporating cut-out monkeys flanked by guardian figures. The side niches have carvings of Englishmen, a rhinoceros and fighting elephants. Bracket figures appear beneath the cornice that runs around the building. Carvings are also seen on the interior doorway leading to the main shrine. The underground chamber beneath the domed hall was once used for yogic instruction. The nearby **Nageshvara Temple** presents a small octagonal sanctuary capped with a brightly painted lotus dome. The adjoining hall has a decorated flat stone ceiling. There is the usual open wooden hall in front. The entrance gate to the compound is surmounted by a chamber for musicians.

No tour of Old Pune would be complete without a visit to the **Parvati Temple**, on the summit of the small hill south of the city. This popular shrine was begun in 1748 by the third Peshwa, Balaji Balajirao. It stands in a polygonal walled compound that looks like a fortress. Indeed, the complex served occasionally as a lookout; from here the last Peshwa viewed the defeat of his forces by the British. A long flight of steps ascends to the Temple. The shrine dedicated to Parvati has a polychromed tower with a central spire surrounded by four lesser pinnacles. The copper pot-shaped finials are replacements of the gilded originals stolen by the Nizam when he raided Pune in 1763. A golden image of the goddess is worshipped within. **Lal Bagh**, not far from the base of the hill, is the largest garden in Old Pune. A popular shrine to Ganapati, elevated on a small rise, stands in the middle.

B. New Pune

British-period Pune, known at that time and since as Poona, extends across both the Mutha and Mula Rivers to the north and west. Much of this area was laid out as a **Cantonment**, with basalt barracks and service buildings for army contingents and verandahed bungalows set in spacious grounds for officers. Civic and religious buildings line the broad, shady streets in this part of the city. **Viddhant Bhavan**, built as the Council Hall in 1870, stands in a well-maintained garden on Manekji Mehta Road. The rectangular red-brick block has an entrance porch on the west, surmounted by an Italianate-styled tower, 25m high, topped with an arcaded loggia and a pyramidal tiled roof. The double-height hall within is surrounded by a gallery on cast-iron brackets. Painted portraits of 19C worthies are on display. **St Paul's Church** stands nearby; begun in 1863, this somewhat severe Neo-Gothic building is relieved by an arcaded porch with animated gargoyles and a single octagonal corner spire. Stained-glass windows frame the marble altar inside.

The **Ohel David Synagogue** on Laxmi Road is the largest synagogue in Southern India. Constructed by David Sassoon in 1863, it presents a plain red-brick exterior with finely carved stone columns and Neo-Gothic arched windows. The solid square tower is topped in church-like fashion with a pyra-

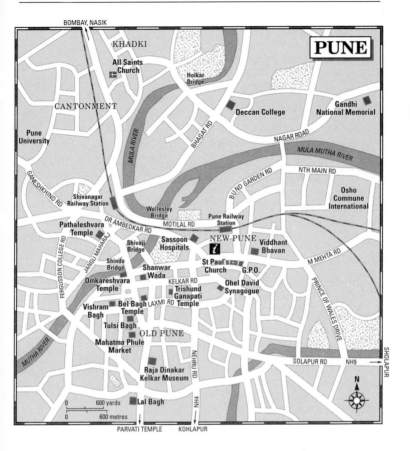

BOMBAY, NASIK

KHADKI

PUNE

All Saints
Church

Holkar
Bridge

CANTONMENT

Deccan College

Gandhi
National Memorial

Pune
University

MULA RIVER

BHAGAT RD

NAGAR ROAD

MULA MUTHA RIVER

GANESHKHIND RD

NTH MAIN RD

BUND GARDEN RD

Shivanagar
Railway Station

Wellesley
Bridge

Pune Railway
Station

Osho
Commune
International

DR AMBEDKAR RD

MOTILAL RD

Pathaleshvara
Temple

Shivaji
Bridge

Sassoon
Hospitals

NEW PUNE

Viddhant
Bhavan

M MEHTA RD

JANGLI MAHARAJ

FERGUSSON COLLEGE RD

Shinde
Bridge

St Paul's
Church

G.P.O.

Omkareshvara
Temple

Shanwar
Wada

KELKAR RD

PRINCE OF WALES DRIVE

Ohel David
Synagogue

Vishram
Bagh

Bel Bagh
Temple

LAXMI RD

Trishund
Ganapati
Temple

Tulsi Bagh

OLD PUNE

Mahatma Phule
Market

MUTHA RIVER

NEHRU RD

SOLAPUR RD

NH9

SHOLAPUR

Raja Dinakar
Kelkar Museum

N

0   600 yards   Lal Bagh

NH4

0   600 metres

PARVATI TEMPLE   KOHLAPUR

midal spire. The interior arcades carry wooden columns and a flat wooden ceiling. The Ark has finely carved wooden doors, while the central podium is surrounded by a polished brass balustrade. **David Sassoon's Tomb** in front is conceived as a Neo-Gothic chapel roofed with an octagonal pyramid surrounded by corner turrets.

Another foundation of the Sassoon family is the similarly Neo-Gothic complex of the **Sassoon Hospitals**, funded by Sir Jacob Sassoon from 1867 onwards, on Dr Ambedkar Road. This thoroughfare leads to **Wellesley Bridge**, opened in 1875, which crosses the Mutha River. Vidyapeth Road, on the other side, is lined with the Neo-Gothic **Engineering College** and **District Courts**.

A short distance south, on Jangali Maharaj Road, is the rock-cut **Pathaleshvara Temple**, the only pre-Maratha-period monument in the city. Assigned to the Rashtrakutas, the Temple consists of an open rectangular court excavated into a basalt outcrop. The free-standing circular pavilion in the middle, entirely monolithic in execution, faces an unadorned colonnaded hall containing three shrines. The Temple was reinvested for worship in the 18C.

Further along Vidyapeth Road is the **College of Agriculture** of 1911, designed by George Wittet. The campus of **Pune University** beyond occupies the grounds of former Government House. The original building is recognised by the high watertower capped by an open iron dome. Other British-period buildings stand in Khadki Cantonment, near the Mula River. **All Saints Church,** consecrated in 1841, is worth visiting for the tablets and brasses commemorating the officers who died in service.

The **Holkar Bridge,** which crosses the Mula River, leads to the **Deccan College**. The original buildings of this institution, designed by Henry St Clair Williams in 1864, present battlement façades and arcaded ranges. The **Gandhi National Memorial,** 1km east of the College, was originally the Aga Khan's palace. Mahatma Gandhi was held under house arrest here in 1942, during which time his wife Kasturba died. Her memorial stands in the spacious grounds.

Pune achieved a certain notoriety in the 1980s when Bhagwan Rajneesh, the controversial spiritual teacher, was deported from the United States and returned to set up his *ashram* here. Known as **Osho Commune International,** the *ashram* continues to attract international visitors, even though its founder died in 1990. It is situated at 17 Koregaon Park, in the eastern part of New Pune.

C. Karla

Karla lies 10km south of **Lonavla,** a popular hill resort 64km northwest of Pune. The site overlooks a forested valley in the Sahyadris through which run NH4 and the Bombay–Pune line.

The rock-cut features at Karla are reached by a steep climb of more than 350 steps. By far the most important excavation is the 1C *Chaitya* **Hall** of the Kshatrapa period, the largest and best-preserved such monument in Maharashtra, comparable to the examples at Kanheri [2D] and Ajanta [5F]. The Hall is approached through an excavated court, on the left side of which stands a monolithic column with a quartet of lions forming the capital. A small Hindu shrine to the right, dedicated to the goddess Ekvira, may be built over the base of another similar column. Though lacking in antiquity, the shrine is the chief attraction for most visitors today.

The *Chaitya's* façade is dominated by a large horseshoe-shaped window, complete with stone imitations of wooden ribs. Panels depicting stately pairs of donors are positioned between three doorways headed by arched motifs. The Buddha images are insertions of the 5C–6C. The side walls are sculpted with the foreparts of three elephants supporting reliefs of vaulted buildings with arched windows and railings. The magnificent apsidal-ended interior is divided into aisles by two rows of columns, most of which have octagonal shafts with pot-shaped bases and fluted capitals. Pairs of seated elephants ridden by embracing couples are carved on the blocks above. The curved vault has original teak ribs set into the rock. The monolithic *stupa* at the end is raised on a double circular drum carved with railing friezes. The hemispherical drum is topped with an inverted stepped finial and a unique wooden umbrella, its underside carved with delicate petalled patterns.

D. Bhaja

The Buddhist antiquities at this site are situated in the cliffs opposite Karla. The Bhaja excavations date back to the 2C BC Satavahana period, making them among the earliest rock-cut monuments in Maharashtra. Most of the 20 monasteries here have a verandah and a hall with small cells provided with benches; two exceptional examples have circular cells. Many monasteries are associated with cisterns. One excavation has 14 rock-cut *stupas* bearing the names of religious teachers.

Rock-cut chaitya *hall, Bhaja*

Cave 12 is possibly the oldest known apsidal-ended *chaitya* hall, the dependence on wooden models being particularly noticeable throughout. Socket holes indicate that a wooden façade was originally inserted into the horseshoe-shaped opening over the entrance. The interior is divided into three aisles by octagonal columns that incline slightly inwards. The roof is fashioned as a curved vault with notches for teak beams, now lost. An unadorned hemispherical *stupa* stands at the end.

Cave 19, a short distance south, is an irregularly shaped hall approached through a columned verandah. Two doors are flanked by guardian figures; the pierced stone window above admits additional light. The verandah roof has an unusual half-vault complete with timber-like ribbing. Supporting columns have part-octagonal shafts. Sculptural compositions are seen either side of the doorway leading to the cell right of the verandah. The left panel depicts a royal personage, possibly Surya, attended by two women driving an aerial chariot. The four horses pulling the chariot trample a demon. The right panel represents a majestic figure, probably Indra, riding a mighty elephant in the company of an attendant holding banner and spear. Dancers, a man and a horse-headed woman appear beneath. The interior of the hall has four side cells with doorways framed by horseshoe-arched motifs.

A path with steps leads for about 1.5km to **Lohagad Fort**, sited spectacularly at the top of the escarpment. Established by Shivaji, it preserves well finished ramparts and an arched gate. The only feature of interest inside is a circular well, partly rock-cut. From here there are fine views over the valley, also to nearby **Vishapur Fort**.

E. Bedsa

The small group of Buddhist excavations at this site, 9km southeast of Karla, is assigned to the 1C Satavahana era. Two excavations are of interest.

Cave 7, a well-preserved *chaitya* hall, is reached through a narrow passageway cut into the cliff. The exterior is richly embellished. The four large columns in the verandah have octagonal shafts, pot-shaped bases and inverted bell-shaped capitals. The blocks above are fashioned as paired animals ridden by couples. The main doorway is flanked by pierced stone windows; the large arched opening above displays timber-like ribs. The side walls are covered with architectural façades complete with arched windows and railings. The hall interior has octagonal columns, inclining slightly inwards, creating triple aisles. An unadorned hemispherical *stupa* is located at the rear. The timber ribs of the vault have vanished.

Cave 11 consists of a verandah with subsidiary cells giving access to an apsidal-ended vaulted hall. Nine small cells cut into the side walls have arched motifs over the doorways, linked by railings in shallow relief.

F. Rajgurunagar

Previously known as Khed, this small town on the Bhima River, 44km north of Pune on NH50, was the headquarters of Dilawar Khan, the commander of the Ahmadnagar forces in the struggles against the Mughals. The **Mosque and Tomb of Dilawar Khan**, dating from 1613, are important examples of Nizam Shahi architecture. The Mosque has triple arches of lobed design, with lotus medallions in the spandrels, sheltered by eaves on curved brackets. The petalled base of the dome is partly concealed by the parapet with domical finials. The interior is divided into six bays, the central two bays unusually roofed with a single dome. The adjacent Tomb has its outer walls divided into double tiers of recesses, pointed arches alternating with lobed arches. The corner finials resemble miniature pavilions.

G. Bhimashankar

This site, 48km northwest of Rajgurunagar, is celebrated for the **Mahadeva Temple**, the site of one of the 12 *jyotirlingas*, or luminous emblems of Shiva. The village of Bhimashankar is situated at more than 1100m altitude, just beneath the wooded heights of the Sahyadris. The Bhima River, which rises nearby, trickles into a small cistern known as the **Moksha Kund**. The Temple dates back to Yadava times, but only the Nandi pavilion of the original 12C–13C monuments survives. The main structure belongs to the Peshwa period, being completed only in 1800 by funds supplied by the widow of Nana Phadnavis. Shivaratri is a popular festival held in February–March, attracting many thousands of devotees.

The Mahadeva Temple is built in a revivalist mode, with a curving tower surrounded by a cluster of half-towered elements. Like the main shaft, these lesser elements are crowned with circular ribbed elements and pot-like finials. The adjacent hall has triple sets of lobed arches. The squat tapering lamp column outside the entrance displays 12 diminishing tiers of curved brackets.

H. Junnar and Shivneri

Junnar lies a short distance west of NH50, some 90km north of Pune, on the way to Nasik. This town was a flourishing Buddhist centre during the Satavahana and Kshatrapa periods, between the 2C BC and the 3C AD. Junnar's significance derived from its location on a trade route leading through the Nana Pass in the Sahyadris, 30km west, down to the Arabian Sea port of Broach, now in Gujarat.

Little is known about Junnar until it became an outpost of the Bahmanis of Gulbarga [24A]. In 1486 the town was taken by Ahmad, the founder of the Nizam Shahi kingdom, and in later times it was disputed by the Mughals and the Adil Shahis of Bijapur [23A], who came into conflict with local Maratha commanders. Jijibai, wife of the Maratha general Shahji, took refuge here, and in 1627 gave birth to Shivaji, the future founder of the Maratha state, an event for which Junnar is best known today. Shivaji actually never lived here as an adult, and the town did not pass into his hands. Junnar was taken in 1705 by Aurangzeb, who halted here for more than seven months before marching on Bijapur. In 1716 Shahu obtained Junnar for the Marathas, in whose possession it remained until 1818, when it was ceded to the British.

The town is enclosed by irregular arcs of basalt outcrops with steep escarpments and flattish tops. **Shivneri** is the name given to the triangular hill that rises 300m above Junnar immediately to the west. A line of about 50 Buddhist caves, mostly simple excavations, are cut into the cliffs on its eastern flank. The fortifications protecting the hill on the south date mostly from the 15C–16C. They are joined by cross walls to a sequence of **Gateways** lining the approach road. The arched entrances are relieved by lion blocks and the occasional double-headed eagle motif.

A flight of rock-cut steps climbs to a domed tomb and a prayer wall on the flat crest of the topmost hill. Buildings of greater interest are seen to the north. They include the small **Kamani Mosque**, which dates from Nizam Shahi times. A flying arch connects the corner minarets; Persian inscriptions are set into the rear wall. The Mosque, which looks down on the houses of Junnar, can be reached directly from the town by a steep flight of steps. The two-storeyed **Pavilion** nearby is pointed out as Shivaji's birthplace. A balcony with arched windows projects from the east wall. The Pavilion forms part of a palace complex, now ruined. The adjacent modern **Bhavani Temple** commemorates the spot where Jijibai is supposed to have worshipped.

Tulja Hill lies 2km west of Shivneri. The Buddhist caves here span the Satavahana and Kshatrapa periods. Known as the **Tulja Lena Group**, they consist of 11 excavations. **Cave 3**, the most important, has an unusual circular *chaitya* hall with 12 tall octagonal pillars surrounding a plain hemispherical *stupa*. The roof is fashioned as a rock-cut dome.

Lenyadri Hill is located 4km north of Junnar. The **Ganesha Lena Group** in the southern escarpment, of a similar date to the previous group, consists of 26 excavations, two of which are chapels, the others being monasteries. **Cave 7** has a verandah with doorways and windows. The octagonal columns have bell-shaped capitals and seated animals. 19 small cells open off the hall within; a later Ganesha image has been placed in one of these. The adjacent *chaitya* hall, **Cave 6**, has similar columns to Cave 7. The main façade is marked by a blind *chaitya* arch. The vaulted interior of the hall has rock-cut ribs, the devotional focus being a hemispherical *stupa* raised on a plain drum.

Three groups of caves are excavated into the north and west sides of **Manmodi Hill**, 2km south of Junnar. Of the 50 or so excavations, four are *chaitya* halls. **Cave 40**, the largest, has a well-preserved façade. The horseshoe-shaped arch over the entrance contains petal-shaped compartments filled with reliefs of Lakshmi, elephants and devotees. The finial of the arch is flanked by relief *stupas* as well as a winged animal-headed figure (left) and a *naga* deity (right). The whole composition is framed by arched façades. The hall interior is incomplete.

Several Nizam Shahi monuments are scattered around the town, the most impressive being a large **Tomb** 1.5km to the east. The founder of this mausoleum is unknown. Finely carved medallions surround the south doorway. The large dome is partly concealed by a brick parapet of interlaced battlement motifs; the corner finials have miniature domes. A smaller pyramidal tomb stands to one side. **Afiz Bagh**, a garden mansion with balconied windows, lies 1km further east.

I. Sasvad

This picturesque town, 31km south of Pune, is the ancestral home of Balaji Vishvanath, the first of the Peshwas. In 1719 Balaji fled to Sasvad for safety, and died here in the following year. Several fortified **Palaces**, known as *wadas*, residences of the Peshwas and those in their service, stand in the middle of the town. Each consists of a quadrangle of bare high walls with rounded corners, entered through arched portals on one side. Dilapidated wooden structures preserve finely carved columns, brackets and beams. Small shrines are built up to the outer walls.

The **Sangameshvara** and **Changla Vateshvara Temples** are located west of Sasvad. The Sangameshvara Temple occupies a platform with steps leading diagonally down to a point where the Karha River joins one of its tributaries; the Changla Vateshvara Temple, 1.5km further west, stands near the south bank of the Karha. The Temples are virtually identical. The *linga* sanctuaries have multiple projections between cardinal niches. The brick towers above rise in diminishing tiers of Mughal-styled arches. They are crowned by bulbous domes with petalled fringes framed by quartets of inward-curving tusks. The adjacent halls have brick parapets with corner domical finials framing petalled domes. Tortoises are carved in shallow relief on the floors within. The open verandahs in front have columns with elaborate brackets; seated Nandis are placed inside. Pairs of lamp columns with projecting curved brackets occupy the corners of the terraces.

J. Purandhar

This celebrated citadel, 15km west of Sasvad or about 40km south of Pune via NH4, occupies one of the highest points in the Sahyadris, the summit rising 1475m above sea level. A road climbs about 500m from the plain to a lower terrace, but the remaining 350m ascent to the main entrance of the stronghold has to be made on foot.

> Purandhar was fortified by the first Bahmani rulers, remaining in their hands until 1486, when it was taken by Ahmad, the founder of the Nizam Shahi kingdom. Shivaji captured the fort in 1670, but it succumbed to Aurangzeb in 1705. Soon after, Purandhar was granted to Pant Sachiv, an influential officer under the first Peshwa, Balaji Vishvanath. The treaty signed here in 1776 between Nana Phadnavis and the East India Company granted Salsette Island in Bombay to the British. After the capture of Sinhagad in 1818, Purandhar was occupied by the British, who used it as a sanatorium and detention camp.

The Purandhar **Citadel** occupies an L-shaped ridge with precipitous sides, approached from the north by way of a steep road. After passing through an austere arched **Gate**, the road arrives at a grassy terrace with an abandoned **Church** surrounded by dilapidated barracks. From here can be seen the line of **Walls** hugging the crest of the hill above. These fine examples of Bahmani fortifications have prominent round bastions and square crenellations.

An overgrown path climbs upward from the terrace, partly by way of rock-cut steps, to the **Delhi Gate** at the eastern extremity of the Citadel. This is the first of a sequence of three arched entrances at successively higher levels arranged along a narrow ridge. From here there are fine views of **Wazirgad**, the fortified lower hill immediately to the east, and of the plains beneath. The path leads from the gates to an overgrown **Complex**, with ruins of residences, barracks and stores, possibly dating back to Bahmani times. Further on, beyond several rock-cut cisterns, is a long rectangular chamber, possibly a **Prison**, with a single doorway and a curving brick vault. The small **Mahadeva Shrine** crowns the summit of the rise in the middle of the Citadel. Another defensive entrance to the fort is seen immediately below.

K. Jejuri

This popular place of pilgrimage, at the eastern end of the Purandhar ridge, 16km south of Sasvad, is famous for its fairs held in April and December. These honour the god Khandoba, a warrior form of Shiva, who killed Malla, a local demon.

The Khandoba cult, supported by pastoral and mercantile communities throughout Maharashtra and northern Karnataka, rose to prominence in the 17C–18C. In 1662 the Khandoba Temple was the setting of the reconciliation between Shahji and his son Shivaji, the father bringing offers of peace from Bijapur. Aurangzeb was driven away from Jejuri by the miraculous appearance of a swarm of hornets, after which the emperor bestowed on Khandoba a diamond worth 125,000 rupees. The Temple was substantially enlarged by the famous queen Ahilyabai, widow of Malhar Rao Holkar's son, and her general, Tukoji.

The **Khandoba Temple** is reached only after passing through the streets of the town and climbing a long flight of **Steps** punctuated by arched portals and subshrines containing effigies of donor figures. Throughout the ascent, vendors offer brass masks of Khandoba, recognised by his staring eyes and curling moustache, as well as bright yellow tumeric powder used in rituals of worship; musicians sing devotional songs. The steps are lined with tapering **Lamp Columns** with curving brackets, the donations of pious individuals. The **Gate** at the top has a lobed arched opening beneath a pointed arch. The Temple stands in the middle of a polygonal fortified **Enclosure**, defined by deep arcades, some looking out over the town and the plain beyond. Other gates are located on the east and west.

Four massive **Lamp Columns** stand in front of the main Temple. On the ground nearby is a **Tortoise**, almost 7m in diameter and sheathed in brass. The Temple, much renovated in recent years, has a Tamil-styled tower capped with a hemispherical roof and flanked by minaret-like towers. The sanctuary doorway is concealed by an embossed silver frame. The effigies within consist of two stones clad with brass masks of Khandoba and his consort Mahlasa, embedded in tumeric powder and sheltered by a gilded domed canopy. The **Panchalinga Shrine** at the rear is distinguished by an octagonal tower with triple tiers of niches topped with a decorated dome. The adjacent hall stores the ceremonial palanquins used at festival times.

The smaller **Mahadeva Temple**, west of Jejuri town, was erected by Malhar Rao Holkar II in 1800. The hall interior is dominated by a large dome adorned with painted figures; a tortoise is carved in the middle of the floor. The chief object of worship is a *linga* accompanied by the donor and his three wives, all in white marble. The square **Tank** nearby was laid out somewhat earlier by Tukoji.

L. Sinhagad

The nearest hill fort to Pune, Sinhagad lies about 30km southwest of the city; it is most easily reached via NH4. Like Purandhar, Sinhagad stands on a high point of the Sayhadris, 1315m above sea level, rising more than 700m above the plain. A metalled road reaches almost to the top, marked by a communications tower.

The history of Sinhagad, known originally as Kondhana, goes back to 1340, when the forces of the Delhi emperor Muhammad Tughluq marched against it. In 1486 it was one of several forts in the Pune region that fell to Malik Ahmad, the founder of the Nizam Shahi dynasty. Shahji, father of Shivaji, was Regent of Kondhana under the kings of Ahmadnagar. In 1647 Shivaji held the stronghold, renaming it Sinhagad, Lion Fort. The citadel subsequently changed hands on several occasions between the Marathas and the Mughals. It was the scene of a daring exploit in 1670, when it was captured by Shivaji's forces under the direction of Tanaji, who used ropes to raise troops and animals up the sheer sides of the hill. Aurangzeb laid siege to Sinhagad in 1701–03, but could not hold it for long. It was thereafter disputed by different Maratha factions until 1818, when it surrendered to British troops. The fort was later used as a warm-weather retreat for the European residents of Pune.

The three-pronged **Fort** of Sinhagad is ringed with steep cliffs from which rise sheer walls of basalt more than 40m high, reinforced by **Ramparts** with regularly spaced towers. On the west flank, the Ramparts seal the mouth of a steep gorge. The hill top is reached by a tortuous path from the northeast, passing through three **Gates**. The first Gate, flanked by a conical tower on the outer face, has a pointed arched recess and battlements. The second Gate is similar, but ruined; the third Gate is complete, with intact towers and a barbican wall. The undulating and irregular interior of the Fort retains few buildings of interest. **Tanaji's Monument**, near the gorge, commemorates the 1670 exploit. Several British-period bungalows are dotted about.

M. Rajgad

One of the most spectacular forts of the Maratha series, Rajgad occupies a formidable triple-pronged hill with sheer drops on all sides. The incomparable views over the surrounding crests of the Sahyadris include distant prospects of hill forts at Torna, 10km west, Sinhagad, about the same distance north, and Purandar, 30km east. Rajgad citadel lies no more than 50km in a direct line from Pune, but is difficult to reach. A climb of two hours is required from **Vajeghar**, a small hamlet reached from **Nasrapur** on NH4, a total of about 50km from Pune.

> Little is known about the history of this remote and rugged region until 1646, when Shivaji captured Torna from the Adil Shahis. With the treasure that he obtained, Shivaji bought arms, cannon and ammunition to strengthen another hill nearby, naming this Rajgad, King's Fort. In the following year he built up Rajgad, making it the seat of his government. The task of fortifying the site was undertaken by Moro Pingle, one of his most loyal commanders. Shivaji returned to Rajgad in 1666 after a successful series of campaigns, and from here mounted his expedition to the Konkan. In 1672 he was persuaded by his father, Shahji, to shift his capital to Raigad [7C]. Like other forts in the Pune region, Rajgad was taken on several occasions by the Mughals and then recaptured by the Marathas. However, it declined in importance in the 18C and was already abandoned in 1818 when the British stormed Purandhar.

Rajgad is approached by a steep path from the north, passing through an **Arched Gate**, tucked into the walls at the extreme end of the northern spur, known as **Padmapati Machi**. Ruined stores, granaries, residences and reception halls are scattered around the level terrace of this spur.

An additional climb is required to scale the **Bala Kila**, or inner fort, which occupies the triangular rise that forms the summit in the middle of the hill, 1317m above sea level. A pointed arched gate on the east is surrounded by sculpted panels and flanked by polygonal bastions. On the level top are a few cisterns, partly rock-cut, and the overgrown remains of **Shivaji's Palace**. This consists of a series of rectangular structures, each with a verandah and a long chamber raised on a platform, standing within a walled compound.

Two very long and narrow spurs fan out from the Bala Kila to the southeast and southwest. They are reinforced with **Fortifications** that follow the curving edges of the cliffs to create sinuous lines of walls. The walls are doubled with a trench between at the extreme ends of the spurs. Round bastions occur irregularly, some with internal steps giving access to outworks beneath. An arched gate in the middle of the east side of the fort, immediately beneath the Bala Kila, leads to a staircase that descends to the plain.

4 · Nasik

Although this city forms part of the Bombay-Pune-Nasik industrial triangle, Nasik still retains its status as one of Maharashtra's most holy cities. The sanctity of Nasik derives partly from the Godavari River, considered as blessed as the Ganga, which flows through the middle of the city. The Kumbha Mela festival, held here every 12 years, last in 1990, attracts huge numbers of visitors, but large crowds can be seen at most times bathing in the river and visiting nearby shrines. A few hours should be sufficient to enjoy these sights [A].

Half-day excursions to **Pandu Lena** [B], with its rock-cut Buddhist monasteries, the pilgrimage temple at **Trimbak** [C], near the source of the Godavari River, and the ruined monument at **Sinnar** [D] are easily made from Nasik. A trip to see the temple at **Jhodge** [E] and the tombs of the Faruqi kings at **Thalner** [F] will take up a full day and more.

■ **Transport**. Nasik lies 130km northeast of Bombay [1], from which it is reached by road on NH3 or by rail to Nasik Road. An air service between the two cities is also available. Pune [3] lies 209km south via NH4. Indirect road connections link Nasik with Aurangabad [5] and Ahmadnagar [6]. All the places described here are easily accessible by bus.

■ **Accommodation**. New hotels at Nasik (STD code 0253), such as the *Holiday Cottages* (☎ 522376) and *Regency* (☎ 562442), have been built on the busy highway near Nasik Road station, 8km east of the city centre. The *Holiday Plaza* (☎ 573521) and *Panchavati Complex* (☎ 575771) are more centrally located.

■ **Tourist Information**. The MTDC office is situated at the Golf Club, Old Agra Road (☎ 570059).

A. Nasik

Nasik's religious status derives from its association with the *Ramayana* legend. Here, it is believed, Rama, Sita and Lakshmana spent part of their exile wandering through the forest, fighting demons and meeting with local sages.

Inscriptions at Pandu Lena indicate that in the 2C–1C BC Nasik was a trading centre with flourishing merchant guilds. Little is then heard of Nasik until the 14C, when the city came under the Delhi Viceroy at Daulatabad [5C]. In later times Nasik passed from the Bahmanis to the Nizam Shahis, and from them to the Mughals. In 1751 Nasik came under the sway of the Peshwas of Pune, who made it one of the headquarters of their expanding kingdom. The Peshwas remained in power until the British took over in 1818.

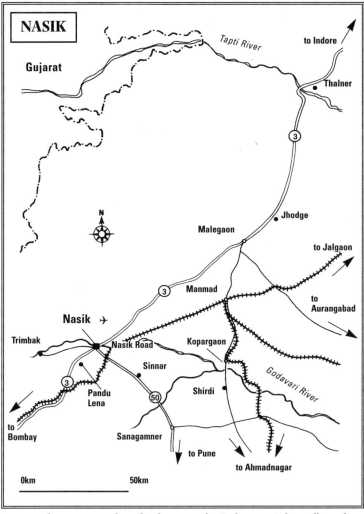

In spite of vigorous modern development, the Peshwa period is still much in evidence at Nasik, as can be seen in the brick mansions with carved wooden fronts and the sandstone temples with soaring spires. The most interesting sights cluster picturesquely on the banks of the Godavari River. The **Ghats** lead down to the river, which is divided into ponds by narrow walkways. The **Rama Kund** is believed to be where Rama performed the funerary rites in memory of his father; a dip here is considered particularly auspicious. The modern **Clock Tower** and marble **Gandhi Memorial** stand somewhat incongruously on the edge of the water. The scene is completed by minor shrines, shops, stalls and a local vegetable market. Brightly painted sculptures of Hanuman are set up at various points.

Sundara Narayan Temple, Nasik

The **Sundara Narayan Temple** stands on the elevated west bank of the Godavari. Dating from 1747, it was subjected to damage and repairs in later times. Wall projections of the sanctuary are enlivened with small carvings of Hanuman (south), Narayana (west) and Indra (north), all sheltered by prominent eaves. The curving spire is of the clustered type, capped with a circular ribbed element. The adjoining hall is entered through three porches, some damaged, each with balcony seating, lobed arches and slightly bulbous domes. The hall roof has a larger but flattish dome with complex bulbous elements. The doorways inside the porches are headed by angled eaves and serpentine pediments.

The **Narashankar Temple**, on the east bank of the Godavari River, near Rama Setu Bridge, stands in an arcaded compound with circular corner bastions topped with domed pavilions. The entrance gate, roofed with a curving vault, is approached by steps from the river. The main shrine and its tower resemble the Sundara Narayan Temple in most respects. Among the few differences are the animals on the upper tiers of the roof. A large bell of Portuguese workmanship is set in the middle of the west compound wall.

The narrow streets east of the Narashankar Temple lead to the **Kala Rama Temple**, also known as Ramji's Temple. This popular place of worship dates from 1782, though it has been remodelled recently. The building stands in the middle of a walled enclosure entered on the east through an arched portal. In front of the main Temple is a long pavilion with lobed arches in the Neo-Mughal style, used for sermons and devotional chanting. A small shrine inside the hall houses a standing image of Hanuman. The smooth surfaces of the curving spire of the main Temple attains a height of 27m. The dome over the adjoining hall is crowned with a triple set of ribbed motifs and a pot finial. Smaller domes cap the porches on three sides. Modern murals within the hall illustrate *Ramayana* scenes. Black stone images of Rama, Sita and Lakshmana are displayed on an embossed silver throne inside the sanctuary.

B. Pandu Lena

The Buddhist monuments at this site are among the oldest in Maharashtra. Pandu Lena refers to a group of rock-cut monasteries located high up on the north face of a hill 8km south of the city, just off NH3. The 24 excavations of this group are accompanied by donative inscriptions belonging to the Satavahana and Kshatrapa periods, spanning the 2C BC to the 3C AD. Buddha images were added to many of the caves in the 5C–6C.

The path ascends partly by way of steps to the middle of the line of excavations. **Cave 3**, towards the right end of the group, is the largest and most elaborate of the monasteries. The octagonal columns of the verandah have bell-shaped capitals carrying pairs of seated elephants, bulls and fantastic animals with riders. The balcony walls have dwarfs which appear to support railing reliefs, now worn. Imitation rafters and railings adorn the ceiling inside. The doorway to the hall is framed by a relief representation of a decorated wooden gateway with rolled ends. Guardian figures are positioned at either side, and inscribed panels above. Small cells, each with a rock-cut bed, open off the large hall. The rear wall has a *stupa* in relief, flanked by female worshippers.

Cave 10 is similar to Cave 3, but there is no balcony, the verandah columns being fully exposed, revealing their pot-shaped bases. An inscription with large letters is incised on the porch wall. A Buddha figure is cut into the *stupa* panel in the rear wall of the hall.

Cave 18, towards the left end of the group, is the only *chaitya* hall at Pandu Lena. Its façade has finely carved details. The entrance is framed by a horseshoe-shaped arch containing ribs interspersed with auspicious emblems and animals; a single guardian stands on the left. A similarly shaped, but larger, arch above has timber-like ribs. This forms part of an elaborate façade with railings, columns, *stupas*, cornices and windows, all in shallow relief. The interior is plain except for octagonal columns with pot-shaped bases. The wooden ribs of the vaulted ceiling have vanished. The focal *stupa* has a high drum crowned with a railing; the finial is an inverted stepped pyramid.

The *chaitya* hall is flanked by two monasteries, **Caves 17** and **20**, linked to it by access staircases, preserved only on the left. Cave 20 was enlarged in later times when images of teaching Buddha and Bodhisattvas were added in the rear shrine. The pot-like bases and capitals of the porch columns, however, are original features. **Cave 19**, immediately beneath Cave 20, is a small monastic excavation, with pierced windows in the porch and decorated railings and arches over the cell doorways.

C. Trimbak

This small town, 31km west of Nasik, is famous for the sanctuary enshrining one of the *jyotirlingas* of Shiva. The town is dramatically framed by an amphitheatre of cliffs; the wooded lower slopes conceal a small spring identified as the source of the Godavari River. The fairs held here in October–November and February–March are attended by large crowds.

The imposing **Trimbakeshvar Temple,** begun by the third Peshwa, Balaji Bajirao, was completed in about 1785. It is built in a revivalist manner, harking back to earlier traditions in Gujarat. The deep-red sandstone building stands in a spacious compound entered through an arched gate on the north. The Nandi pavilion in front has lobed arches containing pierced stone screens and a pyramidal roof with miniature ribbed elements.

The main Temple is entered through a hall with triple porches and balcony seating decorated with lotus medallions. The outer walls of the hall have small niches filled with sculptures. Above rises a bold pyramid of ribbed motifs, with triangular vertical faces on three sides. The adjoining sanctuary is laid out on a complicated plan approaching a circle. Numerous wall projections are carried into the imposing tower, where they are transformed into model elements clustering around the central shaft. Each element is crowned with a part-circular ribbed motif. Both hall and sanctuary are roofed with lofty domes decorated with ribs and central lotuses. The intermediate chamber has a corbelled vault; the wall niches here are capped with fighting elephants. The sanctuary floor, reached by descending a few steps, has a circular pedestal filled with Godavari water. Three diminutive *lingas* here are worshipped as Brahma, Vishnu and Shiva.

A curving market street lined with shops leads to **Ganga Sagar.** This 17m square tank, which traps water from the Godavari spring, is surrounded on three sides by arcades. The small shrine at the southeast corner has carvings on its outer walls. A stepped path leads from this reservoir to the small shrine that marks the source of the Godavari River.

Distant views may be had of the **Fort**, which occupies a sheer scarp above the town. Though associated with events in Maratha history, it is of little architectural importance.

D. Sinnar

This quadrilateral walled town, with arched gateways on four sides, lies 27km southeast of Nasik on NH50. It is best known for the 11C monument, the best preserved from the Yadava period, standing 1km northeast of the town.

The **Gondeshvara Temple** stands isolated against a backdrop of distant hills. The main shrine, its associated Nandi pavilion and four smaller corner shrines are all elevated on a high plinth. This complex stands in the middle of a walled compound with entrances on the east and south. The main Temple consists of a hall with triple porches and a towered sanctuary, both with articulated wall projections. The basement has friezes of elephants, interrupted by a *makara* spout on the north. Sculptures adorn the walls, but the axial niches are empty. The sanctuary spire has tiers of model towers arranged either side of central bands filled with meshes of archlike motifs. The hall is roofed with a pyramid of masonry. The hall interior has four central columns with figural brackets supporting a corbelled dome with a lotus in the middle. The dome is set within a square vault with curving corbels. Minor shrines repeat many of these features on a smaller scale. They preserve the circular ribbed capping elements which are missing on the tower of the main Temple.

From Sinnar it is possible to proceed to Shirdi [6C], about 90km east via Sanganmer.

E. Jhodge

The small town is situated just off NH3, 115km northeast of Nasik. Like the monument at Sinnar, the **Mahadeva Temple** is one of the better-preserved examples of the Yadava style. The abandoned 12C building stands in a spacious landscape west of the town. It has triple sanctuaries, two of which were originally porches, opening off a common hall. Though damaged, the exterior presents a dignified composition dominated by the soaring curved spire over the principal sanctuary. The walls beneath have multiple projections covered with carvings of celestials and attendants, framed by basement and cornice mouldings. The tower above has central tapering bands filled with mesh-like motifs and flanked by eight superimposed tiers of model towers. The whole is capped with a massive circular ribbed element. The pyramidal roof over the hall is incomplete, but the corbelled dome within preserves its supporting brackets fashioned as maidens and musicians. The porch on the west has balcony slabs and carved columns.

F. Thalner

This insignificant village on the north bank of the Tapti River, just off NH3 about 70km north of Jhodge, was once the capital of the Khandesh kingdom on the frontier between Maharashtra and Madhya Pradesh.

> The history of Khandesh begins in 1370 when Firuz Shah Tughluq, ruler of Delhi, granted Malik Raja Faruqi an estate on the southern border of Gujarat, including the fort at Thalner. By the time of Malik's death in 1399 Khandesh was virtually independent of Delhi, with Thalner as its capital. Malik's successors came into repeated conflict with Gujarat, whose kings invaded Khandesh, laying waste the countryside and sacking Thalner. In 1498 Mahmud Shah Begra, the Ahmedabad king, occupied Khandesh, granting some of its territories to one of his nobles. A further battle between Thalner and Ahmedabad took place in 1566. Akbar absorbed Khandesh into the Mughal empire in about 1600, later shifting his headquarters upstream to Burhanpur, now in Madhya Pradesh. The French traveller Francois Tavernier, who passed through Thalner in 1660, described the town as a thriving commercial centre on the route linking Burhanpur with the Arabian Sea port of Surat in Gujarat, both with European factories. Because of its strategic location, Thalner attracted the Marathas, who occupied the town until it was made over to the British in 1818.

The **Fort**, built on a rise overlooking the north bank of the Tapti River, has mostly collapsed, with only a single wall still standing. The 15C **Tombs of the Faruqis**, clustered in a group west of the village, are of greater interest. These buildings show affiliations with traditions of the Malwa region to the north, best seen in the combination of solid cubic forms and flattish domes on high drums. Smaller domes of the same type are placed at the corners of one example. The decoration is fairly restrained, with shallow arched recesses and angled eaves carried on corbelled brackets.

The octagonal, but domeless, **Tomb of Miran Mubarak**, who died in 1457, is the most elaborate of the Thalner group. Each side is marked by a pointed arched opening decorated with fringes of lotus buds. The opening on the south frames a doorway with jambs and lintel. The outer surfaces are almost entirely covered with shallow arabesques, stylised foliation and lotus medallions.

5 · Aurangabad

Aurangabad is familiar to most visitors as a base from which to visit the cave-temples at Ellora and Ajanta, Maharashtra's most famous antiquities. Yet the city [A] and sites in the vicinity [B] deserve attention for the Mughal buildings, the finest in Southern India, as well as for an early set of Buddhist excavations. A full day should be set aside to tour these sights.

The nearby citadel at **Daulatabad** [C], the tombs at **Khuldabad** [D] and the caves at **Ellora** [E] can be covered in a single day, though more time is recommended. The excursion to **Ajanta** [F] will occupy another full day; an overnight stay permits an early morning visit of the caves before the crowds arrive. Ellora and Ajanta are both closed on Mondays.

Adventurous travellers with additional time may be attracted by the outlying sites of **Pitalkhora** [G] and **Ghatotkacha** [H], both with Buddhist excavations, as well as by the ruined temple at **Anwa** [I].

A journey to see the mosques and tombs of **Jalna** [J] and the unique crater lake at **Lona** [K] can be combined in a long day trip. The remains at **Paithan** [L] may be seen on the way to Ahmadnagar [6].

■ **Transport**. Aurangabad is linked by air and road to Bombay [1]; however, the train connection, via Manmad, is inconvenient. Aurangabad lies 212km east of Nasik [4], via Sangamner and Nevasa, and 110km northeast of Ahmadnagar. Buses connect Aurangabad with Daulatabad, Ellora and Ajanta, but alternative arrangements, such as hiring a car, must be made to reach the remoter sites.

■ **Accommodation**. Aurangabad (STD code 02432) is well developed as a tourist centre, with numerous hotels in all categories. The finest are the *Taj Residency* (☎ 333501), *Welcomegroup Rama International* (☎ 485441) and *Ajanta Ambassador* (☎ 485211). An attractive alternative is the *Khuldabad Guest House*, on the ridge of the hill above **Ellora**, or the pleasant *Hotel Kailas* (☎ 41063) next to the caves beneath. For those wishing to spend more time at Ajanta, there is the *MTDC Holiday Resort* at **Fardapur**, 6.5km from the site.

■ **Tourist Information**. The Government of India tourist office is located at *Krishna Vilas*, Station Road (☎ 81217). The MTDC maintains information booths at the *Holiday Resort* (☎ 23298), further east on Station Road, and also at the airport.

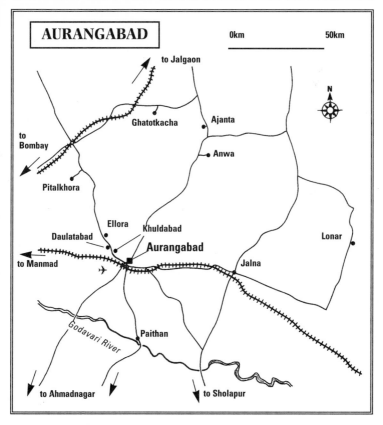

A. Aurangabad

The rock-cut monuments on the outskirts of Aurangabad testify to a Buddhist settlement in the vicinity going back to the 1C AD.

The city itself, however, was only founded in 1610, when Malik Ambar, Prime Minister of Murtaza of Ahmadnagar, chose the village of Khirki for his headquarters. This soon grew into a populous city, attracting the attention of the Mughal invaders. In 1621 Khirki was pillaged and burnt by the Mughal troops under Shah Jahan. Malik Ambar was succeeded as Prime Minister by Fateh Khan, who changed the name of the city to Fatehnagar in 1626. The city was captured once again by the Mughals in 1633. 20 years later, when Prince Aurangzeb was Viceroy of the Deccan provinces, Fatehnagar was renamed Aurangabad. The city was threatened by Maratha bands in 1668 and again in 1681, after which the Viceroy Khan Jahan Bahadur ordered new walls and gates to be built. In 1683 Aurangzeb shifted the Mughal court to Aurangabad, which then assumed the dimensions of an imperial capital, a position it maintained until the Emperor's death in 1707. In 1723 the city became the chief post of the Mughal Prime

Minister Nizamul Mulk, who successfully separated the Deccan provinces from Delhi. His son, Nizam Ali Khan, who succeeded him in 1762, was responsible for shifting the capital of the breakaway Asaf Jahi state to Hyderabad [26], upon which Aurangabad was reduced to a provincial centre of the Nizams.

The crowded streets and markets of Aurangabad are contained within a circle of fortifications laid out on the east bank of the Khan River. The **Walls**, which date from the Mughal era, are about 4.5m high, with crenellated parapets and slit holes for guns, and regularly spaced round bastions. The four principal **Gates** have imposing arched openings surmounted by lines of prominent battlements. The entrances are flanked by polygonal bastions topped with domed pavilions. The **Bhadkal Gate**, on the west side of the city, is an earlier monument, dating from Nizam Shahi times. It displays tiers of shallow arched recesses, with lotus medallions in the spandrels carried on curving brackets in relief. The dome over the interior passageway is carried on eight intersecting arches.

Aurangabad benefits from an ingenious **Hydraulic System** first established by Malik Ambar. This conveys water from distant springs and wells into the city by means of an extensive network of aqueducts, channels and pipes, some more than 4km long. Many features are cut into the bedrock and roofed with masonry. Pressure is regulated by ventilation towers built of lime masonry in which water is forced up into a tank and then down again; such towers are still visible. **Panchakki**, the water mill overlooking the Khan River just outside the west walls of the city, has a tower of this type. Water falling freely from the tower drives a large wheel for grinding grain. The cistern in the middle of the court-yard in front forms the roof of a large subterranean chamber. (At Panchakki, see also the Dargah of Baba Musafir which is described below.)

Important examples of religious architecture are found throughout the walled city. The **Kali Mosque**, erected by Malik Ambar in 1600, is the oldest. Its triple-bayed prayer chamber has arches with lotus medallions on curving brackets in the spandrels. The octagonal corner buttresses are decorated with ornamental niches and topped by domical finials. A fluted dome rises over the middle of the façade. The interior bays are roofed with domes on faceted pendentives. The **Chauk Mosque** of 1662 was built by Shaista Khan, the maternal uncle of Aurangzeb. The steps ascending to its raised terrace are framed by an arched gate. The prayer chamber is five bays wide, with a single central dome and octag-onal buttresses at the corners. The **Lal Mosque** of 1665, the work of Zain al-Abidin, a government official, is similar in layout, but has lobed arches carried on fluted columns.

The **Shah Ganj Mosque** of 1720 occupies the great market square laid out by Aurangzeb, now marked by a modern clock tower. The Mosque is raised high above the street level, with shops built into its sides. Flights of steps on the north and south ascend to a spacious terrace with a large cistern in the middle. The prayer chamber on the west presents a line of lobed arches with finely polished plasterwork. The small *mihrab* in the rear wall is partly octagonal.

Several Mughal-period tombs enshrine the remains of holy personalities. The **Tomb of Hazrat Qadar Auliya**, near Jaffa Gate, has a central chamber roofed with a bulbous dome carried on a high drum. The chamber is surrounded by arcaded porticos roofed with curving vaults. The **Tomb of Nizamuddin Auliya** is a simple cubic chamber with a prominent *mihrab* on a leafy acanthus base. Its corner finials are conceived as miniature pavilions. The **Tomb of Pir Ismail** stands in the well-maintained garden adjoining the Maulana Azad College, beyond the Delhi Gate on the north side of the city. The mausoleum is a flat-roofed arcaded building with domed corner pavilions. The central octagonal chamber accommodates the grave of Aurangzeb's tutor. The complex is entered on the south through a gate with triple arches and rooftop pavilions.

Aurangzeb's citadel, the **Kila Arrak**, laid out in 1693 immediately north of the city, is provided with its own walls. The **Shahi Mosque**, erected by the emperor for his private use, has unusual trilobed arches and triple vaults with curved cornices. The open pavilion, with a curved roof and corner pyramidal vaults that served as the emperor's **Audience Hall**, is located at the highest part of the Kila Arrak, now part of the Government School of Art. The terraces, ponds and fountains in the garden are original features. The Hall is aligned with **Naubat Gate,** the main entrance to the citadel beneath, now unused and dilapidated.

The **Jami Mosque**, a short distance south of the Kila Arrak, was founded in 1615 by Malik Ambar; its prayer chamber was enlarged in Mughal times. Eleven undecorated arches are overhung by eaves on sculpted brackets. The court in front, with a large cistern in the middle, is partly surrounded by domed chambers. The nearby **Kaudiya Luti Mosque**, standing just inside the city walls, is of greater architectural interest. This Mughal building has pierced stone windows set into the walls of the prayer hall. The doorways to side chambers are framed by curved cornices in relief plasterwork. The lobed arches carry domes, that in front of the *mihrab* being elevated on a high drum.

The ***Dargah* of Baba Musafir**, enshrining the remains of Aurangzeb's spiritual guide, stands in a walled complex next to Panchakki, the water mill already mentioned. The tomb is a modest pink stone structure with fluted columns and lobed arches built up to the rear of a mosque. The latter has finely polished plaster piers, lobed arches and corner rooftop pavilions in the finest Mughal manner. The triple domes rise on bands of acanthus leaves. Tomb and mosque, together with *madrasa* and *sarai* (resting place), face onto a delightful garden crowded with flowering shrubs, water channels and fountains bordered by the Khan River.

B. Around Aurangabad
Additional monuments of historical importance are located outside Aurangabad, on the sweeping plain that rises north of the city. The road leading north from Panchakki passes by the campus of the University, in the grounds of which stands the **Soneri Mahal**. This two-storeyed pavilion was erected by a Rajput warrior from central India who accompanied Aurangzeb into the Deccan; it now houses the Archaeology Department. Little is left of the golden tinted murals after which the building was named. The pavilion faces east onto a neglected garden.

Bibi-ka Maqbara, Aurangabad

The road continues north for another 1.5km until it arrives at the **Bibi-ka Maqbara**, the monument for which Aurangabad is best known. The mausoleum, surrounded by sweeping vistas of rugged basalt escarpments, was erected in 1650–57 by Azam Shah, son of Aurangzeb, to entomb his mother, Begam Rabia Durani. The Maqbara stands in the middle of a large walled garden, 457m by 274m, entered on the south through an imposing gateway. The arabesques in the spandrels over the entrance arch and the faceted decoration inside the corner niches are executed in finely modelled plaster; traces of murals can be seen inside. The brass-clad doors are inscribed with the name of the architect, Ataullah, and the date 1661. The garden is demarcated by high crenellated walls with bastions topped by open pavilions on three sides. It is divided into 32 plots by 12 waterways, with sandstone platforms containing ponds and fountains at the crossings; carved stone screens line the axial walkways.

Though the Bibi-ka Maqbara is obviously modelled on the Taj Mahal, comparisons with the Agra monument fail to acknowledge the inventive design and distinguished surface ornamentation of the Aurangabad tomb. Brass-clad doors with elegant embossed designs of flowering plants mark the steps ascending to a broad terrace that overlooks the garden. The tomb itself is a grandiose and strictly symmetrical structure. Each façade is dominated by a lofty portal with a pointed arch flanked by double tiers of smaller arched niches of similar design. A great dome with a pronounced bulbous profile and a brass pot finial crowns the whole composition; the corners are marked with lesser domes and slender finials with miniature domical pavilions. Doorways lead to an inner octagonal gallery bounded by stone screens from which it is possible to view the grave at a lower level, a feature unique to this monument.

The tombstone is enclosed by an octagon of perforated marble screens carved with considerable delicacy. Corner squinches carry the lofty dome above. White marble cladding alternating with delicately moulded plasterwork is used throughout. Like the Taj, the mausoleum is framed by four tapering minarets that stand freely at the corners of the terrace; the examples here, however, are octagonal rather than circular; they are topped by diminutive domed pavilions. The small mosque on the terrace west of the tomb displays finely finished lobed arches and corner minarets. Small recesses with lotuses and arabesques embellish the façade. The interior is roofed with shallow fluted domes.

A distant prospect of the Bibi-ka Maqbara may be had from the **Buddhist Caves** 2km north. The basalt hills here present precipitous scarps, the sides of which have rock-cut monuments divided into two groups, those on the west (Caves 1 to 5) separated from those to the east (Caves 6 to 9) by about 1km. The earliest of the Aurangabad series is **Cave 4**, assigned to the 1C Satavahana era. It is a rectangular *chaitya* hall containing an apsidal-ended colonnade, with a monolithic *stupa* at the rear. Much of the façade and many of the columns have deteriorated, but the finely carved ribs on the ceiling are relatively complete. All the other excavations belong to the 5C–6C Vakataka era.

Cave 1 seems never to have been completed, except for its entrance verandah and porch. **Cave 2** has a small sanctuary surrounded by an ambulatory passageway and preceded by a columned verandah. Bodhisattvas flank the doorway to the shrine, inside which is a seated Buddha in teaching posture, with devotees at his feet. **Cave 3** is the largest and most important of the western group, with a central columned hall approached through a pillared verandah. The antechamber and sanctuary extend beyond the rear wall of the hall, while small cells are aligned along the side walls. The 12 columns inside have multi-faceted shafts with medallions containing seated couples; the capitals are of the pot-and-foliage type. All these elements are embellished with scrollwork, foliation and jewelled garlands. Friezes on the beams above illustrate *Jataka* scenes. The interior of the sanctuary presents a remarkable sculptural tableau of devotees, some with folded hands, others with floral offerings, kneeling before preaching Buddha. Little remains of **Cave 5**, in which Jains appear to have repainted the image of Buddha as a Tirthankara.

Cave 6, the first to be visited in the eastern group, consists of a sanctuary entered directly from the verandah and interior porch. Some of the subshrines in the surrounding passageway have Buddha images; finely carved Bodhisattva figures with attendants and flying celestials appear on either side of the sanctuary doorway. The teaching Buddha within is accompanied by a congregation of kneeling devotees, a later version of the arrangement in Cave 3. Traces of a painted ceiling can be made out in the verandah.

Cave 7, the finest of the eastern group, resembles Cave 6 in many respects. Columned shrines at either end of the verandah house images of Panchika and Hariti (right) and a panel of six goddesses with Padmapani and Shakyamuni (left). The passageway doorway is flanked by bold figures, including Avalokiteshvara surrounded by scenes of rescue (left). Goddesses with attendant and dwarfs adorn the sanctuary doorway, with the usual preaching Buddha within. The side walls have seated Buddhas accompanied by Avalokiteshvara and Tara (right) and female dancer and musicians (left). **Cave 9** consists of three unfinished sanctuaries with porches opening off a common verandah. Among the numerous Buddhist carvings is a Parinirvana scene, now damaged, as in Cave 26 at Ajanta.

The British **Cantonment** lies 2km west of Aurangabad, on the road to Ellora. Several old bungalows can still be sighted. **Holy Trinity Church** of 1879 is a modest Neo-Gothic structure with steep gables and pointed arched openings. The **British Cemetery**, 1.5km beyond, is dominated by an elaborate obelisk that serves as a memorial of Richard Seyer of the Bengal army, who died in 1853.

C. Daulatabad

The most spectacular hill fort of Maharashtra, associated with almost all its rulers in the 12C–18C, lies 14km north of Aurangabad. The site is overshadowed by a mighty rock that rises dramatically 183m above the plain. Its artifically excavated sides create a partly vertical profile, easily distinguished from the natural hills.

Originally known as Devagiri, Hill of the Gods, the citadel was capital of the Yadavas, the most powerful rulers of Maharashtra in the centuries prior to the conquest of the Delhi forces in 1296. Renamed Daulatabad, Abode of Prosperity, the fort served as the main stronghold of the Tughluqs in the Deccan. In 1327 Muhammad Shah shifted his court from Delhi to Daulatabad, which for several years after served as the principal centre of Tughluq power. It was here in 1347 that the Bahmanis declared their independence from the Tughluqs, shifting soon after to Gulbarga [24A]. The stronghold remained under Bahmani control until the end of the 15C, when it was taken over by the Nizam Shahis. In 1601 Daulatabad became the seat of the remnant of the Nizam Shahi kingdom after Ahmadnagar was lost to the Mughals. It succumbed in its turn in 1633, and over the next 20 years was used by the Mughals as their principal headquarters in the Deccan. When Nizamul Mulk asserted his autonomy from Delhi, Daulatabad became a part of his dominions; it was eventally absorbed into the breakaway Asaf Jahi state of Hyderabad.

The first feature to be noticed when arriving from Aurangabad is a **Pavilion** with raised vaulted chambers and overhanging balconies, dating from Bahmani times. The nearby ***Dargah* of Hazrat Shah Bahauddin Ashri** is a small garden tomb, also of the same period. The road continues for about 1.5km before passing through a gap in the outer fort and running beside Fortifications until it arrives at the Outer Gate.

Daulatabad is divided into three distinctive zones: the conical hill itself, known as **Balakot**; an almost circular walled area below that adjoins the base of the hill on its north and east sides and forms an inner fort, **Kataka**; and an outer fort, **Ambarkot**, defined by walls that create a vast area fanning out from Kataka for almost 2km to the north and south. The **Fortifications** of both Kataka and Ambarkot employ double circuits of massive walls set at a marked angle and lined with slit holes and battlements. The lower outer walls of Kataka have both polygonal and round bastions; the higher inner walls are provided with box-like guard rooms and both square and round bastions. Deep moats offer additional protection. The frequent use of 12C–13C temple materials indicates that these works post-date the Yadava period; they constitute the most substantial example of Tughluq military architecture in Southern India.

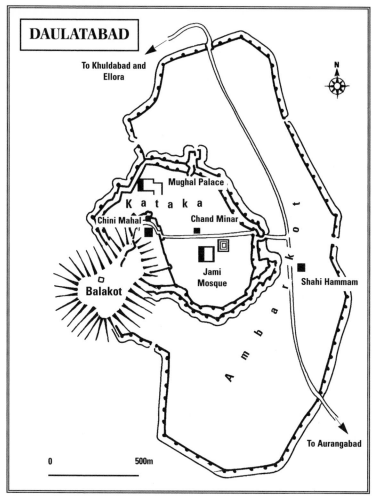

The **Outer Gate** on the east is the one used by most visitors. It presents a
sequence of arched entrances and courts shielded by curving outworks that
project almost 80m beyond the Fortifications. The entrances preserve wooden
doors with great iron spikes; the chambers within have shallow domes with
traces of plaster decoration. Cannons with 'VOC' markings, taken from Dutch
ships, and musketry with finely worked animal heads are on display.

On passing through the Outer Gate, visitors arrive at the beginning of a
Street that traverses Kataka, proceeding west towards Balakot. The royal and
religious structures on either side are now reduced to overgrown piles of rubble.
Excavations here have revealed vestiges of courtly residences, service structures
and waterworks, some belonging to the Bahmani era. The road passes beside a
large square **Tank**.

Immediately west is the **Jami Mosque**, founded in 1318 during the occupation by Qutbuddin Mubarak, the Khilji ruler of Delhi. The vast square court of
the Mosque, some 80m by 60m, is the largest in Southern India. It is entered on
three sides through domed chambers, that on the east approached by a flight of
steps. The spacious prayer hall on the west has a columned façade interrupted
by a trio of arched portals. The interior consists of 25 aisles, five bays deep,
roofed with shallow domes. An enlarged dome rises over the bay immediately in
front of the central *mihrab* in the rear wall. Though many columns have figural
and floral shafts carved on their shafts, they do not all seem to come from
dismantled temples; some were obviously newly fashioned for this project.
Abandoned for many years, the Mosque has recently been converted into a
temple by installing an image of Bharata Mata.

Although the Jami Mosque has no minaret, the **Chand Minar**, standing
freely a short distance away on the north side of the main Street, probably
assumed the function of a prayer tower. It seems also to have served as a victory
monument. Its 30m high shaft is divided into four stages, separated by diminishing circular balconies on projecting brackets. The Chand Minar dates from
the Tughluq occupation, but the third fluted section was added by Alauddin
Hassan, founder of the Bahmani kingdom, to celebrate his break with Delhi. A
brass crescent moon protrudes from the bulbous dome-like summit of the tower.
The small structure at the base includes a diminutive mosque of 1445 adorned
with glazed tiles, a few of which remain in the walls, and sculpted brackets
supporting balconies.

An overgrown path behind the Chand Minar proceeds east to a restored
Mughal-styled **Pavilion**. The path continues to the collapsing remains of the
Mughal Palace immediately north of Balakot. Pavilions with lobed arches are
grouped formally around two large courts, each with a four-square garden. Two
brick built *hammams* form part of the complex.

A small **Mosque** stands beyond Chand Minar, on the north side of the main
Street. Its unadorned prayer chamber is raised on a high plinth. The imposing
Inner Gate nearby functions as the only access to Balakot. Its arched entrance
is flanked by tapering round buttresses. Walls with prominent curved battlements create a discrete fortified zone that forms the lower part of Balakot. The
dilapidated and overgrown buildings here are all that remain of the royal residences of the Bahmanis and Nizam Shahis. The best-preserved feature is the
Chini Mahal, so-called because of the blue-and-white tiles set into its plastered
façade. The double-storeyed hall within is roofed with transverse arches. The
ruined **Bahmani Palace** opposite has triple chambers with arched doorways
opening onto an inner court. The plaster medallions here have finely worked
geometric and arabesque motifs. Fragments of wooden beams and brackets
project from the walls; the windows above have perforated designs in plaster-
covered brickwork. Steps nearby ascend to a circular **Bastion**, on top of which
is a cannon covered with geometric patterns and lions in full relief; the opening
is fashioned as a ram's head.

Access to **Balakot** is possible only after crossing over a trench artifically cut into
the base of the hill. This was originally crossed with a heavily guarded drawbridge, replaced in recent times with a footbridge. The ascent passes through
rock-cut chambers and tunnels, some of which are reworked excavations

contemporary with those at Ellora. The path climbs up the wooded upper slope of the hill, passing by a Mughal **Pavilion** with a part-octagonal arcade, offering magnificent vistas. A magazine and remnants of artillery are seen at the summit. From here, visitors must descend by retracing the Street back to the Outer Gate.

The **Shahi *Hammam***, almost directly opposite the Outer Gate, is a Mughal-period structure. Its chambers are roofed by shallow domes with circular holes on faceted pendentives. The smaller chambers in the corners have baths.

The road proceeding north from Daulatabad passes through the **Delhi Gate** in the outer walls of Ambarkot. Its austere arched opening is relieved by sculpted lions in the spandrels. The road then ascends an escarpment, giving excellent views over the whole site.

Funerary monuments from different eras dot the hills southeast of Daulatabad. The whitewashed ***Dargah* of Sayyid Mohmin Arif Ballal** is popular with devotees. The adjacent ruin has stone screens in the doorway and windows; the corner finials are conceived as miniature domed pavilions. About 750m south of the *Dargah* is a Mughal-styled garden tomb. The walled enclosure has corner octagonal pavilions with fluted corner domes and a dilapidated entrance structure on the west. Square flower plots surround the graves raised on a dais in the middle.

D. Khuldabad

This small settlement lies 8km north of Daulatabad, 4km by road from Ellora, just beneath the crest of the cliff into which the famous caves have been excavated.

> Several Sufi teachers of the Chishti order chose to reside in Khuldabad, Abode of Eternity, during the first occupation of Daulatabad by the Tughluqs; the practice continued into later times. As a result, numerous legends grew up about the site, including the miracle of the staff which sprouted leaves, carried by the pious disciple. Khuldabad's reputation reached its height under the Mughals; Aurangzeb gave orders to be buried here next to the tomb of his favourite saint. Other royal figures also chose Khuldabad as their final resting place: Ahmad Nizam Shah, first of the Ahmadnagar rulers; Malik Ambar, the founder of Aurangabad; Azam Shah, builder of the Bibi-ka Maqbara; and Nizamul Mulk, first of the Asaf Jahi line, the future Nizams of Hyderabad.

The village of Khuldabad is contained within a square of brick **Walls** topped with a line of battlements dating from Aurangzeb's reign. This emperor was also responsible for the **Gateways** on the north and south, which have arched entrances surmounted by pavilions with curving cornices set between polygonal bastions. The principal monuments of Khuldabad face onto the street connecting these Gateways.

The ***Dargah* of Hazrat Khaja Seyed Zainuddin**, on the east side of the street, is entered through an austere domed chamber dating from Bahmani times. This gives access to an inner court surrounded by Mughal-styled arcades, with a mosque on the west. The tomb of the saint, who died in 1370, stands in a small enclosure to the north. This unadorned structure has sloping walls, a parapet of battlements and a flattish dome. The grave of the Mughal emperor in the southwest corner is surrounded by a superbly worked marble screen added in 1921 by the Nizam of Hyderabad; the southeast corner is occupied by the graves of Azam Shah and his family. Relics of the Prophet are displayed in a small chamber nearby.

Opposite, on the west side of the street, stands the **_Dargah_ of Hazrat Khaja Burhanuddin**. This, too, is entered through an early-styled domed chamber, next to which is a two-storeyed structure with Mughal-styled pavilions. The spacious court within is surrounded by arcades. A doorway in the rear wall leads to the tomb of the saint, who died in 1344. This is a modest structure with corner pilasters; a pierced stone window with an inscribed panel above is seen on the east. The tomb is is aligned with a small mosque to the west. This has lobed arches and a central flying arch in front of the dome, a feature typical of Nizam Shahi architecture. The graves of Nizamul Mulk and his descendants are surrounded by red sandstone screens.

Immediately south is **Lal Bagh**, a funerary complex laid out by Khan Jahan, Aurangzeb's foster-brother. The dilapidated octagonal tomb in the middle of the four-square garden preserves traces of yellow tilework. The stone gateway facing the main street is similarly embellished.

Leaving the town by the north Gateway, the road climbs for about 1km, passing through another gate and winding around a _dargah_ and several small tombs before arriving at a group of funerary monuments dating from Nizam Shahi times. The most imposing is the **Tomb of Malik Ambar**, who died in 1626. It displays crisply worked arched recesses, the central ones filled with geometric screens of great variety and beauty. The walls are overhung by a bold cornice on ornate brackets; the corner turrets are conceived as miniature pavilions. The flattish dome rises on a fringe of petals. The smaller tomb nearby is that of Malik Ambar's wife.

An **Unidentified Tomb** stands inside a walled compound a short distance to the northwest, perched on the crest of the hill. This unadorned building has double tiers of arched recesses, the central ones being open. No graves are preserved within. The garden of the adjacent Guest House offers a grand panorama of the plain below. A path from here descends steeply to the Ellora caves, passing by the excavated court of Cave 16.

E. Ellora

The celebrated **Cave Temples** at this site, 26km northwest of Aurangabad, are scooped out of the vertical face of a linear basalt escarpment to face west across the Deccan plain. Buddhist monuments (Caves 1 to 12) occupy the southern part of Ellora, while Hindu monuments (Caves 13 to 29) are located in the middle; Jain excavations (Caves 30 to 33) occupy the northern extremity of the site. The dramatic focus of the site is the magnificent achievement of Cave 16, the celebrated Kailasa. Most visitors begin their tour of Ellora here, though it is also possible to leave the approach road by a path that arrives directly at Cave 1. The site is closed on Mondays.

The rock-cut monuments span a period of almost 400 years. The earliest caves at Ellora are believed to be the minor excavations of the Ganesha Lena group, assigned to the 6C Kalachuri era, above Cave 28, at an original holy spot next to the Girija stream that traverses the site, forming a waterfall in the rainy season. Cave 28 opens directly onto the pool formed beneath the waterfall. Dhumar Lena (Cave 29) is the grandest of the monuments belonging to this early phase and is stylistically related to the Cave Temple at Elephanta [2A]. Another Kalachuri monument at Ellora is Rameshvara (Cave 21). The Vishvakarma (Cave 10) and twin Do Thal and Tin Tal (Caves 11 and 12) date from the 7C–8C Early Chalukya period. The next phase of activity coincides with the Rashtrakuta era in the second half of the 8C, continuing into the 9C–10C. Two records link these rulers with Ellora: the inscribed grant of Dantidurga on Dashavatara (Cave 15) and a set of copper plates discovered in Gujarat, mentioning the involvement of Krishna I in the excavation of Kailasa (Cave 16). The Jain group is also assigned to the Rashtrakuta period.

The first nine caves at Ellora are all variations on the standard monastery layout, with a columned verandah leading to a central hall, with cells opening off the sides and a Buddha shrine at the rear. **Cave 2** has a verandah with images of Panchika with Hariti at the end (right). Guardians flank the entrance, next to which there is a profusion of Buddha figures and divinities. The square hall is defined by fluted columns with cushion-shaped capitals. The side walls have sculptures of seated Buddhas flanked by Bodhisattvas and celestials. A similar but larger Buddha occupies the end shrine. Porches lead from the sanctuary to small side cells. The right porch displays a relief of the miracle at Sravasti.

Cave 4 is a two-storeyed exavation, now mostly ruined. **Cave 5**, a larger excavation entered at a higher level, consists of a long hall divided into three aisles. The benches carved out of the floor may have been used for reading and eating. The porches in the middle of the side walls are flanked by small cells. The columns are delicately carved with medallions surrounded by exuberant foliage.

Cave 6 has a rectangular columned hall with smaller side halls, each with two cells. The columns here have large pot-and-foliage capitals. A columned antechamber leading to a small shrine has its walls covered with Bodhisattva figures and goddesses. The shrine doorway is guarded by large Bodhisattvas with river goddesses on pilasters. The seated Buddha within is flanked by multiple smaller Buddhas, attendants and devotees.

Cave 8 has a shrine surrounded by a processional passageway on three sides (as at Aurangabad). The passage way has three cells on the left, an incomplete columned gallery at the rear and two columns in front. Its sculptures include Panchika and Hariti.

Cave 9, approached through the hall of Cave 6, consists of an open terrace with a balcony. The façade is enlivened with Buddhist deities and an unusual scene of Tara rescuing devotees from the perils of snake, sword and elephant (left), and fire and shipwreck (right).

Vishvakarma (Cave 10), one of the finest *chaitya* halls of the rock-cut series, is named after the mythical architect of the gods. A gateway raised on a basement enlivened with animals leads to an excavated court. The hall at the end has two galleries arranged on two levels. The columns of the lower level have partly

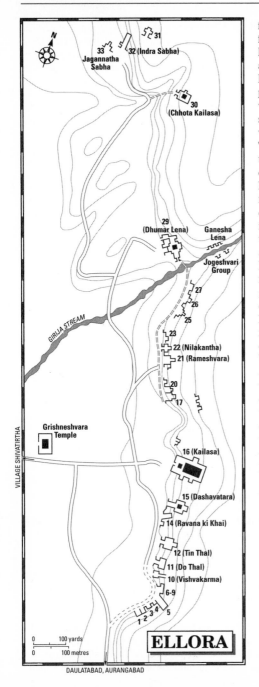

Map labels:

N

31

33   32 (Indra Sabha)
Jagannatha
Sabha

30
(Chhota Kailasa)

29
(Dhumar Lena)   Ganesha
Lena

Jogeshvari
Group

27

26

25

23
22 (Nilakantha)
21 (Rameshvara)

20

17

GIRIJA STREAM

Grishneshvara
Temple

VILLAGE SHIVATIRTHA

16 (Kailasa)

15 (Dashavatara)

14 (Ravana ki Khai)

12 (Tin Thal)
11 (Do Thal)
10 (Vishvakarma)
6-9
1 2 3 4   5

0   100 yards
0   100 metres

ELLORA

DAULATABAD, AURANGABAD

fluted shafts and pot-and-foliage capitals; a long hunting frieze appears above. The upper gallery has a verandah with a parapet wall embellished with amorous couples and scrollwork. The main verandah has end shrines. The antechamber walls of the shrine to the right are covered with reliefs of Buddha and goddesses; a figure of Lokeshvara is enshrined within. The hall itself is entered through three doorways. Access to an upper gallery is by steps left of the verandah. The façade behind this upper gallery has a central doorway flanked by Buddhist figures. The pediment over contains a three-quarters circular window between arched motifs adorned with flying celestials, *naga* deities with coiled bodies and scrollwork. The side niches, containing Bodhisattvas with female attendants, are capped with pyramidal pediments composed of arch-like motifs. Beams are cut out of the ceiling above.

The upper verandah of Cave 10 leads to an internal gallery (above the front bays of the hall) with a balustrade adorned with embracing couples and maidens. The spacious apsidal-ended **Hall** is divided into three aisles by slender octagonal columns. Two central columns of the front row have pot-and-foliage capitals. A frieze of dwarfs and panels showing preaching Buddhas are seen above the column brackets. Curved ribs springing from seated dwarfs accentuate the soaring vault of the interior. A teaching Buddha carved on the front of the votive *stupa* sits within a frame adorned with flying attendants; Bodhisattvas stand at either side. The *stupa* is raised on a tall drum and topped with a multi-tiered finial.

Both **Do Tal (Cave 11)** and **Tin Tal (Cave 12)** have three storeys. (Cave 11 is erroneously named Do Tal, or Two Storeys, because its ground floor was once buried.) Each is entered through a spacious excavated court reached by a passage cut through the cliff. The lowest level of Cave 11 has two cells and a central sanctuary. A flight of steps at the north end of the verandah ascends to the intermediate level. This consists of five excavations, of which the first is incomplete and the last is a cell with a rock-cut bed; the remaining excavations have sanctuaries housing Buddha images attended by Bodhisattvas. The uppermost level has a porch leading to a long columned hall. In the middle of the rear wall is a Buddha shrine, while to the left is a second sanctuary. Images of Durga and Ganesha indicate that this monument was later converted to Hindu worship.

The lowest floor of Cave 12 consists of a long hall with three rows of columns. An antechamber leading to the Buddha shrine is recessed into the rear wall. Steps from the southwest corner of the hall ascend to the topmost level, which consists of a verandah, a hall with four rows of columns and an antechamber and shrine. Five large Bodhisattvas flanked by attendants are carved on each of the side walls; seven Buddhas, meditating or touching the earth, with flying figures above, appear either side of the antechamber entrance. Twelve goddesses seated on lotuses held by *nagas* appear inside.

Ravana ki Khai (Cave 14) consists of a verandah, square hall and small sanctuary surrounded by a passageway. Large guardians and river goddesses flank the sanctuary doorway; a broken image of Durga is seen inside. Figures carved on the side walls include (left wall, front to back) Durga, Lakshmi bathed by elephants, Vishnu as Varaha, seated Vishnu with Shri and Bhudevi, and Vishnu with single consort; (right wall, front to back) Durga, Shiva and Parvati playing dice, dancing Shiva, Ravana shaking Mount Kailasa, and Shiva spearing Andhaka.

Begun as a Buddhist monastery, **Dashavatara (Cave 15)** has an open court with a free-standing monolithic pavilion in the middle. This has pilastered walls with shallow niches and pierced windows overhung by eaves. The entrance is flanked by river goddesses; other female figures are carved on the walls. Reclining lions and seated dwarfs animate the roof. A flight of steps left of the entrance ascends to a spacious hall on the upper floor of the two-storeyed temple at the rear of the court. Shrines are recessed into the middle of three sides of the hall. That at the rear, housing a *linga*, is approached through a porch flanked by guardians.

Large panels, now worn, occupying the space between the wall columns, illustrate a wide range of mythological topics: (in clockwise sequence, from the front of the left wall) Shiva spearing Andhaka, Nataraja, Shiva and Parvati playing dice, the marriage of Shiva and Parvati, and Ravana shaking Kailasa; (rear wall, left side) Shiva emerging from the *linga* to rescue Markandeya, and Shiva receiving Ganga in his hair; (antechamber walls) Ganesha, Parvati and musicians, Lakshmi bathed by elephants, and standing Karttikeya; (rear wall, right side) Shiva emerging from the *linga*, and Shiva in the chariot destroying the demons of the triple cities; (right wall) Krishna holding up Govardhana, Vishnu sleeping on Shesha, Vishnu on flying Garuda, Vishnu as Varaha, Trivikrama with one leg kicked up, and Narasimha disembowelling Hiranyakashipu. A stepped path between Caves 15 and 16, ascending to the Guest House at the top of the cliff, offers elevated views of the Kailasa Temple.

Cave 16, with its central monolithic Kailasa Temple, represents the climax of the rock-cut phase of Southern Indian architecture. This monument was first patronised by Krishna I (756–73), and later by successive figures of the Rashtrakuta dynasty. The Kailasa Temple is obscured from the outside by a screen wall, in the middle of which is a two-storeyed **Gateway** with an upper gallery overhung by eaves. The flanking walls have shallow pilasters framing the Dikpalas and river goddesses. Carved panels of Durga (right) and Ganesha (left) are seen within the passageway. The inner face of the enclosure walls has figures of Durga on the lion and Shiva in the chariot. A free-standing **Nandi Pavilion** stands at the entrance of the Temple. Lakshmi seated in a crowded lotus pond, being bathed by elephants, faces the Gateway. The **Monolithic Columns**, 17m high, at either side have bold mouldings adorned with lotus friezes, garlands and sculpture niches. Three-dimensional elephants, their trunks broken, stand nearby.

The rock-cut **Kailasa Temple** is influenced by Early Chaluyka structural traditions, as at Pattadakal [22D]. The west-facing Temple is raised on a solid basement sculpted with frontal torsos of elephants gathering lotuses in their trunks. Staircases ascend to the upper level, where there is a columned hall with three porches. An antechamber at the rear (east) leads to the principal sanctuary, which is surrounded by an open terrace with five small shrines. Bridges connect the west porch of the hall with the Nandi Pavilion and, in turn, with the upper storey of the entrance Gateway. The high basement of the hall and sanctuary appears to rest on the elephants beneath. Slender wall pilasters frame carved panels and pierced stone windows. A parapet of miniature roof forms is seen above.

The pyramidal mass of the tower rises more than 32m above the pavement. The superstructure is divided into three receding stages and is capped with an octagonal-domed roof. The arched projection on the front face shows seated Shiva surrounded by dwarfs and jewelled garlands. The subsidiary corner shrines have similar but smaller towers. In the middle of the flat roof over the hall is a large lotus surrounded by a quartet of heroic striding lions carved in full relief. The cut-out pilasters at the corners of the Nandi pavilion have dwarfs on top. The porches have intricately decorated columns overhung by curved eaves. The balconies are adorned with pot motifs and foliate friezes.

The sculptural scheme of the Kailasa Temple is elaborate throughout. The staircases at the lower level are flanked by walls covered with narrative friezes depicting episodes from the *Mahabharata* epic (above) and Krishna's birth and youthful exploits (below) on the north staircase. Battle scenes with monkey armies on the south staircase illustrate scenes from the *Ramayana*. Large-scale panels on the lower storey of the Temple show Shiva dancing within the skin of the elephant demon, the same god as Dakshinamurti (both beneath the bridge linking the hall with the Nandi Pavilion), and Ravana disturbing Shiva and Parvati seated in the mountain home (middle of south wall). Shiva spearing

Andhaka (north), the same god appearing out of the *linga* (west), and Jatayu attacking Ravana (south) appear on the upper storey. The outer walls of the sanctuary have icons of Shiva framed by pairs of pilasters supporting foliated *makaras* or arched motifs containing miniature temple towers, attendant maidens and amorous couples.

The hall of the Kailasa Temple is entered through a doorway flanked by pairs of guardians with attendants. To the left is a panel showing Shiva in the scene of the descent of Ganga; on the right, Shiva emerges out of the *linga*. 16 decorated columns inside the hall support a ceiling embellished with an icon of Nataraja. Further depictions of Shiva and Parvati occur within the antechamber. The sanctuary doorway is highly ornamented, with river goddesses at either side; the *linga* within stands on a circular pedestal. Fragmentary murals survive on the porch ceilings: flying figures with dwarfs amid clouds, a deity riding a mythical beast, and battle scenes with elephants, horses and infantry (west porch).

The vertical walls that form the sides of the great court of Cave 16 accommodate sanctuaries, halls and porticos. The **Shrine of the River Goddesses**, left of the entrance Gateway, has delicately worked images of Sarasvati, Ganga and Yamuna, each framed by an arches issuing from open-mouthed *makaras*. The **Lankeshvara Temple**, immediately right, is reached by a staircase with an image of Lakshmi on the wall of the intermediate landing. The Temple has a columned hall with balcony seating on two sides and a sanctuary surrounded by a passageway at the rear. A seated Nandi image is set into a recess in the west wall. The columns are adorned with jewelled bands and large pot-and-foliage motifs with fluted cushioned-shaped capitals. The balcony slabs are enlivened with amorous couples between pilasters. Panels on the side walls depict Ganesha, Narasimha, the trio of Brahma, Shiva and Vishnu, and Parvati, Varaha and Surya (left wall). River goddesses and guardians flank the sanctuary doorway. The *linga* inside stands before a relief depiction of a triple-headed bust of Shiva.

The portico that wraps around the eastern half of the court shelters repeated images of Shiva and Vishnu. The **Hall of Sacrifice** on the south is notable for its remarkable three-dimensional sculptures. Seated Durga, Chamunda and Kali, the last in front of an emaciated prostrate body, appear on the right, the seven Matrikas with Ganesha, and Parvati at the rear, and female attendants on the left. The three-storeyed temple to the left has a doorway flanked by female guardians and attendants.

Cave 17, a short distance further north, is entered through a projecting porch, mostly collapsed, set in a small court. This leads to a columned hall and a *linga* sanctuary with a surrounding passageway. Among the deities represented in the wall panels are Ganesha (left) and Durga and Vishnu (right). An unusual image of Brahma is seen outside the court (left wall).

Rameshvara (Cave 21) is notable for the sensuous beauty of its carvings. A court with a monolithic Nandi in the middle leads to a verandah with side shrines. Female figures adorn the brackets of the verandah columns; amorous couples animate the balcony wall. A gracefully posed Ganga is seen left of the verandah; Yamuna appears in the corresponding position to the right. Panels within the verandah depict Karttikeya, the marriage of Shiva and Parvati in the presence of the gods, Durga (left end shrine), Shiva and Parvati disturbed by Ravana, Shiva and Parvati playing dice with Nandi beneath (rear wall), dancing

Shiva, the seven Matrikas with Ganesha and Virabhadra, and skeletal Kala and Kali (right end shrine). Guardians flank the doorway of the *linga* sanctuary opening off the verandah.

Nilakantha (Cave 22) is distinguished for its free-standing Nandi pavilion, now damaged, and separate shrines for the Matrikas. Three entrances guarded by seated lions give access to the columned interior of **Dhumar Lena (Cave 29)**. The columns of the spacious hall have fluted shafts and cushion-shaped capitals. A square *linga* sanctuary at the rear of the hall is detached from the walls. Its four doorways are flanked by pairs of tall guardian figures with female attendants. Large-scale wall panels depict Shiva impaling Andhaka and the divine couple disturbed by Ravana (west), Nataraja and Lakulisha (north), and the marriage of Shiva and Parvati in the presence of the gods, and the couple playing dice (south). River goddesses are positioned outside the north and south entrances.

The **Ganesha Lena** and **Jogeshvari Groups** are situated in a ravine about 90m above Cave 28. The last cave in Ganesha Lena has traces of paintings showing Shiva appearing out of the *linga* and the scene of the churning of the ocean.

A walk of almost 1km is required to reach the Jain group. **Chhota Kailasa (Cave 30)** is a small but incomplete replica of Cave 16, with a monolithic shrine standing freely in the middle of an excavated court. This shrine has a columned hall entered through a porch with balcony seating adorned with pots, pilasters and elephants. Carved ornamentation is mostly restricted to Jain saints and goddesses. Various Tirthankaras are seen inside the hall; the sanctuary enshrines Mahavira seated on a lion throne.

Indra Sabha (Cave 32), the largest of the Jain series, also has a monolithic shrine in the middle of an open court. Miniature Jina figures adorn the arched niches of the roof projections. A free-standing elephant and column, the latter with four figures on top, stand nearby. The vertical sides of the court are embellished with lion and elephant friezes, as well as with Tirthankaras. A double-storeyed temple is cut into the rear of the court, but only the upper hall is complete. The verandah has carved images of Indra (left) and Ambika with a child seated on her lap, a lion beneath and a spreading tree above (right). Panels within the hall show Indra seated on the elephant as well as various Tirthankaras. Exuberant foliation and garlands, partly cut out, adorn the fluted column shafts. Fragmentary ceiling paintings show flying couples and maidens.

The sustained reputation of Ellora through the centuries as a religious site is demonstrated by the **Ghrishneshvara Temple**, the most popular place of workship for most visitors today. This enshrines one of the self-manifested *jytotirlingas*. Erected in the late 18C by Ahilyabai, the Holkar queen, the Ghrishneshvara Temple is located 750m west of the Kailasa Temple.

The Ghrishneshvara Temple is a revivalist monument notable for its finely worked details. Its sandstone walls are articulated by deeply cut horizontal mouldings defining the plinth and basement. The brick-and-plaster tower above is divided into diminishing tiers of miniature elements, with bands on four sides, terminating in a fluted dome on petals. The frontal projection shows an encrusted arch framing Shiva and Parvati riding on Nandi. The corner finials are conceived as miniature pavilions. The adjoining open hall, sheltering a sculpted Nandi, has porch projections with balcony seating on three sides. The columns are enlivened with carvings of divinities, as well as horsemen and hunters with guns; the cubic brackets are fashioned as crouching dwarfs. Male worshippers must remove their upper garments before worshipping the circular *yoni* and *linga* set into the sanctuary floor. The chamber is roofed by a lofty dome.

Two small **Tombs** outside the Temple compound have finely carved lotus decoration and pierced stone screens typical of the Nizam Shahi style. A further 400m west of the Temple is a small pond known as **Shivatirtha**, also the work of Ahilyabai. This finely finished water monument comprises a square well surrounded by steps and eight diminutive *linga* shrines of different designs.

F. Ajanta

The Ajanta caves (closed on Mondays) are renowned for their paintings. They lie 102km northeast of Aurangabad, the nearest railhead being 55km north at Jalgaon. **Ajanta Village**, 6km southeast of the ancient site, is a well-preserved fortified settlement dating from 1730, and is the work of Nizamul Mulk. The village is contained within a square of crenellated walls reinforced by part-octagonal bastions. The principal gate on the south is approached by an arched bridge over the Vaghora River. The mosque within the walls and the octagonal caravanserai beyond the north gate are the principal features of interest.

The Buddhist excavations at Ajanta were accidentally discovered in 1819 by Captain John Smith, who was out on a hunting expedition. The site then attracted the attention of Major Robert Gill, who lived in the caves in 1849–55, copying the paintings and photographing the ruins. Since then the monuments have been studied extensively and much restored. The fragile condition of the paintings means that the caves are closed from time to time for conservation.

Ajanta's natural setting is incomparable, especially during the rainy season. The monuments are cut into the rocky sides of a crescent-shaped gorge, at the head of which is a waterfall feeding a natural pool, the source of the Vaghora River. A viewpoint above the middle of the gorge giving a panorama of the whole site marks the spot where Smith first glimpsed the caves. 30 Buddhist excavations, some unfinished, are divided into two distinct phases separated by a period of more than 500 years. The earlier Hinayana monuments date from the 2C–1C BC Satavahana period. Among these are Caves 9 and 10, both *chaitya* halls, and several monasteries (Caves 8, 12, 13 and 15A). The later Mahayana monuments, assigned to the 5C, include two more *chaitya* halls (Caves 19 and 26) and a number of monasteries (Caves 1, 2, 16 and 17). These are the work of the Ashmakas and Rishikas, feudatories of Harishena (460–78) and other rulers of the Vakataka dynasty.

Cave 1 is one of the finest monasteries. A verandah with cells and porches at either end has three doorways leading into the hall; 20 columns are arranged in a square around an open space with small cells on three sides. An antechamber in the rear wall gives access to the principal shrine, where a seated Buddha is flanked by Bodhisattvas and flying figures holding garlands.

The sculptural treatment is elaborate throughout. The columns have medallions adorned with scrollwork and flutings with jewelled motifs; circular ribbed motifs serve as capitals. The brackets have flying couples framing scenes from Buddha's life. Figurative friezes over the verandah columns include the sick man, old man, corpse and saintly man encountered by Siddhartha (left porch). The doorways are embellished with *naga* deities, musicians and amorous couples; maidens beneath trees are positioned above.

The **murals** of Cave 1 are among the greatest at Ajanta. *Jataka* scenes cover the hall walls. Left of the front doorway is the *Sibi Jataka*, where the Bodhisattva as a king rescues a pigeon from a hawk. The next panel depicts the conversion of Nanda, who abandoned his wife Sundari. The palace scene which forms the end panel belongs to the *Samkhapala Jataka*. This narrative is continued beyond the corner onto the left wall, where the Bodhisattva as a serpent king listens to an ascetic; to the right, his wounded snake-body is dragged by hunters. Beneath is Alara, the householder who delivers the serpent king by offering his oxen as ransom. The remainder of the left wall is occupied by the *Mahajanaka Jataka*. On the right is the shipwreck of King Mahajanaka, with a queen and her attendants tempting the prince with wordly pleasures on the left. Next, Mahajanaka comes out of a city gate to meet an ascetic in a rocky shelter. He then announces his decision to renounce the world, and finally leaves his capital on horseback.

Paintings of graciously posed Bodhisattvas with elaborate headdresses flank the antechamber doorway in the middle of the rear wall of Cave 1. Padmapani (left) and Avalokiteshvara (right) are accompanied by attendants, divine musicians and flying figures. Further right, another Bodhisattva is offered a tray of flowers by a king. The antechamber side walls record the assault and temptation of Mara (left) and the miracle of Sravasti, when the Master multiplied himself (right). Incidents from the *Champeyya Jataka* occupy the right end of the rear wall. The serpent king Champeyya is captured and made to perform by a snake-charmer. Champeyya's wife begs the ruler of Varanasi to release her husband. Both kings are seated with ladies and attendants in the final deliverance scene. Right of the front doorway, foreigners with peaked caps and beards offer gifts to a seated ruler, sometimes identified as the Vakataka ruler Harishena. The hall ceiling is covered with panels filled with floral and leafy motifs, as well as embracing couples, drinking figures, dwarfs, elephants and geese.

Cave 2 repeats the basic scheme of the previous example, though with additional carvings. The end shrines of the verandah contain a seated *naga* king with *yakshi* attendants (right) and Hariti with a child on her lap (left). The subsidiary shrines in the rear wall of the hall house Panchika and Hariti (right) and corpulent *yakshas* with attendants (left). The monastery is remarkable for the painted ceiling, with numerous compartments filled with a variety of large medallions with delicate bands of lotus ornament, scrollwork and geometric patterns.

Nativity episodes, such as the dream of Maya, the interpretation by priests and the birth of Gautama, are painted on the left wall of the hall in Cave 2. *Jataka* stories cover the remainder of the walls. In the *Hamsa Jataka*, the Bodhisattva as a goose is captured, then released at the order of a royal couple, to whom he delivers a final sermon (left wall). A large portion of the right wall is devoted to the *Vidhurapandita Jataka*, especially the courtly scene with the princess Indrati in a swing, Punnaka's proposal of marriage, the game of dice in which Punnaka defeats Vidhurapandita, the Bodhisattva in an earlier birth, and the final happy union. The conversion of Purna and the rescue of Purna's brother from ship-

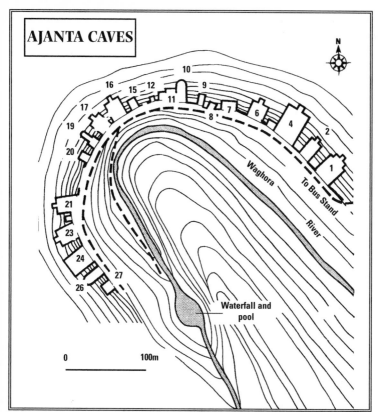

AJANTA CAVES

N

Waghora River

To Bus Stand

Waterfall and pool

0   100m

wreck are seen beneath. Miniature seated Buddhas are painted on the side walls of the shrine and antechamber, also in the hall (left side). Buddha and Bodhisattva figures flank the doorways to the antechamber and sanctuary. Processions of gracefully posed female devotees carrying offerings adorn the walls of the subsidiary shrines. Seated Buddhas cover the walls of the central shrine.

Cave 4, the largest monastery at Ajanta, was never completed. The verandah has eight octagonal columns, with cells at both ends. Three doorways lead into the hall, where part of the ceiling has collapsed. The central doorway is embellished with guardians, couples, flying figures and maidens clutching trees (jambs), and Buddhas and garland-bearing dwarfs (lintel). A panel right of the doorway depicts Avalokiteshvara surrounded by worshippers suffering torments; the miracle of Sravasti is shown on the left. Only a few of the cells are complete. The shrine has the usual arrangement of a teaching Buddha attended by Bodhisattvas. The antechamber is provided with additional standing Buddhas, two of which are unfinished.

The next monastery, **Cave 6**, is excavated on two levels. The lower hall has 16 octagonal columns arranged in four rows, without any central space. The shrine doorway has an ornamental arch springing from open-mouthed *makaras*. Mural fragments on the antechamber walls include the temptation of Mara (right) and the miracle at Sravasti (left). A flight of steps ascends to the upper level. Buddha figures are sculpted in the verandah shrines, as well as on the walls of the hall, antechamber and shrine.

Cave 7, another monastery, has two small porticos with squat octagonal columns. Fluted cushion-shaped capitals support eaves relieved by ornamental arches. The cells are positioned at a higher level at both ends. The focal shrine houses the usual arrangement of Buddha and Bodhisattvas. The side walls are carved with scenes of the miracle at Sravasti.

Cave 9 is the first of the earlier series of monuments in the numbered sequence. The outer elevation of this *chaitya* hall has a large horseshoe-arched window, complete with ribs imitating timbers. The doorway and two windows beneath are surmounted by similar but smaller arches in relief. The Buddha figures are later additions. The rectangular hall has two rows of octagonal columns. The central nave is roofed with a curved vault, but the wooden ribs are lost. The hemispherical *stupa* at the end is raised on a high drum and crowned with an inverted stepped pyramid. Traces of paintings survive in two layers, the earlier being contemporary with the excavation. Left of the doorway, the heads of two ascetics are superimposed on an earlier composition of a *naga* deity and attendants seated in a rocky shelter. On the left wall (left end) a procession of devotees makes its way towards a *stupa* and monastery. The remnant of another older mural survives in a thin band above the left colonnade. The Buddha figures higher up are later additions.

Cave 10, in the middle of the site, is one of the first discovered by Captain Smith, and is possibly the oldest excavation at Ajanta. It is a *chaitya* hall with an apsidal-ended interior. The central aisle has a curved vault, while the side aisles are roofed with half-vaults displaying rock-cut ribs. The votive *stupa* has a double-storeyed drum. The façade, presumably in wood, has vanished. As in the Cave 9, there is evidence of two phases of paintings. The fragments on the left wall include the worship of the bodhi tree and *stupa* by a royal figure accompanied by soliders, musicans and women.

The *Sama Jataka* is illustrated on the right wall. The composition begins with a king shooting an arrow toward Sama, the Bodhisattva, who holds a pitcher on his shoulder. It continues with the penitent king, the sorrowing parents of Sama, the restoration of Sama to life and the reconciliation of the king and Sama. The remainder of this wall illustrates the *Chhaddanta Jataka*, in which the Bodhisattva assumes the form of a royal elephant. The main events here are Chhaddanta's pleasurable life in the Himalayas, the queen of Varanasi ordering that he be killed, his tusks being cut off to satisfy the queen, who subsequently swoons, and the royal couple approaching a *chaitya* hall. Traces of later Buddha figures are seen on the columns and aisle ceilings. The cave also preserves a number of inscriptions.

Cave 11 is a clumsily executed and partly incomplete monastery. The high plinth and parapet of the exterior are decorated with railings. The verandah columns and doorway are painted with decorative motifs. The ceiling paintings, including foliation, birds and animals, are better preserved. Sculpted Bodhisattvas with attendants appear either side of the doorway. Four columns with pot-shaped capitals stand within the hall. The shrine, without an antechamber, has a Buddha sculpted against an unfinished *stupa*.

Caves 12 and **13** belong to the earlier phase at Ajanta. Their façades have completely collapsed, exposing their interior square cells with rock-cut beds. The doorways in Cave 12 have arched motifs connected by friezes of railing motifs. **Cave 14** was planned on a large scale, but was never finished. The hall doorway is adorned with attendants and maidens clutching branches.

The verandah of **Cave 15** has mostly fallen. A *stupa* sheltered by a canopy of serpent hoods is seen above the entrance. Buddha images appear in the shrine and on the rear wall of the hall. **Cave 15A**, reached by descending a flight of steps, preserves only portions of the front wall. The doorway beyond is flanked by elephants in relief and a delicately modelled seated *naga* deity.

Cave 16, one of the largest monasteries at Ajanta, is provided with a donative inscription of Varaha Deva, a feudatory of Harishena. The ceiling of the front aisle of the hall is carved in imitation of wooden beams, the ends supported by dwarfs, musicians and flying couples. The narrow side aisles, with richly adorned columns, are later additions. Only portions of the hall have paintings. The left wall is covered with scenes depicting Nanda's wife fainting, Nanda's efforts to practice self-control and his journey to heaven in the company of Buddha. On the rear wall of the hall, on either side of the shrine, is the miracle of Sravasti and a fragment of an elephant procession.

Incidents from the life of the Master cover the right wall of the hall: Buddha begging, Bimbisara's visit, Gautama's first meditation, Gautama at school and (at the extreme right) the sleeping figure of Maya and a royal couple in a circular pavilion. *Jataka* narratives occur on the front wall of the hall (left side). In the *Hasti Jataka*, the Bodhisattava appears as an elephant who throws itself off a cliff to provide food for hungry travellers. Episodes from the *Maha Ummagga Jataka* illustrate the legend of Mahosadha, in which the wise Bodhisattva settled disputes over the motherhood of a child and the ownership of a chariot.

Like Cave 16, which it resembles in overall layout, **Cave 17** dates from the period of Harishena. The monastery preserves the greatest number of **murals** at Ajanta, among which are many outstanding compositions. A row of eight seated Buddhas above amorous couples is seen over the doorway in the verandah. The incomplete panel to the left shows Indra flying through the clouds accompanied by celestial women and musicians. Further left are successive scenes of a princely couple seated in a pavilion drinking wine, proceeding towards a city gate and finally distributing alms to a large assembly. An unusual Wheel of Life occupies the left wall of the verandah. Celestial maidens right of the verandah doorway include one beauty with her eyes cast to the side, her jewelled necklace askew. Further right is a panel showing Buddha subduing the furious elephant sent by Devadatta to crush him. The verandah ceiling has a lobed medallion surrounded by delicate foliation. Similar motifs decorate the interior ceilings.

Jataka subjects cover the hall walls of Cave 17. The *Chhaddanta Jataka*, immediately left of the entrance, is recognised by scenes showing the royal elephant. The *Mahakapi Jataka*, in which the Bodhisattva appears as a monkey, is seen further to the right: the king on horseback, together with his retinue, shoots arrows at the monkeys; the monkeys escape over the stretched body of the Bodhisattva; the monkeys preach to the king. The entire left wall is devoted to the *Vessantara Jataka*. The episodes include the farewell of Prince Vessantara, his drive with his family in a chariot, their life in the hermitage, his gift of his children to a brahmin in a forest hermitage, the redeeming of the children and the return of the family to the capital.

The *Jataka* in which the Bodhisattva as the lioness Sutasoma cures a prince of cannibalism is illustrated on the wall left of the antechamber doorway in Cave 17. Its scenes show the education of the prince, the cutting and cooking of human flesh, the appeal to the prince to give up cannibalism, and the final banishment to the forest. Paintings within the antechamber depict Buddha preaching, descending from heaven accompanied by Indra, and addressing an assembly (left wall, top to bottom). The shrine doorway beyond is profusely sculpted with Buddhas, female guardians, river goddesses, scrollwork and lotus petals. Four *Jataka* stories appear on the wall of the hall right of the antechamber doorway. The scenes of the elephant refusing food and later bathing with other elephants derive from the *Matiposaka Jataka*. The youth carrying his blind parents in slings from bamboo rods refers to the *Sama Jataka*.

The paintings on the right wall of Cave 17 are mostly devoted to the story of Simhala's conquest of Sri Lanka. This begins (bottom right end) with the shipwreck of Simhala and his merchants, and continues with Simhala accepting the aid of the Bodhisattva, born here as a horse, and leading an expedition against the demonic forces of the ogress, after which he is crowned king of the island. The pilaster beyond contains the celebrated composition of a princess with maids and a female dwarf. Returning to the front wall (left of the entrance), there are a number of forest scenes in which a king and his retinue appear, possibly from the *Ruru Jataka*, in which the Bodhisattva assumes the form of a deer. The *Nigrodhamriga Jataka* occupies the remainder of this wall; the episodes depict the Bodhisattva as a deer offering himself for slaughter to the palace cook, to save a pregnant doe.

Cave 19 is one of the two *chaitya* halls belonging to the later series. Its richly carved façade has an elegant portico. Pilasters on the flanking walls, decorated with foliation, scrollwork and jewelled band, frame standing and seated Buddhas. The façade is dominated by a large horseshoe-shaped window flanked by corpulent *yakshas* with elaborate headdresses. The side chapels have columns with luxuriant pot-and-foliage capitals. A fully modelled *naga* couple seated on a rock is sculpted on the left wall. Seated Buddhas, riders, flying couples, hermits and musicians adorn the column capitals within the hall. The panels above show Buddhas surrounded by bands of scrollwork. The central aisle has a vault with rock-cut ribs; the ceilings in the side aisles are flat. The Buddha image on the votive *stupa* stands beneath an arch springing from open-mouthed *makaras*. A monolithic tier of umbrellas with supporting figures rises above. The ceiling paintings depict floral motifs, figures and animals.

Cave 20 is a small monastery with an antechamber protruding into the hall. The verandah columns and brackets are delicately carved. The roof has rock-cut beams. **Caves 21** and **Cave 23** are almost identical in layout, though incomplete. Richly ornamented columns are seen in the verandahs and halls. Hariti and attendants (right) and a court of a *naga* king (left) appear above the side shrines of the verandahs.

Cave 26, another *chaitya* hall, is larger than Cave 19, but is otherwise similar in arrangement and decoration. A columned verandah, partly collapsed, extending across the façade, has chambers at both ends. The court in front has subsidiary shrines, cells and verandàhs. The hall is enlivened with carved Buddhas. The focal *stupa* has an image of the Master seated in a pavilion. Compositions are carved on the walls (left aisle). The dignified Parinirvana scene shows a 7m long figure of Buddha reclining on a couch, his eyes closed in undisturbed sleep, accompanied by mourning disciples. In the temptation of Mara, Buddha is assaulted by elephants, demonic forces and dancing maidens. **Cave 27**, to the left, is reached by way of a partly collapsed chamber.

G. Pitalkhora

This remote site, 40km northwest of Ellora, has 13 Buddhist excavations, mostly monasteries, cut into the side of a secluded ravine. Dating from the 2C BC to the 1C AD, they constitute the largest group of Satavahana monuments in Maharashtra. Two monuments are of special interest.

Cave 3, a *chaitya* hall, is conceived and executed on a large scale, though its original façade has now collapsed. The apsidal-ended interior is divided into three aisles by octagonal columns. The half-vaults in the side aisles have rock-cut ribs, but the timbers of the central nave are lost. The *stupa* has a monolithic base and a structural drum, now disintegrated. Painted fragments indicate that the hall was in use until the late 5C.

Cave 3 shares a common court with the adjacent monastery, **Cave 4**. The basement of its monolithic outer wall is sculpted with elephants and attendant figures. The doorway is flanked by guardians in foreign dress, armed with spears and shields. The two elephants that once framed the Lakshmi image above have been removed to the Prince of Wales Museum, Bombay [1B]. A covered flight of steps ascends to the monastery. The upper part of the façade, now badly weathered, has traces of ornamental horseshoe-shaped arches. The interior columns have mostly crumbled. The cell doorways are topped with arched motifs, railings and pilasters with decorated capitals. Six cells have vaulted ceilings with rock-cut beams and rafters.

H. Ghatotkacha

The two rock-cut features at this isolated site, some 40km northwest of Ajanta, can be reached only by jeep. The Ghatotkacha monuments are historically related to Cave 16 at Ajanta, since they share the same 5C donor, Varaha Deva. They are scooped out of the rocky sides of a forested ravine, overlooking a waterfall.

The **Monastery**, the more important of the Ghatotkacha excavations, has a verandah and four columns, now broken. The central doorway is enlivened with amorous couples and river goddesses. Seated Buddhas are positioned above the side windows. The long inscription near the left doorway gives the genealogy of the patron. The shrine extending beyond the rear wall of the hall houses a seated Buddha with devotees; deer flanking a wheel are carved on the pedestal beneath. The antechamber columns have medallions adorning the shafts, with pot-and-foliage capitals above. At the right end of the front aisle is a *stupa* with Buddha images. A pilaster in the left aisle has a Buddha and an inscription of about the 8C.

I. Anwa

This small village lies 10km east of Golegaon on the main road to Ajanta, a total of 75km northeast of Aurangabad. It is notable for its Yadava-period monument, the 12C **Madha Temple**, which consists of a sanctuary, an inner closed hall and an open outer hall, the last with porch projections on three sides. The high basement displays deeply cut mouldings. The walls are divided into projections that rhythmically expand outwards. Niches with images of Vishnu occur at the cardinal directions, with ascetic figures in the side recesses. The balconies of the open hall and porches are relieved by flat pilasters with stylised lotuses. The interior doorways are embellished with Vaishnava divinities in the company of Ganesha. The columns have panels with celestial dancers, but the bracket figures above are mostly lost. Concentric rings of delicately worked petalled lobes create corbelled domes. The Nandi and *linga* are later insertions.

J. Jalna

This city, 60km east of Aurangabad, was a provincial centre under the Nizam Shahis and the Mughals, attaining importance in the early 18C, when it became the seat of Kabil Khan, one of Aurangzeb's generals. Nizamul Mulk was responsible for fortifying Jalna in 1723. Several complexes dating from the Nizam Shahi era survive.

The **Kali Mosque** of 1578, in the middle of the city, is surrounded by a rectangle of walls, with an arched gate on the south flanked by pierced stone windows. The prayer chamber within has octagonal columns carrying six small domes. The corner finials display fluted domical tops. The adjacent *Hammam*, added in 1583, has domed chambers on faceted pendentives. The **Jamshid Sarai** opposite, now an active school, has a large square court surrounded by arcaded chambers, with a pond in the middle.

The ***Dargah* of Zacha and Bacha**, west of Jalna, is also assigned to the late 16C. It consists of a bold but simple cubic tomb, with pierced stone screens set into arched recesses on three sides. Sculpted lotuses adorn the doorway on the south. The dome rises over a parapet with corner octagonal finials. The ***Dargah* of Jam Allah Shah**, 1km east of the city, is a popular monument that dates from 1681. Double tiers of recesses display both pointed and lobed arches. The dome above has a petalled base, repeated within the interior. A small mosque, tank and dilapidated wooden colonnade occupy the remainder of the enclosure.

K. Lonar

The **Crater Lake** outside Lonar, a small town 85km east of Jalna via Mantha, is one of Maharashtra's most extraordinary natural features. Scientists have recently identified the Lake as a meteorite impact crater, the largest in India. The circumference of the rim is almost 6km, with sloping sides rising more than 130m. The collision which created the Lake is calculated as having occurred approximately 50,000 years ago. Far from being a sterile wonder, however, the Lake is filled with water and blanketed in dense vegetation. This provides an ideal habitat for a large array of birds, especially peafowls, as well as langur monkeys, chinkaras and deer.

Dilapidated Yadava-period **Temples** dot the edge of the Lake. These picturesque 12C ruins have decorated columns with sculpted blocks, many overturned, defining halls and porches.

The **Daitya Sudana Temple**, within Lonar, is better preserved. Begun in the 13C but never completed, it presents an imposing pile of intricately carved blocks. The walls of the principal sanctuary and attached hall are raised on a high basement enlivened with bands of stylised foliation. Multiple projections treated as niches display figures of Vishnu and Krishna. Pavilion-like niches sheltering icons project outwards on three sides of the sanctuary.

L. Paithan

Built on the north bank of the Godavari River, 51km south of Aurangabad, Paithan owes its reputation to Shalivahana, the Satavahana ruler who made this city his capital in 78 AD. This date is fixed in Indian history as the starting point of the Shaka era, a widespread chronological system that is still current. Paithan disappears from history after the Satavahanas, but emerges again in the 18C as an important centre disputed by the Marathas and Nizams of Hyderabad. The city is known today for its woven silks and cotton fabrics.

Excavations carried out in the 1930s in the sandy mounds near **Nag Ghat**, on the river bank south of the city, revealed a Satavahana settlement with brick structures, drains and wells. These features are still partly visible. Among the associated finds were copper coins, shell objects, beads of semi-precious stones, terracotta figurines and pottery utensils with incised marks.

Paithan is best known today as the birthplace of the Hindu saints Eknath, Dhondinath and Mukteshwar. The *Samadhi* of Eknath Maharaj, near the Godavari River, is a popular shrine with a large fair held in March. The *Samadhi*, contained within a wooden colonnade, marks the spot of Eknath's cremation after death by ritual drowning in 1598. It stands in the middle of a court surrounded by wooden arcades and entered through an arched portal on the east. A path to the west leads to the bathing *ghats*, from where there is a distant prospect of the earthen embankment of **Nath Sagar**, a recently completed hydro-electric project.

The **House of Eknath Maharaj**, in the middle of Paithan, has an arcaded court used for devotional readings; a small chamber at the rear accommodates the deified image of the saint. Modern wall paintings illustrate episodes from Eknath's life. Another traditional mansion which also serves as a place of worship is the **House of Dhondinath Maharaj**. A path from here leads down to the river, where stands the abandoned **Koti Mosque.**

The only monument at Paithan of any antiquity is the **Tirthakambha**, an 11C decorated victory column belonging to the Yadava era. The **Jami Mosque** of 1630, immediately to the north, is believed to occupy the site of the Satavahana palace. Its fortified enclosure has tapering fluted bastions at the corners. The prayer chamber is of little interest.

Funerary complexes mark the eastern fringe of Paithan. The ***Dargah* of Maulana Moazuddin** crowns a small rise overlooking the Godavari River. An arched gateway with triple arcade over leads to a flight of steps. The walled compound at the top of the hill contains the domed tomb of the Chishti saint after whom the *Dargah* is named. The adjacent hall with wooden columns conceals stone remnants of a Yadava shrine.

6 · Ahmadnagar

While it is possible to reach Ahmadnagar (also spelt Ahmednagar) as a day trip from Pune [3], 116km southwest, or from Aurangabad [5], 110km northeast, and even from Nasik [4], 145km north, an overnight stay is recommended. This will permit sufficient time to visit the great Circular Fort and the most important mosques, tombs and palaces in and around the city [A and B], all linked with the Nizam Shahi rulers. Another day may be set aside for a trip to the pilgrimage town of **Shirdi** [C].

■ **Transport**. Frequent buses link Ahmadnagar with Pune, Aurangabad and Nasik. Connections are also possible by narrow-gauge train, running between Manmad on the Bombay–Delhi line and Daund on Bombay–Madras line. Buses link Ahmadnagar with Shirdi.

■ **Accommodation**. A cluster of new hotels and restaurants is located on the Nasik road, 4km north of Ahmadnagar (STD code 0241). The best are the *Hotel Panchashil* and the *Premdan*. The *Ashoka Hotel* (☎ 23607), immediately west of the Circular Fort, is more central.

■ **Tourist Information**. None.

History

Ahmadnagar is linked with the career of Ahmad Nizam Shah (1496–1510), originally a commander in the service of the Bahmanis of Bidar [25A]. In 1496 Ahmad declared independence and, with the aid of local Maratha chiefs, managed to seize Daulatabad [5C] and Panhala [8B]. One of his outstanding achievements was to found a new city, which he named after himself and which came to serve as the capital of the newly launched Nizam Shahi dynasty.

On the death of Ahmad the throne passed to the infant Burhan (1510–53), whose able ministers resisted attacks from the Imad Shahis of Achalpur [10E] and the rulers of Gujarat. The Shia sect was adopted as the state religion, bringing Ahmadnagar into sympathetic relations with Iran. In the wars against Bijapur [23A], Burhan allied himself with Vijayanagara [20B–C] and Golconda [26E]. Burhan's son and successor, Husain (1553–65), secured the frontiers of Ahmadnagar and for a time enjoyed an accord with Goa [11]. Husain's forces joined those of Bijapur, Bidar and Golconda to counter the threat of Vijayanagara, participating in the victory of 1565. Murtaza (1565–88), the next ruler, annexed the Berar region to the northeast in 1574, but his reign was marked by plots and assassinations as well as by renewed assaults from Bijapur. The appearance of the Mughals in 1586 presented a new threat.

The last years of the 16C witnessed a succession of weak rulers and the intervention of the Mughals. The invaders were checked for a time by Chand Bibi, the sister of one of the deceased kings. Malik Ambar, Chand Bibi's able commander, managed to expel the Mughals in 1600 and became the effective ruler of the kingdom, heading successful expeditions against

Bidar and Golconda. After his death in 1626 the Mughals intensified their efforts, permanently occupying Ahmadnagar in 1636. The city passed from the Mughals into the hands of the Nizams of Hyderabad [26A], from whom it was taken by the Marathas in 1760. In 1808 Ahmadnagar surrendered to Arthur Wellesley, later Duke of Wellington. Under the British the city served as the headquarters for a military contingent. Jawaharlal Nehru was among the Indian freedom fighters confined here by the British; *The Discovery of India*, his most popular book, was written within the walls of the great Circular Fort.

A. Ahmadnagar

The tour of Ahmadnagar begins at the **Circular Fort**, concealed in the scrub-lands east of the city. This ring of well-finished masonry, some 1800m in diameter, dates from 1563. The 20m high walls were erected at the orders of Husain to replace the mud ramparts thrown up by Ahmad more than 60 years earlier. 22 semicircular bastions are positioned at regular intervals; one example in the northeast quadrant has triple lobes. Rectangular openings for cannon, originally crenellations, were filled in when a new brick parapet was added during the first Mughal siege in 1586. A 10m wide moat shielded by an earthen embankment encircles the walls. It is crossed by a bridge on the north which leads to a powerful bastion-like barbican. This contains two arched gates, with spiked wooden doors giving access to the interior. Nothing is preserved of Ahmad's palace within. The temples are additions of the Maratha period.

Damri's Mosque, 500m northeast of the Fort, is a small but exquisitely decorated building dating from 1568. Its triple arches are enlivened with delicately carved interlaced strapwork. Lotus brackets carry overhanging angled eaves with a fringe of lotus buds. The square corner buttresses display panels with deeply sculpted niches and medallions. The parapet of cut-out trefoil elements above has finials topped with miniature octagonal pavilions and domical pinnacles; a flying arch connects the inner pair of finials. The flat slabs that roof the six-bayed prayer chamber reflect the pattern on the floor beneath. The rear wall has three niches, polygonal on the sides and square in the middle, surrounded by geometric ornament, with additional foliation filling the central niche. The side windows, also ornamented, are missing their balcony slabs.

The ***Dargah* of Hazrat Shah Sharif** stands in a shady garden about 1km to the east. Founded in 1596, this simple structure has double tiers of alternating pointed and lobed arched recesses. The corner finials are conceived as miniature pavilions with domical tops. The central dome within rises on faceted pendentives.

The tour of Ahmadnagar continues with a selection of religious monuments located in the crowded heart of the city. The **Jami Mosque**, one of the earliest Nizam Shahi projects, has 15 bays roofed with shallow domes on alternating octagonal and circular bases. The building was altered in later times. The **Mecca Mosque** of 1525 is the work of Rumi Khan, a Turkish officer under Ahmad, who was responsible for casting the cannon known as Malik-i Maidan, Lord of the Plain, mounted on the Sharza Bastion at Bijapur. The Mecca Mosque stands on top of a vaulted rest house reached by a steep flight of steps. The triple arches are supported on circular columns of polished granite, supposedly shipped from

Mecca. The finials have clusters of curved brackets carrying miniature eaves and fluted domical tops. The interior is roofed with unusual transverse flat and barrel vaults. The nearby **Tomb of Rumi Khan**, who died in 1568, stands in the grounds of a student hostel. It displays double tiers of triple arched recesses with doorways and windows in the middle of each side. The pavilion-like corner finials, now missing their domical tops, are crowned by a large dome with a petalled base.

Kotla, in the northern part of Ahmadnagar, was erected by Burhan in about 1537 as a Shia educational college. The complex consists of a large square compound surrounded by arcaded rooms for students. It is entered from the east through an arched gate and a domed rest house, now partly fallen. A large platform in the middle of the court marks the site of a covered cistern. The prayer chamber on the west has 15 bays roofed by alternating pyamidal vaults and shallow domes. The arcaded façade is overhung by deep eaves carried on brackets; additional angled struts imitate carved woodwork.

The nearby **Farhad Khani Mosque** of 1569 has three plain arches shaded by overhanging eaves. A lobed arch with ornamental minarets surmounts the entrance gate to the compound. The **Tomb of Sharza Khan**, known fancifully as Do Boti Chira, Two Fingerhold, is a unique miniature building dating from 1562. Its central domed bay is flanked by curved vaults.

Bagh Rauza, on the west side of Ahmadnagar, is a garden complex containing the imposing **Tomb of Ahmad**, the only funerary monument associated with a Nizam Shahi ruler. Dating from 1509, the Tomb stands in a walled compound entered through a domed gate on the south. The cubic building has double tiers of arched openings flanked by arched recesses, with column-like jambs flanking the entrance. The façade is decorated with relief panels of different designs, in addition to calligraphic medallions and lotuses. A brick frieze of arched recesses is overhung by angled eaves on sculpted brackets joined by suspended beams. The corner and intermediate finials are capped with domical tops. The interior is lavishly embellished with plaster arches, some with lobed interiors, surmounted by a calligraphic band. Traces of painted cartouches filled with arabesques are seen in the dome above. The **Tomb of Shah Tahir**, Ahmad's Prime Minister, occupies the southwest corner of Bagh Rauza. The small building has a distinctive pyramidal vault. Just outside the enclosure stands the **Tomb of Malik Ahmad**, the king's astrologer.

B. Around Ahmadnagar

A towered mausoleum and the ruins of two garden palaces are located at sites around the city.

The **_Dargah_ of Alamgir**, 8km east of Ahmadnagar on the road to Paithan [5L], is a small arcaded structure marking the spot where Aurangzeb collapsed and died in 1707. 2km further east, on the summit of a hill rising more than 1000m above sea level, stands the **Tomb of Salabat Khan**. Known also as Chand Bibi's Mahal, this austere tower commemorates Salabat Khan, Murtaza's Prime Minister. The Tomb stands on a spacious terrace with commanding views across the plain to Ahmadnagar. The graves of the patron and one of his wives are housed in an octagonal basement chamber. Above rises a three-storeyed octagon of impressive dimensions, each side marked by triple tiers of arched openings, the uppermost ones with projecting balconies. The double-height octagonal chamber inside is surrounded by domed bays on eight sides.

The great pavilion that forms the centrepiece of **Farh Bagh** can be seen from the road leading to Sholapur [9A], 4km south of Ahmadnagar. Reconstructed by Salabat Khan in 1583, this palace complex is distinctly Iranian in conception, with an emphasis on ceremonial portals and axial symmetry. The pavilion is in poor condition; its bare walls and decaying vaults give little idea of the sumptuous ornamentation with which it was once furnished. Even so, it is an impressive composition, especially since it anticipates by almost 50 years the scheme of the Taj Mahal at Agra, though without the crowning domes. The double-storeyed structure stands in the middle of a square pool approached from the north by a 72m long causeway. It is laid out as an irregular octagon, with four main façades displaying double-height arched portals flanked by tiers of smaller arched recesses, repeated on the angled corner faces. The portals have half-domes plastered with multiple facets and lotus petals. The interior chambers, with similarly decorated vaults at both levels, open onto or look down into the central double-height chamber, which is roofed with a lotus dome rising 18m above an octagonal fountain set into the plaster floor.

Another Nizam Shahi palace, **Hayat Behisht Bagh**, is located 6km north of Ahmadnagar, on a lane running between the Aurangabad and Nasik roads. The focus of this ensemble is a two-storeyed octagonal pavilion standing in an octagonal pond. The pointed arched openings on two levels are decorated with plaster roundels in the spandrels; similar but smaller openings mark the corners. The central chamber is surrounded by an arcade and overlooked by windows from the upper level. The dome above is carried on faceted pendentives. A monumental portal on the south bank of the pond incorporates a *Hammam* with two chambers, roofed by perforated brick vaults. The adjoining rooms for bathing, with cisterns for hot and cold water, can still be seen.

About 500m south of Hayat Behisht Bagh is an **Underground Water Palace** with a unique ventilation tower. This Iranian feature, known as a *badgir*, consists of a chimney-like tower with angled vents at the top. These were designed to create a draught to cool the domed chambers arranged around a subterranean pool. Terracotta pipes set into mortar are evidence of the extensive water system with which the complex was once provided.

C. Shirdi

This small town, 85km north of Ahmadnagar or 25km from Kopargaon, the nearest railhead, from which there are frequent bus services, is celebrated as the residence of Sai Baba, the much-revered saint.

After moving to Shirdi in 1872, Sai Baba attracted both Hindu and Muslim devotees because his teachings embraced both religious traditions. Sai Baba was an expert in Yatha Yoga, but most of his time at Shirdi was spent in a mosque. The number of followers has grown steadily since his death in 1918, and a fair held here in his honour each March–April is attended by huge crowds. The image of Sai Baba showing the saint in a seated posture, one leg resting on the other, his head cloaked in a long white cloth, is a familiar icon throughout Southern India. An indication of his continuing influence is the success of Sai Baba of Puttaparthi [33E], a teacher who claims spiritual descent from the Shirdi saint.

The **Sai Baba Temple** is the chief feature of interest at Shirdi. Devotees worship a full-height image of the saint, sculpted in white marble and elevated on a silver-plated throne, flanked by gilded lions. A glass chamber to the left exhibits articles used daily by the saint, including a gramophone and an umbrella. The black marble **Samadhi**, or tomb, within the Temple contains the mortal remains of Sai Baba, his head lying to the north and his feet to the south. The small mosque within the precincts marks the original residence of the saint.

7 · Mahabaleshwar

A stay at this verdant hill station [A], the highest and most extensive in Maharashtra, may be combined with itineraries for Pune [3] and Kolhapur [8]. Mahabaleshwar provides an attractive base from which to visit the mountain strongholds at **Pratapgad** [B] and **Raigad** [C], both linked with Shivaji, founder of the Maratha state. They can be combined in a full-day journey through the rugged crests of the Sahyadri ranges west of Mahabaleshwar.

Another day may be be taken up with an excursion along the Konkan plain to the island fort of Suvarnadurg, reached from **Harnai** [D], and to the sleepy port of **Dabhol** [E], once a flourishing emporium.

The temples at **Wai** [F] and **Mahuli** [H] on the Deccan plain east of Mahabaleshwar can be visited together with **Satara** [G] in another full-day trip.

■ **Transport.** Mahabaleshwar is linked by road with Bombay [1], 247km northwest via Mahad on NH17, and Pune, 120km north on NH4, the latter providing convenient rail and plane connections with Bombay. Routes from both these cities pass by some of the sites described here before ascending through the wooded Ghats to Mahabaleshwar. Kolhapur lies 193km to the south. When the Konkan Railway is completed, Mahabaleshwar will be accessible from Poladpur, 38km west at the base of the Sahyadri range. Buses link Mahabaleshwar with most of the places described here; day excursions to Raigad, Suvarnadurg and Dabhol are only possible with a car.

■ **Accommodation.** Mahabaleshwar (STD code 021686) is a popular resort, especially between November and May, when it is crowded with Bombayites; for this reason, it is advisable to book accommodation in advance. There is a large variety of hotels and guest houses to chose from, many set in flowering gardens with panoramic views over the wooded hills. The *Dreamland Hotel* (☎ 60228), *Regal Hotel* (☎ 60001), *Dina Hotel* (☎ 60246) and *Frederick Hotel* (☎ 60240) are among the most attractive. The *MTDC Holiday Resort* (☎ 60318) offers further accommodations. An alternative place to consider is **Panchgani** (same STD code), a smaller hill resort 18km east of Mahabaleshwar on the Pune road. The *Hotel Five Hills* (☎ 40301) and the *Aman Hotel* (☎ 40211) are the best available.

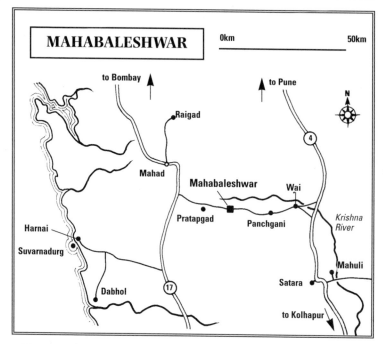

- **Tourist Information**. The MTDC maintains an office at the Kedar Complex on Station Road (☎ 22935).

A. Mahabaleshwar

This hill station spreads over a wooded undulating plateau that tops one of the spurs of the Sahyadris. With an average height of about 1375m, Mahabaleshwar offers welcome relief from the humidity of the coast and the heat of the plains; the monsoon rains, however, are severe. The promontories that protrude north and west offer magnificent views of the precipitous edges of the Sahayadris and the valleys below. Streams issuing from springs at the heads of the ravines form waterfalls in the wet season. Here rises the Krishna River, one of Southern India's greatest and most sacred rivers.

The history of Mahabaleshwar goes back to the days of Shivaji, who visited the sacred spot that marks the source of the Krishna in 1653. The hill was one of the first territories that Shivaji acquired from his fort at nearby Pratapgad. However, it was not until British times that the hill was developed to any extent. General Peter Lodwick explored the region in 1824, with the idea of transforming the hill into a health resort. Lodwick persuaded the ruler of Satara, whose territory it was, to invite Sir John Malcolm, then Governor of Bombay, to visit the site in 1828. The next year, a treaty delivered the hill into British hands. The station was at first called Malcolm Peth, after Sir John, but this name is now restricted to the main bazaar street. Roads were laid out and the resort developed quickly with the construction of bungalows, churches and a club, as well as a polo ground and race course. Mahabaleshwar continues to grow and is now the most populous hill station in Maharashtra.

Malcolm Peth, crowded with shops and new hotels, marks the commercial core of Mahabaleshwar. Above the bazaar is the **Civic Hospital**, near to which stands an **Obelisk** in memory of Sir Sidney Beckwith, who succeeded Malcolm as Governor of Bombay in 1830, and who died at Mahabaleshwar in 1831. The **Roman Catholic Church** and the more impressive Anglican **Christ Church**, now deserted, but with fine stained glass, stand near the bus station. The **Mahabaleshwar Club** still flourishes.

Yenna Lake lies 1.5km northeast of Malcolm Peth, via a winding road that passes by many guest houses. Its pleasant tree-lined shore is ringed with popular walks and pony trails. Mahabaleshwar's lookouts provide more dramatic scenery. **Bombay Point**, 2km southwest of the bazaar, offers an extensive view of the Konkan. **Sidney Point**, 4km west of the bazaar, is marked by a 7.5m high pillar crowned by an urn commemorating Lodwick.

The **Lingamala Falls**, 4km east of Malcolm Peth, are the finest in the area. The cascade has a sheer descent of 165m, unbroken after heavy rain. From Lingamala it is only a short walk to **Wilson Point**, at 1435m the highest peak in Mahabaleshwar. It is named after yet another Governor of Bombay.

Old Mahabaleshwar, 6km north of Malcolm Peth, is the site of the **Mahabaleshvar Temple**, after which the hill station is named. Founded in earlier times but rebuilt in the 19C, this simple black basalt structure enshrines a natural rock saturated with spring water, symbolising the source of the Krishna River. The **Atibaleshvar Temple,** in an adjacent walled compound, has pyramidal roofs with tiers of undecorated eave-like mouldings.

The nearby **Temple of Krishnabai** was erected in 1888 by the ruler of Ratnagiri on the Konkan coast. It consists of an arcaded court, originally open but later roofed over, with a high stone wall at the rear. Water flowing out of five holes at the base of this wall is identified as the Panchaganga, the five sacred rivers, which include the Krishna. The chutes unite before passing through a stone spout carved as a cow and falling into a square stepped cistern; the over-flow is then conveyed into a second identical cistern. Bathing in the water is considered particularly auspicious, and the Temple is usually crowded.

Other lookouts are located beyond Old Mahabaleshwar: **Elphinstone Point** lies 3.5km west, and **Arthur's Seat** is 3km north, across the valley of the Gayatri and Savitri Rivers. The cliffs at these two sites rise more than 800m above the plain. From Arthur's Seat, named after Sir George Arthur, another Governor of Bombay, it is possible to make out the hill forts at Rajgad (1317m) [3M] and Torna (1535m).

B. Pratapgad

This citadel occupies Par Ghat, the hill that guards the stategic pass in the Sahyadris 13km west of Mahabaleshwar.

Par Ghat was unoccupied until 1656, when it was fortified by Moro Pingle, Shivaji's trusted general, thereby opening up a strategic route that descended to the Konkan plain. Four years later, Pratapgad was the scene of Shivaji's treacherous encounter with Afzal Khan, the commander of the Bijapur [23A] army, whom Shivaji brutally murdered. The fort remained an important outpost throughout the 18C, being used by Nana Phadnavis, the chief minister of the Peshwas, as a refuge from intrigues at the Pune court. Pratapgad surrendered to the British in 1818.

The **Grave of Afzal Khan**, beside the main road below the hill, is sheltered by a modern roof; it marks the spot where the commander's head was buried. A path from here climbs to the citadel that crowns the hill, rising 1080m above sea level. To the west and north are sheer precipices, in some places with a vertical drop of up to 250m. The south and east flanks of the hill have double lines of **Fortifications**, with 12m high circular towers and bastions. The walls follow the curving lines of the escarpment, creating lower and upper forts. On passing through the **East Gate**, the outworks of an impressive tower are seen to the right; to the left is the path to the upper fort. The **Temple of Bhavani**, founded by Shivaji and recently remodelled, overlooks the east flank of the lower fort. The Temple enshrines a black stone image of the same goddess worshipped at Tuljapur [9C]. Two squat lamp towers with curved brackets stand on the terrace. A further attraction is the equestrian bronze statue of Shivaji, installed in 1957 and unveiled by Jawaharlal Nehru.

C. Raigad

This hill fort, 25km north of Mahad on NH17, and about 60km northwest of Mahabaleshwar, spreads over the top of a great wedge-shaped block that rises 940m above sea level. The bluff is separated from the main crest of the Sahyadris by a deep valley on the east. The ascent requires a climb of about 300m on foot from the spur where vehicles are parked.

Under the name of Rairi, this fort was held successively by the Bahmanis and Nizam Shahis. In 1636 it was made over to the Adil Shahis, who entrusted it to the Siddis of Janjira [2I]. Shivaji captured Rairi in 1656, thereby opening up the Konkan routes for the extension of Maratha power. In 1672 he selected Rairi as his new capital, renaming it Raigad, Royal Fort. Two years later Shivaji made Raigad his seat of government, striking coins for the first time in his own name. In June 1674 Shivaji was crowned here with much splendour as Chhatrapati, Lord of the [Royal] Umbrella. English embassies visited Raigad to congratulate his successor, Sambhaji, when he assumed the throne in 1681. But this ruler did not enjoy Raigad for long, because in 1689 the Mughal forces besieged the citadel. It was thereafter handed over to the Sidis, with orders to defend it against the Marathas. In spite of repeated attempts, the Marathas were unable to retake Raigad until 1734. The fort remained in Maratha hands until 1818, when it was captured by the British. Sir Richard Temple, the Governor of Bombay, visited Raigad in 1885 and ordered the restoration of some of its buildings. In 1896 Lokmanya Tilak, a popular leader, initiated an annual ceremony to commemorate Shivaji's death.

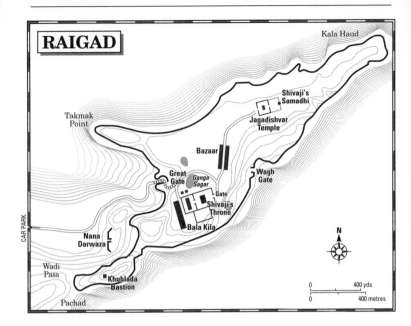

The discontinuous **Fortifications** ringing the Raigad plateau are built of massive basalt blocks laid without any mortar, but reinforced by round bastions. The walls that shield Takmak point, the jagged northwestern promontory of the fort, are particularly strong, as are the walls defending the **Great Gate** that serves as the principal entrance to the fort from the west, and which is used by most visitors. The arched opening, concealed by curving outworks, is adorned with lotus medallions, panels showing lions crushing elephants, and a battlemented parapet.

The path ascends from the Great Gate until it arrives at the comparatively level top of the hill. The first feature of interest to be seen is the circular **Ganga Sagar**, Raigad's chief reservoir. To the south rise the walls of the immense **Bala Kila**, Shivaji's citadel. Two ruined 12-sided towers with multiple tiers of arcaded openings stand freely outside the walls. An arched entrance in the walls leads to a long flight of steps, which ascends to a passageway. Doorways on the right give access to six rectangular enclosures, believed to have accommodated female members of Shivaji's court. The zone at a lower level to the left has five residential suites, possibly for Shivaji's officers. Each suite has a rectangular chamber standing in the middle of a square compound. The walled zone at a higher level on the left was the setting for ceremonies and official business. All that can now be seen are the stone foundations of formally arranged columned halls and colonnades. The platform in the middle supports **Shivaji's Throne**, the remains of which can be viewed through a glass panel and are still held in honour. The restored platform supports a modern, delicately worked cast-iron canopy in a Neo-Mughal style.

The **Granary** and **Treasury** are located north and south of the Throne. A small fountain in front (east) is overlooked by the **House of Justice**. The **Main**

Gate on the east side of the enclosure has a lofty arched opening with upper panels showing lions clawing elephants. The interior passageway is roofed with a corbelled vault.

A path leads north from the Main Gate of the Bala Kila to the **Bazaar**. This comprises two lines of 22 shops facing each other across a broad north–south street. The **Temple of Jagadishvar**, erected in 1674, the year of Shivaji's coronation, stands in a high-walled compound 500m northeast of the Bazaar. Its somewhat austere exterior is relieved by a parapet of trefoil elements framed by corner finials with domical tops. A plastered dome on petals rises over the *linga*; the adjoining hall is roofed with a pyramidal vault.

An arched gate in the east wall of the Temple compound leads to the **Samadhi of Shivaji**, an eight-sided plinth on which the Chhatrapati's body was cremated in 1680. A bust of Shivaji, erected in 1926, commemorates the event. **Waghya's Samadhi** nearby is dedicated to Shivaji's faithful dog that died with its master on the same pyre. It consists of a sculpted animal raised on a 4m high pillar. A path running east from here, following one of the spurs of the hill, leads to the remains of extensive **Barracks**.

D. Harnai

This Arabian Sea port is located 130km southwest of Mahabaleshwar via Khed on NH17, a future station on the Konkan Railway. Harnai is worth visiting for the picturesque fort of **Suvarnadurg**, built on a small island some 500m offshore. The sea around Suvarnadurg is shallow, and it is only possible to reach the island at high tide. There are no regular ferry services, but private boats can be arranged. The fort is more of interest for its striking location than its architectural features.

Suvarnadurg was the second coastal citadel after Vijayadurg [8C] to be extensively renovated by Shivaji, in a bid to counter the influence of the Sidis of Janjira. The walls of the island, as well as its name, Golden Fort, date from 1669. In 1696 it was used as a naval base by Kanhoji Angre of Alibag [2G]. Under Kanhoji's successor, Tulaji, Suvarnadurg became one of the chief posts of the Angre fleet which threatened European and Indian shipping. After a joint attack on the island by the British and the Marathas in 1756, Suvarnadurg was made over to the Peshwas. In 1801 Bajirao, the last Peshwa, fleeing from Yeshwantrao Holkar, sought refuge in Suvarnadurg. The island was finally taken by the British in 1818.

Suvarnadurg is surrounded by **Fortifications**, now much overgrown, that follow its irregular outline. The walls are partly cut out of solid rock and partly constructed of 3–4m square basalt blocks. They are relieved by round bastions and broken by a single roughly fashioned gate just above the high tide mark. A tortoise is carved on a stone at the gate's threshold; on the walls to the left is an image of Hanuman. **Tanks** and a small step-well with abundant water are seen inside the Fortifications. A plastered stone building is identified as the **Magazine**. The extensive foundations beyond are all that remains of the residences of the Angres.

E. Dabhol

This historic port, 37km south of Harnai, is situated on the north bank of the Vaishishti River, 3km from its confluence with the Arabian Sea.

Dabhol was an important centre of shipping when it came under the control of the Bahmanis and Adil Shahis. The Portuguese attempted to capture it in 1514, but were repelled. In the middle of the 16C Dabhol attracted traders from Gujarat and Malabar, as well as from Aden and Ormuz. Large quantites of textiles, grains and vegetables were exchanged here for imported copper, quicksilver, vermilion and horses. The Portuguese raided Dabhol successfully in 1547, but held it only for a few years, after which seaborne trade declined. The port was taken by Shivaji in 1660 and 1666. In the 18C it came under the joint governorship of the Marathas and Sidis, except for a period of 11 years when it was occupied by the Angres. By 1818, when Dabhol passed into the hands of the British, virtually all shipping had ceased.

The only building of interest to be seen at Dabhol today is the **Jami Mosque**, which stands in coconut groves near the water. This was erected in 1649 by Pir Ahmad Abdullah, an officer of the Adil Shahis. The building is raised on a terrace with a small pond, the arcades beneath being reserved for shops. The triple arches of the prayer chamber are sheltered by angled eaves on sculpted brackets. The parapet is interrupted by two finials conceived as miniature pavilions with domical tops. The corner octagonal buttresses have rows of petals, repeated at each of the five stages. A dome rises over the central bay.

F. Wai

This charming town lies 40km east of Mahabaleshwar, 6km from NH4, on the banks of the Krishna River, which here issues from the wooded slopes of the Sahyadaris. At the west end of Wai, the river is traversed by a weir that forms a pool; bathing *ghats* line the banks for about 500m downstream. Nearby temples and shrines were erected by the Rastes, a local family that rose to prominence under the Peshwas in the second half of the 18C. Only the most interesting are described here.

The **Ganapati Temple** on the north bank, constructed by Gangapatrao Raste in 1762, is the most striking of the series. Its 22m high plastered brick tower takes the form of a fluted cone capped with a smaller fluted dome; diminutive conical finials mark the corners. The spacious rectangular sanctuary within, roofed with a pyramidal vault, enshrines a 2m large stone sculpture of Ganesha. The rear west face of the Temple has angled walls to buttress the building in times of flood.

The adjacent **Kashivishveshvara Temple**, at a slightly higher level, was erected in 1757 by Anandrao Bhikaji Raste. It stands in a fortified enclosure, entered on the east through an arched gate. The walls of the Temple are featureless, except for small pierced windows, one with knotted snakes. The 12-sided spire over the sanctuary rises in three diminishing tiers of plastered niches, with a seated figure in each; similar niches framing Durga, Ganesha and Sarasvati form a parapet above the doorway to the hall. The domed interior has a tortoise engraved on the floor. Steps descend to the *linga* sanctuary, which is roofed with a curved vault. The detached Nandi pavilion, with lobed arches on four sides, is flanked by a pair of tapering octagonal lamp columns.

Another project of Anandrao Bhikaji Raste is the **Mahalakshmi Temple**, dating from 1778. It, too, is contained within a walled compound, but faces, more unusually, west. The entrance to the hall is through a series of lobed arches. The spire over the sanctuary consists of five diminishing tiers, each with 12 plastered niches framing divinities and attendants arranged in circular fashion. The tower is crowned with a fluted dome; similar but smaller domes cap the finials of the lowest stage.

Wai is dotted with many fine mansions dating from the 18C. The **Moti Baug** (permission required to visit), the residence of one of the Rastes, is fronted by a double-height verandah leading to wooden panelled rooms. Wall panels frame brightly coloured paintings depicting diverse courtly and mythological topics, surrounded by delicately toned floral bands. The paintings over the doorways are set in lobed recesses. The large garden at the rear of the house has a brick tower with a water wheel.

G. Satara

This city is located on NH4, 30km south of Wai, between Pune, 110km north, and Kolhapur, 120km south.

In 1699 Rajaram, the grandson of Shivaji, made Satara the headquarters of Maratha power, thereby alerting the Mughals, who besieged it in 1700 and 1706. After retaking the city in 1708, Shahu was formally crowned here, thereby confirming Satara as centre of the rapidly expanding Maratha empire. Upon Shahu's death in 1749 the city was occupied by the Peshwa Balaji, who then proceeded to Pune, making this the principal Maratha capital. Satara continued to serve as the residence of a local family who gradually emerged as independent rulers, assuming the title of Chhatrapati. Pratapsinh of Satara was recognised by the British after the fall of Pune in 1818, and the princely state of Satara survived until Independence.

The chief focus of Satara is the royal complex in the central **Square**. The west side of the Square is occupied by the residences of Pratapsinh and Appa Saheb, now the **Pratapsinh High School** and **District Judge's Court**, or New Palace, respectively. They are built in traditional style, with wooden columns, brackets and arches set into brick walls, and sloping roofs with terracotta tiles. The great columned hall inside the Court, now crowded with judicial officers and petitioners, was originally used for public ceremonies. A smaller interior hall in the northeast corner of the Palace has fanciful wooden brackets carrying an upper walkway. Wall paintings at the lower level show mythological scenes, including *Ramayana* illustrations, such as Rama receiving Hanuman, and the scene of the churning of the cosmic ocean. The vividly toned figures are set on a bright yellow background.

Adalat Wada, the Old Palace (permission required to visit) beneath the Fort, south of the city, was used by Shivaji and the later Peshwas. The Palace is currently the residence of the descendants of the Satara Chhatrapatis. Several of Shivaji's own weapons are reputed to be stored here. The **Fort** occupies a triangular flat-topped hill that rises steeply for 300m above the Palace. Its walls and circular bastions can made out from below. There is little of interest on top, except for two gates, a few barren ponds and a dilapidated residence. The **Shrine of Manglai Devi**, the guardian deity of the Fort, is situated in the northeast tower.

The **Shri Chhatrapati Shivaji Maharaj Museum**, near the bus stand in the city, has a small but interesting collection of memorabilia associated with Maratha history. This includes weapons, costumes and regalia, and a model of Rajgad Fort. Musical instruments, games, seals, brass figurines, metalwork, drawings, paintings, some on glass, and fresco fragments are also on display.

Vishveshvara Temple, Mahuli

H. Mahuli

The *Chhatris* of the Satara rulers are located at a picturesque site on the west bank of the Krishna River, 6km east of Satara. The nearby riverside shrines, associated with Pant Pratinidhis, the Viceroys of the Peshwas, are among the finest examples of 18C Maratha architecture.

The largest of the Mahuli monuments is the **Vishveshvara Temple**, erected in about 1735 by Shripatrao. This occupies an irregular polygonal terrace, with an octagonal lamp column at the top of the steps that descend to the water. The east-facing Temple consists of a sanctuary with angled wall projections carried up into the tower. The lower taller stage of the tower has axial niches with curved cornices set between octagonal buttresses capped with domical finials; the upper shorter stage displays an octagon of niches topped with a bulbous fluted dome. A smaller spire repeating some of these elements rises over the antechamber. The adjoining open-columned hall has porch projections with balcony seating on three sides. A European bronze bell with the date 1744 hangs inside. Turrets treated as miniature pavilions enliven the roof and that of the detached Nandi pavilion in front.

The nearby **Sangameshvara Temple** stands at the confluence of the Yenna and Krishna Rivers. Its spire presents a simple curving scheme, with central panels curving up on four sides of the domical roof.

The **Rameshvara Temple**, on the opposite bank of the Krishna River, occupies a large rectangular terrace with steps between corner circular bastions at river level. Only one of a pair of lamp columns stands complete. The main shrine consists of a towered sanctuary, entered through a small porch with a Nandi pavilion in front. The rear arcade conceals a small sanctuary roofed with a dome.

8 · Kolhapur

This commercial and educational city is also a place of historical interest. Kolhapur's palaces and temples [A] may be combined with the military and civic structures of nearby **Panhala** [B] in a single day of sightseeing.

An additional day or two will have to set aside to reach the Arabian Sea strongholds of **Vijayadurg** [C] and **Malvan** [D], the latter celebrated for its island citadel of Sindhudurg.

Kolhapur may be conveniently combined with itineraries for Pune [3], Mahabaleshwar [7] and Sholapur [9]. Journeys can also be arranged linking Kolhapur with Panaji [11] in Goa and Belgaum [21A] in Karnataka.

■ **Transport**. Kolhapur is situated on NH4, 185km south of Pune and 108km north of Belgaum. Air connections are available with Bombay [1]. NH17 runs along the Konkan plain about 60km to the west. When completed, the Konkan Railway will provide convenient rail links with Bombay and Goa. Buses run constantly from Kolhapur to Panhala, but day excursions to Vijayadurg or Malvan are only possible by car.

■ **Accommodation**. By far the best place in Kolhapur (STD code 0231) is the architecturally distinguished *Shalini Palace* (☎ 650401); the *Pearl* (☎ 650451) is another possibility. Attractive hilltop accommodations are available at **Panhala**, 20km northwest of Kolhapur; the finest are the *Hotel Hilltop* (☎ 5054) and the *MTDC Holiday Resort* (☎ 5048). For visitors touring the coastal forts, there is the simple *Nathapi Sevaganga* at **Malvan**.

■ **Tourist Information**. The MTDC maintains an office at the Kedar Complex on Station Road (☎ 652935), and has an information counter at Mahalaxmi Dharamshala on Tarabai Road.

A. Kolhapur

Formerly the capital of the princely state of Kolhapur, this city is attractively located in the plains east of the Sahyadri ranges, in the extreme southwestern corner of Maharashtra.

> Kolhapur traces its history back to the Satavahana period, with remains dating from the 2C BC to the 2C AD. The discovery of Greek-styled figurines and medallions indicates early seaborne contacts with the Mediterranean. Kolhapur attained importance in later centuries, serving as the headquarters of the Shilharas, the most powerful rulers of western Maharashtra in the 11C–12C. The city emerged again in the 18C as the residence of a line of Maratha commanders who achieved autonomy from the Peshwas of Pune.

The tour of Kolhapur described here begins at the **Palace Square** in the middle of the Old City. This is entered through elaborate **Gateways** dating from the

19C. That on the north has an imposing lobed arch flanked by finely detailed balustrades, windows and small balconies carried on elephant tusks. A statue of a wrestler standing inside the Gateway refers to the wrestling academies, or *khushtis*, for which Kolhapur is famous. The east Gateway of the Square has an upper pavilion with curving cornices flanked by towers. The **Government Offices**, in the middle of the Square, occupy the Old Palace, a traditional 18C structure with wooden colonnades, brick infill walls and sloping tiled roofs. A doorway on the east gives access to what was once an open court surrounded by colonnades, later roofed in. A small chamber on the west functions as a shrine for the goddess Bhavani.

A short distance west of the Palace Square is the **Mahalakshmi Temple**, the largest and most popular in Kolhapur. This relic of the Shilahara period was severely damaged at the time of the Delhi invasion at the beginning of the 14C, but was restored in 1722 by the local ruler, Sambhaji. The Temple stands in a walled compound, entered through arched portals on four sides, that on the west being the highest. A pair of lamp columns stands inside. A hall with re-used supports and a long inscription is built against the walls immediately to the left. The west-facing Temple is entered on the north through a porch with inclined balcony slabs decorated with figurines. This is partly concealed by a later structure with wooden columns and a tiled roof. The porch gives access to a sequence of spacious halls with finely carved stone columns and corbelled domed ceilings, partly repaired.

The halls lead to the shrine of Mahalakshmi, whose gorgeously attired image is set in a silvered frame. Subshrines dedicated to Mahakali (north) and Sarasvati (south) open off the innermost hall. The outer walls of all three shrines preserve their complicated faceted outlines, echoed in the high plinth and basement mouldings, as well as in the pilastered niches and overhanging eaves. Most of the niche carvings have been remodelled in plaster, but a few original stone sculptures of maidens can be made out in the recesses. The five pyramidal towers, topped with domical finials that rise above the roof, are 19C additions. The Sheshashayi sanctuary, next to the east entrance, is of interest for the columns, doorway and corbelled dome taken from a dismantled 11C–12C Jain temple.

The next feature of interest in the city is the **Kolhapur Museum** (closed Mondays) on Bhausingji Road, 1km east of the Temple. This sombre Neo-Gothic structure was built as the Town Hall in 1872–76 by Charles Mant, well known for his projects in Madras [36F]. The frontal porch of the Museum is flanked by towers with steeply pyramidal metal roofs. Two European cannons are on display here; the example dated 1609 is engraved with a relief of the god Mars. The Museum houses Satavahana-period items discovered in excavations at nearby Brahmapuri Hill. They include figurines of the Greek god Poseidon, riders on an elephant, and a medallion with Hellenistic figures (replicas only). Pottery fragments, coins and beads from Brahmapuri are also shown. Graceful female musicians are among the sculptures rescued from the Mahalakshmi Temple. The finest sculpture is a female attendant bearing a fly-whisk from Panhala. A bronze bell displayed here was brought from Vasai [2E] in 1739 to be installed in the Mahalakshmi Temple. The raised gallery at one end of the Museum is given over to arms. The **Chhatrapati Pramila Raja Hospital**, opposite the Museum, was built by Mant in 1881–84. Its entrance porch has exuberant Corinthian columns with monkeys and demonic heads incorporated into the arches above.

Mant's masterpiece at Kolhapur, however, is the **New Palace**, 1.5km further north on Bhausingji Road. Completed in the same year as the Hospital, this complex presents a novel blend of disparate features in contrasting basalt and sandstone. The principal south façade presents a double-storeyed range, with Neo-Mughal lobed arches beneath and temple-like columns and brackets above. This scheme is interrupted by trefoil arches capped with curving cornices and small domes. The same elements cap the octagonal corner towers. The central porch is marked by a pronounced curved cornice. To one side rises a 45m high clock tower capped with an octagonal domed pavilion.

The interior of the New Palace accommodates the **Shahaji Chhatrapati Museum**, given over to memorabilia of the Kolhapur rulers. Its furnished apartments and corridors are crammed with arms, howdahs, paintings and photographs. The **Darbar Hall** occupies a double-height space in the middle of the Palace. The side walls display lobed arches filled with stained glass illustrating scenes from the life of Shivaji; carved columns with temple-like brackets support the cast-iron balcony above. A raised throne is placed at one end of the Hall.

The tour of Kolhapur continues with a visit to **Panchaganga *Ghat***, 1.5km northwest of the Palace Square. Brahmapuri Hill, the Satavahana-period site from which objects in the Museum were recovered, overlooks the south bank. Nothing can now be seen of the brick remains uncovered here during the excavations. The *Ghat* itself is lined with funerary structures of the Kolhapur rulers. The **Memorial of Shivaji III**, the largest of these, dates from 1815. It stands with others in a walled compound entered on the east through an arched gate. The Memorial has a sandstone portico with lobed arches. The faceted walls are capped with a brick-and-plaster tower with tapering bands in the middle of four sides. Delicately worked lotus ornamentation covers the interior doorway. The adjacent Memorials are surrounded by a cluster of lamp columns.

The last feature in Kolhapur to be described is the **Shalini Palace**, now a hotel, facing onto Rankala Lake, west of the city, built in 1931–34 as a private guest house for the Kolhapur ruler. Its arcades and balconies rise in three stages, dominated by a central clock tower topped with a domed pavilion, recalling that of the New Palace. The interiors are distinguished by Belgian glass etched with Maratha motifs and the Kolhapur crest.

B. Panhala

This imposing fort, 20km northwest of Kolhapur, is built on an outlying spur of the Sahyadris, rising more than 400m above the plain. The strategic importance of Panhala, guarding one of the principal routes through the Western Ghats, can be judged from its long and varied history.

After serving as the headquarters of the Shilahara ruler Bhoja II (1178–1209), the site subsequently passed into the hands of the Yadavas. It was a favourite outpost of the Bahmanis of Bidar [25A]; Mahmud Gawan, the powerful Prime Minister, encamped here during the rainy season of 1469. By the beginning of the 16C Panhala was absorbed into the kingdom of Bijapur [23A]. The Adil Shahis were responsible for strengthening and rebuilding the ramparts and gateways. The fort was raided by Shivaji in 1659, but it was not until 1673 that he was able to occupy it permanently. In 1701 Panhala surrendered to Aurangzeb, and it was here that the Mughal emperor received the English Ambassador, Sir William Norris. Within a few months the fort was retaken by the Maratha forces under Ramachandra Pant Amatya, who asserted his autonomy by founding an independent dynasty. In 1782 these rulers shifted their head-quarters to Kolhapur. After a local rebellion in 1844, Panhala was taken by the British.

More than 7km of **Fortifications** define the approximately triangular zone of Panhala fort. The walls are protected for long sections by steep escarpments, reinforced by a parapet with slit holes. The remaining sections have 5–9m high ramparts, strengthened by round bastions. Unfortunately, the East Gate, through which the road passes on arrival at the fort, was demolished by the British. A green-and-white-painted ***Dargah*** overlooking a tank is seen to the left of the entrance.

The road continues west for about 400m until it arrives at the **Tin *Darwaza***, or Triple Gate. This elaborate example of military architecture is assigned to the Adil Shahi era. The innermost entrance displays an arched recess framing a lobed arch. A nine-domed chamber gives access to an inner rectangular court lined with arcades. The intermediate entrance is topped with a lintel set within a lobed arch. This frames a plaster composition with lions and an image of Ganesha, additions of the 19C. The side panels have intricately etched patterns of interlocking battlements and stylised arabesques. Prominent battlements are seen above. The west side of the court is overlooked by an elevated guardroom with triple arches separated by decorated jambs. A passageway beneath leads to the outermost entrance. A slab with a Persian inscription of Ibrahim Adil Shah is set into the arcaded recess over the lintel.

A short distance west of the Tin *Darwaza* is a **Step-well** built into the inner portion of a bastion. The chambers at the upper level are arranged on three sides of the deep well. The road continues north for almost 1km until it arrives at the irregularly shaped **Bala Kila** in the middle of the comparatively flat top of Panhala hill. This fortified zone is defined by high walls with bastions, now much dilapidated and overgrown. Three great rectangular **Granaries**, capable of provisioning an entire army, stand freely within the walls. The largest, some 42m by 10m, has 16 chambers roofed with flat vaults rising about 8m above the ground, each with a square hole. Steps on the outside give access to the roof. A domed pavilion is set over the balconied entrance at the east end of the building. Decaying foundations and plinths hidden in the undergrowth are all that remain of the surrounding palaces and barracks.

The road continues north for about 500m before arriving at **Sajja Koti**, a pleasure pavilion set into the ramparts. This two-storeyed structure has an upper chamber with flattish domes on vaults decorated in the typical Bijapur style. An arcaded balcony on the west looks down into the fort. The chamber on the east enjoys fine views of the approach to Panhala from the plains beneath. The **Jyotiba Temple** crowns the summit of a small hill some 5km to the east.

C. Vijayadurg

This isolated but magnificently located fort overlooks the mouth of Vaghotan Creek, 146km southwest of Kolhapur, via Talera on NH17. The route descends through the rugged bluffs of the Sahyadris before crossing the Konkan plain. Vijayadurg's harbour, one of the finest on the Arabian Sea coast, is now little used. The fort here occupies a rocky promontory rising almost 40m above the water, joined to the mainland by a narrow neck of land on the south. The sleepy settlement here gives little indication that this was once a great port.

Vijayadurg dates back to the 16C, when it was first occupied by the Adil Shahis. It was much strengthened by Shivaji, to whom it owes its finest features as well as its name, Victory Fort. Vijayadurg assumed a crucial significance in Shivaji's naval campaigns against the Sidis of Janjira [2I]. In 1698 the Maratha admiral Kanhoji Angre of Alibag [2G] used Vijayadurg as a base from which to attack European and Indian shipping. These disruptive activities continued until 1756, when a flotilla of British and Maratha vessels managed to take Vijayadurg. The port was subsequently held by the Peshwas, but piracy flourished as vigorously as before. Vijayadurg passed into British hands with the conquest of the Maratha territories in 1818.

Vijayadurg takes the form of an irregular circle ringed by three concentric lines of **Fortifications** set at different levels, rising sheerly out of the water. The outermost and innermost rings, both of which are complete, have massive round bastions with slit holes and openings for cannon. The intermediate ring serves as an additional reinforcement on the landward side only. Visitors enter Vijayadurg by passing across a moat, now filled in, cut into the narrow neck of land on the south. The path leads through curving outworks, but the gateway inside is lost. A small domed Hanuman shrine stands within. Steps cut into the rock descend to the harbour to the right. Straight ahead lies a gate with an arched opening. This gives access to a passageway, which runs between the curving second and third lines of Fortifications until it arrives at the **Main Gate**, on the east side of the innermost citadel. Steps ascend between curving outworks to the Gate, which preserves its wooden doors and traces of plaster decoration.

Dilapidated structures within the fort are attractively shaded by mango and banyan trees. To the left of the Main Gate is a vaulted **Magazine**, entered through a doorway set beneath a lobed arch. Steps climb to a **Flag Tower**, from which a path follows the top of the innermost and highest ring of walls, with dramatic panoramas of the ocean below. The path passes by multi-storeyed structures, possibly **Residences**, with balconies but no floors or roofs.

A path running from the right of the Main Gate leads to the **Barracks**, a long rectangular structure, approximately 40m by 10m, with two doorways below and window openings above. The intermediate wooden floor on posts has disappeared. A large tank is partly excavated into the rock nearby. The path continues to the northern extremity of the fort, where there is another tank. This is overlooked by a **Granary** divided into four vaulted chambers, entered on the east through a single doorway. The pavilion on top of the Granary is a British-period addition. From here there are sweeping vistas of both the ocean and the harbour.

D. Malvan

This charming port lies 75km south of Vijayadurg by way of a scenic back road running along the Konkan plain. Malvan can also be approached from Kassal on NH17, 34km east, site of a future station on the Konkan Railway. Malvan is a traditional fishing port, with many old wooden stores and residences crowding the busy waterfront, which faces a curving palm-fringed bay, sheltered from the ocean by rocks and reefs. The formidable citadel of Sindhudurg occupies the largest island on the perimeter of the bay, about 1000m south of Malvan. Access is by local boat (check timings). The collapsing relics of **Padmagad**, a lesser citadel on an islet to the east, can be approached by a causeway at low tide.

In about 1665 Shivaji chose Malvan as his coastal headquarters, fortifying the islands and installing members of his family as Governors. Three years were required before the walls of Sindhudurg were completed; some 6000 workmen, including Portuguese experts, are supposed to have been employed. With the division of Shivaji's dominions between the Maratha chiefs in 1713, Malvan came under the sway of the Kolhapur rulers. The port was taken by the Portuguese in 1746, and 20 years later by the British, who then returned it to Kolhapur. Like Vijayadurg, Sindhudurg was notorious for its aggressive attacks on European shipping. The port was finally ceded to the British in 1812.

Sindhudurg is the most remarkable of Shivaji's coastal citadels. Its **Fortifications** extend for more than 3km, following closely the outer indentations of the irregular island. The walls, some 4m thick and up to 10m high, are partly damaged by the sea on the west. More than 50 round towers, spaced at regular intervals, have slit holes and rectangular openings for cannon. The citadel is entered through a single **Gate** near the northeast corner of the island. This is concealed by curving outworks on top of which is a guardroom with arched windows. The Gate has a single opening bridged by a lintel set in an arched recess. Lime impressions of handprints and footprints, popularly believed to be those of Shivaji himself, are seen on the inner face of the tower immediately north of the Gate.

The interior of Sindhudurg is mostly empty, except for rubble walls, small step-wells and coconut groves. A path leading west from the Gate arrives at the **Shivarajeshvar Temple** erected in 1695 by Rajaram, Shivaji's second son. The Temple is of particular interest, since it enshrines a much venerated sculpted portrait of Shivaji himself. The great warrior is shown in a seated posture, wearing a gilded mask. The shrine, which is approached through a hall with triple vaulted aisles, later extended, is topped with a stepped pyramidal tower capped by a domical finial.

The path continues to the **Mahadeva Temple**, originally a well, with a small *linga* placed in one of the surrounding niches. The **Bhavani Temple** lies beyond. The Fortifications skirt a small beach at the southwest corner of the island, an ideal picnic spot.

9 · Sholapur

This lively manufacturing centre, best known for its machine-woven blankets, sheets and shawls, is also a place of historical significance, with an outstanding example of military architecture standing in the middle of the city. A half day should be sufficient to see the Fort and other sights [A].

Sholapur makes a convenient base from which to visit the stronghold at **Naldurg** [B], the pilgrimage shrine at **Tuljapur** [C] and the ancient site of **Ter** [D], all of which can all be reached in a single-day outing.

The temples at **Ambajogai** [E] lie further afield and will require additional time. The fort at **Parenda** [F] can be combined with the popular temple at **Pandharpur** [G] in another full-day excursion.

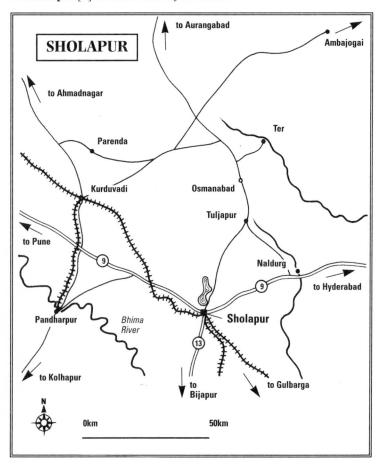

■ **Transport**. Sholapur benefits from excellent communications with Bombay [1], Bangalore [14] and Hyderabad [26], from which it is almost equidistant. Road transport links Sholapur to Pune [3], 265 km to the northwest on NH9, Aurangabad [5], 304km north, Ahmadnagar [6], 207km northwest, and Kolhapur [8], 208 km southwest. Sholapur is near the frontier with Karnataka, within easy reach of Bijapur [23], 101km south via NH13, and Gulbarga [24] 208km southeast. The Bombay-Madras line provides rail links with both Pune and Gulbarga. Frequent buses link Sholapur to all the places described here.

■ **Accommodation**. Sholapur (STD code 0217) is beginning to be developed as a tourist centre, the newest hotels being the *Pratham* (☎ 29581), *Surya* (☎ 29501) and *Vikram Palace* (☎ 28935). **Tuljapur** and **Pandharpur** also offer simple hospitality for pilgrims.

■ **Tourist Information**. None.

A. Sholapur

The strategic significance of Sholapur through the centuries may be judged from the numerous battles fought over its occupation.

Founded by the Bahmanis in the 14C, it was disputed by the rulers of both Ahmadnagar and Bijapur. In 1523 Burhan Nizam Shah and Ismail Adil Shah met at Sholapur to sign a treaty of friendship, but war broke out soon after and the city passed into the hands of Bijapur. In 1623 Malik Ambar successfully besieged Sholapur, but the fort was returned to the Adil Shahis by the Mughals after their conquest of Ahmadnagar. Even so, the Mughals reclaimed the city in 1668. Aurangzeb camped at Sholapur in 1686 while planning the final assault on Bijapur. Nizamul Mulk took control of the city in 1723 in a bid to throw off his allegiance to the Delhi emperor, thereby absorbing it into the newly founded Asaf Jahi state. Sholapur then remained in the possession of the Nizams of Hyderabad until the British assault in 1818.

Sholapur's impressive **Fort** stands in the middle of the city, surrounded on three sides by a tree-lined park incorporating a small zoo; an artificial lake extends to the east. The double-layered **Walls** define an irregular quadrangle, some 320m by 175m. The outer lower walls, which date from Bahmani times, have sloping sides, polygonal bastions and prominent guardrooms and battlements. The moat in front is now mostly filled in. The inner higher walls added by the Adil Shahis, separated from the outer layer by a gap of 10m to 20m, display round bastions with towers, occasionally dismantled. The main **Gate**, at the northeast corner of the Fort, is reached by a timber walkway crossing the moat. The innermost entrance, with a 10m high arched opening, has an inscription of Ali Adil Shah flanked by carved lions. A small **Jami Mosque** with re-used temple columns is seen immediately on the left after passing through the Gate. The interior of the Fort is now a public garden with fountains, much patronised by the local population.

The other significant feature of Sholapur is the **Siddheshvara Temple**, which stands in the middle of the lake east of the Fort, from which there are fine views of the ramparts. This religious complex commemorates a saint who died here in 1167, and who came to be worshipped in deified form as Siddheshvara. It is believed that the city achieved prosperity under his auspicious blessings. The saint is particularly revered by members of the Lingayat sect. The Temple, of no great antiquity, reached by causeway on the south, stands in a fortified enclosure with an arched gateway on the west. The garden within contains the **Samadhi**, in which the saint is entombed, as well as altars for fire offerings. A wooden colonnade surrounds the square sanctuary of the Temple, accommodating small *lingas* covered with gilded brass face masks representing Siddheshvara. A painted plaster spire rises above. The Neo-Classical gable on the front displays a large clock.

Sholapur is furnished with fine civic buildings. The Neo-Gothic **City Corporation** stands in a small park on the main road near the central stadium. Its polished basalt columns, interlaced pointed arches, projecting balconies and octagonal pavilions are painted in striking pastel colours. The similarly styled **N.G. Mills** has a tall octagonal tower.

B. Naldurg

This small town, overshadowed by a magnificent fortress, lies 45km east of Sholapur on NH9. Like Sholapur, Naldurg served as the headquarters of the Bijapur rulers on their various military campaigns. It was later occupied by the Mughals and the forces of the Nizams.

The **Fort**, at the east end of the town, is impressively sited on basalt bluffs that rise sheerly up to 60m above the Bori River. The **Ramparts** define an approximately quadrangular plateau to the west, from which a long promontory extends north into a great bend in the river. Walls cut off the constricted neck by which these two zones are joined. A third enclosure on the other side of the river, roughly circular in shape, is connected with the northern promontory by a wall thrown across the river. This creates a dam that ensured the Fort with adequate water supply.

Sloping **Walls** with slit holes present a line of massive circular bastions with guardrooms on top. Two bastions on the west take variant square and lobed shapes. The battlemented parapet has mostly fallen. The principal **Gate** to the Fort, on the west, is set between bastions in double lines of walls. **Domed Structures**, possibly stables, now much dilapidated, stand immediately inside. From here a street runs east through the quadrangular Fort. The **Mosque** in the middle dates from 1560, in the early years of the Adil Shahi occupation. Its arches display both pointed and lobed profiles, with ornate arabesque ornament in the roundels above.

To the north are the remains of a Neo-Classical **Villa**, built for the representative of the Nizam, but occupied for several years by Colonel Meadows Taylor, the British Resident, formerly of Shorapur [24G], after he took command of Naldurg in 1853. Delicately worked friezes with Greek patterns contrast with the massive stonework of the ramparts up against which the Villa is built. One room leads to a balcony jutting out over the river. A **Palace** set into the east walls of the Fort, a short distance away, consists of domed chambers with balconies projecting over the tops of the walls and a small *hammam*, all opening off a court with a fountain.

A walk of almost 500m is required to reach the promontory extension to the north. Almost at the end is a remarkable **Lookout Tower**, built as an isolated circular bastion more than 30m in diameter. A long flight of steps ascends to the summit, from where a fine panorama may be had of the entire Fort. A cannon with an animal head is mounted on top. The large **Granary** immediately to the east has pointed vaults roofing two long chambers, with domes at the ends. A small **Viewing Pavilion** is set into the west walls of the promontory extension. The **Dam** on the Bori River serves as a causeway to the smaller circular fort. A balcony beneath the causeway indicates a **Water Palace** built into the dam wall.

C. Tuljapur

This popular pilgrimage centre is located 40km northeast of Sholapur, and almost the same distance directly from Naldurg. The **Bhavani Temple** here attained fame in the 17C as the shrine of the goddess who rewarded Shivaji with the legendary sword, thereby inspiring him to victory. (A sign in the Temple indicates that this weapon is now on display in the British Museum, but there is no record of it in London.) Shivaji sought the blessings of Bhavani before embarking upon any important expedition; her name is supposed to have been shouted as a battle cry by the Maratha troops. Two fairs held here every year, one in September–October, the other in April, attract huge crowds from all over Maharashtra.

The Bhavani Temple dates mainly from the Maratha period, but has been substantially remodelled in recent years. It occupies the west slope of a hill, beside a small stream. Steps descend from the crowded bazaar at the top of the hill past an attractive fountain, the **Gomukh Tank**, named after the sculpted cow head out of which water gushes. An open pond nearby, the **Kallol Tank**, is surrounded by steps. **Gateways** with plain arched openings arranged in a descending sequence lead to the main enclosure.

The **Main Shrine** is surrounded by arcades that follow the polygonal outline of the enclosure. The east-facing sanctuary is of little interest, except for its tapering 12-sided spire. This is divided into three stages and capped with double petalled domes, all brightly painted; the plaster niches are filled with deities and sages. The sanctuary is approached through a closed hall with doorways set into arched recesses, and an outer open hall with 16 columns and balcony seating on three sides. The pavilion has arched openings standing freely in front, topped with a shorter but similar spire; it is used for fire sacrifices. An arched gate in the west wall of the compound gives access to a flight of steps that descends to the village in the plain beneath.

D. Ter

This small town (sometimes spelt as Thair), 80km northeast of Sholapur via Osmanabad, rose to prominence under the Satavahanas in the 1C–2C.

Ter's commerce with the Mediterranean is confirmed by the many Roman coins unearthed here. The town is even mentioned in the famous Roman travel work, the *Periplus of the Erythrean Sea*, as one of the two premier centres in this part of India, the other being Paithan [5L]. Ter rose again rose to prominence in the 11C–12C, when it served as the headquarters of a branch of the Shilahara rulers.

Excavations in and around the town have yielded old bricks, pottery fragments, beads, garlands, combs, dolls, conch shells and artistically worked ivories. A selection of these finds are on display in the **Ramalingappa Lamture Museum** (closed Mondays) at the entrance to the town. The display includes Satavahana items: terracottas, pots, beads, jewellery, coins and lamps; portions of a limestone railing from a Buddhist *stupa*; and finely worked stucco heads and stone figurines of goddesses. (The celebrated ivory *yakshi* from Ter is generally stored in a bank.) A superbly modelled, though damaged standing Narayana, dating from the 7C–8C Early Chalukya era, comes from the Trivikrama Temple. A remarkable item is a Shilahara period wooden temple doorway adorned with stylised foliation and a row of divinities.

The most important of Ter's surviving monuments is the **Trivikrama Temple**, near the river at the north end of the town. The Temple dates back to Satavahana times, making it the oldest standing structure in Maharashtra. Though substantially renovated over the centuries, it preserves its original apsidal-ended plan and curving vault, features familiar from rock-cut *chaitya* halls. The shrine was originally a Buddhist foundation, but was later converted to Hindu usage. It is built of plastered brickwork without internal columns, the roof consisting of a smoothly curved vault. The large horseshoe-shaped arch on the front frames a later image of Hanuman. The damaged, but impressive, 1.5m high stone image of Trivikrama placed in the sanctuary probably dates from the Early Chalukya period. It shows the god with one leg kicked up high. A comparable image of Karttikeya riding the peacock is worshipped in a side shrine.

E. Ambajogai

This small town, 163km north of Sholapur via Osmanabad, is known for its many temples attractively situated on both banks of the Jayanti River. Ambajogai was an important centre in Yadava times, judging from the number of 12C–13C vestiges. One example, the **Sakaleshvara Temple**, lies west of the town amidst collapsed blocks overgrown with wild bushes. 12 central columns of the hall, complete with figural carvings on the shafts, still stand. The **Kholeshvara Temple**, north of the town, is also a Yadava monument. Though much rebuilt, it preserves its original doorway decorated with river goddesses and guardians.

The **Jogai Temple**, after which the town is named, stands in the middle of the settlement, but is of little artistic interest, unlike the **Yogeshvari Temple** in the fortified compound on the west bank of the Jayanti River. This Temple is entered through a gateway on the south, surmounted by a gallery for musicians. In addition to the goddess Yogeshvari, the temple enshrines Mahakali and Bhavani. The brick-and-plaster spire over the central sanctuary belongs to the Maratha period. Its lowest square stage has corner pavilion-shaped finials; above rises a 12-sided tower of four stages, each face treated as an arched niche with figures.

The **Hattikhama Caves** on the river bank, some 500m northeast of the Yogeshvari Temple, are assigned to the 11C. The complex consists of a line of rock-cut square chambers approached through a long columned hall with a court in front. Two huge stone elephants face the entrance. In the middle of the court is an elegantly carved hall, partly collapsed, with an image of Nandi inside. Several **Jain Caves** are excavated into the hills opposite.

F. Parenda

This small town, 96km northwest of Sholapur via Barsi, is famous for its **Fort**, one of the most perfect specimens of military architecture in Maharashtra.

> The fort was laid out during the late 15C by Mahmud Gawan, the Prime Minister of Muhammad Shah of Bidar. In 1600, Parenda was taken from the Bahmanis by the Nizam Shahis. The site passed several times between them and the Adil Shahis until it was taken by the Mughals in 1657. It eventually came into the hands of the Nizams of Hyderabad.

Parenda's Fort comprises a quadrangle of double **Walls**, the faces of which incline inwards slightly. They are topped with battlemented parapets with regularly spaced box-shaped guardrooms. The outer lower line has polygonal bastions, doubled at the corners; the inner higher line displays circular bastions on the west, where a polygonal bastion accommodates a small mosque. Many bastions are still mounted by cannon. A moat shields the Walls from the outside. The main **Gate**, at the northeast corner of the Fort, consists of a sequence of three arched openings separated by intermediate courts. The first entrance projects into the moat, where it was originally approached by a drawbridge. The robust teak doors have iron plates and spikes. The cannon placed on the corner bastion rising over the Gate has Persian calligraphy in cartouches, friezes of palmettes and reliefs of lions.

The **Armoury** is situated immediately to the right on entering the Fort. Some 300 stone cannonballs are stored in one of its vaulted chambers. To the south is the rectangular compound of the **Jami Mosque**, entered through an arched gate on the north as well as through a domed entrance on the east. A tank and a covered cistern occupy part of the court. The 27-bayed prayer hall is roofed with flat slabs decorated with lotus medallions. The three bays at the north end are screened off. The temple-like columns have blocks, capitals and brackets decorated with stylised ornament. The outer row is sheltered by angled eaves. Triple stone windows are placed in the end walls. The *mihrab* is of delicately worked polished basalt.

The domed ***Hammam***, west of the mosque, now a depository of loose stone carvings, opens off a small court with a raised area on the south. A short distance west is a deep octagonal **Step-well** surrounded by arcades. The ruined **Palace** nearby is entered through an arched gate. Only the raised floor facing towards an open court can now be made out.

The ground to the south and east within the Fort permits access to the tops of the walls. Overgrown piles of rubble indicate numerous collapsed and buried structures.

G. Pandharpur

This pilgrimage town, the most frequented in Maharashtra, lies on the bank of the Bhima River, 74km west of Sholapur via Mohol on NH9. Pandharpur is crowded with shrines, monasteries, rest houses and shops which cluster around the Vithoba Temple. This faces a busy street that leads to the bathing *ghats*, about 400m east.

In spite of the antiquity of the cult of Vithoba, known as Vithala in the 13C (this name has been recently revived), little that predates the Maratha period can now be seen. The shrines at Pandharpur were much developed in the middle of the 17C during the time of Shahji, Shivaji's father, and also under the Holkars and Shindes in the second half of the 18C. While there is never any shortage of visitors to the Temple, the crowd reaches maximum proportions during festival time in June–July. On this occasion, holy figures are carried on planquins to Pandharpur from their respective homes all over Maharashtra by singing devotees belonging to the Wakari sect.

The **Vithoba Temple** is dedicated to Vishnu in the form of a standing figure with two hands resting on the hips. Though barely 1m high and probably no older than the 17C, this unique image is held in great veneration. According to legend, the original icon was removed in the early 14C, to save it from the sacrilege of the Delhi invaders, after which it was taken to Vijayanagara [20B].

The Temple occupies a rectangular walled compound, 106m by 52m. The main entrance, on the east, is through a columned porch and arched gate, beside which are traces of a 13C structure. The large court within is surrounded by arcades, partly occupied by a lofty wooden structure of recent construction. Two stone lamp columns, more than 10m high, stand near a pipal tree. The main shrine is approached through two halls, both with columns embellished with carved blocks on the shafts, circular capitals and ornate brackets. Other halls open off to the side, that on the south with elaborate columns. The doorways are covered with embossed silver sheets. The exterior plinth and walls of the sanctuary are enlivened with sharply cut mouldings; projecting niches framed by pilasters enshrine images of Venugopala (north), Krishna on Kaliya (west) and Anantashayana (south). The spire has multiple projections rising in stages, marked by plastered niches that contain seated deities. Lesser subshrines for Rukmini and Mahalakshmi occupy the west corners of the court to the rear of the main sanctuary. Both have vividly coloured spires.

Steps descend to the sandy river bed, where many of Pandharpur's holiest shrines are located. **Pundalika's Temple** is an octagonal funerary monument commemorating the spot where a disciple of Vithoba spent the last years of his life. After his death he was buried here, and a *linga* was set into his tomb. The Temple has a slender octagonal spire capped with a brass finial. Nearby **Tukaram's Temple**, built in memory of another holy figure, has an arcaded sanctuary topped with a 12-sided tower rising in three stages. **Vishnupad's Temple**, reached by a small causeway, is notable for the *shraddha*, funeral ceremonies performed by pilgrims. Its columned hall shelters three rocks with carved footprints, believed to be those of Krishna and a cow.

Other important temples stand in walled compounds next to the Holkar and Shinde mansions that crowd the high bank of the Bhima River. The **Dvarkadishvara Temple** has massive circular bastions at the corners of its fortified enclosure. The central sanctuary is topped with a slender polygonal spire. The **Ramachandra Temple**, to the north, enshrines white marble images of Rama, Lakshmana and Sita. A figure to the left represents the royal patroness, Ahilyabai.

10 · Nagpur

Nagpur is the major industrial and commercial centre of northeastern Maharashtra, a hilly and wooded region known as Vidarbha, the habitat of the indigenous Gond peoples. The city is famous for its orange cultivation and cotton and silk weaving, but there are also several historical features associated with the Bhonsale rulers, for which a few hours of sightseeing should suffice [A]. Half-day trips may also be made to the sacred hill at **Ramtek** [B], north of Nagpur, and to the Gandhi Memorial near **Wardha** [C], to the south.

Longer journeys will be required to reach the national park at **Navegaon** [D], east of Nagpur, or the historic town of **Achalpur** [E], the nearby hill station of **Chikaldara** [F] and the fort at **Narnala** [G] a further distance to the west.

■ **Transport**. Nagpur enjoys excellent communications by plane or train with Delhi, Bombay [1] and Hyderabad [26]. The city's somewhat remote location is immediately apparent from the long road distances: Nasik [4] lies 705km west of Nagpur via NH6 and NH3, while Hyderabad is 512km south on NH7, and Jabalpore in Madhya Pradesh is 360km north on the same route. Local transport is available to all the sights described here, but an excursion to Achalpur, Chikaldara and Narnala will not be feasible in a single day.

■ **Accommodation**. Nagpur (STD code 0712) is yet to be developed as a tourist centre, but there are several adequate hotels. The finest are the *Tuli International* (☎ 534784), *Hotel Centre Point* (☎ 520901), *Rawall Continental* (☎ 523845) and *Jagsons Regency* (☎ 228111), the last two near the airport. Basic accommodation is available at **Wardha**. For those wishing to visit Achalpur and Narnala, an overnight stop is possible in the *MTDC Cottages* at **Chikaldara**.

■ **Tourist Information**. The MTDC office is situated at Sankrutik Bachat Bhavan, Normal School Area, Sitabaldi (☎ 533325).

A. Nagpur

Spreading along the north bank of the Nag River, Nagpur was founded at the beginning of the 18C by the Gond chief Bakht Buland.

In 1740 the city became the headquarters of the Bhonsale chiefs, a Maratha family which rose to prominence under the Peshwas of Pune [3A]. Nagpur was sacked by resurgent Gonds in 1765, after which it came under the protection of the East India Company. The Bhonsale troops rebelled in 1817, but the British forces prevailed and Nagpur was secured as capital of the Central Provinces.

The **Mahal**, the core of Old Nagpur in the southern part of the city, still has its arched entrance gates. The **Police Station**, originally the Queen's Palace, is a vestige of the Bhonsale period. It is built in a sombre Neo-Mughal manner, with double-storeyed arcades framed by corner towers with domed pavilions on top. The nearby **Post Office** occupies another royal structure. A walled compound in the vicinity contains the east-facing **Raghurajeshvari** and **Rukmini**

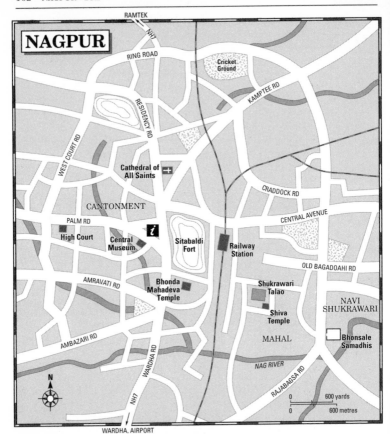

Temples, typical examples of the 18C Maratha style. Both Temples are approached through wooden halls with lobed arcades. The yellow sandstone sanctuaries have complicated star-shaped plans with multiple angled corners. The basements are decorated with sharply cut friezes of animals, attendants, monster heads and petalled designs. Further figures fill the wall niches. Small sculptures of Krishna with *gopis* act as brackets beneath the overhanging eaves. The curving towers repeat the angles of the walls beneath. The central bands have flat geometric patterns flanked by tiers of miniature model towers, capped with circular ribbed elements. A marble pavilion in front of the Rukmini Temple houses a kneeling Garuda.

Another series of Bhonsale monuments is located in **Navi Shukrawari**, southeast of Old Nagpur, where a group of royal memorials dating from the 18C and early 19C stands in a tree-lined compound. The **_Samadhi_ of Raghuji I**, who died in 1755, has a central *linga* shrine topped with a circular pyramidal tower divided into shallow facets. The shrine is surrounded by a vaulted verandah with pointed arches, projecting as porches on four sides. Domed pavilions with curving cornices crown the porches and corner bays of the verandah. The carvings at the base of the monument show mythological figures and courtly processions. The adjacent **Samadhi of Raghuji III** is crowned by a square tower with gently curving sides divided into horizontal facets. The verandah displays lobed arches. The **Samadhi of Kasibai**, a smaller structure nearby, is the only one with a brick-and-plaster tower.

Other Bhonsale features are scattered throughout the city. The **Shukrawari Talao** is a large rectangular reservoir in the central part of Nagpur. The **Shiva Temple**, at the southeast corner, has a red sandstone sanctuary with a star-shaped plan topped by an intricately worked tower. Densely worked ornamentation frames the upper chamber on the east face. The buff-coloured sandstone pavilion in front has lobed arcades, partly concealed by concrete additions. The **Bhonda Mahadeva Temple**, south of Sitabaldi Fort, is a small but intricately decorated building. Ramayana and Krishna scenes are carved in flat relief on the curving bands of the tower. The wall panels in the frontal porch show unusual yogic forms of Shiva (right) and Vishnu (left).

British-period monuments are concentrated in the western part of Nagpur. **Sitabaldi Fort** (access restricted to visitors), established by the British when they occupied Nagpur, extends over a low scrubby hill. It has two rings of defences, with occasional bastions for gun emplacements. The inner enclosure is occupied by barracks and administrative buildings. The **Cantonment**, to the north, is dominated by the **Cathedral of All Saints**, a bland Neo-Gothic project of 1851. Its stone tower with double corner pinnacles was added in 1879.

One of the oldest British structures still in use is the nearby **Central Museum** of 1863 (closed Mondays). The archaeology and sculpture galleries display antiquities brought from 11C–13C temple sites in the vicinity. One of the finest exhibits, Vishnu and Lakshmi riding on Garuda, comes from Mandla in Madhya Pradesh. The sculpted doorway surrounded by miniature figures is from Narasingpur, also in Madhya Pradesh. Items from other parts of Southern India include Buddhist bronzes from Nagapattinam [40M]. The art gallery displays metal and ivory objects, as well as miniature paintings from the Bhonsale collection. Wooden memorial posts with striking carved designs, erected by Gond and Korku peoples, are shown in the anthropology section.

The **High Court**, about 1.5km north of the Museum, is an imposing Indian-styled Neo-Classical edifice that dates from the last years of British domination. The yellow sandstone complex was built in 1937–42 by Henry Medd, who had worked with Edwin Lutyens in New Delhi. The Court is dominated by a central entrance portico with four Ashokan-type columns, approached by a broad staircase. Above the cornice rises a high circular drum with corner domed pavilions; this carries a smooth hemispherical dome, relieved by bands of *stupa*-like railings. The colonnaded galleries extend to either side.

B. Ramtek

The Hill of Rama, as this red sandstone outcrop is known, lies 48km north of Nagpur, a short distance east of NH7. Rising 150m above the town of Ramtek to the west, the hill derives its sanctity from the belief that the god Rama permanently resides here. Today, Ramtek is a popular pilgrimage destination, especially during the fair held in October–November.

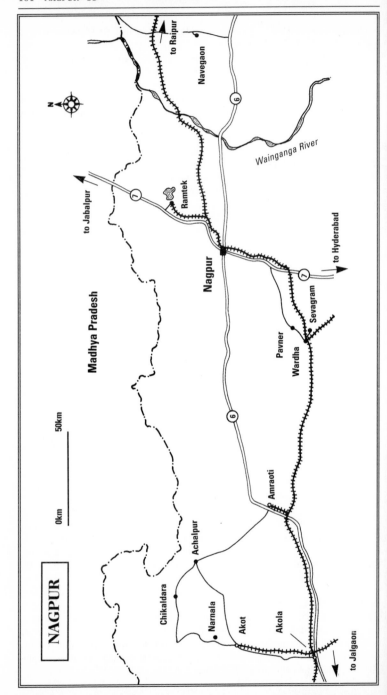

Ramtek is associated with the 4C–5C Vakatakas, who had their capital at Nandavardhan, 5km southwest of the hill. Portions of temples, sculptures and inscriptions at Ramtek are assigned to these kings. In the 12C–13C it came under the sway of the Yadavas, who built the temples at the summit of the hill. These monuments suffered at the hands of the Delhi invaders and were virtually abandoned until the 18C, when the Bhonsales of Nagpur undertook major restoration work. Raghuji I had the images of Rama and Sita installed here in about 1750, thereby reviving religious rituals at the site.

The visit to Ramtek begins at **Ambala Lake**, towards the southern extremity of the hill, 2km southeast of the town. The road passes through an arched **Gate** framed by round bastions and topped with a crenellated parapet. The Lake beyond is ringed with shrines and memorials, most from the Bhonsale period, with curved or pointed towers and sometimes also domes.

The route ascending directly from the Lake to the Citadel at the summit of Ramtek is now little used; a new, more steeply climbing road is preferred. This winds upwards until it arrives at the **Kalidas Memorial**, a modern 12-sided structure with a circular roof. The interior provides a setting for painted illustrations of scenes from the poetry and plays of Kailadasa, the famous Sanskrit author, who spent time at the Vakataka court at Nandavardhan. From here there is a fine panorama of the walled Citadel.

Near to the Memorial stands the **Kevala Narasimha Temple**, a modest structure in bright red sandstone, much restored in later times. This enshrines a 5C image of seated Narasimha, with the right hand of the god resting on a disc. An inscribed slab of the Vakataka era is set into the walls. A path through the undergrowth leads to the nearby **Rudra Narasimha Temple**, which houses an almost identical image.

From here it is but a short distance to the arched opening of the **Varaha Gate**. Just outside stands a small **Mosque** with triple domes, erected in memory of one of Aurangzeb's courtiers. Immediately on the right after passing through the Gate is an open pavilion that shelters a large sculpture of **Varaha**, dating from the 5C. Steps to the left of the Gate arrive at the **Bhogarama Temple**, a small Vakataka structure, much altered. Its twin sanctuaries house 19C images of Rama and Vishnu; a marble image of Krishna is placed in the central niche of the porch.

The path winds around to the **Simha Gate**, the entrance to the first and lowest enclosure of the **Citadel**. This quadrangular compound is contained by massive walls with prominent corner bastions, all dating from the Bhonsale period. In the middle of the west side of the enclosure is the **Bhairava Gate**, the entrance to the second intermediate enclosure, built at a slightly higher level and also contained by massive walls. The Gate has a lobed arch with Mughal-styled niches at either side. The small **Radha Krishna Temple** stands in the southeast corner of the enclosure; a deep rectangular tank and the small **Dasharatha Temple** occupy the southwest corner. The latter is fronted by a porch with sculptures, now worn and whitewashed.

To the right of the Dasharatha Temple is the **Gokul Gate**, the entrance to the third and highest enclosure of the Citadel, extending over the level top of the hill. The triple-storeyed Gate has interior columns supporting upper galleries, partly blocked up. The structure is assigned to the 12C–13C, contemporary with the Temples beyond. These Yadava-period features were substantially renovated by the Bonsales.

The **Lakshmana** and **Rama Temples**, standing one behind the other at the west end of the third enclosure, are the largest and most important at Ramtek, and are invariably crowded with devotees. Each Temple is approached through a hall with triple porch extensions. The adjoining sanctuary has complicated faceted plans, the curving tower above displaying clustered miniature elements. The original carved decoration, damaged through the centuries, is obscured by thick whitewash. The subshrines built into the sides of the enclosure are similarly whitewashed.

The tour continues by retracing the route back to the Varaha Gate. The **Trivikrama Temple**, crowning a small rise 200m to the east, consists of a damaged 5C image of Vishnu with his leg kicked up high. The sculpture stands in front of a dilapidated shrine of the same period. From here there are fine vistas of the Jain Complex and Khindsi Tank beneath the north flank of the hill.

The **Jain Complex**, 2km north of Ramtek town, is assigned to the Bhonsale period. The central west-facing **Shantinatha Temple** has recently been renovated and is now entirely cloaked in marble. It enshrines an enormous polished stone Tirthankara, almost 4m high. The side shrines, dedicated to other Jinas, preserve their original 19C stonework, with intricately carved details on the faceted walls and towers. A short distance west of the complex is the **Kalanka Devi Temple**, a rare example from the 8C–9C Rashtrakuta period. Its barrel-vaulted roof is raised on a sequence of eave-like mouldings.

C. Wardha

The railway junction at Wardha, 62km southwest of Nagpur, is of historical significance because of Mahatma Gandhi's assocation with the area. In 1934 Gandhi selected Wardha as the headquarters of his mission, taking up residence in a nearby village from where he organised political gatherings over the next 13 years. Many decisions of national importance, including deliberations such as the Quit India Proposal, were prepared and adopted here. Among the eminent national leaders whom Gandhi attracted to Wardha was Vinoba Bhave, the social reformer.

A small settlement 8km east of Wardha, renamed **Sevagram**, Service Village, was chosen by Gandhi for his home. **Bapu Kuti**, Gandhi's abode, is a simple cottage with mud walls and tiled roof. Hand-spinning, initiated by the Mahatma, is still practiced in the Village; meetings are held at the open air multi-faith **Prayer Ground**. 3km from Sevagram is the ***Ashram*** of **Vinoba Bhave.** Loose sculptures dating from the 5C, some showing *Ramayana* and Krishna scenes, have been assembled here.

10km north of Wardha, on the Dham River, is **Pavnar**. The **Gandhi Memorial**, an umbrella-shaped construction, commemorates the spot where Gandhi's ashes were immersed after having been brought from Delhi, where the Mahatma was cremated.

D. Navegaon National Park

Maharashtra's finest nature reserve can be reached from Nagpur. The Navegaon National Park is located 132km east of the city, a short distance south of NH6; the nearest railhead is 1km away. The Park is ringed by forested ranges through which narrow roads wind. Strategically placed watchtowers enable visitors to view the varied wildlife. Boats can also be hired to sail across the 11 sq km lake, the area around which is known as the **Dr Salim Ali Bird Sanctuary**. Each winter the lake is home to huge flocks of migrating ducks, as well as to scarlet minivets, paradise flycatchers and kingfishers. Langurs, sloth bears and even the occasional bison and leopard are sometimes sighted. A deer park and an aviary have been set up within the Park.

E. Achalpur

This city, about 200km west of Nagpur via Amraoti, the nearest railhead, attained historical importance as Ellichpur, the capital of Berar.

Originally a province of the Bahmani kingdom of Bidar [25A], Berar emerged as an independent state at the end of the 15C, under the leadership of Fathullah Imad Shah. In 1491 he was encouraged by the Governors of Ahmadnagar [6A] and Bijapur [23A] to proclaim his independence, thereby initiating the Imad Shahi dynasty. Alauddin, who succeeded Fathullah in 1510, participated in the struggles of the era, for a time aligning himself with the Nizam Shahis in an effort to combat the armies of Bijapur and Golconda [26E], and to withstand attacks from Gujarat and Malwa to the north. Burhan assumed the throne in 1562 and three years later participated in the famous battle against Vijayanagara [20B–C]. Berar's independence came to an end in 1572, when it was annexed by Ahmadnagar, but the Nizam Shahis were in control only until 1590, when they were ousted by the Mughals. Claims on the region continued to be made by Ahmadnagar, and Achalpur was occupied for a time by Malik Ambar in 1620. The city succumbed finally to Shah Jahan in 1636, after which Berar was absorbed into the Mughal empire and came under the control of the Sultan Khans, subordinates of the Nizam of Hyderabad.

Achalpur's short-lived role as the Imad Shahi capital is borne out by the dearth of monuments from this era. The oldest building is the **Idgah** of 1347, dating back to the time of the Tughluq conquest from Delhi. The Idgah has a raised domed pavilion over the middle of the wall; only one of the corner minarets survives. The **Jami Mosque**, a 15C Bahmani structure, has an unadorned façade of 11 arches, with 108 pillars inside.

Of greater interest is **Hauz Katora**, a ruined Imad Shahi palace 3km west of the city. The centrepiece of this complex is a triple-storeyed ocagonal tower with arched openings on each side. The interior comprises two superimposed domed chambers. The tower stands in the middle of a circular pond. The **Tomb of Dulha Shah**, 1.5km east of the city, is a popular shrine commemorating a saint who died in Delhi. The building is no earlier than the 18C.

F. Chikaldara

This resort occupies a 1200m high plateau in the Satpura ranges, 28km north-west of Achalpur. Attractively ringed by gently wooded slopes, this hill station was established by the British in the 19C as a sanatorium and a site for coffee plantations. With its array of colourful birds and animals, including oriole, magpie, barbet, chitah, sambha and langur, Chikaldara is a popular destination for nature lovers. The **Melghat Tiger Reserve** nearby contains a wealth of sloth, bear, hyena, gaur, sambhar, nilgai, four-horned antelope, boar, and even the occasional tiger.

Hurricane Point offers fine views of the fort at **Gavilgad**, 3km to the south-west, at a slightly lower elevation. This citadel was established in 1425 by the Bahmani Governors, and later became the principal stronghold of the Imad Shahis. Double walls with round bastions define the **Inner Fort**, approached from the south, where the hill is steepest. The **Outer Fort**, with a third ring of walls, shields the Inner Fort on the north and northeast. The Inner Fort is entered through three **Gates** flanked by guardrooms. One Gate is of interest for the carvings of a lion grasping five elephants in its claws; another carving shows a half-human figure with two heads devouring two tigers. A **Mosque** of large dimensions, now dilapidated, occupies one of the high points within the Inner Fort. Other structures were mostly dismantled in 1858, when the site was occupied by British troops.

G. Narnala

This remotely situated **Citadel** lies about 40km southwest of Chikaldara, at the summit of a 1000m high wooded hill, cut off from the main Satpura range.

Narnala dates back to Bahmani times, having been laid out in 1425 by Ahmad Shah of Bidar. The Citadel was occupied successively by the Imad Shahis, Nizam Shahis, Mughals and Marathas, before being taken by the British in 1818.

Narnala consists of three contiguous zones. The **Inner Fort** encloses the upper plateau of the hill, with two smaller **Outer Forts** protruding at opposite angles. The battlemented walls, varying from 8m to 13m high, are punctuated by 67 round towers. The Inner Fort is dotted with decaying buildings, including fragments of an aqueduct and stone drains, ruins of a palace and a mosque, and overgrown piles identified as the mint, arsenal, powder magazine and stables. Four curious stone cisterns are covered by a masonry platform with small apertures, with the remains of arches on top. A large cannon with a Persian inscription of 1670 lies on the west side of the hill.

The most striking architectural feature at Narnala is the sequence of three arched **Gates** built in pale cream sandstone, providing access to the Inner Fort from the south. The innermost entrance, the **Mahakali Gate**, was erected by Fathullah Imad Shah in 1487, four years before he asserted his autonomy from the Bahmanis. It is profusely decorated, with calligraphic designs and lotus medallions, and is topped by an elaborate parapet. The guardrooms projecting from the sides have arcaded balconies filled with delicately worked stone screens.

Goa

The splendid beaches and well-developed facilities of the Union Territory of Goa attract large numbers of visitors each year. Most tourists arrive in **Panaji** [11], from where they head for the coastal resorts in the vinicity of **Mapusa** [12] or **Margao** [13], in the northern and southern parts of the state respectively.

The most important relics of the Portuguese period are the 16C–17C churches of **Old Goa** [11B], a short distance from Panaji, upstream along the

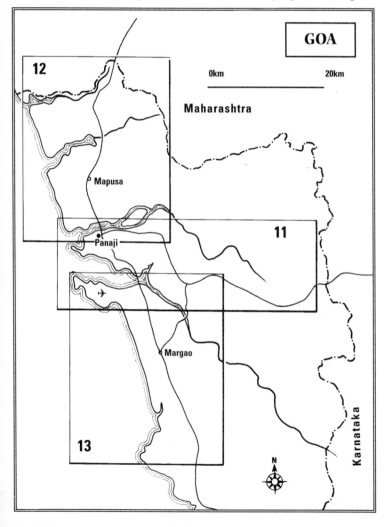

Mandovi River. Here can be seen the tomb of St Francis Xavier, still venerated by local Christians.

Temples built in unique local style with church-like towers abound in the villages around **Ponda** [11L].

Other attractions of Goa include the Portuguese forts of **Aguada** [12A] and **Chapora** [12D], and the 18C Rococo churches at **Moira** [12E] and Margao.

11 · Panaji

Historical sites are scattered all over the densely populated central districts of Goa that lie between the Mandovi and Zuari Rivers.

Panaji [A] and **Old Goa** [B], the present and past capitals, preserve religious and civic monuments spanning some 400 years of Portuguese rule. One full day should be reserved to follow the tours described here. A short excursion from Panaji may also be made to the nearby headland of **Cabo Raj Niwas** [C].

A longer trip is to follow NH17 south of Panaji, taking in the imposing cathedral at **Santan** [D], the seminary at **Pilar** [E] and the chapel at **Agassaim** [F]. The highway continues to Margao [13A].

NH4A, the route running east from Panaji through Old Goa, arrives at Ponda, a predominantly Hindu district dotted with temples built in a unique local style.

At least one day should be set aside to visit a selection of shrines, such as those at **Mangeshi** [G], **Mardol** [H], **Velinga** [I], **Bandora** [J] and **Quelem** [K]. **Ponda** itself [L] has a small mosque, the oldest in Goa. An attractive side trip is to the rural temple at **Savoi Verem** [M].

Another full day will be required to reach the Wildlife Sanctuary near Molem [N] and the remote temple at **Tambdi Surla** [O], the best preserved monument of the pre-European period. From here NH4A continues to **Hubli** [21] in Karnataka. Because of the short distances involved, many of the sights described in the itineraries for Mapusa [12] and Margao [13] are easily accessible as day trips from Panaji.

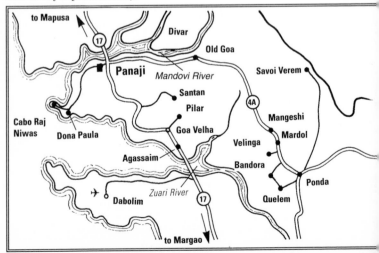

■ **Transport**. The airport at Dabolim, 28km south of Panaji, is now an international destination for planes arriving directly from the UK and other European countries. Flights within India link Goa with Delhi, Bombay [1], Pune [3], Bangalore [14], Madras [36], Tiruvananthapuram [46] and Kochi [47]. A hydrofoil service provides a daily sea link between Bombay and Panaji; the journey takes seven hours.

Bus services are available between Panaji and many cities within Maharashtra and Karnataka, the nearest being Kolhapur [8], Belgaum [21A], Hubli and Mangalore [17]. At present, trains runs only between Margao and Hubli, and points further east in Karnataka. The Konkan Railway, under construction at time of publication, will eventually link Goa with Bombay and Mangalore, as well as with Mapusa and Margao. The nearest station to Panaji will be at Verna.

Touring around central Goa is relatively easy, with frequent bus services reaching all the destinations described here. The roads pass through attractive villages with whitewashed churches and brightly painted houses, all in a characteristic Goan style, interspersed with rice fields and palm groves.

■ **Accommodation**. Compared with tourist developments at the beaches in northern and southern Goa, the state capital (STD code 0832) offers only a limited range of hotels. The finest are the *Mandovi* (☎ 224405), *Fidalgo* (☎ 226291) and *Nova Goa* (☎ 42631). An architecturally distinguished setting marks *Cidade de Goa* (☎ 221133), designed by Charles Correa, a Goan by birth and one of India's leading architects. The hotel is located at **Dona Paula**, a secluded beach on the Zuari estuary, 6km southwest of Panaji. For those interested in exploring the wildlife in the sanctuary near **Molem**, it is possible to stay in the *Tourist Resort* operated by the Goa Tourist Department.

■ **Tourist Information**. The office of the Goa Tourism Development Corporation is located in the Trionara Apartments, Dr Alvares Costa Road (☎ 223459). Another information outlet is the *Tourist Home*, Patto Bridge (☎ 225535). The Government of India Tourist Office has an information centre in the Communidade Building, Church Square (☎ 243412). The Karnataka State Tourist Development Corporation maintains an office nearby in the same Square.

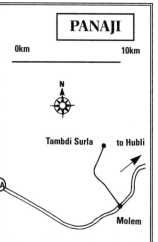

■ **Travel agents and tour companies**. Among the companies offering services for hotel bookings and travel arrangements are *Citizen World Travel*, F4, Gomes Building, C. Alberquerque Road (☎ 227087), *Sita*, 101 Rizvi Chambers, C. Alberquerque Road (☎ 221418) and *Travel Corp*, Sukerkar Mansion, Mahatma Gandhi Road (☎ 225152).

History

Little is known for certain about Goa until the 11C–13C, when this part of the Konkan coast came under the sway of the Kadambas. These rulers established themselves at Govapuri, on the north bank of the Zuari River, a site marked today by the straggling village of Goa Velha. Govapuri became a major port where horses from Arabia were exchanged for pepper, cardamom and other spices. Govapuri was twice raided by the Delhi troops in the early 14C, and was subsequently occupied by the Bahmanis of Gulbarga [24A]. But the Bahmani hold on Govapuri was to last only a few decades. In 1378 the city was conquered by the forces of Vijayanagara [20B–C] and subsequently absorbed into their expanding empire. Struggles for Govapuri continued, however, and the port was retaken by the Bahmanis in 1470. By this time, however, the Zuari had begun to silt up and the Bahmanis decided to shift their headquarters to Ela, on the south bank of the Mandovi River, the site known today as Old Goa. At the end of the 15C the Bahmanis were displaced by the Adil Shahis of Bijapur [23A]. Yusuf, the founder of the new dynasty, was responsible for developing Ela into a splendid city, reputedly with great mosques, houses and gardens.

In 1498 Vasco da Gama completed the first voyage from Europe to Asia, thereby opening up the direct sea link with India. The Portuguese made contacts with the Vijayanagara rulers, who encouraged them to expel the Adil Shahis from Goa. Led by Alfonso de Albuquerque, grandiosely titled Governor of India, the Portuguese attacked in Goa in February 1510, but held the port for only a few months. Not to be deterred, Albuquerque returned soon after with ten additional ships, and the city was finally captured on St Catherine's day, 25 November 1510.

Now known simply as Goa, the port was much expanded by Albuquerque, who provided it with defensive ramparts. He also set about establishing outposts at Aden, Ormuz and Malacca, to which Goa was linked by regular shipping routes. Albuquerque died in Goa in 1515, and his body was returned to Portugal shortly after. Under later Governors, known as Viceroys, Goa was developed as the premier trading post in Asia, unsurpassed in wealth and grandeur. It was for a time the largest European settlement in Asia, with a population of more than 200,000. Goa also served as a base from where Catholic teachings were disseminated. Goa's most famous missionary, the Spanish Jesuit Francis Xavier, landed in 1542. In the same year a programme of religious persecution and enforced conversion was initiated. The Inquisition was imported to Goa in 1560, and remained until its abolition in 1774.

The Portuguese were challenged on occasions by both Vijayanagara and Bijapur, but the European grasp on Goa remained firm. By 1543 the Portuguese had expanded their territories to the districts around their capital, thus completing what came to be known as the Old Conquests. The Adil Shahi threat continued after the fall of Vijayanagara in 1565, and Goa was besieged for almost 12 months by the Bijapur forces in 1570–71. In 1580 Portugal was absorbed into Spain, the enemy of England and Holland, both of whom attempted to expand their interests in Arabian Sea trade. Though the Dutch seized other Indian possessions of the Portuguese, they did not pursue their interest in Goa. After gaining independence from Spain in 1640, Portugal signed a treaty of friendship with England, and there was no further claim on Portuguese territories.

The rise of Maratha power in the later decades of the 17C signalled a new challenge to the Portuguese. In 1680 Goa was occupied by a contingent of Maratha forces under Sambhaji, Shivaji's son. Fortunately for the Portuguese, the Marathas retreated soon after, to deal with the Mughal advance into Maharashtra. A further incursion in 1739 resulted in a ruinous settlement for Goa. Additional lands were bequeathed to Goa towards the end of the 18C by the British, in return for Portuguese assistance in subduing Haidar Ali of Srirangapattana [15C]. These gains, known as the New Conquests, included territories with predominantly Hindu populations. By this time, however, Goa had lost most of its commercial impetus and there was little attempt to convert these new populations. The silting up of the Mandovi River forced ships to dock further downstream at Panaji, to which the Viceroys eventually shifted. This port remained the capital of Portuguese possessions in India until 1961, when Goa was absorbed into the Indian Union.

A. Panaji

Formerly called Panjim, following the Portuguese pronunciation, this attractive city overlooks the south bank of the Mandovi River, a short distance inland from its confluence with the Zuari River. Panaji preserves a distinctive Portuguese atmosphere; its streets are lined with with brightly painted houses and shops, many with cast-iron balconies and sloping tiled roofs. Before the Viceroys moved their residence here in 1759, Panaji was little more than a ceremonial landing

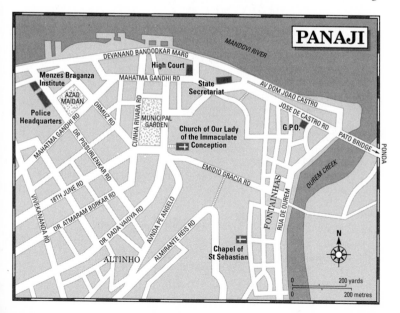

place with a riverside palace and a large church. In 1843, it became the official capital of Goa.

The tour of Panaji begins at the **State Secretariat**, facing the Mandovi River. This marks the site of the palace erected by Yusuf Adil Shah at the end of the 15C, known to the Portuguese as Idalcao's Palace, after a corruption of Adil Khan, one of Yusuf's titles. After the Portuguese arrived, the palace was used by the Viceroys before they proceeded upstream to Old Goa. In time it came to be entirely remodelled, and was even provided with a private chapel. After 1918, when the Viceroys was shifted to Cabo Raj Niwas, the chapel was demolished and the Palace was converted into governmental offices. As it stands today, the Secretariat is an 18C structure. Its whitewashed Neo-Classical façade frames carved stone portals.

The small square west of the Secretariat has a statue of Abbé Faria, the Goan priest who became celebrated as a hypnotist in Paris, dying there in 1819. Further west is the **High Court** of 1878, recognised by its Neo-Gothic windows. The **Municipal Garden** is located inland from the Mandovi River, south of the High Court. This shaded open space is attractively planted with tropical trees and colourful flowers. A monumental column was set up here in 1898 to commemorate the 400th anniversary of Vasco da Gama's landing in India. Da Gama's bust has now been replaced by the lion capital that serves as India's national emblem.

The brillantly whitewashed **Church of Our Lady of the Immaculate Conception** is built into the side of a small hill near the northeast corner of the Municipal Garden. The Church stands on an elevated terrace approached by double flights of balustraded steps, the only example of this feature in Goa. Founded in 1540, but entirely rebuilt in 1619, the Church presents a severe façade, with pilastered bays flanked by single-storeyed square towers. The belfry was added in 1871 to accommodate a bell brought from Old Goa. The plain roofed interior is enhanced by the

Church of Our Lady of the Immaculate Conception, Panaji

richly gilded main altar. This shows an arch flanked by triple sets of columns framing the tabernacle. A small statue of the Virgin occupies a blue painted niche above the arch. Modern altarpieces are placed in the side corners. The pulpit in the north wall has delicately carved details; so, too, the underside of the canopy. A feast takes place here on 6 December.

Returning to the river, the second turn on the left beyond the Hotel Mandovi brings the visitor to the **Menzes Braganza Institute**, incorporating the Central Library. The Institute was founded in 1817 by a wealthy philanthropist to promote arts and sciences. The entrance hall to the building is lined with blue-and-white *azulejos* tiles, dated 1935. They illustrate scenes from a literary work by Luis de Camões, the famous Portuguese author who visited Goa in the 16C. On the south, the Institute flanks the **Police Headquarters**, constructed in 1832 as barracks and administrative offices. This forms the west side of a square known as the **Azad Maidan**. The domed Neo-Classical pavilion in the middle of the Maidan was erected in 1847, its slender Corinthian columns removed from a ruined church in Old Goa. The statue of Albuquerque which once stood here has been replaced by the tomb of Dr Tristao de Braganza Cunha, hero of the Goan struggle for freedom. A modern memorial to this freedom fighter is seen nearby.

The tour of Panaji continues by returning to the Secretariat and proceeding east towards Ourem Creek. A small square here is overlooked by the **Church of St Thomas**. The **Post Office**, originally the Tobacco Exchange, and its neighbour, the former Mint, also face onto the square. Roads running south lead to **Fontainhas**, a picturesque quarter with typical Portuguese-styled houses. One residence has been converted into a hotel, the **Panjim Inn**. The **Chapel of St Sebastian** stands at the end of a lane running towards the Creek. Built in 1888, its Neo-Classical façade has boldly superimposed pediments. Gilded altarpieces are on display, as well as a painted wooden crucifixion taken from the dismantled chapel of Idalcao's Palace.

A winding road ascends from Fontainhas to **Altinho**, the highest part of the city, from where fine views may be had over the Mandovi River. The area is dotted with spacious villas, some with beautiful gardens. The grandiose **Patriarchal Palace** occupies the summit of Altinho.

B. Old Goa

NH4A runs east from Panaji along the south bank of the Mandovi River for 10km before arriving at Old Goa, known to the Portuguese as Velha Goa. The site is celebrated for its 16C–17C cathedrals, churches and monasteries, the largest and most elaborate examples of Baroque architecture and art in Southern India. The monuments stand in a lush garden-like setting, many in excellent condition, having been maintained by the archaeological authorities or by private religious orders. A few have collapsed to form picturesque overgrown piles of rubble. Virtually nothing can now be seen of the defensive walls, civic buildings and grand mansions with which this great trading city was once furnished.

The **Basilica of Bom Jesus**, on the south side of the Square in the middle of Old Goa, houses the tomb of St Francis Xavier, the most venerated Christian shrine in Goa. Unlike other churches, the Basilica has had its plaster coating removed.

The west façade presents a sombre composition, with basalt blocks set into laterite. Superimposed Corinthian, Doric and Ionic pilasters frame doorways at the lowest level, rectangular windows at the intermediate level and circular windows flanked by scrolls and palmettes at the top. The pedimented gable over the central bay bears the letters IHS, a characteristic Jesuit motif. The letters are ringed by angels, some clutching ropes, and surmounted by a royal crown and a cross. The free-standing bell tower is placed at the rear of the building, south of the chancel. The flying buttresses on the sides are modern reinforcements. The **Professed House**, attached to the west façade of the Basilica, was used as monastic quarters until its destruction by fire in 1633. A small teaching establishment is still run here by the Jesuits. The carved panel over the doorway repeats the IHS motif.

Bom Jesus is unusually laid out on a cruciform plan with prominent transepts. Two piers at the west end of the nave, supporting a choir gallery, have Portuguese and Latin inscriptions recording the foundation of the building in 1594 and its consecration in 1605. The heavily gilded alterpieces, among the finest of the period, contrast with the otherwise plain interior. The altar on the left immediately on entering has a polychrome wooden sculpture of St Francis swaying in ecstasy. The high altar in the vaulted chancel is dominated by the three-dimensional figure of St Ignatius Loyola, the founder of the Jesuit order. He contemplates the sunburst above, complete with the IHS monogram held by flying cherubim. The Holy Trinity appears in the uppermost tableau. The whole composition is framed by gorgeously decorated twisted columns headed by a broken pediment. Similarly ornate altars beside the chancel show the Virgin (left) and St Michael (right). The pulpit, set into the south wall of the nave, is supported by seven angels with foliate bodies. Similar figures cover the back wall and canopy of the pulpit; the sides are carved with the four Evangelists and Four Doctors of the Church in the presence of Christ.

The south transept of the Basilica accommodates the **Chapel of St Francis Xavier**. The body of the saint, who died on a journey back from Japan in 1552, made its way to Goa via Malacca, and was interred here in 1624. The Chapel is an addition of 1655, a few years before Xavier's canonisation in 1662. The tomb itself is the gift of Cosimo III, Grand Duke of Tuscany and a member of the famous Medici family. It was designed and manufactured by Giovanni Battista Foggini in Florence, from where it was shipped to Goa in 1698. The polychrome marble base is enlivened with inset bronze plaques depicting the missionary activities of St Francis. The scene visible from the nave shows St Francis preaching in the Moluccas; one of the side panels shows the saint swimming to safety from the natives of the island of Morro.

The silver casket above, in which the saint's body rests, is Goan work dating from 1636; the precious stones once set into its intricately worked sides and top are lost. The remains of St Francis are celebrated for their remarkable state of preservation. They are exposed once every ten years on 3 December, the anniversary of the saint's death, most recently in 1994. However, not all of St Francis's body is intact: one toe found its way to Lisbon, while a section of one arm was despatched to the Church of Il Gesù in Rome.

A **Passageway**, with tombstones of Goan grandees set into the floor, leads past the Chapel of St Francis, the tomb being viewed through windows on four sides. The **Sacristy**, which opens off the Passageway, is entered through magnif-

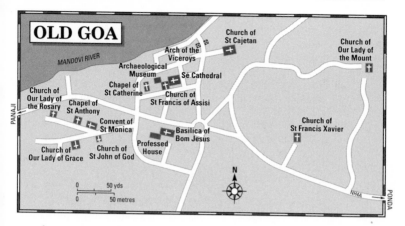

icently carved wooden doors surrounded by a sculpted stone bands; the IHS monogram appears in the pediment. The Sacristy, roofed with a coffered vault, is lined with carved chests with brass plaques, containing clerical vestments. The apse accommodates a Crucifix set in bright blue *azulejos* tiles of Portuguese manufacture; polychrome tiles decorate the altar in front. Steps to one side of the Sacristy ascend to the **Art Gallery** (closed Fridays), where paintings illustrating the life of St Francis by a modern Goan artist are on display. From here it is possible to look down upon the tomb within the Chapel of St Francis. Double-storeyed arcades of noble proportions surround the adjoining **Cloister**.

The tour of Old Goa continues by crossing the Square in order to reach the group of religious buildings on its north side. The **Sé** (Cathedral) to the right, reputedly the largest church in Asia, was begun in 1562 by the Dominican order, apparently on the site of Yusuf's demolished mosque; some 90 years passed before the Cathedral was completed. Its principal east façade presents three austere bays on two levels, with an additional pedimented stage in the middle framed by low volutes. The central door is flanked by pairs of fully modelled Corinthian columns. Only one of the square corner towers still stands; that on the north collapsed after being struck by lightning in 1776. The triple-vaulted nave has deep side chapels separated by plain buttresses. The baptismal font in the side chapel, to the right immediately on entering, bears the date 1532; it is believed to have been used by St Francis.

The third chapel on the right, dedicated to the The Cross of Miracles, has a carved wooden screen of exceptional workmanship. The high altar at the west end of the vaulted chancel has sculpted and gilded wooden panels portraying the life and martydom of St Catherine, to whom the Cathedral is dedicated. The panels are framed by richly embellished Corinthian columns. Christ on the cross flanked by saints appears above; Christ with the Evanglists and Church leaders below. Gravestones bearing 17C and 18C dates are set into the floor in front of the chancel.

The **Church of St Francis of Assisi** stands a short distance to the west. The present structure of 1662 replaces an earlier one, consecrated to the Holy Spirit in 1521. The west façade is flanked by unusual octagonal towers. The doorway, re-used from the original building, is the only example at Old Goa fashioned in the ornate Manueline style, named after Dom Manuel I (1495–1521). The entrance is headed by triple-lobed ribs, with pendant pomegranates and rosettes in panels. Although the Church is no longer used for worship, it retains its finely worked altarpieces and coffered ceiling. The pulpit has intricate carved foliation, the density of which reflects indigenous taste. Oil paintings from the life of St Francis line the chancel walls. A splendid, though faded, high altar fills the rear wall. The panel in its pedimented top shows St Francis standing on a pedestal, being embraced by Christ on the cross. The central portion of the altar is opened up to create a miniature vaulted chamber accommodating the tabernacle. Figures of the Evangelists in niches are set between Corinthian columns at either side. Equally fine carvings are seen in the side altars of the nave. The floor of the Church is almost entirely paved with tombstones.

The Franciscan monastery to the north, with which the Church was once linked, now houses the galleries of the **Archaeological Museum** (closed Fridays), the most important in Goa. The bronze statue of Albuquerque in the entrance hall was cast during the lifetime of the commander; it was originally displayed in Panaji. The similarly impressive metal portrait of Luis de Camões was recently removed from the Square outside the Museum. The carved figures in the first gallery are assigned to the 11C–12C Kadamba period. They include an elaborate icon of Vishnu surrounded by miniature incarnations, Durga decapitating the buffalo demon, and the benign goddess Lakshmi. Hero stones depict martial exploits and naval battles. One example shows a royal personage sitting inside a palace, with warriors beneath. Coins and other objects from the excavations at Chandrapura, near Chandor [13F], dating from the 3C–4C, are also on display.

The upper gallery of the Museum is dedicated to wooden carvings removed from various churches and monasteries. There is also a complete series of Viceregal portraits, the earliest dating from 1547. Even Vasco de Gama makes an appearance here, having briefly served as Viceroy in 1524. The oils are of interest for the static poses and elaborate costumes. Additional carved items are on display in the adjacent cloister, including temple images, hero stones and inscribed panels. A bronze statue of St Catherine, removed from the Arch of the Viceroys, stands in the middle of the court, sheltered by a small pavilion.

The nearby **Chapel of St Catherine** marks the site of the first church, erected by Albuquerque in 1510. This was dedicated to St Catherine, on whose special day the Portuguese scored their decisive victory. A plaque from the original building is set into the side wall of the present Chapel, which dates from the middle of the 16C. The unusually north-facing building has small flanking towers linked to the central pediment by volutes. A portion of the crumbling laterite walls of the city is seen nearby, leading down to the Mandovi River.

The tour of Old Goa now continues by returning to the front of the Sé Cathedral and passing by it on the way to the river landing. A short distance north stands the **Arch of the Viceroys**, the ceremonial riverside entrance to Old Goa. This is a modern replacement of the Arch erected in 1599 by the Viceroy Francisco da Gama, incorporating a portrait of Vasco da Gama, his great-grandfather. The inscribed plaques inside the Arch record various restorations. The plaque on the west is a memorial to Dom Joao IV, the first Portuguese king after the liberation from Spanish rule. A dilapidated stretch of the city wall can be made out in the undergrowth east of the Arch, but nothing remains of the Customs House nearby. The road passing through the Arch leads to the ferry crossing to **Divar** on the other side of the Mandovi River. The wooded rise in the middle of the island is capped with the whitewashed bulk of the Church of Our Lady of Compassion.

A path leading east from the Arch of the Viceroys leads to the Pastoral Institute and the **Church of St Cajetan**. Immediately inside the compound is a free-standing stone **Doorway**, with finely worked jambs flanked by pierced screens. This 12C–13C temple fragment is believed to have come from Yusuf Adil Shah's palace. The Church was built in 1656 by friars of the Italian Theatine order, who lived in Goa for several years. The west façade is modelled on St Peter's Church in Rome, though at a smaller scale and with domical towers instead of side wings. The sombre composition is dominated by a pedimented portico with Corinthian columns; the wall niches accommodate statues of the Apostles. The lofty dome that rises on a circular drum over the crossing, the only example in Old Goa, is supported on four great piers. Directly beneath is a covered well.

The richly carved high altar at the east end of the nave is consecrated to Our Lady of the Divine Providence. The angels here are larger than human size. A small crypt at the base of the altar has lead caskets, in which the embalmed bodies of the Viceroys were stored before being shipped back to Portugal for burial. The subsidiary altars at the ends of the transepts and in the corner bays are in the monumental Baroque manner; so, too, is the pulpit with its supporting beasts and birds. The exuberant woodwork contrasts with the starkly plain walls, coffered vaults and dome.

A short distance east of St Cajetan is the whitewashed **Gate of the Conception**, all that survives of the College of St Paul, erected in 1543 to train new converts. St Francis Xavier lodged at this College during his visits to Goa. It was in the nearby **Chapel of St Francis Xavier**, just north, that his remains were kept before being interred in the Basilica. The Chapel was entirely rebuilt in 1884.

The dilapidated **Church of Our Lady of the Mount** stands at the top of a wooded hill, 300m further north. A plaque on the side wall at the west end of the building records that Yusuf Adil Shah's troops gathered on this hill in preparation for battle with Albuquerque. The building is of little interest, but the panorama of the site is exceptional.

The tour of Old Goa concludes with the religious complexes on the hill west of the site. The first feature to be seen is the **Church of St John of God**, begun in 1685 and now abandoned, unlike the adjacent Convent, which is still in use. On the slope opposite is the large **Convent of St Monica**, founded in the 17C but substantially remodelled and buttressed in later times. A formal garden in the middle of the Convent is surrounded by a vaulted cloister with paintings on the walls and ceiling. The associated church is entered on the south through double doors headed by pediments showing a ship (left) and a double-headed eagle (right); the inscribed slab in the middle gives the date 1636. The altar in the nave is divided into nine round-headed niches filled with figures, St Monica appearing in the middle. The small Crucifix in front of the altar is credited with miraculous powers. Blue-and-white *azulejos* tiles line the lower portions of the chancel walls.

The **Church of Our Lady of Grace**, on the hill above the Convent, is now an overgrown ruin. Its surviving walls and vaults, however, are still impressive. The Church is dominated by a portion of a tower, one of a pair that flanked the west façade; its five stages rise dramatically to a height of 46m. The Church dates from 1602, but the attached monastery is earlier, having been founded by the Augustinians in 1572. The complex fell into ruin after being abandoned in 1835, and the bell from the belfry was transferred to the Church of Our Lady of the Immaculate Conception in Panaji. The **Chapel of St Anthony** stands on the other side of the road. Though dating from 1534, it was entirely reconstructed in 1961, with an unusual curved apse that serves as the entrance.

The road from the Convent ascends gradually to the **Church of Our Lady of the Rosary**, at the western extremity of the hill. The terrace here provides splendid views of the Mandovi River from Divar to Panaji. The site is believed to mark the spot where Albuquerque witnessed the progress of his successful battle. The Church dates from 1549, making it the oldest complete structure still standing in Old Goa. The west façade has full-height round towers at the corners, with a part-circular bell tower to one side. The towers are enlivened with sculpted bands fashioned as twisted ropes, a vestige of the Manueline style. The chief object of interest within the Church is the finely chiselled marble slab, set into the side wall of the chancel, which commemorates Caterina a Piro, the first Portuguese woman to arrive in Goa. The slab has a pilastered frame and frieze of vases hanging from chains, exactly like Muslim gravestones in Gujarat, from where, no doubt, it was brought. The geometric designs in sepia and white plasterwork on the chancery walls are probably 19C.

One unusual feature which has yet to be noted is the **Pillory** formed of re-used temple columns, set up a short distance south of the Square, in the middle of the site.

C. Cabo Raj Niwas

The headland overlooking the confluence of the Mandovi and Zuari Rivers, with a distant prospect of the Arabian Sea, is one of the most spectacular sites in Goa. Here stands **Cabo Raj Niwas**, the residence of various Archbishops and Viceroys, now the home of the Governor of Goa (permission required to visit).

This comfortable villa, with verandahs on all sides, houses a splendid collection of black rosewood furniture, china and glass, mirrors and chandeliers. The building incorporates portions of a Franciscan monastery and chapel, the latter dating from 1594. Its interior is graced by an intricately carved pulpit.

D. Santan

The imposing Baroque monument at Santan is reached by following NH17 south from Panaji for 10km, then proceeding east for about 5km. The grand scale of the **Church of St Anne** strikingly contrasts with the diminutive settlement that bears its name. A legend that St Anne, mother of the Virgin Mary, appeared to the local population led to the dedication of the present structure in 1659.

The east-facing Church has corner square towers divided into five stages and topped by balustraded parapets with pinnacles. The imposing façade has three broad cornices, with the central bays flanked by pairs of Corinthian columns. The pedimented top stage is framed by fan-shaped volutes; the recess here accommodates a figure of St Anne. The central pair of doors bears the date of the building's completion. The aisle-less interior is of majestic proportions. The nave is lined by deep semicircular niches with shell-shaped tops supporting an upper gallery. Lighting is achieved by three tiers of windows in the niches and gallery above. Raised foliate medallions decorate the plastered barrel vault and the underside of the arch supporting the choir.

The high altar is an imposing composition of carved and gilded woodwork flanked by trios of twisted columns. The central portion is cut away to create a chamber accommodating the tabernacle, lit dramatically by a rear window. The topmost panel of the altar, headed by a broken curved pediment, contains a sculpted tableau of St Anne, the Virgin and the Christ child. The side altars are equally ornate. The pulpit on the south wall is supported by six figures with fish-like bodies. The sides, rear panel and canopy are all richly embellished.

E. Pilar

The straggling settlement of **Goa Velha** lies 11km south of Panaji on NH17. A signboard beside the highway identifies this as the site of Govapuri, the head-quarters of the Kadambas in the 11C–13C. Nothing, however, is visible of the ancient settlement.

A side road winds for about 500m through the fields before ascending a small hill to the **Pilar Seminary**. In Kadamba times this was the site of a temple dedicated to Shiva in the form of Goveshvara, from which the name Govapuri was derived. Evidence for this vanished monument comes from stray sculptures discovered nearby. The Seminary was founded by the local Missionary Society of St Francis Xavier in 1890. A revered member of the Society was Agnelo de Souza, who achieved fame as a spiritual teacher until his death in 1927. The present Seminary is a large modern structure. The new chapel has fine stained-glass windows imported from Germany according to designs by a Goan artist. The central panel depicts Our Lady.

Just beneath the Seminary stands the **Church and Monastery of Pilar**, founded in 1613. The plain, unpretentious building has a frontal porch sheltering a finely carved doorway, with a statue of St Francis of Assisi set into a small niche above. This leads to the **Tomb of Father Agnelo**, a major attraction for local pilgrims as this teacher is now in the process of beatification. A passageway connects the Tomb to a charming planted **Court**, surrounded by a two-storeyed arcade. Frescos depict the lives and deaths of various saints, including St Francis of Assisi. The unusual fountain in the middle has an octagonal dais with bird-like figures and monster heads.

The Church interior is dominated by an ornately carved and painted wooden altar. The central panel shows Our Lady of Pilar standing on a short pillar, flanked by angels. Another depiction of Our Lady occurs in a glassed-in niche set into the side wall of the nave. This contains a delicately carved wooden statuette said to have been brought from Spain. The pulpit above is covered with gilded scrollwork, with a painting of Our Lady on the rear panel.

F. Agassaim

This village is located 15km south of Panaji on NH17, just before the highway crosses the Zuari River. Agassaim is notable for the **Church of St Lawrence**, consecrated in 1564. Its plain exterior gives no hint of the remarkable 18C altar inside, one of the finest examples of Rococo art in Goa. The altar, set within a barrel-vaulted chancel painted bright blue, is an exuberant composition with leafy pilasters and capping volutes, all in bright gold on a white background. The figure of St Lawrence holding a grid-iron appears in the central niche, with a domed tabernacle beneath and a risen Christ within a sunburst above. Candles are incorporated into the overall composition. Similar but smaller altars are positioned on either side of the chancel.

G. Mangeshi

The **Mangesh Temple**, one of the largest and most popular Hindu shrines in Goa, stands beside the small settlement that bears its name. This is situated on NH4A, 8km southeast of Old Goa and 12km north of Ponda. The Temple was founded in the middle of the 18C with income from land donated by a local ruler under the Marathas. When the administration of Ponda district was transferred to Goa as part of the New Conquests, the Portuguese agreed not to interfere with the monument and its endowment; the estate is still intact.

The Mangesh Temple is approached from the east along a path lined with balustrades, passing by a large square tank. The water is surrounded by arcaded chambers, the west side marked by a tower with a pointed tiled roof. Steps ascend to a spacious court at a higher level, looking down on the tank. The first feature to be noticed within the court is the octagonal **Lamp Tower**. This is a white-washed structure of seven storeys, the corners marked by Neo-Classical pilasters, with bold cornices in between. Windows with round and trilobed tops are seen at each level, except the bottom. The Tower is crowned with a small dome. Nearby stands a wooden chariot, its octagonal frame covered with carvings and leaping *yali* brackets. Service structures run around the periphery of the court.

The Temple itself is entered on the east through an octagonal pavilion topped with a combination vault and dome displaying bulbous finials; the porches to the north and south are roofed with smaller fluted domes. The hall is painted in ochre and white, with details picked out in bright blue, including the jambs of the trilobed windows. The sanctuary walls form the lower parts of an octagonal tower, complete with Neo-Classical colonettes, cornices and balustraded parapet. The tower is capped with a circular lantern and gilded finial.

The interior of the Temple has a marble floor and tiled walls. Arcades on squat circular columns divide the hall into three aisles. Ornate glass chandeliers hang from the flat wooden roof. Both the antechamber and sanctuary doorways are embellished with embossed silver sheets. These create gleaming frames for the small stone *linga* covered with a brass mask that represents Mangesh. Gilded guardian figures with clubs are set in the open recesses flanking the outer door, with stone images of Durga [right] and Ganesha [left] beyond.

H. Mardol

1.5km south of Mangeshi on NH4A lies the village of Mardol with its celebrated **Mahalasa Temple**, another popular shrine. The court in which the Temple stands is entered from the east through an arched tower with a tiled roof. Immediately to the right stands a seven-storeyed octagonal lamp tower, virtually identical to that at Mangeshi. Near the tower and directly on an axis with the Temple itself is an unusual brass lamp column with a tortoise base and 21 circular trays. The Temple is preceded by a newly completed hall with elaborate stone columns and a concrete roof. This obscures the front of the original hall, a timber structure with a sloping metal-clad roof. Carvings in a curious flat style beside the porch entrances on the north and south show warriors and musicians in vigorous postures; the brackets in between are fashioned as monkeys and *yalis*.

The interior of the Temple is distinguished by intricately carved columns. The 16-sided shafts are covered with stylised foliation and miniature figures in niches; cut-out ribs adorn the double circular capitals. The brackets are of the lotus type, or show crouching lions. The central part of the ceiling is raised up on panels, with brightly painted gods arranged in niches. The periphery of the hall has high wooden seating, with open balustraded screens admitting light and air. Embossed silver doorways give access to the sanctuary, which accommodates the stone image of Mahalasa, a female aspect of Vishnu. The octagonal tower above has arched niches containing plaster figures; the enlarged parrots, however, are modern. The bulbous dome above is roofed with metal shingles.

Immediately south of the Mahalasa Temple stands the **Lakshmi Shrine**, smaller but similar to the main Temple. The bright ochre exterior is topped by a dome on an octagonal tower. The sanctuary within houses twin stone images of Vishnu and Lakshmi. An arched gate at the rear (west) of the court leads to a delightful tank, with rice fields and palm groves beyond.

I. Velinga

This secluded village just off NH4A, 2km south of Mardol or 4.5km north of Ponda, is the setting for the **Lakshmi Narasimha Temple**. Though comparatively little visited, the monument is distinguished by the high quality of its decoration. The court in which the Temple stands is entered on the north through a double-storeyed gate. The hall of the Temple has 28 circular columns carrying a sloping tiled roof; there are no outer walls, only balustraded screens. The hall abuts the original entrance porch of the sanctuary, marked by a steeply pyramidal roof; the porches on the north and south are similarly roofed. The masonry walls of the sanctuary are topped with a double-staged tower, both square and octagonal, complete with Neo-Classical pilasters, niches and balustraded parapet. The somewhat reduced dome above has unusual vertical sides. The interior (access restricted to visitors) has carved columns and silver embossed doorways comparable to those in the Mardol Temple.

The charm of the Lakshmi Narayana Temple derives partly from its peaceful wooded setting, with groves of palm trees on the hill above. Immediately east of the Temple is a large square tank surrounded by steps and arcades, interrupted by doorways roofed with curving cornices. The east side of the tank is overlooked by a tower with a projecting timber balcony and a pyramidal tiled roof.

J. Bandora

Bandora is a small, sprawling settlement 1.5km west of NH17, about 2km north of Ponda, with two important Hindu shrines. The first to be visited when coming from Ponda is the **Nagesha Temple**, almost hidden by groves at the bottom of a small valley. The complex is entered on the east through a Neo-Classical portal. Columns from a dismantled Kadamba monument are set up nearby. Another Kadamba relic is a sculpted pedestal, now missing its image, placed at the west end of the compound. A five-stage octagonal lamp tower stands just inside the portal. Brighly painted images of deities fill the arched niches on each side, and cobras rear up at the corners.

The Temple presents the usual arrangement of front and side porches with pyramidal roofs adjoining a long hall with a gabled roof. Neo-Classical details typical of the 18C, such as pilasters and round-headed windows, are picked out in pink and ochre. These colours blend with the terracotta tiles of the roof and the ceramic lions arranged on the ridge. Finials mark the corners of the balustraded parapet that tops the octagonal tower over the sanctuary. The flattish dome above is enlivened with a band of interlocking serpents at the base and a brass pot-like finial at the apex. The marble-clad interior has circular columns carrying arcades. The wooden ceiling is raised on panels decorated with painted gods in niches. The sanctuary houses a *linga* set into the floor, behind which is a sculpted image of the deity. Nandi appears in the entrance porch. A rectangular tank in front (west) of the Temple is surrounded by coconut palms. It is overlooked by an entrance tower with a tiled roof.

The **Mahalakshmi Temple**, 1.5km west of the Nagesha Temple, is the second place of worship in Bandora. The Temple is of the standard type, except for the fluted dome that crowns the double-stage tower over the sanctuary. Similar fluted domes in combination with smaller smooth domes roof the side porches.

K. Quelem

The road south of Bandora runs through the hamlet of Quelem, about 2km distant. The route passes by the **Ramnatha Temple**, a characteristic monument in the local style, with a predominance of Neo-Classical features betraying its renovation date of 1905. Small domes top the sanctuary and side porches. The interior is particularly elaborate, with ornate glass chandeliers suspended from the ceiling. Silver sheets embossed with monkeys, deer and birds intermingling with stalks and leaves cloak the sanctuary doorway. The arch above is filled with figures of Shiva and Parvati looking down on Rama with Sita, Lakshmana and Hanuman. Guardian figures with elephants beneath are set at either side. The principal cult object within the sanctuary is a Shiva *linga*, said to have come from a dismantled 16C temple, accompanied by a gorgeously decked image of Vishnu.

The **Shantadurga Temple** is situated barely 1km to the east, in a delightful setting on the edge of lush rice fields. This popular shrine was founded in 1738 by Shahu, the ruler of Satara [7G], a small Maratha principality in Maharashtra. In spite of its attested date, the Temple has been totally remodelled in more recent times, as is obvious from the bold Neo-Classical manner of the wall pilasters and the rounded concrete hoods of the windows. The Temple is comparatively vertical in proportions. Both the hall and porches have steeply pyramidal tiled roofs. The tower over the sanctuary, one of the highest of the series, has a triple-stage octagonal drum with a balustraded parapet topped with a flattish dome and a small lantern. The marble-clad interior is enriched by glass chandeliers and embossed silver screens containing small niches filled with guardian figures. The sanctuary displays the seated image of Shantadurga in white marble, flanked by icons of Shiva and Vishnu, all sheltered by a richly gilded canopy.

The court in which the Shantadurga Temple stands has a huge wooden chariot with an octagonal base covered with carvings. A spreading fig tree stands to one side. Stone blocks beneath the tree are fashioned as sculpture niches.

The road from Quelem continues east for about 2km to Ponda.

L. Ponda

This small town lies on NH4A, a total of 30km southeast of Panaji, at the junction with the road to Margao, 17km south. The only historical feature to be seen at Ponda is the **Safa Mosque** on NH4A, 1km north of the town centre. Built in 1560 under the patronage of the Adil Shahi rulers, the Mosque is the oldest such structure still in use in Goa. It stands on one side of a rectanglar laterite tank. Six flights of steps separated by arched chambers descend to the water. The prayer hall has plastered walls divided into shallow arcaded recesses, with the entrance on the east. The gabled roof is a timber structure covered with tiles and topped with pot-like finials. The rear wall within has an arched *mihrab* flanked by shallower side niches. Free-standing columns placed around the hall suggest an exterior colonnade, now lost.

M. Savoi Verem

This small village is reached by way of a picturesque route running 16km north from Ponda, with distant views of the wooded valley of the upper Mandovi River. The modest **Ananta Temple** here is built on a hillside, next to a fishpond and a small tree shrine. Its hall has a double-tiered tiled roof, the entrance on the east being marked by a tower capped with a pyramidal roof. This is evidently a replacement for the sanctuary tower, which is absent here. The attached open hall is modern. Ornately carved wooden columns and brackets, all brightly painted, are seen within the original interior. A similarly decorated wooden door is placed between two columns. The sanctuary is home to a finely carved slab depicting Vishnu reclining on Ananta.

N. Molem

This hamlet on NH4A, 28km east of Ponda, is the stopping-off point for the **Bhagwan Mahaveer Wildlife Sanctuary**, the largest in Goa. The Sanctuary covers more than 200sq km of undulating territory, climbing the foothills of the Western Ghats. A few tigers may be seen in the flatlands, but the uplands offer black panthers, herds of bison and different varieties of deer. Chattering monkeys, elsewhere rare in the state, are also to be seen. Even if few animals are glimpsed, the birdlife and wooded landscape are a constant delight.

O. Tambdi Surla

A side road running 9km north of Molem leads to the **Mahadeva Temple**, a wonderfully isolated monument standing in the dense forest that cloaks the lower ridges of the Western Ghats. The 12C–13C date and the comparatively complete state of preservation make this the most important example of Kadamba architecture in Goa. The Temple consists of a towered sanctuary and columned hall, the latter partly open on the east as a porch, where it is roofed with steeply sloping slabs. The walls rise on a sharply modelled basement, featureless except for a frieze of shallow pilasters. The triple-stage tower has parapet elements incorporating carvings of Brahma (south), Shiva (west) and Vishnu (north). The capping roof has a dome-like top. Stylised lotuses decorate the inclined balcony slabs in the porch. Four columns in the hall, with sculpted scenes on their shafts, support a ceiling with nine star-shaped designs containing lotuses. The doorway to the antechamber has sharply cut pilasters flanked by latticed screenwork.

12 · Mapusa

Mapusa, the largest town in the territory north of the Mandovi River, is situated on NH17, 14km north of Panaji. The town itself is of little interest, but from here it is possible to reach the popular beaches of Aguada, Calangute, Baga and Vagator. Any of these makes a convenient base from which to visit the historical locations in North Goa.

The most important sites are the coastal forts at **Aguada** [A], **Reis Margos** [B], **Chapora** [D] and **Terekhol** [H], and the churches at **Calangute** [C] and **Moira** [E]. Inland temple sites abound, those at **Naroa** [F] and **Pernem** [G] being the most interesting. At least two days should be set aside to visit a selection of these destinations, all of which are accessible from the beach resorts, via Mapusa where necessary.

Because of the short distances involved, day trips are also possible from the Mapusa area to Panaji [11A], Old Goa [11B] and Ponda [11L].

■ **Transport**. Frequent bus services connect the beaches to all the sites described here, as well as to Panaji and other points south. When completed, the Konkan Railway will link Mapusa with Panaji and Margao [13A].

■ **Accommodation**. The beaches of North Goa are dotted with an abundance of hotels in all price ranges. The most luxurious are the *Fort Aguada Beach Resort* (☎ 276201), *Holiday Village* (☎ 276201) and *Aguada Hermitage* (☎ 276201), near Candolim (STD code 083288), all managed by the Taj Hotel Group. The *Hotel Baia Do Sol* (☎ 721141) at **Baga** (STD code 083288) and the *Sterling Vagator Beach Resort* (☎ 273276) at **Chapora** (STD code 083226) are less extravagant but also comfortable. An unusual place to stay is at the *Hotel Terekhol Fort Heritage* (☎ 220705), at the northern extremity of the state.

■ **Tourist Information**. None.

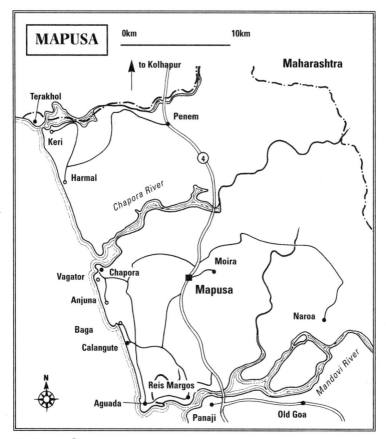

A. Aguada

The **Fort** at Aguada, 10km west of Panaji after crossing the Mandovi River, is built on a headland commanding the Arabian Sea to the north and west, and the estuary of the Mandovi and Zuari Rivers to the south. Part of the site now provides a setting for the Fort Aguada Beach Resort. A restored stone **Jetty**, extending into the sea beneath the Resort, once provided landing facilities as well as a base for cannon. Remnants of walls are seen nearby.

The **Citadel** occupies the highest point of the headland, accessible by a road which winds upwards for about 1km from the Resort. From here there are sweeping panoramas of the ocean and rivers. The Citadel, which dates back to 1617, was besieged on many occasions by the Dutch and Marathas, but never succumbed. It was, however, temporarily occupied by British toops in 1798 during their struggles against Tipu Sultan of Srirangapattana [15C].

The Aguada Citadel is the finest example of Portuguese military architecture in Goa. It consists of an irregular quadrangle of laterite **Walls** with attenuated angled corners. The Walls have a broad walkway shielded by battlements with openings for cannon. The surrounding moat is deep and largely rock-cut. The path beyond the moat is protected by a large sloping earthen embankment.

The southeast corner of the Citadel is extended to accommodate the **Main Gate**, the doors of which are lost, and the vaulted **Magazine**. Here, too, stands the massive circular bulk of the triple-stage **Lighthouse**, added in 1864. (Since 1976 this has been superseded by a modern structure built outside the Walls.) The central part of the Citadel is empty, except for a large **Cistern** with steps descending to arched vaults. This once supplied the Fort with fresh water, hence the name Aguada, Portuguese for watering place.

A flight of steps climbs from the Main Gate to the entrance to the Lighthouse. The steps also give access to the walkway that runs along the top of the Walls. A line of ramparts following the steep side of the hill descends to the water, to protect the river landing at the Citadel.

The Church of St Lawrence crowns a small rise 1.5km east of the Citadel. Completed in 1634, it displays a pedimented gable flanked by square towers. The altar inside shows St Lawrence clasping a boat, a reminder that this saint is the protector of sailors.

B. Reis Margos

The **Fort** at Reis Margos occupies an elevated location overlooking the Mandovi River, 4.5km upstream from Aguada. Though this Fort is earlier than that at Aguada, having been begun in 1551, it was totally rebuilt in 1707. The Fort (access restricted to visitors) presents a somewhat forbidding spectacle of overgrown walls. As at Aguada, these are laid out in quadrangular formation, though at a smaller scale. The angled bastions at the corners are topped with circular domed turrets for firing.

The **Church of the Magi Kings**, beneath the entrance to the Fort, dates from 1555, but was entirely remodelled in 1771. The Church is approached by a broad flight of steps with balustraded sides. Carved *yali* balustrades, removed from a dismantled temple, flank the bottom steps. The imposing east façade is articulated by slender Corinthian columns. The Portuguese coat of arms, surmounted by a three-dimensional half crown, is placed beneath the central pediment framed by volutes. Faded paintings adorn the walls of the nave. At the west end is the elaborate high altar, recently modified to create a recessed chamber for the tabernacle, surrounded by figures and flying angels. The richly worked blue-and-gilt woodwork of the altar is headed by a painted panel depicting the three Magi presenting gifts to the Christ child. The gravestone of the Viceroy Dom Luis de Ataide, who died in 1581, is set into the floor of the corridor north of the nave. It is embellished with the royal coat of arms in bold relief. The feast of Reis Margos is held here on 6 January each year.

C. Calangute

This beachside town, 6km north of Aguada or 8km directly southwest of Mapusa, provides the setting for the 18C **Church of St Alex**, a typical example of the Goan Rococo style. The double-storeyed façade of the Church has an intriguing false dome, complete with arcaded drum and capping lantern, rising over the central bays. The dome is flanked by square towers topped with pyramidal arrangements of pinnacles. The white-and-gold interior, much remodelled, preserves its original elegance. The nave is lined with window niches headed by shell-shaped half-domes. The side altar is delicately painted, and the canopy is enlivened with tassels and flowers. The high altar presents an exuberant composition of flattened pilasters, swirling brackets and extended sunbursts.

D. Chapora

This **Fort** overlooks the mouth of the Chapora River to the north and Vagator Beach on the west, a spectacular situation that once marked the northern limit of the Portuguese possessions. Chapora can be reached from Mapusa, 10km east, or directly from Calangute, 10km south.

> The Fort dates back to the Adil Shahi occupation of Goa in the years prior to the arrival of the Portuguese, but was rebuilt in 1717. Chapora fell to the Marathas in 1739, being held for two years by the ruler of Pernem on the other side of the Chapora River. The Fort was returned to the Portuguese at the end of the 18C, but lost its military significance with the acquisition of the New Conquests.

The Fort is built on a level-topped hill with steep sides. Roughly hewn laterite **Walls** and dry ditches dug in front follow the irregularities of the contours. Crudely built lookout posts with domical tops punctuate round bastions with large openings for cannon. The **Main Gate**, at the top of a steep approach track, is small and unpretentious. It leads to a vast emptiness, with no indication of the church, barracks and housing that once stood here.

E. Moira

This village, 4km east of Mapusa, is worth visiting for the small **Church of Our Lady of the Immaculate Conception**, one of the finest examples of the Rococo style in Goa. The Church dates back to 1636, but its façade and interior altars were added at the end of the 18C. It faces northeast onto a spacious terrace looking out over rice fields and forests. An unusual outdoor pulpit is built to one side. The double-storeyed façade of the Church is divided into niches with shell-shaped half-domes, those in the middle being higher and lobed. The central tower presents a part-octagonal drum, dome and lantern on the frontal face only. The square side towers have flattish domes framed by small pinnacles.

The nave of the Church is lined with window niches headed by the same half domes as those on the façade. The chancel, painted entirely in blue, is roofed with a decorated vault. The gilded altar has a central arched recess flanked by pilasters, with angel heads on the capitals and leafy volutes at the sides. The recess is filled with a tiered pedestal accommodating a glassed receptacle enshrining an image of the Virgin. The altars on either side of the chancel are consecrated to St Sebastian and Christ on the Cross. A pleasant cloister with a small garden opens off to one side of the nave.

F. Naroa

This small settlement is located 25km east of Mapusa, via Bicholim, not far from the river crossing to Divar Island. The road passes by Maem Lake, a favourite boating spot. The **Saptakoteshvara Temple** at Naroa is of historical significance, having been founded by Shivaji when the Marathas first took possession of this part of Goa. Begun in 1668, the building was later renovated. An inscribed slab giving the Temple's history is placed over the doorway within the porch.

The exterior of the east-facing Temple has pilastered walls, large square windows and a prominent triangular frontal gable, all roofed with a sloping tiled roof. The octagonal tower over the sanctuary has arched niches between pilasters, a balustraded parapet and a flattish dome. The sanctuary is a plain square chamber accommodating a small *linga*. A nine-tiered lamp column on an octagonal dais stands in front.

G. Pernem

This small town lies on NH17, 18km north of Mapusa, in the middle of the wooded hills that mark the boundary between Goa and Maharashtra. Pernem is worth visiting for several small temples with unusual features, as well as a grandiose palace.

The **Bhagavati Temple**, in the middle of Pernem, is a brightly painted monument of little merit, except for its well-proportioned octagonal tower. A greater attraction is **Deshprabhu House**, 300m north of the town centre (permission required to visit). This sprawling complex is still inhabited by the descendents of the local rulers of Pernem, who trace their origins back to Maratha times. The House is entered through an arched gate between polygonal towers. The reception rooms in the central Neo-Classical block are notable for the collection of Goan furniture, Chinese ceramics, silvered palanquins and memorabilia.

The modest **Mulvir Temple** at Malpem, 2km east of Pernem, is set in a delightful grove of palm trees, with a spring-fed tank nearby. Though the Temple is only a simple arcaded structure with a tiled roof, paintings cover the arches of the hall and the sanctuary walls. The faded compositions, with sketchy black linework, illustrate the development of a pictorial tradition in the region during the 18C–19C. The best-preserved scenes show Vishnu on Shesha (over shrine door), *Ramayana* episodes (arches of side aisles), the churning of the ocean, Krishna holding up Govardhan mountain, a *Ramayana* battle and Vishnu's incarnations (shrine walls).

The **Mauli Temple**, standing in a forest clearing 1km west of Pernem, is similar in date and layout to the Mulvir Temple, except for a polygonal porch extension at the front (west). The masonry vaults of the arcaded hall are covered with stylised lotuses and scrollwork executed in *sgraffito* technique, by which reddish plaster is chipped away to reveal a white background. The sanctuary is dedicated to the warrior form of Devi; the black stone image shows the goddess armed with sword and shield. Immediately west of the Temple is a small stream. A fierce image of Durga is set up near the water.

H. Terekhol

This coastal **Fort** surveys the confluence of the Terekhol (Tiracol) River and the Arabian Sea. It is situated on the north bank of the river, accessible by ferry from Keri on the south bank, 15km west of Pernem.

The Fort was founded in the early 18C by the Maratha chiefs of Sawantwadi, a nearby town in Maharashtra, and was only captured by the Portuguese in 1788. It was contested by the British, to whom it was temporarily surrendered in 1835. Terekhol attained fame during the freedom struggle against the Portuguese; several demonstrators were killed here in 1955.

The road from the ferry leads through the tiny village of Terekhol, with its modern chapel dedicated to St Anthony, up the hill to the main gate of the Fort. Laterite walls define a small irregular zone on top. The triangular bastions, with lookout posts headed by domical turrets, offer magnificent panoramas of the river and ocean.

The inner court of the Fort is dominated by the **Church of St Anthony**, patron saint of the army and Portugal's national saint. The façade of this modest structure has an ornate pediment, with voluted sides flanked by open square towers. The *Hotel Terekhol Fort Heritage* occupies the former garrison quarters of the Fort.

13 · Margao

Margao, also known as Madgaon, the leading centre of the rich agricultural zone south of the Zuari River, is situated on NH17, 33km south of Panaji [11A]. In spite of the city's architectural charm, most visitors will prefer to stay at one of the nearby beach resorts, from where it is possible to make excursions to various historical sites.

Portuguese vestiges are evident in the churches at **Margao** [A], **Colva** [B], **Sancoale** [C], **Rachol** [D] and **Courtorim** [E], all of which can be reached in two half-day trips. An excursion to **Chandor** [F] provides an opportunity for viewing one of the great mansions of Goa.

Temples are a comparative rarity in South Goa, the finest being those at the summit of **Chandranatha Hill** [G]. The citadel at **Cabo de Rama** [H] to the south is now much decayed, but the journey skirts some of Goa's most beautiful beaches.

Panaji, Old Goa [11B] and Ponda [11L], though described in an earlier chapter, are easily accessible from Margao. Ponda, for instance, lies only 17km northeast.

■ **Transport**. The airport at Dabolim, 28km north of Margao, is convenient to the beach resorts of South Goa. At present, Margao is linked by train to Hubli [21] and Hospet [20] in Karnataka. The future Konkan Railway will run between Margao and Panaji as well as to points south, such as Mangalore [17]. Bus services already connect Margao with all these destinations, as well as with all the sites described here.

■ **Accommodation**. The beaches of South Goa are served by luxury hotels, such as the *Oberoi* (☎ 513291) at **Bogmalo**, 4km from Dabolim, the *Majorda Beach Resort* (☎ 220025), *Resorte de Goa* (☎ 745066) and *Goa Renaissance* (☎ 245208) at **Varca**, and the *Holiday Inn Resort* (☎ 746303) and *Leela Beach Hotel* (☎ 246363) at **Cavelossim**. A profusion of more modest accom-

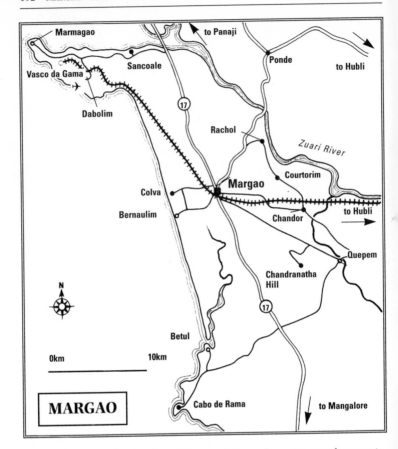

MARGAO

modations is to be found at **Colva** and **Benaulim**, two popular resorts, among them the *Penthouse Beach Resort* (☎ 731010) and *Colmar* (☎ 721253) at Colva. The STD code for all these locations is 0834.

■ **Tourist Information**. The Government of Goa Tourist Information Centre operates an office in the *Tourist Hostel* at Margao (☎ 222513). A counter is also maintained at **Dabolim Airport**.

A. Margao

Margao, the largest city in South Goa, preserves many of its Portuguese period houses and civic buildings. The well-maintained and shady **Jorge Barreto Park** serves as a favourite meeting place in the middle of Margao. It is overlooked on the south by the **Municipal Council Building** of 1905. The redpainted structure, with prominent arcades and balconies, accommodates the Municipal Library. The **City Market**, the liveliest in Goa, is located a short distance east.

The streets running north from the Park lead to the **Church Square**, onto which face traditional houses with brightly painted façades and ornate cast-iron balconies. The whitewashed **Cross** in the middle, shaded by spreading mango trees, is the largest and most ornate in Goa. This Rococo edifice displays curving acanthus leaves; it supports a plain stone cross with crudely engraved emblems.

The **Church of the Holy Spirit** occupies the southwest corner of the Square. Founded in 1565 on the site of a demolished temple, the Church was substantially rebuilt in 1675. The west façade, the only one to be plastered, presents pedimented windows in three stages. A canopied niche in the middle of the topmost stage frames a relief composition of the Virgin in the company of the Apostles. The balustraded towers at the corners, slightly set back, are topped with flattish domes with lanterns. A half-arch on the north side of the Church leads to a courtyard formed by residences intended for the clergy, now a school. The nave of the Church is lined with deep window niches topped by shell-shaped half-domes. The barrel vault is coffered throughout. The elaborate altar at the east end is richly carved and gilded. The Crucifix in the topmost recess is framed by angels on ornate columns. Free-standing Corinthian columns placed against the side walls of the chancel carry a cut-out foliated

The Cross in the Church Square, Margao

arch. The side altars are equally ornate, especially those consecrated to the Archangel and the Virgin. The pulpit is carried on unusual animal brackets. The Sacristy, which opens off the nave on the north, has a finely finished vault. A feast takes place here on 9 December.

The road running east from the Church of the Holy Spirit leads to **Sat Burnzam Gor**, one of Goa's largest private mansions (permission required to visit). The name refers to seven roofs, of which only three are now preserved, each a steep pyramid of tiles, rising over the long line of doors and windows that distinguishes the street façade. The Viceroy's secretary, Inacio Silva, commissioned the house in about 1790, and his descendants still live in several of the apartments. The grand reception room at the upper level preserves magnificent furniture; there is also a private chapel. The house next door is of interest for the Neo-Gothic tracery of its windows. A porch shelters a grand staircase leading to the front door.

The small **Damodar Temple**, occupying an old house, is found in one of the streets leading south of the Church Square. A brass face-mask of Shiva covers a small *linga* set into the floor.

B. Colva

This town, 5km east of Margao, is of interest for the **Church of Our Lady of Mercy**, a fine example of the 18C Rococo style, standing 1km inland from the ocean. The triple-bayed west façade, with pedimented doors and windows, is surmounted by a panel containing the IHS monogram of the Jesuits. Animals are seen in the volutes; pinnacles crown the capping pediment. A single bell tower rises to one side. The charming blue-and-white-painted chancel frames a four-tiered altar with the Virgin Mary on top. The Corinthian columns set against the side walls carry an arch with leafy tracery. The Church is famous for the image of Menino (Boy) Jesus, which is credited with miraculous powers. The original statue was removed in 1834 to the College at Rachol; its replacements are believed to retain the supernatural attributes of the original. Menino Jesus appears in two side altars and in a painted panel over the pulpit. The crowned youth holds an orb and a flag. The Church is attached to a school with an attractive arcaded courtyard.

C. Sancoale

The elaborate, but fragmentary, east façade of the **Church of Our Lady of Health**, the only portion of this monument to survive, soars over a forested grove on the south bank of the Zuari River, 19km northwest of Margao, off NH17. Built by Jesuits in 1606, the Church was destroyed by fire in 1834. Pilasters with enlarged Corinthian capitals frame round-headed doorways below and rectangular pedimented windows above. The topmost stage has a circular opening headed by a small niche enlivened with pinnacles. Plaster compositions over the side doorways show bearded figures, one holding a sword, the other a book, standing in ornate frames; angels adorn the central doorway. The volutes are arranged symmetrically around the circular opening above.

D. Rachol

The **College of All Saints** at Rachol, a small village 8km northeast of Margao, dates back to 1574. Originally called after Ignatius Loyola, the founder of the Jesuit order, its name was altered after the expulsion of the Jesuits in 1759. The College is renowned throughout Goa for its high standard of learning and training. A press was set up here to print a biblical digest in Konkani, the local language. The translation was by Father Thomas Stephen, the first recorded Englishman to have visited Southern India, who arrived in Goa in 1579. Apart from an extension in the 19C, most of the present College dates from the rebuilding of 1606–10.

The College, sited on top of a small rise, was once encircled with laterite walls and a moat, of which only a segment remains. This contains the semicircular-headed **Gate**, flanked by Doric columns through which the road passes. The Gate is painted in contrasting bands of colour. The College beyond is approached from the east. A lofty but plain doorway leads to the **Entrance Hall**, distinguished by the use of a central column supporting a vault that arches down at the corners. Murals, now faded, adorn the walls. They include a scene of fiery hell.

The main rooms of the College are arranged on two levels around a large **Court**. The raised platform in the middle of the Court conceals a subterranean cistern divided into eight cross-vaulted chambers. Remnants of Hindu sculptures discovered here suggest that this may originally have been a temple tank. Paintings of different saints are seen above the doorways to the rooms at the rear (west) of the Court. The Last Judgement and Biblical scenes cover the walls of the hall leading to the Sacristy on the south side of the Court.

The **Church** beyond presents a spacious interior decorated with polychrome carved panels. Those on the chancel walls show different saints, surrounded by angels in foliation. The naive style of these panels contrasts with the gilded magnificence of the high altar and the pulpit. The famous statue of Menino (Boy) Jesus, taken from Colva, is exhibited in the altar to the left. Bone relics of Constantine the Great, brought from Rome in 1782, are kept in a side altar left of the main entrance. The **Gallery** over the east end of the nave houses a pipe organ, reputedly the oldest in Asia, shipped from Lisbon at the end of the 17C. The corridor outside the entrance to the Gallery, running the full length of the Church, is lined with mural portraits of founders of the various religious orders, including St Francis of Assisi. The oil paintings in the **Main Hall** beyond portray Goan Archbishops and the youthful Dom Sebastiao, the royal founder of the College, on horseback. The adjacent library is amply stocked with rare books.

A side wing of the College has recently been converted into the **Museum of Christian Art** (closed 13.00–14.00). The collection of religious art objects, the finest in Goa, is attractively displayed. Many of the objects, which date mainly from the 17C–18C, were removed from Old Goa. The wooden carvings include images of St Ursula and St Margarite. Among the silver reliquaries and other ritual items is a remarkable 40cm high monstrance, fashioned as a pelican with a casket set into its chest. Embroidered vestments and capes are also on display. The ivory statuettes are of outstanding quality, particularly an exquisitely made 12cm high figure of Christ as the Good Shepherd, with a forest scene beneath. Larger ivories show the Infant Christ and Christ on the cross. Painted wooden panels are also exhibited, some set in enamelled frames. An inlaid chest with figural legs is the most elegant of several articles of furniture.

The isolated **Church of Our Lady of the Snows** stands 1km east of the College, on the edge of rice fields extending to the Zuari River. Its modest façade displays Rococo volutes on the uppermost stage; only one tower is preserved. The interior has the usual array of ornate wooden altars. Among the gravestones set into the floor of the chancel is a memorial commemorating the burial site of five missionaries killed in 1583. A carved and painted panel of the Last Supper adorns the front altar.

E. Courtorim

This small hamlet, 5km east of Rachol, provides an idyllic setting for the **Church of St Alex**, which faces west towards a large tank covered with water lilies. The Church opens on to a terrace with a small **Cross**, complete with twisted colonettes and exuberant plasterwork. The façade of the Church dates from the rebuilding of 1647. The side towers have unusual octagonal uppermost stages with small domes and lanterns; wavy volutes flank the central stage. The interior demonstrates the Goan Rococo style at its most exuberant. The chancel is framed by free-standing Corinthian columns supporting a foliated arch. The triple-tiered altar at the end contains images of St Alex with other saints, flanked by foliated and gilded bulbous columns. The tabernacle in front is conceived as a miniature building. The ornate side altars are consecrated to St Sebastian and St Michael. The cast-iron gallery was added in the 19C.

F. Chandor

The road from Courtorim winds southeast through pleasant countryside for about 4km before arriving at Chandor, a sprawling settlement, also accessible from Margao, 13km west. At the heart of Chandor is a long narrow Square, at the east end of which is the **Church of Our Lady of Bethlehem**. The original façade collapsed in 1949 and was subsequently rebuilt in an unsympathetic Neo-Gothic style. Of greater interest are the free-standing memorials that dot the square, which include an elaborate Neo-Gothic edifice erected in 1885 by Francisco Xavier Braganza, a member of the family whose house occupies the south side of the square.

The **Braganza House** is one of the few privately owned mansions in Goa open to the public. It dates back to the 16C, but the structure assumed its present large dimensions only in the course of the 18C. The exceptionally long façade consists of 25 bays with window openings, mostly trilobed in shape and partly filled with stained glass. These open on to a balustraded verandah that runs the full length of the building. The lower level has simple openings for kitchen, stores and servants' quarters. A central gable marks the staircase ascending to the residential apartments at the upper level, now divided into two separate apartments. These give the best possible idea of the gracious living style enjoyed by Goan aristocratic families in the 19C.

Both apartments have grandiose reception rooms with tiled floors, painted walls and timbered ceilings, off which open smaller galleries for leisure and dining, as well as bedrooms with private balconies. The rooms are furnished with locally carved wooden furniture, among the finest to be seen in Goa, as well as imported glass chandeliers and porcelain; paintings, photographs and other personal items crowd tables and chests inlaid with brass or mother-of-pearl. The east apartment has its own private chapel, adorned with a carved and gilded altar in the Rococo style. A library of more than 5000 books is to be seen in the west apartment. This was formed by Luis de Menezes Braganza, a journalist and newspaper proprietor at the turn of the 20C.

1.5km east of the Square at Chandor lies the village of **Cotta**, beyond which which is the archaeological site of **Chandrapura**. Excavations undertaken here in 1929 recovered pottery fragments going back to the 2C–1C BC, the earliest such finds in Goa. An inscribed copper plate dating from the 3C–4C AD is the oldest historical document in the state. (Some of these items are displayed in the Archaeological Museum in Old Goa.) The decayed brick walls and overturned stone footing blocks at Chandrapura formed part of an east-facing shrine dedicated to Shiva, as indicated by the large but headless Nandi still to be seen nearby. The structure dates from the 12C–13C Kadamba era.

G. Chandranatha Hill

The **Chandreshwar** and **Bhutanatha Temples** on the summit of Chandranatha Hill are reached by following a winding road for about 5km from Paroda, a small village 12km southeast of Margao. The road climbs almost 400m through increasingly dense forest inhabited by monkeys; the last part of the ascent is by a flight of stone steps. The temples occupy the level top of the Hill, with fine views of the plain beneath and the ocean beyond. Though the Temples are no earlier than the 18C, they mark the site of a Kadamba period foundation going back to the 12C–13C.

The Chandreshwar Temple presents a rectangle of plain walls with open porches sheltering balcony seating; that on the south is topped with a small dome, that on the east has a pyramidal roof. A dome on a high octagonal tower rises above the sanctuary. A natural rock forms the ritual focus of the Temple, against which are placed small *lingas* representing Chandreshwar. The original shrine consists of a small domed chamber built up to the south face of the rock. This was later entirely encased within the structure that stands today, the tower being supported on a vault built on top of the rock. Kadamba-period sculptural fragments are assembled in the sanctuary and surrounding corridor. The Temple has recently been renovated; vividly painted panels adorn the ceiling of the hall in front of the shrine.

The adjacent Bhutanatha Temple is a simple vaulted chamber that enshrines an unshaped stone set at an angle into the ground. The *linga*, sculpted out of a large boulder and covered with a brass mask, represents Chandreshwar.

A **Chariot** is parked in the shelter south of the Temples. Completed in 1983, this painted wooden structure has carved panels interspersed with fully carved *yalis* and monkeys.

H. Cabo de Rama

Cabo de Rama is a promontory which lies about 30km south of Margao, half this distance on NH17. The **Fort** here, though of little architectural interest, offers splendid ocean views north along the beach towards Colva, and south to Goa's last headland before Karnataka.

The Portuguese occupied Cabo de Rama between 1763 and about 1835, after which it was abandoned. The dilapidated entrance to the Fort is reached by crossing a dry moat. The small chapel inside is still occasionally used. The remains of barrack blocks are seen nearby.

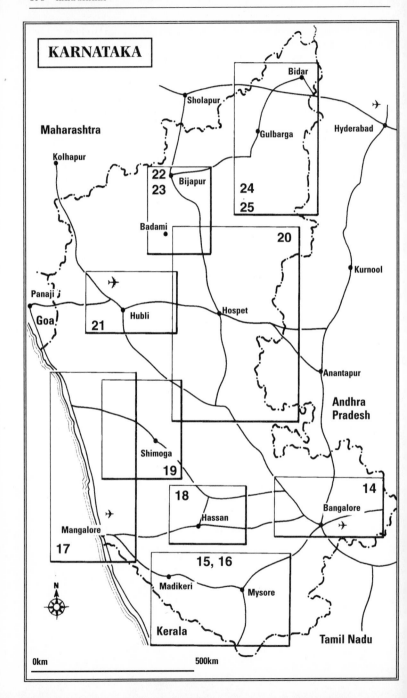

Karnataka

Most visitors to Karnataka arrive at **Bangalore** [14], a modern city that preserves much of its British heritage.

One popular route proceeds southwest from Bangalore to **Mysore** [15], the capital of the former Wodeyar state, only a short distance from the island citadel of **Srirangapattana** [15C], the scene of the British victory over Tipu Sultan at the end of the 18C.

The route west continues to **Madikeri** [16] in the wooded hilly region of Kodegu, beyond which lies the port of **Mangalore** [17].

Karnataka's coastal region is of interest for its 15C–16C temples, as at **Udupi** [17B] and **Mudabidri** [17C]. The coastal road that runs north from Mangalore to **Margao** [13] in Goa is the most attractive in the state.

The itinerary west from Bangalore or north from Mysore leads to **Hassan** [18], from where the 12C–13C Hoysala monuments at **Belur** [18A] and **Halebid** [18B] may be reached. The remote shrine at **Sringeri** [19H] is accessible from **Shimoga** [19].

Hospet [20] is the principal tourist centre of central Karnataka, and is the stopping-off point for **Hampi** [20B] and **Kamalapuram** [20C], on the edge of the magnificent ruins of Vijayanagara, the capital of Southern India's most powerful dynasty in the 14C–16C.

Further north lies **Badami** [22], with its 7C–8C Chalukya temples, the earliest and best preserved in the state. **Bijapur** [23], yet further north, the residence of the Adil Shahis in the 16C–17C, is renowned for the Gol Gumbad, the largest domed mausoleum in Southern India.

Mosques and tombs spanning the 14C–16C Bahmani and Baridi periods stand at **Gulbarga** [24] and **Bidar** [25], in the northern extremity of Karnataka. From here it is possible to continue on to **Sholapur** [9] in Maharashtra or to **Hyderabad** [26] in Andhra Pradesh.

14 · Bangalore

Bangalore, the capital of Karnataka, is situated at the extreme southeast corner of the state, on the southern edge of the Deccan plateau. Its elevation of just over 1000m guarantees an agreeable mildness of climate. The city has in recent years emerged as a leading manufacturing and commercial centre, renowned for its computer and communication industries.

In spite of rapid development, vestiges of the past are still to be found. Isolated monuments from the period of the Gowdas and the interregnum of Haidar Ali and Tipu Sultan dot the streets of **Old Bangalore** [A]; the British presence is more in evidence in **New Bangalore** [B]. A full day should be sufficient to cover all the sights noted here.

An excursion to the rock citadel at **Shivaganga** [C] can be combined with visits to the little-known temple at **Sibi** [D] and the unusual tomb at **Sira** [E], both of which are on NH4. This highway continues to Chitradurga [20K], recommended stop-over on any journey from Bangalore to Hospet [20] or Hubli [21].

NH7 leads north from Bangalore to the hill fort at **Nandi** [F], from where it is possible to continue into Andhra Pradesh to visit the ceiling paintings at Lepakshi [33G]. Both Nandi and Lepakshi may be reached in a full-day excursion. The temples at **Kolar** [G] and **Kurudumale** [H] are accessible on NH4 east of Bangalore. The highway continues into Andhra Pradesh and Tamil Nadu.

■ **Transport**. Bangalore is connected by air to Delhi, Bombay [1], Panaji [11], Hyderabad [26], Madras [36] and Thiruvananthapuram [46]. In the future the city will also be served by an international airport. Trains and buses connect Bangalore to all of these cities, as well as to Mysore [15] and a host of lesser centres in Karnataka, Andhra Pradesh and Tamil Nadu. Local buses reach all the destinations described here.

■ **Accommodation**. An abundance of hotels in Banglaore (STD code 080) caters for all categories of visitors. The most luxurious are the *West End Hotel* (☎ 2255055), *Sheraton Windsor Manor* (☎ 2269898), *Taj Residency* (☎ 5584444), *Gateway Hotel* (☎ 5584545) and *Oberoi Bangalore* (☎ 5585858), followed by the *Ashoka Hotel* (☎ 2269462) and *Holiday Inn* (☎ 2262233). All these hotels are located near the Racecourse or the Mahatma Gandhi Road commercial area. Less expensive accommodations are also to be found in these parts of the city. The *Mayur Pine Top* (☎ 78624) is available for visitors wishing to spend a night at the summit of **Nandi Hill** (STD code 08156).

■ **Tourist Information**. The Government of India Tourist Information Office is located in the KFC Building, 48 Church Street (☎ 5585417). The headquarters of the Karnataka State Tourist Development Corporation (KSTDC) are at Mitra Towers, 10/4 Kasturba Road, Queen's Circle (☎ 2272580). Other KSTDC centres are maintained at 64 St Mark's Road, the City railway station and Bangalore airport.

■ **Travel agents and tour companies**. Among the companies offering services for hotel bookings and travel arrangements are *Mercury*, Infantry Road (☎ 577730), *Sita*, St Mark's Road (☎ 578091) and *Thomas Cook*, 55 Mahatma Gandhi Road (☎ 5586742).

History

Bangalore was founded as Bangaluru in 1537 by Kempe Gowda, a local chief in the service of the emperors of Vijayanagara [20B–C]. The Gowdas rose in importance after the destruction of Vijayanagara in 1565, and by the turn of the 17C they were in control of a large portion of southeastern Karnataka. On their western flank, however, the Gowdas were challenged by the Wodeyars of Mysore and the Nayakas of Ikkeri [19C]. Bangalore was raided several times by the Adil Shahis of Bijapur [23] and the Marathas, eventually being taken by the Wodeyars in 1687. The English established a garrison at Bangalore in the early years of the 18C, but were ousted in 1758 when the city came under the control of Haidar Ali; three years later he usurped the Mysore throne, retaining Bangalore as one of his outposts. Haidar Ali's aggressive campaigns were continued by his son, Tipu Sultan. After the defeat of Tipu at Srirangapattana [15C] in 1799, Bangalore was

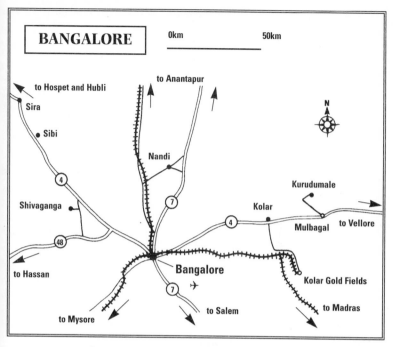

incorporated into the reconstituted princely state of Mysore. The city, however, retained its importance for the British, who continued to maintain a significant military presence until Independence.

A. Old Bangalore

The tour of historical Bangalore described here begins at **Tipu Sultan's Palace** on Albert Victor Road, just west of the junction with Krishnarajendra Road. The Palace marks the site of the original Gowda residence that stood in the middle of the Fort, the walls of which were dismantled and rebuilt at the end of the 18C. Only the north-facing audience hall of the Palace still stands. This consists of double-height wooden columns with lobed arcades carrying a flat wooden roof; chambers with balconies on three sides look down into the hall. Though now somewhat shabby, the Palace would once have been ornately furbished in a mannner akin to Daria Daulat Bagh at Srirangapattana.

The **Venkataramana Temple**, immediately east on Krishnarajendra Road, is a 17C complex dating from the Gowda period. The outer walls of the main shrine are covered with rows of gods in procession; a pyramidal brick tower rises over the sanctuary. The open hall in front is distinguished by *yalis* projecting from the outer piers. Quartets of identical animals adorn each of the central four columns of the hall.

A fragment of the stone **Fort**, constructed by Haidar Ali in 1761, may be seen a short distance north of the Venkataramana Temple. The **Delhi Gate** has prominent arched entrances with fine plasterwork, which give access to a barbican shielding an isolated round bastion. Steps in the side walls of the

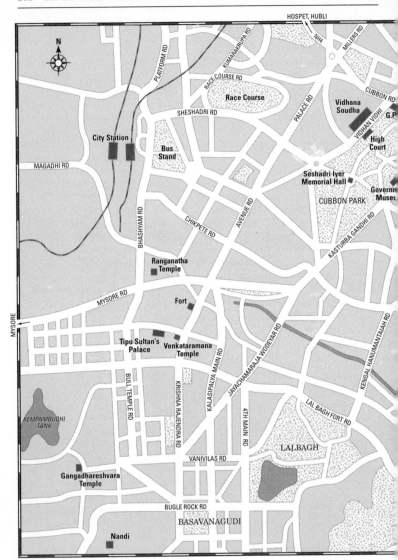

barbican lead to the crenellated walkway that once ran along the top of the ramparts.

The **City Market**, immediately north of the Fort, marks the heart of Old Bangalore. The regularly planned narrow streets, crowded with traffic, are original features, as are the brick houses with internal courts surrounded by colonnades. Among the religious monuments to be found here is the **Ranganatha Temple**. Like the Venkataramana Temple, it has sculpted *yalis* on the columns of the entrance porch. An inscribed slab set up here is dated 1628, in the reign

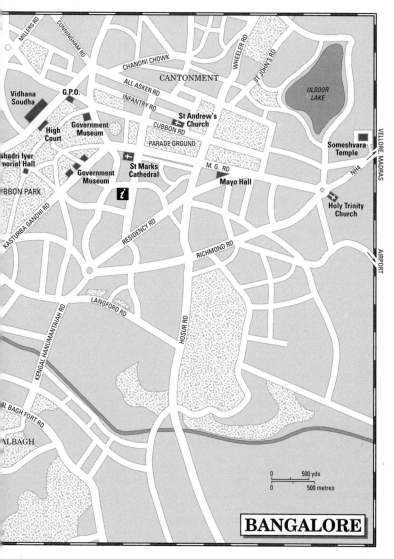

BANGALORE

of Kempe Gowda II. The columns and doorways inside the temple are finely finished.

1.5km east of Tipu Sultan's Palace is **Lal Bagh**, a garden of about 250ha, originally established as a pleasure resort in the time of Haidar Ali. It was converted into horticultural gardens in 1856, with a professional superintendent being sent out from Kew Gardens in London. Lal Bagh contains a rare and valuable collection of tropical and subtropical plants, together with indigenous and foreign fruit trees. The spacious **Glass House**, with its delicate cast-iron frame, dates from 1889. Lotus ponds, lakes and shaded avenues are interspersed with natural boulders. The entrance to the park is marked by a handsome equestrian statue of Chamaraja Wodeyar of Mysore.

Gavipur, 2km west of Lal Bagh, was once an independent village but is now absorbed into suburban Bangalore. The **Gangadhareshvara Temple**, with its main shrine set into a natural rocky crevice, is of interest for the unique granite pillars which stand freely in the court. Two of these support great discs, almost 1.5m in diameter, representing the sun and moon; the other two have a Nandi and trident on top. **Basavangudi**, less than 1km south, is named after a picturesque hill strewn with boulders, one of which is fashioned as **Nandi**. Dating back to Gowda times, the 4.5m high seated bull is ceremonially decked with garlands and bells. The animal is sheltered from the weather by a later structure. A small **Ganesha Temple** is situated at the base of the hill.

Other vestiges of Old Bangalore survive at the eastern extremity of the city, beyond the end of Mahatma Gandhi Road, the principal commercial thoroughfare. **Ulsoor** is a traditional settlement, with old houses facing onto regular lanes. The great **Tank** established by the Gowdas in the 17C lies to the north. The same rulers were responsible for the **Someshvara Temple**, in the middle of Ulsoor. The monument, the largest in Bangalore, is approached from the east through an imposing *gopura* with sculpted walls and a pyramidal brick tower. An ornate lotus medallion is carved on the ceiling over the passageway. A lofty lamp column stands in the street outside. The Temple within has an entrance porch decorated with *yalis* and colonettes on the outer columns. Carvings of deities relieve the otherwise plain walls. The altar and flag column in front have finely finished basements.

B. New Bangalore

The tour of the city continues with a description of the main sights of New Bangalore. By far the largest and most important building in this area is the **Vidhana Soudha**, completed in 1956, accommodating both the Secretariat and State Legislature of Karnataka. The imposing polished granite complex is designed in a revivalist style; the columns with corbelled brackets, projecting balconies, curving eaves and dome-like towers are all derived from temple architecture. These elements are assembled in multi-storeyed wings that fan symmetrically outwards from grandiose porticos in the middle of each side. The Vidhana Soudha faces onto Vidhan Vidi, a broad ceremonial avenue, on the opposite side of which stands the **High Court**, known locally as the Attara Kacheri. This Neo-Classical stone building, completed in 1868, is painted deep red. Its central Ionic portico is headed by double pediments. An equestrian statue of Sir Mark Cubbon, the Commissioner of Bangalore in 1834–61, stands in front.

Cubbon Park, at the back of the High Court, is named in honour of the Commissioner. This expanse of more than 120ha of pleasant greenery in the heart of Bangalore was laid out in 1864. The Park is dotted with statuary: a portrait of Chamarajendra Wodeyar overlooks the pond near an octagonal cast-iron bandstand; a formidable marble sculpture of Queen Victoria, erected in 1906, announces the entrance to the Park at the beginning of Mahatma Gandhi

Road; a matching sculpture of Edward VII stands a short distance away. **Seshadri Iyer Memorial Hall**, in the middle of the Park, commemorates the Prime Minister of Mysore State in 1883–1901. The building was erected in 1913 to accommodate the City Central Library. Its red-painted Neo-Classical front is marked by a gable-topped portico. A statue of Seshadri Iyer stands in front. A large semicircular wing extends from the back of the Hall.

Kasturba Gandhi Road lines the east flank of the Park. Here stands the **Government Museum** (closed Mondays), another Neo-Classical building with fully modelled Corinthian columns, all painted bright red, dating from 1876. The sculpture gallery displays carved limestone fragments from the 2C Buddhist site at Sannathi [24H]. The 12C images of standing Surya, dancing Shiva and Krishna playing the flute all come from Halebid [18B]. An impressive item is the 9C granite icon of Durga from Avani. The main hall has double-height Corinthian columns supporting an upper gallery. Archaeological mate-rials shown here include items

Queen Victoria in Cubbon Park, New Bangalore

from megalthic burial sites and 1C pottery from Arikamedu [39B]. The remainder of the space is devoted to Tipu Sultan memorabilia, with arms, prints and a relief model of Srirangapattana. Hero stones showing mounted warriors and foot soldiers engaged in battle are displayed at the base of the circular cast-iron staircases. Among the paintings that line the upper gallery are fine exam-ples of the 19C Mysore school, illustrating mythological topics. Next door is the **Visvesvara Industrial and Technological Museum**, and on the other side the **Venkatappa Art Gallery**, the latter devoted to contemporary painting and sculpture.

The oldest building to back onto Cubbon Park is **Raj Bhavan** (permission required to visit), the former British Residency, dating from 1831. This white-washed Neo-Classical villa, with a prominent colonnaded porch, is set in beau-tifully landscaped grounds. The **General Post Office**, a short distance away, has an imposing corner entrance portico that imitates the Vidhana Soudha.

Mahatma Gandhi Road was laid out as part of the British **Cantonment**, with parade grounds and barracks to the north and churches and bungalows in well-tended gardens to the south. Many of these buildings still stand, giving an idea of Bangalore in former times; they are, however, overshadowed by high-rise office buildings, apartment blocks and hotels. Proceeding east from Cubbon Park along Mahatma Gandhi Road, the first historical feature is **St Mark's Cathedral**. This 1812 structure presents a simple Neo-Classical scheme, with an imposing but unpedimented portico on the front and an apsidal apse at the rear. A shallow dome marks the internal crossing. **St Andrew's Church** on Cubbon Road, which runs parallel to Mahatma Gandhi Road, is a simple Neo-Gothic building dating from 1867. Its lofty square tower is relieved by octagonal turrets.

Mayo Hall, on the angled intersection of Mahatma Gandhi Road and Brigade Road, was opened in 1883 as a tribute to Lord Mayo, the Viceroy assassinated at Port Blair [49A] three years earlier. The Hall, which now houses a variety of public offices and courts, presents a handsome Italianate façade with pedimented upper windows and vase-like pinnacles. The **East Parade Church** of 1863, a short distance east, has prominent Ionic portico, now painted bright grey, but no tower. **Holy Trinity Church**, a project of 1851, frames the eastern extremity of Mahatma Gandhi Road. This, too, is fronted by an Ionic portico, but here the entrance is topped by a triple-stage tower with Neo-Greek palmettes at the corners. Ulsoor, the traditional quarter already noted in Section A, lies further east. **St Patrick's Church**, on Residency Road near the corner of St Mark's Road, dates from 1887, rebuilt in 1894–99. The impressive Neo-Classical façade displays superimposed colonettes in the middle. The twin towers have pedimented windows. The interior is of interest for the wooden-panelled barrel vault.

This tour of New Bangalore concludes with a visit to **Bangalore Palace**, 3km north of the Mahatma Gandhi Road area. This was constructed in 1880 for a British merchant, and was then taken over and extended by the Wodeyars.

The Palace faces east onto extensive grounds, partly converted into a formal garden with axial paths and garden plots. The main building is built entirely in granite, and presents an unsymmetrical, but agreeable, clutter of towers and turrets. The formal apartments in the south block are entered through a low arch framed by polygonal towers with exaggerated battlements. A grand double staircase is situated outside the building to the rear (west). An internal curved flight of steps with elegant wooden balustrades ascends to the grand reception room at the upper level, which is adorned with Neo-Gothic stained-glass windows and panelled ceiling. Other parts of the Palace (access restricted to visitors) are given over to private apartments, many with their original furnishings intact. The central block has a circular room at rooftop level, with part-circular arcade and cast-iron balcony beneath; a circular staircase tower with a battlemented top rises to one side. The north block is double-storeyed with polygonal corner towers, and adjoins dilapidated service structures, a conservatory, stables and stores.

C. Shivaganga

This spectacular citadel is situated 50km northwest of Bangalore, via Dobbspet on NH4. In the 16C Shivaganga became one of the chief headquarters of the Gowdas, who retained this outpost after Bangalore was lost to the Wodeyars. The site is dominated by the dramatic sugarloaf-shaped crag of Shivaganga Hill, rising more than 100m above the plain, protected by arcs of massive walls.

The settlement at the base of the hill has a large **Kalyana Tank** with carvings on the stepped sides. A lofty lamp column stands beside the entrance *gopura*, leading to a line of rock-cut steps. This passes through two more *gopuras*, one with six steep storeys supporting a vaulted roof with arched ends. The steps arrive at the **Gangadhareshvara Temple** which, together with the adjacent Honnadevi shrine, is built into a natural cavern. Metal portraits of the Gowadas are placed here. The shrine is approached through an ornately carved doorway, in front of which is a seated Nandi surrounded by lathe-turned columns. The south entrance is treated as an elaborate porch, with horses and riders carved on the front columns and friezes of deities on the rear walls. The double-curved eaves are topped by a parapet crowded with plaster figures.

A gateway with a porch and an unfinished tower give access to **Kempe Gowda's Hall**, a detached structure commanding an extensive panorama of the surrounding landscape. This hall has animal columns, doubled at the corners. A tall column headed with a quartet of brackets stands nearby. Steps from here ascend to the summit of the hill.

D. Sibi

The small **Narasimha Temple** beside NH4, 95km northwest of Bangalore, just before Sibi village, was erected at the end of the 18C by a local official under Tipu Sultan. The monument is worth visiting because of its well-preserved ceiling paintings, among the finest of the Wodeyar period. Mythological topics with bright red backgrounds and formally posed figures contrast with courtly portraits and processions depicted in a provincial Mughal manner. The panel over the central passageway of the entrance gate to the Temple shows a rocky landscape populated with wild beasts, hunters and ascetics in caves. Krishna appears at the summit of a hill playing the flute, with herdsmen and *gopis* beneath. The supporting beams have lines of soldiers in red coats with muskets, artillery, flag-bearers, elephants, camels and foot-soldiers. The paintings over the side chambers show receptions with turban-clad courtly figures and sexual scenes with concubines.

The Temple compound is surrounded by a colonnade with an ornate plaster parapet. Niches with multiple aspects of Narasimha have pointed arches and temple-like towers above. The paintings inside the entrance porch of the Temple are arranged in nine panels. Over the central aisle: Shiva and Devi with Ganesha and sages surrounded by aspects of the god; Vishnu as Vishvarupa, with the map of the universe on his body; a triple niche containing Narasimha with Lakshmi flanked by Shiva and Brahma, surrounded by the story of Narasimha, continuing on the supporting beams. *Ramayana* episodes form the subject of the three panels to the right; Krishna scenes occupy the corresponding panels to the left. The front panels in both rows portray battles, with heroes in chariots hurtling towards each other. The sides of the supporting beams beneath the frontal eaves show fighTing figures in the company of musicians, flag-bearers and courtiers. The undersides of the beams are enlivened with stylised lotus designs.

A pleasant grove of pipal trees near to the Temple shelters a cluster of *naga* stones. The grove overlooks a stepped tank.

E. Sira

This town lies further along NH4, a total of 123km northwest of Bangalore.

> Sira gained importance under the Bijapur rulers, from whom it was
> captured by Aurangzeb in 1687. It subsequently served as an outpost of the
> Mughals and the Asaf Jahis of Hyderabad [26A]. Haidar Ali began his
> career here before serving under the Wodeyars. The town declined after
> Tipu Sultan forcibly removed a large number of families from it to
> Sriringipattana.

The **Tomb of Malik Rihan**, which dates from 1651, is seen beside the highway
on the south side of the town. Arcades capped with angled eaves on sculpted
brackets surround the central chamber. The three-quarter spherical dome rises
on an upper storey, with corner domical finials in the typical Adil Shahi manner.
The **Jami Mosque** inside the town, dating from 1696, is more Mughal in style.
The prayer chamber has five arches with lobed profiles and an ornate parapet
flanked by octagonal buttresses. There are three diminutive domes, the central
one higher than the side ones. Remnants of the walls and fort of the **Fort**
nearby, headquarters of the Mughal commanders, can still be made out.

F. Nandi

This rock fort, 50km north of Bangalore, just off NH7, was a favourite retreat of
Tipu Sultan, from whom it was captured by the British in 1791. The monuments
at the summit of the hill, which rises abruptly 600m above the plain, and in
Nandi Village beneath, date back to the 9C. The cool climate and magnificent
scenery make Nandi a favourite picnic spot for Bangalorians.

An arched **Gate** is reached after a drive of about 20 minutes from the foot of
the hill. This is set into the fortifications that girdle the upper fort. **Tipu Sultan's
Summer Palace**, a modest structure with a small verandah just inside the Gate,
overlooks a delightful garden with a large tank. A path ascends to a wooded park
at the summit. The nearby **Yoganandishvara Temple** is of interest for the delicately cast brass door frame in front of the principal sanctuary.

Descending to the foot of the hill, the road winds around the base of the rock
for about 4km before arriving at **Nandi Village**. Here stands the **Bhoganandishvara Temple**, actually a pair of shrines dedicated to Bhoganandishvara (north) and Arunachaleshvara (south), built in a simple massive
style associated with the 9C–10C Nolamba rulers of Hemavati [33H]. The outer
walls have regularly spaced pilasters with pierced stone windows animated with
figures of dancing Shiva (south wall of Arunachaleshvara), Durga standing on
the buffalo head (north wall of Bhoganandishvara) and dancers in scrollwork.
A row of dwarfs supports the parapet. The pyramidal multi-storeyed towers
display pilastered walls, eaves and parapets. Black stone sculptures of Shiva and
Nandi are placed in the upper level of the Bhoganandishvara tower, the roof of
which is square. Columns with carved panels on circular shafts adorn the
Temple interior. The hall in front has a ceiling panel with Shiva and Parvati
surrounded by Dikpalas. Large polished black stone *lingas* are housed in both
sanctuaries. Nandis are seated in small pavilions in front.

The Bhoganandishvara Temple was substantially enlarged in later times. The first extension took place under Vijayanagara in the 16C, with the construction of a small pavilion between the two main shrines. The ornate columns with attendant maidens are intricately carved in grey-green granite. The ceiling is a dome-like composition with dancing figures surrounding a central lotus. The next building phase took place under the Gowdas in the 17C, at which time the small Maheshvara shrine was added behind the open pavilion. A procession of gods and sages adorns its outer walls. A wall joining the two Nolamba shrines was skilfully worked to resemble the 9C originals. At the same time, a spacious columned hall was built in front of both shrines. The whole ensemble is set within a large compound surrounded by colonnades, entered on the east through an unfinished *gopura*. The two goddess shrines at the rear have friezes of celestials, similar to those on the Maheshvara Temple. The compound located to the north has a large hall with *yali* columns and a central dais for displaying images. A large square tank with stepped sides lies beyond.

G. Kolar

Kolar, 40km east of Bangalore on NH4, preserves monuments dating from different periods. The **Dargah**, on the west side of the city, is associated with Haidar Ali, who had long-established connections with Kolar, being born some 16km distant. The *Dargah* of his family members (he is buried at Srirangapattana) consists of a simple tomb with an ornate parapet and corner finials with domical tops. The adjacent mosque has similar features, as has the small gate on the south side of the complex. The nearby **Idgah**, also dating from Haidar Ali's period, has a long wall with niches flanked by tapering octagonal buttresses shaped like minarets.

Other historical buildings are found on the east side of Kolar. The **Kolaramma Temple**, after which the city is named, is a foundation of the 11C, when the Cholas of the Tamil zone occupied this part of Karnataka. The Temple stands within a rectangular compound, entered through an imposing gate. The central shrine has wall niches headed with part-circular frames filled with foliation. The columns within the hall display fluted shafts and cushion-shaped capitals.

The 17C **Someshvara Temple**, immediately south, is the most elaborate monument from the Gowda era. The highly sculpted *gopura* on the east is crowded with images of various gods. The tower above rises in five diminishing storeys crowned with a barrel-vaulted roof. The passageway within is roofed by a central lotus surrounded by tiers of cut-out petals; the jambs and lintels display delicate creeper motifs. The Temple within is preceded by a spacious columned hall, with colonettes and *yalis* on the outer supports. The shrine at the rear (west) has bold pilasters interspersed with single pilasters standing in pots. Friezes of animals decorate the lowest moulding of the basement. The pyramidal tower, restored in later times, is capped with a hemispherical roof. The ceremonial pavilion, in the southwest corner of the compound, has outer columns adorned with *yalis* and pairs of maidens. The raised dais within is treated as an independent pavilion, with an ornately worked basement, columns and eaves.

The celebrated **Kolar Gold Fields** (permission required to visit) are located 38km south of the city. The mines, which extend some 2400m below the surface, are the oldest and deepest in Southern India.

H. Kurudumale

This small village, 18km northwest of Mulbagal, some 30km east of Kolar on NH4, is worth visiting for the artistic **Someshvara Temple**, a 12C monument dating from the brief period of Chola domination of southern Karnataka. The Temple stands within a partly collapsed walled compound with a flight of steps on the south. The Tamil influence is seen in the restrained treatment of the basement and pilastered walls, and in the sombre designs of the niches. Entry to the east-facing building is from a side porch reached by transverse flights of steps flanked by *yali* balustrades. The columns here have blocks with delicately modelled icons of Shiva, including the god in dance posture (right column). A large sculpture of Ganapati is placed on the ground in front. The carvings on the interior columns include deities and saints. A pyramidal tower with a hemispherical roof crowns the sanctuary. A rectangular goddess sanctuary capped with a barrel-vaulted roof stands immediately to the north.

The **Vinayaka Temple**, accommodating a much-revered monolithic image of Ganapati, stands within Kurudumale village, about 350m south of the Someshvara Temple. This 12C foundation was extended in later times, with the addition of a square hall in front. The interior columns illustrate diverse aspects of Shiva, such as Bhairava and Bhikshatanamurti; other icons are arranged along the wall shelf. An unfinished *gopura* stands east of the Temple.

15 · Mysore

The former capital of the Wodeyar rulers, Mysore is a charming city pleasantly situated at an elevation of 750m, surrounded by well-watered fields and wooded hills. It has been developed as a prominent educational centre, with the largest university in Karnataka. The city is known for its ivory work, sandalwood carving and silk weaving. A full day may be spent here, visiting palaces and civic buildings [A].

Half-day trips may be made to the shrine on **Chamundi Hill** [B], the fort at **Srirangapattana** [C] and the intricately sculpted temple at **Somanathpur** [D], the last two usually combined in a single excursion. Religious sites in the vicinity, such as **Talkad** [E], **Nanjangud** [F] and **Melukote** [G], will require additional journeys.

For those interested in wildlife, the sanctuaries at **Bandipur** [H] and **Nagarhole** [I] are the finest in Karnataka; both are approached from Mysore.

The city is also a convenient stopover on any journey from Bangalore [14] to the hill station of Madikeri [16], the coastal town of Mangalore [17], the temple centre at Hassan [18] or the resort of Udhagamandalam (Ooty) [43C] in the Nilgiri Hills of Tamil Nadu.

■ **Transport**. Mysore is connected by frequent bus and train services with Bangalore, 138km northeast, the nearest airport and principal railhead. Local buses reach all the destinations described here.

■ **Accommodation**. The *Dasaprakash Paradise* (☎ 515655) and *Green Hotel* (☎ 512536) are attractively situated on the fringes of Mysore (STD code 0821) ; the *Quality Inn Southern Star* (☎ 27217), *King's Court* (☎ 25250) and

Metropole (☎ 520871) are more centrally located, as are a host of lesser accommodations. The *Lalitha Mahal Palace* (☎ 571265) at the foot of Chamundi Hill offers an architecturally distinguished setting.

It is also possible to be based near **Brindavan Gardens**, 19km northwest of Mysore, at the *Hotel Krishnaraja Sagar* (☎ 57222).

Visitors wishing to spend time at the wildlife sanctuaries in the region can stay in the *Forest Department Lodges* at **Bandipur** or the *Kabini River Lodge* (reservations ☎ 520901), near **Karapur**, 60km southwest of Mysore.

■ **Tourist Information**. The KSTDC Office is situated in the Old Exhibition Building, Irwin Road (☎ 22096). Information counters are also maintained at the railway station (☎ 30719) and central bus terminal.

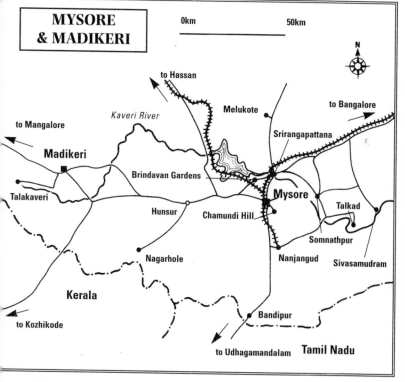

History

Mysore is associated with the Wodeyars, originally the Governors of southern Karnataka under the emperors of Vijayanagara [20B–C]. The first Wodeyar, Timmaraja, was responsible for laying out a fort here in 1524. This he named Mahishuru, after the demon Mahisha killed by the goddess Chamundeshvari, worshipped on top of a nearby hill. After the sack of the Vijayanagara capital in 1565, the Wodeyars asserted their independence.

In 1610 Raja Wodeyar occupied Srirangapattana, a nearby fort on an island in the Kaveri river, making this the second capital of the Mysore kingdom. From here the Wodeyars waged wars on the Gowdas of Bangalore and the Nayakas of Ikkeri [19C].

The Wodeyar throne was usurped in 1761 by Haidar Ali who, together with his son, Tipu Sultan, expanded the Mysore kingdom by pursuing aggressive campaigns against the Peshwas of Pune [3A] and the Nizams of Hyderabad [26A]. This policy brought Haidar and Tipu into direct conflict with the British. In 1793 Tipu had Mysore levelled in order to built an entirely new capital, but these plans never materialised, because he was killed at Srirangapattana in 1799. Two years later the British re-established the Wodeyar line by crowning the infant Krishnaraja III under the watchful eye of a Resident. This king and his successors, particularly Krishnaraja IV, who ascended the throne in 1902, were exemplary monarchs. They ruled a model state renowned for its enlightened policies of social reform and vigorous building programmes. The Mysore kings revived Dasara, the spectacular royal festival dating back to Vijayanagara times, which is still celebrated each September–October.

A. Mysore

The tour described here begins at the **Amba Vilas Palace**, in the middle of the city. The Palace is contained within a quadrangular fort, roughly 450m square, built by the Wodeyars in the 18C, of which portions of stone walls remain. The main Palace block, a replacement of an earlier residence, was begun in 1897 according to an imaginative design by Henry Irwin, and then later expanded. The building presents a grey granite exterior, with corner towers crowned by quartets of painted metal-clad domes. The central wing, conceived as a great seating gallery for viewing the Dasara parades, is emphasised by a higher tower crowned with a central dome surrounded by turrets. The façade is illuminated on occasions by many thousands of lightbulbs. The Palace faces onto a vast parade ground, entered on the east through the **Elephant Gate**, which has a trio of lobed arches, the central one 20m high.

The wings of the Palace are built around an inner court with colonnades relieved by temple-like brackets with sculpted figures. The armoury, library, lifts and other services are located on the north. A staircase on the east lined with wooden panels ascends to the upper level. A pair of silver-clad doors with embossed panels depicting miniature deities opens on to the magnificent turquoise and gold **Public Darbar Hall**. Its 47m long arcades have fluted columns with slightly bulbous shafts; the broad lobed arches support shallow domes decorated with blue skies and golden stars. The murals on the rear wall, against which the throne was once positioned, show a line of goddesses, with Chamundeshvari, the protective divinity of the Wodeyars, in the middle. The paintings were executed by Ravi and Raja Varma, celebrated artists from Kerala. The adjacent **Private Darbar Hall** is smaller, though equally elaborate. It makes use of similar columns and arches, but the central space is entirely roofed with stained glass imported from Glasgow.

It is necessary to descend to the lower level in order to visit the **Kalyana Mandapa**, on the south side of the inner court. This double-height octagonal chamber was first used for marriage ceremonies in 1910. Slender cast-iron

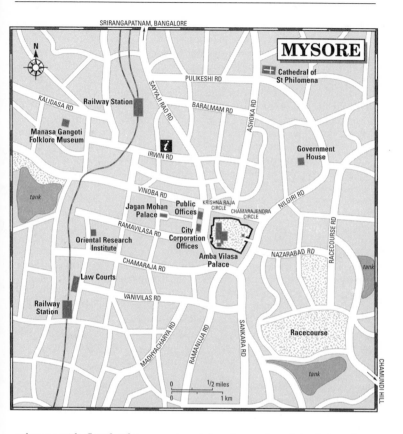

columns with fluted sides support metal arches and a stained-glass dome animated with brightly coloured peacocks. Stone patterns are inlaid into the floor. The **Museum**, in the rear block of the Palace, houses a collection of arms, including 'tiger claws', fearful iron talons. The upper level displays paintings of the Mysore school, mostly of mythological subjects, but also of royal geneaologies. The private quarters of the Wodeyar descendants are situated on the north side of the complex. The **Department of Archaeology**, occupying an annex to the south, has a modest collection of architectural fragments and carvings.

Small shrines stand within the fort walls of the Palace. The **Venkataramana** and **Lakshmi Ramana Temples**, reputedly early Wodeyar foundations, have 19C brightly coloured pyramidal towers rising over their *gopuras* and sanctuaries.

Handsome public buildings and monuments erected under the Wodeyars grace the spacious tree-lined streets of Mysore. Immediately west of the Amba Vilas Palace are the **City Corporation Offices**, which have lobed arcades and octagonal towers with balconies and domes. The adjacent **Public Offices** are built in a style closer to that of the Palace. Several blocks west is the **Jaganmohan**

Palace, erected for the installation ceremonies of Krishnaraja III, which were performed by Lord Curzon. The Palace partly obscures an 1861 Neo-Classical structure, now the **Chamarajendra Art Gallery**, which houses an agreeable mix of royal memorabilia and local crafts. The upper levels preserve fine murals, including illustrations of royal pastimes.

Mysore's principal commercial thoroughfare, Sayyaji Rao Road, begins at **Krishnaraja Circle**, near the northwest corner of the Palace. A statue of Krishnaraja Wodeyar sheltered by a hexagonal pavilion stands in the middle, with curving wings of offices and shops on four sides. **Chamarajendra Circle**, a short distance east on Albert Victor Road, has a marble portrait of Chamarajendra Wodeyar beneath a finely worked domed kiosk.

Nearby **Government House** (access restricted to visitors), the home of the British Residents from 1805, has a central court surrounded by a columned arcade. A curving verandah leads into the garden. The **Cathedral of St Philomena**, a short distance north, is a large French Neo-Gothic monument completed in 1959.

Imposing public monuments in the western part of the city include the **Law Courts** and **Krishnarajendra Hospital**, as well as the departments of **Manasa Gangotri**, the campus of Mysore University. The **Oriental Research Institute** houses an important library of Sanskrit manuscripts. All these buildings display an individual Neo-Classical manner, with whitewashed colonnades and arcades, curving metal-clad vaults and mansard roofs, and focal domes raised over pedimented porches. The **Folklore Museum** at Manasa Gangotri is home to one of the largest ethnographic collections in Southern India. Its holdings include toys, puppets, masks, household objects and an impressive series of wooden *bhuta* figures from Mekkekattu [17I].

The ornamental **Brindavan Gardens**, a popular picnic spot for Mysorians, are laid out below the Krishnarajasagar Dam on the Kaveri River, 16km north of the city. Formal lawns and planting line a central channel with a sequence of spectacular fountains, which are illuminated for one hour three nights a week.

B. Chamundi Hill

The road leading to the base of Chamundi Hill, 3km southeast of Mysore, passes by the **Lalitha Mahal**, designed in 1930 as a private royal guesthouse, and now a hotel. This Neo-Classical scheme has a severely whitewashed façade dominated by a dome rising on a colonnaded drum. Double-height colonnades terminating in secondary domed pavilions flank the central porch, with a pedimented balcony above. The twin banqueting rooms, one still used for dining, are roofed with stained-glass vaults.

A **Nandi Monolith** is seen beside the road about halfway up Chamundi Hill. This bull, sculpted in 1659 out of a single boulder 7.5m long and 5m high, shows a seated animal decked with ceremonial bells and garlands.

The road climbs until it arrives at the summit, from where fine views may be had of the city, some 300m below. The **Chamundeshvari Temple** here was founded by the Wodeyars in the 17C, but was remodelled in later times. It is entered through a *gopura* topped with a pyramidal tower of brightly coloured plasterwork. The doors within the gate, as inside the Temple itself, have embossed silver panels depicting different goddesses. The sanctuary accommodates a richly attired Chamundeshvari, the focal point for the annual Dasara celebrations. The nearby **Rajendra Vilas Palace**, completed in 1938, was intended as a summer retreat for the Wodeyars. It is built in a revived Rajput style, with domical pavilions on the roof.

C. Srirangapattana

Known to the British as Seringapatam, this island citadel on the Kaveri River is situated 15km northeast of Mysore, beside the Bangalore road. The name of the island is derived from the temple of Sri Ranganatha, located within the walls of the **Fort**.

> The headquarters of the Wodeyars and their usurpers, Haidar Ali and Tipu Sultan, Srirangapattana became celebrated for the battles fought here by the British forces under Lord Cornwallis and General Harris in their attempt to subdue Tipu. In 1799 Harris successfully stormed the citadel and killed Tipu, thereby confirming British supremacy in Southern India.

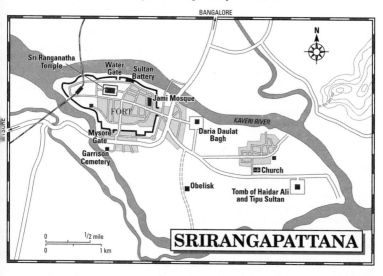

In their zeal to wipe out all vestiges of Tipu Sultan's power, the British demolished the palace and military structures within the Fort. However, they spared the **Bridges** with stone pylons across the two arms of the Kaveri River, from where fine views may be had of the bathing *ghats* and of the **Ramparts** beyond. The walls define an irregular zone at the west tip of the island. The polygonal bastions and turreted parapets surrounded by broad moats on the east and south are the work of French engineers in the service of Tipu Sultan. The **Mysore and Elephant Gates** on the south have double circular headed entries and flanking guardrooms. The vaulted dungeons of the **Sultan Battery** on the north are where Tipu had British prisoners confined in appalling conditions. Near to the **Water Gate** is a simple enclosure that marks the spot where Tipu was killed.

Religious monuments within the Fort are still in use. The **Sri Ranganatha Temple** was substantially restored in the 19C. This large complex, with two concentric enclosures, is entered on the east through an imposing *gopura* with a five-storeyed pyramidal tower. The rectangular sanctuary within accommodates a reclining image of Vishnu. The god is approached through a succession of columned halls and an open court with a gilded lamp column. A large chariot with carved wooden panels is parked outside the Temple walls. The minarets of the **Jami Mosque**, at the east end of the Fort, are visible from the Bangalore road. The Mosque, erected by Tipu Sultan in 1787, has a raised prayer chamber flanked by substantial minarets. These rise in two stages, topped by cornices with pinnacles and bulbous domes. Pierced openings on the sides ventilate the internal staircases.

Daria Daulat Bagh, 500m south of the Fort, still on Srirangapattana Island, was built in 1784 by Tipu as a pleasure resort. The main pavilion, which stands in the middle of a well-maintained garden bounded by the river, has triple arcades in the middle of each side surrounded by a verandah with lofty columns. The double-height reception rooms within are overlooked by chambers with balconies. The influence of Mughal art is seen in the carved woodwork and painted designs. The rear walls of the verandah are entirely covered with murals, restored in 1855. They depict battles, including Haidar Ali's victory over the British at Pullalur in Tamil Nadu in 1780 (west wall). The British troops surrounded by the Mysore forces form a hollow square, with Colonel Baillie seated in his palanquin in the middle. Daria Daulat Bagh is now a museum (closed Fridays) displaying maps, portraits and topographical scenes associated with Tipu.

The road from Daria Daulat Bagh continues south for 1.5km before passing by the **Church** of Abbé Dubois, a French missionary who worked here in 1799–1823. Dubois' description of Southern Indian peoples and customs remains a standard reference. Memorials to British soliders are seen in the **British Cemetery** nearby. The **Tomb of Haidar Ali and Tipu Sultan**, also known as the Gumbaz, is located 1km further south. The monument stands in a formal garden with avenues of cypresses, entered on the east through an arched gate. The Tomb consists of an imposing domed chamber surrounded by a verandah roofed with angled eaves and a parapet displaying finials and minaret-like turrets. The dome, on a petalled drum, is raised high on a square chamber; it, too, is framed by a parapet with ornamental turrets. Father and son are buried together, their bodies resting in a crypt beneath the cenotaphs. The ebony and ivory doors were donated in 1855 by Lord Dalhousie, the Viceroy of India.

D. Somnathpur

The **Keshava Temple** at this site, 35km east of Mysore, is one of the best-preserved examples of the Hoysala style. The Temple was erected in 1268 by Somanatha, a general of the Hoysala king Narasimha III. The triple-sanctuaried shrine stands in the middle of a rectangular court, approached from the east through a doorway with an open portico. An inscribed slab set up here records Somanatha's benefaction.

The shrines of the Keshava Temple are laid out on star-like plans that approx-

Keshava Temple, Somnathpur

imate circles, opening off a columned hall which extends east as a screened porch. Both shrines and hall are elevated on a plinth that repeats the complicated outlines of the plan. Carved elephants project from the deeply cut plinth, and processions of elephants, horses and riders, scrollwork, mythological scenes, *makaras* and geese cover the sanctuary basements. The walls above consist entirely of sculpted panels set at angles to each other. Most depict Vishnu in his various forms and incarnations, together with consorts. Among the finest compositions are Vishnu and Lakshmi on Garuda, Indra and Shachi on the elephant, and dancing Ganesha. The figures are richly encrusted with tassels, jewels and crowns; they stand beneath frames headed by scrollwork or over-hanging trees; labels beneath identify the artists. The panels are sheltered by angled eaves with petalled fringes. The pyramidal towers over the sanctuaries have vaulted frontal projections. Each diminishing storey has pot-like motifs and flattened roof forms; foliated arches frame miniature seated dwarfs and musicians. Dome-like roofs crown the summits.

The basement of the hall of the Keshava Temple is enlivened by friezes of temple façades and towers interspersed with amorous couples. The pierced screens above are set between columns and sheltered by angled eaves. The hall interior has magnificent columns with lathe-turned and multi-faceted shafts. The corbelled dome-like ceilings are surrounded by lobed motifs, pendant buds and looped bands. A life-size icon of Krishna playing the flute, surrounded by attendants, *gopis* and herds, is installed in the south shrine; Janardhana, a form of Vishnu, occupies the north shrine. The image in the west shrine is a modern replacement.

The Keshava Temple is not the only Hoysala monument at Somnathpur. The dilapidated **Panchalingeshvara Temple** was also built by Somanatha in 1268, but in a contrasting unadorned style. It was intended as a memorial to his family members, represented by five sanctuaries housing Shiva *lingas* arranged in a row. Each sanctuary has a small pyramidal tower with a hemispherical roof.

E. Talkad

The capital of the Gangas, the rulers of southern Karnataka in the 5C–10C, and subsequently an important centre for the Cholas and Hoysalas, Talkad is today an insignificant village on the north bank of the Kaveri River, 45km southeast of Mysore via Tirumakudal Narsipur. The site is of interest for the structures now partly buried by sand dunes from the river bed. However, only a few of these dilapidated structures, including the modest **Pataleshvara Temple**, date from Ganga times; the more interesting monuments belong to the 12C–13C. Talkad is famous today for the Panchalinga Darshana, a bathing festival that takes place at intervals ranging from 4 to 14 years.

The **Vaidyeshvara Temple**, the principal place of worship at Talkad, is laid out according to a complex plan, with numerous projections in the typical Hoysala manner. The exterior, partly reconstructed, displays angled wall slabs treated with slender pilasters. Niches with figural carvings are overhung by eaves with stone chains at the corners. The south porch has a doorway with guardians. The interior columns, with sharply defined capitals and curving brackets, carry a ceiling with a pendant lotus surrounded by a ring of figures.

The nearby **Kirti Narayana Temple**, reached by a short walk over the dunes, is less ornate. Its outer walls are supported on sharply defined basement mouldings. The pilastered projections and niches with pediments are devoid of sculptures. The pyramidal tower, partly restored, is capped with a domed roof. The adjoining hall was originally open, with balcony seating on three sides. The interior columns have slender multi-faceted and fluted shafts.

About 20km downstream from Talkad, at **Sivasamudram Falls**, the Kaveri River branches into two streams, each making a descent of about 125m in a succession of picturesque rapids. The Falls are surrounded by densely forested hills.

F. Nanjangud

This flourishing town, 23km south of Mysore, is situated on the Kabini River, a tributary of the Kaveri, surrounded by rice fields and coconut and banana groves. It is home to a three-day car festival every March. The **Nanjundeshvara Temple** was one of the major foundations of the early Wodeyars, but little can be seen of the original 17C structure other than a small gate and a fluted lamp column incorporated into later colonnades. The sanctuary was maintained during the period of Haidar Ali and Tipu Sultan, both of whom made donations to the god; a small *linga* shrine within the complex is named in Tipu's honour. The monument was substantially enlarged by Krishnaraja III, from whose time the outer enclosure walls, measuring 127m by 53m, were added, together with the principal *gopura* on the east.

G. Melukote

This religious spot occupies a rocky ridge rising abruptly 150m from the plain, 54km north of Mysore. Melukote is associated with Ramanuja, the famous Vaishnava philosopher, active in the 11C–12C, who established the temple and its associated monasteries here. These religious institutions have been supported through the centries by successive Hoysala, Vijayanagara and Wodeyar kings; they are still active today.

The road ascending Melukote Hill passes by the large **Kalyani Tank**, which is surrounded by colonnades and overlooked by a numerous small shrines and rest-houses. A short distance east is a rocky hill with two unfinished **Rock-Cut Temples** excavated into the sides, and a 2.5m high **Monolithic Ganesha**. Steps climbing to the **Narasimha Temple** at the summit arrive at a *gopura* with a lofty pyramidal tower. This leads to a terrace, from which there are sweeping views of the plain beneath. The shrine of the Temple lies beyond.

The road continues south until it reaches the **Narayana Temple**, the most important at Melukote. This stands in a rectangular enclosure, surrounded by colonnades surmounted by a fanciful plaster parapet. The main shrine is approached through a towered entrance *gopura* and two successive halls. Fine bronzes of Vishnu and Ramanuja are installed in the sanctuary and in the lesser shrines of the surrounding corridors. The most artistic part of the complex is the hall in front of the goddess shrine on the north side of the complex, added in 1458 by a Vijayanagara general. The hall columns are intricately worked with cut-out pilasters, jewelled garlands and miniature animals and figures; the mythological scenes include *Ramayana* episodes and the story of Narasimha attacking Hiranyakashipu.

A short distance south of the Narayana Temple, at the summit of a rocky rise, is a massive but **Unfinished Gate**, dating from the 15C. The passageway is of interest for the treatment of the doorway jambs, with maidens standing on *makaras* and guardians leaning on clubs. The chambers on either side have columns with sculpted divinities on the shafts; crouching figures and striding elephants are seen beneath.

The road continues to Sravana Belgola [18E], about 50km northwest.

H. Bandipur

Bandipur Wildlife Sanctuary lies 80km south of Mysore, on the road to Udhagamandalam. Covering some 874 sq km of deciduous forest, mostly teak and scrubland, on the lower slopes of the Nilgiri Hills, the Sanctuary was established by the Wodeyar ruler in 1931 and is now open to the public. It is noted for its elephants, bison, sambar, spotted deer and bears; tigers and leopards are now rare. Birdlife includes the crested hawk and the serpent eagle.

Jeeps, vans and riding elephants are available through the Forestry Department; viewing is from raised platforms near watering places. The best months to visit are May–June and September–November.

I. Nagarhole

Nagarhole Wildlife Sanctuary, another reserved forest of the former Wodeyars, lies 96km west of Mysore, via Hunsur. The Sanctuary covers 570km of gentle hills bordering Kerala on the south. The Kabini River flows through a moist and tropical deciduous forest, with an upper canopy reaching 30m. The timber here is valuable, some 5000ha being devoted to plantations of teak and rosewood.

Local species of animals are plentifully represented at Nagarhole, especially wild elephant, bison, sambar, spotted deer and wild pig; tigers and panthers are only ocasionally sighted. Birds include black woodpecker, Indian pitta, pied hornbill, whistling thrush and green imperial pigeon. Butterflies abound, also waterfowl and reptiles.

Jeeps, vans and guides may be rented from the Forestry Department.

16 · Madikeri

Madikeri, formerly called Mercara, is the headquarters of the Kodagu district (known to the British as Coorg), an area of Karnataka unsurpassed for its natural beauty. The highlands of Kodagu occupy both sides of the Western Ghats, offering delightful panoramas of verdant valleys, ravines, fast-flowing streams and lofty peaks rising to about 1700m above sea level.

Driving through Kodagu, with a stop in Madikeri, forms an attractive part of any itinerary linking Mysore [15] with Mangalore [17] or Kannur [48G] in Kerala. Other than the sights of **Madikeri** [A], for which a few hours should suffice, a half-day trip may also be made to **Talakaveri** [B], the source of the Kaveri River, which flows from here through southern Karnataka and central Tamil Nadu to the Bay of Bengal.

Kodagu is home to a community with a distinctive mode of life, still evident in local customs, festivals, dress and language. Coffee is the chief produce, with about one-third of all plantations in Southern India being located here. The district is also celebrated for its oranges, as well as for its crops of cardamom and pepper.

(See location map, p 211.)

■ **Transport**. No trains run through Kodagu, but regular bus services link Madikeri with Mysore, 96km east, and Mangalore, 122km northwest. Local buses within Kodagu connect Madikeri with Talakaveri.

■ **Accommodation**. The *Chitra Lodge* (☎ 27311) and *Hotel Mayura Valley View* (☎ 26387) are the best of the small range of hotels available in Madikeri (STD code 08272).

■ **Tourist Information**. The KSTDC bureau is located in the PWD Travellers Bungalow (☎ 26580).

History

In 1681 Madikeri became the headquarters of a line of local chiefs, who successfully resisted the domination of the Nayakas of Ikkeri [19C] and the Wodeyars of Mysore. Madikeri was overrun by Haidar Ali in 1773 and subsequently occupied by Tipu Sultan. In 1790 Virarajendra, the local ruler, allied himself with the British against Tipu who, according to a treaty of 1792, was excluded from Kodagu. Later figures, such as Lingarajendra, remained loyal to the British. Even so, Kodagu was annexed by the British in 1834, but remained independent until its absorption into the state of Karnataka.

A. Madikeri

Madikeri is a delightfully situated town dominated by a **Fort** which crowns a small hill. This is shielded by an irregular hexagon of walls with bastions at each angle, surrounded by a ditch. The circuitous entrance on the east is guarded by three successive gates. The **Palace** inside the fort, begun in 1812, was for a time the residence of the Kodagu rulers; it now houses Government Offices. Its sombre whitewashed façade has double arcades capped with a sloping tiled roof. The clock tower at one corner was added in 1933. There is a small court in the middle. A temple of Virabhadra nearby was removed in 1855 to make way for **St Mark's Church**, which is built in a plain Neo-Gothic style, with a prominent spire.

The **Omkareshvara Temple**, situated in a hollow east of the Fort, was established by Lingarajendra in 1820. The main shrine is capped with a three-quarters dome framed by four turrets. A gateway with a tiled roof in front leads down to a tank with a small pavilion in the middle, reached by a causeway.

Of greater architectural interest are the **Tombs of Virarajendra and Lingarajendra**, which stand in a compound enclosed by embankments on a high spot north of the city. Modelled on the mausoleum of Haidar Ali and Tipu Sultan at Srirangapattana [15C], they are identical structures, with bulbous domes raised on octagonal drums. The main chambers beneath have plain walls, with Neo-Classical arched openings overhung by angled eaves. The corner finials with square and octagonal sections are crowned by miniature domes.

Raja's Seat, at the western edge of Madikeri, is a small pavilion commanding a breathtaking view of the valley, through which the road descends to Mangalore.

B. Talakaveri

This pilgrimage spot, about 35km southwest of Madikeri via Bhagamandale, is situated on the wooded slopes of Brahmagiri, a peak rising 1355m above sea level. Two small shrines, dedicated to Ishvara and Ganapati, stand here, with two square tanks between them. The smaller tank is particularly sacred, since its contents are identified with the Kaveri River. An upsurge in the water level, signifying the annual rebirth of the river, is observed during the Tula Shankaramana festival in October, an event that attracts crowds of worshippers.

17 · Mangalore

A tour of Kanara, as the narrow coastal strip of Karnataka is known, offers visitors one of the richest and most attractive landscapes in Southern India. The architecture is unique in this region; so, too, are the *bhuta* ceremonies and Yakshagana theatre performances.

While a few hours are probably sufficient to view the sights of **Mangalore** [A], the largest city in Kanara, two or three days will have to be set aside to reach all of the temple sites described here, such as **Udupi** [B], **Mudabidri** [C], **Karkala** [D], **Venoor** [E], **Vittal** [F] and **Dharmasthala** [G], many with Jain monuments. The village of **Mekkekattu** [I] is of interest for its animistic *bhuta* cult.

Towns on NH17, the coastal highway connecting Goa with Kerala, include **Barkur** [H], **Bhatkal** [K] and **Gokarna** [L], also of interest for their shrines. The pilgrimage sanctuary at **Kollur** [J] is remotely sited in the wooded foothills of the Western Ghats.

■ **Transport**. Flights from the airport situated halfway between Mangalore and Udupi, 58km distant, offer connections with Bombay [1] and Bangalore [14]. Trains link Mangalore directly with Bangalore, 363km east, and Kozhikode [48], 239km south. The Konkan Railway will eventually link Udupi and

Mangalore with Panaji [11] and Kozhikode. Buses connect Mangalore and Udupi with most centres in southern Karnataka, the trip from Bangalore providing an opportunity for passing through Madikeri [16]; Hassan [18] is 142km east on NH48. All the sites described here can be reached by local bus from Manglaore or Udupi.

■ **Accommodation**. Mangalore (STD code 0824) is a thriving port, and many hotels here cater for businessmen. The *Hotel Poonja International* (☎ 440171) and *Hotel Moti Mahal* (☎ 441411) offer comfortable accommodation in the middle of the city. Some tourists may prefer to relax at the *Summer Sands Beach Resort* (☎ 467690) at **Ullal**, 12km south. **Udupi** (STD code 08252) also has acceptable places to stay, the *Kediyoor Hotel* (☎ 22381) being recommended.

For visitors who wish travel up the coast from Mangalore to Goa, it is possible to break the journey at the *Murdeshwar Temple Guesthouse* (☎ 08385 8517), spectacularly sited on an island reached by a causeway, just off NH17, 18km north of **Bhatkal**.

■ **Tourist information**. The KSTDC office is located at the *Hotel Mayura Netravathi*, Nadri Hills (☎ 411192).

A. Mangalore

Attractively located on the estuary of the Netravati and Gurpur Rivers, Mangalore is surrounded by undulating terrain cloaked in groves of palms, with distant views of the Arabian Sea. It is today a busy commercial centre, trading in timber, roof tiles and groundnuts, with a new port situated to the north.

The cosmopolitan mix of Mangalore's population was observed as early as 1342 by the North African traveller, Ibn Batutta, who commented on the presence of Persians and Yemenis. These merchants were attracted by the crops of rice and pepper for which Kanara was famous, and conducted their trade with both Hindus and Jains. At this time Mangalore was one of the main ports of Kanara, coming under the sway of the emperors of Vijayanagara [20B–C]. In 1526 and 1547 the port was raided by the Portuguese, who levied tribute on the Vijayanagara governors. However, it was not until 1670 that the Portuguese made a treaty with the Nayakas of Ikkeri [19C] permitting them to build a factory here. The Nayakas were displaced in 1763 by Haidar Ali, who made Mangalore his naval headquarters. The city was taken from Tipu Sultan, his successor, by the British in 1784, after which it was absorbed into the Madras Presidency.

Virtually the only vestige of the fortifications with which the city was once provided is **Sultan's Battery**, a watchtower attributed to Tipu. The **Lighthouse** on top of a hill in the north part of the city is modern. Numerous churches dot the city. The **Jesuit College of St Aloysius**, completed in 1885 in the Italianate style, has extensive murals. **St Joseph's Theological Seminary**, built in 1879, has a pair of weathered towers. The **Church of the Most Holy Rosary**, recently renovated, is the only one with a dome. Muslim monuments include the **Jami Mosque of Zinad Baksh**, remodelled by Tipu at the end of the 18C. The interior wooden columns and *mimbar* (stepped pulpit) are delicately carved.

British remains are mostly confined to the graves and obelisks in the cemetery adjoining the **Church of St Paul**. Erected in 1843, this simple structure is dominated by a triple-stage tower.

The **Government Museum**, in the northern part of the city, has a small collection of antiquities, including a remarkable bronze bell, complete with a miniature Lakshmi shrine, *yalis* and devotee. There are also wooden carvings of divinites, such as Bhairava and Hanuman, as well as *bhuta* figures from Mekkekattu. Stone sculptures discovered at Barkur date back to the 13C; later sculptures portray local warriors.

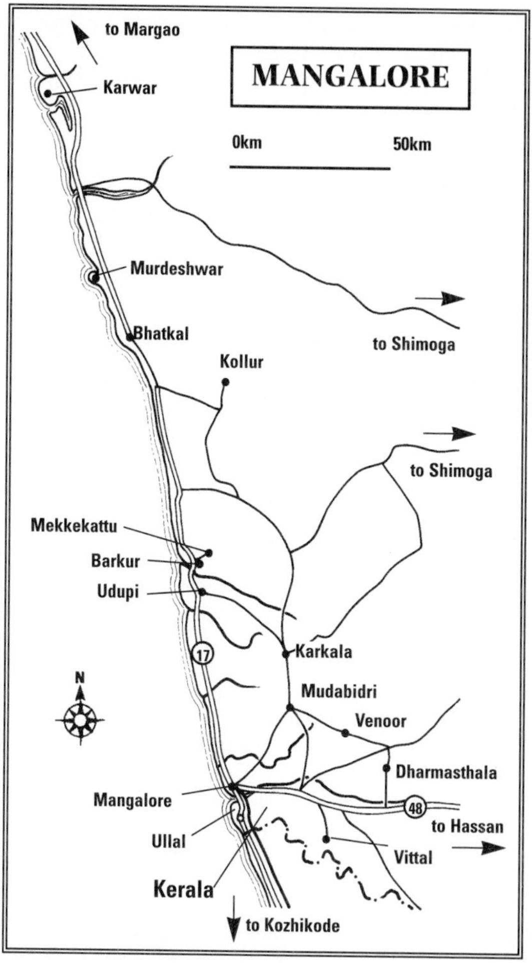

The **Manjunatha Temple**, 3km north of the centre of

MANGALORE

0km   50km

to Margao
Karwar
Murdeshwar
Bhatkal
Kollur
Mekkekattu
Barkur
Udupi
Karkala
Mudabidri
Venoor
Dharmasthala
Mangalore
Ullal
Vittal
Kerala
N
17
48
to Shimoga
to Shimoga
to Hassan
to Kozhikode

Mangalore, stands at the foot of Kadri Hill, a wooded rise with caverns reputedly inhabited by local *yogis*. The Temple mostly dates from the Nayaka period, though its history is much earlier, as it is associated with Hindu saints such as Matsyendranath and Gokarnath. The rites focus on the Shiva *linga* in the sanctuary, while at the same time paying respect to the Buddhist deities installed in the verandah. The Temple is contained within a rectangular compound, entered on the east through a gateway in front of which is a tall lamp column. Steps from here ascend to sacred spots on the hillside. The Manjunatha shrine, a modest square chamber, is roofed with a pyramidal tower.

The concrete screens of the surrounding verandah, replacements of timber originals, are overhung by angled eaves and projecting lotus corbels. The three Buddhist images kept here are among the largest such bronzes in Southern India. They are assigned to the 10C–11C, and were probably cast in the Tamil zone before being shipped to Mangalore. The image of Lokeshvara, 1.6m high, is dated 968. This three-faced figure with six arms is seated within an elaborate frame, with diminutive guardians at either side. The exceptional quality of Manjushri, another bronze, is evident in the delicately modelled face and headdress.

B. Udupi

The religious significance of this town, 50km north of Mangalore on NH17, is enhanced by the fact that this was the birthplace of Madhava, a famous 12C Vaishnava teacher. The urban focus of Udupi is an open **Square** surrounded by temples and *mathas* with ornate wooden verandahs. The latter serve as head-quarters for eight different monastic orders.

The **Krishna Temple**, on the north side of the Square, supposedly founded by Madhava, is a celebrated place of pilgrimage, especially during the Pargaya festival in January. The core sanctuary has a gilded metal screen through which Krishna holding the spear can be viewed. This image is said to have been mirac-ulously rescued from a ship wrecked on the coast nearby. The Temple is built in traditional style, with a wooden hall and sloping roofs clad in copper sheets; it faces east towards a large tank. Chariots with three-quarter spherical tops created from brightly coloured ribbons tied to bamboo frameworks are parked outside the entrance to the Temple.

The **Chandramauleshvara Temple**, dedicated to Shiva, stands in the middle of the Square, surrounded by shops that crowd up to its compound walls. The small square sanctuary within the compound has a pyramidal roof divided into two tiers with metal and terracotta tiles, topped with a brass pot finial. Similar materials roof the columned hall in front. The west side of the square is occupied by the **Ananteshvara Temple**, consecrated to Vishnu. Its apsidal-ended sanctuary and adjoining columned hall are surrounded by a walled passageway, the latter covered with sloping stone slabs. The roofs over the sanc-tuary and hall are sheathed in copper. The frontal gable has wooden struts with hanging hands and a monster mask at the apex. The rear panel, also of wood, shows a *linga* flanked by elephants, guardians, peacocks and lotuses. A stone altar with a finely sculpted base is located immediately outside the east entrance to the Temple.

Manipal, 3km east of Udupi, is a progressive industrial and educational centre, famous for its Medical College. The **House of Vijayanath Shennoy** is a small museum displaying household objects in a typical architectural setting.

C. Mudabidri

This town, 35km northeast of Mangalore, is situated in the midst of wooded hills with distant views of the Western Ghats. That this was a Jain centre of some importance is indicated by the many temples, known as *bastis*, interspersed with monasteries, or *mathas*. Many of these shrines and institutions were sponsored by local Chauta chiefs and their families in the 15C–16C.

The largest and most elaborate monument at Mudabidri is the **Chandranatha *Basti*** of 1429. This stands in a compound at the west end of the main street of the town, entered through an imposing entrance portico. The main unit consists of a rectangle of walls containing the sanctuary, and two interconnecting columned halls. The columned interior is massive, with doorways flanked by guardian figures and pot-and-foliage motifs. Several fine bronzes of Jinas in ornate frames are on display in the inner hall. The surrounding open verandah has full-height columns carrying the the stone tiled overhang. Two additional sloping roofs above the sanctuary are coated with copper tiles on angled wooden brackets. The roof over the frontal hall has been altered, but its

Chandranantha Basti, Mudabidri

triangular gable is intact; it shows guardian figures and female attendants holding flowers beneath a Jina flanked by elephants. The struts are fashioned as hanging hands, and there is a brass monster mask at the apex.

The detached **Hall** in front of the Chandranatha *Basti*, an addition of 1452, is notable for its magnificently carved columns, which display a variety of designs with miniature figures, knotted patterns and lotus motifs. The central bay is roofed with an ornate lotus medallion ceiling. A 16.5m high lamp column with animals and figures on the double capital stands freely in front.

The **Jain *Matha***, near the entrance to the Chandranatha Basti, is home to an important collection of manuscripts (permission required to visit). Other temples scattered throughout the town present smaller but comparable schemes to the Chandranatha. The **Settara** and **Shantinatha** *Bastis* are laid out according to the standard rectangular plan, with surrounding verandahs. Each Temple has an additional subshrine to accommodate images of the 24 Tirthankaras arranged on a very long stone pedestal. Exactly this type of Tirthankara shrine forms the main unit of the **Derama Setti *Basti***, which has a long sanctuary approached through a broad columned hall. The temple is roofed with double tiers of sloping stone slabs with a flat area in the middle, with log-like stone strips covering the joints.

The **Guru *Basti***, almost as large as the Chandranatha *Basti*, presents the standard rectangular scheme with three halls leading to the main sanctuary, where a 2m high image of Parshvanatha is under veneration. The columns in the outer hall are finely worked, as are those in the entrance structure. The latter has sloping stone tiers on four sides of a raised flat roof marked by a battlemented parapet. A lofty lamp column stands outside the temple compound on the other side of the street. The **Kote** and **Vikrama Setti *Bastis***, dedicated to Neminatha and Adinatha respectively, present simpler and smaller schemes, with long entrance structures.

The remains of the **Chauta Palace** are located on the western fringe of Mudabidri. The dilapidated apartments are of interest for the carved wooden doorways and columns showing mythological scenes, attendant figures, animals, birds and foliation. **Jain Memorials** stand at the east end of the town.

These curious laterite structures present undecorated stone pyramids with three, five and even seven diminishing tiers of mouldings. The **Badagu *Basti*** is situated just north of Mudabidri, on the road to Karkala. The temple, which overlooks an idyllic landscape, is a simple rectangular building with a sloping roof. The frontal wooden gable has a panel showing a seated Jina.

D. Karkala

This town is situated 18km north of Mudabidri, 35km southeast of Udupi, from where it may also be approached. Visitors arriving in Kanara from the Malnad region may descend the Ghats by a road leading directly from Sringeri [19G], 32km northeast.

Karkala is an important centre of Jainism in Kanara, most of the older temples being *bastis* connected with the local Bhairavasa rulers. The most interesting monuments are situated outside the town. About 1km east is a granite outcrop, on top of which is the famous **Gommateshvara Monolith**, reached by a flight of rock-cut steps. The 13m high image was completed in 1432, in obvious imitation of the earlier and larger example at Sravana Belgola [18E]. It shows a naked figure, the face staring straight ahead with a serene expression, the arms hanging limp to the sides. The free-standing image is surrounded by a low railing. A column set up outside the enclosure is topped with a seated figure of Brahma.

The **Chaturmukha *Basti***, at the base of the hill, dates from 1587 and is strictly symmetrical in layout. The sanctuary in the middle of the columned hall has doorways on four sides, through each of which three stone images may be viewed; in this way, a set of 12 Tirthankaras receive worship. The surrounding verandah has projecting porches in the middle of four sides. The *Basti* is roofed with sloping stone slabs, the overhang being supported on the outer colonnade. Log-like strips cover the joints of the flat slabs on top. The columns are mostly unadorned, except for those near to the doorways, which have multi-faceted shafts and fluted capitals.

The **Neminatha *Basti*** is situated at the foot of a densely wooded hill about 1km west of the Gommateshvara Monolith. The sanctuary and double halls of this temple are surrounded by a rectangle of walls sheltered by a verandah. The subshrines are aligned with an open hall in front. The column that stands east of the complex is the finest at Karkala. A triple set of basement mouldings supports a fluted column adorned with bands. An ornate double capital carries a diminutive pavilion.

The **Anantapadmanabha Temple**, founded in about 1567, is located at the east end of Karkala's main street. This shrine is dedicated to Vishnu, with a reclining image of the god placed inside a square sanctuary, surrounded by a double passageway. The shrine doorway is surrounded by delicate friezes of lotus ornament and miniature warriors. The open hall in front is raised on a basement enlivened with frieze of elephants, extended as seating on three sides. The columns here have fluted shafts and pronounced double capitals. The roof above has two sloping tiers of stone slabs, with a frontal gable imitating timberwork. The pyramidal roof over the shrine is sheathed in copper tiles and has a pot finial. The **Venkataramana Temple**, located in the same street, is more popular. It has been much renovated in recent years.

E. Venoor

Another side trip from Mudabidri is to the small settlement of Venoor, 15km east, a total of 80km from Mangalore. This Jain centre was headquarters of the local Ajila chiefs, who were responsible for commissioning the **Gommate-shvara Monolith** in 1604. Similar to but not quite as as high as the Monolith at Karkala, this example also stands in a compound, outside which is a column with a seated icon of Brahma on top. The nearby **Parshvanatha *Basti***, a contemporary structure, follows the standard rectangular layout already noted for temples at Mudabidri.

The **Kalli *Basti***, the largest at Venoor, is dedicated to Shantinatha. This 17C temple presents an imposing colonnade carrying the overhang of the stone roof. Interior steps lead to an upper chamber provided with its own sloping roof and capping pavilion. The long structure to one side enshrines a line of 24 Tirthankara images. Beyond the entrance structure is a lofty column standing on a triple basement. Its fluted shaft with decorated bands carries an ornate double capital with cut-out animals at the corners. The miniature pavilion on top is complete with a stone finial.

F. Vittal

This town is reached from Mangalore by continuing a short distance beyond Puttur, 50km to the east. The **Panchalingeshvara Temple** is built in a style current in southern Kanara and northern Kerala. The building is apsidal in plan, with a sanctuary surrounded by double passageways approached through twin halls preceded by a porch. The Temple is entirely roofed with copper tiles arranged in three sloping tiers carried on wooden struts. The tiers wrap around the rear of the sanctuary, giving the building a heavy, almost ship-like appearance. The roof overhang is carried on columns partly concealed by wooden screens. An elaborate gable rises over the porch. The building stands in the middle of a spacious rectangular compound surrounded by a colonnade. An open pavilion sheltering a large Nandi image, an altar and flag column stand in front (west), with minor shrines for Ganapati and Durga nearby to the south.

G. Dharmasthala

This attractive site, surrounded by forested hills, rice fields and areca (palm) plantations, is located 75km east of Mangalore, a short distance from the Netravati River, a bathing centre for pilgrims. Dharmasthala is linked with the influential Heggede family, followers of Jainism and patrons of the **Manjunatha Temple**, in which a *linga* was installed in 1780; curiously, the priests of the sanctuary are Madhava Vaishnavas. The sponsorship of the Heggedes continues to this day, as can be seen in the finely executed **Gommateshvara Monolith**, set up here in 1973.

The small but interesting **Manjusha Museum** is located opposite the entrance to the Temple. All manner of religious objects are on display here, including carved and painted panels, bronze sculptures and bells. There is even a selection of ethnographic household objects. Two temple chariots covered in wooden figures stand in front.

H. Barkur

This town, just off NH17, 74km north of Udupi, was one of the richest ports of Kanara in the 15C–16C. However, the river on which Barkur was situated silted up, and the modern port is now situated 4km west. The town's past prosperity is reflected in the many religious monuments that dot the town. The largest, the **Panchalingeshvara Temple**, is situated beside a tank at the south end of Barkur. It is approached through an entrance structure with projecting porticos on two levels; hero stones are set up beside the steps. The inner compound has two east-facing *linga* shrines, one apsidal-ended (south), the other rectangular (north), both with Nandi pavilions in front. Though extensively renovated, the sloping terracotta roofs are original features. The roof wraps around the curving end of the sanctuary in the south shrine. Pilastered niches with different pediments and false doors can be made out on the outer walls of the north shrine.

The **Ganapati Temple**, in the northern part of Barkur, also consists of two east-facing shrines within a compound. Consecrated to Shiva and Ganapati, these rectangular structures are of almost equal size. The Shiva shrine has two storeys with shallow niches and false doors. Both levels are overhung by sloping tiles. A large entrance structure running the full width of the compound has a continuous sloping stone roof. The interior columns are elaborately carved with deities, dancers, musicians, creepers and buds. The rear walls are enlivened with modern murals. A short distance further north, on the outskirts of the town, is an **Earthern Fort**, dating from the 17C Nayaka era. It is laid out as a square, with an entrance on the east.

Other monuments in Barkur include the simpler **Someshvara** and **Somanatheshvara Temples**, both with focal sanctuaries in the middle of small compounds. The Someshvara Temple has deities carved on the wooden brackets carrying the angled upper roof. The frontal gable is ornate, with an embossed metal mask at the apex. The Somanatheshvara Temple is the only example at Barkur to preserve stone carvings of guardians beside the doorway.

I. Mekkekattu

This small settlement, 8km north of Barkur, is of interest for the **Nandikeshvara Temple**, dedicated to the *bhuta*, or spirit, cult. This shrine was totally renovated in the 1960s, with the result that the original wooden sculptures were dispersed, some to the Folklore Museum in Mysore [15A]. The new set of some 170 *bhuta* images comprises the largest and most complete set in Kanara. They are carved out of the wood of the jack-fruit tree and are painted in bright red, with boldly modelled faces outlined in white and black. The two shrines at Mekkakattu are arranged one above the other: the lower shrine accommodates a winged bull, Nandikeshvara, surrounded by warriors; the upper shrine displays Nandikeshvara's consort on the bull, with female attendants. A seated magician accompanied by a monkey is placed outside the main entrance. A shed to one side is crowded with large and fierce guardians holding swords, mounted warriors, female attendants, bulls and even a tiger. Donor figures, also in brightly painted wood, occupy a subsidiary shrine.

J. Kollur

This pilgrimage temple, 106km north of Mangalore via the port of Kundapura on NH17, is picturesquely situated at the foot of the Western Ghats, on a road that climbs through the forest to Shimoga [19A]. Though the **Mukambika Temple** here has a long history, the present building was erected in 1616 by Venkatappa, one of the Ikkeri Nayakas. The shrine is dedicated to the goddess Mukambika, who takes the form of a *jyotirlinga* incorporating aspects of Shiva and Shakti. The small sanctuary is topped by a pyramidal tower with an arch-shaped frontal projection; this is surmounted by a square roof sheathed in gilded copper. The building stands in a small compound surrounded by subsidiary structures with arched openings, angled overhangs and battlemented parapets. *Yalis* adorn columns either side of the entrance portico on the east.

K. Bhatkal

This town is located on NH17, 155km north of Mangalore. Bhatkal is an important port with a large Muslim population; even so, it is well provided with Jain and Hindu monuments dating from the 16C–17C. Two important Jain temples face onto the main street of the town. The **Chandranatheshvara** *Basti* consists of three east-facing shrines (with intermediate walls missing) adjoining a pair of long halls. The surrounding verandah has peripheral supports carrying a double-tiered sloping stone roof. An additional square hall in front has stone screens with circular and leaf-like perforations between peripheral supports with capitals and brackets. The screens are overhung by angled eaves. The double-storeyed entrance structure on the east has chambers on either side of a central passageway. Sloping roofs shelter both storeys. The **Parshvanatha** *Basti* is located a short distance south, set back slightly from the street. Its location is marked by a tall lamp column that stands outside the temple compound. It is similar in layout to the schemes already noticed at Mudabidri.

Bhatkal also has several interesting Hindu shrines. The 17C **Choleshvara Temple** within the town is a diminutive square structure with intricately pilasters standing in pots, as well as niches framing flattish carvings of divinities. The pyramidal tower is crowned with a square roof. The treatment is ornate throughout. The **Raghunatha Temple** resembles the Choleshvara Temple, except that its interior is more ornate, with guardian figures on either side of the shrine doorway.

The next group of monuments to be described lies on the other side of NH17, 2km east of the centre of Bhatkal. The most interesting is the **Khetapai Narayana Temple**, a shrine consecrated to Vishnu, named after a local chief who erected it in 1540. This small, but finely finished, building consists of a sanctuary and hall enclosed in a rectangle of stone screens carved to imitate wood. The screens are raised on a basement with reliefs illustrating *Ramayana* episodes and other mythological topics. The supports and intermediate pilasters are carved with figures and decorative motifs. Cut-out *yali* balustrades with rolled ends mark the main entrance on the west. The doorway is flanked by guardian figures carved in full relief; the lintel is partly concealed by a beam with part-circular cuts, decorated with relief carvings. Similar beams surmount the slatted screens. The sloping stone roof rises steeply on four sides, the upper part being flat with log-like strips.

The interior of the Temple has squat columns with lathe-turned shafts. The ceiling over the central bay has a central lotus panel with Dikpalas in the corners. The Temple stands in the middle of a small compound, outside which is a lofty column. Carvings of a donor figure, Agni, Varuna and Kubera adorn the base. An adjacent small structure has a sanctuary and open hall, both with peripheral supports carrying pyramidal roofs with angled stone slabs.

The **Santappa Nayaka Tirumala Temple**, a short distance south of the Khetapai Narayana Temple, resembles it in overall layout. The outer screens are, however, supported on blocks rather than a sculpted basement. The beam running across the outer doorway has three lobes, with a foliated mask in the middle and riders on monsters at either side. The interior shrine doorway is flanked by images of Hanuman and Balakrishna (left), and Garuda and Krishna holding up Govardhana (right). *Ramayana* friezes cover the beams supporting the central ceiling.

L. Gokarna

This town lies 62km north of Bhatkal on NH17, with a deviation of 9km to the coast. From here it is 115km north via Karwar to Margao [13A]. Gokarna owes much of its charm to the traditional brick houses with tiled roofs facing onto narrow streets that run inland from a magnificent beach.

The principal historical feature is the **Mahabaleshvara Temple**, an ancient foundation destroyed by the Portuguese in 1714 and subsequently rebuilt. The Temple stands in a high walled compound, entered on the west from the direction of the ocean. The pilastered walls with battlemented parapets and the octagonal domed tower over the sanctuary reflect the influence of Maratha practice. Triple porches give access to a spacious hall, the floor of which is engraved with a giant tortoise. A doorway decorated with embossed brass sheets frames the small stone *linga*, the principal object of devotion. This is mostly concealed by a brass face mask that sits on serpent coils and is sheltered by serpent hoods.

18 · Hassan

A market town of no historical interest, Hassan makes a convenient base from which to visit sites associated with the Gangas and Hoysalas, rulers of central Karnataka in the 9C–13C. The intricately worked temples at **Belur** [A] and **Halebid** [B], the finest of the Hoysala series, may be combined in a half-day trip. The lesser monuments at **Dodda Gaddavahalli** [C], **Arsikere** [D] and **Aralaguppe** [E] will require additional time. Another half-day excursion from Hassan is to the Jain sites of **Sravana Belgola** [F] and **Kambadahalli** [G]. The barefooted climb to the summit of the hill at Sravana Belgola is best made in the early morning.

■ **Transport**. Hassan is most conveniently reached by road from Bangalore [14], 174km east, partly on NH48, also from Mangalore [17], almost the same distance west along the same highway. It is also approached by road from Mysore [15], 112km south. Shimoga [19] lies 157km north. Buses reach all the destinations included here.

■ **Accommodation**. The *Hotel Hassan Ashok* (☎ 68731) is the best in Hassan (STD code 08172), but acceptable alternatives like the *Hotel Amblee Palika* (☎ 66307) also exist. It is also possible to stay at **Belur** (STD code 08177) in the *Hotel Mayura Velapuri* (☎ 22209) and other smaller places, such as the *Sri Gayatri Bhavan* (☎ 22255). The KSTDC maintains tourist cottages at **Halebid**. Simple accommodation for pilgrims is available at **Sravana Belgola**.

■ **Tourist Information**. The KSTDC maintains a tourist bureau at Vartha Bhavan, B.M. Road (☎ 68862).

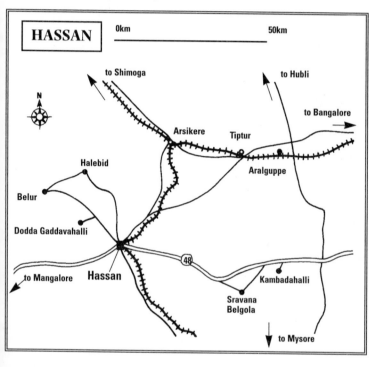

A. Belur

This small but lively town, 39km north of Hassan, is celebrated for the **Chennakeshava Temple**, an outstanding example of Hoysala architecture and art, erected in 1117 as a victory monument by Vishnuvardhana, the Hoysala king.

The Temple complex is entered through a 16C Vijayanagara-styled *gopura* that dominates the main street of the town. The Temple, built entirely in grey-green schist, consists of a sanctuary with minor shrines on three sides and a columned hall partly open as a porch in front. Both the sanctuary and hall are raised on a terrace that repeats the complicated star-shaped plan of the building. The hall is approached by double flights of steps on three sides, which are flanked by model shrines with pyramidal towers. The doorways are headed by arches framed by pairs of *makaras* with profusely foliated tails sitting on pilasters. Icons of Vishnu, Narasimha or Varaha, each with Garuda beneath, are carved on the lintels.

The porch is enclosed by (later) pierced stone screens with geometric designs incorporating miniature figures. One composition (east of the main doorway) shows Vishnuvardhana, the royal patron of the monument, seated with ministers, courtly women and attendants. The friezes of elephants, meandering lotus stalks, garlands, couples and musicians on the walls beneath are carved with remarkable precision; angled brackets sculpted as female musicians are sheltered by the overhanging eaves. These masterpieces of Hoysala art depict sensually modelled dancing maidens beneath intricately worked trees and foliage. The figures appear as a huntress and dressing (north), plaiting hair, gazing into a mirror and holding a parrot (east). Label inscriptions identify the various artists. The sanctuary walls are raised on carved rows of elephants, lions and horses. The panels with elaborate pediments depict incarnations of Vishnu seated with consorts. No tower has been preserved.

The interior of the Chennakeshava Temple is dominated by polished multi-faceted and lathe-turned columns. The central supports have brackets fashioned as gracefully posed female attendants standing in ornate frames carved on the shafts. The ceilings above have ornate domes with concentric corbelled rings decorated with scrollwork and lotus buds. Large guardian figures with richly jewelled costumes dominate the sanctuary doorway. The lintel shows Vishnu and Lakshmi seated within an arch, flanked by *makaras*.

The 12C **Ammanavara Temple** occupies the northwest corner of the Chennakeshava enclosure. Sculpted panels set into the walls show maidens and divinities beneath trees. Additional carvings are seen in the **Kappe Chennigaraya Temple** to the south. A stepped tank with minor shrines is found in the northeast corner of the complex.

B. Halebid

This site, 14km east of Belur, or 42km north of Hassan by another route, is identified with Dorasamudra, the Hoysala capital.

> The first great ruler of Dorasamudra, Vishnuvardhana (1108–41) was responsible for expanding the Hoysala kingdom. He subdued the Late Chalukyas of Basavakalyana [25D] to the north, and secured the south against the Pandyas of Madurai [44A]. The reigns of Ballala II and Narasimha, which spanned 1173–1235, were marked by a series of military triumphs which established the Hoysalas as the most powerful dynasty of Southern India. The territories under their control encompassed most of Karnataka and even substantial parts of the Tamil lands. The last of the great Dorasamudra monarchs, Narasimha III and Ballala III, spent much of their reigns battling against the Yadavas of Devagiri, later renamed Daulatabad [5C]. Both the Hoysalas and Yadavas succumbed to the Delhi invaders at the beginning of the 14C.

The overgrown and crumbling **Ramparts** of the Hoysala capital at Halebid enclose an approximate half circle almost 4km across. The granite walls have gateways with bent entrances interspersed with square bastions. The Ramparts on the east overlook **Dorasamudra**, a vast tank after which the capital was

named. Several monuments stand inside the walls, including the remains of a palace, yet to be excavated.

The double-shrined **Hoysaleshvara Temple**, begun in 1121, but not completed until after the middle of the 12C, represents the climax of the Hoysala achievement. Like the monument at Belur, it is built entirely in grey-green schist. Each shrine consists of a central sanctuary, with three subsidiary chambers opening off a columned hall laid out on a stepped plan. The halls, which are linked to form a spacious interior, are partly open, with porches and balcony seating at the peripheries. In front (east) of each hall is a detached pavilion sheltering a large Nandi image. The animals, adorned with bells and jewels, face towards the Shiva *lingas* inside the sanctuaries. Both shrines and pavilions are raised on a high plinth that repeats the complicated outlines of the building itself. The basement is enlivened with friezes of elephants, lions, horses, scrollwork, epic scenes, *makaras* and geese with foliated tails. The precision of the carving and the vitality of the compositions are unsurpassed. Scenes from the *Ramayana* and *Mahabharata* (west side) include Rama killing the golden deer, Rama and Sita with the monkeys, and Bhishma dying on a bed of arrows. Krishna with *gopis* or fighting demons is seen on the east. These epic subjects are interspersed with courtly scenes, hunting expeditions and military exploits.

Divinities in animated poses cover the outer walls of the Hoysaleshvara Temple. The figures wear richly decorated costumes and headdresses, and stand beneath luxuriant scrollwork or foliage. Among the finest panels are Shiva dancing inside the flayed skin of the elephant demon, Krishna holding up Govardhana to protect the herds, and the same deity playing the flute (south side); Shiva dancing on the dwarf, and Ravana shaking the mountain (north side). The hall doorways are approached by flights of steps flanked by miniature shrines with pyramidal towers; these suggest the forms of the superstructures over the main shrines, which were never completed. Swaying guardians encrusted with jewels and tassels are positioned either side of the doorways. The lintels are intricately fashioned with dancing icons of Shiva in foliated frames terminating in *makaras*. Pierced stone screens with geometric designs set between peripheral columns are overhung by projecting eaves. The brackets on lathe-turned columns are fashioned as three-dimensional dancing maidens and musicians.

The corbelled ceilings within the Temple incorporate friezes of miniature figures, such as dancing Shiva surrounded by the Dikpalas and musicians. Guardians with ornate costumes and headdresses are positioned beside the sanctuary doorways.

The attractively landscaped grounds of the Hoysaleshvara Temple serve as an open-air **Archaeological Museum**. Among the many 12C–13C sculptures gathered here is a large image of seated Ganesha and a fine Nandi. The foundations of two recently cleared temples are seen to the west.

A road running south for about 500m leads to the group of **Jain *Bastis***. The three 12C temples here present exteriors with sharply moulded pilasters, preceded by columned halls. The only carvings are striding elephants beside the steps and an enlarged figure of Parshvanatha in the central shrine. The hall ceilings present three rotating octagons filled with scrollwork, with a central panel of Krishna. The road continues for another 300m to the 13C **Kedareshvara Temple.** This star-shaped shrine has a moulded basement and a set of carved panels. Pierced stone screens illuminate the hall interior.

C. Dodda Gaddavahalli

This small village is reached after turning west off the Belur road, 10km north of Hassan. The **Lakshmidevi Temple** of 1113, an early example of the Hoysala style, stands in the middle of a large walled court. It consists of a central hall, off which open four shrines, dedicated to Kali (north), Mahalakshmi (east), Bhairava (south) and a Shiva *linga* (west). The shrine walls have shallow niches headed by pediments representing different temple towers. The two-storeyed superstructure over the Bhairava shrine presents a sequence of intricately carved elements arranged in pyramidal fashion and capped with a multi-faceted square roof. The other three shrines have pyramidal arrangements of horizontal mouldings with similarly shaped roofs. Prancing *yalis* are positioned on the frontal projections of the towers. The doorway to the Kali sanctuary is protected by extraordinary skeletal figures displaying daggers and skulls. The goddess within is an imposing seated figure brandishing weapons.

D. Arsikere

The 13C **Shiva Temple** at this town, 44km north of Hassan, is the most remarkable example of the star-like scheme perfected by Hoysala architects. The outer walls of the sanctuary present numerous angled projections approximating a circle. These angles are repeated in the overhanging eaves and roof elements that rise in pyramidal fashion above, giving the tower a clustered, three-dimensional appearance. The adjoining hall, partly open on the east, has angled buttresses concealing the rectangular interior space. A platform leads to an open pavilion with a central octagon surrounded by 12 additional supports, also laid out on a complicated star-shaped plan. The polished lathe-turned shaft columns support a dome-like lotus ceiling. The adjacent **Vira Ballaleshvara Temple**, a slightly earlier structure, is of lesser interest.

E. Aralaguppe

This insignificant village, 52km northeast of Hassan via Tiptur, is of interest for its monuments, dating from the Nolamba and Hoysala periods.

The 9C **Kalleshvara Temple** is a modest structure, unadorned on the exterior except for pilastered walls and perforated stone windows. The inner hall is roofed with a small but exquisitely crafted ceiling panel, the masterpiece of Nolamba art. The ceiling is divided into nine panels, with dancing Shiva in the middle surrounded by Dikpalas, all smoothly modelled in high relief. Flying attendants carrying garlands are positioned at the corners.

The **Chennakeshava Temple**, a short distance away, is assigned to the 13C. The columns here are elegantly treated in the typical Hoysala manner. Richly carved friezes on the basement, though worn, shows episodes from the Krishna story. Sculptures are positioned between the wall pilasters above.

F. Sravana Belgola

This celebrated Jain pilgrimage town, dominated by the Gommateshvara Monolith, lies 36km east of Hassan, just off NH48 via Nelamangala.

> Sravana Belgola was established in the 9C–10C under the Gangas, the powerful kings of southern Karnataka at this time. The site benefitted from the patronage of Chamundaraya, the minister of Rajamalla IV (974–85), both converts to Jainism. The temples dating from the 12C are associated with Gangaraja, the commander of the Hoysala army. Sravana Belgola was further developed during the Vijayanagara and Wodeyar periods, and continues to flourish today. In 1981, on the thousandth anniversary of the installation of the Gommateshvara Monolith, a great commemorative festival, Mahamastakabhisheka, took place in which the statue was ritually bathed with milk, water, coconut milk, rice water, sandalwood paste, turmeric, vermilion and flower petals. Lesser consecrations take place every four years, and a major festival every 12 years, the next being due in 2005.

Most of the features at Sravana Belgola are clustered on two granite hills overlooking the village. The visit described here begins with an ascent of **Vindhyagiri**, the granite outcrop south of the town, rising 143m above the plain. A long line of rock-cut steps climbs the shoulder of the hill. The first building to be seen is the triple-shrined **Odegal *Basti***, which houses images of Adinatha (south), Neminatha (east) and Shantinatha (west). The plain exterior is buttressed by angled props. The nearby **Brahmadeva Mandapa** shelters a circular column erected by Chamundaraya, with leafy scrollwork incised on the shaft. A boulder carved with rows of miniature Jina figures is seen next to the

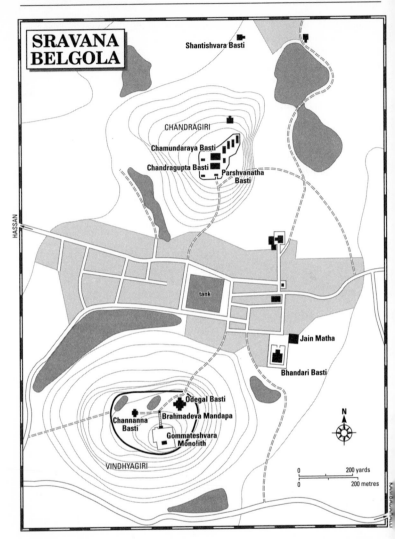

Akhanda Gateway at the top of the last flight of steps. The **Siddhara *Basti***, inside the Gateway to the right, has inscribed memorial pillars set up beside the doorway. A little further on is the **Channanna *Basti***, a simple 17C structure preceded by a tall lamp column.

The **Gommateshvara Monolith**, representing Bahubali, the son of the first Tirthankara to seek enlightenment, is located at the summit of Vindhyagiri. At 17.7m high, this is the largest free-standing sculpture in Southern India. The naked saint stands immobile, his glance fixed steadfastly ahead, creepers winding around his legs and arms. The figure has extended shoulders and elongated arms; the modelling of the body is uniformly smooth. The facial features are delicately carved, as are the coils of hair. Snakes and ant-hills are sculpted out of the rock beneath, where inscriptions record the benefactions of Chamundaraya and subsequent donors. The Monolith stands in a compound surrounded by a colonnade sheltering additional Tirthanakara images. The ceiling panel over the entrance shows Indra surrounded by the Dikpalas.

The tour continues by descending the same steps. The chief place of interest within the town below is the **Jain *Matha***, a short distance east of the staircase. Formerly the residence of the chief pontiff of Sravana Belgola, this mansion has chambers opening off a verandah running around a central court. An important collection of Jain bronzes is displayed here, many items dating from the Ganga era. A remarkable series of brightly coloured murals from the

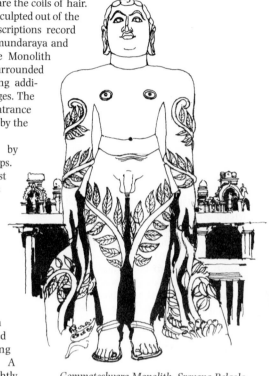

Gommateshvara Monolith, Sravana Belgola

18C–19C covers the rear walls of the verandah. The murals illustrate the past and present births of Parshvanatha, including the story of Marubhuta and his wicked brother Kamatha, and incidents from the legend of Nagakumara. One animated composition shows the annual fair at Sravana Belgola, complete with stalls and crowds. The adjacent **Bhandari *Basti***, substantially rebuilt in recent times, enshrines 24 Tirthankaras arranged in a row on a long pedestal. A stone column topped with a small pavilion stands in front.

For the next part of the tour of Sravana Belgola it is necessary to cross the town, passing by a large tank on the north, opposite which a path climbs **Chandragiri**. The monuments and inscriptions on this hill are contained within a single walled compound. The temples have plain exteriors, relieved only by regularly positioned pilasters, elaborate parapets and multi-storeyed towers. The 10C **Chamundaraya *Basti***, named after the patron of the Gommateshvara Monolith, houses an image of Neminatha. Its hollow tower, capped by an octagonal dome, serves as an upper shrine for Parshvanatha. Miniature sculptures adorn the parapet elements. The interior ceiling shows a seated Jina in the company of the Dikpalas.

The adjacent 12C **Chandragupta *Basti*** is notable for its carved stone screens with miniature figural panels. These depict incidents from the lives of Bahubali and Chandragupta, his royal disciple. A hall links this monument to its neighbour, the Kattale *Basti*. The exterior of the **Parshvanatha *Basti*** has slender pilasters. The sanctuary houses a huge 5m high image of the Tirthankara. A 17C lamp column capped with a small pavilion stands in front.

The **Shantishvara *Basti***, about 300m north of Chandragiri, is the only temple at Sravana Belgola to have been built in the ornate Hoysala manner. Though dilapidated, the wall panels preserve Jina figures standing in niches headed by tower-like pediments. They are flanked by attendant maidens, musicians and dancers beneath panels of decorative scrollwork. A Jina figure seated on a throne is enshrined within the sanctuary.

G. Kambadahalli

This village lies 15km east of Sravana Belgola, also just off NH48. The Jain monuments here form an ensemble of two coordinated groups within the same compound. The 10C shrines are typical of the Ganga style, with clearly articulated basement mouldings, pilasters and pyramidal towers crowned with square or dome-like roofs.

The triple-shrined **Panchakuta *Basti*** houses images of Adinatha (south), Shantinatha (east) and Neminatha (west). The adjacent double-shrined **Shantinatha *Basti*** has a later porch with several fine carvings, including a superbly modelled seated Jina accompanied by guardians. The ceiling inside the Shantinatha shrine shows Dikpalas around a seated Jina. A lofty stone column north of the compound has a pot-bellied *yaksha* seated on the double capital.

19 · Shimoga

Shimoga is the principal centre of the Malnad, the forested region of western Karnataka, renowned for its rocky peaks and spectacular waterfalls, such as those at Jog. **Shimoga** [A] makes a convenient base from which to visit the monuments associated with the local 16C–17C Nayaka rulers.

The temples at **Keladi** [B] and **Ikkeri** [C] may be combined in a single day, with another day for the more remote forts at **Nagar** [F] and **Kavaledurga** [G].

The pilgrimage temple at **Sringeri** [H] can be visted en route to Karkala [17D] in Kanara. Additional time will have to be set aside to reach the earlier temple sites at **Balligave** [D], **Banavasi** [E] and **Amritpur** [I].

■ **Transport**. Shimoga is linked by road with Bangalore [14], 274km southeast, as well as with Mangalore [17], 197km southwest, Hassan [18], 157km south, and Hospet [20], 194km northwest. Express routes from Bangalore to Goa usually pass through Shimoga and Jog. Local buses reach all the sites described below.

■ **Accommodation**. The well-established *Rock Diamond* is the principal hotel in Shimoga (STD code 08182), but there are newer places, such as the *Hotel Samman* (☎ 23319). It is also possible to stay in more picturesque surroundings at Jog; the *Tourist Rest House* here offers fine views of the 250m cascades of the Sharavati River (best viewed in October and November). It is also possible to find accommodation in **Sagar**, a town known for carving in sandalwood and ivory. Simple pilgrimage hostels are available at **Sringeri**.

■ **Tourist Information**. The KSTDC Tourist Bureau is situated on Balaraj Urs Road.

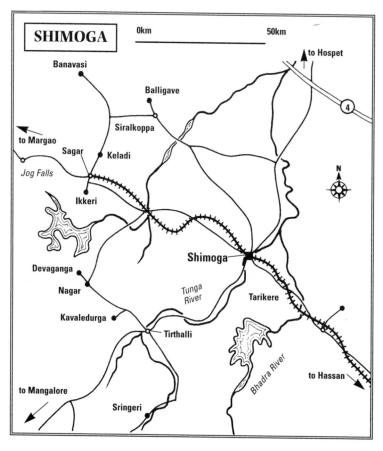

A. Shimoga

This city, on the bank of the Tunga River, was one of the most important possessions of the Nayakas. In 1763 Shimoga was taken by Haidar Ali, but by the beginning of the 19C it had been absorbed into the kingdom of the restored Wodeyars of Mysore [15A]. Shimoga is today a lively market centre noted for its trade in areca nuts and groundnuts, paddy rice and pepper.

The only historical feature in Shimoga is **Shivappa Nayaka's Palace**, which overlooks the river. Though named after a prominent 17C Nayaka ruler, this recently restored structure belongs to the time of Haidar Ali in the latter half of the 18C. The **Darbar Hall** is a two-storeyed structure with massive wooden columns connected by lobed arched panels. Raised side chambers with balconies look down into the Hall. Sculptures brought from nearby temple sites are displayed in the Palace grounds. The Hoysala-period panels include one example showing Shiva and Parvati seated beneath an ornate frame, which comes from Balligave. The hero stones belong to later times.

B. Keladi

This small town, 6km north of Sagar, 72km northwest of Shimoga, is associated with the Nayakas, the rulers who began their careers under the emperors of Vijayanagara [20B–C]. The first known member of the family, Chaudappa, was active here in 1506. The next ruler, Sadashiva, who reigned in 1513–63, gained renown in the campaigns against the Adil Shahis of Bijapur [23A] and was granted the ports of Kanara in reward.

Chaudappa and Sadashiva were responsible for the **Rameshvara** and **Virabhadra Temples**, the principal monuments at Keladi. The Rameshvara Temple is generally assigned to Chaudappa, while the adjacent Virabhadra Temple, with which it is connected, was added by Sadashiva. Both shrines have small east-facing sanctuaries roofed with pyramidal towers capped with square roofs. The walls are plain, except for shallow pilasters. A unique motif is the architect's measuring rod carved in shallow relief on the rear (west) wall of the Virabhadra shrine. Its length (78.5 cm) is scaled into halves, quarters and eighths. In front of both shrines are open columned halls with central spaces. The peripheral columns are decorated with riders on horses; intermediate slabs serving as balcony seating have friezes of temple-like façades. The angled overhangs are surmounted by battlemented parapets. The ceiling inside the hall of the Virabhadra Temple is adorned with elaborate geometric patterns, some derived from textiles, as well as looped and knotted designs, Surya with the Dikpalas, and the double-headed eagle, *gandabherunda*, the emblem of the Keladi rulers.

The **Parvati Temple** stands within the same compound as the Rameshvara and Virabhadra Temples. Its attached hall has finely carved wooden columns and ceilings, dating from the 17C. The entrance to the complex is a traditional structure, with wooden columns and a sloping tiled roof.

The **Keladi Museum**, immediately in front of the Temples, is home to a modest collection of artefacts and documents connected with Nayaka history.

C. Ikkeri

This site, 3km south of Sagar, served as the second Nayaka capital.

Doddashankanna was responsible for moving the Nayaka headquarters here soon after 1563, from where he ruled together with his brother. The two next powerful figures, Ramaraja and Venkatappa, whose reigns spanned 1570–1629, were monarchs of an increasingly autonomous kingdom. In 1614, Venkatappa declared his independence from Vijayanagara. Many victories are attributed to Venkatappa, who extended the Nayaka kingdom into central Karnataka and northern Kerala. Ikkeri lost importance in about 1639, when the Nayaka capital was shifted to Bidnur, later renamed Nagar.

Nothing remains of the palace at Ikkeri described by Pietro della Valle, an Italian who travelled in this part of Karnataka in the early 17C. The only monument to survive is the grandly conceived **Aghoreshvara Temple**, which is assigned to the reign of Doddashankanna in the second half of the 16C. The outer walls of the passageway around the north-facing sanctuary are raised on a high plinth with sharply defined basement mouldings. The stone tower above rises in a succession of storeys capped with a three-quarter spherical roof. The spacious hall in front of the sanctuary is entered by doorways on three sides, with access steps flanked by *yali* balustrades. The wall slabs imitate balcony seating with friezes of temple-like towers; the arched widows with pierced screens above are sheltered by angled eaves. The spacious interior of the hall has 16 impressive columns, the shafts and double capitals of which are divided into multiple facets. Rings of concave lotus petals alternating with deeply carved scrollwork decorate the central ceiling panel. The sanctuary houses a huge pedestal that supports a polished basalt *linga*.

An open pavilion stands immediately in front of the Temple. The large sculpture of Nandi inside is glimpsed through arched openings separated by slender pilasters and overhung by angled eaves. A battlemented parapet with finials conceals the roof.

A subsidiary shrine, possibly for Devi, stands next to the main Temple. Prancing *yalis* are carved on the porch columns, with decorated balcony slabs between them. Perforated stone windows illuminate the hall within.

D. Balligave

This small village, 2km north of Siralkoppa, 70km northwest of Shimoga, was once an important centre of learning, with *mathas* belonging to devotees of different theological schools. Balligave is also known for its 12C–13C monuments from the Hoysala period.

The **Kedareshvara Temple** consists of three shrines opening off a common hall. The west and south sanctuaries have *lingas*, one of which is worshipped as Brahma; the north sanctuary houses a statue of Vishnu. The ornate pyramidal towers of these shrines have dome-like roofs and frontal projections with ornate arches topped by monster masks. The hall projects outwards as a porch, with peripheral seating slabs enlivened with rows of miniature temple towers. The central ceiling shows dancing Shiva surrounded by the Dikpalas. The stone screens beside the doorways are carved with interlocked serpents.

The **Tripurantaka Temple**, northeast of the village, is now somewhat dilapidated. The hall stands on a plinth adorned with figures and animals, some illustrating *Panchatantra* fables; others are shown in animated sexual positions. Hero stones are set up beside the entrance steps. The hall has a magnificent lintel over the doorway to the main sanctuary, which shows Shiva dancing inside the skin of the elephant demon, with Brahma, Vishnu and a host of miniature figures on either side.

A short distance from this monument is the Jiddikera tank, overlooked by a number of small shrines and a 10m high **Commemorative Column**. This was erected by one of the Late Chalukya kings as a victory monument. The sculpted double-headed eagle, or *gandabherunda*, on top is a 19C replacement. The original is now kept in a small shrine at the column base.

E. Banavasi

This site, overlooking the Varada River, 38km northwest of Siralkoppa, was the capital of the Kadamba rulers in the 10C–11C, and then an outpost of the Late Chalukyas. But its history goes back to earlier times, for it was to Vanavasi, as the site was once known, that a Buddhist teacher was deputed in the 3C. **Buddhist Antiquities** were excavated here in the 1920s. The archaeologists revealed several brick *stupas*, including one with a diameter of about 30m, unfortunately no longer visible.

The chief monument of interest at Banavasi is the double-shrined **Madhukeshvara Temple**, which stands within a compound extending to the river. Two shrines dating from the 12C stand next to each other, set at a slight angle. They are approached through open porches with balcony seating sheltered by steeply sloping roofs, added in the 17C. The interiors are notable for the lathe-turned and multi-faceted columns typical of the Late Chalukya style. An ornate image of Shiva and Parvati is placed beside the doorway of the larger shrine. Another item of interest is a stone bed with ornate columns and a canopy, displayed in a chamber on the south side of the court.

F. Nagar

Nagar is somewhat remotely located in the forested hills of the Western Ghats, 86km west of Shimoga, via Hosanagara.

In 1639, during the reign of Virabhadra, the Nayaka capital was shifted from Ikkeri to the fort at Bidnur, later renamed Nagar. This move was necessitated by an invasion of troops from Bijapur, as well as by incursions from Mysore and Goa. Shivappa (1645–60) developed Bidnur into an impregnable citadel and managed to recover territories lost to the Wodeyars and Portuguese. But the Nayaka kingdom deteriorated in later times, and was eventually absorbed into the dominions of Haidar Ali.

Shivappa Nayaka's Fort, at the end of the town, is named after the ruler who did the most to improve and enlarge it. The Fort presents a formidable exterior of overgrown laterite ramparts, enhanced by European-styled battlements with musket holes and cannon mouths. The entrance, flanked by two circular buttresses, is reached by crossing a causeway over the moat. Little is preserved inside the walls, other than the crumbling chambers and column blocks of the audience hall. An octagonal well and several small tanks testify to the need for providing the inhabitants with water. A few modest shrines in the town beneath the Fort date from Nayaka times, the most important being the **Nilakanteshvara Temple**.

The pleasure resort known as **Devaganga** is located in delightful wooded surroundings 2.5km north of Nagar. This Nayaka complex consists of tanks and fountains connected by a water channel fed by a natural spring. The largest tank, 25m by 18m, has a small pavilion in the middle, reached by a bridge; other smaller ponds have circular, star and lotus shapes. At the south end is a bathing place paved with slabs. A small Shiva shrine is elevated on an earthen bank overlooking the complex. There are no other royal structures. The road from Devaganga continues through the Ghats before descending to Kollur [17J].

G. Kavaledurga

This isolated **Citadel**, also known as Bhuvanagiri, was one of the chief outposts of the Nayakas in the 16C–17C. It is located 25km southwest of Nagar, or 90km west of Shimoga via Tirthalli. Kavaledurga occupies one of the most elevated points in the Malnad. The ascent follows a stone pathway passing through a set of gates, each marking a circuit of walls at successively higher levels protecting the innermost fort.

The crumbling **Ramparts**, overgrown by trees and vines, present a picturesquely ruined spectacle. The remains of walls and column blocks indicate decaying courtly structures; wells and tanks are located nearby. From the summit, 969m above sea level, there are spectacular views over the peaks of the Western Ghats to the Arabian Sea. A rectangular granary and small shrine are situated here.

The **Kashivishvanatha Temple**, the most complete monument at Kavaledurga, occupies the innermost fort of the Citadel. This Nayaka-period building stands in a small compound, with an unusual pair of lamp columns outside. The Temple itself has plain walls overhung by angled eaves and a parapet of trefoil battlements with corner finials. The pyramidal tower over the sanctuary is capped with a square roof. The arched entrance to the hall is flanked by columns sculpted with rearing *yalis*.

Similar, but smaller, shrines are seen in the town below Kavaledurga. They include the **Anjaneya** and **Virupaksha Temples**, the former with animals and figures carved in relief on the walls of the sanctuary.

H. Sringeri

This small town is located 103km southwest of Shimoga via Tirthahalli, the road to it winding beside the upper reaches of the Tunga River. Beyond Sringeri, the road follows the river to its source and then passes over the ridge of the Western Ghats before descending to Karkala.

The celebrated *matha* at Sringeri was founded in the 9C by Shankara, the originator of the Advaita Vedanta school of Hindu philosophy. The pontiffs of Sringeri attained considerable renown as advisors to the Vijayanagara emperors. The *matha* has maintained its religious importance through the centuries, and is today a popular pilgrimage centre.

The main complex at Sringeri is picturesquely situated on a terrace overlooking the forested banks of the river. The 16C **Vidyashankara Temple** enshrines a Shiva *linga* worshipped as the *samadhi*, or memorial, of Shankara himself. The unusual appearance of the building is partly explained by the influence of earlier Hoysala traditions. The Temple has a double apsidal-ended plan created by multiple setbacks, echoed in the high plinth on which the building is elevated. The outer walls contain an east-facing sanctuary surrounded by antechambers and a passageway, approached through a spacious columned hall. The high basement displays superimposed friezes of animals and figures, including the story of Arjuna fighting Shiva disguised as the hunter. *Yali* balustrades flank the steps ascending to each of the six doorways.

The walls are composed of angled panels carved with various divinities, the most important being accommodated in niches headed by shallow temple towers. The aspects of Shiva include Nataraja, the god slaying the elephant demon, shooting an arrow at the demons of the triple cities, and appearing out of the *linga* to rescue Markandeya. All of Vishnu's *avataras* are present, including Krishna playing the flute and Rama seated with Lakshmana. The tower over the sanctuary has two multi-faceted storeys crowned with a hemispherical roof and pot finial. The massive piers inside the hall are treated as rearing *yalis* with riders, doubled at the corners. They carry heavy brackets and ceiling slabs with a central dome-like lotus. Fine bronzes are displayed in the sanctuary.

The **Sharada Temple**, a short distance north of the Vidyashankara Temple, is a modern structure built in the Tamil style. The focal shrine is surrounded on four sides by a grandiose corridor flanked by piers with animal brackets.

I. Amritpur

This small village, some 50km southeast of Shimoga via Tarikere, is notable for the **Amriteshvara Temple**, erected in 1196 by a general of Ballala II. This outstanding example of the Hoysala style is remarkable for its clearly articulated architectural ornamentation. The outer walls of the *linga* sanctuary are carved with rare refinement, as is evident in the unfinished niches and single pilasters headed by fully articulated temple towers of different designs. Delicately incised creeper ornament occupies the intervening wall spaces. The pyramidal tower presents ascending sequences of elegantly carved parapet elements, each headed with a monster mask. Multiple images of Shiva occupy the arches in the middle of three sides, ascending to the dome-like roof. The tower's frontal projection is capped with a fully sculpted warrior battling with a *yali*, a typical Hoysala motif. The spacious columned hall extending outwards with projections in the middle of each side is partly open as a porch. The peripheral seating is decorated with panels showing hunters, dancers, musicians and diverse Krishna scenes and *Ramayana* episodes. Models of temples with complicated towers are seen beneath. The lathe-turned columns are overhung by generous curving eaves.

20 · Hospet

The remains of **Vijayanagara**, the capital of the greatest of all Southern Indian empires, present a spectacle of ruins dispersed in a remarkable rugged landscape traversed by the Tungabhadra River.

Most visitors will use **Hospet** [A] as a base from where they will tour the temples in and around **Hampi** [B] and the royal structures near **Kamalapuram** [C]. At least two full days are recommended.

Another day will have to be reserved for an excursion north of the Tungabhadra River, to take in the traditional town of **Anegondi** [D] and the nearby megalithic site of **Hiriye Benekal** [E] nearby.

The journey west from Hospet to Hubli [21], in the direction of Goa, passes near the Late Chalukya temples at **Kukkanur** [F] and **Ittagi** [G]. Further monuments attributed to these rulers as well as to their successors, the Hoysalas, are located at **Bagali** [H], **Kuruvatti** [I] and **Harihar** [J], southwest of Hospet. The road continues to Shimoga [19].

NH13, which runs south from Hospet, meets NH4 at **Chitradurga** [K], the

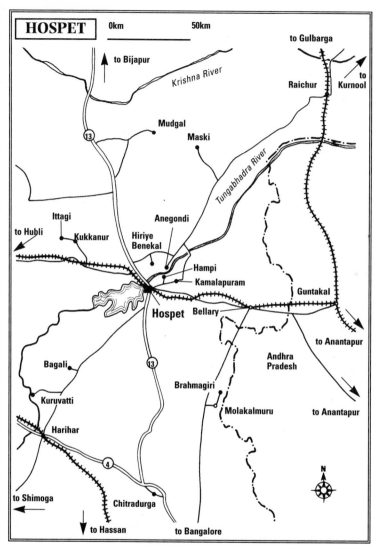

most imposing citadel in central Karnataka. From here it is possible to continue to Bangalore [14]. An excursion to **Brahmagiri** [L], with its prehistoric vestiges, is possible on the way.

The route northeast from Hospet may take in the prehistoric site at **Maski** [M] as well as the fortified city of **Raichur** [N]. The road from Raichur continues to Kurnool [32] in Andhra Pradesh.

From Hospet, NH13 runs north towards Bijapur [23] passing near to the spectacular fortress at **Mudgal** [O].

■ **Transport**. Hospet is reached most conveniently by overnight train from Bangalore or Hyderabad [26], the town being connected to Guntakal on the main Bombay–Madras line. Hospet lies 337km northwest of Bangalore, via Chitradurga on NH4. Lesser routes connect Hospet with Shimoga [19], 194km south; Hubli, 116km west; and Badami [22] and Bijapur [23], 150km and 207km north respectively. All of the sites included here can be visited by local bus, but because of the distances involved outlying places such as Chitradurga, Brahmagiri, Maski and Raichur cannot be reached as day excursions. A car is recommended.

■ **Accommodation**. The *Malligi Tourist Home* (☎ 48101) and *Hotel Priyardashani* (☎ 48838) are the best in Hospet (STD code 08394), while the recently opened *Mayura Bhuvaneshvari* (☎ 51374) at **Kamalapuram** offers accommodation on the edge of the Vijayanagara site. The *Hotel Mayur Vijayanagara* (☎ 48270) is inconveniently located 5km southwest of Hospet on the edge of the Tungabhadra Dam. Simple lodgings are also available at **Hampi**, where visitors can enjoy the authentic atmosphere of a pilgrimage site. A trip to **Raichur** (STD code 08532) will involve an overnight stay, which is possible at the *Hotel Nrupatunga* or *Hotel Priya* (☎ 20531).

■ **Tourist Information**. The KSTDC maintains a Tourist Bureau at the Taluk Office premises near the bus stand.

History

Vijayanagara was founded in 1336, when the Sangamas seized control of the territories of the Hoysalas, whose power had already been eroded by an invasion of Karnataka by the Delhi army in 1311. The Sangamas, sons of a local chief, first established themselves at Hampi, a modest religious site on the Tungabhadra, before shifting their headquarters 2km south to a fortified capital which they named Vijayanagara, City of Victory. From this citadel they planned the campaigns that brought almost all of the peninsula south of the Tungabhadra River under their control. Bukka (1354–77) and Harihara II (1377–1404) were among the early prominent Sangamas.

Vijayanagara was not the only state to be founded in the 14C. Several commanders of the invading Delhi army remained at Madurai [44A], in the south of Tamil Nadu, from where they declared their autonomy. Simultaneously, the Bahmanis to the north established an independent kingdom from their headquarters at Gulbarga [24A]. While the Sangamas managed to extinguish the Madurai dominion, thereby ending any challenge to their authority from the south, their struggles with the Bahmanis were ongoing. Even so, the Sangamas maintained their position as mighty rulers. Abdul Razzaq, Persian envoy to the court of Devaraya II (1424–46) describes the spectacular ceremonies of the Mahanavami festival at Vijayanagara, to which all of the governors and lesser chiefs of the empire were summoned.

Sangama influence waned in the second half of the 15C, and in 1485 the Vijayanagara throne was usurped by Narasimha Saluva, the governor of Chandragiri [35C]. At about the same time the Bahmani kingdom disintegrated into five smaller states, including those of Bijapur, Bidar [25A] and Golconda [26E]. The Saluvas did not stay in power for long, and were displaced by the Tuluvas in 1505. Under Krishnadevaraya (1510–29) and his brother-in-law, Achyutadevaraya (1529–42), Vijayanagara attained the height of its power. Both emperors toured extensively throughout the empire, subduing rebellious chiefs and making donations to prominent temples in Andhra Pradesh and Tamil Nadu. They conducted battles against the sultans of Bijapur and Golconda, and against the kings of faraway Orissa. The arrival of Europeans on the west coast brought Vijayanagara into contact with the Portuguese, who profited from shipments of horses from Arabia. Accounts of Vijayanagara by Portuguese traders confirm the magnificence of the capital and the ostentation of the court. Their vivid accounts of the Mahanavami make for entertaining reading.

Sadashiva succeeded Achyutadevaraya, but was prevented from taking power by Ramaraya, the commander of the imperial forces. Ramaraya kept Sadashiva virtually prisoner while effectively controlling state business. But Ramaraya's policies antagonised the sultans to such an extent that they formed an alliance intent on destroying Vijayanagara. This led inexorably to the great battle of January 1565 on the bank of the Krishna River, not far from Aihole [22E], where Ramaraya faced the combined armies of Bijapur, Bidar, Golconda and Ahmadnagar [6A]. The Vijayanagara forces were defeated and Ramaraya's head was paraded before the troops, who fled in panic. Ramaraya's brother, Tirumala, rushed back to the capital, where he collected Sadashiva and the imperial treasury before escaping to Penukonda [33D] in Andhra Pradesh. Left undefended, Vijayanagara was thoroughly sacked and burnt. So complete was the devastation that the site was never reoccupied. Except for the Virupaksha Temple at Hampi, which still flourishes as a religious centre, the Vijayanagara monuments stand dilapidated and deserted.

A. Hospet

This lively commercial town was once a royal suburb of Vijayanagara, when it was called Hospattana. The most important monument is the **Anantashayana Temple**, 1.5km northeast of Hospet, on the road to Hampi and Kamalapuram. Dating from the period of Krishnadevaraya, this impressive building stands in a walled compound, entered from the road through a large, unfinished *gopura*. The Temple has a partly open columned hall, with rearing *yalis* carved on the outer supports. The rectangular sanctuary within was intended for a reclining image of Vishnu, now vanished. The tower above, more than 24m high, is roofed with an unusual double-apsidal-ended roof constructed in corbelled brick.

An unfinished 15C Muslim **Tomb** in the southern part of Hospet is another vestige of the Vijayanagara era. A massive earthen **Dam Wall**, about 1km south of the town, over which passes the road to Chitradurga, dates from the time of Krishnadevaraya. A Portuguese visitor observed that human sacrifices were performed when the wall broke.

The **Tungabhadra Dam**, 3km southwest of Hospet, is the largest in Karnataka and a popular attraction. Regular supplies of water and electricity generated by this project have brought prosperity to Hospet and the Vijayanagara area. Mining of iron ore in the hills nearby is the most important local industry.

B. Hampi

This small village on the south bank of the Tungabhadra River, 13km northeast of Hospet, has a longer history than Vijayanagara, having been a sacred spot as early as the 8C–9C. It remains an active place, with crowded shops and stalls lining Bazaar Street, which leads up to the **Virupaksha Temple**. Together with other large religious complexes, lesser shrines and monolithic sculpted images, the Temple overlooks a rocky gorge through which the river makes its way in a northeasterly direction.

Many features in the landscape are identified with episodes in the *Ramayana*, especially those in which Rama enlists the aid of the monkey king Sugriva and his general Hanuman. In spite of these *Ramayana* associations, the Virupaksha Temple is dedicated to an aspect of Shiva. The deity here is commonly referred to as Pampapati, Lord of Pampa, the goddess equated with the Tungabhadra itself. The legend of Pampa being betrothed and married to Virupaksha is celebrated in the great chariot ceremonies that still take place in Bazaar Street each March–April and November–December.

The Temple is entered on the east through a lofty whitewashed *gopura*, a 19C renovation of an earlier structure. Its diminishing brick-and-plaster storeys create a pyramidal tower rising almost 50m high, until recently the highest in Karnataka. 15C carved blocks are set into the lower walls. The *gopura* gives access to the outer enclosure of the Temple, on the opposite side of which is a smaller *gopura*, dating from the time of Krishnadevaraya. This emperor was also responsible for extending the main shrine that stands at the west end of the inner enclosure, and the open hall that he added in 1510 still stands. Its outer columns are transformed into sculptural compositions showing *yalis* with riders. The animals are sheltered by deeply curving eaves; the brick-and-plaster parapet above is a 19C replacement.

The spacious interior is defined by 16 columns with rearing animals and riders. 19C ceiling paintings have been restored to reveal deities on bright red backgrounds. The composition is divided into two pairs of matching panels, showing the marriage of Rama and Sita (front) and that of Shiva and Parvati (end), both couples standing with trees in the background, flanked by divinities. Shiva shooting an arrow at the demons of the triple cities (right) and Kama aiming a similar arrow at Shiva (left), are balanced on either side of the central lotus.

At the east end of the hall is a long panel depicting a procession with Vidyaranya, the pontiff of Sringeri [19H], carried in a palanquin, accompanied by soliders and musicians. The enclosed hall beyond, usually entered through side porches, leads to the focal *linga* sanctuary. The subshrines to the north house Bhuvaneshvari and Pampa, two aspects of Shiva's consort. The intricately worked grey-green schist columns and ceiling are taken from a dismantled 11C–12C structure.

The *gopura* on the north gives access to the **Manmatha Tank**, just outside the enclosure wall, overlooked on the west by a group of early shrines. These include a structure with squat columns and sloping roof slabs. A sculpted panel showing a warrior battling with a *yali*, a typical Hoysala emblem, is placed inside the hall. The Tungabhadra River lies a short distance beyond.

The crowded, colonnaded **Bazaar Street**, which stretches 750m east from the Virupaksha Temple, serves as Hampi's market. Persian and Portuguese chroni-

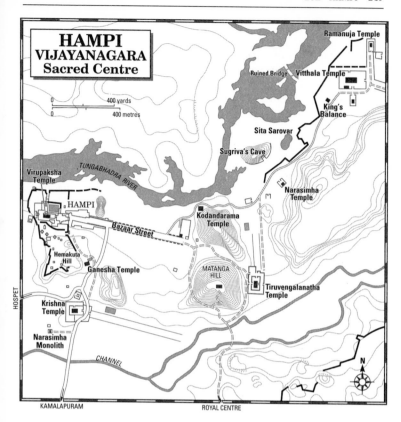

clers remarked upon the jewels and courtesans that were once available here. Today, squatters occupy double-storeyed mansions that were once the homes of the Vijayanagara elite. The restored structures at the end of the Street include a hall with reused schist columns and a **Monolithic Nandi** with a defaced head, sheltered by a pavilion. A stepped path from here leads over a ridge to the Tiruvengalanatha Temple.

The temples on the sloping shelf of **Hemakuta Hill** overlook Hampi from the south. They are built in a massive, unadorned style, typical of the 14C. Several have multiple sanctuaries topped with pyramidal stone towers divided into horizontal layers. One triple-sanctuaried example was erected by a local chief as a family memorial just prior to the foundation of Vijayanagara. Multi-storeyed open gateways define a path leading to the summit. The **Ganesha Temple** beyond occupies an elevated ridge. An elegant portico with slender columns leads to an impressive 4.5m high sculpture of Ganesha, sculpted out of a single boulder. A similar but smaller Ganesha monolith nearby is housed within an open pavilion.

The **Krishna Temple** is located a short distance south of the Ganesha sculptures. The colonnaded street of this monument extends east into groves of sugar cane. A rectangular tank to one side is picturesquely surrounded by neglected colonnades. The Temple itself is entered through a massive *gopura* with a frontal verandah. The brick tower, though mostly collapsed, is of interest for the battle scenes fashioned in plaster. These may illustrate Krishnadevaraya's conquest of Udayagiri [34D], an event commemorated in the construction of the Temple in 1516.

The main shrine is approached through a spacious open hall, with outer columns fashioned as *yalis*, and an inner hall with porches. A dark passageway surrounds the sanctuary, its outer walls divided into bays by pilasters and niches. The brick tower over the sanctuary is capped with a hemispherical roof. Small subshrines cluster around the main unit; some have their walls covered with inscriptions. A **Granary** with six domes stands in the outer enclosure to the south.

The road in front of the Krishna Temple passes through a triple-bayed gateway before continuing south to Vijayanagara and Kamalapuram. A few metres off this road just south of the Krishna Temple is the **Narasimha Monolith**, a remarkable representation of the man-lion form of Vishnu seated in yogic posture. This 6.7m high sculpture, the largest at the site, was a commission of Krishnadevaraya in 1528. The ***Linga* Shrine** nearby shelters a large rock-cut emblem of Shiva. Recent irrigation work has caused it to be flooded.

The tour described here continues by returning to Hampi and proceeding east along the Bazaar Street. A path turning off to the north to follow the Tungabhadra River provides majestic vistas of the surrounding rocks and hills. **Chakra Tirtha,** an auspicious bathing spot at a bend in the river, marks the place where Lakshmana, Rama's brother, crowned Sugriva. The **Kodandarama Temple** here is of interest for its carvings of the *Ramayana* heroes on a large boulder built into the sanctuary. Rocks with **Multiple *Lingas*** cut into their upper surfaces in geometric formation are situated nearby. Here, too, is a fine image of **Ananta- shayana**.

The path continues to the **Tiruvengalanatha Temple**, a large-scale complex erected in 1534 by the brother-in-law of Achyutadevaraya. This double-walled complex is approached from the north along a colonnaded street. A pair of *gopuras* of almost equal size give access to two concentric walled enclosures. The shrines of the inner compound are much dilapidated. The columned hall in the outer compound has carvings on the column blocks, showing ascetics and seductive maidens among divinities. A path leads from the rear (south) of the Temple to the irrigated valley that separates Hampi from the Palace Zone of Vijayanagara [C]. Steps from a path that runs along the side of the valley ascend to the summit of **Matanga Hill**. This affords a magnificent prospect of the whole site, including an aerial view of the Tiruvengalantha Temple.

The **Narasimha Temple** is the next monument to be encountered on the riverside path. This 14C structure stands within a small compound entered through a double-storeyed gateway. The main shrine has a pyramidal stone roof resembling those on Hemakuta hill. **Sugriva's Cave** in front (north), a natural cleft marked by painted ochre and white stripes, is hallowed as the spot where Surgriva hid the jewels that Sita dropped when she was abducted by Ravana. A shallow pond known as **Sita Sarovar** lies in a rocky depression to one side. The river at this point is crossed by a **Bridge**, of which only stone pylons survive. The

Purandara Dasa Mandapa nearby is named after the famous musician at the Vijayanagara court.

The path continues beside an exposed rock strewn with small mounds of stones assembled by pilgrims to ensure fertility and good fortune. Further along is a double-storeyed gateway and an unusual portal known as the **King's Balance**. This consists of two columns and a lintel from which a metal balance or swing was suspended. Here the Vijayanagara kings had themselves weighed against gold and jewels, which were then distributed to the brahmins.

The **Vitthala Temple,** the finest of the Vijayanagara series, is located at the end of the path, about 1.5m northeast of Hampi. The Temple is sometimes thought to have been erected to house the celebrated image from Pandharpur [9G] in Maharashtra, which was removed for safety during the period of the Nizam Shahis. The foundation date of the Temple is not known. The main shrine stands in a rectangular compound entered through *gopuras* on three sides. Free-standing halls with internal platforms for displaying images of divinities are arranged around the east-facing main unit. This presents a somewhat severe exterior, concealing an inner passageway around the focal sanctuary and an adjoining enclosed hall with porches.

The glory of the Temple is the open **Hall** in front, an addition of 1554. This is elevated on a basement decorated with friezes of lions, elephants and horses, the last with Portuguese attendants; miniature shrines house the incarnations of Vishnu. The hall columns present different combinations of cut-out colonettes, figural sculptures and rearing *yalis*, carved in a virtuoso manner. (Contrary to popular belief, the tones emitted from the colonettes when lightly struck do not form part of a musical scale.) The outer piers are deeply overhung by curving eaves with ribs and rafters on the undersides. Ceiling slabs with spans of no less than 10m, carried on massive beams, once roofed the central hall; most have fallen. Those *in situ* are carved with elaborate lotus medallions. The Garuda shrine immediately in front of this hall is conceived as model chariot, with four decorated stone wheels. Its walls have cut-out colonettes and delicate creeper motifs. The brick tower is lost.

Colonnaded Streets run east and north from the principal *gopura* of the Vitthala Temple. The latter leads to the dilapidated **Ramanuja Temple**, which is contained in a rectangle of walls, entered on the south through a *gopura* with a portico with animal columns. The shrine within is approached through a hall with rearing *yalis* defining the central square space. The other colonnaded street runs past a large **Tank** to an open pavilion with a central dais, 900m to the east. The road from here proceeds south to Kamalapuram and north to Talarighat, the river crossing to Anegondi.

C. Kamalapuram

This village, situated at the edge of the Palace Zone of Vijayanagara, lies about 12km northeast of Hospet. Kamalapuram itself is of little interest, except for a dilapidated 18C **Fort** in the middle of the village and a large **Tank**, dating from Vijayanagara times, outside the village to the south.

The **Archaeological Museum** (closed Fridays) is worth visiting for the instructive large-scale model of the Vijayanagara site that occupies a central court. Sculptures in the surrounding galleries include slabs carved in a vigorous manner, with Virabhadra, Bhairava, Hanuman and serpent deities. Two headless figures appear to represent a royal couple. Jewellery, weapons and manu-scripts are also shown. Hero stones collected from all over the site illustrate scenes of battle and of the hero being received in heaven.

The road leading northwest from Kamalapuram in the direction of Hampi arrives within 1km at the fortifications of the **Palace Zone**. This part of the site is identified closely with the Vijayanagara emperors, their family members, nobles and commanders. Some buildings stand relatively complete, having been erected entirely of masonry, including their roofs and towers. The openings, balconies, vaults and domes have an Islamic appearance, due to the adoption of forms and techniques borrowed from contemporary Bahmani architecture, as seen at Gulbarga and Bidar. Other buildings must have been fashioned out of wood, terracotta and plaster, and were almost totally destroyed in the sack of the city. Only their masonry foundations and footing blocks, recently revealed by excavators, survive.

The first monument to be seen after leaving Kamalapuram is the **Queen's Bath**, a pleasure pavilion with balconies, overlooking a central square pond, now empty. Little of the original plasterwork survives, except in the vaults in the arcaded passageway. The pavilion is surrounded by a water channel; the collapsed remains of an aqueduct are seen nearby. The **Chandrasekhara Temple**, 100m northeast, stands in the middle of a rectangular compound with collapsing walls. A *gopura* marks the entrance on the east. The two sanctuaries that open off a common hall present unadorned basements and pilastered walls; the towers have both square and rectangular roofs.

Returning to the Queen's Bath, the road proceeds around the outer walls of the **Royal Enclosures** of the Palace Zone. The enclosures, mostly irregular in shape, are defined by tapering walls with granite blocks ingeniously fitted together without any mortar. Though certain enclosures are known as the Zenana and Mint, these identifications are not based on historical or archaeo-logical evidence.

The first enclosure to be visited is the largest. Here stands the elevated floor of the **Hundred-Columned Hall**, probably the audience hall where the Vijayana-gara emperor dispensed justice. Immediately south are the remains of smaller columned halls, some facing onto paved courts with wells. The functions of these structures are unknown, though presumably they were linked with the public activities of the king. An **Underground Chamber** with re-used schist slabs and columns of a dismantled temple may have served as a subterranean treasury.

The northeast corner of the enclosure is occupied by the **Mahanavami Platform**, a unique monument laid out in ascending levels. The slightly sloping sides are covered with reliefs of hunting scenes, performances of music and dance, wrestling matches and the reception of prisoners. Elephants, horses and camels also appear. Staircases provide access to the top of the platform, that on the west flanked by intricately worked schist slabs. The monument is associated with the Mahanavami festival, mostly on the basis of Portuguese accounts, which describe the Vijayanagara emperor ascending a platform to make sacrifices to a goddess and to witness the processions of animals, soldiers and courtly women.

The **Bathing Tanks** south of the Platform include a remarkable square pond surrounded by steps and landings, all fashioned out of schist. Numbers and

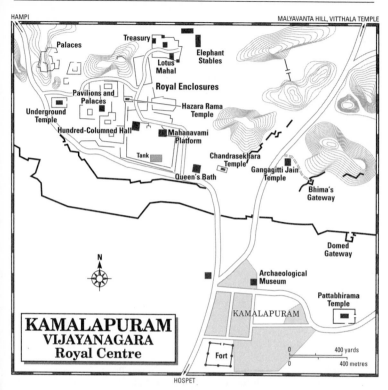

HAMPI

MALYAVANTA HILL, VITTHALA TEMPLE

Treasury

Palaces

Elephant
Stables

Lotus
Mahal

Royal Enclosures

Pavilions and
Palaces

Underground
Temple

Hazara Rama
Temple

Hundred-Columned Hall

Mahanavami
Platform

Tank

Chandrasekhara
Temple

Gangagitti Jain
Temple

Queen's Bath

Bhima's
Gateway

N

Domed
Gateway

Archaeological
Museum

Pattabhirama
Temple

KAMALAPURAM

KAMALAPURAM
VIJAYANAGARA
Royal Centre

Fort

0   400 yards

0   400 metres

HOSPET

letters on the blocks indicate directions and levels. The aqueducts nearby formed part of a complex hydraulic system that transported water to the Palace Zone from the Tank at Kamalapuram.

Returning to the entrance to the enclosure, the road passes through two massive **Gateways**, of which only the lower masonry portions remain, arriving at the **Hazara Rama Temple**. This shrine served as the place of private of worship for the Vijayanagara kings and is the finest example of 15C religious architecture at Vijayanagara. The Temple faces onto a plaza where many of the roads of the capital converged. Directly opposite are a collapsed lamp column and a small Hanuman shrine. A road leading noprth-east is lined with dilapidated sanctuaries built in different styles.

The Hazara Rama Temple is contained within a rectangle of walls, the outer faces of which are covered with friezes of elephants, horses being led by bearded, possibly Arab, attendants, soldiers in contrasting formations and female dancers and musicians. These parades correspond to the Persian and Portuguese descriptions of the Mahanavami festival. A modest gateway with a pillared portico gives access to the compound. The friezes on the inner face of the enclosure walls portray episodes from the *Ramayana*. They begin with the Shravanakumara prologue (right side of north gate), recognised by the youth carrying his parents in baskets.

The outer walls of the main shrine are raised on a moulded basement and divided into projections and recesses by pairs of pilasters. This scheme is relieved by single pilasters in ornate pots and niches capped with roof forms. The brick tower over the sanctuary has been restored. The attached **Hall** has elegant porches, that on the east contained within a later extension. The outer walls are covered with sculptures arranged in three tiers, relating the main events of the *Ramayana*. The story begins with the fire sacrifice of Dasharatha (north end of west wall) and ends with the enthronement of Rama together with Sita (south end of west wall). Scenes on the front (east) wall show Rama shooting the golden deer, and the battle with Ravana.

The interior of the hall is remarkable for the polished granite columns covered with carvings of different aspects of Vishnu. No icons have been preserved inside the sanctuary, but the pedestal has slots for a trio of images, possibly Rama, Lakshmana and Sita. A smaller double-shrined temple stands immediately to the north. This, too, has finely finished mouldings and sculpture panels illustrating the continuation of the *Ramayana*. Additional scenes depict the story of Narasimha.

A path leads west from the Temple to a series of enclosures still being cleared by excavators. Here can be seen the remains of a **Royal Residence**, with an inner court defined by verandahs on three sides, leading to a set of small chambers at the top. Circular brick-lined depressions in the court to the north may have been for plants or trees. A newly discovered stepped pond to the rear has an unusual bull-headed water spout. The **Nine-Domed Pavilion** in the adjacent enclosure is a reception hall divided into vaulted bays. It is overlooked by a **Two-Storeyed Octagonal Pavilion**.

Returning to the Hazara Rama Temple, the path continues some 150m north until it arrives at the enclosure of the **Lotus Mahal,** the most individual of all courtly structures at Vijayanagara. Laid out symmetrically with projections in the middle of each side, the double-storeyed building has openings framed by lobed arches overhung by curved eaves. A staircase tower provides access to the upper level. The Mahal is roofed by nine pyramidal towers, that over the centre being raised up. In spite of its fanciful and unhistorical name, the Lotus Mahal probably served as a place of reception for the king or military commander. Ruined residences are seen nearby.

In the northwest corner of the enclosure is a **Treasury**, with a long gabled roof partly concealed by the ornate perforated parapet. The building is entered through a single doorway, while light and air are admitted only through small openings. **Watchtowers** built into the walls of the enclosure survey the approaches on all sides. The example near the treasury has a square staircase tower with balconies on four sides. That in the southeast corner is octagonal in plan, with double arcades at the top surmounted by a pyramidal tower.

A doorway in the east wall of the Lotus Mahal enclosure leads directly to the **Elephant Stables**. This imposing structure consists of 11 chambers, each accommodating one or two of the animals used by the Vijayanagara rulers for state occasions. The stables are roofed with alternating domes and 12-sided vaults, arranged symmetrically about a raised upper chamber for drummers and musicians. The arched openings and arcades of the principal façade are

Elephant Stables, Kamalapuram (Vijayanagara)

Bahmani in style. The stables face west onto an open space, probably used as a parade ground. An **Arcaded Structure** on the north side has a raised verandah which may have been for courtiers to review troops and animals. The internal court would have been suitable for martial sports and animal fights.

A path behind the stables leads to a complex of ruined religious structures. These face on to the road, now buried, that begins in front of the Hazara Rama Temple. Among the shrines is a dilapidated 15C **Jain Temple**.

The tour of the Palace Zone concludes by returning to the Hazara Rama Temple and continuing west in order to reach the **Underground Temple**. Dedicated to Virupaksha, the same deity worshipped at Hampi, this temple derives its name from the fact that it was discovered almost completely buried under washed out soil. The irrigation of nearby fields is responsible for the water that constantly floods its inner halls. Though overlaid by numerous extensions, the original shrine is a 14C structure resembling those on Hemakuta Hill. The complex is entered through a simple *gopura*, missing its brick tower.

On the opposite side of the road is another **Royal Residence**, with its characteristic inner court surrounded by verandahs with small chambers at the upper level. About 50m to the north is a complex of similar residences uncovered by archaeologists in recent years. Labelled as the **Noblemen's Quarter**, this area is crowded with royal residences of the type previously noted. The density of the planning, with narrow lanes between the different structures, together with the many water channels and wells, gives the best possible idea of a royal suburb of the capital.

The road proceeds west until it joins with the main route linking Kamalapuram and Hampi. The tour of the sights around Kamalapuram, however, continues with the **Pattabhirama Temple** 1km east, a monument notable for its grand scale. The towered *gopura* on the east is the best preserved at the site. To the rear of the temple is the **Domed Gateway**, with its circular drum elevated on four soaring arches. Unfortunately, almost nothing can be made out of the plaster decoration with which it was once decorated. Its masonry arches contrast with the unmortared blocks of the fortification walls.

Further features are seen outside the Palace Zone of Vijayanagara, on the road running north from Kamalapuram to Talarighat. The **Gangagitti Jain Temple**, about 500m north of Kamalapuram, is a severe building erected in 1385 by an officer of Harihara. It has double sanctuaries and halls, with squat columns and double capitals. A lofty lamp column stands outside. A lane to one side leads to **Bhima's Gateway**, named after the epic hero brandishing a sword, carved on a loose slab placed inside. Massive walls define a passageway that makes a number of turns before passing through a gateway roofed with lintels on decorated brackets.

A short distance further north is a fork in the road, overlooked by **Malyavanta Hill**, 150m east. This is supposed to be the spot where Rama waited while Hanuman went in search of Sita. The *Ramayana* associations are confirmed by images of Rama and his retinue carved on a boulder inside the sanctuary of the **Raghunatha Temple**, situated at the summit of the Hill. The rock is topped with a small tower. The 100-columned hall to the south is provided with a rear stage for performances of sacred dance and theatre. The adjacent *gopura* has a delicately carved basement, a pair of imposing *yalis* with riders on the frontal portico, and a pyramidal brick tower with much of its plaster details intact. A doorway in the west wall of the compound leads to a cistern with Nandis and *lingas* carved on the sides. From here there is a fine panorama of the Palace Zone.

The remains of an Islamic quarter may be seen further north, just off the road leading to Talarighat. A **Mosque** and **Tomb**, the latter domed, were erected by a military commander of Devaraya II. Muslim graves are seen on a nearby ridge. The road continues north, passing through the **Talarighat Gate** set into the fortifications. This has an upper chamber with arched openings and a crenellated parapet.

D. Anegondi

Situated on the opposite bank of the Tungabhara River 4km downstream from Hampi, Anegondi is also accessible by a roundabout road from Hospet, more than 30km distant. It is, however, quicker and more enjoyable to take the short coracle ride from Talarighat. Anegondi was an important settlement prior to the foundation of Vijayanagara. After the destruction of the capital it continued to thrive under a local line of rulers that continues to this day.

The visit to Anegondi starts at a monumental **Gate** on the Tungabhadra River, from which a path begins towards the town, 1km north. The path passes by a dilapidated *Matha*, a religious structure with re-used schist columns and bare traces of paintings on the ceilings. A short distance further on are the stone **Walls** with circular bastions that encircle the town.

The dilapidated **Palace** in the heart of Anegondi is no earlier than the 17C–18C. The main square is dominated by the **Gagan Mahal**, now the headquarters of the town council, a contemporary structure that recalls the Lotus Mahal at Vijayanagara. The Gagan Mahal faces west towards the **Ranganatha Temple**, of little interest except for its re-used schist columns and colonnades painted vivid green. The **Gate** nearby, now in danger of collapse, is a 14C structure with finely finished columns. Lanes on the east side of the town lead to the **Bathing Ghats**. At the south end of the steps is a picturesque group of shrines with fine views of the river, which here makes a turn north.

Anegondi's **Citadel** is located 1km west of the town. The rocky hill is ringed by massive walls dating partly from Vijayanagara times. Fortified gates protected by round bastions give access to enclosures with barracks, wells and other military structures.

E. Hiriye Benekal

This prehistoric site is located just off the Hospet–Gangavati road, 42km northeast of Hospet, partly via NH13. About one hour's walk through boulder-strewn territory is required to reach the groups of **Megaliths**, dating back some 2000 years. Where standing complete, these consist of quadrangular burial chambers defined by upright slabs laid on edge, up to 2m high, capped with large circular slabs. A smaller group of Megaliths at a lower level is distinguished by unusual holes cut into the side slabs. The larger group at a higher level, with more than 50 Megaliths, is called Murar Mani, Old People's House.

Local help will be needed to locate two rock shelter nearby with paintings on the overhangs. The faint ochre compositions show horsemen with spears, figures brandishing clubs, and antelopes, horses and bulls.

F. Kukkanur

This small town, 48km northwest of Hospet, via Koppal, is renowned for its temples assigned to the Rashtrakuta and Late Chalukya periods.

The 9C **Navalinga Complex** consists of a cluster of nine shrines built in sandstone, each with a multi-storeyed square tower, opening off three interconnected columned halls. In spite of the presence of votive *lingas*, the shrines were originally consecrated to female divinities. The niches in the unadorned pilastered walls are headed by *makaras* with foliated tails and parapets of roof forms in relief. The lintels over the shrine doorways are elaborately conceived; the one in front of the west shrine has cut-out *makaras*, looped garlands and flying figures. The shrines stand in the middle of a large compound, together with smaller structures and a tank. The two entrance gateways are 16C additions.

A short distance away is the 10C **Kalleshvara Temple.** The square sanctuary of this shrine has a triple-storeyed tower with a frontal projection. The walls are adorned with temple-like reliefs of different designs. The capitals of the lathe-turned columns inside the adjacent hall are intricately worked. Rectangular Ganesha and Durga subshrines face each other across the middle of the hall.

G. Ittagi

This village, 5km west of Kukkanur, dates back to Early Chalukya times. An 8C portal with a sculpted lintel stands in between two mud-clad houses on the main street. The chief monument at Ittagi is the **Mahadeva Temple**, erected in 1112, an outstanding example of the Late Chalukya style. The Temple, which faces east onto a large square tank, comprises an open outer hall with triple porches, an inner enclosed hall and a towered sanctuary. The carving of the schist blocks is exceptional throughout; so, too, is the mastery of complicated architectural elements. The walls display pilastered projections expanding outward in the middle of each side of the sanctuary and inner hall. The niches, now empty, are headed by tower-like pediments. The parapet has deeply cut arch-like motifs surrounded by foliation and monster masks, repeated in diminishing tiers on the pyramidal tower. Both lathe-turned and multi-faceted columns crowd the porches and halls. The lintel over the sanctuary doorway shows dancing Shiva flanked by *makaras* set in elaborate scrollwork. The ceiling panels are conceived as corbelled domes with ribs and intricate lotus designs.

H. Bagali

This small village is located 55km southwest of Hospet on the Harihar road. The **Kalleshvara Temple**, northeast of the settlement, dates back to Rashtrakuta and Chalukya times. The original 10C monument consists of a sanctuary and adjoining hall, articulated by boldly modelled basement mouldings and wall pilasters. Remarkable sexual acts are carved on the cornice blocks above the sanctuary walls: coitus between two and sometimes three figures, women displaying their vulva, male figures with enlarged phalluses, some engaging in self-fellatio. A triple-storeyed tower rises above.

The 11C extensions to the Temple include the south doorway to the hall. This is surrounded by bands of finely carved miniature figures, including couples, with Lakshmi flanked by elephants in the middle of the lintel. The spacious open hall, laid out on a stepped plan, with balcony seating all around, is another addition. This gives access to a Narasimha shrine on the north. The sharply moulded basement and varied shapes of the interior columns are typical of the Late Chalukya style, as are the sharply angled eaves and ornate parapet. Loose sculptures brought from dilapidated temples in the vicinity are assembled here. A small detached shrine to the east accommodates a finely worked image of Surga.

I. Kuruvatti

This village overlooks the Tungabhadra River, 90km southwest of Hospet via Harpanahalli. Kuruvatti is of interest for the 11C **Mallikarjuna Temple**. Slender pilasters on the outer walls of the sanctuary and hall frame niches capped with towered pediments. The multi-storeyed tower has a dome-like roof and a frontal projection with an arched face. The inclined bracket figures on the pilasters framing the east doorway of the hall are masterpieces of Late Chalukya art; they show fully modelled female dancers and intricate foliage backgrounds. A large Nandi faces towards the hall doorway. The columns within have finely worked shafts, both lathe-turned and multi-faceted. A lintel suspended in front of the sanctuary doorway is carved with Brahma, Shiva and Vishnu. These divinities stand inside an ornate arch flanked by *makaras* with flowing foliated tails.

J. Harihar

This small town, overlooking the east bank of the Tungabhadra River, lies on NH4, 107km southwest of Hospet. The town takes its name from the **Harihareshvara Temple**, erected here in 1224 by a minister of the Hoysala king Narasimha II. The extensive building has its outer walls articulated by slender niches headed by miniature towers in relief. The superstructure rising above is a later restoration. The open hall in front, with multiple projections on three sides, has inclined balcony slabs decorated with friezes of temple-like towers in relief. The interior aisles are flanked by lathe-turned columns with sharply cut details. The main shrine houses a 1.3m high image combining Vishnu (right) with Shiva (left).

The large number of inscribed slabs set up in the compound shows the continued significance of the Temple in Hoysala and Vijayanagara times.

K. Chitradurga

This city is located 180km south of Hospet on NH13, or 200km from Bangalore on NH4, at the foot of a rugged chain of granite hills rising to 1175m above sea level.

The strategic importance of Chitradurga is revealed by the the Late Chalukya and Hoysala occupation of the site in the 11C–13C, after which the site came under the sway of Vijayanagara. A line of local Nayakas declared their independence from Vijayanagara in 1602, bringing a period of autonomy to Chitradurga. The fort was taken from the Nayakas by Haidar Ali in 1779, but was captured by the British some 20 years later. The stronghold provides a range of monuments associated with almost all of the later occupants of Citradurga; other vestiges of the past are apparent in the city itself.

The visit to Chitradurga described here begins at the entrance to the **Fort**, at the west end of the city. Four successive lines of walls gird the rocky hill. They are constructed of great blocks of granite fitted between the boulders, rising 5m to more than 12m high. The walls are strengthened by bastions of different shapes and sizes; there is also a moat at the bottom. The walls enclose an irregular elevated zone, comparatively flat, but strewn with rugged boulders to create a rocky wilderness.

A sequence of massive **Gates** provides access to the Fort from the east. The first Gate, which dates from the Vijayanagara period, is approached through a barbican which creates three bends. Sculptures of a double-headed eagle, serpent and Ganesha are carved on the walls. At the south end of the elevated ground within is a **Cave Temple** with a headless seated goddess. A **Powder Factory** nearby has a pit with four large grinding stones, 1.5m in diameter. Passing by a stone trough, the path leads through the second and third Gates, both with guardrooms, set into the 15m thick ramparts. A small **Ganesha Shrine** and an **Oil Pit** are found within the third Gate.

The monuments of greatest interest within the Fort comprise a sequence of two free-standing Gateways and a number of lamp columns and swing portals lining the path between the **Hidimbeshvara** and **Sampige Siddheshvara Temples**. Both shrines were founded by generals of the Hoysala kings in the second half of the 13C. The Hidimbeshvara Temple, to the north, is built at the summit of a rocky hill, facing onto a boulder. Its columned hall and projecting porch are typical Hoysala features, but the brick parapet is a later addition. The two **Gateways** already noted are independent structures erected by the Nayakas in the 17C. They have double colonnaded storeys and upper pavilions with pyramidal towers and dome-like roofs.

The Sampige Siddheshvara Temple, to the south, is entered through yet a third, double-storeyed gateway with a rooftop pavilion. This example has an ornate brick parapet continuing on to the enclosure walls at either side. A square platform inside the temple compound is where the Nayakas performed their coronation ceremonies. The sanctuary at the southwest corner consists merely of a porch leading to a natural cavern, where a Shiva *linga* is worshipped. Another monument nearby, the **Ekanatheshvara Temple**, founded by the Nayakas, is of lesser interest.

Tanks and **Wells** are scattered about. They include a circular well 7m in diameter, with two flights of steps leading down to the water, and a large tank in a natural crevice. The rubble and mud remains of residential quarters and storage granaries associated with the **Nayaka Palace** occupy the south part of the Fort.

City walls enclose the **Old Town** of Chitradurga in a rectangle on the eastern flank of the Fort. Several gates still stand, including one with guardrooms that now house the local **Museum**. The 17C **Ucchalingamma Temple**, enshrining the protective goddess of the Nayakas, faces onto the principal street. It is entered through an entrance structure flanked by a high basement supporting a double-storeyed portico. A lofty lamp column stands in the middle of the street in front. The shrine within is a modest unadorned structure approached through a double hall. It is crowned with a pyramidal tower capped with a dome-like roof resembling the towers of the Gateways within the fort.

That Chitradurga was of importance in earlier times is demonstrated by artefacts discovered at **Chandravalli**, 1.5km northwest of the city, at the foot of the Fort. Excavations here conducted some years ago uncovered lead coins, Roman silver coins, ornaments of gold, silver and copper, and painted and polished pottery shards, all associated with the 2C–3C Satavahana period. (Some of these items are shown in the Government Museum, Bangalore [14B].) Faint traces of brick walls were also discovered. An inscription on a rock giving information about the town at this time is located near the **Bhairaveshvara Temple**. This Hoysala-period monument has been much renovated in recent times. Prehistoric remains were also discovered in the natural caverns in the nearby hills.

L. Brahmagiri

The distant site of Brahmagiri, 8km north of Molakalmuru, a small town about 120km southeast of Hospet via Bellary, is of importance for its prehistoric and early historic remains. Under the name Isila, Brahmagiri seems to have had contacts with Northern India in the 3C BC. **Ashokan Inscriptions** of the Maurya emperor were found on two boulders less than 1km apart on the western perimeter of Brahmagiri; a third document is located 5km to the north-west. These imperial records are the earliest historical documents to be discovered in Karnataka.

The central part of Brahmagiri is bounded on the east by the Chandreshvara tank, on the north by the Chinna Hagar River, and on the south by a hill with caves and rocky shelves bearing evidence of habitation. The most conspicuous items to be seen here are the remains of megalithic **Burial Chambers**. These consist of stone circles and slabs defining small stone cists, some as large as 2m by 1.6m, capped with circular slabs up to 2.6m in diameter. Archaeologists believe that these Chambers were constructed over many centuries, including the Maurya era. **Rubble Structures** all around indicate a settlement of considerable size. Pottery fragments, stray bricks, stone tools, copper coins and iron slag are among the stray finds.

Modest **Temples** belonging to the Rashtrakuta and Chalukya eras are located on the hill above the prehistoric site.

M. Maski

This small town, 113km northeast of Hospet, lies near another series of **Prehistoric Sites**. Maski is flanked by a long chain of granite hills with natural caverns in the sides and extensive flat surfaces on top.

Some 17 Sites have been explored since the late 19C, yielding an abundance of artefacts. They included Neolithic implements, such as stone axes and hammers, as well as funerary urns of burnt clay. Beads of crystal, amethyst, carnelian, lapis lazuli and agate testify to trade with distant places. So, too, does the proliferation of products made from conch shells. Metal finger-rings, earrings, bangles and necklaces were also among the remains. These finds have been dated approximately to the 5C–3C BC.

Maski is also known for its **Ashokan Inscription**, which was discovered on a boulder inside a cave on the west slope of the hills. Unlike the records at Brahmagiri, this example mentions the 3C BC emperor by name. Iron slag, furnaces and grinding stones found at the foot of the hills indicate early smelting activity. A large field of **Menhirs**, arranged in regular avenues, is located to the southwest. Inscriptions from the 10C–16C are also found at Maski.

N. Raichur

This provincial headquarters lies 185km northeast of Hospet by road, and about the same distance south of Gulbarga, but is more conveniently reached by rail, being situated on the main Bombay–Madras line. It also possible to approach Raichur from Hyderabad, about 200km northeast.

> Raichur was a city of considerable importance under the Kakatiyas of Warangal [28A] before being seized by the Delhi forces in 1312. Soon after, it was absorbed into the Bahmani kingdom, giving its name to the richly irrigated triangle of land between the Krishna and Tungabhadra Rivers, over which so many wars were fought between Gulbarga and Vijayanagara. After passing into the hands of the Adil Shahis, Raichur was captured by Krishnadevaraya in 1520, only to be retaken by Bijapur 22 years later. It remained under the control of Bijapur until the Mughal conquest in 1686. The city then became part of the Mughal domains, and was in time assimilated into the territories of the Nizams.

Raichur is dominated by two irregularly shaped and concentric citadels. The **Outer Fort**, assigned to the 14C–15C Bahmani period, has tapering walls reinforced by a mix of quadrangular and round bastions protected by a broad moat. The **Inner Fort**, encompassing a smaller area, belongs to the 12C–13C Kakatiya era. It is built with extremely long blocks, finely jointed without any use of mortar, strengthened by square bastions. Both Forts incorporate a rocky hill on the south side of the city, which overlooks a large tank beyond the walls.

Raichur's most important monuments date from the Bahmani and Adil Shahi periods. They are located on a crowded commercial street that runs just over 1km from west to east. The tour begins at the **Mecca Gate** in the Outer Fort, a Bahmani structure with a plain arched opening surmounted by a Persian inscription dated 1470. The Gate is topped with a small pavilion roofed with a pyramidal vault. The **Sailini Gate**, a short distance east, is set between two massive bastions of the Inner Fort. Its arched opening is framed by a parapet of rectangular battlements with curved backs. A small mosque and *dargah* dating from Adil Shahi times are built into the Gate. Unusual shallow **Engravings** can be made out on the Fort walls on the opposite (south) side of the road. They include a 1294 record of the Kakatiya commander of Raichur, and a scene depicting large stone slabs being transported by bullock carts.

A path leading off the main street, just opposite the Post Office, leads south towards the the **Kali Mosque**. This modest structure of six bays incorporates re-used temple columns of polished black basalt. The overhanging angled eaves are partly obscured by a concrete extension in front. The path continues towards the **Dargah of Mian Babu** and its accompanying mosque before arriving at a dilapidated staircase. This ascends to the **Bala Hisar** at the summit of the rocky hill. This citadel consists of a simple triple-bayed hall and a detached prayer chamber. A circular platform with a cannon is placed nearby.

Returning to the main street, the **Fort Jami Mosque** stands a short distance east of the Post Office. Its simple prayer hall, roofed with domes and vaults, has artistically worked inscribed panels set into the rear wall. The compound in front is entered through a small domed chamber on the east. The **District Prison** diagonally opposite is believed to mark the site of the Kakatiya palace. The **Daftar-ki Mosque** nearby is of little interest.

The street continues east, making a bend around the **Sikandar Gate** in the Inner Fort. This structure has a well-preserved arcaded passageway framed by a handsome arched portal capped with a battlemented parapet. A small Adil Shahi mosque is built into the walls nearby. To reach the **Naurang Gate** it is necessary to turn off the main street here and proceed north, following the walls of the Inner Fort. This Gate served as the principal north entrance to the Outer Fort, but is now in disuse. It has a large central court surrounded by arcades into which are built sculpted blocks showing female stick-dancers, gods and goddesses, *yalis* and squatting lions, motifs familiar from Vijayanagara art. Arched portals are positioned on two sides.

The tour of Raichur proceeds by returning to the main street and continuing east to the **Ek Minar Mosque**, so-called because of the single cylindrical minaret that stands detached from the small prayer chamber. This feature dates back to the first years of Bahmani occupation. The **Kati Gate**, a short distance away, marks the eastern extremity of the Outer Fort. It is set between massive round bastions and is headed by a lintel and an inscribed panel set into an arched recess. The **Jami Mosque**, about 350m east on the same street, is a Bahmani foundation. Its prayer chamber consists of 33 arcaded bays employing re-used Kakatiya columns. The octagonal buttresses with ornate bases at the corners are Adil Shahi additions.

7km south of Raichur is the small village of **Maliyabad**, with its remarkable 12C–13C Kakatiya fort. The inner walls of finely fitted granite blocks are partly rectangular in layout. Two life-size stone statues of elephants stand inside the walls.

O. Mudgal

Located 109km north of Hospet via NH13, this historical site is of exceptional interest for its well-preserved military architecture.

Mudgal was a strategic outpost contested by the Vijayanagara and Gulbarga rulers, whose commanders occupied it succesively in the 14C and 15C. The fort here came under the permanent control of Bijapur after the middle of the 16C.

Mudgal's **Citadel** adjoins the west side of the modern town. The ramparts define an approximately elliptical zone, some 800m along the greater north–south axis, with major entrances on the north and east. The massive **Walls** are doubled throughout. The outer line, built in the early 17C at the orders of Ibrahim Adil Shah, is noticeably angled and displays prominent round bastions; it is shielded by a broad moat. The inner line, assigned to the 15C–16C Vijayanagara era, is more vertical and shows square bastions. The battlements, with rounded merlons on top of both circuits, are inscribed with records of various governers.

The **Fateh Darwaza**, or Victory Gate, the eastern entrance to the Citadel, is reached after passing through a bent entryway flanked by bastions and ramparts. A hall flanking the inner passageway is dated 1560, and has a column showing the defaced relief of a courtly figure. The same date is inscribed on the outer face of the wooden doors, which are studded with iron spikes.

The southern portion of the Mudgal Citadel occupies elevated rocky terrain. Within this zone stands an inner fort, or **Kila**, whose walls are reinforced with square bastions. A dilapidated pavilion and a round platform intended for cannon are the only features of interest. A large rectangular tank is seen nearby.

21 · Hubli

The largest city in northwestern Karnataka, Hubli is a leading manufacturing centre. Dharwad, 21km distant, the home of Karnatak University, is smaller and quieter.

While there is little of historical interest in either city, visitors tend to pass through Hubli on the way from Bangalore [14] to destinations in Maharashtra or when travelling between Goa and Hospet [20]. Such journeys provide opportunities to visit the fort at **Belgaum** [A] and the rare Kadamba-period shrine at **Degamve** [B], both on the way to Kolhapur [8] in Maharashtra.

The Late Chalukya temples at **Gadag** [C], **Dambal** [D] and **Lakkundi** [E] may be combined as a half-day excursion from Hubli, or visited en route to Hospet. The monuments of the Hubli area include the exquisite mosque at **Lakshmeshwar** [F].

■ **Transport**. Hubli is within easy reach of the airport at Belgaum, 81km northwest on NH4, from where there are flights to Bombay [1]. Kolhapur is located 109km further along NH4. Bangalore lies in the other direction, 418km southeast. Both rail and road link Hubli with Margao [13], 189km west, and Hospet, 116km east. It is possible to travel from Hubli directly to

Badami [22] and Bijapur [23], 100km and 198km north respectively. Local buses reach all the sites described here.

- **Accommodation**. The *Ashok Hotel* (☎ 62271) and *Hotel Kailash* (☎ 52235) are the best available in Hubli (STD code 0836). The *Hotel Dharwad* (☎ 41725) is the only recommended place in **Dharwad** (same code as Hubli).

- **Tourist Information**. None.

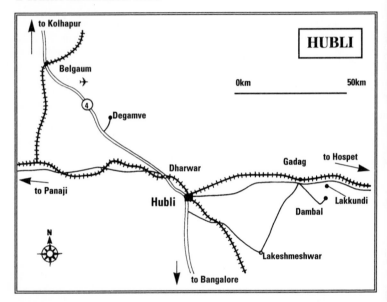

A. Belgaum
Belgaum lies 95km northwest of Hubli on NH4, on the border with Maharashtra.

> Belgaum rose to prominence under the Adil Shahis of Bijapur. Asad Khan, the governor of the city in the first half of the 16C, was the outstanding personality of the era. The city fell to the Marathas in 1673 and was absorbed into the Mughal kingdom soon after, serving for a time as a provincial centre. It was taken by Haidar Ali and then in 1818 by the British, who used the city as a military outpost.

The **Cantonment**, with many of its buildings still preserved, is located in the west part of the city. **St Mary's Church**, begun in 1864 in a Neo-Gothic style, preserves flying buttresses and stained-glass windows.

The **Fort** stands east of the city. Its stone walls, surrounded by a ditch, define an elliptical zone almost 1km across. Blocks taken from dismantled temples are set into the walls. The main gate on the north was added by a Bijapur commander in 1631. The **Safa Mosque** nearby is the work of Asad

Khan. Three dilapidated **Jain Temples** in the vicinity are Late Chalukya monuments of the 12C. The north-facing Temple preserves a pyramidal roof, and there is an ornate corbelled dome-like roof over the adjacent hall. The shrine doorway is richly carved. The smaller south-facing Temple, now missing its sanctuary, has a verandah with seating slabs carved with panels of figures.

B. Degamve

This village lies 5km north of Kittur, a small town on NH4, 58km northwest of Hubli. The chief feature of interest is the **Kamala Narayana Temple**, erected in the 12C by a queen of one of the Kadamba rulers. The monument has double shrines, now consecrated to Vishnu and Mahakali, and an intermediate chamber housing an image of Lakshmi Narayana. These divinities all face into a long columned hall, open on the east as a porch. The outer row of columns carries the angled overhang of the eaves. The balcony seating below is adorned with fully modelled temple towers. The interior columns and doorways are enlivened with carved panels.

C. Gadag

This city, 53km east of Hubli, is of interest for its Late Chalukya monuments. The 11C–12C **Trikuteshvara** and **Sarasvati Temples** stand next to each other in the same compound in the south part of the city. The sanctuary of the Trikuteshvara Temple houses a pedestal with three *lingas* facing into a large open hall with projecting sides and balcony seating all around. A second sanctuary, directly opposite the first, faces west into the hall. The Sarasvati Temple is also incorporated into this scheme, its north-facing shrine opening into the same hall. The Temples have their outer walls adorned with pairs of pilasters carrying temple towers in relief. The porches have balcony seating enlivened with figural panels overhung with steeply angled eaves. The columns also have sculpted figures, many arranged in shallow niches. The towers over the sanctuaries are incomplete.

The **Someshvara Temple**, in the middle of Gadag, though abandoned and neglected, is intricately decorated. Figural panels headed by foliation partly conceal slender pairs of pilasters capped with pediments conceived as model towers. The parapet is encrusted with carved elements. The doorways to the hall are surrounded by densely carved figures and foliation; that on the south is approached through a small porch. The adjacent **Ramesvara Temple** is similar, but more ruined.

D. Dambal

This village, 21km southeast of Gadag, is renowned for the **Dodda Basappa Temple**, one of the finest examples of the Late Chalukya style. The *linga* sanctuary has numerous angled projections that almost approach a circle in plan. The walls display elongated pilasters, singly or in pairs, terminated by tower-like motifs. The pyramidal superstructure, which continues the wall projections beneath, culminates in an unusual star-shaped roof. The interior columns of the adjoining hall have gleaming lathe-turned shafts and capitals. The doorways are surrounded by bands of stylised foliation, with miniature figures beneath. The hall attached to the east end of the Temple shelters an unusually large polished stone image of Nandi, known locally as Dodda Basappa, after which the temple is named.

E. Lakkundi

This village is located 11km east of Gadag, directly on the main road from which its temples may be glimpsed. Lakkundi preserves both Jain and Hindu monuments, dating from the 11C–12C. These Late Chalukya structures are built entirely of grey-green schist. The basements have deeply cut mouldings; slender wall pilasters frame niches headed with tower-like pediments of different designs. The halls and porches have lathe-turned and multi-faceted columns supporting decorated beams and corbelled ceilings enlivened with finely carved detail. The richly encrusted doorways are flanked by perforated screens incorporating figures and foliate motifs. The open porches have balcony seating overhung by steeply angled eaves.

The **Jain *Basti***, the largest and most prominent temple at Lakkundi, stands near the road on the northern edge of the village. Its sanctuary walls rhythmically expand outwards in shallow projections, repeated in the parapet of miniature roof forms above. The five-storeyed pyramidal tower is capped with a square roof. Enclosed and open halls adjoin the sanctuary, the latter enlarged by projections on three sides.

The nearby **Kashivishvanatha Temple**, the other major monument at Lakkundi, consists of two sanctuaries facing each across a porch, now mostly collapsed. The basement is adorned with friezes of elephants and lotus petals. The walls have pairs of pilasters capped by *makaras* with flowing tails or with temple-like reliefs of different designs. Niches with curved tower-like forms mark the most prominent projections; they contrast with the pyramidal shape of the tower of the temple itself, which is preserved incompletely over the west sanctuary. The doorways are surrounded by bands of stylised foliation with guardians beneath.

Another feature of interest at Lakkundi is the **Stepped Tank**, on the other side of the main road. This consists of a square pond surrounded by landings and miniature shrines. A two-storeyed colonnade serves as a bridge.

F. Lakshmeshwar

This small town, 48km southeast of Hubli or 38km directly south of Gadag, is renowned for its ornate Adil Shahi monument. The **Kali Mosque** of about 1617 resembles similarly elaborate projects at Bijapur. The Lakshmeshwar complex has an imposing entrance gate, with an arched recess framing a doorway with temple-like jambs and lintel. The doorway is topped by a parapet with finials in shallow relief. Sculpted brackets carry the overhanging eaves above, which is a cut-out parapet of luxuriant design with intermediate domical pinnacles. The composition is flanked by slender minarets.

The prayer hall of the Mosque itself presents a triple-arched façade, the central opening having lobes cut into the outer plane. Crisply worked plaster roundels fill the spandrels. The arches are overhung by sloping eaves on sculpted brackets, with hanging stone chains in between. The intricately worked parapet shows cut-out interlaced battlement motifs. The intermediate pinnacles are conceived as diminutive pavilions, complete with miniature eaves and domes.

The façade is framed by octagonal minarets rising high above the roof line. Stone chains hang from miniature pavilions at the intermediate stages, as well as from lotus petals beneath the domical tops. A small dome rises over the central rear bay of the hall.

Several 11C period temples stand just outside the town. Though much damaged, they preserve traces of the crisp carving characteristic of the Late Chalukya style. The **Someshvara Temple**, the largest of the group, stands in an open court entered on the south through a gateway, anticipating the *gopuras* of later times. The main shrine has wall niches topped with model temple towers. This adjoins an almost free-standing columned hall with multiple projections, entered on three sides. Another interesting monument is the **Lakshmilingeshvara Temple**, which gives its name to the town. Here, triple *linga* sanctuaries opening into a common hall adjoin a much larger hall on a stepped plan, also with triple doorways. Unfortunately, the outer walls have been substantially rebuilt.

22 · Badami

The Early Chalukya temples in and around Badami are celebrated for their varied forms and splendid carvings. There is also the natural beauty of the Malprabha River Valley, in which the temples are set.

Two days will be needed to visit the monuments at **Badami** [A] and nearby holy spots at **Banakshankari** [B] and **Mahakuta** [C], as well as the villages of **Pattadakal** [D] and **Aihole** [E].

■ **Transport**. Badami can be reached by train, on the branch line running between Gadag [21C] and Bijapur [23]. It can otherwise be approached by road from Hospet [20], 207km southeast, Hubli, 100km south, or Bijapur, 136km north. The nearest airport is at Belgaum [21A], about 140km west. Bus services are available from Badami to all of the temples included here.

■ **Accommodation**. The newly opened *Hotel Badami Court* (☎ 65230) is the best available at Badami (☎ 08357), but the *Hotel Mayura Chalukya* (☎ 65046) is an alternative. An alternative place to stay is the simple *Tourist Lodge* at **Aihole**. Some visitors may prefer make an overnight stop at the *Durga Vihar Hotel* at **Bagalkot**, some 35km northwest of Aihole.

■ **Tourist Information**. None.

History

Badami is associated with the Early Chalukyas, the dominant rulers of Karnataka in the 6C–8C. Originally called Vatapi, the town was their headquarters, and from here they conquered substantial parts of Maharashtra, Andhra Pradesh and Karnataka. The first great king of this line, Pulakeshin I, was already on the Badami throne in 543. He was succeeded by his son, Kirttivarman I (556–97). Civil war broke out during the reign of Kirttivarman's son, Mangalesha. Pulakeshin II (609–54), the next great ruler, was instrumental in expanding the Chalukya kingdom. In 612 he conducted a daring raid on Kanchipuram [37F], the capital of the Pallavas in the Tamil zone. The Pallavas retaliated and occupied Badami in 654. Pulakeshin lost his life in the ensuing battle.

Vikramaditya I was the ruler responsible for expelling the Pallavas and restoring the fortunes of the Chalukya kingdom. In 681 he was succeeded by his son, Vinayaditya (696–733), whose reign was the longest and most peaceful; that of Vikramaditya II (733–44) was more aggressive, due to wars waged against the rival Pallavas. Vikramaditya's son, Kirttivarman II, was the last of the Early Chalukyas; he was overthrown by the invading Rashtrakutas in 753.

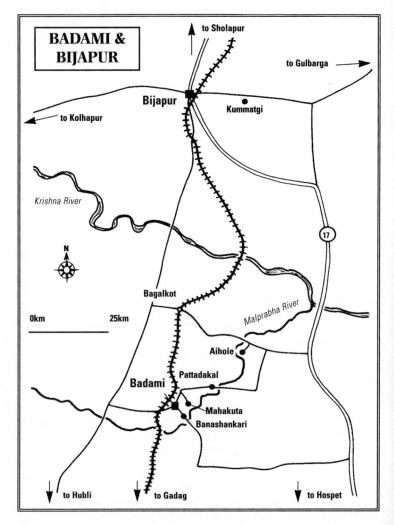

Badami remained in the hands of the Rashtrakutas until the middle of the 10C, after which it was absorbed into the territories of the Late Chalukyas, a line of kings only vaguely related to their earlier namesakes. In later centuries, Badami came successively under the sway of the Hoysalas, Tuluvas and Adil Shahis, the last of whom were responsible for the gates and forts that still stand in and around the town. Badami was an important outpost for the Marathas, from whom it was seized by British troops in 1818.

A. Badami

Badami is surrounded by a horseshoe of rugged red sandstone cliffs, with forti-fied headlands to the north and south. The narrow streets of the town are concentrated to the west of a dam wall which contains a tank with bright green water.

The tour described here begins with the 6C **Cave Temples**, excavated into the sheer escarpment of the south headland. The deep-red sandstone is here streaked with purple veins, giving the Caves a colouristic quality. These are the finest **rock-cut monuments** in Karnataka, much admired for their robust sculptures. Access steps and landings offer spectacular views over the town and tank.

Cave 1 is entered through a porch which gives access to a columned hall with a small square sanctuary set into the rear wall. The column shafts are decorated with jewel-and-garland motifs and small medallions containing figures and foli-ation. The capitals are fluted. Sculpted panels at either end of the porch depict Harihara (left) and Shiva with Nandi (right). The ceiling panels show a deeply modelled coiled *naga* divinity in the middle, with Shiva and Parvati in the company of flying couples at either side. Outside the porch to the right is a small shrine housing images of Durga, Karttikeya and Ganesha. A magnificent 18-armed icon of dancing Shiva is carved on the cliff face nearby.

Cave 2 repeats the scheme of the previous example, except that the deities are all Vaishnava. Panels at either end of the porch show Varaha (left) and Trivikrama (right), both with friezes of dwarfs beneath. The brackets are fash-ioned as figures emerging from open-mouthed *makaras*. The ceiling panels include a wheel of radiating fish and a design incorporating swastika motifs and flying couples. Gracefully posed warriors guard the porch entrance.

The next monument, **Cave 3**, is laid out in accordance with the others, but at an enlarged scale and with a greater emphasis on ornamentation. Its historical importance is confirmed by an inscription dated 578. Panels crowded with animated dwarfs animate the basement of the Cave, and the interior columns present a variety of multi-faceted and fluted designs. Medallions on the shafts show amorous couples encased in delicate lotus ornament. The brackets of the outer row of columns are fashioned as embracing couples or maidens beneath trees; rearing beasts project outwards to carry the curving overhang of the eaves. An image of Garuda is carved on the inner face of the eaves. Fragmentary paintings at either side show courtly figures.

Major figural compositions are carved on the porch walls: Vishnu seated on the coiled serpent (end panel), Varaha and standing Vishnu (side panels) to the left; Narasimha (end panel), Harihara and Trivikrama (side panels) to the right. The last deity forms the climax of an enlarged scene, with Vamana and other figures. The uppermost parts of the walls have epic friezes, including the churning of the ocean and Krishna vanquishing demons. The porch ceiling is decorated with medallions showing Vishnu flanked by Lakshmi and Garuda (middle), Karittikeya (left), and Shiva, Indra and Varuna (right). Other figures are seen on the hall ceiling, such as Brahma with the Dikpalas.

The topmost **Cave 4**, the last of the series, is a Jain monument. It is smaller in scale and less elaborate than its predecessors. Both seated and standing Tirthankaras adorn the walls; the full modelling of these figures distinguishes them from later insertions of small standing Jinas.

It is not possible to proceed further, and visitors must return to the base of the cliffs. Near to the entrance of Cave 1 stands a red sandstone **Tomb**. This finely executed building belongs to the Adil Shahi period. The prominent cornice, ornate trefoil parapet and three-quarter spherical dome are all typical features of Bijapur's architecture. Visitors should proceed along the path that runs beside the dam wall.

The **Yellamma Temple**, overlooking the tank, is a Late Chalukya project. Its walls and multi-storeyed tower are divided into narrow projections framed by slender pilasters; the secondary pilasters are capped with miniature roof forms. Turning left soon after brings visitors to a central crossing. The nearby

Bhutanatha Temple, Badami

Jambulinga Temple is approached through a passageway between two houses. This Early Chalukya building, which dates from 699, is of interest for the three sanctuaries opening off a common hall. That they were once dedicated to different deities is suggested by the different ceiling panels, which show Shiva, Vishnu and Brahma. Other compositions depict a coiled *naga*, a wheel with fish spokes, and swastikas with flying couples. The adjacent **Virupaksha Temple** is assigned to the Late Chalukya era.

The tour of Badami proceeds through several of the town's gates until the **Archaeological Museum** (closed Fridays), on the north side of the lake, is reached. Among the sculptures exhibited here is a Jain goddess seated beneath a tree. Two panels from Pattadakal show Shiva spearing the demon and riding in a chariot, shooting arrows. An icon of Lajja Gauri shows a squatting female divinity with a lotus head. A path following the tank passes by the **Mallikarjuna Group**, a cluster of Late Chaluyka shrines with open porches and pyramidal squat towers with layers of deeply set tiers.

The **Bhutanatha Temple** is picturesquely sited at the east end of the lake. The sanctuary and inner hall belong to the Early Chaluyka era, but the open porch with balcony seating overlooking the water is later. The caverns in the rocks nearby display carved images, the largest of which is an impressive figure of a Jina seated on a throne. There is also a depiction of Vishnu sleeping on Ananta, attended by Lakshmi.

The tour continues by returning to the Archaeological Museum, passing through an arched gate and climbing up a stepped path that ascends the northern headland. This route partly follows a deep gorge with dramatic overhanging bluffs. The first monument to be seen, the **Lower Shivalaya**, is situated on a rocky promontory overlooking the town. Only the tower, with a dome-like roof, survives. The small pavilions opposite may have been ceremonial structures used by the Early Chalukya kings. The next features to be noticed are crenellated fortifications and conical granaries, probably no earlier than the 18C.

The **Upper Shivalaya**, at the summit of the headland, may be the first structural temple of the Early Chalukyas. Though not all of its 7C fabric is preserved, the building is impressive for the proportions of its elevation. The tower over the sanctuary is capped by a square domical roof. Angled slabs cover the surrounding passageway. The basement has friezes of animated dwarfs and scenes of the Krishna legend (south). Other Krishna panels are carved on the pilastered walls.

The final monument to be described, the 7C **Malegitti Shivalaya,** can only be reached by taking a side path near the bus stand on the main street. Sited on top of a huge boulder, out of which it seems to grow naturally, the temple presents a simple combination of towered sanctuary, columned hall and entrance porch. The outer walls have clearly articulated basement mouldings, pilastered walls and overhanging cornices. Pierced stone windows, with *makaras* and garlands above, flank sculpted panels of Vishnu (north) and Shiva (south). The tower has an octagonal domed roof.

B. Banashankari

This pilgrimage spot, 5km east of Badami, is celebrated for the **Banashankari Temple**, the most popular place of worship in the vicinity. A chariot festival takes place here in January–February, attended by a busy market and fair. The Temple itself is of little interest architecturally, but faces east towards an attractive square tank of impressive proportions, surrounded by arcades. Much of the complex dates from the 18C Maratha period.

C. Mahakuta

This attractive wooded site lies 8km beyond Banashankari, along a road that passes beneath a rocky outcrop, or about the same distance on another road that turns off the route from Badami to Pattadakal.

The Mahakuta shrines stand within a walled enclosure, grouped around a rectangular tank fed by a natural spring. A small pavilion in the middle of the water shelters a four-faced Shiva *linga*. The principal shrine, the **Mahakuteshvara Temple**, belongs to the late 7C, later than the Badami monuments, but earlier than those at Pattadakal. It consists of a sanctuary surrounded by a passageway, approached through a columned hall with a small porch. The walls are raised on basement mouldings with intricate friezes illustrating epic subjects interspersed with foliate panels. Pierced stone windows with ornate pediments are placed either side of niches with Ardhanarishvara (north) and Shiva (north and west); guardian figures appear on the east wall. A storeyed tower capped with an octagonal domical roof rises over the sanctuary. A small Nandi pavilion stands in front.

Almost exactly the same scheme is followed in the **Mallikarjuna Temple**, on the south side of the tank. The interior has fine ceiling slabs, all of which are nine-panelled compositions with different deities in the middle. The adjacent **Sangameshvara** and **Mahalinga Temples**, on the west side of the tank, are small structures with curving spires. Delicately carved panels in the wall niches depict Harihara (north), Ardhanarishvara or Narasimha (west) and Lakulisha and Varaha (south).

A dilapidated **Gateway** outside the complex, abutting its southeast corner, has remarkable skeletal guardian figures, identified as Kala and Kali. A fallen sandstone column discovered nearby has been removed to the Archaeological Musuem at Bijapur.

The **Naganatha Temple** stands at the head of a ravine, about 2km southwest of Mahakuta. This monument may be compared with similar examples at Aihole. Perforated screens light the passageway surrounding the sanctuary and adjoining columned hall. Embracing couples beneath trees are carved on the porch columns.

D. Pattadakal

This village lies 16km northeast of Badami, overlooking the Malprabha River at a point where the water flows north. The road from Badami passes by a dilapidated 9C **Jain Temple**, assigned to the Rashtrakuta era. Its outer walls have slender pilasters, but no sculptures. The stepped tower has a square roof. Unusual elephant torsos carved in full relief are placed either side of the inner doorway where they are framed by *makaras* with ornate tails.

The main group of monuments is located 500m further east, at the edge of Pattadakal village. The temples and subshrines, all facing east toward the river, stand in a landscaped compound entered at the northwest corner. The monuments are remarkable for their variety, demonstrating the meeting of different architectural styles; they represent the climax of the Early Chalukya achievement in the first half of the 8C. They are described here in sequence from north to south.

The **Kadasiddheshvara** and **Jambulinga Temples** have curved spires adorned with horseshoe-shaped arched motifs and ribbed elements. Worn sculptures on the outer walls of the sanctuaries are framed by pilasters. The frontal (east) faces of the towers have circular panels containing Nataraja images.

The **Galaganatha Temple** presents a more evolved, though not necessarily later, version of the same scheme. The monument may be compared with those at Alampur [32B], with which it is contemporary. The most striking feature is the well-preserved curved tower, with horizontal tiers covered with horseshoe-shaped motifs; ribbed elements are positioned at the ends and at the summit. Porches once projected outwards on three sides, but only that on the south survives. It shelters a carved panel showing Shiva energetically spearing Andhaka. Damaged river goddesses and an icon of dancing Shiva adorn the sanctuary doorway.

The **Sangameshvara Temple**, a foundation of Vijayaditya, was never completed. The finely proportioned exterior displays walls divided into projections and recesses by pairs of pilasters, a parapet of miniature roof forms and a multi-storeyed tower capped with a square roof. Most of the sculpture panels are incomplete. The intermediate perforated stone windows have bold geometric designs.

The **Kashivishvanatha Temple** is the only example in this group to be assigned to the Rashtrakuta period in the second half of the 8C. The wall projections have pediments and arch-like motifs. Similar designs cover the

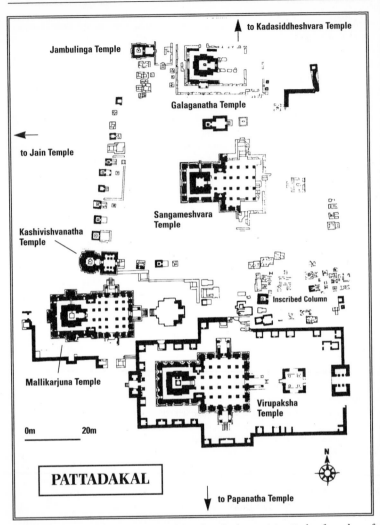

to Kadasiddheshvara Temple

Jambulinga Temple

Galaganatha Temple

to Jain Temple

Sangameshvara
Temple

Kashivishvanatha
Temple

Inscribed Column

Mallikarjuna Temple

Virupaksha
Temple

0m   20m

PATTADAKAL

N

to Papanatha Temple

tower, especially the central vertical bands, which consist entirely of meshes of these motifs. A dancing Shiva is positioned on the front (east) face.

The neighbouring, almost identical, **Virupaksha** and **Mallikarjuna Temples** were erected by two queens in about 745 to commemorate Vikramaditya's victory over the Pallavas. The Temples each have a *linga* sanctuary surrounded by a passageway that opens on to a columned hall, divided into five aisles and entered through three porches. An open pavilion to the east in the Virupaksha Temple shelters a large image of Nandi. Walls enclose the Temples in rectangular paved courts, with subshrines and entrance gates on the east. The diagonal arrangement of the two enclosures is unique.

The Virupaksha and Mallikarjuna Temples show a marked stylistic evolution in the increase in scale and complexity of design. There are slight differences between the two monuments: the wall projections in the Virupaksha Temple are flanked by two sets of pilasters, while three sets are employed in the Mallikarjuna Temple; a square roof caps the multi-storeyed tower of the Virupaksha Temple, while that over the Mallikarjuna Temple is hemispherical. Both towers have horseshoe-shaped frontal projections framing icons of dancing Shiva.

The vitality of Early Chalukya art is amply illustrated by carvings on the outer walls showing Shiva and Vishnu in diverse aspects. The panels on either side of the east porch of the Virupaksha Temple are among the finest; they show Shiva appearing out of the *linga* (left) and Vishnu as Trivikrama (right). Other notable sculptures are dancing Shiva (east end of south wall), Bhairava (south wall of sanctuary) and Vishnu with Durga beneath (north wall of sanctuary).

The panels on the Mallikarjuna Temple are less well preserved and are partly unfinished, as in the vigorous Nataraja on the rear (west) wall of the sanctuary. Perforated stone windows with delicately carved foliate motifs are inserted into the wall recesses. Both sculptures and windows are surmounted by arch-like pediments filled with figures or *makaras* with foliated tails. Divinities and embracing couples are carved on the porch columns: those in the Virupaksha Temple include Shiva subduing Ravana (south porch) and Vishnu riding on Garuda (north porch). The side panels of the east doorway of the Virupaksha Temple show auspicious pot-bellied attendants. The ceiling panel here portrays Surya riding in a horse-drawn chariot. Figures with clubs guard the doorways.

The interior columns of the Virupaksa and Mallikarjuna Temples have bands of narrative friezes depicting epic stories, as well as decorative scrollwork and lotus ornament. The wall columns are enlivened with graceful courtly couples. the ceilings raised over the central aisles are carved with *naga* divinities, dancing Shiva and scenes of Lakshmi bathed by elephants. The doorways to the sanctuaries have river goddesses and attendants beneath at either side, and *makaras* with foliated tails raised above. A remarkable fully modelled icon of Durga is placed in the minor north shrine within the Virupaksha hall. The sanctuaries house polished granite *lingas* on high pedestals. The large Nandi image within the open pavilion of the Virupaksha complex is naturalistically carved and cere-monially decked with garlands and bells. The circular columns have projecting brackets and delicately applied foliate decoration. A gate on the east side of the enclosure leads down to the river.

A path from the Virupaksha Temple follows the Malprabha south for about 200m to the **Papanatha Temple**, on the other side of Pattadakal village. Two interconnecting columned halls lead to a sanctuary with blind porches on three sides. Elements derived from different styles are combined in the elevation: the tower over the sanctuary resembles the superstructures of the Kadasiddheshvara and Jambulinga Temples, while the parapet of roof forms and the *makaras* with foliated tails on the pilasters flanking niches and doorways recall similar elements on the Virupaksha and Mallikarjuna Temples.

The basement of the front porch of the Papanatha Temple is carved with struggling elephants and lions. The friezes on the outer walls illustrate episodes from the *Mahabharata* and *Ramayana*; the latter is easily recognised by the processions of monkeys (south wall). The porch columns are adorned with courtly couples, maidens and guardians; similar figures appear on the peripheral columns inside both halls. The wall niches within the outer hall are occupied by images of Durga and Ganesha. The columns have cushion-shaped capitals and ornate brackets decorated with monster masks and foliation. An upper tier of brackets carrying transverse beams is fashioned as open-mouthed *makaras* disgorging lions. The ceilings are carved with fine Nataraja figures and coiled *naga* deities.

E. Aihole

The Hindu and Jain monuments in this somewhat isolated town, 50km northeast of Badami, belong to both the Early and Late Chalukya periods, as well as to the intervening Rashtrakuta era, a period spanning the 6C–12C. The temples are dotted around the town, the houses of which are contained in an incomplete circle of fortifications, as well as in the surrounding fields and on top of a nearby hill.

Only the most important temples at Aihole are described here, especially those assigned to the 7C–8C. The names by which they are known are derived from their temporary inhabitants in recent times, rather than the divinities worshipped there. The monuments are described according to a visit that begins and ends at the **Durga Temple**, the largest and most elaborate at Aihole, a royal foundation of Vikramaditya II. The name of this shrine is misleading: it refers not to the goddess Durga, but to the fact that it once served as a defensive outpost (*durg*). The actual dedication of the Temple remains unknown. The apsidal-ended plan of the Durga Temple imitates *chaitya* halls of earlier Buddhist architecture. The semi-circular sanctuary and adjoining rectangular hall are approached through a porch with seating, all surrounded by an open colonnade. An incomplete tower rises over the sanctuary.

The sculptures in the Durga Temple are among the masterpieces of Early Chalukya art. The columns at the entrance are carved with amorous couples and guardian figures; those inside the porch are adorned with medallions, garlands and jewels; the ceiling panels here have a coiled serpent and fish wheel. The hall doorway is flanked by river goddesses and guardians. Pierced stone windows alternating with niches with pediments of different designs embellish the colonnade that runs the full length of the building. The carved panels in the niches show (in clockwise sequence) Shiva with Nandi, Narasimha, Vishnu with Garuda, Varaha, Durga and Harihara. Only traces of the flying couples carved on the sloping ceiling slabs survive. (The two finest examples are now in the National Museum, New Delhi.) In contrast to the rich treatment of the exterior, the hall interior is plain. A circular pedestal devoid of any image is placed in the sanctuary.

The adjacent **Archaeological Museum** (closed Fridays) is home to a number of stray sculptures, including a damaged image of Ambika seated on a lion, surrounded by figures.

A short distance south of the Durga Temple is a group of monuments arranged around a tank, with sculpted figures set into its stepped sides. The **Surya Narayana Temple** presents a simple combination of towered shrine, columned hall and porch. A later image of Surya is placed in the sanctuary. The **Ladkhan Temple** is of interest for its obvious reliance on timber models. A spacious columned hall is roofed with sloping strips of stone slabs in two tiers;

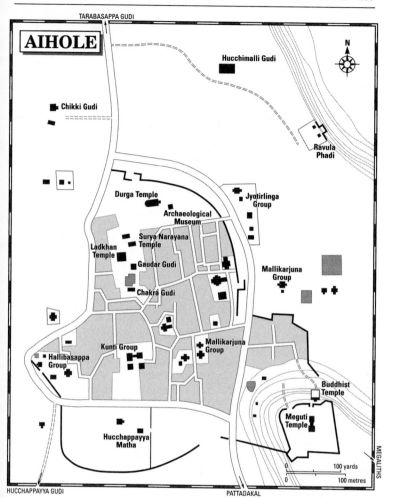

log-like strips protect the joints. A small chamber rises over the middle of the roof; this has damaged carvings of Vishnu, Surya and Ardhanarishvara on the outer walls. River goddesses and couples embracing beneath trees are carved on the outer columns of the porch. The inclined balcony seating is decorated with pot-and-knot motifs. The hall interior is austere. A small sanctuary is positioned against the rear wall; perforated stone screens on three sides illuminate the interior.

The nearby **Gaudar Gudi** is set at a lower level, suggesting an earlier date than the Ladkhan Temple. The Gaudar Gudi is a simple quadrangular colonnade comprising an inner hall and sanctuary. The inclined balcony slabs set between peripheral supports are decorated with pot motifs. The roof slopes on four sides. The niches with triangular pediments on the sanctuary walls are empty, but the doorway is elaborately carved. The adjacent **Chakra Gudi** is ruined, except for the well-preserved curving tower over the sanctuary, which is capped with a circular ribbed element.

A short walk through the streets of Aihole is required to reach the **Kunti Group**, another interesting ensemble. Four temples built close together, dating from different periods, consist of partly open halls with sloping roofs and overhanging eaves. Each temple has a small sanctuary positioned against the rear wall. The southeast example, probably the first to be built, is entered from the north, where the columns are carved with amorous figures. The northwest temple also has sculpted figures. The interior is enlivened by three finely carved ceiling panels of Shiva with Parvati, Vishnu on the serpent and Brahma on the lotus. Guardians flank the sanctuary doorway. The two remaining structures are assigned to the Rashtrakuta era, as is evident from the columns, which have squat proportions and triangular panels of lotus decoration. A free-standing portal with animal brackets links the two north temples.

The **Hucchappayya Matha** lies further south, beyond the houses of the town. Its severe exterior is relieved by sculpted columns flanking the east porch, showing embracing couples, including a woman with a horse's head. The hall is roofed with ceiling panels depicting the same trio of divinities noted in the Kunti Group.

For visitors with additional time and interest, there is an optional excursion along a path that runs beside the Malprabha River. The path leaves Aihole near the **Hallibasappa Gudi**, a Rashtrakuta temple recognised by the unusually large figures of river goddesses beside the entrance, and then crosses a small stream and continues for almost 1km before arriving at the **Hucchappayya Gudi** (not to be confused with the temple previously described). This well-preserved temple has a sanctuary with a curving tower adjoining a rectangular hall and small porch. Couples and guardians are carved on the porch columns, and guardians flank the sanctuary doorway. Unfortunately, the trio of ceiling panels carved with Shiva, Vishnu and Brahma has been removed to the Prince of Wales Museum, Bombay [1B]. The nearby **Galaganatha Group** belongs to the Rashtrakuta era. The main temple is entered through a portal with a lintel decorated with *makaras* and looped garlands. The doorway inside is carved in imitiation of earlier designs.

It is necessary to return to Aihole in order to climb the flat-topped hill to the southeast. The most convenient route is to follow the main road north and then branch off at the **Mallikarjuna Group**. The central temple here is an Early Chalukya foundation, but the tower with horizontal mouldings is later. The entrance portal here is adorned with *makaras* and auspicious emblems.

A stepped path leads upwards from the Mallikarjuna Group. Just before reaching the top of the hill, the path passes the 6C **Buddhist Temple**. This has massive colonnades in front of rock-cut chambers at two levels. A ceiling panel at the upper level shows a seated Buddha. The doorways are surrounded by delicate reliefs. Beyond lies the **Meguti Temple**, from where fine views may be had of Aihole and the Malprabha Valley as far as Pattadakal. This temple is a Jain foundation with an inscription of 634, making it the earliest dated structure in Southern India. The exterior of the Temple is divided simply into a basement, pilastered walls with deep niches, now empty, and a cornice. The chamber over the sanctuary is a later addition, as are the porch and hall in front (north). An impressive seated Jina figure is placed within the sanctuary. An interesting group of **Megaliths** is seen on the level top of the hill southeast of the Meguti Temple. They comprise chamber tombs with circles of stone slabs supporting capping pieces. These features are some 2000 years old.

The tour of Aihole continues by descending the hill and following the road that runs around the ring of fortifications. The **Jyotirlinga Group** consists of several modest Early Chalukya shrines concealed by later additions. A track through the fields leads to **Ravula Phadi**, a sanctuary excavated into a sandstone outcrop northeast of the town. This 6C cave temple is preceded by three small shrines with primitive towers. A broken fluted stone column stands on an axis with the cave entrance. Ravula Phadi comprises a *linga* sanctuary and two side chambers, partly incomplete on the right, opening off a central hall. Delicately modelled figures on the walls of the hall depict Ardhanarishvara, Harihara and Shiva with Ganga. The antechamber preceding the *linga* shrine is enlivened with deeply carved panels of Varaha and Durga. An elaborate composition around the walls of the left side chamber shows ten-armed Shiva dancing in the company of Parvati, Ganesha and the Matrikas; all the figures wear pleated costumes. Guardians in foreign dress flank the entrance to the monument.

The tour proceeds along a track in front of Ravula Phadi in order to reach the **Hucchimalli Gudi**. This rectangular building combines a columned hall with a sanctuary and surrounding passageway lit by small windows. Sloping slabs roof the outer aisles, and a curved tower rises over the sanctuary. The porch ceiling contains a unique depiction of Karttikeya riding on the peacock. The track eventually meets the main road proceeding north from the town. Almost opposite, set back from the road, is the **Chikki Gudi**. This temple is laid out in a similar fashion to the previous example, but without any tower. Finely executed lotus ornament cloaks the columns and beams inside the hall. Two elaborate ceiling compositions show Shiva dancing and spearing Andhaka, and Vishnu sleeping on the serpent and kicking his leg up as Trivikrama. The adjacent ruined structure has an apsidal-ended in plan. The Shiva *linga* on a circular pedestal placed here may be original. The tour of Aihole concludes by returning to the main road and proceeding to the Durga Temple, a short distance away.

The itinerary described here does not include the **Tarabasappa Gudi**, beside the main road 1km north of the town. This temple follows the standard tripartite layout, with sanctuary, hall and porch. The sanctuary has pilastered wall niches and a fully preserved curved tower.

23 · Bijapur

Bijapur stands in the middle of a desolate plain that provides a striking contrast to the magnificent fortications, gateways and noble monuments of the city. Celebrated for the splendid mosques, tombs and palaces erected by the Adil Shahi rulers in the 16C–17C, Bijapur is a rewarding stop-over on any tour of northern Karnataka. Today, it is a thriving market town and a centre for the outlying regions.

A visit to Bijapur may conveniently be combined with itineraries for Hospet

[20], Badami [22] and Gulbarga [24], even with that for Sholapur [9] in Maharashtra.

At least one full day will be taken up with the monuments of **Bijapur** [A] and its immediate **environs** [B] described here. An excursion to the royal resort at **Kummatgi** [C] will occupy another half day. The location map for Badami and Bijapur is on p 268.

■ **Transport**. Bijapur can be reached by rail, being situated on the branch line linking Sholapur with Gadag [21C], with connections to Hospet and Hubli [21]. Road transport is, however, quicker and more frequent. Sholapur is 101km north of Bijapur on NH13; the same highway leads in the other direction to Hospet, 207km south. Badami is situated 136km south of Bijapur, and Hubli 198km. Gulbarga lies 98km northeast via Jevargi.

■ **Accommodation**. The *Hotel Mayura Adil Shahi* (☎ 20934) is probably the best in Bijapur (STD code 08352), but there are also new places, such as the *Hotel Madhuvan* (☎ 25571) and *Hotel Samrat* (☎ 21620).

■ **Tourist Information**. The KSTDC maintains a bureau at the *Hotel Mayura Adil Shahi*.

History

Bijapur was already well established in 1294, when it was annexed by the invading Delhi army. The city subsequently became a provincial centre under the Bahmanis. At the end of the 15C, Bijapur was under the governorship of Yusuf Adil Khan. This able officer, of Central Asian origin, served under Mahmud Gawan, the influential Prime Minister of Bidar [25A]. Yusuf was posted to Bijapur, from where he proclaimed his independence in 1490, thereby transforming the city into the capital of a new kingdom. He did not, however, assume the title of Shah, but continued to profess allegiance to the Bahmanis.

Almost all the Adil Shahis succeeded each other in direct father-to-son line. The most prominent figures were Ali I (1558–80) and his successor Ibrahim II (1580–1627). The careers of most rulers were taken up with the struggles between the rival states of Bidar and Golconda [26E]. The Adil Shahis also waged wars with neighbouring Vijayanagara [20B–C], lending their support to the army that defeated this great empire in 1565. The Adil Shahis benefited greatly from the victory, seizing much of Vijayanagara's wealth and territories.

The greatest fortunes of the Adil Shahis and the period of their greatest monuments coincided with the second half of the 16C and first half of the 17C. Muhammad I (1627–56) was on the throne when the Mughals first besieged Bijapur in 1636. However, it was not until 1686 that the Mughal forces under Aurangzeb succeeded in invading the the kingdom, occupying the capital and bringing to an end the Adil Shahi line. The city quickly declined under the Mughals.

Constant warfare did not prevent the Adil Shahis from patronising art and literature, and many painters and poets flocked to the Bijapur court, where a distinct school of miniature painting was developed. Their patronage extended also to religious learning, especially to the Sufi *dargahs*, where the intellectual climate of Bijapur was further developed. The Bijapur kings were also well acquainted with Hindu mythology and astonomy. Ibrahim II, for instance, even adopted a traditional Indian title, Jagatguru, Preceptor of the World.

A. Bijapur

The city of Bijapur is strongly fortified, being contained within a circuit of **Outer Walls** that define an elliptical zone, some 2.5km along the greater east-west axis. The Walls were erected in 1565 under Yusuf Adil Khan and are fairly complete, reaching a height of 10m. The outer faces are reinforced by 96 round bastions with intermediate projecting guardrooms and a prominent battle-mented parapet. A broad pathway runs continuously along the top of the Walls. The bastions were modifed in later times with the introduction of artillery, and many fine guns are still in place. The most famous is the Malik-i-Maidan, Lord of the Plain, which sits on the **Sharza Bastion**, surveying the approaches to Bijapur from the west. The Walls are broken by six major **Gates** that define the principal roads of the city. The Gates follow a standard pattern, with lintels on corbelled brackets surmounted by lofty arches and battlemented parapets.

Only the most important monuments are described here. The tour begins at the east end of Bijapur, with the **Gol Gumbad**, the Tomb of Muhammad I. This faces south onto Mahatma Gandhi Road, the principal east–west street of the

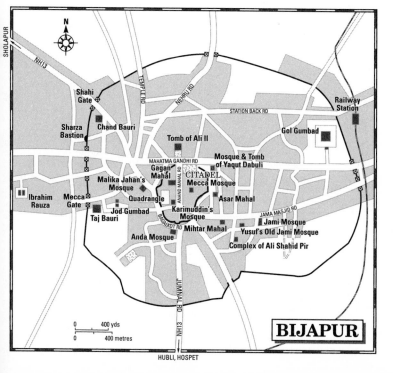

city, a short distance from the railway station. Completed at the time of Muhammad's death in 1656, this is the major achievement of the Adil Shahis and one of the greatest structural triumphs of Indian architecture.

The design of the Gol Gumbad is strikingly simple, with a hemispherical dome, nearly 44m in external diameter, resting on a cubical mass 47.5m square. The exterior is majestic, with triple sets of arched recesses on three sides. Medallions on brackets are etched into the plasterwork in the spandrels. The central recesses are filled with stone screens pierced by doorways and windows. An overhanging cornice, cantilevering outwards for more than 3m, is supported by tiers of sculpted brackets and surmounted by an arcade and parapet of trefoil elements. The corner octagonal towers have open stages, each marked by arcades, concealing staircases. They are topped by bulbous domes on petalled bases, imitating at a smaller scale the great dome that serves as the climax of the whole composition.

The interior of the Gol Gumbad is dominated by eight arches in overlapping squares that form interlocking pendentives. These curve inwards to create a circular gallery, from which the dome rises. The austere quality of the chamber emphasises the overall structural system. A cenotaph slab in the floor lies over the true grave in the basement. A part-octagonal bay projecting outwards in the middle of the west side indicates the direction of Mecca.

The Gol Gumbad stands in the middle of a formal garden. To the west is a small but handsome mosque, with a restrained façade of five arches flanked by slender minarets wih domed turrets. The finely finished gateway on the south has an upper vaulted chamber intended for musicians. The building now serves as the **Archaeological Museum** (closed Fridays). Early Chalukya temple sculptures and an inscribed pillar from Mahakuta [22C] are displayed here, as well as elegantly worked calligraph slabs from the Adil Shahi period. The upper rooms house a collection of Chinese porcelain, some discovered in the Chini Mahal, and carpets. An interesting 17C watercolour map of Bijapur shows the concentric rings of walls and all the major buildings and waterworks.

The **Jami Mosque** is reached by proceeding west and south from the Gol Gumbad. Begun by Ali I in 1576, this great project was never completed. The corner buttresses indicate where tall minarets would have risen on either side of the prayer hall. This presents a row of nine arches, only that in the middle is lobed, with medallions in the spandrels. The overhang is carried on sculpted brackets. The parapet was never begun. The great hemispherical dome at the rear rises on a cubic clerestory relieved by arched recesses and a pierced parapet with prominent finials.

The interior of the Jami Mosque is impressive for its monumental simplicity. The nine bays in the middle are roofed with a single lofty dome. Two intersecting squares of arches with intermediate faceted pendentives create an octagonal space over which the dome appears to float, the first appearance of this structural device at Bijapur. The treatment of the stone *mihrab* is sumptuous, with receding sculpted planes of stylised foliation framing the central arch, and traces of gold and other pigments. The prayer chamber faces on to a court, only partly surrounded by arcades. The detached gateway on the east was added by Aurangzeb at the beginning of the 18C.

Continuing west along the same street as the Jami Mosque, visitors will arrive at **Yusuf's Old Jami Mosque**. Dating from 1513, this is one of the earliest Adil

Shahi monuments in the city; it anticipates the mature Adil Shahi style in its use of a hemispherical dome on a tall circular drum rising on a ring of lotus buds with petals. The prayer chamber has three bays, the central one wider than those on the sides. A short distance south, down a side street, stands the **Complex of Ali Shahid Pir**, assigned to the reign of Ali I. This consists of a small mosque, little more than 10m square, superbly decorated with sharply cut plaster. The waggon-vaulted roof running parallel to the façade is a rarity in Adil Shahi architecture.

The **Mihtar Mahal** stands on the same street as the Jami Mosque. This complex, which belongs to the period of Ibrahim II, is entered through a multi-storeyed gate opening directly on to the street. The projecting balconies with arched openings are overhung by angled eaves. The angled struts are decorated with relief and cut-out stylised lions, geese and foliation, in imitation of timber-work. Slender finials with bulbous domes rise above the parapet. The gate gives access to a mosque, notable for the elaborate brackets carrying the overhang and the ornate trefoil battlements of the parapet. Slender minarets flank the façade.

The **Asar Mahal**, reached by taking a turn north, is situated just outside the Citadel (see below), to which it was once linked by a great bridge, portions of which still survive. The building was original intended as a Dad Mahal, or Hall of Justice, but was later converted into a sacred reliquary to house two hairs of the Prophet, thereby ensuring its preservation over the centuries.

The Asar Mahal gives the best possible idea of a typical Adil Shahi palace. Its east front consists of a double-height portico with slender timber columns carrying a ceiling with inlaid wooden panels. The portico surveys a formal garden with a central pond. To the rear of the portico are chambers on two levels, connected by staircases at either end. The upper chambers were orna-mented with murals depicting courtly scenes, but these have mostly faded. Elegant compositions with vases and blue flowers on leafy stems can still be made out in the south chamber. The chambers are entered through inlaid wooden doors with geometric screens above. The ruined **Jahaz Mahal**, another palace, stands to the north.

The tour of Bijapur continues with a visit to the **Citadel**, in the middle of the city. This is contained within a circle of **Inner Walls**, no longer continuous but occasionally doubled, repeating many of the features of the Outer Walls already noted. The Inner Walls, which date mostly from the reign of Ali I, are surrounded by a moat with water on the west only; it was filled in elsewhere. The **South Gate** to the Citadel, the only one to be completely preserved, is reached only after crossing a causeway that passes beneath a broad arch. The Gate is shielded by a curved wall that creates a bent entryway.

The first feature to be noticed after passing through the South Gate is **Karimuddin's Mosque** of 1310, erected during the occupation of Bijapur by the Delhi army. The Mosque, entirely built out of pillaged temple materials, has a long columned hall with a raised clerestory in front of the *mihrab*.

The remains of the palace area of the Adil Shahis lie immediately west. The core of this zone is a spacious **Quadrangle** surrounded by arcades, today occu-pied by administrative offices, including the judicial court. On the south is the **Chini Mahal**, so-called because of the blue-and-white tiles found in the vicinity.

This contains a ceremonial hall almost 40m long, flanked by suites of rooms. The **Sat Manzil**, at the northwest corner of the Quadrangle, overlooks the Walls and moat. Only four out of the original seven arcaded storeys still stand. Water basins and traces of murals suggest that this building was intended as a pleasure pavilion. The **Jal Mandir**, immediately north, is a curious miniature pavilion standing in a small pond. Its architecture is intricately formed, especially the dome on a petalled drum.

The **Gagan Mahal**, a short distance further north, served as the audience hall of Ali I. Its great central arch is flanked by two smaller ones that face north towards an open area, where the public once assembled. The spandrels are filled with stucco medallions of stylised ornament supported on fish-like brackets, a characteristic emblem of the Adil Shahis. Little is left of the chambers decorated with ornate woodwork that once opened off the main hall. Immediately east of the Gagan Mahal is another similar hall, the **Anand Mahal**, completed in 1589. Its triple-arched façade has been retained in the conversion of the hall into municipal offices.

The **Mecca Mosque** of 1669, in the east part of the Citadel, stands within a high walled compound, suggesting that it may have been reserved for courtly women. The finely finished prayer chamber has a sombre arcade topped with a hemispherical dome. A pair of minarets is incorporated into the complex. The ruined structures nearby have been identified as stables and granaries.

The tour proceeds by leaving the Citadel and visiting a number of monuments located on its periphery. The **Tomb of Ali II** stands a few metres north of the Citadel, a few metres off Mahatma Gandhi Road. This monument presents imposing lines of open arcades surrounding the central square chamber, of which only the lower walls were completed. The whole building is elevated on a lofty plinth, approached by steps on the south. The **Mosque** and **Tomb of Yaqut Dabuli**, a short distance east, just off the same street, are named after one of Muhammad I's African slaves. These two modest structures have prominent cornices, but the Mosque is devoid of any dome.

Malika Jahan's Mosque, on the west side of the Citadel, is an exquisite building erected in 1586 by Ibrahim II in honour of his wife. Three unadorned arched openings lead to the six-bayed prayer chamber. The treatment of the brackets carrying the overhang is elaborate, with cut-out curving struts, suspended beams and wall panels carved in luxuriant detail with lotus motifs and leafy arabesques. The cornice and parapet above have pierced interlocking designs. The intermediate finials are conceived as miniature pavilions with domical tops.

The **Anda Mosque** stands on the south side of the Citadel, only a short distance from the South Gate already noted. This Mosque is the only one at Bijapur to be raised on an upper level. The apartment below is closed by a single door, from which a staircase concealed in the walls ascends to the prayer chamber above. These unusual features suggest that the building may have been reserved for women. The triple-arched façade of the mosque has delicately worked medallions in the spandrels and brackets above; the parapet is notable for its lace-like treatment. Four elegant finials with their own projecting cornices cluster around a central dome with fluted sides.

The **Jod Gumbad**, to the west of the Anda Mosque, comprises a pair of matching octagonal tombs housing the remains of Khan Muhammad, the commander of the Adil Shahi troops, and his spiritual advisor, Abdul Razzaq Qadiri. Both structures have tall elegant façades, capped with cornices on brackets and corner finials with domical tops. The slightly bulbous domes display well-defined petalled flutings at the bases.

Further west is the **Taj Bauri**, one of Bijapur's principal water monuments. This consists of a large square tank with stepped sides, surrounded by arcades with central chambers. A broad flight of steps on the north descends to the water. These are framed by a monumental arched portal with octagonal towers capped by characteristic domes on petals. The **Mecca Gate** in the Outer Walls stands nearby. Another reservoir, the **Chand Baur,** is located a short distance north, just within the **Shahi Gate.**

Ibrahim Rauza, Bijapur

The tour of Bijapur concludes with the **Ibrahim Rauza**, the most splendid of all Adil Shahi monuments. This complex, situated 350m beyond the Outer Walls on the west side of the city, was intended for Ibrahim II's queen, Taj Sultana, and was then converted into a mausoleum for the sultan and his family. The scheme was completed in 1626. The complex consists of a paired **Tomb** and **Mosque** in the middle of a formal garden, 140m square, entered through a gateway on the north. A raised pathway leads to the plinth on which the Tomb and Mosque are elevated. Arches of uneven spacing support the flat roof of the verandah that surrounds the cenotaph chamber.

The exterior of the Tomb is a majestically conceived pyramid of turrets and finials, crowned with a three-quarter spherical dome raised high on a frieze of petals. The cornice surmounting the verandah is carried on ornate brackets, in between which were stone chains for lamps. The cornice wraps around corner octagonal buttresses capped with domical finials on petals. The finials have miniature arcaded storeys, cornices and bulbous domes. The outer walls, doorways and windows of the cenotaph chamber, as seen within the verandah, are decorated with superbly executed panels of geometric and calligraphic designs, both in shallow relief and as cut-out screens. The chamber itself is roofed with a vault, with curving sides divided into nine squares.

The Mosque opposite, facing east towards the tomb, repeats the overall scheme of the mausoleum, but at a smaller scale. The corner buttresses are carried up beyond the roof line so that they look like slender minarets. Arcaded balconies project outwards from the side walls of the prayer chamber.

B. Around Bijapur

The immediate environs of Bijapur are dotted with Adil Shahi remains. Ibrahim II was actively involved in the expansion of Bijapur, and in 1599 began work on a twin circular city called **Nauraspur**. This idea never came to fruition, but parts of the unfinished fortifications can be seen 3km west of Bijapur. Among the few completed, though now ruined, structures at Nauraspur is the **Nauras Mahal**, a slightly smaller copy of the Gagan Mahal inside the Bijapur Citadel.

The monuments at **Ainapur**, 3km east of Bijapur, are better preserved. The **Tomb of Ain-ul Mulk** is built in a style reminscent of Bahmani architecture. The cubic mausoleum has double tiers of arched recesses. The crenellated parapet is enlivened with pavilion-like turrets at the corners; the dome has flattish proportions. The adjacent **Mosque** is a small structure with remarkable ornamentation. The refinement of its plaster tracery is particularly noteworthy in the medallions in the spandrels. These plaster details contrast with delicately carved stone brackets, cornice and parapet.

A short distance further east is the unfinished **Tomb of Jahan Begum**. Judging from its surviving corner turrets and connecting arcades, this was intended as a replica of the Tomb of Muhammad, but at a lesser scale, the inner chamber being intended to carry a dome of about half its diameter. This architectural reference is appropriate, since Jahan Begum was one of Muhammad's principal queens. Five graves on a double platform include that of the queen and her family members.

C. Kummatgi

The small village of Kummatgi, 16km east of Bijapur, is of interest for the remains of a pleasure resort dating from Adil Shahi times. A cluster of structures with tanks and cisterns overlooks a large lake. The **Double-Storeyed Tower** stands in the middle of a square pond, reached only by a small bridge. Vaults with interesting designs are seen within; pipes opening outwards, embedded in the walls, created cooling sprays. Water was raised manually and by bullock to a cistern on the roof, from where it flowed through pipes. Water also descended through a perforated rose sprinkler set into the ceiling of the upper chamber.

The **Painted Pavilion** faces the Tower. This low, long structure is divided into bays roofed with vaults carried on fan-like pendentives. Unfortunately, only the faintest traces of the murals with which this pavilion was once adorned can now be made out. They show scenes of courtiers hunting, drinking, listening to music, playing polo and enjoying wrestling matches.

24 · Gulbarga

The largest centre in northern Karnataka, Gulbarga is also a historical place and a popular pilgrimage spot, the city being best known for the *Dargah* of Hazrat Gesu Daraz. Gulbarga is dotted with a profusion of structures dating from the Bahmani and Adil Shahi periods. At least one day should be set aside to visit the most important mosques, tombs and shrines [A].

Half-day trips may be made to the *dargahs* at **Holkonda** [B] and **Aland** [C]. A visit to the ruins of the palace city of **Firuzabad** [D], south of Gulbarga, will occupy another half day.

A journey further south, taking in the mosque and shrine at **Gogi** [E], the prehistoric remains at **Bhimarayanagudi** [F] and the palaces at **Shorapur** [G], can be achieved in a full-day excursion. A visit to the isolated Buddhist site at **Sannathi** [H] is in the nature of an expedition.

Though it is possible to make a full-day return trip to Bidar to see the architectural remains of the later Bahmanis and their successors, an overnight stay is recommended. This city is described in a separate itinerary [25].

■ **Transport**. Gulbarga lies is on the main Bombay–Madras line and is easily accessible by train. By road, Gulbarga is 98km northeast of Bijapur [23] and 97km southwest of Bidar. The city may also be approached from Hyderabad [26], 223km east, or Sholapur [9], 208km northwest, Local buses run from Gulbarga to all the sites included here. The journey to outlying places like Firuzabad and Sannathi, however, can be tedious.

■ **Accommodation**: the *Pariwar* (☎ 21522) is the most comfortable place to stay in Gulbarga (STD code 08472); the *Hotel Mayura Bahmani* (☎ 20644), an older establishment, is an alternative.

■ **Tourist Information**. None.

History

Gulbarga was chosen as capital of the newly founded Bahmani kingdom by Alauddin Hasan Bahman Shah, soon after he proclaimed his independence from Delhi in 1347. Though the Bahmanis waged wars with the neighbouring kings of Vijayanagara [20B–C] in the second half of the 14C and during most of the 15C, they built up an extensive kingdom encompassing much of northern Karnataka, western Andhra Pradesh and almost all of Maharashtra. Tajuddin Firuz (1397–1422), an outstanding figure, established a close relationship with the Chishti saint, Hazrat Gesu Daraz, but this turned sour after the saint predicted that Firuz's brother, Ahmad, would inherit the throne; this, in fact, turned out to be true. In order to avoid conflict with Firuz's immediate descendants, Ahmad promptly shifted the Bahmani capital to Bidar in 1424, upon which Gulbarga was reduced to a provincial centre. After the fragmentation of the Bahmani kingdom towards the end of the 15C, the city came under the sway of the Bijapur kings. In 1658 it was absorbed into the Mughal dominions, from where it passed into the hands of the Nizams of Hyderabad.

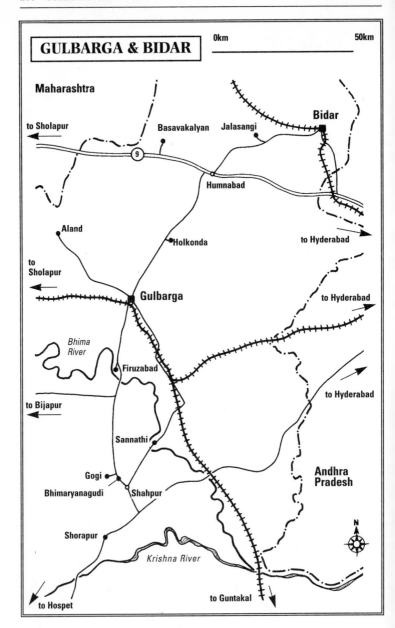

GULBARGA & BIDAR

A. Gulbarga

The tour of Gulbarga described here begins at the **Fort** that once served as the headquarters of the Bahmanis and the governors of the later Adil Shahis. The tapering stone walls with massive round bastions define an irregularly shaped circle about 250m across, with entrances in the middle of the east side and at the northwest corner. The **East Gate**, the principal entrance, reached at the end of a causeway crossing the moat, has a pointed arched opening flanked by bastions. Mounds of overgrown uncleared rubble within the Fort suggest the remains of courtly and military structures. The Fort is dominated by the **Bala Hisar**, a solid keep with turrets devoid of openings, from the top of which there is a fine view of the surroundings. The entrance on the north is reached by a long flight of steps.

The **Jami Mosque**, immediately south of the Bala Hisar, was erected in 1367. Unlike any other mosque in Southern India, this example is entirely roofed over, without any internal court. The hall presents receding perspectives of broad arches with angled profiles. They define bays roofed alternatively with pointed vaults and shallow domes on faceted pendentives. An enlarged chamber in front of the *mihrab* in the rear wall is roofed with a lofty dome

Jami Mosque, Gulbarga

on pendentives; the corner arches display curious elongated lobes. The external arcades were once filled with screens. Steps ascend to the roof, where the pattern of domes and vaults may be seen to advantage. The bold battlements and finials of the parapets are characteristics of the early Bahmani style.

A **Bazaar Street**, dating from Bahmani times, runs west from the Mosque. It consists of two lines of small chambers roofed with pyramidal vaults; the arched entrances are sheltered by angled eaves. The **Northwest Gate**, at the end of Bazaar Street, is shielded by massive curving outworks fitted into the Fort walls. Funerary monuments associated with the first Bahmani rulers stand abandoned in the fields about 400m west of the Fort. The **Tombs of Alauddin Hasan** and **Muhammad I** probably date from the deaths of these sultans, in 1358 and 1375 respectively. They have massive cubic chambers with slightly sloping walls, low flattish domes and corner finials. The only features of interest are the arched doorways in the middle of one side. The later **Tomb of Muhammad II**, who died in 1397, follows the same scheme. The **Chor Gunbad** is built at the top of a rising on a slope about 1.5km further west. This tomb was

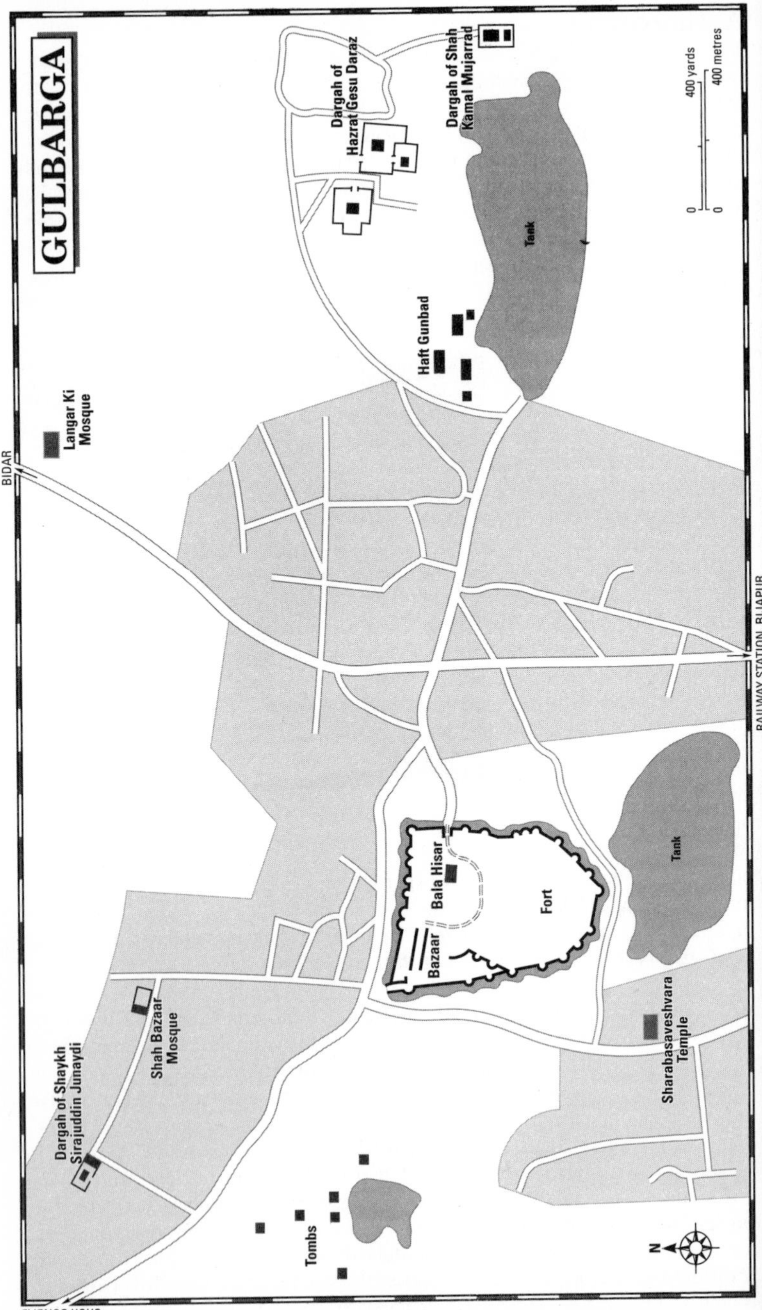

GULBARGA

Dargah of Hazrat Gesu Daraz

Dargah of Shah Kamal Mujarrad

Tank

Haft Gunbad

Langar Ki Mosque

BIDAR

RAILWAY STATION, BIJAPUR

Bala Hisar

Fort

Bazaar

Tank

Dargah of Shaykh Sirajuddin Junaydi

Shah Bazaar Mosque

Sharabasaveshvara Temple

Tombs

CHOR GUNBAD

N

400 yards
400 metres

0

erected in 1420 by a merchant for Hazrat Gesu Daraz; the saint, however, declined to use it. The domed mausoleum has double tiers of arched openings on its outer walls. Unusual miniature domed pavilions mark the corners.

About 500m north of the Tombs is the ***Dargah* of Shaykh Sirajuddin Junaydi**, the spiritual preceptor of the early Bahmanis. The main compound houses a simple tomb in the early Bahmani manner and a small unadorned mosque. Yusuf Adil Khan added a monumental **Gateway** to the complex in the early 16C. This impressive structure stands freely to the east, providing a focal point for a long street. It consists of double arcades with a central portal raised slightly above the roof line. This symmetrical composition is flanked by impressive minarets, whose cylindrical shafts are interrupted by two intermediate balconies and capped with flattish domes.

The **Shah Bazaar Mosque** stands at the east end of the same street. The monument, which dates from the period of Muhammad I (1358–75), has a more conventional layout than the Jami Mosque in the Fort. It is entered on the east through a domed chamber that serves as a gateway. Its plain walls, single arched opening and battlemented parapet are typical early Bahmani characteristics. The prayer hall at the west end of the court inside has 15 aisles, each with six domed bays.

One building not associated with the Bahmanis stands beside the tank south of the Fort. This is the **Sharabasaveshvara Temple**, a 19C construction that enshrines a Shiva *linga*. The Temple is built in a Maratha-influenced style, with a brick-and-plaster polygonal spire covered with sculpture niches. The sanctuary is approached through a hall with Neo-Mughal columns and arches. Another feature of interest is the **Government Museum** (closed Fridays), which occupies a small domed tomb opposite the Government Hospital nearby. A small collection of sculptures is housed here, including some from the Buddhist site of Sannathi.

Though the ring of fortified walls that once contained the city is no longer preserved, the **Bazaar Crossing** in the commercial heart of Gulbarga can still be seen. This consists of two streets meeting at right angles, with shops and stores accommodated in arcaded chambers, now partly hidden behind modern shop fronts.

The first group of monuments to be described on the eastern edge of the city is the **Haft Gunbad**, another royal funerary complex. The **Tomb of Alauddin Mujahid** (1375–78) has sloping walls devoid of any decoration, flattish domes and fluted corner finials. The five graves within are those of the king, his wife and sister. The **Tomb of Dawud I** (1378), is a double mausoleum, with two domed chambers linked by a narrow corridor.

The **Tomb of Tajuddin Firuz** is the largest and most elaborate of the Haft Gunbad series. Like that of Dawud I, this is a double mausoleum with two domes rising more than 9m above the parapet of trefoil elements. Important innovations signify the mature Bahmani idiom: the walls are no longer plain and tapering, but are divided into arched recesses with angled profiles in multiple planes; the upper recesses are filled with geometric patterns in pierced masonry; similar panels appear above the entrances marked by angled eaves on brackets.

The bands of foliate and arabesque patterns, as well as roundels filled with geometric designs, are executed in finely cut plaster. Similar bands and roundels decorate the interior.

The **Dargah** of **Hazrat Gesu Daraz** stands about 500 northwest of the Haft Gunbad, beyond the city limits. The complex is crowded with prayer halls, schools, rest houses, stores and gateways, testifying to the significant role that this saint played in the history of Islam in Southern India. The *Dargah* remains a popular place of pilgrimage for devout Muslims, attracting thousands of people for the annual *urs* festival held in his honour. The mausoleum of the founder dates back to the death of the saint in 1422. The tomb has a double-storeyed façade divided into arched recesses. Exterior decoration is confined to a frieze of indented squares at the top of the walls, surmounted by an elaborate parapet with domical finials. Sumptuous designs are painted onto the dome within. The canopy over the grave, decorated in mirrorwork and mother-of-pearl, is later. Similar tombs nearby are also assigned to Bahmani times.

The small **Mosque** in the south court of the *Dargah* is of later origin, having been erected in the second half of the 16C by Afzal Khan, a general under Muhammad Adil Shah. This finely finished building is provided with fully sculpted brackets carrying a prominent overhang, as well as clusters of domical finials and a dome raised on a petalled frieze. An immense **Ceremonial Arch** springs from high towers positioned at the two south corners of the court. This 17C structure has unusual carved roundels containing heraldic animals on fish-like brackets. The arch is surmounted by a gallery with rows of brackets. The small chamber that stands freely beneath the arch has a curved vaulted roof in the Mughal manner.

Another interesting complex is the **Dargah** of **Shah Kamal Mujarrad**, some 250m southeast of that of Gesu Daraz. This funerary complex commemorates another saint who resided in Gulbarga. The complex has a plain tomb with a lofty dome, as well as a mosque, rest house and stables. The stucco ornamentation of the prayer hall is exuberant, with multi-lobed bands of richly encrusted plaster framing the arches; similarly decorated roundels fill the spandrels. The rest house has a central domed chamber entered through a graceful portico, contrasting with the stables, a long building with ten shallow domes.

The last monument worth visiting at Gulbarga, the **Langar Ki Mosque**, lies 1.5km north of the city, beside the road to Bidar. This mosque and its accompanying tomb belong to the first half of the 15C. The prayer chamber is entered through triple arches, each with pointed lobes. The interior is distinguished by the transverse pointed vault with imitation timber ribs. Fine stucco ornamentation is seen in the wall niches, especially the *mihrab*.

B. Holkonda

The funerary complex at this site is reached from Gulbarga by following the Bidar road north for about 30 km, then turning right. Seven Bahmani tombs are preserved here, five within an enclosure where there is also a collapsing mosque. The complex is entered through a lofty **Entrance Portal**, marked by a pointed arch and headed by a parapet of trefoil battlements. The **Tomb of Dilwar Khan** is seen on the right. This octagonal building has pointed arched recesses on each side topped with a battlemented parapet with bulbous finials.

Further west is the **Tomb of Shaykh Muhammad Mayshakha**, the saint to whom the whole complex is dedicated, is an imposing late 14C structure with plain tapering walls. These are interrupted only by the entrance on the south, which is framed by an arched recess in triple planes. The **Tombs of Azam Khan** and **Khair Khan**, beyond, display double tiers of arched recesses. The latter is notable for the finely worked stucco roundels in the spandrels.

C. Aland

This town, 42km northwest of Gulbarga, is of interest because of the *Dargah of Ladle Sahib*, which is dedicated to the Chishti Sufi saint who was the spiritual guide of Gesu Daraz. The most impressive aspects of this complex are the two 16C **Gateways** that define a processional path leading to the main tomb. The outer Gateway has a central arched flanked by lofty minarets on octagonal bases. The cylindrical shafts of the minarets are interrupted by single arcaded galleries; bulbous domes mark the summits. The inner Gateway is a more conventional structure, with similar-styled minarets at the two outer corners. The main tomb inside the complex is of little architectural interest.

The nearby **Kali Mosque** of 1642 is a modest structure with three rectangular bays, each roofed with a dome on extended pendentives.

D. Firuzabad

The *Dargah* **of Khalifat al-Rahman**, a saint about whom little is known, faces directly onto a road running south from Gulbarga, about 30km away. The complex dates from the early Bahmani era, as is evident from the blank sloping walls with raised portals in the middle of each side, and the battlement parapet with bulbous finials. The central domed chamber is approached through vaulted galleries on four sides. A smaller domed gateway on the west leads to the court of a small mosque, provided with six shallow domes. The *Dargah* is contemporary with the nearby **Palace City** of Firuzabad, named after its founder, Tajuddin Firuz Shah. The ruins of the city are situated 2km south of the *Dargah*, on the east bank of the Bhima River. The site is approached by an unpaved route leading off the main road.

Tajuddin established Firuzabad in 1400, to commemorate a victory over the Vijayanagara forces and to serve as a base for future campaigns. The city seems also to have functioned as a royal pleasure resort. It did not, however, survive the lifetime of its royal founder.

Firuzabad is laid out as an irregular square, almost 1km across, defined by massive ramparts on three sides. The city is entered by way of Firuzabad village, on the bank of the Bhima River. Two lines of small vaulted chambers defining a **Bazaar Street** are visible behind the mud walls of the houses. The **West Gate** has an arched entrance flanked by polygonal bastions. A path leads from here to the **Jami Mosque**, the largest feature within the city and once the grandest of all Bahmani mosques. Only its domed entrance chamber, with a finely worked stone doorway, and its perimeter walls still stand. These enclose an immense rectangle, about 95m by 55m. Nothing is left of the prayer chamber within, except overturned piers and fallen plaster vaults. Steps inside the walls of the

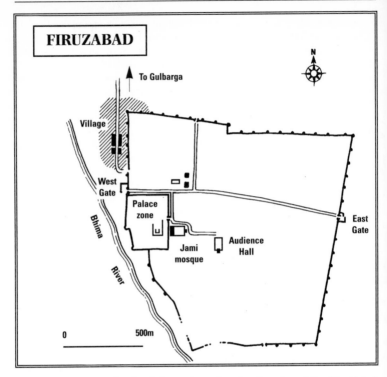

mosque ascend to rooftop level, from where there is a fine view of the dilapidated **Palace Zone** to the west. This presents a confusing mass of enclosure walls, collapsing structures and piles of overgrown rubble. The main entrance is a lofty portal south of the Mosque, with traces of royal animals in stucco in the spandrels. Among the ruined structures here are two double-storeyed chambers, possibly the residences of Tajuddin's queens.

The **Hammams** are of particular architectural interest, as they are the oldest in Southern India. The one on the south side of the Palace Zone has a dome surrounded by smaller pyramidal vaults. The interior chambers preserve their original plasterwork, the finest at the site. Another more decayed example is located outside the Palace Zone, north of the Mosque. The double-height **Audience Hall** to the east stands freely in the middle of the site. Its floors and vault collapsed long ago. A path proceeding from the mosque leads to the **East Gate**, which has a ribbed vault over its passageway and an extensive barbican shielding the outer entrance.

E. Gogi

This small town, 45km south of Firuzabad, is worth visiting for its mosques and tombs. The finest, the **Kali Mosque**, commissioned by the sister of Ibrahim I of Bijapur, is entered through a gateway decorated with interlaced bands surrounding the arched opening. The interior displays a flat vault enlivened with timber-like ribs. The prayer chamber within presents a triple arcade with ornate plasterwork in bands around the openings and in the roundels of the spandrels. Elegantly curved brackets carry the overhanging eaves. The octagonal corner buttresses have domical finials. The interior consists of a single chamber with a small dome suspended over the middle, carried on eight intersecting arches with faceted pendentives in between. The polygonal *mihrab* projecting from the rear wall serves as the base of a hollow tower crowned with a small dome rising above the roof.

The ***Dargah* of Hazrat Chanda Husayni**, a short distance west, is a popular place of worship. The complex is entered on the north through an arched gate. The focal building is the open tomb of the saint, surrounded by modern stone screens. To the rear (west) stands the domed mausoleum of the royal patroness of the nearby Mosque. It is built in a simple style, with double tiers of triple arched recesses on four sides. That this site was important for the Adil Shahi rulers is indicated by the simple arcaded structure nearby, which shelters the graves of the first four Bijapur kings. A gateway on the west of the complex leads to a large lake.

A small and much rebuilt **Jain Temple** tucked away in a side street of Gogi is worth visiting, in order to view a beautiful image of Parshvanatha in polished schist, dating from the 8C–9C.

F. Bhimarayanagudi

This modest settlement, 5km east of Gogi, preserves a **Prehistoric Site**, one of the largest in Karnataka. Stone alignments are here combined with Neolithic ash mounds. Overgrown granite boulders and collapsed menhirs in both basalt and reddish granite are arranged in long lines stretching more than 150m. Archaeologists date these remains to the beginning of the Christian era.

G. Shorapur

This historic town, 100km south of Gulbarga, was the capital of the Bedars, a line of local chiefs whose domain comprised much of the territory between the Bhima and Krishna Rivers.

> The Bedars battled with Aurangzeb in the last years of the 17C, rising to prominence under the Nizams of Hyderabad. Colonel Meadows Taylor, author of the celebrated *The Confessions of a Thug*, was posted here as a British Political Agent in 1841. Shorapur was the scene of an uprising by the Bedars in 1857.

The **Walls** surrounding Shorapur are almost intact, with arched gates providing access on four sides. In the middle of the town stands the **New Palace** of about 1840. Its unadorned façade contrasts with the decorated though dilapidated interior apartments. The three levels of reception rooms employ intricately worked wooden columns, brackets and beams. The fanlights over the windows are Neo-Classical. The 18C **Old Palace** nearby, now a primary school, has a small court with a fountain overlooked by a Mughal-styled loggia.

The **Venugopala Temple** of 1709 stands on an elevated terrace rising above the centre of the town. It has a large open hall, with decorated balcony seating on three sides. The outer row of columns, which stand clear of the balcony, have sculpted elephants at their bases. A pyramidal tower with a hemispherical roof crowns the plain sanctuary behind.

A path ascends the hill to the residence of Meadows Taylor, now the **PWD Guest House**, perched on a rocky eminence. Dating from 1844, this simple villa has a gracious colonnaded verandah giving access to two circular reception rooms.

H. Sannathi

This village on the east bank of the Bhima River, some 60km south of Gulbarga, can only be reached by a poor road via Wadia, a station on the Gulbarga–Raichur line. Sannathi is best known today for the **Chandralamba Temple** overlooking the river, which here makes a great bend. Dedicated to a form of Devi, this 11C shrine is visited by large numbers of pilgrims, especially in March–April. The sanctuary faces east and is unusually circular in shape. A 3C BC inscription of Ashoka, the Maurya emperor, was recently discovered on a slab used as a pedestal for a goddess image in a subshrine. It is now displayed in the Temple compound.

Sannathi is of considerable archaeological importance, being the largest **Buddhist Site** in Karnataka. Unfortunately, the monuments have been much denuded, with its carved limestone blocks being re-used in later temples and houses. Slabs with fine carvings have been removed to the State Museums at Gulbarga and Bangalore [14B].

Sannathi attained importance in the 1C–2C, at a time when the Satavahanas held sway over northern Karnataka; the site declined after the 3C. The remains of brick fortifications indicate a settlement of some size. The walls and the curving river bank delimit a roughly quadrilateral zone some 600m across. An elevated walled area, referred to as the **Citadel**, has a high density of surface finds, including Satavahana coins and pottery. Mounds outside the walls indicate Buddhist **Stupas**, originally coated in limestone slabs. One example, 500m south of the Chandralamba Temple, preserves traces of the paved pathway that surrounded the circular plinth, no less than 25m in diameter. Several undecorated pillars were found in the fields nearby. Another *stupa*, about 2km north of the village, has a mound measuring 70m in diameter and more than 8m high.

25 · Bidar

This historic city in the northern extremity of Karnataka is celebrated for its magnificent fort, mosques, tombs and *madrasa*, associated with the Bahmanis and their successors, the Baridis. Though most of Bidar's surviving monuments date from Bahmani and Baridi times, fine arts continued to flourish here in later centuries, as is evident from the intricately worked inlaid metalwork, named *bidri* after the city itself.

All the important monuments in **Bidar** [A] and its **environs** [B] may be covered in a single day, either as an excursion from Gulbarga [24] or Hyderabad [26], but an overnight stay is recommended. This will permit an excursion to the temple at **Jalasangi** [C] and the spectacular citadel at **Basavakalyan** [D]. The location map for Gulbarga and Bidar is on p 290. (See location map, p 288)

■ **Transport**. Bidar is most conveniently reached by road from Gulbarga, 98km southwest, also from Sholapur [9] in Maharashtra, 149km west, and

Hyderabad, 145km southeast, both on NH9. The rail link is unsatisfactory, as Bidar is situated only on a branch line from Hyderabad. Local bus services are available from Bidar to Jalasangi and Basavakalyan.

■ **Accommodation**. The *Bidar International* and *Hotel Mayura Barid Shahi* (☎ 20571) offer only basic accommodation in Bidar (STD code 08482).

■ **Tourist Information**. Nothing is available in Bidar itself, but there is a KSTDC Tourist Bureau at **Basavakalyan**.

History

Bidar served as the capital of the later Bahmanis, after Ahmad I (1422–36) shifted his headquarters here from Gulbarga in 1424. During the reigns of his successors, Alauddin Ahmad II (1436–58) and Shamsuddin Muhammad III (1463–82), the Bahmani kingdom reached its greatest extent, stretching from the Arabian Sea to the Bay of Bengal. The outstanding personality of the era was Mahmud Gawan, Muhammad's Prime Minister, the effective ruler of the kingdom. He strove to maintain a balance between the Dakhnis, the well-established Muslim nobles and commanders, and the recent emigrés from the Persian world, known as Afaqis, but in the end was unable to prevent internal conflict.

As the Bidar court disintegrated into factions towards the end of the 15C, several powerful figures emerged. They included Yusuf Adil Khan and Nizamul Mulk, the future founders of the kingdoms of Bijapur [23A] and Golconda [26E] respectively, and also Qasim Barid I, first of the Baridi dynasty. His son, Amir Barid (1504–43), gained control of the Bidar territories, much diminished after the fragmentation of the Bahmani kingdom. Ali Barid (1543–80) was an active patron of architecture and a participant in the 1565 battle against Vijayanagara [20B–C]. But Bidar continued to decline under his rule and that of his successors. In 1619 the city was conquered by Ibrahim Adil Shah and the Baridi territories were annexed by Bijapur. The city was occupied by the Mughals in 1656, from whom it passed into the hands of the Nizams of Hyderabad.

A. Bidar

The description of Bidar begins with the **Fort**, now an archaeological zone, at the north end of the walled city, where it occupies a promontory of land that falls sharply to the plains on the north and east. Though originally laid out by the Bahmanis, the Fort and its various features were remodelled under the Baridis. The **Double Walls** that contain the Fort are protected on the south by a triple moat hewn out of the rock. The Walls are reinforced by both round and polygonal bastions, many with gun emplacements, interspersed with projecting guardrooms on triple brackets. The Walls are topped with a bold parapet of arched battlements. There are seven gateways in the Walls, all strongly defended.

The tour of the Fort begins by passing through a line of three **Gates** in the southeast quadrant of the citadel. The intermediate Sharza Gate, so-called because of the sculpted animals set into the façade, has polygonal balconies projecting from the sides. It is further adorned with polychrome tiles on the relief

Gumbad Gate, Bidar

parapet over the arched entrance. The innermost Gumbad Gate, reached only after passing across the causeway, has double arches with pointed contours capped with a flattish dome.

An ensemble of royal buildings occupies the southern part of the Fort. Though now in ruins, they give the best possible idea of formal courtly planning in the 15C–16C. The first features to be noticed on entering this zone are a multi-domed **Bath** on the right and the **Rangin Mahal** on the left (permission required to visit). The latter, one of the best-preserved palaces at Bidar, dates mainly from the period of Ali Barid. An arched gate gives access to a rectangular court with a small pond in the middle. The six-bayed hall on the south has intricately worked timber columns, brackets and beams, a rare survival of a vanished wooden tradition. The side walls are partly covered with polychrome tile mosaic in bold geometric and arabesque patterns. A suite of vaulted chambers opens off to the south. The doorways here have polished basalt bands inset with delicate mother-of-pearl designs. The kitchen opens off the west side of the court.

The next important building to be seen, the **Solah Khamba Mosque**, served as the principal place of worship within the Fort. This was founded in 1327, during the occupation of Bidar by the Delhi forces, but was later extended. Only the prayer chamber stands now. Its long line of 19 arched openings is relieved by a parapet of interlocking pierced battlements. The flattish dome is raised on a circular drum ornamented with trefoil merlons in relief. The long hall is five bays deep. The circular columns with petalled elements at the top of the shafts carry flattish domes on faceted pendentives. The *mihrab* recessed into the rear wall is

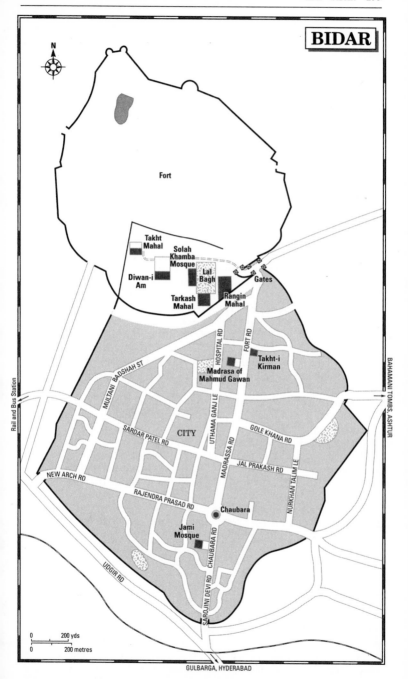

BIDAR

N

Fort

Takht Mahal
Solah Khamba Mosque
Diwan-i Am
Lal Bagh
Tarkash Mahal
Rangin Mahal
Gates

Rail and Bus Station

HOSPITAL RD
FORT RD
Takht-i Kirman
Madrasa of Mahmud Gawan

MULTANI BADSHAH ST

UTHAMA GANJ LE

SARDAR PATEL RD
CITY
MADRASSA RD
GOLE KHANA RD

NURKHAN TALIM LE

BAHAMANI TOMBS, ASHTUR

JAL PRAKASH RD

NEW ARCH RD

RAJENDRA PRASAD RD
Chaubara

Jami Mosque

CHAUBARA RD

SAROJINI DEVI RD

UDGIR RD

0   200 yds
0   200 metres

GULBARGA, HYDERABAD

framed by a lobed arch. A dome roofs the enlarged bay in front, partly enclosed by walls; the supporting squinches incorporate decorative struts fashioned as elephant trunks.

The Mosque faces east onto a rectangular garden, known as **Lal Bagh**, with a central lobe-fringed pond. Channels conducted water from the **Tarkash Mahal** on the south to a bath on the north, the latter now serving as a small **Museum**. The Tarkash Mahal receives its name from the Turkish princess who is supposed to have lived there. Only the dilapidated arcades of this complex are now seen. The **Gagan Mahal**, which lies beyond, is an elaborate residential complex with vaulted chambers.

The **Diwan-i Am**, the public and ceremonial focus of the Bahmani and Baridi rulers, stands a short distance west of the Mosque; it was originally entered through a vaulted gate on the north. A large rectangular court, flanked by high walls with arched recesses, is overlooked on the south by a spacious hall. The timber columns that once supported its roof have vanished, but their locations are indicated by finely worked stone footings. The chambers opening off the hall on three sides had polychrome wall panels, but these have sadly decomposed. The floors in some chambers preserve geometric designs in stonework.

Further west is the **Takht Mahal**, or throne chamber, where the Bidar rulers held private audience. It, too, has a columned hall facing north onto a rectangular court. This is entered through a structure with a bent entryway at the northeast corner. One chamber at the rear (south) of the hall has a complicated plan with curving sides; another is furnished with a small lotus-shaped pond. The Takht Mahal is dominated by a monumental portal on the west side of the court. This has a high arch with a markedly pointed profile. Hexagonal tiles in the spandrels, now mostly lost, depicted royal tiger and sun emblems. A dilapidated pavilion southwest of the complex offers fine views of the lower part of the Fort.

Visitors must retrace the path back to the entrance to the Fort in order to enter the **City**. This is contained within a circuit of high walls with strongly defended gateways. The tour proceeds south along the axial street. The first building of interest is the **Takht-i Kirmani**, an imposing gateway dating from the period of Shihabuddin Ahmad I. Its arched entrance is flanked by smaller arched openings and capped with a line of trefoil battlements. Bands and roundels of foliate and arabesque designs are intricately modelled in plaster relief. Nothing can now be seen of the mansion which originally stood behind the gateway.

The next important building to be encountered is the celebrated *Madrasa* of *Mahmud Gawan*, named after its founder, who completed it in 1472. This grandiose, though ruined, monument testifies to the pervasive influence of the Shia doctrines propagated by the Afaqis. The building is clearly modelled on contemporary Central Asian models. Four great arched portals, surmounted by domes raised high on circular or octagonal drums, face onto a central square court. Triple tiers of arched openings at either side of the portals lead to teaching chambers and the library; additional domed chambers occupy the corners. The principal east façade was flanked by a pair of tall cylindrical minarets, of which only one now stands. It has two intermediate stages cantilevering outward as balconies; the summit is domed. The minaret and frontal arcade are ornamented with sumptuous cut tiles in blue and white, with touches of yellow and green. Some panels have bold calligraphic and geometric motifs.

The **Chaubara**, the next structure to be seen, is a squat circular tower standing at the crossing of the two principal thoroughfares of the city. The **Jami Mosque** is seen a short distance south. This plain, but elegant, structure dates from the first decades of the 15C, but was restored in later times. Seven arches are decorated with fiely worked plaster bands and roundels with foliate and arabesque designs. The angled eaves on the brackets are surmounted by a parapet of trefoil battlements. The interior employs pointed arches and pendentives rising from plain piers.

B. Around Bidar

Royal and saintly funerary complexes surround Bidar. The mausoleums at **Ashtur**, 3km northeast, are reached by leaving the city by one of the gates in the east walls. The first monument to be glimpsed from the road is **Chaukhandi**, the tomb of the Shia saint Khalil Allah, who died here in 1460. The complex is entered through a large gateway with an imposing pointed arch. The mausoleum within consists of a square domed chamber surrounded by a free-standing octagonal screen wall. This outer wall is provided with arched recesses flanked by panels that include diagonal squares, all outlined in masonry bands. The south doorway is headed by a majestic Koranic inscription, probably the finest such calligraphic example in Karnataka. It is in overlapping cursive script set against a foliate background incised in black basalt. Like the saint, the calligrapher came from Persia.

A short distance further east along the road lies the necropolis of the later Bahmani kings, with the mausoleums arranged in a single line. The **Tomb of Ahmad I**, at the east end, is the earliest and one of the grandest of the group. Its impressive square domed chamber is provided with three tiers of pointed arched recesses, four on each of the middle and lower registers, and seven at the top. The ornamentation is restricted to a series of superb calligraphic bands and plaster roundels in the spandrels. The battlemented parapet has corner finials, repeated on the 16-sided drum on which the dome is raised. Remarkable foliate, geometric and arabesque designs of obvious Persian inspiration are painted on the internal walls and dome. They still preserve their original brilliant gold, vermilion and turquoise colouring. Unlike the other royal tombs, that of Ahmad is under veneration.

Traces of polychrome tiles are discerned on the adjacent **Tomb of Alauddin Ahmad II**. The façades here employ five arched recesses of unequal height, symmetrically disposed about the central, largest niche. The arches have gently double-curved contours outlined in stone bands, in contrast to the more angled arches of earlier monuments. The diagonal square panels above the outer niches are unusual. The parapet is further elaborated, as are the corner finials. The later **Tomb of Shamsuddin Muhammad** recalls earlier schemes in its triple tiers of arched recesses and bold parapet. There is a complete absence of decoration. Two small tombs nearby have unusual pyramidal vaults.

The site where the later Baridi rulers chose to be buried lies 2km west of Bidar. The **Tomb of Qasim Barid**, the first of the line, is a small unremarkable building with a plain conical dome. The **Tomb of Amir Barid**, his successor, was left incomplete, with two storeys of arched recesses but no dome.

The masterpiece of the Baridi series, and the largest of the group, is the **Tomb of Ali Barid**, dating from 1577, three years before the death of this ruler. The Tomb comprises a lofty domed chamber, open on four sides, standing in the middle of a four-square garden. Each façade has a central arched opening flanked by double tiers of smaller recesses; the five horizontal bands above were intended for tilework, but this was never added. The parapet and base of the dome, both with trefoil battlements or petals, are elaborately treated; an octagonal finial marks the summit. The bands and panels of coloured tiles inside the dome chamber include Koranic quotations. The pendentives, with net-like patterns creating numerous facets, are decorated with arabesque plasterwork. The sarcophagus is of polished black basalt.

The garden in which the Tomb stands is entered on the west through a gateway with wide low arches and upper rooms decorated with a profusion of small lobed niches. A small mosque beyond has three broad arches in triple planes. Elaborate arabesque decoration fills the plaster roundels in the spandrels. An elegant pierced parapet of interlocking battlements surmounts the angled eaves on small brackets. Two minarets with domical tops flank the façade.

The **Tomb of Ibrahim**, Ali Barid's son, who died in 1587, has carved door jambs employing temple-like pilasters. The **Tomb of Qasim Barid II**, completed in 1591, reverts to earlier schemes, with a squat façade and two tiers of arched recesses flanking the larger, higher recesses in the middle. The parapet and bands at the base of the dome are elaborate.

Funerary monuments are also located south of Bidar. The **Dargah of Hazrat Shah Abul Faid**, 1.5km beyond the city walls, stands beside the road leading to Zahirabad on NH9, making it the first monument to be seen when arriving from Hyderabad. The saint commemorated in this complex, who died in 1474, exercised considerable influence on the Bidar rulers and is held in great reverence today. The tomb is a mature Bahmani building, its façades divided into tiers of arched recesses. The imposing dome that rises above is the largest at Bidar. The arched entrance to the tomb chamber is outlined by a stone frame set in panels of magnificent polychrome cut tiles painted with fanciful arabesque designs. Of the three graves inside, the one in the middle is of the saint himself. Tombs of lesser religious figures are clustered around.

C. Jalasangi

This insignificant village, 22km southwest of Bidar, 1km west of the road to Humnabad, is worth visiting for its small 11C **Shiva Temple**. Though damaged and partly rebuilt, the Temple has refined carvings which are among the finest examples of Late Chalukya art. Only the walls of the sanctuary and antechamber stand complete; the tower is missing. The sculptures on the outside walls of the sanctuary and antechamber include deities in axial niches, such as Shiva (south), Narasimha (west) and Durga (north), and maidens in the side recesses. The female figures on the south side are particularly alluring. One holds up a slate on which she inscribes the name of Vikramaditya, the royal patron of the Temple. A dancing Ganesha is seen to the right. The fully modelled figures contrast with the flat relief of the architectural decoration and the deeply cut mouldings of the basement. A frieze of mythical beasts is positioned beneath the cornice. A few original columns and an ornate doorway are seen in the adjoining hall.

D. Basavakalyan

This city and its nearby **Citadel** are located 6km north of NH9, about 55km southwest of Bidar via Humnabad.

Known in ancient times simply as Kalyan; this Citadel served as capital of the Late Chalukyas and Kalachuris, the most powerful rulers in northern Karnataka in the 10C–13C. The Citadel was substantially rebuilt after the devastation caused by the Delhi army in 1308–10. It then served as an outpost for the Bidar and Bijapur rulers. After being occupied successively by the Marathas and Mughals, it eventually came under the control of the Nizams of Hyderabad. In the 19C, Kalyan was home to a series of influential local governors who did much to alter and improve the Citadel.

The *Gadigges*, or memorial shrines, in and around Basavakalyan are consecrated to the Virashaiva teachers who launched radical social and religious reforms here in the 12C. Though suppressed by the Late Chalukya rulers, this movement was revived in the 18C–19C, when most of these structures were erected. The *Gaddiges* consist of arcaded courts overlooked by vaulted and domed halls that resemble mosques.

The Citadel, at the north end of the city, is approached along the main bazaar street. Before entering the Citadel, it is necessary to cross an arcaded **Ceremonial Court**, dating from the 18C–19C. The entrance structure at the southwest corner is plain but elegant, with an inscribed panel over the arched opening and slender octagonal finials above. Re-used temple materials make up the niches and doorways in the side walls. A square platform with a small fountain stands in the middle of the Court, axially aligned with timber-columned pavilions on the south and west. A cannon with a fine Persian inscription lies on the ground north of the platform. An arched gate at the northwest corner of the Court leads to the Citadel itself (closed Mondays).

The **Outer Walls** define an elliptical zone, varying from 650m to 550m in diameter, surrounded by a deep stone lined moat, mostly empty, protected by an earthen embankment. The Walls, which date from Bahmani times, are strengthened by massive round and polygonal bastions, with guardrooms projecting outwards on corbelled brackets and a line of tall battlements on top. The Walls incorporate an abundance of reused Late Chalukya temple materials. A sequence of three **Gates** with arched entrances and vaulted passageways is located at the south end of the Citadel. The wooden doors have metal spikes for repelling elephant attacks. A 30m long causeway protected by a rectangular barbican leads to the first Gate. Discarded temple sculptures assembled between this and the second Gate include representations of Hindu and Jain deities, as well as a charming *naga* couple with entwined serpentine bodies.

The second and third Gates are connected by a stepped path that ascends to the open and raised area of the **Lower Fort**. Among the overgrown collapsed structures here are a powder magazine to the right and a rectangular barracks block to the left. The path continues until it meets the base of the **Inner Walls**. These are assigned to the Adil Shahi era, though improved in later times, and are distinguished by the massive bulk of their round bastions. The rectangular openings at the top are for cannon, many of which are still in place.

A flight of steps wrapping around one of the bastions ascends to the **Upper**

Fort, which contains residential, religious and ceremonial complexes mostly dating from the 18C–19C. The **Raj Mahal** is seen immediately on the left after passing through the arched gate in the Inner Walls. This palace has a small court with a pond in the middle, overlooked by triple arcades on the north, decorated with plaster roundels displaying ornate designs on fish-like brackets. The vaulted interior is enlivened with further fine plasterwork. A re-used temple doorway is set into the west side of the court. Steps to the left of the entrance to the Raj Mahal climb to a higher palatial complex at the topmost level of the Citadel. The court here is lined with lobed arcades on the south and a restored pavilion on the east, the latter looking over the Walls onto a square tank below. Returning to the arched gate in the Inner Walls, a path to the right leads to the **Government Museum**, which occupies a whitewashed pavilion fronted by a Corinthian colonnade. The small collection includes 11C–13C depictions of kneeling Garuda and standing Vishnu. Excavated items from Maski [20M] and Sannathi [24H] are also on display, as are several small cannon and other arms.

Immediately north stands the **Rangin Mahal**, with an arcaded pavilion of delicate workmanship facing onto a small garden with a central fountain. A passageway gives access to a small triple-bayed **Mosque**, which is roofed with a bulbous dome raised high on a petalled drum. Further apartments beyond lead via a domed **Granary** to the **Darbar Hall**. This comprises a pavilion with lobed arches facing east onto a rectangular court with a line of fountains running down the middle. The court is overlooked by balconies on three sides framed by curving cornices. Steps ascend to a bastion at the east end of the court, where a roughly cast 7.5m long cannon is situated.

Andhra Pradesh

Incorporating much of the former domains of the Nizams, Andhra Pradesh is the second largest state in Southern India. **Hyderabad** [26] and the adjacent fort of **Golconda** [26E] are dotted with mosques, tombs and ceremonial gates, such as the Char Minar, dating from the 16C–17C Qutb Shahi period. They make an obvious starting point for any tour of the state.

Day trips beyond Hyderababad should include a visit to the Buddhist site of **Nagarjunakonda** [27H], with its incomparable collection of 2C–4C sculptures. A journey north leads to the circular city of **Warangal** [28], the capital of the 13C–14C Kakatiya rulers, while the route east terminates at **Vijayawada** [29] at the head of the Krishna Delta, not far from other Buddhist spots such as **Amaravati** [29K].

The highway running north from Vijayawada passes by **Rajahmundry** [30]

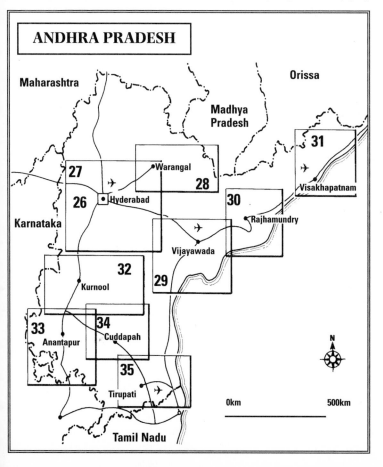

and **Visakhapatnam** [31]. The latter is the finest port on the Bay of Bengal coast, with access to temples at **Simhachalam** [31B] and **Mukhalingam** [31H].

The southern half of Andhra Pradesh is particularly dense in Hindu religious monuments. **Kurnool** [32] lies near the 8C Chalukya temples at **Alampur** [32B], as well as the 16C pilgrimage centres of **Srisailam** [32C] and **Ahobilam** [32F] in the Eastern Ghats.

The intricately decorated sanctuaries at **Tadapatri** [33B] and the painted halls at **Lepakshi** [33G], also assigned to the 16C, are best reached from **Anantapur** [33], while **Cuddapah** [34] gives access to the grandiose fort at **Gandikota** [34C]. The most famous shrines in Andhra Pradesh are those in and around **Tirupati** [35], from where the stronghold at **Chandragiri** [35C] may also be visited.

Visitors should be aware that Andhra Pradesh has been a 'dry' state since 1994.

26 · Hyderabad

The capital of Andhra Pradesh has a long and illustrious history. Together with Golconda, Hyderabad served as the headquarters of the Qutb Shahis and their successors, the Asaf Jahis, better known under their title of the Nizams. A splendid courtly culture and building tradition flourished here for more than 400 years. The British were responsible for developing the twin city of Secunderabad as a military base.

In spite of the rapid growth which has transformed Hyderabad and Secunderabad into a metropolis with a population of nearly 5 million, the third largest in Southern India, architectural remains of the Qutb Shahis and the Nizams and their nobles are visible everywhere.

At least one full day will be taken up with mosques, palaces and museums in both **Old Hyderabad** [A–B] and **New Hyderabad** [C].

Another half day may be set aside for a tour of **Golconda** city and fort [E] and the tombs nearby [F] on the western fringe of the city. A few hours may also be spent at **Secunderabad** [D], northeast of New Hyderabad, seeking out vestiges of the British occupation.

Hyderabad is an obvious starting point for any tour of Andhra Pradesh, a suitable base from which to plan trips to Warangal [28], Vijayawada [29], Kurnool [32] and other historical centres in the state. Full-day excursions beyond the capital are described in the following itinerary [27].

■ **Transport**. Hyderabad is connected by air to Delhi, Bombay [1], Nagpur [10], Bangalore [14] and Madras [36], as well as to Vijayawada, Visakhapatnam [31] and Tirupati [35]. The airport is located between New Hyderabad and Secunderabad. Trains from Secunderabad provide rail links with all these cities and other points within Andhra Pradesh, such as Warangal, as well as Hospet [20] and other destinations in Karnataka.

Both NH7 and NH9 pass through Hyderabad, joining the city by road with Nagpur, 512km north, Vijayawada, 270km east, Kurnool, 219km south, and Sholapur [9] in Maharastra, 303km west. Express buses follow all these routes.

Sholapur [9] in Maharashtra, 303km west. Express buses follow all these routes. An excellent city bus service reaches all the monuments and museums in and museums in and around Hyerabad.

■ **Accommodation**. The commerial and industrial importance of Hyderabad (STD code 0842) is reflected in the many hotels with which the city is furnished. The most luxurious are located in the Banjara Hill area, west of Hussain Sagar, the great lake that separates New Hyderabad and Secunderabad. They include the *Taj Residency* (☎ 399999), *Krishna Oberoi* (☎ 392323), and *Krishna Holiday Inn* (☎ 393939). Some visitors may prefer the somewhat old-fashioned, more centrally located *Ritz Hotel* (☎ 233571). A cluster of hotels of diverse standards dots the Abids zone in the middle of New Hyderabad.

■ **Tourist Information**. The headquarters of the Tourism Department is located at Gagan Vihar, Mahatma Gandhi Road (☎ 843994). The Andhra Pradesh Travel & Tourism Development Corporation (APTTDC) has its main booking office at Yatrinivas, S.P. Road, **Secunderabad** (☎ 843942). Counters are also maintained at the airport and at Secunderabad railway station. The Government of India Tourist Office is at Sandozi Building, Street No 1, Himayatnagar, Hyderabad (☎630037).

■ **Travel agents and tour companies**. Among the companies offering services for hotel bookings and travel arrangements are *Mercury*, Public Gardens Road (☎ 234441), *Thomas Cook*, Saifabad (☎ 222689), and *Trade Wings*, Public Gardens Road (☎ 230545).

History

The hill fort of Golconda was a major outpost of the Kakatiyas of Warangal in the 12C–13C. It was famous for its wealth, and was noted by Marco Polo in 1291. In 1364 Golconda was ceded by the Kakatiyas to the Bahmanis of Gulbarga [24A], who had earlier declared their independence from Delhi. Golconda was retained as an important citadel commanding the eastern tracts of the Bahmani kingdom. However, it was not until the emergence of the Qutbi Shahis that Golconda became a dynastic capital. Quli Qutb al-Mulk (1494–1543), the founder of this line, rose to power under the Bahmanis of Bidar [25A]. Though never formally declaring his autonomy, he was an outstanding military leader and strategist who steadily consolidated his gains over rival rulers, including the emperors of Vijayanagara [20B–C] and the kings of Orissa. The territories under his control equalled those of the Adil Shahis of Bijapur [23A]. Golconda was strongly fortified, and the city was furnished with civic, military and religious structures.

Golconda reached the height of its power under Ibrahim Qutb Shah (1550–80). This ruler reorganised the Qutb Shahi state, appointing Hindu officials to high military, administrative and diplomatic positions. But these were unstable times, and Ibrahim frequently came into conflict with the competing kingdoms of Bijapur and Ahmadnagar [6A]. These difficulties were set aside to create an alliance that resulted in the defeat of the

Vijayanagara forces in 1565. This confederation soon disintegrated, and by 1569 Golconda was already quarrelling with Bijapur over lands previously held by Vijayanagara. In 1579 Golconda and Ahmadnagar joined forces to raid the Bijapur kingdom.

The threat of Mughal expansion into Southern India began to be felt during the reign of Muhammad Quli Qutb Shah (1580–1612). Ahmadnagar fell to the Mughals in 1600, leaving the Qutb Shahis and the Adil Shahis to bear the impact of attacks from the north. Meanwhile, Venkatapatideva, one of the later Vijayanagara kings of Chandragiri [35C], proved a potential enemy on the southern borders of the kingdom. It was during Muhammad Quli's reign that it was decided to expand the congested Golconda capital. A bridge was thrown across the Musi River in 1578, permitting the move of the city to the east. The plans for Hyderabad were made in 1591, and over the next few decades the principal monuments, parks and gardens were laid out. Though affairs of state were conducted thereafter in the new capital, Golconda continued to be used as a fortified citadel, with an international reputation as an emporium of the diamond trade.

Under Muhammad Qutb Shah (1612–26), Golconda enjoyed a period of comparative peace, though the Mughals continued to threaten the frontiers. Contacts were maintained with Persia and Europe. It was at this time that the factories of the Dutch, French and English merchants were first established on the east coast of the Qutb Shahi kingdom. In 1636, during the reign of Abdullah Qutb Shah (1626–72), Aurangzeb was appointed Viceroy of the Mughal province of the Deccan. From this time on, Golconda-Hyderabad was under the surveillance of the Mughals, who were attracted by its prodigious wealth and famous diamond hoards. Maratha military power emerged as an additional threat in the period of Abul Hasan Qutb Shah (1672–87). Golconda-Hyderabad finally succumbed to the Mughals in 1687, thereby losing its status as a capital. However, the Mughal hold on the former Qutb Shahi territories was repeatedly challenged by the Marathas.

In 1723 Nizamul Mulk, Prime Minister of the Mughal emperor Muhammad Shah, was sent to Aurangabad [5A] to crush rebel forces. He stayed on, and soon after proclaimed himself independent of Delhi, thereby initiating the Asaf Jahi dynasty. Within a few years Nizamul Mulk shifted his headquarters to Hyderabad, which became home to a new line of rulers. The Nizams recovered the fortunes of the earlier Qutb Shahi capital, resisting the encroachment of the British and French, and even occasionally joining forces with the Europeans, as in 1790 and 1792, during the wars against Tipu Sultan of Srirangapattana [15C]. In the course of the 19C the Nizams became allies of the British, concluding treaties by which they retained virtual autonomy, although a Resident was appointed to oversee the Hyderabad court. The Nizams continued in power for some years after Independence, but in 1956 Hyderabad was absorbed into the newly constituted state of Andhra Pradesh. Descendants of the Nizams continue to live in the city.

A. Old Hyderabad

Old Hyderabad, on the south bank of the Musi River, was laid out with two principal streets intersecting at right angles; these survive today as crowded commercial thoroughfares. The crossing is dominated by the **Char Minar**, built in 1592 as the chief landmark of the newly established capital and a monumental entrance to the Qutb Shahi palace. The Char Minar presents imposing portals on four sides, each spanning more than 11m. Arcaded storeys and geometric screens are seen above. The four corner minarets, after which the monument is named, rise to a height of 56m above the ground and are capped with domical finials. They contain spiral staircases (access restricted to visitors) which ascend to triple tiers of balconies, from which there are fine views over Old Hyderabad. The upper levels were used as a *madrasa* and mosque, from where royal proclamations were read out to the assembled public. The rear wall of the mosque is indicated by blank niches framed by petalled ornament.

Char Minar, Old Hyderabad

The **Jami Mosque** of 1598 stands immediately northeast of the Char Minar. It is entered through a narrow lane flanked by shops, above which its whitewashed minarets can be seen. The east façade of the prayer hall has three lobed arches on either side of a central pointed arch. The interior is roofed with shallow domes, except in front of the *mihrab*, where there is a rectangular vault. Inscriptions in cut basalt flank the polygonal *mihrab* niche. The rear wall of the prayer hall almost touches one of the Four Arches of the **Char Kaman**, erected in 1594 to define a great open square a short distance north of the Char Minar. The West Arch served as a ceremonial gateway to the parade grounds where Muhammad Quli reviewed his troops; his drummers were housed in a chamber elevated on the East Arch. The square is now mostly occupied by buildings, through which run two main streets. A portion of the octagonal cistern, the Gulzar Hauz, is still to be seen in the middle.

The **Lad Bazaar**, one of the original market streets of the city, runs west from the Char Minar, marking the main route connecting Hyderabad with Golconda. The street terminates in a square, where a large 19C clock tower looms over a delicate white mosque of the same period.

Immediately south of the Char Minar is the **Mecca Mosque**, begun in 1614 by Muhammad Qutb Shah. The Mosque takes its name from the belief that the bricks inserted over the central arch were baked out of clay brought from Mecca.

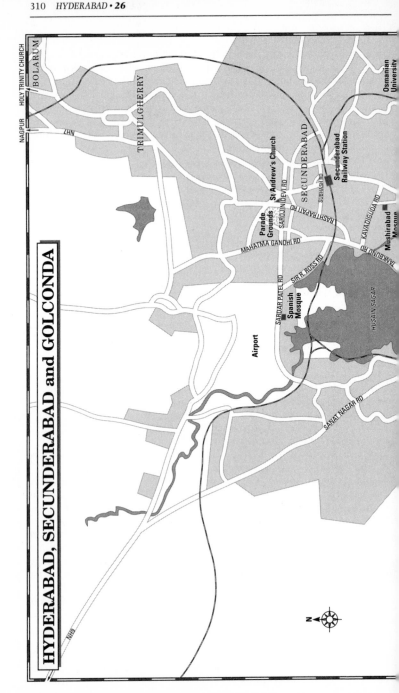

HYDERABAD, SECUNDERABAD and GOLCONDA

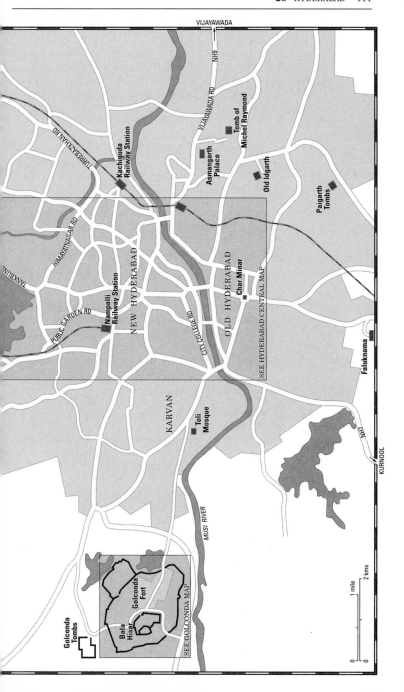

VIJAYAWADA

NH9

VIJAYAWADA RD

Tomb of
Michel Raymond

TURREBAZKHAN RD

Kachiguda
Railway Station

Asmangarth
Palace

Old Iqgarth

Paigarth
Tombs

HIMAYATNAGAR RD

NEW HYDERABAD

OLD HYDERABAD

Char Minar

SEE HYDERABAD CENTRAL MAP

TANKBUNL

Nampalli
Railway Station

PUBLIC GARDEN RD

CITY COLLEGE RD

Faluknama

KARVAN

Toli
Mosque

NH7

KURNOOL

MUSI RIVER

Golconda
Tombs

Golconda
Fort

Bala
Hisar

SEE GOLCONDA MAP

0   1 mile

0   2 kms

Its grandiose, but undecorated, prayer chamber, the largest in Hyderabad, is 74m long and 59m deep. It is entered through five lofty arches carried on solid stone piers. The façade is topped with boldly overhanging eaves. The polygonal minarets at either end have octagonal galleries and Mughal-styled domes, added by Aurangzeb in 1687. On the south side of the large paved court onto which the Mosque faces is a long arcaded pavilion. This accommodates the tombs of the later Nizams and their family members. (The first Asaf Jahis are buried at Khuldabad [5D].)

The **Chau Mahalla**, the principal residence of the Nizams (permission required to visit), is located to the rear of the Mecca Mosque. A fine aspect of the vast walled complex may be had from the roof of the Mosque. The Chau Mahalla comprises a linear arrangement of state reception halls and residential suites, separated by formal gardens with pools and fountains. Public audiences, entertainments and banquets were held here up until British times, the last royal host being Mir Osman Ali Khan Bahadur, the seventh Nizam (1911–48). The main entrance to the Chau Mahalla is on the west through an arched gateway topped by a slender clock tower.

The **Khilwat Mahal**, at the north end of the complex, is a double-height *darbar* hall, having arcaded façades with lobed arches and balustraded parapets, all richly encrusted with plaster. The corner chambers at the upper level are roofed with open octagonal pavilions surrounded by turrets and finials. The other buildings tend to be more Neo-Classical in design, generally with tall porticos on the north.

The next group of monuments to be described is situated near the Musi River, which is crossed here by the **Afzal Ganj Bridge**, reconstructed after floods in 1908 to serve as the major link between Old and New Hyderabad. The **High Court**, west of the Bridge, was erected in 1916 as the first major project of Vincent Esch, a British architect in the service of the Nizams. The outer walls of the Court are enriched with panels of relief decoration in red sandstone, used also for the columns, arches, balustrades and eaves. The building has a central portal, 18m high. The dome above is surrounded by smaller domes, all cloaked in blue tiles and topped with gilded finials. The Court faces across the river to the Osmania General Hospital.

The nearby **Badshahi Ashurkhana** was intended as a congregational hall for Shia Muslims to gather during the Muharram festival, held each year in April–May. Dating from 1596, this is one of the oldest such buildings in Southern India. The inner hall, with double-height timber columns, is enhanced by tile mosaics applied to the walls in 1611. Though partly damaged by floods, the original brilliant yellow, orange, blue and turquoise colours are intact. The arched panels, filled with hexagonal tiles, illustrate flowering designs and calligraphic *alams*, the latter representing ceremonial standards. The outer hall is a later extension. Metal *alams* are displayed on Thursdays and during Muharram.

The **Diwan Deorhi**, a short distance east of the Badshahi Ashurkhana, on the other side of the main road leading to Afzal Ganj Bridge, was once home to Hyderabad's Prime Ministers. Nothing remains of this palatial complex except two outer gates, one with a Neo-Classical parapet and side windows, the other with Neo-Mughal arcades. It was here that Salar Jung assembled his celebrated collection of art objects. In 1968 this was shifted to a new Museum overlooking the Musi River. (The collection is described in [B].)

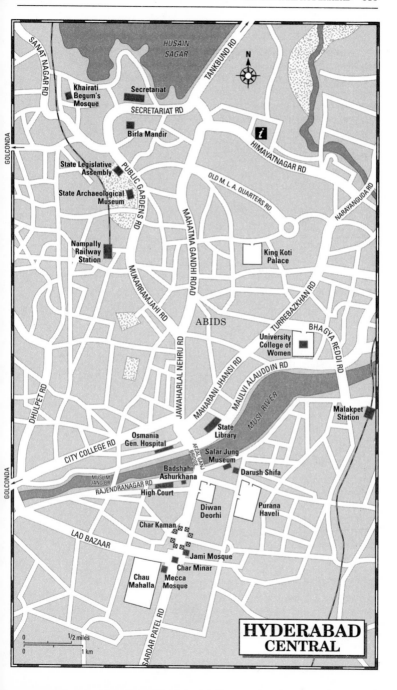

Purana Haveli, 1km east of Afzal Ganj Bridge, another favoured Ministerial residence, now houses the Azamth Jah Educational Institute (permission required to visit). The central part of the palace consists of two long wings with double Ionic colonnades, facing each other across a garden. Octagonal towers with octagonal domes and lotus finials mark the north ends of the wings. The villa at the south end of the garden, the home of Mahboob Ali Khan Bahadur, the sixth Nizam (1869–1911), is conceived as a European bungalow. Its verandahs, which give shelter to French and Italian marble statuary, are surmounted by balustraded parapets with corner vases. The entrance portico has a broken pediment on Corinthian columns.

The **Darush Shifa**, House of Cure, about 250m north of Purani Haveli, was founded as a hospital and caravanserai in about 1530. It no longer functions as such, its outer chambers, facing onto the street, being occupied by mechanics and small businesses. The central court is overlooked by double-storeyed arcades. A small *ashurkhana* in the middle of the court, a later addition, is home to a fine collection of *alams*. The **Mosque** immediately outside the north entrance to the Darush Shifa has a triple-arched façade framed by graceful minarets with open galleries, now partly hidden by a large concrete extension. Coloured tiles decorate the medallions in the spandrels.

Other historical features are located on the peripheries of Old Hyderabad, now contained within sprawling suburbs. A curiosity is the **Tomb of Michel Raymond**, set on a terrace at the summit of a rocky eminence 3km east of the Char Minar. An obelisk marks the grave of this French adventurer, who served in the Nizam's army and who died in Hyderabad in 1789. A small Neo-Classical pavilion stands in front. The nearby **Asman Garh Palace** houses the Birla Archaeological Museum (permission required to visit). This unusual Neo-Gothic building with a castelated round tower dates from the early 20C.

The **Paigarh Tombs**, 3km southeast of Char Minar, comprise a virtual city of the dead, with streets lined with funerary structures. These serve as graves for the family of nobles who rose to prominence under the last Nizams. The earliest Tomb dates from 1786, the most recent from 1968. The central group is attractively set in a well-maintained garden. A line of flat-roofed arcaded pavilions is decorated with exquisitely worked plaster. Geometric and foliate patterns adorn the arches, while clusters of vase-like pinnacles enliven the parapets.

The **Old Idgah** of 1610 stands a short distance south of the Paigarh Tombs. This consists of a prayer hall of five bays, the arches surmounted by an open gallery and a battlemented parapet. The façade is framed by massive minarets of unusual stunted proportions, topped with bulbous finials.

Undoubtedly one of the most remarkable sights of Hyderabad is the **Falaknuma**, the Sky-Touching [Palace], perched on a small hill 3km south of Char Minar (permission required to visit). The main block was begun in 1884 for Nawab Sir Vikarul Umra Bahadur, a Paigarh noble, but in 1897 it was purchased by the sixth Nizam for his personal use. The main gate presents a pyramidal composition of superimposed Neo-Classical storeys framing a broad arch. The road from here ascends to the main block, where a grand Palladian vista greets the visitor. A rusticated basement pierced by arches supports a long terrace, reached by a majestic double flight of steps. The main block consists of open colonnades, Ionic below and Corinthian above. The entrance hall is provided with an Italian white marble fountain and curved benches. The frescos on the walls and ceiling have flowering garlands and flying cherubs on a vivid blue background. Residential apartments with bathrooms open off to either side. The doors at the rear lead to a sweeping staircase flanked by Italian marble figures holding candelabras.

The formal reception rooms on the upper level of the Falaknuma have French tapesteries, ornate inlaid furniture from Kashmir and Victorian bric-a-brac. The throne room is in the French manner, with heavily draped mirrors on the walls, extravagant chandeliers and a geometric parquet floor. A smoking room, billiard room and card room, connected by arched openings with curtains, lead to the banqueting hall, where a long oval table is surrounded by 101 seats. Curved wings added to the rear of the complex served as the residence for female members of the royal household, separated from the front range by a large court. A pavilion nearby, distinguished by its pinnacled roof, was used for coronation anniversaries.

Just north of the entrance gate are the ruins of **Jahannuma Palace** and its extensive gardens, laid out in 1823.

B. Salar Jung Museum

The vast numbers of objects accumulated by Yusuf Ali Salar Jung (1889–1949), the Prime Minister to the Nizam, are of considerable interest not only for their intrinsic artistic worth, but also because they reveal the eclectic taste of the wealthiest Indian collector in the first half of the 20C. The Museum (closed Fridays) is still growing with the purchase of new objects. The courts and verandahs between the different galleries, though unsympathetic in style, are filled with European statuary, most of it belonging to the academic schools of the 19C–20C. Only the most interesting Rooms are noted here.

Room 2, the Founder's Gallery, shows paintings, furniture, porcelain, documents and other objects associated with Salar Jung and his forebears. **Room 3** is dedicated to sculptures and textiles. Among the Hindu and Jain bronzes from the Tamil zone are larger and more imposing Nataraja and Somaskanda figures from the 15C–16C, and a dancing Ganesha of the same date. A variety of *kalamkari* cloths, produced by a mixture of printing and dyeing techniques, includes a long composition illustrating the Shiva Purana, dated 1840. Painted cloth scrolls known as *patas*, a speciality of Andhra Pradesh, are also on display. **Room 3A** is devoted to stone sculptures. Among the highlights is an elegant limestone Buddha wearing a fluted costume, assigned to the 2C–3C Satavahana period, from Nelakondapalli in eastern Andhra Pradesh, and a 5C sandstone-face *linga* showing a head of Shiva, from the Gupta site of Kausambi in Northern India. Other fine pieces are the 12C polished black basalt figures of Mahavira and Parshvanatha from Karnataka.

Furniture and minor arts in wood, many from Karnataka, are on display in **Room 4**. They include ostentatious cabinets and tables intricately fashioned from sandalwood and rosewood. Religious carvings include panels of different divinities, taken from temple chariots. **Room 6** presents a sumptuous selection of printed and embroidered fabrics, such as 18C appliqué temple hangings from Rajasthan. Their vivid compositions contrast with the subtle motifs incorporated into contemporary muslins from Dhaka in Bangladesh. **Rooms 8–11**, the children's section, has a marvellous assemblage of toys from all over the world, including a unique 1939 model of a flying boat. **Room 14** contains ivory chairs and tables manufactured in Visakhapatnam, as well as figurines and inlaid boxes, many from Mysore [15A].

European statuary, including the 'Veiled Rebecca', made in Italy in 1876, a particular favourite of Salar Jung, is seen in **Room 15**. The 19C gilded clock immediately outside is a great attraction because of the mechanical figures which move on the hour.

The armaments on display in **Room 16** include guns, daggers, swords and shields. They give a good idea of the refinement of metal casting in the 17C–18C. Some are identified as belonging to the Mughal emperors and their commanders. **Room 17** is dedicated to ornately decorated metalware, including splendid ewers, basins, trays, spice boxes, and *huqqa* bases executed in the inlaid *bidri* technique. The 20C Indian paintings in **Room 17A** include oils by Ravi Varma and Abanindranath Tagore.

Miniatures form a significant part of the Salar Jung collection. **Room 18** shows a representative selection of Mughal, Rajasthani, Pahari and Deccani paintings, illustrating the full variety of the different schools. 16C Jain manuscripts from Gujarat and 18C miniatures from Shorapur [24G] are also on show. 18C–19C European painting is displayed upstairs in **Room 20**, but there is little of quality, other than works by Canaletto and Guardi and the High Victorian artists Frederick Leighton and Lawrence Alma-Tadema. A large assemblage of European porcelain, furniture, bronzes and glass is seen in **Rooms 21–24**. The jades in **Room 26** are the finest on view in any Southern Indian collection. One masterpiece is Shah Jahan's archery ring, in green jade inlaid with gold. The European bronzes in **Room 27** are mostly 19C copies of Classical figures. Of greater interest are the clocks in **Room 28**.

Illuminated Islamic manuscripts constitute a significant section of the Museum. **Room 29** has several magnificent 9C Korans in bold Kufic script, from North Africa. Another Koran, dated 1288, displays the autographs of Jehangir, Shah Jahan and Aurangzeb. Later treatises on history, astronomy and mathematics, as well as historical romances, come from Persia. One 17C manuscript combining Arabic and Indian scripts was commissioned by Ibrahim Adil Shah II of Bijapur. The largest book is a Koran dated 1730, from Arcot [38B]. There is even an example of a female calligraphic hand, that of a famous courtesan in 18C Hyderabad.

Chinese and Japanese porcelain and statuary can be seen in **Rooms 31–36**.

C. New Hyderabad

The commercial heart of New Hyderabad lies north of the Musi River. The tour of this part of the city begins with the monuments overlooking the river. The **Osmania General Hospital**, another project of Esch, dating from 1925, faces the High Court, from which its domed silhouette is best viewed. Like the Court, it is designed in a Neo-Mughal manner, its long wings roofed with high domes surrounded by pavilions. The **State Central Library**, begun in 1891, some 750m downstream, stands opposite the Salar Jung Museum. It was designed by Indian architects and anticipates the style developed by Esch. The Library houses a notable collection of manuscripts and rare books.

The **University College for Women**, backing onto the river 1km further east, occupies the old British Residency (permission required to visit). This grandiose mansion was constructed in 1803 for James Achilles Kirkpatrick, the first Resident to consolidate the British presence in Hyderabad. Designed by Samuel Russell, the Residency is conceived on Palladian lines. The main building, containing the *darbar* hall, is entered from the north through a double-height portico, approached by a grand flight of steps flanked by stone lions. Eight massive Corinthian columns are surmounted by a triangular pediment framing the seated lion and unicorn, the arms of the East India Company. This leads into a stately reception hall with 22 columns supporting an upper storey, with large rooms all around. Costly chandeliers and large mirrors add to the splendour of the effect.

The entrance from the river is through a triumphal arch and past colonnaded loggias accentuating the axial plan of the complex. The extensive but overgrown gardens include a small cemetery at the rear, where some of the Residents are buried. Kirkpatrick's own grave is marked by a domed canopy. Near to the outer walls are the remains of the Rang Mahal, where Kirkpatrick's Muslim wife, Khair-un-Nissa, lived.

That the area around the Residency was intended as the abode of British officials and Eurasian subordinates is indicated by the imposing bulk of **St George's Church**. This dates from 1844 and presents an unimaginative Neo-Gothic design, with buttressed side aisles and a frontal tower. The nearby **Christ Church** is a later structure of 1867.

King Koti Palace, about 1km north, was the principal home of the seventh Nizam (permission required to visit). Its original owner was Kamal Khan, a wealthy businessman, who had his initials incised on the walls and doors of his new mansion, built in a Neo-Classical style. After it was taken over by Mir Osman in 1899, before he assumed the Hyderabad throne, it was decided to retain these initials by renaming the palace King Koti. The east block of the complex, now serving as a hospital, includes a grand reception room used for official and ceremonial purposes. The west block contains the main residential buildings, known as Nazri Bagh. The street entrance to Nazri Bagh always has a curtain draped across it and is consequently known as the Purdah Gate. The tallest structure is a clock tower, meticulously maintained over the years. Mir Osman continued to live in Nazri Bagh until his death in 1967. He is buried in a corner of the Palace grounds.

The **Public Gardens**, on Mahatma Gandhi Road in the middle of New Hyderabad, are approached through an arched gate flanked by castellated octagonal towers. The small **Mosque** standing immediately inside was used by the last Nizam. Its horseshoe-shaped arches and triple domes with moulded designs reflect the influence of Egyptian Islamic architecture.

The **State Archaeology Museum** nearby (closed Fridays) houses an important collection of early Buddhist antiquities. These represent art traditions in Andhra Pradesh during the 1C–4C Satavahana and Ikshvaku periods. Prominent among the sites represented is Amaravati [29K], from where several slabs carved with lotus medallions and pot-and-foliage motifs have been brought. The reliefs of *stupas* include that sheltered by tree-like parasols from Chandavaram. Fully sculptured Buddha figures in white limestone have elegantly modelled fluted robes. 11C–12C Kakatiya sculptures from Patancheru include a 3m high standing image of Parshvanatha and a smaller seated dwarf. The same era is represented by two columns with *Ramayana* scenes, from a temple at Katangur, and a composition with courtly maidens, from Warangal. Panels from Nalgonda depict unusual scenes of ritual suicide. A columned hall with an ornate ceiling composition from Ghanapur [28D] has been re-erected in the garden, as has a wooden temple chariot with carvings of monster heads on the beams.

The rear wing of the Museum accommodates a valuable collection of bronzes. Hindu divinities and saints from Motupalli span the Chola and Vijayanagara periods. The Jain figurines from the 9C–10C site of Bapatla are the finest, especially the icon of Ambika, which stands in an ornate frame. Bronze bells and copper-plate grants are also on display, as well as sets of Roman coins discovered at coastal sites in Andhra Pradesh. Inscribed slabs from temples and mosques are shown in the outside verandah. Copies of murals from the Buddhist caves at Ajanta [5F], a site originally within the Nizam's domains, are exhibited in the upstairs gallery, where there are also Chinese dishes and bowls.

The **State Legislative Assembly**, on the north side of the Public Gardens, dates from 1913, and is built in a revived Rajput style. The double-storeyed arcades, overhung by angled cornices, are topped by rows of domed pavilions with lobed arches. The scheme is dominated by a dome raised high on an octagonal pavilion.

The **Birla Planetarium**, reputedly the finest in India, stands opposite the Assembly on the other side of Mahatma Gandi Road, at the summit of Naubat Pahad. The **Birla Mandir**, consecrated to Venkateshvara, is perched on top of another hill a short distance north. Completed in 1976 and constructed entirely out of white marble from Rajasthan, the temple combines a Southern Indian-styled entrance *gopura* with an Orissan-styled sanctuary. The interior walls of the hall are adorned with *Ramayana* friezes.

Khairati Begum's Mosque, the finest Qutb Shahi monument in New Hyderabad, is situated 750m northwest of Birla Mandir, not far from Hussain Sagar. This monument dates from about 1633, and was built by the daughter of Muhammad Qutb Shah for her tutor, Akhund Mullah Adul Malik. The triple arches of the prayer hall have ribbed fruits at the apexes; the spandrels are filled with tasselled motifs. A galleried cornice and a battlemented parapet are seen above. The elaborate minarets at either side have double tiers of 12-sided galleries carried on petals. Deeply incised geometric patterns cover the upper stages of the minarets. The adjacent domed structure marks the empty tomb of Akhund Mullah, who died while on a visit to Mecca.

The **Secretariat**, of no particular concern architecturally, overlooks the **Hussain Sagar**, the immense reservoir with a 3km long dam wall over which the road runs from New Hyderabad to Secunderabad. The tank, completed in 1562, is named after its builder, Hazrat Hussain Shah Wali. Aurangzeb's forces are said to have encamped on its bank during their siege of Golconda. Recreational facilities, such as the Boating Club and Sailing Club, line the shores. Gateways imitating those at Warangal were erected in 1968 to mark the ends of the road that runs along the dam wall; bronze portraits of cultural and political figures in Andhra's history line the route. The most recent addition is a colossal monolithic statue of Buddha, which stands on a small island in the middle of the water.

Another Qutb Shahi monument worth seeking out stands 1.5km east of Hussain Sagar. The **Mushirabad Mosque**, erected at the same time as the reservoir, is built in an ornate style, as is obvious from the parapet of pierced interlocking battlement motifs interspersed with petalled finials. Triple-tiered minarets flank the composition. The bottom 12-sided stage is enlivened with bold curvilinear designs; the top circular stage has geometric patterns. The intermediate balconies are carried on tiers of petals and buds.

Osmania University is located 3km east of the Mushirabad Mosque. Founded in 1919 as the only institution with Urdu as the principal medium of instruction, this has one of the largest campuses in Southern India, with many impressive buildings distributed in a spacious parkland. The first structure to be built on campus, the Arts College, was completed in 1939 to designs by a Belgian architect. Its faintly North African Islamic style is striking. The central wing of the College, reached by double flights of steps, is emphasised by a trefoil-arched portico and an overhanging cornice with a line of supporting arches. The entrance hall has a decorated domed ceiling. The College forms the focus for a long pond that reflects palm trees on either side. Other buildings in the campus are in a similar style, but less distinguished. A botanical garden is located at the south end of the campus.

D. Secunderabad

Hyderabad's twin city, named after the third Nizam, Mir Akbar Ali Khan Sikandar Jah, was founded as a station for British troops following the alliance between Hyderabad and the British in 1853. Laid out 5km north of Old Hyderabad, from which it was originally separated, it is now linked by almost continuous development with New Hyderabad.

The British presence may still be felt in the **Parade Grounds** in the middle of Secunderabad, which are overlooked on the east by the unpretentious **St Andrew's Church**. The brick **Clock Tower** a short distance south, standing in a small municipal garden near the Station, is capped by a pavilion with triple arcades. Wesleyan, Baptist and Methodist and Catholic places of worship dot the surrounding streets. Another British relic is the **Secunderabad Club**, 1km north of the Parade Grounds, founded in 1878 and still active.

The **Paigarh Palace** on Sadar Patel Road, 2km west of the Parade Grounds, is of greater architectural merit. The entrance to the complex is announced by the **Spanish Mosque** of 1906, built in a curious Neo-Gothic style with exaggerated horseshoe-shaped arches. The palace to the rear (south), now occupied by the Hyderabad Urban Development Authority, is an elegant Neo-Classical villa dominated by a porch with lofty Corinthian columns.

The **Cantonment** at **Trimulgherry**, 3km north of the Parade Grounds, preserves British-period barracks, hospital, military prison and bungalows, all built in an austere style. **Holy Trinity Church**, 3km further north at **Bolarum**, was erected in 1848 with a donation from Queen Victoria, on land given by the Nizam. Its Neo-Gothic exterior is animated by steeples rising above the battlemented parapet. Four additional steeples crown the square tower. The interior has fine stained-glass windows. Metal plaques and stone slabs set into the walls record the British soldiers and civilians who died in Hyderabad, as do the tombs in the well-maintained cemetery.

E. Golconda

The remains of Golconda, the first capital of the Qutb Shahis and one of the greatest citadels of Southern India, lies 5km west of New Hyderabad on an elevated plateau strewn with granite boulders. The highest of these rocky eminences, rising 130m above the plain, forms the core of Golconda **Fort**.

Golconda **City** is delimited by curtain walls that create an irregular circle some 5km in circumference. Round bastions reinforce the massive tapering walls capped with lines of crenellations, rising to an average height of 18m. The broad ditch on the outside is now mostly dry. A roughly quadrangular extension to the northeast, the Naya Kila, or New Fort, dates from 1724; it has an unusual nine-lobed bastion jutting out of the defensive wall.

The **Victory Gate** on the east, through which the conquering Mughal army under Aurangzeb entered the City, is the one most often used by visitors arriving from Hyderabad. It is shielded by massive curving outworks commanded by projecting guard chambers on sculpted brackets. Similar chambers surmount the two arched entrances of the Gate. The inner entrance preserves its wooden doors with iron cladding in geometric designs. A **Bazaar Street** 300m long connects this Gate with the second ring of fortifications, that contains the **Bala Hisar**, or inner fort. The arcaded chambers lining the Bazaar Street, still used as shops and residences, served as the principal market of Golconda. Here stands the *khazana*, or royal treasury, now the **Archaeological Museum** (closed Fridays). A collection of stone sculptures is displayed in the planted central court and surrounding arcaded chambers. A 3m high Jain figure of Parshvanatha is set up in the garden; slabs showing mounted heroes crushing their enemies and scenes of ritual suicide are strewn about. Inscribed slabs dating back to the 11C are also seen here.

The west end of the Bazaar Street is flanked by a pair of **Ceremonial Portals**, each with a dome carried on two walls and two open arches. The elaborately decorated spandrels have fantastic animals, birds and winged figures in pleated costumes; the medallions are filled with tigers. The **Jami Mosque** of Golconda is situated immediately to the rear of the north Portal. Erected by Quli Qutb al-Mulk in 1518, it was the site of his assassination 25 years later. The Mosque is entered on the east through a domed chamber with a re-used temple doorway. The prayer chamber has 15 bays roofed with flattish domes, the central dome distinguished by ribs. A fine calligraphic panel is set into the semi-circular *mihrab*. A cluster of dilapidated and ruined structures is visible a short distance north of the Mosque. The best-preserved structure here is the long **Granary** with 16 domed bays, now used as a carpet-weaving centre.

The **Bala Hisar Gate**, the principal entrance to the Fort on the east, is concealed by a detached barbican wall. The entrance has a pointed arch enlivened with triple rows of foliate motifs. *Yalis* and ornate medallions fill the spandrels. The composition is topped with three projecting guard chambers on curved brackets. The large domed chamber inside the Gate serves as a setting for a small collection of Chinese ceramics, coloured tiles and other objects discovered within the Fort. The Gate leads directly to a portico roofed with a flattish dome that exhibits remarkable acoustics.

The royal *Hammam*, immediately north, comprises a complex of interconnecting chambers roofed with perforated domes. Gardens with axial waterways were once situated nearby. A road flanked by vaulted **Barracks**, stores and

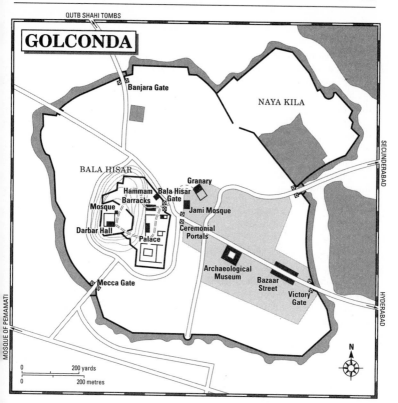

granaries proceeds west towards the stepped path that ascends to the summit of Bala Hisar. The tour described here, however, turns south in order to visit the **Qutb Shahi Palace**. This complex is laid out in a sequence of vaulted chambers interspersed with high-walled enclosures, providing a transition from public to private zones. The buildings are now ruined, with collapsing walls and vaults.

The triple arcades of the **Shilakhana**, the Armoury, dominate the first, outermost enclosure. The second enclosure is overlooked on the west by the **Taramati Mosque**, a small place of worship used by the Qutb Shahi rulers and their nobles. Traces of fine plasterwork are seen on the triple-arched façade. The **Dad Mahal**, or Hall of Justice, faces onto the east half of the enclosure. This comprises a nine-domed hall flanked by residential quarters with small chambers at either side.

An arcade leads by way of a lofty **Audience Hall**, with transverse arches supporting heavy vaults and domes, to the third enclosure, where the private zone of the Palace begins. The paved court here has a 12-sided pool in the middle and a part-octagonal chamber with arched openings at the northwest corner. The **Rani Mahal**, on the south, has a raised terrace, now missing its high wooden columns, opening into a triple-vaulted hall. Delicately worked plaster arabesques fill the roundels above the side arches.

Continuing south, steps descend to a large hall, possibly for courtly assemblies, now ruined except for supporting piers that carried masonry vaults. Beyond, at the lowest level, is the **Shahi Mahal**, a small pavilion standing in the middle of a private garden. This partly fallen structure has portals on four sides raised on a vaulted substructure. Additional residential apartments, now almost totally ruined, are situated to the east. A short distance west is a small mosque with an arcaded court hidden from view by high walls. This was probably intended for the female members of the court.

More than 200 steps from here lead up to the summit of Bala Hisar, passing through walls built of massive granite blocks that climb up and over the boulders. The ascent is lined with stores and granaries, as well as a **Treasury** with six flattish domes, dated 1624. The ruined tanks and water channels beside the steps form part of an elaborate hydraulic system by which water was raised to the uppermost level of the Bala Hisar. Immediately below the summit is the **Mahakali Temple,** built up to a large boulder. **Ibrahim's Mosque**, named after the third Qutb Shahi ruler, stands nearby. Its modest triple-arched prayer chamber is flanked by slender octagonal buttresses. The terrace in front extends on to the ramparts.

The ***Darbar* Hall** of the Qutb Shahis occupies the highest point of the Bala Hisar. The lower level of the Hall is divided into vaulted bays. A chamber with triple openings set into the rear wall was reserved for the king. The rooftop pavilion offers uninterrupted views of the Palace below, as well as of the entire City and its surroundings. Steps descend by another path, returning to the Bala Hisar Gate.

The tour continues by taking the road that proceeds north from the Bala Hisar. This runs near to a large stepped **Tank** before passing through the **Banjara Gate**, the principal entrance to the City from the north. The pointed arched entrance is set between polygonal bastions. The carved blocks set into the side walls depict animals and birds. The road continues northwest for about 750m before arriving at the Qutb Shahi Tombs.

F. Around Golconda

Almost all the Qutb Shahi rulers are buried in the royal necropolis outside Golconda. The ensemble consists of seven royal tombs surrounded by subsidiary funerary structures, a mosque and mortuary chamber, set in a formal garden containing ponds and planted pathways (closed Fridays). As the suburbs of New Hyderabad extend steadily west, the monuments are beginning to lose their splendid isolation.

The first mausoleum to be seen is the **Tomb of Abdullah**, which stands just outside the east gate of the complex. This nobly proportioned building presents a pyramidal arrangement of arcaded storeys, seven arches beneath and five above. Pierced plaster screens are set between the eaves and battlemented parapet. Finials with dome-like summits mark the corners and intermediate points. The composition is crowned with a large dome rising on a petalled base. The richly ornamented details include finely worked plaster and coloured tilework. The diminutive **Tomb of Abul Hasan** (died 1687), the last of the Qutb Shahis, is seen left of the gate.

The **Tomb of Hayat Baksh Begum** (died 1667), the wife of Muhammad Qutb Shah, is seen to the right of the gate after entering the complex. This Tomb repeats the scheme already noted for the Tomb of Abdullah, with additional emphasis of trefoil battlements on the parapet. Sombre arcades with octagonal domes are seen at the lower level. The contemporary **Mosque** to the rear (north-west) has exquisite plasterwork: incised ribbon-like motifs curl outwards from sharply modelled fluted buds at the apexes of the five arches, and calligraphic medallions are placed in the spandrels. Pierced masonry screens with different geometric designs are set between domical finials. The corner minarets have double tiers of 12-sided arcaded galleries on petalled bases and crowning three-quarter spherical finials. The **Tombs of Pemamati** and **Taramati**, two noble-women at the Qutb Shahi court, are situated nearby.

The **Tomb of Muhammad** conforms to the scheme already described, but with an overall increase in scale. The dome, which attains a height of more than 50m, dominates the whole complex. The petals at its base are enlarged and fully modelled. The mausoleum contains the tombs of Chand Bibi, the daughter of Ibrahim Adil Shah of Bijapur, as well as other offspring of the Qutb Shahi family. A **Mortuary Bath**, built into one corner of the complex, has lines of chambers roofed with low vaults. The bodies of deceased monarchs were laid out here on a 12-sided platform and washed before being interred. The **Tomb of Muhammad Quli**, directly south of the Bath, shows yet another variation in design. The central bays on each side are recessed for porticos with slender octagonal granite columns. A heightened parapet runs over a cornice with cut-out floral motifs. Decorated corner finials rise on part-octagonal buttresses. A basalt cenotaph decorated with calligraphy is placed in the middle of the domed chamber, directly above a simple granite grave in the vaulted substructure beneath.

The **Tomb of Quli Qutb al-Mulk** is a modest structure, with only three recessed arches elevated on a low terrace. The black basalt grave is engraved with fine Persian calligraphy. Other graves are laid out on the terrace. The arcaded drum of the dome inside the chamber is recessed behind a narrow gallery with a cut-out balustrade.

The **Tomb of Yar Quli Jamshid** (died 1550), a short distance west, is the only octagonal example at Golconda. It consists of a double-height chamber, with two tiers of arched recesses and a projecting balcony with ornate balustrades. Eight finials cluster around the petalled base of the dome.

The **Tomb of Ibrahim** (died 1580), in the southern extremity of the complex, presents an alternative design influenced by earlier Bahmani architecture. The domed chamber comprises a simple cube, with each façade being divided into double tiers of five arches. Traces of coloured tilework are visible in the bands over the upper arches and beneath the parapet. A square open pavilion nearby contains the remains of Ibrahim's chamberlain.

After finishing the tour of the Qutb Shahi Tombs, visitors may wish to explore other monuments in the vicinity of Golconda. The road running southwest from the Bala Hisar leads to the **Mecca Gate**, of interest for the magnificent inscription that runs continuously around three sides of the outer entrance. The arched opening is set between unusual polygonal bastions. The walls create double barbican enclosures.

About 1km further west are two hills crowned by imposing buildings associated with the two noblewomen buried in the necropolis. The **Mosque of**

Pemamati, the first to be reached, north of the road, is of little worth architecturally, but the terrace in front affords a magnificent panorama of the Bala Hisar. The **Baradari of Taramati,** south of the road, is a simple vaulted pavilion raised on a high terrace.

The road leading east from the Fath Gate towards Old Hyderabad passes by the suburb of **Karvan,** 2km distant from Golconda. The **Toli Mosque,** near the main road, is a highly ornate monument that dates from from 1672. The central arch is distinguished by shallow lobes and ornate lotus medallions in the spandrels. The angled eaves sheltering the arches are surmounted by geometric screens of different designs. The curving brackets carry a cornice, over which runs the parapet of trefoil battlements with domical finials. The part-octagonal buttresses at either end support minarets with triple tiers of arcaded galleries as well as deeply recessed mouldings. The fully modelled treatment of the petalled ornamentation is the most elaborate of the period. The minarets are crowned with the usual three-quarter hemispherical finials topped with brass finials.

The interior of the Mosque is unusual. The prayer chamber is divided into two transverse halls. The outer hall, roofed with a flat vault, has its side walls adorned with elevated balconies, complete with arcades, parapets and corner finials. The inner hall, entered through three arches only, is roofed with triple domes.

27 · Around Hyderabad

The Hyderabad region is dotted with historic localities that can be reached as full-day trips from the capital, or be combined with other itineraries.

The citadels at **Koilkonda** [A], **Medak** [C] and **Bhongir** [D] are associated with the Kakatiya, Bahmani and Qutb Shahi rulers. Examples of ornate temple styles can be seen at **Kandi** [B], **Panagal** [E], **Pillalamarri** [F] and **Nagulapad** [G].

A journey is recommended to the Buddhist site of Nagarjunakonda, now reduced to an island in Nagarjunar Sagar, the largest reservoir in Andhra Pradesh. The *Vijay Vihar Complex,* opposite the boat jetty at **Vijayapuri** [H], serves as a convenient overnight stop.

Warangal can also be reached as a day excursion from Hyderabad, but appears here as a separate itinerary [28].

A. Koilkonda

The **Fort** above this small town lies about 125km southwest of Hyderabad, via Badepalli on NH7, about halfway to Kurnool [32A] further south. Koilkonda Fort is linked with the Qutb Shahis who did much to develop it as a major outpost on the southern fringes of their kingdom.

Perched on a hill rising more than 250m above the plain, the Fort is protected on the west by a deep ravine, while on the east it is guarded by several streams. Visitors approach the Fort from the town, which nestles at the northern foot of the hill. A long flight of steps leads in zigzag fashion to the top, where formidable bastions abut every angle. **Ponds** line the path. The first in a sequence of defensive **Gates** has an inscription of Ibrahim Qutb Shah from 1550. Animals and birds in modelled plaster fill the spandrels above its arched entrance. The passage beyond the Gate is narrow and tortuous.

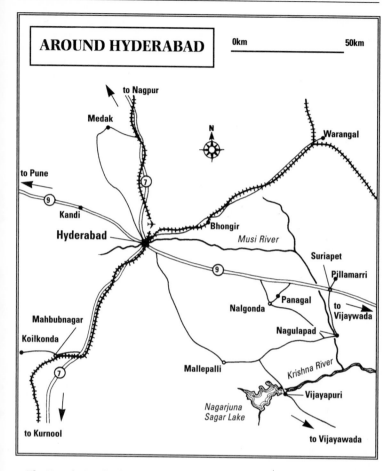

The Fourth Gate leads to a level part of the hill, where there are the ruins of a **Palace** with vaulted apartments. Traces of a water-lift connected with an adjacent tank at the south end of the Palace and a nearby aqueduct indicate the method by which water was raised and transported. **Magazines** and **Granaries** nearby survive in dilapidated condition. These rectangular buildings have thick masonry walls and shallow brick vaults.

A narrow pasageway climbs up through three more Gates before arriving at the top of the hill, from where there is a fine view. A **Mosque** with a prayer hall entered through five arched openings stands here, as does a **Store** of massive dimensions. Another monument of interest within the Fort is the **Idgah**, which has curious circular end buttresses with chambers on top which probably served as lookout posts. Lobed arched recesses adorn the wall.

B. Kandi

Known also as Nandikandi, this village lies about 50km west of Hyderabad on NH9. It is of interest for the **Ramalingeshvara Temple**, dating from the Late Chalukya era. This 11C monument is preceded by an unusual **Portal** with a lintel supported on two posts adorned with icons of Nataraja and Lakshmi. The sanctuary has a star-shaped plan with 16 angles, marked by basement mould-ings and multi-faceted walls. Single pilasters headed by miniature spires and arched frames fill the recesses. Sequences of deeply recessed cornices, headed by relief representations of curved towers, rise above, combining to form a compli-cated superstructure that retains the original star shape as it rises, even to the capping roof piece. A projection on the front face of the tower ends in an arched frame intended for a sculpted icon, now missing.

The shrine of the Ramalingeshvara Temple is approached through a hall with triple porch projections surrounded by balcony seating. The central columns have multi-faceted shafts and capitals covered with minute carvings of divini-ties. The shrine doorway is framed by creeper motifs, with attendant maidens beneath. Large guardians are carved on separate slabs at either side. The niches in the rear walls of the hall house icons of Ganesha and Sarasvati.

C. Medak

This town, 86km north of Hyderabad, 18km west of NH7, is overshadowed by a substantial **Fort**, now much decayed. Founded by the Kakatiyas in the 12C, the site was taken from them by the Bahmanis of Gulbarga [24A], eventually passing into the hands of the Qutb Shahis.

The Medak Fort consists of two lines of walls girding a hill northwest of the town. It is entered along a road that passes through a sequence of **Gates**, the first of which is of little consequence. The **Mubarak Mahal**, inside the second Gate, is of massive construction. The stepped path ascends to the third and largest Gate, distinguished by round bastions. The fourth Gate is less imposing. You will finally arrive at the **Elephant Gate**, named after the animal carved in relief on one side, beyond which is a ruined court. A flight of steps leads from here to the highest part of the hill, more than 100m above the surrounding country. A 3m long brass gun, made in Rotterdam in 1620, commands the plains beneath. Several **Granaries** and **Stores** stand nearby. The small **Mosque** nearby dates from the Qutb Shahi period.

A **Tomb** beneath the Fort is assigned to the Bahmani period; it is not known for whom it was built. By far the most imposing monument in Medak is the Neo-Gothic **Catholic Church**, completed in 1924, one of the largest in Southern India. The prayer hall, which is more than 90m long and 60m high, can accom-modate up to 5000 worshippers. The entrance is dominated by a single soaring tower framed by buttresses. The tall windows have wooden slats and delicate tracery. The Church is remarkable for its extensive use of stained glass.

D. Bhongir

This city, 47km northeast of Hyderabad by both road and rail, is celebrated for the great **Fort** that occupies a dramatically isolated rock rising 120m above the landscape. Though the site dates back to the 10C–11C Late Chalukya period, much building took place here in the 12C under the Kakatiyas of Warangal. The Fort was later occupied by the Bahmanis and Qutb Shahis.

The granite rock on which the Fort is built naturally divides the defences into two parts. The upper Fort crowns the summit, while the lower Fort extends along a lower spur that descends towards the city on the west. A deep cleft between the Forts is dammed up by cross walls to form a descending chain of ponds fed by rock-cut channels. A ruined **Palace** on the upper Fort has a splendid outlook. A small detached bastion nearby supports two **Guns**, one bronze, the other iron. Close to the fortifications on the north lies a mutilated Nandi which, together with stray columns in the lower Fort, indicates one or more dismantled temples.

Portions of the **Walls** and **Gates**, belonging to the Kakatiya period, have massive dry stone masonry and quadrangular bastions. They form a striking contrast to the Bahmani and Qutb Shahi additions, in which walls of rubble set in mortar are strengthened by polygonal and round bastions.

The **Idgah** and **Tombs** dotted around Bhongir date mostly from the Qutb Shahi period.

The road and railway continue to Warangal, 94km northeast.

E. Panagal

Located 3km north of Nalgonda, a district town 112km east of Hyderabad, partly via NH9, the village of Panagal is overshadowed by a Qutb Shahi **Fort**, built on the summit of a nearby hill. A large **Tank** on the edge of the village has a long dam wall. A black tablet found here bears an inscription dated 1551, during the reign of Ibrahim Qutb Shah.

Two Late Chalukya monuments, dating from the 11C, stand next to each other on the edge of the water. The **Pacchala Someshvara Temple** consists of four *linga* sanctuaries, a fifth having been lost, arranged on two sides of an open columned hall. Only two shrines survive with their walls and multi-storeyed towers intact. Carvings of miniature figures set in creeper motifs cover the wall pilasters and intervening recesses. A large variety of divinities appears here, including Shiva and Parvati on Nandi, Vishnu riding on Garuda, Vishnu and Brahma adoring the *linga*, multi-armed Ravana shaking Kailasa, and a lyrical panel with Shiva dancing, the tresses of the god's hair flying outward. The other shrines have unsculpted walls, occasionally relieved by chambers in the middle of each side, complete with balcony seating, columns, eaves and square towers. The columns inside the hall display additional figures on the cubic blocks.

The **Chayya Someshvara Temple** stands in the middle of a compound with an entrance structure on the south. The Temple consists of a trio of shrines, dedicated to Shiva, Vishnu and Brahma, each roofed with a fully preserved pyramidal tower. The sanctuaries open off a common hall, the columns of which have multi-faceted shafts with cubic blocks covered with epic scenes. Six subshrines stand within the compound.

F. Pillalamarri

The **Ekakeshvara Temple**, established in 1208 by the wife of a provincial governor, stands northwest of Pillalamarri, a small village located 5km north of Suriapet, 133 km east of Hyderabad on NH9. Though incompletely preserved, the monument is a fine example of the Kakatiya style. The building is elevated on a plinth with deeply set recessed mouldings. Steps on three sides ascend to the porch extensions of the hall, originally open on the front, with balcony seating all around. The sanctuary has pilastered walls on a sharply cut basement over-hung by a deeply angled eaves. The tower above, missing its upper portion, shows ascending tiers of miniature model forms either side of a central band. The frontal projection has an arched frame.

The almost contemporary **Nameshvara Temple** inside the village, partly restored, has finely worked columns with sharply cut mouldings. The Temple is of unusual interest for the traces of frescos that survive on the beams inside the hall. The best-preserved composition shows the churning of the cosmic ocean, with gods and demons pulling the serpent coiled around the axial mountain. The sculptural ornamentation of the doorways and columns is of high quality. The triple-shrined **Mukkantishvara Temple** stands nearby.

The highway continues from Suriapet to Vijayawada [29], 128km southeast.

G. Nagulapad

Two fine specimens of Kakatiya architecture are to be discovered in this remote village on the east bank of the Musi River, 25km south of Suriapet. They are situated close to each other, partly concealed by houses, with a small mosque in between.

The **Kameshvara Temple**, north of the mosque, is a late Kakatiya structure, dating from 1358. Its hall has porch projections on three sides, each approached by a flight of steps. Parts of the walls and roof of the hall have now collapsed. The exterior of the shrine has alternating projections and recesses, with deeply set horizontal grooves, overhung by a deep cornice with fringes of buds and cut-out ribs and rafters on the undersides. No tower is preserved. Those columns still standing in the hall have precisely cut ridges and bands, with somewhat exaggerated double capitals.

The *linga* sanctuaries of the **Triple-Shrined Temple**, south of the mosque, were consecrated in 1234. The outer surfaces of the sanctuaries are poorly preserved, in striking contrast to the excellent condition of the interior. The ornamentation of the columns, beams and ceilings here is unsurpassed in Kakatiya art. The columns have sharply cut horizontal grooves and bands creating octagonal sections between cubic blocks. The capitals have sharply moulded discs and square upper portions with circular petalled undersides. They carry beams carved with friezes of figures illustrating *Ramayana* and *Mahabharata* episodes. The battle scenes, with armed warriors riding in chariots and royal figures accompanied by retinues, are among the most remarkable of these compositions. The undersides of the beams have finely modelled lotus medallions. The ceilings display lotus flowers surrounded by rings of petals raised on rotated squares. The triangular portions are packed with sharply cut figures of divinities flanked by attendants. The doorways to the shrines are equally embellished.

H. Vijayapuri

The waters of Nagarjunar Sagar, dammed by a stone wall bridging a deep gorge through which the Krishna River flows, have submerged the Buddhist site of Nagarjunakonda. It is possible to visit the lake and the rescued remains of Nagarjunakonda as a day trip from Hyderabad, 166km distant, via Mallepalli. It is, however, crucial not to miss the morning boats from Vijayapuri to the island (check timings), where there is an important museum and a number of reassembled Buddhist monuments. Visitors may continue on to Vijayawada, 175km east.

The ancient site of **Nagarjunakonda** originally covered an area of about 23 sq km on the east bank of the Krishna River, hemmed in by the sparsely wooded hills of the Nallamalai range.

> This riverside location was first occupied by the Satavahanas between the 2C BC and 2C AD. They were succeeded by the Ikshvakus, the most powerful rulers in Andhra in the 3C–4C, who made Nagarjunakonda their capital. That the Ikshvakus were great supporters of Buddhism is evident from the large number of monasteries and shrines erected here to serve the needs of different sects. Inscriptions name some of these religious communities as well as individual donors. The Ikshvakus were ousted by the Pallavas of Kanchipuram [37F] in the 5C.

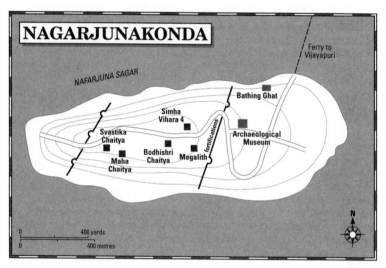

Excavations conducted in 1954–61 brought to light more than 30 Buddhist establishments at Nagarjunakonda. These mostly consisted of formal combinations of hemispherical *stupas*, *chaitya* halls with circular, apsidal-ended or rectangular plans, and monastic complexes with cells arranged in wings around a central court. The *stupas* have concentric or radial infill walls of brick or rubble, the exteriors being coated with plaster or limestone slabs. The halls and monasteries are constructed with finely finished limestone columns set into brick or rubble walls; of these, only the lower portions have survived, including pavement slabs and access steps.

Not one Buddhist monument at Nagarjunakonda survives intact in its orignal location. The flat-topped hill that overlooked the site from the south is now an island in the lake. The **Archaeological Museum** (closed Fridays) here is a major repository of rescued limestone sculptures and relief carvings. Together with similar panels and friezes from Amaravati [29K], these constitute the most important examples of Buddhist sculpture in Andhra Pradesh. Nagajunakonda's art is distinguished by animated carving with vigorously posed figures. Unlike the Amaravati reliefs, which are badly damaged, those from Nagarjunakonda are freshly preserved.

The first group of carvings to be seen in the Museum are capping panels from *stupas*. Some slabs show representations of *stupas* in the company of flying celestials and seated Buddhas. Others depict incidents from the life of the Master: leaving the palace, the gods carrying Siddhartha's crown and the report of the departure, combined on one slab; or the protection of Buddha by Muchalinda, Buddha receiving alms and the first sermon, on another. One double-sided panel shows courtly couples, elephants and ganas. Long friezes, originally capping pieces of railings that surrounded the *stupas*, are also on display. The panels on one frieze illustrate episodes from the *Mandhatu Jataka*. Another example shows the conversion of Nanda, interspersed with amorous couples. A third piece depicts typical scenes from the life of the Master, such as the renunciation, the departure from the palace, the assault of Mara, the enlightenment and the first sermon, all separated by medallions.

Columns, gathered from different monuments, are adorned with lively courtly scenes and dancing dwarfs. There are also a few free-standing sculptures, mostly headless images of Buddha attired in elegantly modelled robes. One impressive figure, complete with head, is more than 3m high. A few 16C items, such as a seated Narasimha executed in granite, show that the site was inhabited in later times.

A short distance north of the Museum, on the edge of the water, is the **Bathing *Ghat***, originally located on the bank of the Krishna River, at the edge of the Nagarjunakonda site. Its steps are entirely constructed of finely finished limestone slabs. 150m to the rear of the Museum is a line of rubble **Fortifications**, dating from the 16C. Simple gateways lead to a number of reconstructed monuments. The first to be seen is a **Megalith**, dating back more than 2000 years. It consists of a stone circle enclosing a heap of stones, concealing a simple burial chamber that once contained four skulls.

Simha Vihara 4, on the opposite side of the path, dates from the Ikshvaku period. It comprises a *stupa* built on a high platform, accompanied by a double *chaitya* hall, one enshrining a *stupa*, the other a monumental standing Buddha. The **Bodhishri Chaitya** nearby presents a simple hemispherical *stupa* raised on a cylindrical drum encased in limestone slabs. The *stupa* is contained within an apsidal-ended brick structure.

With a diameter of 27.5m, the **Maha *Chaitya*** was one of the largest *stupas* at Nagarjunakonda. The radiating pattern made by its internal rubble walls is a particular feature of *stupa* architecture under the Ikshvakus. Projections with columns are positioned at the cardinal directions. The *stupa* once contained a reliquary with a tooth relic. An apsidal-ended shrine stands to one side. The **Svastika *Chaitya***, towards the end of the path, is named after the pattern made by rubble walls inside the *stupa*.

Other reassembled features may be visited on the mainland, 15km south of Vijayapuri by road. The **Stadium**, possibly used for musical and dramatic performances or sporting contests, presents tiered galleries with seating on four sides of a rectangular court. A short distance further along the road is a **Monastic Complex**, which includes the usual shrines and *chaitya* halls, as well as a refectory, store and bath. The principal residence has four wings of cells around a court, within which is a 16-columned hall. The adjacent structure, identified as a convent, has two wings of cells approached through a narrow passageway. Another residence nearby combines double *chaitya* halls with a central 36-columned structure. Three circular chambers are positioned in a row on the west. A **Temple**, comprising a rectangular sanctuary and a columned hall, stands almost at the water's edge.

28 · Warangal

This city is of historical importance, having served as the capital of the Kakatiyas in the 13C–14C; it is today particularly known for its wool trade. A half day should be sufficient to visit the remarkable circular fort and ruined temple at **Warangal** [A], as well as the better preserved religious monument at nearby **Hanamkonda** [B].

The finest examples of Kakatiya temple architecture are the temples at **Palampet** [C] and **Ghanapur** [D]. Both sites may be reached in a half-day excursion from Warangal.

A trip to the pilgrimage shrine at **Bhadrachalam** [F] on the Godavari River, passing by the **Pakhal Wildlife Sanctuary** [E], will take up one full day and more.

■ **Transport**. Warangal is situated on the main line linking Hyderabad [26], 140km southwest, with Vijayawada [29], just over 200km southeast. Road connections exist with both cities, as with all the destinations described here. Warangal is also connected by rail via Khazipet to Nagpur [10] in Maharashtra. All the sites described here can be reached by bus from Warangal or Hanamkonda.

■ **Accommodation**. The *Ashoka Hotel* (☎ 85491) at **Hanamkonda** (STD code 08712) is the best in the Warangal area, though there are simpler alternatives. Lodges catering for pilgrims are available at **Bhadrachalam**.

■ **Tourist Information**. The APTTDC maintains an office in the Tourist Rest House at **Kazipet** (☎ 6201), and one at Kazipet railway junction, 10km from Hanamkonda.

History

The Kakatiyas emerged as the most powerful rulers of the Andhra country at the beginning of the 12C. Rudradeva (1158–95), the first great Kakatiya monarch, had his headquarters at Hanamkonda, from where he waged wars against the Late Chalukyas and Cholas. The next important figure, Ganapatideva (1199–1262), the outstanding personality of the era, extended the Kakatiya dominions as far as the east coast, thereby coming into conflict with the rulers of Orissa. His other campaigns were aimed against the Cholas and their successors, the Pandyas. Ganapatideva's generals even managed to raid Kanchipuram [37K], deep within the Tamil country. It was during Ganapati's reign that the capital was shifted to the newly laid-out city of Warangal.

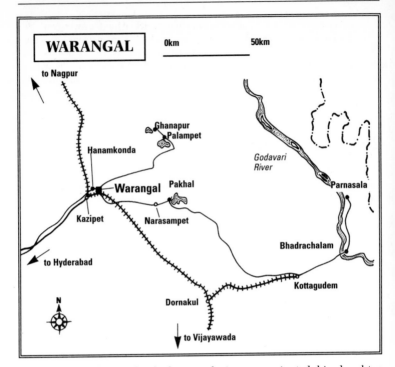

Ganapatideva, who had no male issue, nominated his daughter Rudramadeva (1262–89) as heir. She took an active part in government, and is supposed to have dressed in male garments when holding meetings with ministers and generals. Under her direction, the new city of Warangal was ringed with triple fortifications and many new monuments were constructed. Rudramadevi was succeeded by her grandson, Prataparudra (1289–1323), the last of the Kakatiya line. At first he experienced difficulties with the Yadavas and the Hoysalas, but the invasion of Southern India by the Delhi army removed both these rivals. Prataparudra resisted the first of these conquests in 1303, but in 1323 was compelled to pay tribute in cash and elephants. After his death there was rebellion among the local chiefs, and in 1336 their leader, Kapaya Nayaka, captured Warangal from the Delhi commander. Soon after, this part of Andhra came under the sway of the Bahmanis of Gulbarga [24A], who occupied Warangal in 1366.

At the beginning of the 16C a local chief, Sitapati, who adopted the Persian title of Shitab Khan, was governor of Warangal under the Bahmanis. In 1504 he declared his independence and allied himself with Ramachandra, the ruler of neighbouring Orissa. Shitab Khan was soon threatened by the rising power of the Tuluva emperors of Vijayanagara [20B–C], which bordered the Warangal territories to the southwest. Shitab Khan was vanquished by the Vijayanagara forces in 1510, when they took control of the city. But in 1532, Warangal was seized by Quli Qutb al-Mulk and incorporated into the growing kingdom of Golconda [26E]. With the later transformation of Golconda into the state of Hyderabad, Warangal became part of the Nizam's dominions.

A. Warangal

The modern town of Warangal is situated a short distance north of the Kakatiya capital. The original city was laid out according to a circular plan, with three concentric rings of walls. The **First Ring** of walls, about 1.2km in diameter, constitutes the innermost part of the capital, usually referred to as the **Fort**. The walls are of massive granite blocks, no less than 6m high, laid without any mortar. The rectangular bastions overlook a broad moat, still filled with water. The inner faces of the walls have steps ascending to a path that runs continuously along the top. The watchtowers and lines of battlements here date from the Bahmani period. The four **Gateways** at the cardinal points are preceded by sturdily built barbican enclosures, demanding two turns to the left on entering the city. The identical arrangements of the Gateways create a pattern of rotational symmetry, not unlike a swastika. That these entrances were renovated in Bahmani times is clear from the sculpted balustrades and other blocks re-used from dismantled temples, and the curved protective walls in front of the east and west gateways.

Portal of the Shiva Temple, Warangal

The area contained within the Fort is now partly agricultural, with village houses defining an axial east–west road. The archaeological zone in the middle coincides with the enclosure of a demolished **Shiva Temple**. Only the free-standing entrance **Portals** in the middle of four sides of the enclosure still stand. They consist of pairs of posts with brackets carrying massive lintels, achieving an overall height of about 10m. The treatment of the portals is ornamental, with boldly carved lotus buds, looped garlands, mythical beasts and birds with foliated tails. The absence of religious themes possibly expains why the Portals were spared by the invaders.

Of the Temple itself, nothing remains except overturned slabs and smashed columns, brackets and ceiling panels, now formally displayed. Traces of the original foundation slabs indicate a main shrine facing east towards an open hall laid out on a stepped plan. Recent excavations at the southeast corner of the complex have uncovered the remains of a row of subshrines, each with a votive *linga*. Another small temple nearby has a hall with sharply modelled columns and brackets. The sanctuary is low and plain.

The **Kush Mahal**, 150m west of the archaeological zone, may have functioned as the audience hall of Shitab Khan, but is probably a 14C structure dating from the period of the Delhi invasion. It consists of a rectangular chamber flanked by massive sloping walls, with six vaulted arches admitting light on each of the long sides. The timber roof, on five transverse arches, is lost. Steps ascend to the roof, from where excellent views may be had across the site.

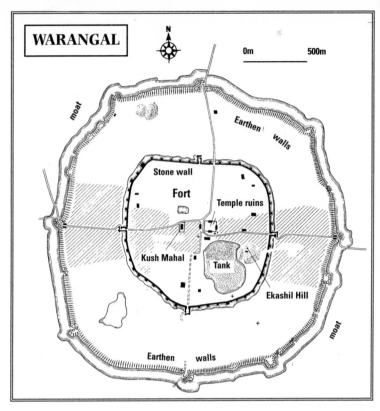

A short distance south of the archaeological zone is a pond used for bathing and washing. It is overlooked from the east by a prominent **Rock** which rises abruptly from the water. This natural feature, known as Orugallu (Single Rock) in Telugu (Ekashila in Sanskrit), gives its name to Warangal. A small temple and other structures occupy the top of this granite outcrop. Further shrines and reservoirs are scattered throughout the Fort. Three long rectangular granaries are seen near the south gate.

Warangal's **Second Ring** of walls, defining a circle 2.4km in diameter, completely surrounds the Inner Ring. These earthen fortifications also have a broad moat, now partly filled in. The area within this circuit is mostly given over to fields, with houses flanking the east-west road that continues to the Fort. The gateways at the cardinal directions are aligned with those of the Fort. Those on the east and west have arched structures dating from the Bahmani period. Their passageways are guarded by massive earthen embankments that protrude beyond the walls.

The **Third Ring** of walls, again of earth, defines a vast irregular circle, some 12.5km in diameter, within which stands the modern city of Warangal. The fortifications are interrupted on the northwest by the rocky hills and earthen walls of Hanamkonda.

B. Hanamkonda

The site of the first Kakatiya capital is located 3km northwest of Warangal, the two cities now being connected by almost continuous development. The principal monument of interest in Hanamkonda, the **Thousand-Pillared Temple**, is located just off the main road. This impressive example of Kakatiya architecture dates from 1163, during the reign of Rudradeva. An inscribed slab set up within the entrance gate on the east gives the historical details of its foundation.

The Temple is built of grey-green basalt and is finely worked throughout. Three shrines, dedicated to Shiva, Vishnu and Surya, lead off a columned hall that opens on the south as a porch. The outer walls of the shrines and hall rise upon a deeply moulded basement. No sculptures remain in the wall niches, which are headed by tower-like pediments. The balcony seating in the porch is sheltered by angled eaves. The hall interior is crowded with columns displaying sharply cut multi-faceted shafts; the capitals are adorned with jewels and petals. The central ceiling panel is an elaborate composition, with scrollwork surrounding an icon of Nataraja. The doorways have cut-out lintels, with deities in the middle flanked by *makaras* and scrollwork. The plinth of the Temple extends south; a magnificent polished Nandi is placed here. Yet further south is another columned hall, less finely worked and now dilapidated, constructed entirely out of granite.

About 1km south of the Temple, on the far side of a rocky outcrop, lie the earthen ramparts and granite entrance portals of Hanamkonda **Fort**. The **Siddheshvara Temple**, inside the south entrance to the Fort, consists of a small *linga* shrine adjoining an open hall with seating on three sides. The infill walls and the spire over the sanctuary are later additions. A mound nearby has bricks and other debris of buried and ruined structures. Rock-cut Jain vestiges are to be found in caverns high up on the nearby rocks.

C. Palampet

This site, 68km northeast of Warangal, is of importance because of the **Ramappa Temple**, built by Recherla Rudra, a general of Ganapatideva. Dating from 1213, this is the best-preserved example of Kakatiya architecture. The main sanctuary and antechamber of the Temple open off a large columned hall laid out on a stepped plan, with balcony seating all around. The whole scheme is raised on a high plinth. The reddish sandstone exerior of the sanctuary has a sharply moulded basement with a miniature frieze of elephants; the slender wall pilasters frame tiers of mutiple niches, now empty, in the middle of each side. Deeply overhanging angled eaves continue around the building. The brick tower is multi-storeyed, with successive layers of pilastered walls and parapets, somewhat restored. A vaulted projection is seen on the front face of the tower.

The front porch of the hall is contained within high balcony walls adorned with pilasters framing female figures and stylised lotus ornament. The polished basalt columns inside have cubic shafts, occasionally covered with carvings, separated by octagonal sections. The double capitals are sharply cut. The peripheral columns have angled brackets fashioned as rearing mythic beasts or as female dancers and musicians. The figures are masterpieces of Kakatiya art, and are notable for the smooth modelling, sinuous postures and curiously elongated bodies and heads. The ceiling panel over the central bays incorporates miniature figures within rotated and ascending squares.

A detached pavilion, with a fully sculpted Nandi, and a subsidiary shrine also stand within the walled compound of the Temple. An inscribed slab giving the historical circumstances of the monument is sheltered by a small pavilion.

The **Ramappa Cheruvu**, the great lake created by Recherla Rudra, lies 1.5km south of the Ramappa Temple. Its waters, which encompass nearly 24 sq km, are surrounded by picturesque forested hills.

D. Ghanapur

The temples at this site, 13km northwest of Palampet, are also associated with a vast lake. The **Ghanpur Cheruvu** has an earthen dam wall more than 2km long and 16m high. It is contemporary with a 13C temple group, now much ruined, constructed during the reign of Ganapatideva, after whom the settlement is named.

The **Kotagullu**, as the complex is known locally, consists of two east-facing Shiva shrines, both with halls on stepped plans with seating all around. A Nandi pavilion stands in front of the larger example. Both temples are raised high on plinths with deeply set mouldings. Their outer walls, now ruined, have regularly spaced projections with pilasters in the recesses. The towers have fallen. The balcony slabs in the porches of one example have friezes of elephants, ducks and stylised flowers, as well as temple towers in shallow relief. The overhanging angled eaves have mostly fallen. The internal columns have cubic blocks separated by sharply cut octagonal bands. A few bracket figures survive. Further sculptural evidence is seen in the richly decorated jambs of the doorways.

The temples stand in the middle of a square compound, with a row of comparatively well-preserved small *linga* shrines near the west perimeter wall, now partly buried. Some shrines have curved towers enhanced by diminutive replicas placed at each level. These multiplied elements are separated by vertical strips in the middle of each side. Other shrines have pyramidal multi-storeyed towers capped with square roofs. Elaborate gateways are seen on two sides of the complex. That on the south is laid out as a large hall, with projections on four sides; only some of its columns still stand.

E. Pakhal

Yet further evidence of the extensive hydraulic works of the Kakatiyas in the 13C may be seen at Pakhal, 42km east of Warangal. The waters of the tank here, encompassing more than 30 sq km, are contained by a 1.2km long earthen dam. The surrounding hills are densely forested and filled with wildlife, such as as bears and deer, and even the odd tiger and leopard. This natural setting forms the core of the **Pakhal Wildife Sanctuary**. December–February is the best time for viewing the animals and birds.

F. Bhadrachalam

The celebrated pilgrimage shrine at Bhadrachalam, on the east bank of the Godavari River, lies 140km east of Pakhal, the road winding its way through forested hills. The site can also be reached from Vijayawada [29A], some 200km south, or from Rajahamundry [30A], about the same distance southeast. Bhadrachalam is of great mythological significance, since Rama and Sita are believed to have spent part of their forest retreat here. The **Shrirama Temple**, which marks the spot where Rama crossed the river, was built by Kancherla Gopanna, governor under the last of the Qutb Shahis in the second half of the 17C. He is is said to have appropriated funds from the imperial treasury for the purpose, and was subsequently imprisoned. After a miraculous rescue, he adopted the title of Ramdas.

Despite the beauty of its natural setting, the Shrirama Temple is of little interest architecturally, having been substantially rebuilt in recent years. It is entered through an impressive *gopura*. The main shrine houses an unusual four-armed icon of Rama; bronzes show the god together with Sita and Lakshmana. The **Ushnagunda**, or Hot Pool, is located in the bed of the Godavari River, only a short distance from the Temple. This consists of a hot spring that emerges when the sand at the bottom of the river is disturbed.

Parnasala, 35km north of Bhadrachalam, is believed to mark the hermitage where Sita was approached by the demon Ravana in disguise as an ascetic; he then assumed his real form and abducted her.

29 · Vijayawada

Strategically situated at the head of the richly irrigated Krishna River Delta, Vijayawada is a thriving business centre and a convenient base from which to visit interesting and varied historical sites.

A few hours will suffice for **Vijayawada** itself [A], with a half-day excursion northwest of the city to the hill fort at **Kondapalle** [B] and the Buddhist remains at **Jaggayyapeta** [C].

The Dutch tombs at **Machilipatnam** [D] and the Buddhist structure at **Ghantasala** [E], southeast of Vijayawada, may be combined in another day trip.

A full-day journey southwest of Vijayawada can take in the rock-cut monument at **Undavalli** [F], the temple at **Mangalagiri** [G], the museum at **Guntur** [H], and the shrines at **Chebrolu** [I] and **Bapatla** [J].

The Buddhist site at **Amaravati** [K], the most famous in Andhra Pradesh, deserves a half day in itself, not only for seeing the sculptures in the local museum, but also the active place of worship overlooking the Krishna River nearby.

Additional time will have to be set aside to reach the remotely located Buddhist vestiges at **Goli** [L], the fort at **Kondavidu** [M] and the unusual early brick shrine at **Cherzala** [N].

■ **Transport**. Vijayawada is linked by air with Hyderabad, Visakhapatnam [31] and Madras [36]. It benefits from being at the meeting point of NH9 and NH5, also a railway junction, with excellent connections to Hyderabad, 270km northwest, Rajhamundry, 180km northeast, Guntur, 32km south, and even Madras, 412km beyond Guntur. The main railway line running south from Vjayawada passes through Kurnool [32], from which one branch continues to Hospet [20] in Karnataka. Local transport reaches most of the localities described here.

■ **Accommodation**. Vijayawada (STD code 0866) is a major business centre, with numerous places to stay. The best is the *Hotel Illapuram* (☎ 61282), but the

Hotel Raj Towers (☎ 61311) and *Hotel Manorama* (☎ 77220) are acceptable alternatives.

■ **Tourist Information**. The APTTDC maintains offices on Gopal Reddy Road, opposite the Old Bus Station (☎ 61220), as well as at the Krishna Veni Motel, Sitanagaram (☎ 75382). There is also a counter at the railway station.

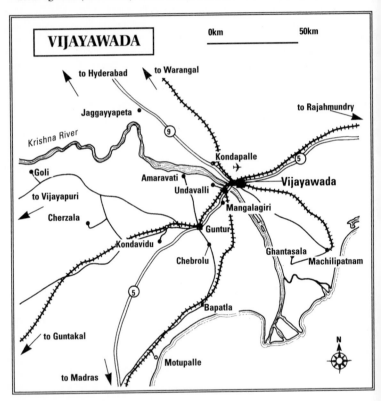

A. Vijayawada

The economic importance of Vijayawada through the centuries is explained by its advantageous location, 70km inland from the Bay of Bengal, commanding the coastal trading routes as well as those following the Krishna River upstream to the interior. The city is picturesquely surrounded by hills on three sides, with the swiftly flowing waters of the river on the south. The 1km long **Prakasam Barrage**, on the outskirts of Vijayawada, is one of the earliest major irrigation projects in Southern India. First finished in 1855, the scheme irrigates nearly one million ha, converting the Krishna Delta into the richest granary in Andhra.

Known in former times as Bezwada, Vijayawada was an important centre of the Vishnukundin rulers in the 5C–6C. In about 605 the city was taken by the Early Chalukyas of Badami [22A], who made it the headquarters of their eastern domains. These rulers eventually became separated from the main line, and are generally referred to as the Eastern Chalukyas. Hiuen Tsang, the Chinese pilgrim, stayed in a monastery at Bezwada in 639 and noted the decline of Buddhism in the area.

Isolated Buddhist vestiges are still to be seen within Vijayawada. They include rock-cut steps on the **East Hill**, believed to indicate the presence of a monastic establishment. It was here that the colossal, but much damaged, statue of Buddha was discovered, now on view in the **Victoria Jubilee Museum** (closed Fridays). Among the other Buddhist antiquities in this collection is a well-preserved standing Buddha from Alluru, dating from the 3C–4C. This white limestone figure is gracefully dressed in a fluted robe; the head is modelled with particular refinement. Prehistoric materials, such as stone tools, microliths and Neolithic implements, are also on display. Coins, arms, metalwork and miniature paintings from the 17C–18C illustrate the arts that flourished here under the Qutb Shahis and Nizams.

The Eastern Chalukya presence in Vijayawada in the 7C is testified to by two groups of excavated monuments at Vijayawada. Five rock-cut sanctuaries at **Mogalrajapuram**, 3km east of the city centre, are located at the extreme end of a row of hills. They have porches with undecorated squat columns. Cave 2 shows an overhanging cornice with artifical windows. Worn images indicate a variety of deities. Two additional cave-temples may be seen in the west part of the city, beneath **Telegraph Hill**. The larger of the two examples has a dipli-dated but spacious colonnade that gives access to a trio of small *linga* shrines.

B. Kondapalle

Kondapalle, 14km northwest of Vijayawada on NH9, is best known today as a place of manufacture of brightly painted wooden dolls.

The picturesque hill fort at Kondapalle was founded by the Eastern Chalukyas in the 8C, before being occupied by the Reddi chiefs in the 14C–15C. The fort was conquered by the Bahmanis in 1471, and from them passed to the Qutb Shahis, who made it into the most important stronghold in the Krishna Delta. Kondapalle was eventually absorbed into the Nizam of Hyderabad's domains, though it also served for a time as an outpost for the British.

The **Lower Fort**, entered through three successive gates at the foot of the hill, is thickly overgrown with jungle and cactus. The **English Barracks** within the walls are now much decayed. Ascent of the hill is by way of a path winding between two ridges, climbing up for more than 1km, mostly by way of a stone staircase. The ruins of an old palace appear dramatically perched on a crest above the path.

The **Upper Fort** is entered through a trio of large entrances, known collec-tively as the ***Dargah* Gate.** They have 5m high stone walls, with lintels up to 4m across. The whitewashed ***Dargah* of Gulab Shah** nearby, which gives its name to the Gate, commemorates a commander who was killed here defending the fort. Immediately above is the **Tanisha Mahal**, a Qutb Shahi structure. The ground floor consists of colonnades divided into separate chambers. A small stone staircase leads to the upper level, where there is a reception hall with subsidiary chambers, and bathrooms with stone cisterns and terracotta pipes set into the walls, all lacking their roofs. Traces of intricately worked plaster decoration can still be made out.

A path leads to a deep **Tank** fed by a natural spring. The **Granary** beyond is supported on high arches, with different compartments serving as separate receptacles, each with an opening in the roof. Near to the Granary are the **Magazines**. The hill all around is strongly defended by **Fortifications**, with towers and ramparts. A path descends from the **Golconda Gate**, on the other side of the Upper Fort.

C. Jaggayyapeta

This town, 77km northwest of Vijayawada on NH9, was once an important Buddhist centre. Relics were discovered here in the 19C on a low hill called **Dhanu Bodu**, which runs parallel to the road leading to the town. As at Amaravati, some 50km southeast, these vestiges suffered from pillaging by local people.

The principal Buddhist remains consist of the **Maha *Chaitya***, as the *stupa* is referred to in the 3C–4C inscriptions, a ruined pillared hall immediately southeast, and a few inconspicuous mounds in the vicinity. The drum portion of the *stupa*, 21m in diameter, stands to a height of about 1.25m and has four cardinal projections. It is faced with greenish limestone slabs fixed to the masonry ring wall containing the brick-and-earth core of the *stupa*. The slabs at the base of the drum are carved with figures showing worship of the *stupa* by devotees bearing garlands. Other items, including a representation of a royal figure, are now in the Government Museum, Madras [36D]. Fragments of Buddha images and the carved plinths of subsidiary votive *stupas* suggest the existence of other Buddhist shrines nearby.

D. Machilipatnam

Known to Europeans as Masuliptanam, this town, 70km southeast of Vijayawada, in the Krishna Delta. In the 17C–18C it was renowned for its cotton textiles, especially finely woven muslins and brightly coloured prints. Trade greatly declined after 1864, when an enormous tidal wave penetrated some 30km inland, drowning more than 30,000 people. In spite of this and other similar calamities since, the town has revived and is once again a thriving textile centre. It is currently a focus for the Church Missionary Society.

> Machilipatnam's commercial history begins with the arrival of the English. The East India Company established an agency here in 1611 and a factory some 11 years later. Except for a brief period in 1628–32, when they were expelled, the English made this port their major headquarters on the Coromandel Coast. Their advantage over rival Dutch and French companies was confirmed by a decree from the Mughal emperor Aurangzeb in 1698, granting them trading monopolies. The French obtained a similar grant from the Nizam in 1753, but were forcibly ousted by the British six years later.

Little can now be seen of Machilipatnam's mercantile past. About the only items of interest are the **Dutch Tombs** in the burial ground. Their handsomely carved inscriptions and coats of arms bear dates ranging from 1649 to 1725.

E. Ghantasala

This somewhat isolated village, 21km west of Machilipatnam, was once a renowned mercantile centre, dependent on seaborne traffic. Roman gold coins and locally produced copper and lead coins with ship motifs, belonging to the Satavahana period, testify to the flourishing Indo-Roman trade. Buddhism played an important part in the life of Ghantasala, but unfortunately the monuments were subjected to large-scale pillage. Decorated limestone **Columns** of various sizes have been discovered in the village and the surrounding fields. They belong to pillared halls associated with 2C–3C monastic establishments. Some columns are still seen lying on the ground near low mounds.

The ruined **Maha *Chaitya*** was excavated in the early part of the 20C. Like other *stupas* in the region, this example has radial and ring walls of rubble, once filled with rammed mud to create a solid hemispherical mass. (One casing limestone slab carved with a relief depiction of the assault and temptation of Mara has found its way to the Musée Guimet, Paris.) The recent find of a coping stone carved with garland-bearing dwarfs suggests that the *stupa* was originally encircled by a high railing.

F. Undavalli

The rock-cut sanctuaries at this site, overlooking the south bank of the Krishna River, lie 2km west of NH5, just 4km south of Vijayawada. Contemporary with similar caves at Vijayawada, the Undavalli examples are assigned to the 7C–8C Eastern Chalukya rulers. The architecture is massive and unrelieved, with undecorated squat columns with angled cuts and curved brackets.

The most impressive sanctuary at Undavalli is the **Triple-Storeyed Cave.** This consists of three halls at different levels, linked by internal staircases with terraces in front. On the outside, these halls present superimposed colonnades, one set back from the other, separated by overhanging curved eaves with false windows. The fully sculpted lions and seated sages in stucco, serving as parapet elements, are later additions, as are many of the carved panels. The hall inside the uppermost level has a large panel of Vishnu reclining on the serpent at one side, now much restored.

Monolithic temple **Models** and other excavated halls are seen nearby.

G. Mangalagiri

This town on NH5, 13km south of Vijayawada and 19km north of Guntur, is overlooked on the south by a wooded hill with a natural cave, which is accorded great sanctity. There are also indications of rock-cut sanctuaries, now greatly worn, going back to Eastern Chalukya times. A **Victory Pillar**, near the foot of the steps which ascends the hill, is inscribed with the account of the capture of Kondavidu fort in 1515 by the commanders of the Vijayanagara emperor Krishdevanaraya.

The main attraction of Mangalagiri is the **Lakshmi Narasimha Temple**. This monument goes back to the time of the Reddi chiefs in the 14C, but was substantially remodelled in the 17C–18C. Entrance *gopuras* in the middle of four sides provide access to the compound. The east entrance presents a steep pyramid of eleven storeys, each marked by a rectangular opening topped with a barrel-vaulted roof. There are no sculptures on the walls beneath or on the tower, merely pilastered projections. The north entrance is shorter, but is covered with plaster figures, now somewhat decayed. The unfinished *gopura* on the west was begun during the Qutb Shahi period, judging from the arches with lobed profiles,

The main east-facing shrine in the middle of the compound is raised on a high terrace marked by rows of pilasters. The outer walls of the sanctuary and adjoining hall have regularly spaced niches and single pilasters standing in pots, all in shallow relief. The double-storeyed tower over the sanctuary is capped with a hemispherical roof. The shrine is approached through an open hall, some of the columns are fashioned as rearing *yalis*. The outer piers are overhung by deeply curving eaves. A small Garuda shrine in front displays wheels on the side walls, suggesting a chariot. Its pyramidal roof is crowned with a lotus finial.

H. Guntur

This city, 32km southwest of Vijayawada on NH5, came into prominence after being granted to the French in the early 18C as a trading depot, developing thereafter as a place of commercial importance. Guntur is dotted with tobacco-curing factories and mills for rice, cotton and oil. There are no historical features of note within the city, but the newly opened **Baudhasree Archaeological Museum** (closed Fridays) is worth visiting. Sculptures discovered at 2C–4C Buddhist sites in the region are displayed here. They include elegantly modelled Buddha figures dressed in flowing robes, and *stupa* slabs showing devotees or scenes from the former lives of Buddha. Associated finds, such as black-and-red polished ceramic fragments, are also exhibited. There is, in addition, an unusual limestone stool with cut-out lotus flowers. Carvings associated with the Eastern Chalukyas include 8C panels of seated Brahma and standing Vishnu. Later art is represented by 15C–16C bronze figurines.

I. Chebrolu

This small town, 10km south of Guntur, has an ancient history, going back to Ikshvaku times. The high **Mound** on which the houses are built has yielded terracotta figures and coins, two of which, in gold, pertain to the Roman emperor Constantine. The standing monuments belong to the 9C–10C Eastern Chalukya period. The finest example at Chebrolu is the **Bhimeshvara Temple**, raised on a solid lower storey, with entrance porches on three sides marked by deeply overhanging eaves. These give access to a corridor running around four sides of the central *linga* shrine. The tower above, with its capping hemisphere, is of a later date.

The nearby **Adikeshvara Temple**, dating from the 12C, has double shrines. The sanctuaries are roofed with multi-storeyed towers, somewhat altered. They are preceded by an enclosed hall, entered through a small porch with columns fashioned as seated *yalis* on squatting elephants. The adjacent **Nageshvara Temple** presents a different arrangement, the main shrine being approached through an open hall with balcony seating all around, now partly obscured by infill blocks. The entrance *gopura* with a steeply pyramidal tower is assigned to the 17C–18C. A Nandi pavilion stands outside the Temple compound.

That Chebrolu flourished in later times is revealed by the unusual 18C

Brahmalingeshvara Temple. This consists of a small shrine surrounded by a colonnade, standing on an island in the middle of a large square tank. The main object of worship here is a *linga* with four images of Brahma carved on its sides, set into a lotus bowl. The *linga* is viewed through doorways on four sides, each with cut-out screens and sharply modelled overhanging eaves. The ceiling inside is delicately worked, with a lotus medallion and corner petals. The soaring tower presents a graceful pyramid of horizontal elements, recently whitewashed. A bridge on the east links the shrine with the bank, where steps lead down to the water. Eight subshrines were originally positioned around the tank facing the Brahmalingeshvara, those at the corners being dedicated to goddesses.

J. Bapatla

This town lies 38km south of Chebrolu, only 7km from the Bay of Bengal. The **Bhavana Narayana Temple** here was erected by the Cholas when they conquered the Krishna Delta region in the 10C. Architectural connections with the Tamil country are seen in the multi-storeyed pyramidal towers of the triple shrines, capped with prominent hemispherical roofs. A standing Vishnu is under worship in the central shrine, with subsidiary divinities in the corners. The Temple, together with minor sanctuaries, stands in a walled compound.

Motupalle, where Marco Polo is supposed to have landed in 1298, is a forgotten port 32km further south along the coast.

K. Amaravati

This small town, 34km north of Guntur on the south bank of the Krishna River, is best known for the **Maha *Chaitya***, or Great *Stupa*, which once stood on its outskirts. The remains of this monument were first noticed in 1796, but systematic investigation did not take place until the middle of the 19C, by which time many limestone portions had been pillaged. Virtually nothing can now be seen of the *Stupa*, other than a low earthen mound, 45m in diameter, surrounded by a pathway defined by upright slabs. The Maha *Chaitya*, probably the largest and most elaborate in Southern India, was founded in the 3C–2C BC during the Satavahana era, and was enlarged on several occasions under the Ikshvakus in the 3C–4C AD. The *Stupa* is celebrated for its finely worked limestone capping pieces and posts and railings, most of which have been removed from the site. The largest collections are in the Government Museum, Madras [36D], and the British Museum, London. Together with sculptures from Nagarjunakonda [27H], those from Amaravati are of outstanding importance for the development of the Buddha figure and the narrative tradition illustrating the life of the Master.

The **Archaeological Museum** (closed Fridays), next to the Maha *Chaitya*, is home to a collection of recently discovered panels, posts, railings and sculptures, dating from both the Satavahana and Ikshvaku eras. The first gallery shows large standing Buddhas, some more than 2m high, with elegantly fluted robes. One item depicts a maiden gracefully posed beneath a horseshoe-shaped arch. Several panels show *stupas* with flying celestials and the worship of Buddha's throne. There is also a fully modelled embracing couple, probably celestials. The second gallery is dominated by a remarkable life-size bull, ceremonially decked with garlands and tassels. This has been reconstituted from fragments discovered in 1980 in the vicinity of the Amareshvara Temple. Nearby is a wheel with cut-out spokes, symbolic of Buddha's teachings, as well as two elegant standing Buddha figures.

A reconstruction of part of the *stupa* railing, reaching an impressive height of almost 6m, stands in the Museum courtyard. It is composed mostly of plaster casts taken from pieces in the Madras collection, incorporating several original cross bars. They show a mixture of full lotus flowers and narrative scenes, such as the birth of Buddha and various miracles. A useful model showing the original scheme of the Maha *Chaitya* is also on view.

The **Amareshvara Temple**, elevated on a mound overlooking the Krishna River, a short distance away, was founded by the Eastern Chalukyas in the 10C–11C, but was largely renovated in the 18C by Venkatadri Nayudu, a local chief. That the monument occupies an earlier Buddhist site is suggested by the curiously shaped *linga* under worship in the upper sanctuary. This actually forms part of a *yupa*, or stone pillar inserted into a *stupa* as a symbolic axis of the universe. The temple is approached by free-standing gateways on the south and east, the former marking the end of the main street of the town. The Temple is surrounded by a double enclosure, the inner compound raised up on retaining walls as a solid structure, with flights of steps on three sides. The shrine exterior is of little interest, but the columns in the outer hall, which has balcony seating all around, have well-shaped cubic blocks and double capitals. Here is placed a brass-clad image of Venkatadri Nayudu, his hands held together in adoration.

The remains of the fort of **Dharanikota**, parts of which go back to the 18C, overlook the Krishna River 1km west of the town.

L. Goli
This small village lies about 100km west of Guntur, a short distance from the route to Vijayapuri, 43km further west, a stopping-off point for Nagarjunakonda. Goli is best known for its Buddhist antiquities, dating from the Ikshvaku era, but other remains are also of interest. They include three **Dolmens** west of the village, and the dilapidated **Malleshvara Temple** in an old fort to the southwest.

An irregular pit with stray bricks marks the site of a small, but profusely decorated, *Stupa*. Most of the limestone sculptures discovered here in 1926 are now on display in the Government Museum, Madras. An exception is the panel showing Nanda's forced ordination, which has made its way to the Metropolitan Museum, New York. One item still to be seen at Goli is a panel with a seven-hooded serpent, presently in worship in a small shed.

M. Kondavidu
The Kondavidu range of hills west of Guntur is dotted with forts of different periods. They are most easily reached by taking a diversion of 5km from Phirangipuram, 27km west of Guntur.

The **Puttakota**, or Lower Fort, dates back to the 11C–12C, when the Gajapatis of Orissa commanded this part of coastal Andhra. It occupies a valley in the middle of the hills, the mouth of which is closed by a high embankment of earth and stone. The area inside, now much overgrown, is filled with remains of temples, pillared halls, wells and stone mortars.

The Upper Fort, or **Kila**, on top of the hill, is reached by a path from Puttakota.

This citadel is associated with the Reddis, for whom it was the principal stronghold in the 14C–15C. The zone is surrounded by battlemented ramparts with high towers. The area inside is filled with disintegrating dwellings, treasuries, magazines and granaries. One structure with a rock-cut chamber may have been used as a store. Overturned mortars are seen everywhere around. There are many springs and three large tanks, one feeding into another. Several shrines have had their sculptures chipped away. One was transformed into a mosque by Ghulab Ghazi, a local commander, whose tomb stands nearby.

The Reddis were repeatedly challenged by the Vijayanagara emperors for supremacy in this part of coastal Andhra. They were finally vanquished in 1515, after which another citadel at Kondavidu, known simply as **Kota**, was built. This is situated beneath the northern flank of the hill. The ramparts, broken by two defensive entryways, remain to a considerable extent. The chief monument of merit inside Kota is the **Gopinatha Temple**, a 16C structure later converted into a mosque. It is entered through a spacious open hall, the outer columns of which have cut-out colonettes and sculpted *yalis* overhung by deeply curving eaves. An inner hall with side porches leads to the principal shrine. The walls, partly concealed by cactus, are relieved by deeply moulded basements and pilastered niches. No tower is preserved over the sanctuary.

N. Cherzala

This remote village, 56km northeast of Guntur via Narasaraopet, is of interest for a number of modest shrines, in particular the **Kapoteshvara Temple**. Though currently in use as a Hindu place of worship, the apsidal-ended plan and vault of the building recall similar, though incompletely preserved, 3C–4C Buddhist structures at Nagarjunakonda. Only 7m long, the Kapoteshvara Temple is built entirely of brick, including the vaulted roof. The frontal arch is ornately treated with plaster decoration framing a temple tower in shallow relief.

Miniature monolithic shrine **Models**, evidently votive in nature, stand in the precincts of the Temple. One example has a columned porch in front of the shrine doorway.

30 · Rajahmundry

The densely populated Godavari River Delta is dotted with historical sites, testifying to the sustained economic significance of this richly watered zone through the centuries.

Rajahmundry, the largest city in the region, only a short distance from the great dam at **Dowleshwaram** [A], makes a convenient halt from which to visit the Buddhist relics at **Guntupalle** [B], a half-day trip, as well as the Eastern Chalukya temple at **Bhimavaran** [C] and the pilgrimage shrine at **Antarvedi** [D] which can be combined in a single excursion.

A full-day journey to the eastern part of the Delta may take in the religious monuments at **Bikkavolu** [E], **Drakasharama** [F] and **Samalkot** [H]. This trip may be extended to include the scanty vestiges of the European presence at the former trading posts of **Yanon** [G] and **Kakinada** [I].

An outstanding feature of the Rajahmundry area is the enchanting scenery. Plantations of rice and sugar cane are traversed by canals and channels, with distant views of the forested ridges of the Eastern Ghats. A full-day launch trip up the **Gorge of the Godavari** [J] is recommended.

■ **Transport**. Rajahmundry is on the main line from Madras [36], as well as on NH5, midway between Vijayawada [29], 180km southwest, and Visakhapatnam [31], 192km northeast. Local transport reaches all the destinations described here.

■ **Accommodation**. The *Hotel Anand Regency* and *Hotel Mahalakshmi* are the finest in Rajahmundry (STD code 0883).

■ **Tourist Information**. None.

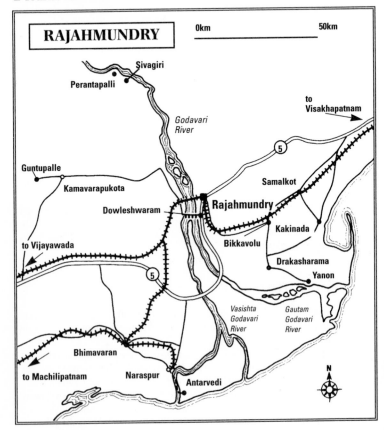

A. Dowleshwaram

The well-watered Godavari Delta draws its wealth from extensive cultivation of rice, sugar cane, areca nut, turmeric and bananas, as well as local industries such as cotton dyeing and printing. These all depend on an immense system of canals and channels that fans out all over the delta. Unfortunately, the Godavari River, the source of the water, is prone to flooding; severe weather poses an additional threat of cyclones, sometimes with devastating tidal waves. There were several attempts to control the river after Rajahmundry was ceded by the Nizams to the English in 1766. Enormous physical difficulties were encountered in harnessing the Godavari River, which here attains widths in excess of 6km. Sir Alfred Cotton was eventually successful in constructing the great **Dam** at Dowleshwaram, 10km downstream from the city. The Dam, more than 4km long, was built in 1848–52, with subsequent repairs and alterations.

B. Guntupalle

This small village lies 87km west of Rajahmundry via Kamavarapukota. (Guntupalle is also accessible from Vijayawada, via Eluru, 35km south of Kamavarapukuta.) A wooded ravine a short distance east of the village preserves Buddhist antiquities dating back to the 2C–1C BC Satavahana era.

Several features stand on a terrace approached by a long flight of steps. A **Circular Complex**, occupying a commanding position, includes an unadorned brick *stupa*, more than 9m in diameter, surrounded by a passageway. Part of the limestone cladding is intact. Standing Buddha images, some up to 2m high, dating from the 3C–4C, are placed here. More than 30 **Stupas** of varying sizes are located nearby; so, too, are the ruins of a **Columned Hall** and an **Apsidal-Ended Shrine**.

Two groups of rock-cut shrines stand a short distance away. The excavated *Chaitya* **Hall** has an unusual circular plan, and a dome-like ceiling with a network of radiating ribs imitating wooden rafters. The entrance is framed by a horseshoe-shaped arch.

C. Bhimavaran

This town, 126km southwest of Rajahmundry, has an important, though somewhat worn and poorly restored, Eastern Chalukya monument. The core shrine of the 11C **Someshvara Temple** houses a 1.5m high *linga*. The outer walls of the passageway surrounding the shrine are severely plain, except for pilasters set in recesses. The pyramidal tower above has flattened model roofs in ascending tiers, capped by an enlarged square roof with a dome-like top.

D. Antarvedi

The pilgrimage shrine at Antarvedi is reached by boat from Naraspur, 112km south of Rajahmundry, on the Vasishta branch of the Godavari River. Naraspur was an important European trading post, but nothing can now be seen of the Dutch, French and English presence. As in the past, small ships are built here; it is also an important centre of lace-making.

It is about 10km by boat from Naraspur to the confluence of the Vasishta River and the ocean. Here is situated **Antarvedi**, the most sacred of bathing spots in the Godavari Delta, sometimes known as Dakshina Kashi or the Southern Varanasi. Great numbers of pilgrims visit the **Lakshmi Narayana Temple** in February–March to attend the wedding festival of the god, identified as Narasimha.

According to local legend, Narasimha manifested himself in an ant-hill, where the existing stone image of the deity was discovered. This was originally kept in a shed and then installed in the Temple, which was erected in 1823. Its brightly painted entrance tower is visible along the sands.

E. Bikkavolu

This village is located about 45km east of Rajahmundry, and is approachable by road or train. The 9C **Chandrashekhara, Golingeshvara** and **Rajarajeshvara Temples**, which stand in a row, are all assigned to the Eastern Chalukya era. Characteristic features are the moulded plinths, pilastered walls with regular projections, parapets of miniature roof forms and multi-storeyed towers crowned with square roofs, some restored. Finely sculpted icons of Ganesha, Karttikeya and Durga are set into the wall niches. Additional images of Vishnu, Surya, Brahma and the Dikpalas appear on the Golingeshvara Temple. The central panels are framed by secondary pilasters that support *makaras* with foliate tails. Each Temple adjoins a columned hall, generally with unadorned walls. Fine carvings of Durga and Virabhadra are placed inside the hall of the Golingeshvara Temple.

Abandoned and dilapidated structures stand on the fringe of the Bikkavolu Temple. These include the **Nakkalagudi** and the **Virabhadra Temples**, both with squat pyramidal towers. The sculpture panels, though worn, compare with those of the Golingeshvara Temple. The slightly later 10C **Kanchanagudi Temple**, now abandoned and overgrown, presents an elegantly heightened triple-storeyed tower.

F. Drakasharama

This locally celebrated pilgrimage spot lies 40km south of Rajahmundry via Ramachandrapuram. The 10C **Bhimeshvara Temple** here is of interest for the enormous 5m high *linga*, believed to have belonged to the demon Taraka. This 10C sanctuary stands in the middle of a hall arranged unusually on two levels. The outer walls have single pilasters and capping cornices at both levels. Columns with sharply modelled capitals are employed within. The pyramidal tower over the *linga* sanctuary is capped with a square roof.

Evidence of European presence at Drakasharama is seen in the **Dutch Tombs** on what is called the Ollandu Dibba, or Holland Mound. They date variously from 1675 to 1728, and have finely carved slabs.

G. Yanon

This former French settlement, no more than 914ha in extent, is located 37km east of Drakasharama, 20km from the mouth of the Gautam Godavari River.

The French built a factory here in 1750, shortly after which they were defeated by the British in the battle at Pithapura. Unlike other French trading posts on the Coromandel Coast, Yanon was only temporarily occupied by the British, in 1802–03, and remained under French control into the 20C. It now forms part of the Union Territory of Pondicherry [30].

Few European remains are to be seen, partly because in 1839 the town was laid waste by a hurricane, accompanied by an inundation of the sea. The **Catholic Church** postdates this catastrophe. A spacious walled **Parade Ground** is laid out on the south side of the town, bordering the river.

H. Samalkot

The 11C **Bhimeshvara Temple** at this town, 47km east of Rajahmundry, is the largest East Chalukya monument in the region. It resembles the slightly earlier monument at Drakasharama, with which it shares the same name. The tower over the central shrine at Samalkot has two distinct storeys capped with a square roof. The columned porches on two levels project outwards on three sides of the hall; the columns are fashioned as seated lions. Supports with finely finished double capitals are seen inside the hall; some of the shafts are enlivened with figural motifs. A double-storeyed colonnade runs around the enclosure walls of the complex. The gateways on the north and south have pilastered walls, but no towers.

Samalkot attained some measure of significance in the 18C, when it became the headquarters of a group of landowners who resisted the European traders. The fort here was also the scene of fighting between the British and French, both of whom occupied it on different occasions in 1759. The fort served as a sanatorium for British troops, but was eventually demolished in 1838. Since then, Samalkot has emerged as a commercial centre, with numerous sugar refineries and distilleries.

I. Kakinada

This busy seaport, 18km south of Samalkot, was renowned for its cotton exports, which attracted European traders.

The Dutch built a factory and mint in 1628 at **Jagannathapuram**, on the south side of the harbour, by decree from the Mughal emperor. The British attacked the settlement in 1781, occupying it for three years. During the wars of the French Revolution in 1789–95, Jagannathapuram was once again captured, only to be returned in 1814. The port reverted finally to the British in 1824. European remains here are confined to a small **Cemetery**. The earliest identifiable graves are those of a Dutch family dated 1775–78. In the course of the 19C the bay silted up, and Kakinada replaced Jagannathapuram as the principal port. A second impulse to seaborne commerce was provided by the American Civil War in 1861, during which Kakinada rose to prominence because of huge shipments of cotton textiles. The town is today an important Christian centre.

The **Protestant Church** possesses one of the finest organs in Southern India. A **Roman Catholic Church** and convent stand nearby.

J. Godavari Gorge

The forested ravine of the Godavari River, which begins about 80km north of Rajahmundry, constitutes one of the most impressive scenic tracts in Andhra Pradesh. Before flowing into the plain of the Delta, the River makes its way through the wooded hills of the Eastern Ghats, the peaks of which here reach almost 1500m high. The configuration of these ranges forces the river through a series of narrow constrictions separated by broad stretches of water. This alternation of gorge and lake has reminded European travellers of Scottish and Italian scenery. Though it is possible to travel part of the way by road, the boat trip from Rajahmundry is more comfortable (check timings).

Small villages line the Godavari River as it passes through the Ghats. One of these, **Sivagiri**, serves as a landing post for the *girijans*, forest hunters with bows and arrows, who inhabit the surroundWing hills. The jungle, which begins at the bank, provides an ideal habitat for tigers and bears, which can be occasionally be sighted drinking at the water's edge. **Perantapalli**, another village 10km further upstream, is reached only after passing through a narrow canyon bounded by jagged boulders heaped at the jungle's fringe.

31 · Visakhapatnam

The Visakhapatnam area is notable for its delightful scenery, with forested hills descending to rocky headlands on the Bay of Bengal coast.

A few hours should be reserved to visit the sights of **Visakhapatnam** [A], with half-day trips to the hill temple at **Simhachalam** [B], the Buddhist relics at **Sankaram** [C] and the curious Dutch tombs at **Bheemunipatnam** [D].

The Buddhist sites at **Ramatirtham** [E] and **Salihundram** [F] will demand a longer journey, especially if this is extended to include the pilgrimage shrines at **Srikurman** [G] and **Mukhalingam** [H]. From here it is possible to continue into Orissa.

The **Borra Caves** [I], with their remarkable limestone formations, are easily reached from Visakhapatnam.

■ **Transport**. Visakhapatnam is linked by air to Calcutta, Hyderabad [26] and Madras [36]. Together with Waltair, the city forms a major junction on the Madras-Calcutta line, with another branch heading north to Raipur in Madhya Pradesh. Visakhapatnam lies on NH5, 192km northeast of Rajahmundry [30] and 426km southwest of Bhubaneshwar in Orissa. Local buses and trains reach all of the destinations described here. Boats occasionally run from Visakhapatnam to Port Blair in the Andaman Islands [49].

■ **Accommodation**. The most comfortable places to stay in Visakhapatnam (STD code 0891) are the *Taj Residency* (☎ 567756) and *Park Hotel* (☎ 554488), both overlooking **Ramakrishna Beach**, 5km from the centre of Visakhapatnam. The *Sarovar* and *Meghalaya* (☎ 555141) are more centrally located.

■ **Tourist Information**. The APTTDC maintains offices at the Nehrunagar Shopping-Office Complex (☎ 563016) and at the VUDA Building, Siripuram.

A. Visakhapatnam

Formerly known as Vizagapatam, or simply as Vizag, this city is a major industrial centre and naval base known for heavy industries, with an oil refinery, zinc smelting plant and specialist steelworks. Visakhapatnam benefits from what was until recently the only deep-water harbour on the Bay of Bengal and the second biggest shipyard in Southern India, after Bombay [1]. The port serves as a major export terminal for bulk iron and manganese.

Little is known of Visakhapatnam's history prior to the arrival of the Europeans. The English established themselves here in 1682 and quickly built up a lucrative commerce in textiles, tobacco and ivory. The city came under the control of the Mughals in 1689; the English were taken prisoner and all of their property was seized. Peace was established in the following year, and trade was resumed again. Except for attacks by local chiefs and an invasion by the French in 1757, Visakhapatnam remained in British hands until Independence.

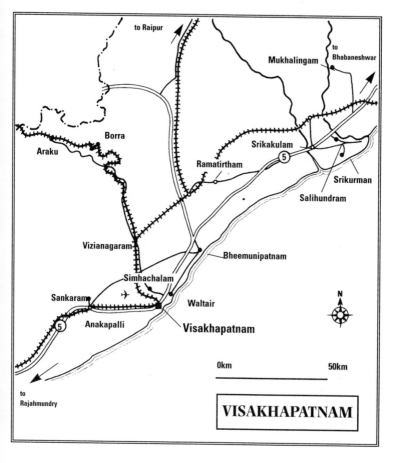

Visakhapatnam benefits from a splendid setting, facing onto a broad bay. Its southern extremity is bounded by a promontory with a hill rising 175m above the sea, known as **Dolphin's Nose**. The lighthouse here has a beam visible more than 60km out to sea. The oldest part of the city, the **Fort**, is separated from Dolphin's Nose by a small river which forms a sandbar. Here can be seen the remains of 18C **Barracks**, an **Arsenal**, the **Court House** and **Protestant**

Church, the last being marked by a graceful circular lantern topped with a dome-like roof. The **Cemetery** nearby contains European graves going back to 1699.

Visakhapatnam is framed by a line of three hills, each topped by a shrine associated with a different religion. The **Venkateshvara Temple**, on the south hill, has a small, steeply pyramidal entrance *gopura*. The central hill is crowned with the **Church of the Virgin Mary**, approached by a path lined with shrines of the Stages of the Cross. Its whitewashed façade is flanked by slender towers. The **Dargah of Isai**, a Muslim saint much venerated by seafarers, is set beneath the north hill. It is roofed with a flattish, bulbous dome.

Waltair, once a separate town but now part of greater Visakhapatnam, is located near Ramakrishna Beach, at the northern extermity of the bay. Originally established as a health resort for British officers, it preserves several churches. The **Church of St Paul** of 1847 is a simple Neo-Classical scheme, with a modest portico displaying a quartet of Ionic columns. A semicircular arch divides the congregation from the altar, with stained-glass in the apse. The **Catholic Pilgrimage Chapel** dates from 1867. Waltair is renowned for the **Andhra University**, one of the largest campuses in Andhra Pradesh, founded in 1931.

B. Simhachalam

The popular **Varaha Narasimha Temple** at Simhachalam is dramatically sited high up in the secluded forest of the Kailasha Hills, 16km north of Visakhapatnam. This shrine is believed to have been dedicated originally to Shiva, but was later transformed into a Vaishnava place of worship after a visit by Ramanuja, the famous teacher, at the end of the 11C. The story is borne out by the principal votive image of the Temple: a *linga*-shaped form, composed of sandalwood paste, concealing a diminutive stone effigy of Vishnu. Dating back to the 8C–9C, the Temple was entirely rebuilt in 1268 by a military commander of Narasimha, the Eastern Ganga king of neighbouring Orissa. That Simhachalam continued to be a place of importance in later centuries is evident from the visit of Krishnadevaraya, the emperor of Vijayanagara [20B–C], in 1516. The growth of nearby Visakhapatnam ensures that the Temple continues to expand.

The Varaha Narasimha Temple is approached by a long winding road that ascends the hill, arriving at a car park from which flights of steps ascend to gateways on the north and west. These take the form of *gopuras* with steeply pyramidal towers, recently renovated. Most visitors enter through the north *gopura*, inside which is a large hall built into the northeast corner of the enclosure. The peripheral supports of polished granite are fashioned as seated lions. The animals support shafts with carved reliefs and sharply modelled double capitals. The internal columns are enlivened with bands of foliation and jewelled garlands. A lofty flagpole stands in front (west) of the porch that gives access to the inner enclosure.

The main Temple consists of two halls, one open the other closed, aligned with the square sanctuary and its surrounding passageway. The outer hall has round columns decorated with figural friezes and garlands. One of these is identified as the pillar out of which Narasimha miraculously appeared. The 12 columns of the inner hall support a ceiling with rotated squares. The sanctuary which lies beyond is roofed with a corbelled vault. The outer walls of the shrine and hall are raised on a high basement adorned with *yalis* and makaras. The wall projections have framing pilasters, with *yalis* in full relief. Icons of gods, ascetics and royal figures stand beneath ornate trees carved in shallow relief.

Major panels in the middle of the sanctuary walls depict Varaha (north), Narasimha disembowelling Hiranyakashipu (east) and Trivikrama (south), each surmounted by a smaller icon of Krishna in the pediment. These sculptures are executed in the finest Orissan style, with smoothly rounded bodies contrasting with delicately etched facial features, costumes and jewellery. The figural compositions are interspersed with exuberant scrollwork and creeper motifs. Windows capped by ornate pediments admit light to the hall. The pyramidal towers over the sanctuary and hall are crowned by circular ribbed elements.

The inner enclosure of the Temple is surrounded by a colonnade into which three small shrines are built. That in the northeast corner is conceived as a chariot, with large wheels carved on the basement. Life-size prancing horses are placed either side of the access steps.

C. Sankaram

The village of Sankaram, 3km north of Anakapalli, 38km west of Visakha-patnam, is known for its 3C–4C Buddhist antiquities, the dilapidated remains of which are seen on two hills just north of the village.

On the level top of the east hill, known as **Bojjanakonda**, are the basement and lower portions of a large *Stupa*, around which are smaller votive *stupas*, partially rock-cut and brick-built. The brick **Monastery** nearby has a central court surrounded by small square cells, with an apsidal-ended shrine in the middle. **Rock-cut Sanctuaries** are cut into the sides of the hill, four with Buddha reliefs. The cave with a monolithic *stupa* has 16 columns. Images of Ganesha and Bhairava in another excavated sanctuary indicate that the site was used in later times for Hindu worship.

Lingalakonda, the east hill, has numerous rock-cut *Stupas* arranged in ascending tiers, dominated by the outlines of a large monolithic *stupa*.

D. Bheemunipatnam

This small, quiet fishing port lies 24km northeast along the coast from Visakhapatnam, the road skirting a series of splendid sandy beaches.

> Bheemunipatnam was once Bimlipatan, one of the major Dutch settle-ments on the Coromandel Coast. The Dutch used this as a port for exports of rice in the 17C. In later times it became famous for jute manufacturing, with large mills operating in the surrounding villages, many still in opera-tion today. Bimlipatan was sacked by the Marathas, who invaded the coastal region in 1754, and was destroyed again in 1781, during the Anglo-Dutch wars. It surrendered to the British in 1795, but was not finally given over to them until 1825.

Hints of Bheemunipatnam's Dutch past are evident in its **Houses**, with colon-naded verandahs and sloping tiled roofs, and the crumbling **Fort** overlooking the beach. Of greater interest are the **Tombs** in the cemetery overlooking the ocean. This has a series of remarkable obelisk-shaped tombs bearing Dutch

Dutch Tombs, Bheemunipatnam

inscriptions, the earliest dating from 1760, as well as a French record of 1785. The Lighthouse nearby is more recent.

British-period monuments include the 19C **Clock Tower** in the middle of the town. The **Church of St Peter**, some 2.5km north, built in 1864, is recognised by its 20m high belfry. The interior is notable for its tiled pavement and wooden furniture.

The small **Krishna Shrine**, on the top of the hill outside the town, is approached by a steep flight of steps.

E. Ramatirtham

This village, 72km northeast of Visakhapatnam via Vizianagaram, is known for its Buddhist remains, dating from the 3C–4C Ikshvaku era. The main group of monuments is located on a hill north of the village, known as **Gurubhaktakonda**. They are dramatically sited on a narrow ledge 165m above the plain, hemmed in by the vertical cliff of bare rock on one side and a deep ravine on the other.

The first feature to be encountered is the **Main Stupa**, 22m in diameter, of which only the base survives. At the foot of the cliff nearby is a tank fed by water dripping from the rocky overhang. Further along is a terrace of boulders, with rows of monastic cells and the ruins of an imposing plastered **Apisdal Hall**, where the apse contains a small brick *stupa* faced with stone slabs. A small relic casket, containing lead coins and clay sealings, one with a legend written in character of the 2C, was discovered here. A columned **Hall** is situated nearby.

Four **Chaitya Halls**, laid out in an irregular line, are all apisdal in plan. Votive *stupas* partly survive in two of the Halls. Two **Monasteries** nearby, bordering the ledge, have long rows of cells, the doorways of each chamber flanked by stone pilasters.

Remains of similar Buddhist structures may be seen on the adjacent hill, called **Durgakonda**. The 8C–9C images of Jain saviours belong to the period when Buddhism had disappeared from the region.

F. Salihundram

The Buddhist remains at this site form an imposing landmark, picturesquely situated on top of a hill overlooking the Vamsadhara River, 8km from its confluence with the Bay of Bengal. Salihundram lies 15km east of Srikakulam, a town on NH5, 101km northeast of Visakhapatnam.

A rubble-paved path, lined by structural remains, ascends to the crest of the hill. Two **Apsidal Sanctuaries** stand immediately inside the gate. One enshrines a seated image of Buddha made of plaster-covered brickwork; the other has a stone-cased votive *stupa* with a brick core. A number of **Stupas** higher up the path include one with eight radial spokes. The **Circular Sanctuary** at the summit is 7.5m in diameter, with walls almost 5m thick, standing to a height of barely 1m. Nothing survives of the roof or the votive *stupa* inside. The **Main Stupa** nearby is made of wedge-shaped bricks around a central hollow shaft. Here, excavators recovered three stone caskets, each containing a crystal reliquary with gold flowers.

Dilapidated walls indicating a group of **Monasteries** are concentrated near the bank of the Vamsadhara River, beneath the hills.

G. Srikurman

The **Shri Kurmanatha Temple** at this coastal village, 13km east of Srikakulam, was founded by the Eastern Chalukyas in the 10C, but was substantially remodelled in the 12C–13C, when the Cholas temporarily occupied coastal Andhra Pradesh. The Temple is unique in having the tortoise form of Vishnu as its principal object of veneration. The main shrine is contained within an enclosure, the walls of which have shallow pilasters. Gateways with columned porches are placed in the middle of the east and south walls. Two lamp columns stand inside. The main shrine is surrounded by a colonnade, with 19C wall paintings depicting Krishna episodes and aspects of Vishnu. Sculpture niches appear in the outer projections of the sanctuary and attached halls. The walls are capped with a parapet of miniature roof forms. The tower over the sanctuary rises in two diminishing storeys, capped with an octagonal-domed roof.

H. Mukhalingam

This remote small town, on the east bank of the Vamsadhara River, lies 46km north of Srikakulam, partly by NH5. Mukhalingam was the first capital of the Eastern Gangas, the royal patrons of 12C–13C religious monuments at Puri and Konarak in neighbouring Orissa.

The 9C **Madhukeshvara Temple**, in the middle of Mukhalingam, is the most important and best-preserved of the group. The Temple consists of a sanctuary and an adjoining rectangular hall, with unusual subsidiary shrines built into the four corners. Sculpted panels between the corner shrines are set into niches with tower-like pediments in shallow relief. Among the numerous icons are finely carved images of Narasimha and dancing Shiva (south). The corner shrines are distinguished by curved towers with horizontal divisions, capped with enlarged disc-like ribbed motifs.

The curving tower over the sanctuary is larger and higher, but is also simpler, with plain horizontal divisions and duplicated disc-like elements. The central projections on each side have arch-shaped niches containing images of different deities. Shiva appears on the east face, as Bhikshatanamurti (above) and

Nataraja (below). The doorways on the east and south have jambs adorned with guardian figures, maidens and gracefully posed amorous couples, all set in delicate but luxuriant foliation. The lintel over the east doorway shows scenes of the Krishna story, as well as miniature friezes of battles, with soldiers and elephants. The south doorway is surmounted by multiple images of Shiva, showing the god dancing with the skin of the elephant demon and spearing Andhaka.

The Temple stands within a rectangular compound with a curious screen wall dividing it into two parts. The corner shrines imitate those already noted for the hall. The detailed ornamentation of the doorways and towers is finely executed, particularly in the panels over the doorways. A sculpted *naga* set near to the north compound wall holds a pot for water to flow into a small basin. The entrance gateway in the screen wall has intricately carved ascetics in meandering creepers on the jambs. The east entrance to the enclosure has a curving vaulted roof with a trio of ribbed finials on the ridge.

The 11C **Bhimeshvara Temple**, 200m southeast, repeats the basic scheme of the Madhukeshvara Temple, but is less well preserved. Most of the original detail has been lost, except for the delicately worked doorways.

The **Someshvara Temple**, a 9C monument with a single sanctuary, stands at the entrance to the town. Its curved tower, about 15m high, is treated with narrow horizontal bands. The main west doorway has panels of scrollwork, with the Navagrahas and a seated Lakshmi figure on the lintel; river goddesses enliven the jambs. The triple niches on each of the side house finely worked panels of Shiva, ten-armed Durga and one-legged Shiva (north), Harihara, Karttikeya and Ardharishvara (east), and Lakulisha, Ganesha and Shiva (south).

I. Borra

The journey by rail or road to the **Borra Caves**, 90km north of Visakhapatnam, winds continuously upwards through densely forested hills. The Caves, discovered in 1807 by William King of the Geological Survey of India, are situated in limestone cliffs overlooking the Gosthani River, at an altitude of 1400m. The impressive interior consists of a series of magnificent spaces enlivened with jagged stalactites and stalagmites, now illuminated by electric lights. Several smaller stalagmites are worshipped as *lingas*, with Nandis placed in front.

The road from Borra ascends to the Araku Valley, 22km further north.

32 · Kurnool

This city lies near the south bank of the Tungabhadra River, 32km upstream from its confluence with the Krishna River. Though there are few sights to draw visitors to **Kurnool** [A], the city makes a convenient stop on the journey from Hyderabad [26] to Anantapur [33] and Bangalore [14] on NH7.

Historical localities accessible from Kurnool include the temples at **Alampur** [B], recently salvaged from the rising waters of the Krishna River, an easy half-day trip. Full-day excursions will be required to reach the more distant but picturesquely situated prilgrimage spots at **Srisailam** [C], **Mahanandi** [D], **Satyavolu** [E], **Ahobilam** [F] and **Yaganti** [G], all east of Kurnool. Allow at least two days for these sites, possibly with an overnight stay at Srisailam or Ahobilam, The citadel at **Adoni** [H] can be visited on the way to Hospet [20] in Karnataka.

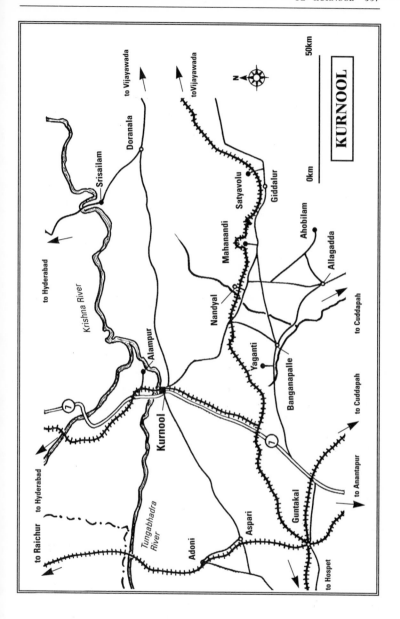

KURNOOL

N

0km   50km

to Vijayawada

to Vijayawada

toVijayawada

Srisailam

Doranala

Satyavolu

Giddalur

Mahanandi

Ahobilam

Allagadda

Nandyal

to Cuddapah

to Hyderabad

Krishna River

Alampur

Yaganti

Banganapalle

to Cuddapah

Kurnool

to Anantapur

Tungabhadra River

Adoni

Aspari

Guntakal

to Raichur   to Hyderabad

to Hospet

■ **Transport**. Kurnool is on the main line from Secunderabad [26E] to Guntakal, rail junction for Bangalore and Madras [36], with a branch line to Hospet and other points in Karnataka. Kurnool is 291km south of Hyderabad and 140km north of Anantapur [33] by road. Cuddapah [34] is about 225km southeast. Local transport reaches all the destinations described here.

■ **Accommodation**. The *Hotel Rajavihar* (☎ 20702) and *Hotel Raviprakash* (☎21116) are the best in Kurnool (STD code 08518). Simple accommodation for pilgrims is available at **Srisailam** and **Ahobilam**.

■ **Tourist Information**. None.

A. Kurnool
The importance of this city as an administrative centre may be judged from the fact that in 1950–56 it served as a state capital.

The history of Kurnool goes back to 1620, when it was conquered by Abdul Wahad Khan, the commander of the forces of Bijapur [23A], whose Tomb remains the chief attraction of the city. Kurnool gained further prominence under the Mughals and their successors, the Asaf Jahis of Hyderabad. A local family of chiefs commanded most of the district, the first member of which, Daud Khan, was installed by Aurangzeb. This line of Khans lasted until the British took over Kurnool at the beginning of the 19C.

About the only historical feature in Kurnool is the **Tomb of Abdul Wahad Khan**, in the east part of the city. This finely finished monument, dating from 1639, consists of a domed chamber surrounded by an arcaded passageway. A battlemented parapet with corner pavilion-shaped finials frames a central dome raised on a circular drum enlivened with petals. A lesser tomb chamber adjoins the building on the east.

B. Alampur
This village, on the north bank of the Tungabhadra River, lies 30km north of Kurnool, and about half the distance on NH7. Alampur was threatened by the rising waters of the recently completed dam of the Srisailam Project, 85km downstream. The barrage erected here has saved the temples, but has deprived them of the river view that they once enjoyed. Other structures in the vicinity have been dismantled and re-erected near the village.

Alampur formed part of the kingdom of the Early Chalukyas of Badami [22A], and was evidently an important settlement, judging from the many temples erected here in the 7C–8C. These comprise the largest and earliest surviving Hindu monuments in Andhra Pradesh. The group of nine temples at Alampur is known as the Nava Brahma, even though they are all dedicated to Shiva. With the exception of the Taraka Brahma, the temples conform to a standard scheme, with east-facing sanctuaries surrounded by passageways and preceded by columned halls, all contained within rectangles of walls. The curved towers above the sanctuaries are divided into tiers adorned with arch-shaped motifs and capped by circular ribbed elements.

The first feature to be seen on arriving at Alampur is the reconstructed **Sangameshvara Temple**, the blocks of which were brought from **Kudaveli**, at the confluence of the Tungabhadra and Krishna Rivers, now a flooded site. The Temple is elevated on a high terrace embellished with a frieze of animals, pilastered projections and a prominent parapet. The niches on the outer walls of the Temple have pediments of different designs, some with pairs of *makaras*. The niches on either side of the entrance frame large pot-bellied *yakshas*. The tower is of the standard type.

The Nava Brahma group stands in the middle of the village, surrounded by houses. They are described from north to south. The **Vira Brahma Temple** has its outer walls divided into projecting niches framed by pairs of pilasters, with triangular pediments of arch-shaped motifs above. The niches are empty, but flying figures embellish the tops of the walls. The tower has pronounced central projections. The **Vishva Brahma Temple** is more elaborate. Pediments of complicated designs based on arch-shaped motifs surmount the niches and windows. The basement blocks are sculpted with dwarfs, musicians, dancers, monster masks and geese with foliated tails. The interior columns have seated lions at the base, fluted shafts and ribbed pot-shaped capitals. The beams are incised with scrollwork. Triple niches appear in the passageway around the sanctuary. The adjacent **Arka Brahma Temple** is partly ruined.

The **Kumara Brahma Temple**, the earliest of the group, has a plain exterior with perforated stone screens lighting the interior passageway. The internal columns and beams are decorated with foliation and miniature figures. The **Bala Brahma Temple**, the only one currently in worship, has its outer walls partly concealed by a later colonnade. Various sculptures, including a series of the Matrikas, are placed here. A gateway to the east once led down to the Krishna River; it now faces the barrage wall. The **Garuda Brahma Temple** is similar to the Vishva Brahma Temple, but is almost devoid of carved decoration. The sanctuary doorway has bands of foliation, a flying Garuda figure and flanking guardians.

The **Svarga Brahma Temple**, dated 689, has a frontal porch of six columns with fluted shafts and pot-and-foliage motifs embellishing the bases and capitals. Additional porches with similar supports shelter the windows on three sides of the passageway. The Temple is notable for its elaborate sculptures, including a complete set of Dikpalas in the corner niches. Other icons show Shiva dancing, appearing out of the *linga*, shooting arrows at the demons of the triple cities, and seated in teaching posture beneath a tree; accessory images include amorous couples and flying figures at the top of the walls, and guardians on the columns. The arch-shaped frontal projection on the tower frames an icon of dancing Shiva.

The **Padma Brahma Temple**, the latest in the series, displays complicated niche forms on the outer walls and inside the passageway. The tower is incomplete, and there is no entrance porch. The **Taraka Brahma Temple** has an unusual multi-storeyed tower with the usual arch-shaped frontal projection. The **Gate** in the wall nearby served as the original entrance to the complex. Carved deities are seen on the ceiling.

The **Archaeological Museum** (closed Fridays), next to the Temples, is home to a fine collection of Early Chalukya sculptures. The masterpiece is an exquisitely refined image of dancing Shiva with multiple arms holding different weapons, trampling on a dwarf; the detached facial expression is noteworthy. Other items include images of Durga and ceiling panels showing dancing Shiva and a coiled serpent. A slab for libations is carved with a squatting figure of Lajja Gauri. Numerous decorated columns and beams are also on display. Among the items assigned to the Late Chalukya period are a polished basalt Nandi ridden by Shiva and Parvati.

That Alampur continued to be an important site in later times is indicated by fortifications and gateways inside the village, and by the **Papanasanam Group**, 1.5km southwest. These small temples are assigned to the 9C–10C, a period of transition between the Rashtrakutas and Late Chalukyas. Most examples display pyramidal multi-tiered towers; one has an unusual apsidal-ended roof. There is little external decoration, but the internal columns are decorated with figurative and foliate motifs. A fine Durga image is preserved in one temple; another shrine has a ceiling panel showing Vishnu's incarnations.

C. Srisailam

A visit to Srisalam, 180km east of Kurnool, can be accomplished as a day excursion, but an overnight stay is advisable. The drive to this site, particularly the last 35km from Doranala, is through the wooded slopes of the Eastern Ghats. Srisailam benefits from a dramatic site overlooking the deep gorge of the Krishna River, some 200m below, from the south. The recently completed **Srisailam Project**, one of the largest hydro-electric schemes in Andhra Pradesh, has dammed the waters all the way back to Alampur. (It is also possible to reach Srisailam directly from Hyderabad, about 190km north.)

The **Mallikarjuna Temple** at Srisailam is a popular place of pilgrimage, especially during the festival of Shivaratri in February–March. The cult of Shiva celebrated here is closely linked with the Chenchus, hunters who inhabit the surrounding forests. Though Mallikarjuna is known to have been worshipped in earlier times, the present monument is no earlier than the 14C–15C. It enjoyed the patronage of the emperors of Vijayanagara [20B–C], several of whom personally visited the site.

The Temple is surrounded by high walls with a crenellated parapet defining a large compound, 208m by 168m. The walls are of particular interest because of the remarkable reliefs carved on the blocks. The bottom course is ornamented with a procession of elephants, some uprooting trees, while the second course is devoted to equestrian and hunting scenes. The panels on the third and fourth courses depict processions of soliders, dancing girls, musicians, sages, pilgrims and mythical beasts. A host of scenes represents Shiva in diverse forms: as the wandering ascetic, as the hunter fighting Arjuna, as the slayer of the elephant demon and as the rescuer of Markandeya, who is shown clutching the *linga*. A large panel of a seated king near the east gateway may represent Krisnadevaraya; a model shrine nearby frames a standing icon of Shiva. Royal motifs on the south wall include a two-headed eagle known as *gandabherunda*.

Modest gateways with columned porticos on four sides, some with pyramidal brick towers, lead into a spacious compound filled with shrines and open halls. The Mallikarjuna Temple consists of a modest sanctuary capped by a pyramidal tower with diminishing tiers. This houses one of the *jyotirlingas* of Shiva. It is approached through a hall with triple porches, an addition of 1405. The pilastered walls and pierced stone windows have been entirely replaced, except for the columns in the porch, which have edicts of the Vijayanagara kings. A small subshrine near the north porch of the Temple shelters a *linga* with multiple miniature replicas carved on to its sides. The other shrines are of lesser interest.

D. Mahanandi

This pilgrimage spot is attractively situated in the wooded foothills of the Eastern Ghats, about 100km east of Kurnool via Nandyal. The Mahanandi monuments belong to the Early Chaluyka period, and are comparable to contemporary structures at Alampur. The **Mahanandishvara Temple** has its core shrine contained within a rectangle of walls that accommodates a spacious columned hall and corridor. The spire that rises over the sanctuary has its curving sides adorned with arch-shaped motifs. A circular ribbed element crowns the summit.

Two subsidiary temples, as well as several shrine models nearby, are of the same age as the main monument.

E. Satyavolu

This village, 30km east of Mahanandi via Giddalur, is the setting for two other Early Chalukya monuments. The **Ramalingeshvara** and **Bhimalingeshvara Temples** stand next to each other, the first being the larger. Both have shrines with wall niches in the middle of three sides, roofed with curving towers of the Alampur type. The frontal projections, with vaulted roofs and arched faces, frame icons of dancing Shiva. The hall attached to the Ramalingeshvara Temple has pierced stone screens and sloping roof slabs. This is preceded by an outer open hall, a later extension of the 14C–15C. The hall and its triple projecting porches are surrounded by balcony seating sheltered by angled eaves. Panels of divinities, accessory figures, animals and birds are seen on the basement. Mythological topics and decorative motifs embellish the blocks of the central four columns.

F. Ahobilam

This somewhat remote pilgrimage site is situated at an elevation of 925m in the forested hills of the Eastern Ghats. Ahobilam lies 148km southeast of Kurnool via Nandyal and Allagadda; it is only 112km north of Cuddapah.

Ahobilam is linked with Narasimha, the Man-Lion incarnation of Vishnu. According to local legend, Narasimha falls in love with a local Chenchu girl and has to undergo tests to prove his valour before marrying her. While the Narasimha cult at Ahobilam was first sponsored by the Reddis of Kondavidu [29M] in the 14C–15C, it was the 16C emperors of Vijayanagara who gave prominence to the site. It has continued since as a significant religious centre, and attracts large numbers of pilgrims. It is presently the headquarters of an important Vaishnava *matha*.

Ahobilam is the name given to two sites 8km apart. **Lower Ahobilam** is a small settlement, offering simple accommodation and facilities for devotees. The

Narasimha Temple here is a grand edifice, dating mostly from the 16C. An ornate pavilion and lamp column stand in the main street, which proceeds west towards the complex. The Temple is entered through two *gopuras*, the outer one lacking its tower. The inner gate has pilastered walls raised high on a double basement, and a five-storeyed pyramidal tower above. The passageway walls are covered with relief carvings of figures, creeper motifs and superimposed temple façades.

The spacious columned hall of the Narasimha Temple appears to have been built in imitation of an almost identical structure in the Vitthala Temple at Vijayanagara. The outer supports are raised on an ornate basement with a frieze of elephants and attendants. Clusters of cut-out colonettes surround the outer columns, with secondary shorter colonettes and squatting dwarfs above. The eaves are replacements. The interior is divided into open areas defined by sculpted columns. That on the north is enlivened by multiple aspects of Narasimha; that to the rear is flanked by riders on *yalis*, as well as by richly attired courtiers. The main shrine is comparatively unadorned and modest in scale. The columned hall in the southwest corner of the compound has slender colonettes and animals on the outer columns, with rearing beasts flanking the central aisle.

Upper Ahobilam is set in a picturesque wooded ravine with a waterfall and stream. The approach path passes by a large square tank with stepped sides. It is overlooked by a 16-columned pavilion with a central dais; the columns display *yalis* and colonettes. The *gopura* that gives access to the **Narasimha Temple** from the west has a freshly whitewashed three-storeyed tower. The interior of the gate is of interest for the friezes of courtly figures and *Ramayana* scenes that enliven the side chambers. The hall of the main Temple is built up to a natural cavern, where the most important image of Narasimha is venerated. The walls here are covered with friezes of deities and accessory figures, especially Chenchu huntresses with bows. The squat columns have double blocks covered with sculptures and extended double capitals and lotus brackets. Other 16-columned halls, resembling that already noted outside the complex, stand to the east. A gateway here leads to the trail that climbs the hill, reaching various caverns and other sanctuaries sacred to Narasimha.

G. Yaganti
This little-visited spot, 90km south of Kurnool via Banganapalle, is delightfully located at the head of a rocky valley framed by a crescent of sandstone cliffs. A cascade feeds a large square tank in front of the 16C–17C **Umamaheshvara Temple**. This pond is surrounded by animated friezes of courtly and mythological scenes carved on the blocks just above water level. The surrounding colonnades and central pavilion are later additions. A towered *gopura*, a short distance west, leads to the main Temple, which has an outer hall with porch projections on three sides, each with balcony seating. The slightly irregular layout is explained by the monolithic Nandi which is accommodated here. The interior columns have figures of deities, many standing in arched niches, and decorative patterns carved on the shafts.

A doorway in the northwest corner of the Temple compound leads to a track that crosses the stream and then climbs up to a number of natural caverns that serve as *linga* shrines.

H. Adoni

This strategically located stronghold, 80km southwest of Kurnool via Aspari, was much contested by the emperors of Vijayanagara and the Bahmanis of Gulbarga [24A].

> In 1568 Adoni was captured by the Adil Shahis of Bijapur [23A], who installed a garrison here under a series of commanders. The Adil Shahi domination of Adoni remained unchallenged until Aurangzeb's generals arrived in 1690. In 1756 the Nizam of Hyderabad, who had by then assumed control of the former Mughal territories, presented Adoni to his brother Basalat Jung, who made it his headquarters. In 1778 Adoni was twice besieged by Haidar Ali of Srirangapattana [15C], but it was not until 1786 that it was occupied by his son, Tipu Sultan, who demolished the fortifications and removed the stores and guns to Gooty [33A]. Adoni was ceded to the British in 1800.

The town is located south of a series of rocky hills that forms the nucleus of the citadel. The imposing bulk of the **Jami Mosque**, erected in 1660 by Madu Qadiri, the Adil Shahi Governor, dominates the streets of the town. This structure is entered through a lofty portal framed by buttresses. The prayer hall overlooks a spacious court. Its five-arched façade is surmounted by angled eaves on sculpted brackets and a parapet of trefoil elements. The corner octagonal buttresses, with stone chains hanging from brackets, rise as minarets. The composition is topped with a dome raised high on a petalled drum. The interior bays are roofed with alternating shallow domes and vaults. The doorways to the side chambers in the outer aisle display temple-like colonettes and pediments. The *mihrab* is conceived as a domed chamber.

The road from the town proceeds north for about 500m before passing through the walls of the sprawling **Lower Fort**. Disintegrating structures are seen beside the road. Better-preserved features are found in the **Upper Fort**, including the **Rangin Mosque**, erected by Masud Khan, the Governor of Adoni in 1662–87, partly out of materials from dismantled temples. The piles of stones nearby are all that remain of what must have been an elaborate Vijayanagara-period monument. The **Venkanna Bhavi** is a large well named after a minister of Sidi Masud Khan. The **Tomb of Malik Raman Khan**, a local holy figure, stands a short distance beyond, on the south edge of the Fort, overlooking the town. Its domed chamber was later extended with the addition of extra funerary chambers.

33 · Anantapur

Anantapur makes a useful stop-over on any journey from Hyderabad [26] to Bangalore [14]. Though there is nothing of historical interest within the city itself, the area around Anantapur is rich in monuments.

The fort at **Gooty** [A] and the ornate Vijayanagara-period shrines at **Tadpatri** [B] can be combined in a single-day excursion north of the city, with the possibility of continuing on to Cuddapah [34] via Gandikota [34C].

A trip southeast of Anantapur can take in the isolated, elegant shrine at **Somapalem** [C], with the option of proceeding on to Tirupati [35].

The fort at **Penukonda** [D] and the temples at **Gorantla** [F] and **Lepakshi** [G], the latter famous for its celebrated ceiling paintings, are located on or near NH7, the highway that leads to Bangalore. The village of **Puttaparthi** [E], renowned as the headquarters of Sri Sathya Sai Baba, is situated nearby.

Additional time will have to set aside to reach the isolated village of **Hemavati** [H], with its Nolamba-styled temples.

■ **Transport**. Anantapur is on the main line from Guntakal junction to Bangalore, with rail links to Hyderabad and Hospet [20] in Karnataka. NH7 connects Anantapur with Kurnool [32], 140km north, and Bangalore, 224km south. Lesser roads lead to Cuddapah, 165km east, and Tirupati, 304km southeast. Buses are available to all the destinations covered here.

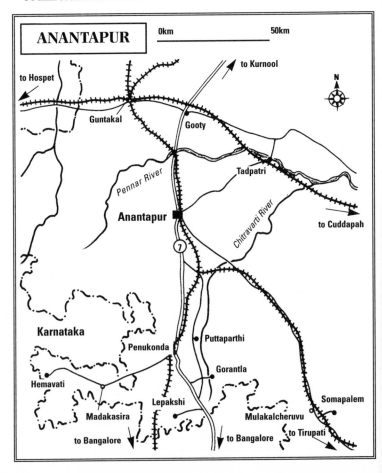

■ **Accommodation**. The *Hotel Sapthagiri* (☎ 2914) and *Swagath Hotel* (☎ 20245) are acceptable places to stay in Anantapur (STD code 08554). The *ashram* at **Puttaparthi** offers accommodation to large numbers of visitors.

■ **Tourist Information**. None.

A. Gooty

The Fort at Gooty, 50km north of Anantapur, occupies a striking granite outcrop that rises more than 300m above the plain.

> First established by the emperors of Vijayanagara [20B–C], Gooty rose to prominence in the 18C, when it became the stronghold of the Maratha commander, Murari Rao. He became well-known to the British, and joined forces with Robert Clive against the Nawab of Arcot [38B] in 1751. Gooty was lost to Haidar Ali in 1773 after a siege of nine months, but eventually came into British hands by way of a settlement with the Nizam after the defeat of Tipu Sultan in 1799.

A tortuous path, shielded from the southwest by a single gate, climbs from the town to the **Fort**. This is contained by walls that run around the rock, connecting 14 massive round bastions. The highest part of the site, reached after passing through two more gates, is occupied by a gymnasium and a powder magazine. A small pavilion of polished limestone known as **Murari Rao's Seat** is perched on the edge of a cliff nearby, with fine views across the surrounding landscape. The ruined ancillary buildings include prisons where British soldiers were held. There are also a number of wells in the rocks.

The **English Cemetery**, at the base of the Fort, has several fine tombs.

B. Tadpatri

This town, on the south bank of the Pennar River, 53km northeast of Anantapur, rose to prominence in the 15C–16C, when it became a provincial outpost of the Vijayanagara empire. The religious monuments erected here at this time are the most ornate of the period. They are built entirely of intricately worked grey-green granite.

The **Chintala Venkataramana Temple**, situated in the middle of the town, is contained within a rectangle of high walls, broken on the east by a soaring *gopura* with a steeply pyramidal tower, partly incomplete. Sculptures enliven the granite basement and walls. A ceremonial swing and tall lamp column stand outside (east). Most visitors enter the monument through a modest doorway on the north, which leads to a rectangular court surrounded by colonnades. The principal Vishnu shrine, which stands in the middle, adjoins a closed hall with side porches and a larger open hall, with a central rectangular space defined by raised platforms. The east end is partly blocked by a small Garuda shrine fashioned as a chariot. The goddess shrine, to the northwest, is connected by way of an open porch with an unusual circular sanctuary.

The outer walls of the principal shrine and its adjoining hall are raised on a finely modelled basement. Sculpted figures on the surfaces between the wall pilasters illustrate episodes from the Krishna and *Ramayana* legends. Leaping *yalis* grace the columns of the porches. The doorway lintels within the porches show Sita's ordeal by fire in the presence of the gods (south) and Rama's final enthronement (north). The multi-storeyed tower over the sanctuary, with later plaster figures, is topped by a hemispherical roof.

The outer supports of the open hall are raised on an ornate basement with crouching dwarfs. Maidens holding offerings, carved almost in the round, grace the central columns on the sides, replaced by *yalis* on the front (east). The Garuda shrine here is treated as a miniature chariot, complete with stone wheels. The interior space is surrounded by piers with leaping *yalis* ridden by warriors. Traces of ceiling paintings are seen over the side bays. The goddess shrine repeats many of these features, but is even more ornate. The eaves overhanging the peripheral columns are animated with carved lizards and playful monkeys. The ceiling is conceived as a dome-like lotus filled with tiers of petals and a central pendant bud. The adjacent circular shrine has a multi-faceted basement and walls.

The **Bugga Ramalingeshvara Temple** is located 1km north of the town, overlooking the sandy bed of the Pennar River. The incomplete *gopuras* on the north and south are the most elaborate in Southern India. The architectural elements are obscured by carved divinities, donors, guardians, sages and dwarfs. The double basement is interrupted by figural niches with lobed and arched profiles; tower-like pediments rise above. Other mouldings are embellished with friezes of jewels and elegant scrollwork. The door jambs in the passageway are carved with maidens clutching luxuriant creepers. Similar maidens bearing lotuses, and riders on horses, decorate the columns between. Fully modelled squatting dwarfs are seen beneath.

The west-facing shrine within the compound houses a *linga* set in a pedestal filled with water, perpetually fed by a small spring. The adjoining hall is entered through side porches with *yali* columns. The outer walls present an elegantly proportioned moulded basement and pilastered niches. The pyramidal tower over the sanctuary has the usual hemispherical roof. The shrine is aligned with a modest gateway leading down to the river. Immediately south are two smaller sanctuaries, dedicated to Parvati and Rama. They open off a common hall with piers showing cut-out colonettes in double sets, one above the other, as well as rearing *yalis* and attendant females. The walls of the two sanctuaries have complicated basement series interrupted by miniature niches. The doorways are surrounded by bands of creeper motifs.

C. Somapalem

This remote village is reached by taking a diversion of about 6km from Mulakacheruvu, a small settlement 132km southeast of Anantapur on the route to Tirupati. The **Chennakeshava Temple** at Somapalem was probably built by a local governor during the Vijayanagara period, towards the middle of the 16C. Just in front (east) of the Temple stands an 18m high lamp column raised on a double basement enlivened with friezes of dwarfs, mock battles and royal animals. The base of the column shows figures in niches, including a courtly donor, while the tapering shaft is covered with bold undulating stalks and scrollwork. A projecting hall with a central dais, right of the ruined gateway that leads into the Temple, has columns sculpted with richly dressed donor figures and attendant maidens. A lobed wall niche is provided with a stone bolster.

The main Temple, within the compound, is approached through an open hall with colonettes on the outer piers. They are overhung by curving eaves, with a brick parapet above showing deep niches devoid of plaster sculptures. A small Garuda shrine, treated as a chariot with small wheels on the side, protrudes into the hall. *Yalis* grace the columns lining the central aisle. Traces of faded paintings, illustrating *Ramayana* episodes, can be made out on the ceiling. An open hall in the southwest corner of the compound contains a small pavilion exquisitely worked in grey-green granite. Its columns show maidens holding lotuses on slender pilasters. The subshrine beyond is entered through a doorway; on the lintel is a frieze of Rama enthroned.

D. Penukonda

This city, 74km south of Anantapur, was a strategic citadel for the Vijayanagara emperors in the 14C–16C.

For about two decades after 1565, when the Vijayanagara capital was sacked and burned, Penukonda served as the chief headquarters of the Aravidu rulers, the successors to the Vijayanagara throne. Repeated raids by the forces of Bijapur [23A] and Golconda [26E] persuaded these rulers to shift their headquarters to Chandragiri [35C]. The Qutb Shahis captured Penukonda in 1610, retaining it as an important outpost, until it was taken by the Mughals and then the Marathas.

The site is dominated by a rocky hill, with walls climbing up its steep sides to create an approximately triangular **Fort**. Vestiges of past occupation lining the path to the summit include gateways, watchtowers, collapsing halls and several shrines. The walls beneath the hill contain much of the **City** in a quadrangle. The major gateways, with bent entrances, are located in the middle of the north and east sides. A large tank provides protection on the south. Religious and royal monuments face on to the north–south road that runs through the middle of the city.

The **Parshvanatha Temple** enshrines a remarkable sculpture from the 12C–13C Hoysala era. This depicts a naked Jain saviour standing in front of an undulating serpent. The nearby **Sher Shah Mosque** belongs to the period of the Qutb Shahi occupation, as is obvious from the plaster decoration on the arcaded façade and the bulbous dome rising on a petalled drum. The vaulted bays of the prayer chamber are defined by lobed arches. The *mihrab* is unusually ornate.

About 250m further south are the twin **Rama** and **Shiva Temples**, which stand side by side. The pilastered walls of their long low façades are covered with carvings depicting *Ramayana* and Krishna legends on the Rama Temple, and scenes from Shaiva mythology on its neighbour. The sanctuaries in both Temples have pyramidal brick towers capped with hemispherical roofs. That in the Shiva Temple is enclosed within a dark passageway with carved icons in wall niches. The hall that precedes this shrine has piers with colonettes. A later hall adjoins the Rama Temple, in front of which are a lamp column and gateway.

The adjacent **Gagan Mahal** is a courtly monument assigned to the period when Penukonda served as an imperial capital. It resembles pavilions in the royal enclosures at Vijayanagara. An arcaded verandah leads to a vaulted hall with chambers at the rear. A domed pavilion above is roofed with an octagonal pyramidal tower capped by a ribbed finial. An adjoining staircase block is capped with an analogous but smaller tower. (These features anticipate the larger and more symmetrical schemes at Chandragiri.) Less than 50m east is a detached **Square Pavilion**, whose unadorned sloping walls are overhung by curving eaves, with a pierced parapet and a capping octagonal pyramidal tower above. Richly worked plasterwork is preserved inside. A **Well** nearby has an ornate entrance fashioned in the semblance of a lion. The *Gopura* in the vicinity is an 18C construction, unattached to any temple.

Penukonda extends north beyond the City walls. The *Dargah* **of Babayya**, about 500m north, was much patronised by Haidar Ali and Tipu Sultan. It remains a popular place of worship, with a great fair in December.

E. Puttaparthi

This village is situated on the west bank of the Chitravati River, about 60km south of Anantapur via Dharmavaram. In spite of its somewhat remote location, Puttaparthi is now a centre of great attention, since it is the abode of Sri Sathya Sai Baba, one of Southern India's most celebrated saintly figures. Sai Baba is credited with spiritual wisdom, and is notorious for his occult powers. His residence is visited by large numbers of disciples from all over the country and abroad. In recent years, devotees of Sai Baba have constructed the **Prasanthi Nilaya**, an *ashram* for the saint and his followers, where many of them live for prolonged periods. Prasanthi Nilaya is a large colony furnished with all possible facilities, including guest houses and dormitories, kitchens and dining halls. There are, in addition, a Sanskrit school, printing press, post office and private hospital.

F. Gorantla

This small town on the east bank of the Chitravati River, 30km southeast of Penukonda, is worth visiting for the **Madhavaraya Temple**, a fine example of the early Vijayanagara style. The monument was erected in 1354 by a local chief, and in spite of its relatively plain exterior preserves interesting reliefs. The compound in which the Temple stands is entered through a massive *gopura*, never completed and now somewhat neglected. The open porch of the Temple has balcony seating on three sides, the peripheral columns partly transformed into *yalis* standing on elephants. The fierce faces of the beasts exhibit protruding eyes and open jaws. The internal columns have their shafts divided into blocks sculpted with Krishna legends and *Ramayana* episodes, scenes from the story of Narasimha, and acrobats, fighters and musicians. The shafts terminate in double capitals and elegant lotus brackets with pendant buds. The ceiling over the central bay of the porch has a large flower surrounded by petals. The doorway leading into the hall is surmounted by a frieze of Rama enthroned.

G. Lepakshi

The small town of Lepakshi lies 12km west of NH7, just near the point where the highway meets the Karnataka frontier, 35km south of Penukonda. (Lepakshi is about 140km from Bangalore, from where it may also be approached as an excursion.) The major attraction here is the **Virabhadra Temple**, erected under the patronage of two brothers, Viranna and Virupanna, who were governors of Penukonda in the middle of the 16C. The monument illustrates the considerable artistic achievements of Vijayanagara architecture, sculpture and painting.

The first feature to be seen on arriving at Lepakshi is the **Nandi Monolith**, 1km east of the town. This imposing sculpture shows Shiva's bull mount seated comfortably to one side. The animal is ceremonially decked with garlands and bells.

Monolithic Naga, *Virabhadra Temple, Lepakshi*

The Virabhadra Temple itself, occupying a rising granite outcrop, stands in the middle of two concentric irregular enclosures. The outer compound is entered through gateways on three sides, that on the north being most often used by visitors. This is somewhat awkwardly positioned in relationship to the outer east gate. It leads directly to an open hall with a large central space. The peripheral columns here are elevated on an ornate basement, with blocks carved as horses and warriors. The columns with slender colonettes are overhung by deeply curving eaves. The central space is defined by massive piers fashioned with trios of figures at the corners: Natesha between Brahma and a drummer (northeast), a dancing maiden between a male drummer and cymbalist (southeast), Parvati between female attendants (southwest), and a drummer between three-legged Bhringi and Bhikshatanamurti (northwest). The intermediate piers show musicians and ascetics.

The ceiling of the hall is almost entirely covered with paintings, which are the most important specimens of Vijayanagara pictorial art. The frescos have been cleaned recently, to reveal the fresh black linework and vibrant ochre, brown and green colours. The compositions are of outstanding interest for the details of costume and facial types. They are arranged in long strips that correspond with the bays that surround the central hall, and illustrate legends from the Puranas and the *Mahabharata* and *Ramayana* epics. The donor brothers of the monument are portrayed worshipping Shiva and Parvati in the company of male and female courtiers (east side). The boar hunt of Shiva is an animated forest scene that forms the climax of the story of Arjuna's encounter with Shiva as the hunter (west corridor).

Steps on the south side of the open hall ascend to an inner enclosed hall. Its outer walls (as visible from the outer hall) are covered with friezes of elephants, as well as the legends of Siriyala and of Arjuna fighting Shiva disguised as the hunter. The central space of the inner hall is defined by piers fashioned as *yalis*. The animals are doubled at the corners, angling outwards, with figures carved on the sides. They include Shiva dancing and spearing the demon, as well an icon of Durga (northwest corner), now worshipped independently. The ceiling above has a large painted composition of standing Virabhadra in the company of one of the sponsors of the monument, Virupanna, and his wife. The principal cult deity of the Temple, a fierce human-sized image of Virabhadra decked with skulls and carrying weapons, is accommodated in the axial north-facing shrine. The side shrines are dedicated to Keshava, Kali, Uma and the *linga*, the last being partly set into a natural cavern. These shrines are modest structures capped with brick towers, visible only from the outside.

Additional features of interest are seen in the outer compound of the Temple. Inscriptions are carved on the blocks of the inner enclosure wall, especially near the northeast corner, where they even extend onto the bedrock. A large, unfinished hall occupies the southwest corner of the inner compound. Its peripheral columns are sculpted with sages, and those in the middle with divinities. No roof slabs seem to have been added. A natural boulder to the east is partly fashioned as a coiled *naga* with a multi-hooded head, rearing up to shelter a polished granite *linga*.

H. Hemavati

This remote village, located 80km southwest of Penukonda via Madakasira, served as the capital of the 9C–10C Nolambas. The temples erected here testify to the distinctive architectural idiom developed by these rulers. Though some sculptures from Hemavati have been removed to the Government Museum in Madras [36D], others survive *in situ*.

The **Doddeshvara Temple** is a modest unadorned structure with regularly spaced pilasters. The perforated stone windows are adorned with standing divinities, including a gracefully posed figure of Ganga (east), as well as foliate designs. The internal columns are decorated with looped garlands. The adjacent **Siddheshvara Temple** has been much reconstructed. Original columns with sculpted panels are seen in the hall in front of the sanctuary, which houses an impressive seated Bhairava image. A finely carved doorway is seen in the **Virupaksha Temple**.

34 · Cuddapah

This city, in the Pennar River Valley, makes a serviceable stop-over on any journey from Vijayawada [29], Kurnool [32] or Anantapur [33] to Tirupati [35], in the southeast corner of Andhra Pradesh. There are only a few historical features in **Cuddapah** [A], for which a few hours will be sufficient.

Worthwhile excursions may be made from Cuddapah to the temples at **Pushpagiri** [B] and the fort at **Gandikota** [C], both of which may be visited in a single day trip west of the town, with the possibility of continuing on to Tadpatri [33B] and Anantapur.

A full-day trip north of Cuddapah can take in the mountain stronghold at

Udayagiri [D] and the rock-cut shrines at **Bhairavakonda** [E]. Visitors travelling directly to Tirupati may pass by the temple at **Vontimitta** [F].

■ **Transport**. Cuddapah is situated on the main line from Guntakal junction to Madras [36], with connections to Hyderabad [26] and Hospet [20], the latter in Karnataka. By road Cuddapah is 215km southeast of Kurnool, 165km east of Anantapur and 140km northwest of Tirupati. Buses reach all the destinations, but an excursion to Udayagiri and Bhairavakonda is only possible with a car.

■ **Accommodation**. The *Pennar Hotel* is the best available in Cuddapah.

■ **Tourist Information**. None.

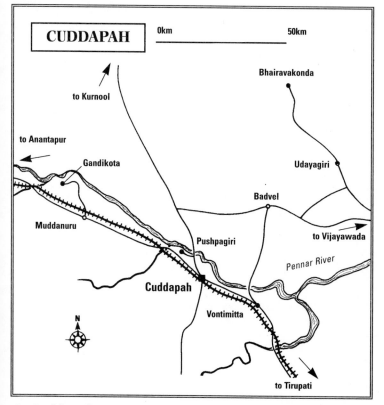

A. Cuddapah

This city derives its importance from its location in the Pennar Valley, a major route leading from interior Andhra Pradesh through the Eastern Ghats to the Bay of Bengal. The Cuddapah region, though somewhat arid, is famous for its crops of turmeric, onions and melons. Quarrying has become a significant industry, and Cuddapah stone is widely exported.

Cuddapah was annexed by the Mughals in 1687. The line of commanders that they installed here assumed an almost independent status under the title of Nawab. The Cuddapah Nawabs were ousted by Haidar Ali in 1776, and the city was ceded to the British after the defeat of Tipu Sultan in 1799.

Isolated vestiges of the Nawabs are scattered throughout Cuddapah. Two **Watchtowers** in the heart of the city are all that survive of the dismantled palace. These slender structures have arched openings and miniature domes sitting on petalled bases. The **Azam Mosque**, dating from the early 18C, is another project of the Cuddapah Nawabs. Its six-bayed prayer chamber is entered through triple arcades overhung by sloping eaves on ornate brackets. The circular buttresses have miniature arcaded balconies and slender finials with miniature domes. About 200m south is the ***Dargah* of Syed Ahmed Sahib**, a cubic building with triple arched recesses on each side surmounted by tiers of arched recesses. The corner buttresses resemble those on the mosque just noticed. The dome is low and flattish.

The **English Cemetery**, on the outskirts of the city, is a reminder of Cuddapah's former foreign population. The tomb of Webb Thackeray, a civil servant in the Madras Presidency and uncle of William Makepeace Thackeray, is dated 1807. Nearby **Christ Church**, erected in 1881, has an arcaded portico with slender columns.

B. Pushpagiri

This somewhat remote village is reached along a dirt track that runs 6km west from the Prodattur road near Chennur, 17km north of Cuddapah. Two groups of temples at Pushpagiri date back to the 12C–13C, when the region was under the sway of a line of Chola rulers remotely connected with those in the Tamil zone. The monuments were substantially renovated under the Vijayanagara kings in the 15C–16C. The village is today the seat of a well-known Vaishnava religious institution.

The main group of temples at Pushpagiri is situated north of the village, near the west bank of the Pennar River. The principal monument here is the **Vaidyanatheshvara Temple**, a typical late Chola building with a small shrine attached to a columned hall. The Temple stands in the middle of an enclosure, entered through a small side gate. Carved panels are set up in the surrounding colonnades. The **Trikuteshvara Temple**, immediately north, has three shrines with plain pilastered walls, each capped with a square-domical roof, opening off a central hall.

The nearby **Bhimalingeshvara Temple** consists of a shrine and hall raised on a double basement, with carvings on the lowest band. The walls have sculpted panels between the niches and pilasters. The pyramidal tower rises in ascending sequences of projections and miniature roof forms, and is crowned by a prominent square-domical roof. The hall is somewhat unfinished on its east front, where double steps flanked by balustrades ascend to a small platform that supports a Nandi sculpture.

The **Chennakeshava Temple**, the most artistic at Pushpagiri, is picturesquely situated beneath a bare hill rising from the east bank of the Pennar River, directly opposite the village. The Temple faces west towards the river, which has to be forded in order to reach the towered entrance to the enclosure. The Chennakeshava Temple consists of three shrines opening off two columned halls. Not all parts of the complex were finished at one time, as is clear from the makeshift walls on the front (west). The basements of the shrines are remarkable for the relief carvings of animals and figures, interspersed with fully modelled pots sprouting foliation, surmounted by circular pilasters. Even the spouts for the outflow of libations are embellished.

The walls of the two west-facing shrines are almost entirely covered with reliefs showing deities, *Ramayana* and Krishna episodes, and the story of Arjuna fighting Shiva as the hunter. There are repeated icons of dancing Shiva in the company of attendant maidens, dancers and musicians. The most important compositions are headed by foliated frames. The pyramidal towers that rise over the shrines have receding storeys, with pilastered projections capped by square or hemispherical roofs. The less-decorated south-facing shrine shows sculptures of Brahma (north) and Dakshinamurti (south) in unadorned niches.

C. Gandikota

This celebrated citadel, 75km northwest of Cuddapah, is reached by turning north at Muddanuru on the Anantapur road, then west just before the bridge across the Pennar River, and following a stony route for about 8km. Gandikota, Gorge Fort, is aptly named, as it is perched about 100m above a rugged gap, no more than 200m wide, through which the river forces its way.

> The history of Gandikota goes back to Vijayanagara times, but the Fort itself mostly dates from the period of the Qutb Shahis, who captured it in 1589. In spite of claims by the Vijayanagara rulers of Chandragiri [35C], the forces of the Qutb Shahis continued to occupy Gandikota, and were still in control when François Tavernier, the famous French traveller, halted there in 1652. Gandikota was captured by Aurangzeb's general in 1687 and by the beginning of the 18C it had come under the control of the Cuddapah Nawabs. Haidar Ali improved and garrisoned the Fort, but it was taken by the British in 1791.

Few strongholds in Andhra Pradesh enjoy such a spectacular natural setting, yet this is not immediately apparent on arrival. The first view of the **Fort** is of a line of massive stone walls with prominent square bastions, topped by a crenellated parapet. The main entrance, on the east, is through a sequence of barbican enclosures that leads to an arched **Gate**. This is surmounted by battlements with six squat finials. A triple-storeyed **Tower** rises above the dilapidated houses of the small settlement inside the Fort. This elegant structure, possibly a remnant of the Qutb Shahi palace, has arched openings below and fretted windows for pigeons above. The imposing prayer chamber of the **Jami Mosque** stands to the north. The triple-arched openings are overhung by sloping eaves, over which rises a parapet with arched openings. The massive circular buttresses at the corners are capped with minarets that are topped by domical finials. A large **Granary** with a vaulted roof stands to the north.

The dilapidated **Ranganayaka Temple**, beyond the Granary, is entered through a collapsing gateway without a tower. The hall inside has finely finished animal piers, but is otherwise in poor condition. An unusual feature is the architect's measure incised on the enclosure walls south of the main shrine. The **Madhavaraya Temple**, west of the settlement, is more impressive. It is recognised by its *gopura*, which has a four-storeyed, steeply pyramidal tower. This incomplete and worn gate has elaborately modelled basement mouldings and crowded wall pilasters. The double chambers flanking the passageway interior have columns with figural carvings. The main shrine inside the compound is preceded by a spacious hall, with elegantly proportioned supports overhung by deeply curving eaves. The interior space is defined by piers fashioned as rearing *yalis* with riders, some in European dress.

D. Udayagiri

The Fort at Udayagiri lies 98km northeast of Cuddapah; the last 47km of the journey from Badvel passes through the forested highlands of the Eastern Ghats. Udayagiri occupies the comparatively level top of two narrow hills that run north–south and rise more than 600m above the plain. The sides of these hills are so precipitous as to be inaccessible, as the rocky bluffs at the top are nearly 300m high in some places. Because of these unsurpassed natural defences, Udayagiri was the preferred citadel for all rulers in this part of Andhra Pradesh.

> The site first enters history as a stronghold of the Reddis of Kondavidu [29M], rivals of the emperors of Vijayanagara [20B–C]. Udayagiri was captured from the Reddis by Krishnadevaraya in 1512. It then came under the command of the Qutb Shahis, who occupied it until the Mughal invasion of 1687. By the time it passed into the hands of the Cuddapah Nawabs in the course of the 18C, it had already fallen into disuse.

At least two hours are required to ascend the **Fort**, the preferred route being from the east. From this path it is possible to view the panorama of ruined bastions, lookout towers and gateways that gird the tops of the hills. In spite of their considerable scope, the ramparts are unremarkable. Of greater interest is the **Mosque**, which forms a conspicuous landmark on the highest part of the south hill. This has an arched opening in front, flanked by two towers. A Persian inscription over the *mihrab* states that it was erected in 1643 by Ghazi Ali, the General of the Qutb Shahi forces. Numerous carved blocks indicate that it was partly built out of re-used temple material. The **Granary** nearby is an earlier structure, possibly a renovated temple hall. A small secondary mosque at the north end of the same hill has an inscription of 1661.

Almost nothing survives of the walls and gateways that once protected the settlement at the base of the eastern flank of the hills. The only historical feature to be seen is the dilapidated 16C **Ranganayaka Temple**, which stands at the end of the main street. Its towerless east gate leads into an outer enclosure which has another, smaller *gopura* on the south, with a virtually intact pyramidal tower. The main shrine within has been despoiled. The **Krishna Temple**, another 16C project, is situated 1km south of the town, overlooking a stepped square tank. Its main shrine is damaged, but several carvings of Balakrishna can be made out on its outer walls. The *gopura* nearby serves as an entrance to an attractively shaded compound. A broken hall here preserves finely finished *yali* columns.

E. Bhairavakonda

Eight **Rock-cut Shrines** at this remote site, about 45km northwest of Udayagiri, are among the earliest Hindu monuments in Andhra Pradesh. They date from the 7C–8C, a period when the Reddi chiefs of Kondavidu controlled the forested ranges of the Eastern Ghats.

The Bhairavakonda Shrines are situated on the bank of the stream at the bottom of a small but wooded ravine, near to a 60m high waterfall. Though excavated at different levels, the Shrines are almost identical. They consist of columned verandahs sheltered by curved eaves, with false windows leading to small sanctuaries with polished black basalt *lingas*. Seated lions are carved on the bases of the outer columns. Icons of Shiva, Vishnu, Brahma and Ganesha are carved on the walls, and guardians with clubs appear on either side of the sanctuary doorways. Some Shrines have Nandis set into roofless courts.

The Shrines face the diminutive **Durga Bhairava Temple**, after which the site is named. This houses an unusual eight-faced goddess.

F. Vontimitta

This town, 28km east of Cuddapah, is notable for the **Kodandarama Temple**, the largest in the region. This 16C monument is contained within a rectangle of walls with three imposing *gopuras*. That on the east, crowned with a steep five-storeyed tower, is approached by a long flight of steps. The unadorned walls of the main Temple contrast with the sculptural treatment of the hall that precedes it. The columns here have cut-out colonettes on which attendant maidens are carved, replaced by Krishna and Vishnu on the central supports on the south. Maidens and deities are combined in triple sets at the corners, a device unknown elsewhere. The central space within the hall is defined by *yali* piers, the animals being doubled at the corners, where they frame attendant figures. The ceiling over the hall is raised on complex brackets with multiple corbels.

35 · Tirupati

This city, in the extreme southeast corner of Andhra Pradesh, is the destination of countless pilgrims, who make the ascent to Tirumala in the nearby hills to worship at the Venkateshvara shrine, reputedly the wealthiest in Southern India. The substantial revenues enjoyed by the local temple management, known as the Tirumala Tirupati Devasthanams (TTD), have funded renovations at many religious sites in the vicinity, as well as supporting civic projects and numerous charitable and educational institutions.

Other than a visit to the temples at **Tirupati** [A] and **Tirumala** [B], which may be accomplished in a single day, a side trip is easily made to the nearby fortress palace at **Chandragiri** [C] and religious monument at **Mangapuram** [D].

Excursions to the small, early shrine at **Gudimallam** [E] and the popular temple at **Sri Kalahasti** [F] follow the Svarnamukhi River on its course east towards the Bay of Bengal. Both places can be reached in a single day.

The lesser-known temples at **Narayanavanam** [G] and **Nagalapuram** [H] can be seen on the way to Madras [36].

■ **Transport**. Tirupati is directly connected by air with Bangalore [14], Hyderabad [26] and Madras. The airport lies 12km south of the city. Trains are convenient, as Tirupati lies on the main line from Bombay [1] or Hyderabad to Madras. A train also runs from Bangalore. Tirupati is most easily approached by road from Madras, 150km southeast, or from Bangalore, 265km west. There are also connections with Anantapur [33], 304km northeast, and Cuddapah [34], 140km north. A continuous bus shuttle links Tirupati with Tirumala, starting before dawn in order to ensure that devotees are in time for the first devotions. Local transport reaches all of the destinations described here, even the faraway village of Gudimallam.

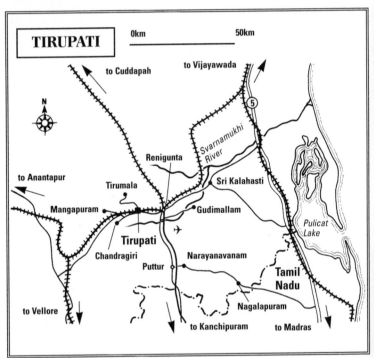

■ **Accommodation**. Hotels at Tirupati (STD code 08574) range from the finely appointed *Bhimas Paradise* (☎ 25747), *Bhimas Deluxe* (☎ 25521) and *Hotel Mayura* (☎ 25925) to simpler and cheaper lodges. The TTD maintains cottages and guest houses on **Tirumala Hill**, which offer a quieter alternative to the busy streets of Tirupati.

■ **Tourist Information**. The APTTDC has its office near Choultry No. 3 (☎ 23208). There is also an information counter at the railway station.

A. Tirupati

Dramatically sited at the foot of the bluff of red sandstone that marks the beginning of the Tirumala Hills, Tirupati is a lively commercial city focused on the Govindaraja Temple. Its crowded streets echo the rectangular plan of the monument, which is laid out on an east-west axis approached along a thoroughfare lined with shops and stalls. This passes through a magnificent free-standing **Gopura**, erected in 1624. Its passageway is flanked by decorated jambs and lintels carried on ornate brackets. Maidens on either side stand on *makaras*, clutching creepers with curling stalks that frame miniature divinities. A carved portait of the sponsor of the *Gopura* appears on the south side of the passageway. This shows Matla Anantaraja, a local chief, in the company of three wives, paying homage to Govindaraja. The seven-storeyed pyramidal tower, which rises almost 50m, is covered with finely finished projections capped with model roof forms, with openings in the middle of each side.

A short distance west are the twin compounds of the **Govindaraja Temple**, one behind the other, linked by modestly scaled gates. The outer *gopura* has *Ramayana* scenes carved on the passageway walls. A tall swing pavilion outside has columns covered with elegant foliation. The twin shrines at the west end of the inner compound are dedicated to Ranganatha, the reclining form of Vishnu, and Krishna with consorts. A minor shrine nearby has an icon of Lakshmi identified with the poetess Andal. The sanctuaries open off a common hall, the piers of which have crouching lions and extended brackets. The hall in the southwest corner has finely finished colonettes on the outer piers, while the central space is lined with *yalis* projecting inwards. An exquisitely finished pavilion in the middle has ornate columns of grey-green granite and a wooden roof.

The Kacheri Nammalvar Temple, immediately north of the Govindaraja Temple, now serves as the **Shri Venkateshvara Museum of Temple Art**. The Museum stands in a colonnaded compound, entered on the south through a small *gopura*. The exhibits of photographs, architectural models, diagrams and metal ritual items are arranged to explain the principles of Vaishnava artistic traditions. They are displayed in the spacious hall that precedes the main shrine.

The **Anjaneya Shrine**, east of the detached *Gopura*, is notable for the trios of *yalis* and horses that mark the outer corners. Similar cut-out animals, with riders on the columns, flank the central passageway. A short distance further east is a large square tank with a central pavilion. Float festivals, in which sacred images are displayed in small boats illuminated by lamps, take place behind the Anjaneya Shrine in January–February.

The **Kapaleshvara Tirtha** lies at the foot of the Tirumala Hills, 2km north of Tirupati. A colonnade runs around three sides of a square pond, fed by a waterfall. A *linga* sheltered by a brass in one of the shrines opening off the colonnade is identified as Kapaleshvara.

B. Tirumala

The wooded crags of the Tirumala Hills, rising 700m above Tirupati, provide a splendid natural setting for the **Venkateshvara Temple**, 22km distant from Tirupati via a winding steep road. Pious devotees make the trip by foot, starting at the modern *gopura* at the base of the hill and then following a picturesque path through the forest. Because of the great crowds, that regularly exceed 10,000 in a single day, worshippers have to wait in line before entering the Temple, in which there is a quite rapid system of entry and exit. Pilgrims come from all over the country and abroad; their offerings in notes and coins, sometimes even gold and silver, are sorted in the *hundi*, or treasury, within the complex. The gross income earned in this manner reached almost 1.3 billion rupees in 1996, and not counting 340kg of gold.

The worship of Venkateshvara, Lord of the Seven Hills, is traced back to the 9C–10C Chola era. It was, however, under the patronage of the 15C–16C emperors of Vijayanagara [20B–C] that the shrine was expanded and Venkateshvara was adopted as the protective deity of the royal family. The promotion of Venkateshvara, known variously as Venkataramana, Tiruvengalanatha and Srinivasa, amounted to no less than an imperial cult, the god appearing together with rulers on their seals and coins. (He is nowadays portrayed with a black face and his eyes covered, to prevent his gaze from scorching the viewer.) Krishnadevaraya visited Tirumala seven times, making lavish gifts and endowments on each occasion. His portrait and those of his queens are still to be seen. Achyutadevaraya, his successor, who began his career at Chandragiri, ordered special ceremonies at Tirumala and Sri Kalahasti before hastening to the Vijayanagara capital, where he was crowned in 1529. The Tirumala shrine continued to attract benefactions from the later Vijayanagara rulers of the Aravidu line in the first half of the 17C.

The Venkateshvara Temple has been renovated extensively to provide facilities for the ever-expanding numbers of devotees, thereby obscuring many original features. The complex is contained within a rectangle of walls, entered in the middle of the east side through a modest 13C *gopura*; the tower is later. The portico immediately inside is a 17C structure, with warriors on *yalis* projecting from the columns. Almost life-size sculptures of the Vijayanagara emperors paying homage to Venkateshvara are displayed here. The brass images of Krishndevaraya and his two queens (right) and a polished granite sculpture of Achyutadevaraya (left) are the finest portraits of the Vijayanagara era. Two halls with columns covered with carvings, those on the front and central aisles displaying rearing *yalis*, stand to the south of the entrance *gopura*. A small pavilion within one hall has ornate supports, with cut-out colonettes overhung by curving eaves. The north part of the compound is occupied by a kitchen where food is prepared for pilgrims; the sweets known as *laddus* are a speciality. A lamp column cloaked in gold sheet stands in front of the *gopura* that gives access to the inner compound. Similar metal covers the threshold and jambs of the doorway itself.

The main shrine, in the middle of the inner compound of the Temple, is a modest Chola-period structure. The tower, with a hemispherical roof covered in gold sheet and topped by a gilded pot finial, has been rebuilt. The preceding hall has sculpted columns overhung by curved eaves cloaked in gold. A portion of the inner space is given over to the *hundi* already noted. The standing crowned image of Vishnu within the sanctuary is ornamented with diamonds and rubies; metal icons of Shridevi and Bhudevi are placed at either side. The remainder of the compound is occupied by colonnades and minor shrines, one 14C example housing an image of Varadaraja, and an office where donations can be made in foreign currency.

A small **Art Museum** is situated in the colonnade outside the Temple, opposite the east entrance. This has a collection of stone, metal and wooden images, paintings and copper-plate inscriptions, many from Vijayanagara times. There are also votive figurines, lamps, musical instruments and arms.

A large **Rectangular Tank**, with stepped sides and a pavilion in the middle of the water, is seen to the north.

C. Chandragiri

This citadel, 11km west of Tirupati, served as an important provincial centre of the Vijayanagara empire.

Chandragiri was the headquarters of Narasimha Saluva, the founder of the second line of Vijayanagara rulers in 1485. It was also the principal capital of the Aravidus in the first half of the 17C. It was from here that Venkatapatideva (1586–1614), the greatest of the Aravidu rulers, presided over the diminishing territories of Vijayanagara. The civil war that broke out at his death hastened the dissolution of the empire.

The royal and religious structures at Chandragiri occupy an impressive site, on the southern flank of a great granite hill. Massive walls with bastions of different shapes, surrounded by a ditch, contain these structures in an irregular quadrangular **Fort**. An east–west road, passing through a succession of gateways, defines three compounds in a row, with the palaces situated in the middle. Further

Raja and Rana Mahals, Chandragiri

massive walls climb up the side of the hill, with lookout towers surveying the approaches from all directions.

The north-facing **Raja Mahal** at Chandragiri, usually associated with Venkatapatideva, is the masterpiece of Vijayanagara palace architecture. It is both larger and more formal in layout than the earlier courtly buildings at Vijayanagara. The Raja Mahal is arranged in three storys of arcades, linked by eaves and walkways. The interior sequence of vaulted chambers is interrupted by a double-height audience chamber in the middle. The building is capped with a domed pleasure pavilion, roofed by a steeply pyramidal tower that forms the climax of the whole composition. Reduced versions of this tower are placed at the four corners. The building is flanked at either end by staircase blocks roofed with similar towers. The fresh plasterwork gives little idea of the original decoration. A tank overshadowed by trees stands to the north.

The nearby **Rana Mahal** is smaller and different in plan. A passageway passes through the lower storey, indicating that the building must have served as a gateway. The upper level has a domed chamber and an arcaded verandah. The end staircase towers are roofed by octagonal pyramids with domes. The tower in the middle of the roof is of the same type as the Raja Mahal, but is slightly higher. The east façade preserves portions of the original exuberant plasterwork, with foliate motifs embellishing arched openings and medallions with geometric designs above. The Rana Mahal faces east onto a court once surrounded by colonnades, now lost. The excavated remains of a royal residence are seen to the north.

Several abandoned, collapsing **Temples** stand in the vicinity of the palaces. These modest 15C–16C structures have small stone sanctuaries capped by pyramidal brick towers with hemispherical roofs. The outer walls have regularly spaced pilasters and small niches, but there are no sculptures.

The **Kodandarama Temple**, at one end of the village of Chandragiri, 1km east of the Fort, is still under worship. Its sanctuary is approached through an outer open hall and an inner closed hall, the latter with triple niches on each side. The finely detailed walls of the sanctuary are visible in the passageway, which was added around the sanctuary later.

D. Mangapuram

The **Kalyana Venkateshvara Temple** at this site, 9km west of Tirupati, has recently been reinvested for worship by the TTD. The monument is of historical interest, having been founded in 1540 by a Governor of Chandragiri. The Temple is entered on the east through an imposing *gopura* with a renovated five-storeyed tower. The shrine that stands in the middle of a rectangular compound is preceded by an open hall with *yali* columns; the animals are tripled at the corners, where riders are also seen. The entrance steps on the front skirt a small Garuda shrine. The walls of the enclosed hall and sanctuary present rows of shallow pilasters, many standing in pots. The pyramidal tower has two storeys capped with a hemispherical roof.

E. Gudimallam

This somewhat remote site on the south bank of the Svarnamukhi River, 30km east of Tirupati, is reached by turning off the Puttur road, about 5km south of Renigunta. The route, which is clearly marked, passes through fields and delightful villages. Gudimallam is famous for the remarkable *linga* venerated within the sanctuary of the **Parashurameshvara Temple**. This 1.5m high cult object, which dates back to the 1C BC, has a well-preserved figure of Shiva carved on to its shaft. The god is shown with matted hair and holding a trident; the lower part of his body is clearly visible beneath the folds of his costume. Excavations indicate that the *linga* once stood freely, surrounded by a low stone railing. In the 9C century it was contained with an apsidal-ended sanctuary preceded by an antechamber, both additions of the Pallava period. The shrine was further extended under the Cholas in the 12C, but the apsidal-ended tower was only added in the 16C. The building was again remodelled a few years ago.

F. Sri Kalahasti

Like Tirupati and Tirumala, Sri Kalahasti is also a celebrated pilgrimage shrine, but the deity worshipped here is Shiva rather than Vishnu. The town is attractively situated on the south bank of the Svarnamukhi River, 33km east of Tirupati, at a point at the foot of the Kailasha Hills where the valley opens up into the plain. While the bathing *ghats* and shrines on the hill attract a steady flow of devotees, religious life is mainly focused on the Kalahastishvara Temple. This complex enshrines the Vayu (air) *linga*, one of the five elemental emblems of Shiva in Southern India. Sri Kalahasti is also associated with Kannappa, the hunter who plucked out his eye in a frenzy of adoration, to offer it to the *linga*. A small shrine consecrated to this saintly devotee of Shiva is located at the summit of the hill above the town.

The villages around Kalahasti are known for the production of *kalamkaris*, brightly coloured cotton fabrics, showing traditional mythological subjects, produced by a mixture of printed and dyeing techniques.

Sri Kalahasti is dominated by an impressive **Gopura** that stands freely at the end of the main street of the town. This towered gateway was erected by Krishnadevaraya in 1516, and is the finest example from his era. The granite walls are raised on a double basement divided into deeply modelled mouldings. The walls have niches alternating with single pilasters standing in pots. The basements and walls terminate in sculpted blocks on either side of the passageway entrances. Vijayanagara dynastic emblems, showing the boar and sword together with the sun and moon, appear here. Maidens on *makaras* clutching creepers are carved on the jambs within the passagway. The seven storeys of the steeply pyramidal tower rise 36.5m above ground level. The pilastered projections capped with miniature roof forms have been recently renovated. The tower has a vaulted roof, with a line of nine pot finials on the ridge and horseshoe-shaped arches at the ends.

A sequence of two gateways, one with a portico, leads to the outer enclosure of the **Kalahastishvara Temple**. This wraps around the main Temple on three sides. On the east is the rocky side of the hill; on the west are found the popular bathing *ghats*, reached through another gopura. Columned halls, pavilions, lamp columns and altars crowd the enclosure. The large hall in the southwest corner is raised on a high basement with finely carved friezes; the outer supports have animal carvings.

The main Temple is contained within a rectangle of high walls, with a single towered entrance on the south. The four shrines inside all date from the Vijayanagara period. The most important is that opening to the west, which houses a curiously elongated *linga* protected by a brass cobra hood. A brass-covered lamp column stands in front. Other shrines, dedicated to Jnanaprasumbha, Dakshinamurti and Ganesha (south), open off a 19C colonnade laid out as a vast quadrangle. The massive piers have leaping horses and riders lining the approach from the south, while animal brackets, corbelling inwards, cover the side aisles. Among the bronzes on display here are processional icons of Shiva and a complete set of the 63 Nayanmars (north corridor). A stone representation of Kannappa as a hunter is placed in the west corridor.

A short distance south of the Kalahastishvara Temple is the dilapidated, overgrown **Manikantesvhara Temple**. This earlier monument dates from the 12C Chola era, and is typically Tamil in style. The Temple stands in a square compound built up to the base of the hill. Its east-facing sanctuary and hall have finely detailed basement mouldings, pilastered walls and niches, the last filled with icons of Shiva. A towered gateway is capped with an enlarged vaulted roof, much renovated in later times.

G. Narayanavanam

This small town, 35km south of Tirupati, just 2km east of Puttur, is famous for its weaving, with looms set up in the main street. The **Kalyana Venkateshvara Temple** was established in 1541, but was extended in later times. The Temple is approached from the east through a large *gopura*, of interest for the relief compositions in the passageway. The ceiling panels show a kneeling soldier with a gun shooting a prancing deer, between a pair of geese and a sexual scene. The central lotus is surrounded by Dikpalas. The doorway lintels have fish and *makaras*, a camel with rider, and Kama and Rati on parrots. The second *gopura*, defining the inner compound, has an entrance portico with cut-out colonettes. The main Temple, approached through a hall with side porches, is roofed with a pyramidal brick tower capped by a hemisphere.

H. Nagalapuram

An important Vijayanagara monument of ambitious proportions stands in this small town, 24km east of Narayanavanam. The west-facing **Veda Narayana Temple** dates back to Chola times, but in the first half of the 16C it became the nucleus of a vast complex, with three concentric enclosures linked by axial gateways.

The complex is entered from the west through a grandiose *gopura*, dating from the reign of Krishnadevaraya. Intended as one of the largest projects of the era, comparable to that at Sri Kalahasti, the gateway was never finished beyond the imposing basement and walls. A path leads to a second, smaller *gopura*, also assigned to Krishnadevaraya, which is raised on a double basement and pilastered walls devoid of niches. The gateway has been much repaired, as can be seen by the crisp whitewashed details of the five-storeyed tower. A lamp column stands on an ornate plinth within. Among the subsidiary structures standing in the second enclosure is an east-facing goddess shrine with finely finished walls. A portico with colonettes and *yalis* on the outer supports gives access to the main Temple. A columned hall lined with animal columns leads to the original shrine. This has an ornate basement embellished with Krishna scenes and other figures. Carved icons of Shiva and Brahma are fitted into the wall niches.

Tamil Nadu

Though Tamil Nadu is a land of temple towns, **Madras** [36], the first port of call for most visitors, is a 17C–18C British creation, as is obvious from the Neo-Classical style of its fort and churches.

Day trips from Madras lead to sites associated with the 7C–8C Pallava kings, particularly the rock-cut sanctuaries at **Mamallapuram** [37A] and the structural temples at **Kanchipuram** [37F].

Imposing religious complexes from the 16C–17C are seen at **Vellore** [38], directly west of Madras, and at **Tiruvannamalai** [38E] and **Chidambaram** [39E], the last most easily approached from **Pondicherry** [39], the headquarters of the former French holdings in Southern India. Pondicherry also serves as a base from which to visit **Gingee** [39F], the state's most spectacular fortress.

The richly irrigated delta of the Kaveri River marks the heartland of Tamil Nadu. **Thanjavur** [40] and **Tiruchirapalli** [41], the largest cities in this zone, have magnificent Hindu monuments dating back to the 10C–11C Chola era. Additional Chola monuments are seen at nearby **Darasuram** [40F], **Kumbakonam** [40G] and **Gangaikondacholapuram** [40J]. The church at **Velanganni** [40N] and Muslim shrine at **Nagore** [40O] are situated in the vicinity.

The hill resorts at **Yercaud** [42A] and **Udhagamandalam** [43C] are reached from **Salem** [42] and **Coimbatore** [43], two industrial centres in interior Tamil Nadu.

Madurai [44] is the largest city in the southern part of the state, celebrated for its temple and palace, linked with the 17C Nayaka kings. Pilgrims journey from Madurai to the celebrated sanctuary on **Rameswaram Island** [44J]. **Kanyakumari** [45M], at the southern tip of Tamil Nadu, lies not too far distant from **Tirunelveli** [45].

36 · Madras

Now renamed **Chennai**, the capital of Tamil Nadu, with a population of nearly 5,500,000, Madras is built on the shore of the Bay of Bengal, but lacks any natural harbour. Even so, from its foundation in 1639 until the middle of the 19C, when it was eclipsed by Bombay [1], Madras was the the busiest and wealthiest seaport in Southern India. Its history is closely identified with European commerce, as testified to by its remaining Portuguese and British vestiges. Madras also incorporates several earlier settlements, complete with temples and markets, which preserve their traditional Tamil character.

Two full days may be occupied with the major sights of **Fort St George** [A], **George Town** [B], **Ponnamallee High Road** [C], **Anna Salai** [E], **Chepauk and Triplicane** [F], and **Mylapore and San Thomé** [G].

Additional time will be required to visit the art collections of the Government Museum in the **Pantheon Complex** [D], as well as the outlying districts of **Adyar** [H], **Guindy and the two Mounts of St Thomas** [I].

Other than monuments and museums, Madras benefits from a lively cultural scene, with regular performances of music and dance, reaching a climax during the December festival, for which the city is famous.

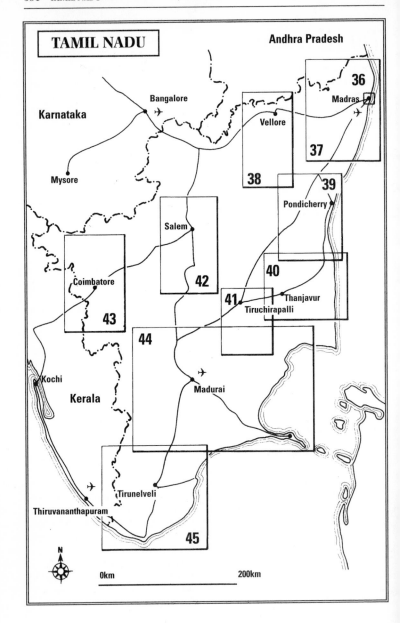

Madras makes a convenient base from which to visit historic localities within an approximate 100km arc of the city. They are described in the following itinerary [37]. It also makes a logical starting point from which to tour Tamil Nadu, and may be combined with itineraries for Vellore [38], Pondicherry [39] and points further south. The temples in and around Tirupati [35] in Andhra Pradesh are more easily approached from Madras than from Hyderabad.

■ **Transport**. Madras is directly linked by air with cities in Europe, Sri Lanka and Southeast Asia, with services arriving and departing from Aringar Anna International Airport. Internal air services from Kamaraj Domestic Airport on the same site connect Madras with Delhi and Calcutta, also Bombay, Pune [3], Panaji [11], Bangalore [14], Hyderabad [26], Visakhapatnam [31], Thiruvananthapuram [46] and Port Blair [49]. Air connections within the state are available to Tiruchirapalli [41], Coimbatore [43] and Madurai [44].

Rail services connect Madras (STD code 044) with all the major cities in Tamil Nadu, as well with major centres in Karnataka and Andhra Pradesh. The two main stations are Madras Central (☎ 563535) and Egmore (☎ 566565). There is also a comprehensive suburban network, and a Metro system is currently being constructed.

Long-distance bus services run from the Esplanade Bus Stand (☎ 561835) and Parry's Esplanade (☎ 566351). City buses are available to all local destinations (☎ 566063). Yellow-topped taxis and auto- and cycle-rickshaws operate throughout the city.

The better car hire companies include Hertz (☎ 8265491), Ashok (☎ 8278884) and Ganesh (☎ 8260666).

■ **Consulates**. The **British** High Commission is at 24 Anderson Road, Nungambakkam (☎ 473136); the **USA** Consulate is at 220 Anna Salai (☎ 473040).

■ **Banks**. The *State Bank of India, Central Bank of India, Bank of America, Citibank* and *Grindlays Bank* all have branches along Anna Salai, and most top hotels have banks on their premises. *American Express* is at Spencer Plaza, Anna Salai, and *Thomas Cook* is at Nungambakkam High Road and Rajaji Salai.

■ **Post Offices**. The main Post Office is at Rajaji Salai in George Town, with other large offices in Anna Salai, Nungambakkam High Road and Pondy Bazar.

■ **Hospitals and Chemists**. The *General Hospital* (☎ 563131), *Apollo Hospital* (☎ 476566) and *Kilpauk* (☎ 8255331) are among the many hospitals, and have chemists on or near the premises. The emergency ambulance telephone number is ☎ 102.

■ **Accommodation**. There is an abundance of hotels of all standards, many situated on or near to Anna Salai, the thoroughfare that marks the commercial heart of Madras. The finest are the *Hotel Taj Coromandel* (☎ 8272827), *Welcomegroup Chola Sheraton* (☎ 8281010), *Hotel Connemara* (☎ 8523361) and *Hotel Ambassador Pallava* (☎ 8554476). The *Residency Hotel* (☎ 8253434), *Hotel Madras International* (☎ 8524111), *Hotel Savera* (☎ 8274700) and *New Woodlands* (☎ 8273111) are also of a high standard. The *Trident* (☎ 2344747) offers luxurious accommodation near the airport.

■ **Tourist Information**. The Tamil Nadu Tourism Development Corporation (TTDC) has its headquarters at 143 Anna Salai (☎ 560820), with the Government of India Tourist Office next door (☎ 8524295). Another TTDC office is at 25 Dr Radhakrishnan Road, **Mylapore** (☎ 840213). Information counters are maintained at Madras Central railway station and at the international and domestic airport terminals. The booking office for the TTDC Hotel Tamil Nadu chain is in the Corporation Building opposite the Central Station.

■ **Travel agents and tour companies**. Among the many companies offering services for hotel bookings and travel arrangements are *Mercury*, 191 Anna Salai (☎ 8522993), *Sita*, 26 C-in-C Road (☎ 478861), *Thomas Cook*, 112 Nugambakkam High Road (☎ 473092), and *Travel Corp*, 734 Anna Salai (☎ 868813).

A. Fort St George

The tour of Madras described here begins at Fort St George, the site of the first settlement of the East India Company in Southern India. This was located on a sandy spit near the estuary of Cooum Creek, on territory ceded to Francis Day in 1639 by Venkatadri Nayaka of Chengalpattu [37C], the representative of the Vijayanagara ruler at Chandragiri [35C].

The first buildings, surrounded by earthen ramparts erected at what was then known as Madraspatnam, were consecrated on St George's Day, 23 April 1640. Known thereafter as Fort St George, they formed the nucleus of a rapidly growing settlement that soon established itself as the principal headquarters of British commerce on the Coromandel Coast. The lucrative trade in textiles and spices soon attracted the attention of the French, and the Fort was temporarily lost to Labourdonnais in 1746 and Lally in 1758; in 1769 it was threatened by Haidar Ali of Srirangapattana [15C]. The original military, administrative and religious functions of the Fort have been retained through the centuries, and the buildings that crowd the 17ha of the Fort are still mostly in use.

Nothing remains of the original walls of Fort St George; the sloping **Ramparts** with battlements for gun emplacements are 18C works constructed after the French attacks. Designed by Bartholomew Robbins, they form an irregular pentagon, with the longest wall running parallel to the Bay of Bengal on the east, now separated from the sands by Kamarajar Road. Two triangular bastions protrude into the moat at the north and south ends of the seaward side; three more bastions are positioned on the landward side. This scheme is further reinforced by a ring of earthen walls provided with numerous angles. The result is the most complete example of British military architecture to be preserved in Southern India. There are five main **Gates**, each with a rounded masonry entry, once approached across drawbridges, now replaced with roads. Most visitors arrive through the Sea Gate on the east.

The first building to be seen on entering the Fort is the **Legislative Assembly** of the state of Tamil Nadu, its long Neo-Classical façade dominating the seaward aspect of the Fort. This building incorporates portions of the original 1694 Government House. The 20 polished black granite Doric columns that grace its front and side porticos come from a dismantled colonnade, constructed in 1732, that runs from the Sea Gate to the Parade Ground within the Fort, demolished in 1910.

Immediately north of the Legislative Assembly stands the **Fort Museum** (closed Fridays), originally the Public Exchange Hall. The Hall of Arms, occupying the original warehouse on the ground floor, contains artillery, regimental flags, weapons and armour associated with various British campaigns. One room displays the silver dishes and ewers presented in 1687 to St Mary's Church by Elihu Yale who, after serving as Governor of Madras in 1684, went on to bequeath his name to Yale University. Finely worked 17C silver dishes and a cup removed from the Church at Pulicat [37I] are also on display, as is an excellent large-scale model of the Fort. A somewhat severe statue of Lord Cornwallis, sculpted in 1800 by Thomas Banks, stands at the foot of the stairs. It shows the Governor General accepting Tipu Sultan's two young sons as hostages.

The first floor, housing the Portrait Gallery, is where merchants daily met for trade and news. The paintings here include portraits of British worthies and Indian nobility of the Madras region, such as the Wallajah Nawabs of Arcot [38B]. The Gallery is overlooked by a wooden balcony at one end. The adjacent room retains items of correspondence of Clive, Wellesley, Cornwallis and Bentinck. The Prints Section, on the second floor, displays early views of Madras. The elegant Ionic **Rotunda**, standing freely near the south end of the Museum, was erected in 1799 as a monument to Cornwallis, whose statue was originally placed here.

A short walk leads to the **Parade Ground**, formerly Cornwallis Square, laid out in 1715 on the site of the first Fort House, the residence of the Madras Governors. The ministerial offices are seen on the east of the open space, with barracks for regiments on the other three sides. **St Mary's Church**, reputedly the oldest Protestant place of worship in Asia, stands near the southeast corner of the Parade Ground. Built in 1678–90 as the religious focus for the growing British population of Madras, the Church is still in worship. St Mary's was built by Streynsham Master, the Governor of Madras, from subscriptions contributed by residents of the Fort, including Elihu Yale. Both Yale and Robert Clive were wedded here. Job Charnock's three daughters were baptised in the Church before the family moved to Bengal, where Charnock founded Calcutta in 1690. Thomas Pitt, subsequently the Governor of Fort St George, Warren Hastings, Lord Cornwallis and Arthur Wellesley, later the Duke of Wellington, were all members of St Mary's congregation.

The Church presents a plain whitewashed façade, broken by arched openings with shuttered windows set into 1.2m thick brick-and-lime walls. The battlemented parapet is a later addition. The restrained Neo-Classical tower was added in front of the west door in 1701; its octagonal steeple was only completed in 1795. Curving staircases ascend to doorways set between the tower and the

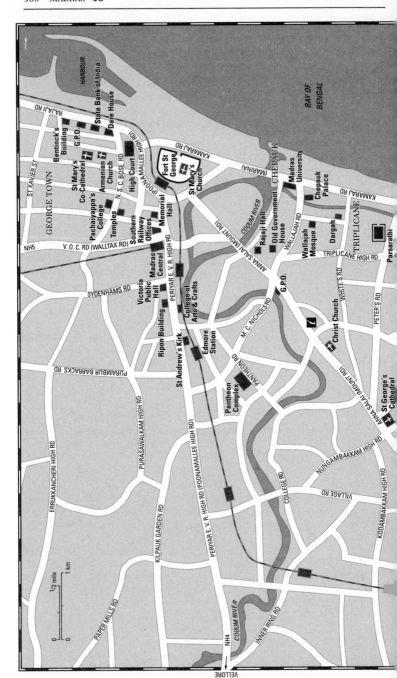

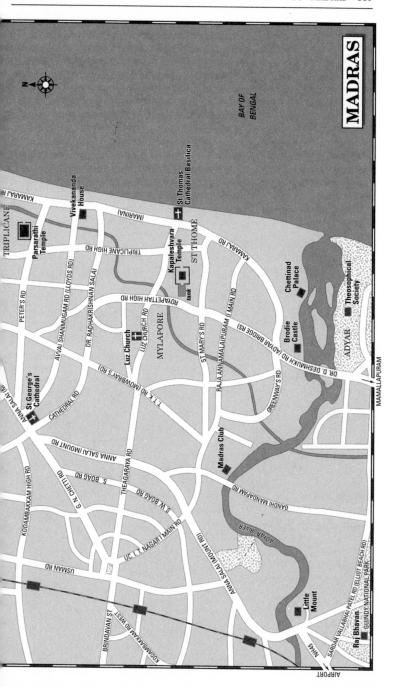

nave. The arcades creating triple aisles support masonry vaults intended to withstand bombing, siege and cyclone. At the west end is a raised gallery with an ornate wooden balustrade, reserved for the Governor and Council. A rich assortment of tombs and memorials is seen in the nave.

The early 19C monuments on the north wall include a panel by John Flaxman, commemorating Josiah Webbe, and another by John Bacon, dedicated to Frederick Christian Schwartz, the distinguished missionary. The Italian oil painting of the Last Supper which serves as the altarpiece in the sanctuary, a 19C extension, is supposed to have been captured in 1761 in a raid on Pondicherry [39A]. An interesting item in the possession of the Church is a Bible printed in 1660. Gravestones removed in 1763 from an earlier cemetery are set into the pavement that surrounds the Church. They include that of Elizabeth Baker, the wife of the first President of Madras. The words inscribed on her tombstone and the date 1652 are the oldest English inscriptions in Southern India.

Immediately west of St Mary's is the office of the Archaeological Survey of India, once **Admiralty House**. This Neo-Classical mansion, with its imposing double-height columned portico, was where Clive, the Steward of the Fort, and his newly wedded wife lived in 1753. State receptions were held here prior to the construction of the Banqueting Hall on Anna Salai.

After finishing the tour of Fort St George, visitors have a choice of routes through the city: north along Rajaji Road to George Town, west along Poonamallee High Road to Egmore and the Pantheon Complex, southwest along Anna Salai, or south along Kamarajar Road, skirting the Marina to Chepauk and Triplicane, with Mylapore and San Thome beyond.

B. George Town

The indigenous population of Madras at the turn of the 18C, estimated at some 300,000, was accommodated in a walled quarter known originally as Black Town, later George Town, immediately north of Fort St George. Much of the wealth and trade of Madras is still concentrated here in the crowded streets and tiny shops. Though the walls have now disappeared, the regular layout of the streets is still evident. George Town is flanked on the east by Rajaji Road, running past the modern harbour, and on the south by N.S.C. Bose Road.

The first feature of interest to be noticed on Rajaji Road is the 38m high **Lighthouse** of 1841. This is conceived as a massive Greek Doric column, its beam visible 25km out at sea. The adjacent red-brick **High Court** of 1888–92, one of the city's most distinguished monuments, was designed by J.W. Brassington, but was revised and completed by Henry Irwin and J.H. Stephens. The imposing complex employs Islamic-styled portals with arched recesses, surrounded by fringes of buds topped with battlemented parapets. The flanking octagonal towers, their corners marked by circular ribs, are capped with square pavilions with bulbous domes painted with stylised arabesques. An octagonal central tower, added in 1912, rises almost 50m over the east block of the Court. Domed pavilions cluster against its base; the summit is marked by a large bulbous dome framed by eight domical finials. Originally intended as a lighthouse with a fine view over the city and the ocean beyond, it now serves as a memorial. One of the chambers inside the tower houses a marble statue by George Wade of T. Muthaswami Iyer, the country's first Indian judge. The interior of the Court is of interest for the liberal use of carved woodwork and stained glass.

Parry's Corner, immediately north of the High Court, where N.S.C. Bose Road runs into Rajaji Road, takes its name from the oldest British mercantile company still operating in Madras. The site is occupied by **Dare House**, erected in 1940 in the International Modern style. Further along Rajaji Road is the **State Bank of India**, built in the 1890s in a manner recalling that of the High Court. The main entrance is marked by a sequence of lobed arches headed by arcaded windows. The square towers at either side have projecting balconies lined with pierced stone balustrades. These serve as platforms for finely worked octagonal domed pavilions. The **General Post Office** next door, which opened in 1884, is the work of Robert Fellowes Chisholm, one of the city's most celebrated architects. Its arcaded ranges are terminated by square towers with curious multi-gabled roofs. The central arched entryway is flanked by larger and higher square towers devoid of roofs.

Bentinck's Building stands a short distance further north along Rajaji Road. This 1793 structure, now somewhat dilapidated, was used variously as the Supreme Court and the Collectorate of Madras. It is one of the few original Neo-Classical projects overlooking the ocean to survive. Its superimposed Doric and Ionic colonnades are emphasised by a part-circular projection in the middle.

Diverse religious and educational buildings are located on or near N.S.C. Bose Road, formerly Esplanade Road. The first to be seen is **Anderson's Church**, recognised by its octagonal tower capped with a gabled steeple. Next comes the **Armenian Church**, entered from a side street through a modest gate bearing the date 1712. Gravestones with Armenian script in curious designs are set into the pavement of the planted court inside. A detached belfry tower with rounded openings is roofed with a petalled dome framed by vase-like pinnacles. The Church itself dates from 1772. It has an octagonal lantern rising over the curving vaults which roof the sanctuary. The interior consists of a long narrow nave with an unusual stepped altar at the east end, incorporating small oil paintings of the life of Christ.

St Mary's Co-Cathedral, immediately north, is a reminder that George Town's population once had more Catholics than Protestants. The date 1642 inscribed over the central door commemorates the year of the first Catholic place of worship in Madras, as distinct from San Thome. A stark Neo-Classical tower of four stages, topped with an octagonal lantern, rises from one corner. Oil paintings within show the Crucifixion and Mary Magdalene.

Pachaiyappa's College, further along N.S.C. Bose Road, is named after Pachaiyappa Muthiar, an interpreter who worked for the East India Company. It opened in 1850, to provide education for poor boys. Built in an authentic Neo-Greek style, the College has an imposing portico elevated on a terrace high above the traffic. Six Ionic columns topped with a bold pediment shelter the grand doorway leading to the school.

The twin **Chennakeshava Perumal** and **Chenna Mallikeshvara Temples** face onto N.S.C. Bose Road a short distance west. Known collectively in the past as the Town Temple, these shrines were consecrated in 1766. They are built in a traditional Tamil idiom, having square towers covered with plaster sculptures and topped by square domical roofs. Two modest **Jain Temples** in nearby Mint Street testify to the long-standing presence of Gujarati merchants in George Town.

C. Poonamallee High Road

The principal route proceeding west from Fort St George is lined with civic structures. At the extreme east end of the High Road stands the **Memorial Hall**, built in 1857 as a thanksgiving for the preservation of Southern India from the Mutiny. Its handsome Ionic portico is now rarely used. The adjacent **Southern Railways Office**, completed in 1922, presents a lively fusion of Neo-Mughal and European motifs executed in local granite. **Madras Central Railway Station** next door was built in 1868–72 according to designs by George Hardinge. Double-storeyed arcades with corner pavilions flank the 40m high central clock tower, which is topped with a pyramidal roof. The nearby **Victoria Public Hall**, completed in 1889, is the work of Chisholm. This red-brick composition is distinguished by its corner tower, with a sloping tiled pyramidal roof relieved by small wooden gables. Next door stands the **Ripon Building**, named after one of the Governors of Madras, accommodating the offices of the City Corporation of Madras, inaugurated in 1688. The Building, which dates from 1913, presents an imposing three-storeyed Italianate façade dominated by a central clock tower.

Further along Poonamallee High Road, on the south side, is the **College of Arts and Crafts**, founded in 1850. It occupies a later mansion built by Chisholm, that still stands in a tree-lined garden. **St Andrew's Kirk**, a short distance west, was erected in 1818–21 by Thomas de Havilland to a design by Lieutenant Grant. This handsomely proportioned Neo-Classical church, perhaps the grandest in Southern India, is entered through a monumental pedimented Ionic portico. This is surmounted by a slender triple-stage tower with a tapering octagonal spire. The outer walls of the unusual circular nave have boldly defined Ionic columns, repeating those of the front portico, with louvred doors set between them. The circular hall within has 16 fluted columns with finely modelled Corinthian capitals. They support a 15m diameter dome painted with golden stars on a blue background.

St Andrew's Kirk, Madras

A footbridge next to St Andrew's Kirk leads to **Egmore Station**, another project of Chisholm. This presents a synthesis of pointed Islamic arches and towers topped with Rajput domed pavilions. The left portico is headed by a tympanum filled with leafy scrolls and the monogram of the South Indian Railway. An imaginative curved vault with triple pot finials rises above. The library and museums of the Pantheon Complex are situated a short distance west.

D. Pantheon Complex

Taking its name from the Public Assembly Rooms that once stood on this site, the Pantheon Complex houses the major cultural institutions of Madras. The collections of the **Government Museum** (closed Fridays) are displayed in four separate blocks. The **Archaeological Galleries** house an important series of stone sculptures brought from sites in Tamil Nadu and Andhra Pradesh. The first room displays 8C Pallava carvings, including a large seated Vishnu. Among the Nolamba period items is a charming 10C ceiling panel from Hemavati [33H], showing Shiva and Parvati on Nandi riding through the clouds. 10C–12C Chola art is best represented by Ardhanari from Tiruchennampundi, Shiva appearing out of the *linga* from Mudiyanar, and Ranganatha from Villupuram. One of the finest examples is the elegant figure of Surya from Uttani, which is placed at the top of the stairs. A finely worked 11C Late Chalukya doorway is also on display. Among the exhibits assigned to the 16C is a somewhat damaged sculpture of seated Balakrishna from Hampi [20B]. The upper balcony that rings this room accommodates epigraphs from different eras, sandstone fragments from the 2C BC Buddhist monument at Bharhut in Madhya Pradesh, and stray 1C–2C AD pieces from Gandhara in northern Pakistan. The connecting corridor at the end of the room is lined with hero stones, some with lively hunters or horsemen, such as the panel from Ipuru.

The next room of the Archaeological Galleries is crammed with figures and architectural fragments, mostly from Pallava and Chola sites. They include a complete set of Saptamatrikas, several Dakshinamurti images and large icons of seated and standing Vishnu. Of particular interest are the limestone posts, railings and drum slabs recovered from the demolished *stupa* at Amaravati [29K]. A plaster model to one side gives an idea of the original appearance of the monument. The carvings, which are mostly assigned to the Ikshvaku era in the 2C–4C, testify to the vitality of early Buddhist traditions in Southern India. Amaravati decorative art is represented by ornate lotus medallions and long friezes of garlands carried by dwarfs. On the reverse sides of the medallions are *Jataka* stories, with crowded scenes palaces, courtiers and mounted riders. The drum panels are adorned with pots filled with lotuses and serpents wrapped around *stupas*. The greatest panel of the Amaravati series depicts a *stupa* in deep relief, complete with railings, side columns supporting sun discs, and flying celestials.

Carvings from other Buddhist sites of the same period include those from Jaggayyapeta [29C], one depicting a royal figure holding a solar disc. One side room displays Jain figures, the largest being a seated Jina from Tuticorin [45G]. Another room presents Buddhist reliefs discovered at Goli [29L], including a frieze of *Vessantara Jataka* scenes, in which the Bodhisattva appears as an elephant. The large seated Kali figure nearby comes from Hemavati. The **Zoological and Geological Galleries** are located beyond.

•

The next portion of the collection is housed in a structure of Italianate design, incorporating a part-circular theatre surrounded by an arcade. The cannons placed around the building include a magnificent example with a tiger head, taken from Tipu Sultan's army at Srirangapattana in 1799. Another example displays the arms of the Dutch East India Company. The **Arms Gallery** within displays many items from Thanjavur [40A]. The finest are the elephant goads, or *ankushas*, in exquisitely chiselled steel, daggers with pierced steel guards and swords with deeply modelled gauntlets. The adjacent **Prehistoric Gallery** shows Iron Age pottery, terracotta burials, stone and metal tools. The most interesting item is a terracotta sarcophagus with six legs and a ram's head, from Markapuram in Andhra Pradesh. Earthenware urns from Adichanallur [450] are displayed, together with their associated iron weapons and other implements. Roman pottery, beads and other ornaments come from Arikamedu [39B].

A grand double **Staircase** leading to the upper level of the building is lined with wooden doors from the Chettinad area [44K] and wooden lintels carved with *Ramayana* episodes, removed from a temple at Kolam [46H]. Further wooden exhibits are seen in the lofty hall at the upper level, distinguished by its stained glass and papered ceiling and vault. The **Ethnographic and Folk Art Galleries** show assorted items from all over Southern India, the most fascinating being ivory boomerangs, brass masks and musical instruments.

The next building within the Pantheon Complex is the **Old Connemara Library** of 1896, designed by Irwin. Its former reading room (permission required to visit) has an intricately worked ceiling, with varied geometric designs carried on curving panels of stained glass. The side arcades are embellished with richly cut acanthus leaves and arabesque motifs in the plaster spandrels. The extensive collection of books and manuscripts was begun in 1861.

The **Bronze Gallery**, to the rear of the Library, houses the largest collection of Southern Indian metal images. The exhibits are contained in glass cases on the sides, arranged in chronological sequence, with several items of outstanding quality displayed freely in the middle. The Chola period is well represented. The Ardhanarishvara from Tiruvengadu is often acknowledged as one of the masterpieces of the era; the blending of male and female physiognomies and dress is unsurpassed. Among the Nataraja icons, complete with flaming halos, is a small delicate example from Kuram. The sets of figures include a paired Shiva and Parvati from Kilaiyur [41G], and the group of Rama with Sita, Lakshmana and Hanuman from Tiruvalangadu. Also of interest are Vishnu from Kamal, and Maheshvari, with flame-like headdress, from Velanganni [40N]. A set of Alvars from Tiruvalangadu includes a finely modelled Somaskandamurti. A cheerful dancing Ganesha is among the later 17C bronzes.

The upper level of the Bronze Gallery shows Chola-period Buddhist figures, many from Nagapattinam [40M]. The finest show the Master standing in an ornate frame, or seated beneath a profuse but delicate tree, flanked by serpent attendants. Several Avalokiteshvara figures are also of merit.

The **National Art Gallery**, formerly the Empress Victoria Memorial Hall, is another project of Irwin, dating from 1909. It is built in pink standstone in a delicate Neo-Mughal style. The main entrance and pierced stone screens above are framed by a recessed pointed arch fringed with buds. The walls are topped with a crenellated parapet, above which stand a cluster of octagonal pavilions crowned with domes, that in the middle being larger and higher. The side rooms, opening off the entrance, accommodate ivory and sandalwood caskets, printed cloths and paintings on glass and mica, with charming secular and mythological scenes. The central hall is hung with imposing oil paintings, of little worth compared to the bronze masterpieces that are also on show. The 11C Nataraja from Tiruvengadu, sometimes considered the greatest of all Southern Indian dance icons, displays perfectly balanced posture and delicately detailed flying hair with snakes. No less impressive is the Rama group from the same site. The **Gallery of Contemporary Art** next door is dedicated to temporary shows.

E. Anna Salai

This thoroughfare, originally known as Mount Road, in reference to St Thomas Mount, to which it proceeds, was once lined with handsome offices and stores. Only a few survive the recent development: Agarchand Mansion, Higgenbotham's and The Mail. Many celebrated landmarks, such as the Neo-Gothic arcades of 1897 of Spencer & Co., have vanished forever. Anna Salai begins on an island in Cooum Creek just south of Fort St George, a site marked by an equestrian statue of Sir Thomas Monro, the Governor of the Madras Presidency in 1819–26. This work of 1839 is by Francis Chantrey. The **Gymkhana Club** nearby, a relic of British military days, is still popular.

A portrait of George V stands in front of the iron gates leading to the **Rajaji Hall**, just off Anna Salai, south of Cooum Creek. This impressive Neo-Classical building was erected in 1802 as a monumental setting for state entertainments according to a design by John Goldingham, the astronomer and engineer to the East India Company. The Banqueting Hall is approached by a broad flight of steps that leads to an arcaded lower storey wrapping around the main hall. This was added in 1875, partly concealing the severe Doric columns of the Hall within. The pediments above were originally adorned with trophies commemorating British victories, now replaced with emblems of the Tamil Nadu state. The portraits of British dignitaries that once lined the interior of the Hall have been removed to the Fort Museum and Raj Bhavan. A fine library of historical materials remains.

Old Government House stands in the estate immediately south of the Rajaji Hall. Originally the residence of a Portuguese merchant, Luis de Madeiros, it was acquired in 1753 by the Governor, but was later damaged during the French wars. The House was entirely remodelled in 1800 by Goldingham, who added a double staircase and reception rooms on the upper floor. The deep verandah with paired Doric columns dates from 1895.

Another vestige of Neo-Classicism is the **Old Madras Club**, known in its heyday as the Ace of Clubs, now a decaying relic within the Express Estate, just off a street running east from Anna Salai. The Club was founded in 1832, and its central reception hall was erected in 1842; it was later extended, with a spacious colonnaded verandah with pedimented ends.

Christ Church, 1km further south on Anna Salai, is a small, graceful structure dating from 1852, whose handsome Ionic porticos shelter doorways on three sides. It is topped by a slender multi-stage tower with an octagonal steeple. More impressive is **St George's Cathedral** on the corner of Anna Salai and Dr Radhakrishnan Salai, also known by its former name of Cathedral Road. This imposing monument was planned by James Caldwell and constructed in 1814–16 by de Havilland. The brilliantly whitewashed frontal portico, with triple side rows of paired Ionic columns, is topped with a plain pediment. The tower, set well back, has a lower square stage and an upper round stage, topped with an octagonal spire that attains an overall height of 42.5m. The side walls have louvred doors headed with semicircular stained-glass windows, the glass repeated in similarly shaped lunettes above. The side doors are sheltered by full porticos. Double rows of nine Ionic columns carry a curved vault decorated with raised plasterwork over the central aisle.

The apsidal chancel accommodates a marble alterpiece of St George crowned with a marble pediment. Among the many fine monuments are Chantrey's memorial of 1830 to Bishop Heber (north wall, east end), and the fully sculpted funerary figures of James Lushington and Reverend Daniel Corrie. A small domed gate once served as the entry to the adjacent cemetery. It now leads to a cluster of graves picturesquely shaded by ashoka trees and an old banyan. Here can found the tombstone of Elizabeth de Havilland, the architect's wife, dated 1818. Some graves are enclosed by a railings made of discarded spears, allegedly brought from Tipu Sultan's arsenal at Srirangapattana.

Anna Salai continues to Little Mount, Raj Bhavan at Guindy, and St Thomas Mount.

F. Chepauk and Triplicane

Kamarajar Road, previously South Beach Road, and the adjacent foreshore serve as a broad Marina that runs beside the Bay of Bengal on the eastern extremity of the city. Planned by Grant Duff, the Governor of Madras in 1881–86, it connects Fort St George with San Thome Basilica, almost 5km distant.

Chepauk is the name given to the quarter now partly occupied by the campus of **Madras University**, founded in 1857 as the major institution of the city, located just south of Cooum Creek. The University is of architectural interest, with many innovative buildings designed by Chisholm, the most unusual being the **Senate House** of 1873. This red-brick building is illuminated by windows with coloured glass in geometric patterns. The windows are set behind lofty arcades carried on solid round pillars and topped with domical finials. The square towers in the middle of the long sides have projecting balconies shaded by angled eaves. The pointed arches in coloured tilework at the top frame triple sets of narrow round-headed windows. The arches merge with domes painted with stylised ornament. The smaller octagonal towers at the corners are capped with domed pavilions. Outside the south entrance is an 1887 Golden Jubilee statue of Queen Victoria seated beneath an ornate cast-iron canopy manufactured in Glasgow.

Chepauk Palace, immediately south, on the other side of Wallajah Road, was designed by the English engineer Paul Benfield in 1768 as the Madras residence of Muhammad Ali of Arcot (1749–95). The complex consists of two long blocks in left formation, both with arcaded ranges. Chisholm added a tower in 1870 to link the two blocks. This curious structure combines disparate features: broad arched entrances at the base, tiers of superimposed balconies in the middle of each side, slender octagonal buttresses at the corners, protruding above the roof line as minarets with domical tops, and a capping small dome on a petalled base. The horizontal striped paintwork gives the tower an almost Byzantine appearance. The Palace was acquired by the Madras Government in 1885, and now serves as the headquarters of various departments; its original name is, however, retained.

The next building of interest on the Marina is **Presidency College**, founded in 1840. As rebuilt by Chisholm in 1864, the architect's first commission in Madras, the complex presents an austere appearance with round-headed windows. The ribbed dome with clocks on four faces is an addition of 1887.

Vivekananda House, about 1km further south, is an architectural curiosity erected in 1842 to store blocks of ice shipped from Boston. Its semi-circular frontage has double rows of arched windows. The rooftop pavilion is headed with a peculiar pineapple-shaped finial. The building was occupied for a few months by Swami Vivekananda (see p 493), hence its name.

Triplicane, a short distance south of Chepauk, is also linked with the Nawabs of Arcot. Muhammad Ali was responsible for the **Wallajah Mosque**, erected in 1795 on what is now Triplicane High Road, near the junction with Wallajah Road. Graves of the Arcot family, as well as the tomb of the saint Maulana Bahrul Uloom, are seen in the adjacent graveyard. The Mosque presents an austere façade with flanking minarets, square at the base, octagonal in the middle and fluted and circular in the upper stages, topped with bulbous finials. The *Dargah* of Hazrat Dastagir Sahib, further south on Triplicane High Road, is another prominent Muslim monument. It is recognised by a bulbous dome of squat proportions framed by a quartet of pinnacles.

It is, however, for the **Parthasarathi Temple** that Triplicane is best known. Identified with the village of Thirupallikeni, this quarter has regularly laid-out streets that echo the rectangular walled compound of the Temple itself. This monument traces its history back to the 9C, and was the scene of many battles, with Dutch and French troops occupying it at various times. It has been extensively renovated in recent years. The twin sanctuaries of Krishna and Rukmini (access restricted to visitors) are approached through *gopuras* with vividly painted towers on both the east and west. A stone colonnade with carved columns leads to the east *gopura*. A decorated wooden chariot is parked nearby. A tank with a small pavilion in the middle is seen further south.

G. Mylapore and San Thomé

Mylapore is located immediately south of Triplicane, only a short distance inland from the Marina. This traditional quarter is dominated by the **Kapaleshvara Temple**, the largest in Madras, surrounded by narrow bustling lanes. The original foundation was damaged by the Portuguese in 1566, but was rebuilt in later times. The Temple is dedicated to Shiva, who is here conceived as a peacock (*mayil*) since the goddess Parvati assumed the form of a peahen in order to worship the *linga*, hence the name Mylapore (Mayilapura).

The Temple complex is entered on the east through a *gopura* with a lofty pyramidal tower crowded with plaster sculptures; nine pot finials line the ridge of the barrel-vaulted roof. Depictions of Shiva in diverse forms appear in the creepers held by maidens carved on the doorway jambs. Small east-facing *linga* and Vinayaka shrines are seen on entering the compound. The principal *linga* sanctuary is, however, entered from a columned hall on the west. The same hall gives access to a rectangular barrel-vaulted shrine on the north, consecrated to Devi. A sequence of Nandi, altar and lamp column stands outside. A smaller gate here leads to a vast tank with stepped sides.

San Thomé Cathedral Basilica, on the Bay of Bengal, marks the legendary burial place of St Thomas the Apostle.

Nestorian Christians from Iran erected a chapel over what they believed to be the grave of St Thomas, possibly as early as the 7C–8C, and the site came to be venerated as a holy shrine. The Portuguese rebuilt the chapel in 1523, calling it San Thome, and used it as the nucleus of their headquarters on the Coromandel Coast. San Thome remained in their hands until 1672, when it was occupied by the French, followed two years later by the Dutch. The British took command of San Thome in 1749, but Portuguese priests remained in charge of the Basilica. The building was demolished in 1893, and a new Basilica was raised three years later in a Neo-Gothic style.

The whitewashed gabled façade, framed by octagonal towers, is dominated by a separate higher tower with a high octagonal steeple that marks the south entrance to the Basilica. The chief attraction of the interior is a small narrow tomb set beneath the floor in the middle of the nave, alleged to contain the remains of St Thomas. The newly completed **St Thomas Museum** (closed Tuesdays), at the rear of the Basilica, houses items dating from the Portuguese period, including tombstones, a baptismal font, receptacles, granite carvings and a map dated 1519. Several pre-European vestiges are also on display. A silver reliquary contains a fragment of the iron spear said to have killed the Apostle.

The Christian character of San Thome is reflected in the numerous places of worship that dot the neighbourhood. A small **Anglican Church** with a Neo-Gothic verandah stands next to the Basilica. A short distances south is **Lazarus Church**, dating back to 1582, rebuilt in 1637 by the prominent Madeiros family, and renovated in 1928. Of greater historical interest is **Luz Church**, west of Mylapore. An inscribed plaque set into the outer south wall of the building records it was erected by a Franciscan monk in 1516, making it the oldest European structure in Madras. The Baroque style is evident in the pilastered façade, adorned with curving volutes and conical finials framing a sunburst motif. The altar within shows the Virgin and Christ crowned by angels. The barrel vault has relief plaster decoration. 17C Portuguese tombstones are set into the pavement.

H. Adyar

This part of Madras is named after the river that marks the southern periphery of the city. **Chettinad Palace** stands in spacious grounds on the north bank of the Adyar River, close to its confluence with the Bay of Bengal. **Brodie Castle** nearby, an imposing white structure with a Neo-Classical portico and a castel-lated round tower, takes its name from the East India Company servant who built it in 1796–98.

The **World Headquarters of the Theosophical Society** occupies the south bank of the Adyar River, reached by the Elphinstone bridge of 1840. Founded in 1875 in New York by Helena Petrovna Blavatsky and Henry S. Olcott, the Theosophical Society shifted to Madras in 1882, taking over the home of John Huddlestone, one of three Madras Government officers sent to negotiate with Tipu Sultan in 1784. During Annie Besant's presidency from 1907, the Society's property was expanded to encompass some 110ha of beau-tifully tended gardens. They include a huge banyan, one of the world's largest trees, estimated at more than 400 years old. The paths are marked by granite columns removed from a temple hall. Small shrines of different faiths are concealed in the gardens.

The **Great Hall** in the main building is enlivened with plaster reliefs depicting world religious figures, and a three-dimensional portrait of Blavatsky and Olcott. The adjacent Museum (access restricted to visitors) displays portraits of the Society's Presidents and a few antiquarian items. The Society's **Library** of more than 165,000 books functions as a centre of postgraduate studies in Sanskrit and Indology.

Vestiges of British recreational life are to be seen further upstream. On the north bank of the Adyar River stands the **Madras Club**, formerly the Adyar Club. Established in 1891 in an 18C villa owned by George Moubray, who arrived in Madras in 1771, the Club stands in gardens sweeping down to the water. The river frontage is embellished with a stately octagonal dome rising over a semi-circular bay. The octagonal room within has an arcaded perimeter.

I. Guindy and the two Mounts of St Thomas

Further historical features are located in the extreme southwest of Madras, towards the airport. **Guindy National Park**, on Sardar Vallabhai Patel Road, leading to Elliot Beach, consists of 270ha of deciduous scrub jungle. This incorporates a sanctuary for spotted deer and black buck, as well as a unique snake park and reptilium. **Raj Bhavan**, at the western perimeter of the Park, was the country residence of the Madras Governors from 1817, first used by Munro (permission required to visit). Sprawling colonnaded wings flank the central hall, the interior of which is enlivened with a bust of Wellington and paintings removed from the Banqueting Hall. The nearby **Gandhi Memorial Pavilion** was erected in 1956.

Little Mount, an outcrop of granite associated with the refuge of St Thomas, stands north of the Park, near Marmalong Bridge across the Adyar River. The **Church of Our Lady of Good Health** was founded in 1551. A roughly carved plaque set into the wall left of the entrance shows a figure of St Thomas and the date 1612. Steps to one side of the altar lead to a small grotto, reputed to be the retreat of the saint. A rocky crevice behind the Church is filled with natural water. The cross cut into the rock here is said to mark the spot where St Thomas preached.

The higher **Mount of St Thomas**, 3km southwest, marks the place where the Apostle is supposed to have been martyred in AD 68, after arriving here from Kerala. The Mount rises 90m above the plain, and can be clearly seen from the airport. The ascent begins in the village at its base, where a whitewashed gate with a central arch is surmounted by an icon of St Thomas and the date 1726. Brick-paved steps climb to the modest **Church of Our Lady of Expectations**, whose west façade has an arched doorway with an inscription of 1707, naming an Armenian donor and bearing the royal arms of Portugal. The barrel-vaulted interior is of interest for the gilded altar. This frames a carved stone plaque showing the celebrated Bleeding Cross, surrounded by a Pahlavi inscription. This was discovered by the Portuguese in 1521, but its antiquity remains uncertain. The building next door was once a Franciscan orphanage and school.

The **Cantonment**, beneath the east flank of the Mount, preserves several 18C Neo-Classical villas, one of which served as the residence of Hastings in

1769–72. The **Garrison Church** of 1830 is an unassuming edifice with an unpedimented Ionic portico. Its slender tower has been truncated, marring its original four-stage design. The interior is furnished with memorials of military officers.

37 · Around Madras

Hindu monuments dating from the 7C–9C Pallava era, the earliest to be preserved in Tamil Nadu, are scattered throughout the Madras region, as at **Mamallapuram** [A], **Chengalpattu** [C], **Kanchipuram** [F] and **Uttiramerur** [G].

Later Vijayanagara- and Nayaka-period temples, dating from the 16C–17C, stand at **Tirukkalukkundram** [B], **Sriperumbudur** [E], Kanchipuram and **Tiruttani** [H], all of which are lively towns frequented by pilgrims.

Mamallapuram and Kanchipuram, the two most popular destinations outside Madras, demand separate full-day excursions, possibly combined with one or more nearby sites. A side trip to the bird sanctuary at **Vedantangal** [D] is an additional option. Another half day will have to be set aside to reach the Dutch cemetery at **Pulicat** [I].

Some excursions may be combined conveniently with other itineraries: Kanchipuram is directly on the highway to Vellore [38]; Chengalpattu is a stop-over on the way to Pondicherry [39] or Tiruchirapalli [41]; Tiruttani may be visted en route to Tirupati [35].

■ **Transport**. Buses run frequently from Madras to all the towns described here.

■ **Accommodation**. Visitors not wishing to stay in Madras may prefer the relaxing seaside accommodation beside the Bay of Bengal. *Fisherman's Cove* (☎ 44304) at **Mamallapuram** (STD code 04113), 57km south of Madras, is the most luxurious. Other attractive hotels there include the *Silversands Beach Village* (☎ 42283), *Temple Bay Ashok Beach Resort* (☎ 42251), *Golden Sun Beach Resort* (☎ 42245) and *Ideal Beach Resort* (☎ 42240). The completion of the *Hotel Baboo Soorya* (☎ 22555) means that it is now possible to stay comfortably in **Kanchipuram**.

■ **Tourist Information**. The TTDC maintains an office in Covelong Road, **Mamallapuram** (☎ 42232).

A. Mamallapuram

The road from Madras to Mamallapuram is lined with artists' studios and work-shops. 12km south of Madras is the **Kalakshetra Academy,** dedicated to teaching and performing classical Southern Indian music and dance, as well as traditional textile designing and weaving. The **Cholamandal Artists' Village**, another active centre, is at **Injampukkam**, 24km south, while 49km south at **Muttakkadu** is the **Dakshinachitra Centre**, where wooden houses typical of Southern India's different regions have been reconstructed. Mamallapuram itself, 60km south, is celebrated for the **Government College of Architecture and Sculpture**, responsible for the revival of traditional carving and bronze-casting techniques. The town is full of shops displaying newly completed artworks.

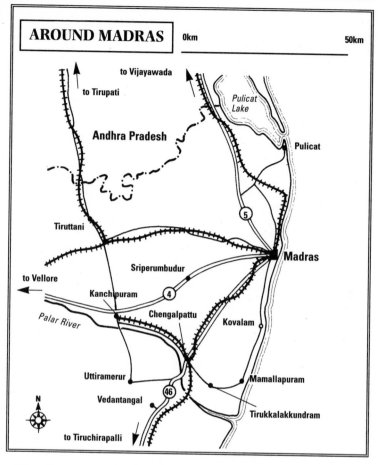

AROUND MADRAS

0km 50km

to Vijayawada
to Tirupati

Pulicat Lake

Andhra Pradesh

Pulicat

5

Tiruttani

Sriperumbudur

Madras

to Vellore

4

Kanchipuram

Palar River

Chengalpattu

Kovalam

Uttiramerur

Mamallapuram

46

Vedantangal

Tirukkalakkundram

N

to Tiruchirapalli

Mamallapuram, previously Mahabalipuram, takes its name from Mamalla (650–68), one of the Pallava kings of Kanchipuram. Its seaside location suggests that it may have served as a port. Mamallapuram's rock-cut and mono-lithic temples are the earliest examples of monumental architecture in Tamil Nadu; its free-standing temples are also the first erected in this zone. The associated sculptures, some of which are large-scale compositions, are the finest examples of Pallava art.

Cave temples and carved panels dating from the 7C and early 8C are cut into the rocky sides of a granite outcrop running parallel to the ocean, about 400m from the shore; they are described from north to south. The **Trimurti Mandapa**, at the north end, consists of a row of triple shrines, each flanked by pilasters, between which stand guardian figures. The rear walls show Brahma (left), Vishnu and Shiva (right), attended by kneeling devotees. A polished stone *linga* is placed before the last image. Beyond the Shiva shrine is a niche with Durga standing on the decapitated buffalo head, framed by a foliated arch springing from *makaras*. The **Kotikal Mandapa**, west of this monument, has a crudely excavated sanctuary preceded by a small verandah. Female figures in relaxed postures flank the doorway.

The **Varaha Cave Temple**, further south, conforms to the same scheme, except that the columns have lion bases; a parapet of roof forms is carved above the eaves. A projecting shrine in the middle of the rear wall is flanked by guardians and Lakshmi (left) and Durga (right). The large-scale carvings on the side walls show Varaha lifting up Bhudevi (left) and Trivikrama (right).

The nearby free-standing **Ganesha Ratha** is a rectangular monolith with a columned verandah, with lion columns flanked by guardians between wall pilasters. An image of Ganesha has recently been installed in the small sanctuary. The upper storey, capped with a vaulted roof, complete with arched ends and pot and trident finials, rises above the parapet. East of the Ganesha Ratha is the **Archaeological Museum**, with sculptures and architectural pieces assembled in an outdoor compound.

Arjuna's Penance, a sculpted relief more than 30m long and 14m high, is situated a short distance south of the Museum. The composition is remarkable for the vitality and naturalism of the smoothly modelled figures and animals. Two large boulders are covered with flying gods, goddesses and semi-divine beings, as well as elephants and other animals, all converging on the central cleft. The gap is filled with a slab sculpted with male and female *nagas*, their hands held together in adoration, over which water once flowed from a tank behind into a basin beneath. Arjuna standing on one foot is seen left of the cleft. Four-armed Shiva, holding the magic weapon which Arjuna hopes to win by his penance, stands nearby. Beneath is a hermitage shrine of Vishnu, in front of which sit sages, two deer and lion; disciples beneath engage in austerities.

To the right of the cleft beneath the elephants is the story of the cat who performed atonement by standing on one leg, thereby tricking a group of rats. The relief is sometimes also thought to illustrate the penance of Bhagiratha, who persuaded Shiva to receive the Ganga in his matted locks. According to this interpretation, the water flowing over the *naga* figures would represent the descent of the celestial river. Immediately right of Arjuna's Penance is a group of monkeys carved in the round.

A short distance south of Arjuna's Penance is the **Pancha Pandava Mandapa**, of which only five columns with lion bases were completed. Still further south is the **Krishna Mandapa**, with a 16C colonnade sheltering a long composition that follow the curving contours of the rocky face. Krishna is shown shielding the herds and *gopis* from Indra's storm by lifting up Govardhana Hill. The naturalistic details, such as the hero milking a cow who licks her calf, are remarkably tender. Other figures, shown in affectionate embrace or playing the flute, are modelled with a fluid roundness.

A short distance in front (east) of the Krishna Mandapa stands the **Sthalashayana Perumal Temple**. This 17C–18C complex is entered through an unfinished *gopura* on the east, which leads to a second, smaller inner *gopura*, recently renovated. The hall between the *gopuras* has pillars with donor carvings. The Vishnu shrine within is of little artistic merit.

The **Olakkanatha Temple** is perched on the rocky summit above the Krishna Mandapa. The lower walls of this free-standing structure have pairs of pilasters framing worn Shiva images; no ceiling or superstructure remain. A

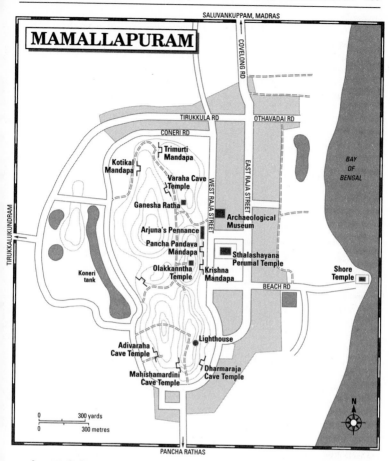

MAMALLAPURAM

SALUVANKUPPAM, MADRAS

COVELONG RD

BAY
OF
BENGAL

TIRUKKULA RD

OTHAVADAI RD

CONERI RD

Trimurti
Mandapa

Kotikal
Mandapa

Varaha Cave
Temple

WEST RAJA STREET

EAST RAJA STREET

Ganesha Ratha

Archaeological
Museum

TIRUKKALUKUNDRAM

Arjuna's Pennance

Pancha Pandava
Mandapa

Olakkanntha
Temple

Krishna
Mandapa

Sthalashayana
Perumal Temple

Koneri
tank

Shore
Temple

BEACH RD

Lighthouse

Adivaraha
Cave Temple

Mahishamardini
Cave Temple

Dharmaraja
Cave Temple

0   300 yards
0   300 metres

N

PANCHA RATHAS

modern **Lighthouse** occupies another prominence further to the south.

Proceeding south along the base of the rocky outcrop, another, unfinished, version of Arjuna's Penance is seen. The adjacent **Dharmaraja Cave Temple** has three empty sanctuaries excavated into the rear wall of an open hall. The architectural elements are unadorned, and the guardians flanking the central doorway have been chiselled away.

Two further cave temples of interest are located at the south end of the outcrop. A path ascends to the **Mahishamardini Cave Temple**, which consists of three shrines, the central one with a projecting porch, all set within a long verandah with slender fluted columns. The end panels of the verandah are among the greatest masterpieces of Pallava art. They show Vishnu sleeping on the coils of Sesha, in the presence of the gods (left), and Durga on the lion, approaching the buffalo-headed demon (right).

The **Adivaraha Cave Temple**, a short distance west, is cut into the base of the rocky outcrop. Partly obscured by a modern structure, this temple consists of a verandah with a shrine in the rear wall. Two columns have seated lions at the base. The doorway to the sanctuary, approached through a porch projecting into the verandah, is flanked by guardian figures; an image of Varaha is enshrined within. The sculpted panels on the verandah walls depict royal and mythological figures. The figures on either side of the sanctuary have been identified as portraits of royal figures. The end panels of the verandah show Lakshmi bathed by elephants (left), and Durga standing on the buffalo head (right).

The **Shore Temple** is built on a sandy promontory overlooking the Bay of Bengal, directly east of the Sthalashayana Perumal Temple. The Shore Temple is approached from the west through ruined courts with Nandi images placed on the walls, in the middle of which are altars with decorated plinths. A small boulder to the south is fashioned as Durga's lion; the goddess is seated on the hind leg of the animal, with the decapitated buffalo head to one side. A newly revealed elliptical pond, with a miniature circular shrine in the middle and a boar carved out of a boulder on one side, can be seen north of the Temple.

Together with the Kailsanatha temple at Kanchipuram, the Shore Temple is the first significant structural project of the Pallava era, dating from the reign of Rajasimha (700–28). In spite of its overall erosion, the elegant proportions of the sanctuaries and towers are still evident. The Temple comprises a complex of three shrines. The original sanctuary is a small chamber that shelters an image of sleeping Vishnu, carved on top of a low granite boulder. A sanctuary facing east towards the ocean houses a multi-faceted polished stone *linga*, with worn images of a Somaskanda group on the rear wall. A smaller sanctuary, facing west, similarly provided with Shaiva icons, abuts the Vishnu shrine. The rows of pilasters with worn lion bases on the outer walls are sheltered by eaves and a parapet. Steeply pyramidal superstructures, with diminishing storeys repeating those of the walls beneath, rise above the two Shaiva shrines. The towers are capped by octagonal domical roofs with basalt finials.

The group of five shrines known as the **Pancha *Rathas*** is one of the chief attractions of Mamallapuram. These monoliths are hewn out of boulders standing in the dunes some 300m south of the main rocky outcrop. These temple-like features date back to the reign of Mamalla, but were never completed. Their purpose remains mysterious: they may have served as models of different building types, and perhaps for this reason were compared with chariots (*rathas*); they are named, inexplicably, after Draupadi and the Pandava brothers.

The Draupadi and **Arjuna *Rathas***, at the north end of the group, are elevated on a common plinth animated with elephants and lions. The Draupadi *Ratha* has a hut-like roof with curved ridges. Female guardians between pilasters flank the west doorway; a *makara* arch is positioned above. Standing images of Durga are seen on the other three sides. A similar representation of the goddess is carved on the rear wall of the shrine. A free-standing lion stands a short distance west.

The Arjuna *Ratha* has elegant pilasters framing guardians and couples, with deities in the middle of each side: Shiva leaning on Nandi (south), Indra on the elephant (east) and Vishnu with Garuda (north). The wall is overhung by eaves with a parapet of diminutive, yet fully formed, roof forms. The upper storey repeats the pilastered walls, eaves and parapet, but at a reduced scale. The

Pancha Rathas, *Mamallapuram*

capping roof is an octagonal dome. The porch (west) gives access to the verandah and empty sanctuary. A finely sculpted Nandi is located to the east.

The Bhima *Ratha*, the next in line, is incomplete in its lower portions, except for the columns with seated lions on the front (west) and the finely modelled eaves and parapet. The temple is dominated by a vaulted roof with arched ends.

The Dharmaraja *Ratha*, the tallest and most elaborate of the group, is a triple-storeyed version of the Arjuna *Ratha*. Columns with lion bases on the first storey flank an entrance porch leading to the unfinished sanctuary. Sculptures framed by pilasters are positioned in the end panels: Ardhanarishvara and Bhima (east), Shiva and the royal patron Mamalla (south), Shiva (west) and Brahma and Harihara (north). The second storey consists of a passageway around a square shrine, enlivened with gods, guardians and attendants. Devotees with Chandra (north) and Surya (east) populate the walls of the third storey. The chamber at this level has a Somaskanda group accompanied by Brahma and Vishnu carved on the rear wall.

West of the other monoliths, the **Nakula Sahadeva *Ratha*** is the only example with an apsidal-ended plan. Its crowning vault has an arched face on the south. A free-standing elephant stands nearby.

Three smaller, less well-finished monoliths are located about 500m west of the rocky outcrop. The twin **Pidari *Rathas*** and the **Vilian Kuttai *Ratha*** each have two storeys capped with square or domed roofs.

Other features of interest are located north of Mamallapuram. The road passing by an **Unfinished Gateway** of the 16C leads to the **Mukundanayanar Temple**, a small 8C structure that imitates the simpler *Rathas*.

The **Tiger Cave** lies 4km north of Mamallapuram, near the village of **Saluvankuppam**. This somewhat fantastic monument consists of a large boulder, out of which a small portico has been fashioned in the middle, possibly for displaying bronze images during festivals in Pallava times. It is surrounded by a ring of fierce *yali* heads, with two additional elephant heads on the left.

B. Tirukkalukkundram

This town, 14km west of Mamallapuram and the same distance east of Chengalpattu, is dominated by the quartet of matching *gopuras* that rise above the outer walls of the **Bhaktavatsaleshvara Temple**. This monument is associated with the Nayakas of Gingee [39E], and is one of their most ambitious projects. The 17C gateways are grandiose structures, with passageways adorned with carved maidens clutching creepers, scenes of *linga* worship and various deities. The ceilings show Kama and Rati on parrots (south *gopura*) and even paintings of royal visitors (west *gopura*). The towers vary from nine storeys on the north and south to seven on the east and six on the west; they are devoid of plaster sculptures. The principal east entrance through the east *gopura* leads to a spacious compound, with a large square tank in the northeast corner and an elaborate marriage hall in the southwest corner. The latter has columns with *yalis* on the periphery, replaced by horses on the central east–west aisle leading to the dais at the highest level.

A lofty columned hall with side aisles is reached after passing through the second east *gopura*. The aisle proceeding north is lined by columns with sculpted horses, and has a Nataraja shrine at the end. The aisle leading west gives access to the principal *linga* sanctuary in the innermost enclosure. This small apsidal-ended structure has finely finished basement moulding, wall pilasters and deep niches occupied by carved images: Ganesha and Dakshinamurti (south), Shiva appearing out of the *linga* (west), and Brahma and Devi (north). The plaster tower above repeats the apsidal-ended scheme, with an ornate frontal arch. The goddess shrine is located in the northwest corner of the intermediate enclosure.

About 400 steps climb to the **Vedagirishvara Temple**, perched on the summit of a 160m high hill northeast of the town. The Temple is of little interest architecturally, but its rooftop terrace offers magnificent views of the Bhaktavatsaleshvara Temple and the great tank to the east. Visitors make the ascent in order to witness priests feeding two sacred vultures who fly down regularly at midday. The path from the Temple descends past the 7C **Orukal Mandapa**. This consists of a *linga* shrine flanked by sculpted attendants and figures of Vishnu (right) and Brahma (left). The end walls show gracefully posed celestials. The shrine is reached through a hall with double rows of pillars. Pallava-period inscriptions are seen on the inner columns, while the outer supports bear graffiti of Dutch visitors; the earliest example is dated 1664.

C. Chengalpattu

Known previously as Chingleput, this town lies 58km southwest of Madras on NH45, 28km west of Mamallapuram and 35km east of Kanchipuram. The town is of historical interest because of its **Fort**, the most important in the region in the 17C–18C.

> Founded by the Qutb Shahis of Golconda [26E], and later occupied by the rulers of Arcot [38A], the Fort was taken by the French and British. Robert Clive secured the surrender of the French garrison in 1752, but temporarily lost the Fort to Haidar Ali of Srirangapattana [15C] a few years later.

Little remains of the Fort, through which the railway now passes, except for the 18C **Raja Mahal**. This courtly structure, now much altered, consisted originally of five storeys. Its small inner room is surrounded by arcades and roofed with a small dome. The **Anjaneya Temple** in the town dates from the 19C.

Near the hamlet of **Vallam**, 3km southwest of Chengalpattu, three **Cave Temples** dating from the Pallava period are cut at different heights into low granite hills. **Cave I**, the most important, bears an inscription of the reign of Mahendravarman I (580–630). Later carvings of Ganesha and Jyeshtha occupy niches either end of the walled-up verandah.

D. Vedantangal

The 30ha marshy site of the **Vedantangal Bird Sanctuary** lies 28km south of Chengalpattu on NH45. The Sanctuary is known for its great numbers of water-fowl; visiting and resident birds include crested cormorants, night herons, grey pelicans, sandpipers, grey wagtails, open-billed storks, ibis, egrets and purple moorhens. An observation tower on the edge of the water assists visitors in sighting birds. The best season to visit is November–February.

E. Sriperumbudur

This town, 40km southwest of Madras on NH4, was the site of the assassination of Rajiv Gandhi 1991. A granite memorial commemorates the tragedy at a site beside the highway, just south of the town.

Sriperumbudur is traditionally known as the birthplace of the Vaishnava saint Ramanuja, who is worshipped in the **Adi Keshava Temple** in the middle of the town. Though this Temple traces its origin back to the Chola era, its architecture mostly belongs to the 16C–17C. The complex is entered on the east through an imposing, but austere, *gopura* of standard design. This is of interest for the *Ramayana* friezes that cover the side walls of the passageway. The gate gives access to the outer enclosure, which is surrounded by colonnades and subsidiary structures on four sides. The Rama and Lakshmi shrines are located at the northwest and southwest corners respectively; the latter is preceded by ornate columns.

Visitors can only enter the inner higher enclosure of the Temple from the entrance porch on the south side. Broad steps flanked by *yali* balustrades climb up to the plinth, which is adorned with sculpted dancers, couples and attendants, as well as Vaishnava divinities and scenes from mythology, such as the story of Narasimha. The columns of the entrance porch have rearing horses with riders flanking the aisle, which leads north to the main doorway. This aisle continues inside the inner enclosure, the horses being replaced with *yalis*. Immediately ahead is Ramanuja's shrine, facing south, while to the left stands Vishnu's sanctuary facing east. Both structures are ornately treated, with pilastered niches set into their outer walls; the eaves have cut-out ribs on their undersides, and pendant stone chains. Hemispherical towers protrude above the roof line. The only other features of interest are the lofty swing pavilion and long marriage hall aligned with the east *gopura* outside the Temple.

F. Kanchipuram

Located 32km west of Sriperumbudur, just off NH4, Kanchipuram is one of the most vibrant religious and cultural centres in Tamil Nadu, also well-known for its flourishing silk industry. No less than 50 temples within the city are dedicated to different Hindu divinities, including major complexes consecrated to Shiva, the Goddess and Vishnu. This profusion of shrines means that religious festivals at Kanchipuram take place at various times throughout the year.

The archaeological vestiges discovered here testify to the popularity of Buddhism and Jainism in earlier times, and at least one Jain religious complex is still in worship. Kanchipuram served as the capital of the Pallavas in the 7C–9C, but continued to maintain its importance during the succeeding Chola, Vijayanagara and Nayaka eras. The religious monuments are distributed in three distinct zones: the Ekambareshvara and Kamakshi Temples and associated sanctuaries in Shiva Kanchi, to the north; the Varadaraja Temple in Vishnu Kanchi, to the southeast; the Jain shrines at Tiruparuttikunram, on the other side of the Vegavati River, on the southern perimeter of the city.

The tour of Kanchipuram described here begins at the **Kailasanatha Temple**, which stands on the edge of open fields about 500m west of Shiva Kanchi. The Temple was begun by Rajasimha, and is the oldest standing building in the city; however, it lacked priests and worshippers until only a few years ago. It is now the site of the annual Mahashivaratri Festival in February. Constructed almost entirely in sandstone, the Kailasanatha consists of a planned complex, with a central sanctuary standing in the middle of a rectangular enclosure lined with small shrines. Two doorways are positioned on the east; a single doorway on the west is now blocked up.

As in the Shore Temple at Mamallapuram, the principal sanctuary houses a multi-faceted *linga*, with a Somaskanda panel carved on the rear wall. The sanctuary is entirely surrounded by a narrow passageway. The walls are raised on a moulded basement relieved by friezes of dwarfs and foliage patterns. The projecting shrines at the corners and in the middle of each side are framed by pilasters with rearing *yalis* at their bases. A large variety of Shaiva images appears here, including Shiva appearing out of the *linga*, flanked by Vishnu and Brahma (south), and Shiva in the chariot shooting arrows, flanked by Durga and Bhairavi (north). The figures are framed by pilasters supporting *makaras* with foliated tails. The pyramidal superstructure above repeats the wall scheme below at diminishing scales; the capping roof form is an octagonal dome. The flat-roofed hall east of the sanctuary was originally a detached structure. The figures on its outer walls have recently been plastered.

The shrines lining the compound walls of the Kailasanatha Temple all have dome-like roofs, and have seated Nandis and elephants between them. Images of Shiva and other divinities, carved in relief within the shrines, are mostly eroded and overlaid with plaster and colourwork. The inner walls were also once painted. Fragmentary scenes of Shiva with Uma and Skanda, and of Shiva accompanied by Vishnu and Brahma are seen on the north and south walls.

At the east end of the compound stands the Mahendravarmeshvara shrine, named after the ruler who succeeded Rajasimha. This free-standing structure has a large vaulted roof with arched ends. In the middle of the outer walls are carvings of Dakshinamurti (south), a Somaskanda group (west) and dancing Shiva (north). A polished granite *linga* is enshrined within. The outer faces of the enclosure walls of the Temple are relieved by pilasters. Additional minor shrines flank the east entrance. A seated Nandi faces the Temple from a platform a short distance east.

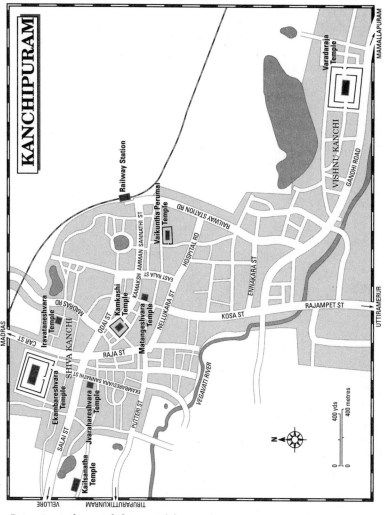

Returning to the crowded streets of the city, the tour continues with a visit to the
Ekambareshvara Temple, the largest in Shiva Kanchi, and the location of the
Panguni Uthiram Festival in March–April. A lofty pavilion with slender columns
stands in the middle of the street leading up to the south *gopura*. This impressive
17C structure has a double series of granite walls, with nine diminishing storeys
in plaster covered brickwork rising above. The tower is surmounted by a vaulted
roof reaching almost 60m above the ground. Its arched ends are enlivened by
monster masks; 11 pot finials adorn the ridge. Smaller *gopuras* on the south and
west lead to the second enclosure. The south *gopura* is elaborately decorated in
the 16C Vijayanagara manner. Its entrance is concealed by a later columned hall
built up to it on the south. A square tank is positioned nearby. In the middle of

the second enclosure stands the main temple, which faces east. It is preceded by a long hall incorporating an earlier *linga* shrine, Nandi pavilion, altar and lamp column. A large stepped tank stocked with fish is set at an angle to the north.

The main Temple, contained within its own rectangle of walls, is surrounded on four sides by a spacious columned corridor enlivened with animal brackets. It houses a stone *linga*, identified as the earth, or *prithvi*, the *linga* worshipped by Kamakshi, the resident goddess of the city. Relief carvings throughout the Ekambareshvara Temple show Kamakshi clutching Shiva's emblem. Smaller multi-faceted *lingas* are displayed in colonnades flanking the corridor; a *sahasra linga* occupies the shrine at the northeast corner. A subsidiary shrine accommodating a large brass Nataraja icon opens off to the north. The Somaskanda shrine, in the southwest corner of the enclosure, is approached through a hall with columns showing 16C carvings of *yalis* with riders. To the rear (west) of the main Temple is an open court with a sacred mango tree, beneath which Kamakshi is believed to have worshipped Shiva. Its spreading branches shelter a raised walkway.

A short distance east of the Ekambareshvara Temple is the 8C **Iravataneshvara Temple**. This Pallava-period monument has a square sanctuary, with a pyramidal tower crowned by a large square roof. The wall sculptures show Shiva as the *yogi* (north), dancing Shiva (west) and Dakshinamurti (south). The figures are flanked by attendant deities and guardians; *makaras* with foliated tails are positioned above.

The **Jvarahareshvara Temple**, facing east onto the road running south of the Ekambareshvara Temple, is one of the few monument at Kanchipuram dating from the 12C Chola era. Its unusual elliptical sanctuary adjoins a rectangular antechamber, columned hall and porch. The outer walls, raised on a finely modelled plinth, have pilasters standing in pots, pairs of pilasters framing niches, now empty, and pierced stone windows. The plaster-decorated brick tower, crowned with an elliptical domed roof, is a recent renovation. In front of the Temple are an altar and a small Nandi pavilion.

A short distance southeast of the Ekambareshvara Temple is the **Kamakshi Amman Temple**, one of the most popular in Shiva Kanchi. Modestly proportioned *gopuras* provide access into the almost square outer enclosure from the middle of four sides. The lower parts of the gateways are 16C. The east *gopura*, the most elaborate, has niches filled with carvings of Ganesha (right) and Subrahmanya (left). An ornate marriage hall stands freely within the outer enclosure, north of the main Temple. This ornate structure dates from the 16C Vijayanagara period. A frieze of *yalis* enlivens the basement; the column shafts have blocks covered with carvings. Cut-out colonettes mark the central aisles in both directions. The raised dais in the middle stands on a tortoise base. A large tank with a central pavilion occupies the north side of the enclosure.

The inner compound, in which the main shrine is situated, is entered on the east (access restricted to visitors). The original entrance, however, was from the south, judging by the altar, lamp column and Nandi pavilion arranged on this side. Kamakshi's sanctuary within is roofed with a rectangular gilded tower that rises above the walls.

A small abandoned **Shiva Temple**, set beneath street level, is seen near the northeast corner of the Kamakshi complex. This dilapidated 12C structure has a hemispherical roof with arched motifs. The **Matangeshvara Temple**, a short distance southeast of the complex, is a small, square 8C sanctuary, with a pyra-midal tower capped by a square roof. This adjoins a columned hall that opens to the west. Columns with seated lions at the base flank the entrance. This scheme is virtually repeated in the **Mukteshvara Temple**, further south.

The **Vaikuntha Perumal Temple**, built by Nandivarman II (731–96), the most important Pallava monument at Kanchipuram after the Kaliasanatha Temple, is located in the east part of Shiva Kanchi, near the railway station. The core building consists of sanctuaries arranged one above the other on three ascending levels. That on the lowest level, accommodating a standing image of Vishnu, is surrounded by a double corridor. The sanctuary at the intermediate level, with a seated image of Vishnu, has a single corridor. No corridor is found in the uppermost level, where Vishnu is shown in his reclining form.

The outer walls of the sanctuaries have pilastered bays, with images of Vishnu and his incarnations on the projections. The topmost sanctuary is capped with an octagonal roof. The lowest sanctuary adjoins a hall on the west, and is surrounded on four sides by a colonnade. The much-worn reliefs on the rear walls of the colonnade, some of which have labels, relate historical events pertaining to Pallava genealogy, including coronation scenes, receptions and battles. The columns in front have lion bases. The entrance hall and gateway, through which the Temple is entered, are later 16C additions.

The tour of Kanchipuram proceeds with a visit to the **Varadaraja Temple**, the focal monument of Vishnu Kanchi. According to local legend, this monument commemorates the site where Brahma performed a *yagna*, or fire sacrifice, to invoke the presence of Vishnu. This rite was carried out on a square altar raised high above the ground. The core of the Varadaraja Temple, elevated on an artif-ical square platform, accords to the description of Brahma's altar. High-towered *gopuras* on the east and west lead into the spacious outermost courtyard of the Temple. The east *gopura*, the finer of the two, was commissioned by Kumara Tatacharya, the spiritual preceptor of the Vijayanagara emperor Venkatapatideva (1586–1614). The tower is raised on a solid granite structure divided into two storeys, both with basements, pilastered projections and wall niches. The passageway entrance is bridged by a broad lintel carried on lotus brackets. The interior is flanked by jambs adorned with maidens clutching creepers. The brick-and-plaster tower presents an impressive pyramid of nine diminishing storeys, each with windows in the middle of the long sides. The capping vaulted roof has arched ends.

The 16C hall that stands freely within the outer court, just inside the west *gopura*, is one of the masterpieces of late Vijayanagara architecture. Its ornate basement is regularly punctuated by small niches; *yali* balustrades flank the staircase on the south. The sculptural treatment is elaborate throughout. Fully modelled warriors on rearing horses, Kama on the swan, and Rati on the parrot appear on the periphery. The horses are doubled at the corners, with *yalis* in between. The columns are overhung by curving eaves, with stone chains for hanging lamps at the corners. Animals with riders appear in multiple form on the piers surrounding the raised dais at the north end of the interior. The column shafts here have blocks covered with carvings of divinities, saints, amorous couples and jesters. Crouching *yalis* and elongated buds serve as brackets carrying the roof beams. North of the hall is a tank with a small pavilion in the middle. Another tank is located at the extreme east end of the same enclosure.

A small *gopura* on the west gives access to the intermediate enclosure of the Varadaraja Temple (access restricted to visitors). This is mostly occupied by columned halls and subsidiary shrines, dating from the 12C. The hall immediately in front of the west entrance to the innermost enclosure has Chola-style columns. The shrine dedicated to Anantalvar is a small 12C structure with simply moulded basements and pilastered walls; the tower has a hemispherical roof.

The shrine to Purundevi Tayar, the chief consort of Varadaraja, stands in the southwest corner. This 17C Nayaka structure has sharply cut pilasters standing in ornamental brackets, and delicately modelled eaves. The paintings on the adjacent swing pavilion illustrate the sports of Krishna: the youthful god steals the clothes of the *gopis* and dances on the hoods of the serpent Kaliya. In the hall opposite the nearby Narasimha shrine, Rati and Manmatha ride in aerial chariots, shooting a profusion of arrows.

The innermost enclosure of the Varadaraja Temple is occupied by a colonnade lining the perimeter walls. The Andal shrine, in the northwest corner, has elaborately carved columns depicting Vaishnava icons. A small gateway and a flight of steps ascend to the raised sanctuary that forms the core of the Temple. This enshrines bronze images of Vishnu flanked by consorts; guardian figures protect the doorway. The rectangular tower above has been renovated recently. The sanctuary is surrounded by a passageway with subsidiary shrines. The 18C paintings on the peripheral walls show presiding divinities of different Vaishnava centres and saintly and holy men. One scene, to the rear (east) of the sanctuary, illustrates shows the Garuda *vahana* being transported, together with parasols, fly-whisks and other insignia. A royal devotee on an elephant plays cymbals and sings the glory of Varadaraja.

The tour of Kanchipuram is only completed with an excursion across the Vegavati River to **Tiruparuttikunram**, southwest of the city, to visit the Jain complex known as **Trailokyanatha.** This consists of two double shrines, each with apsidal-ended sanctuaries, built in the 12C Chola style, with small towers capped by hemispherical roofs. The exteriors have been much renovated, and no sculptures have survived. The shrines, one of which is dedicated to Vardhamana, are preceded by a long hall with slender columns, an addition of the 17C. The ceilings are covered with paintings illustrating stories of the Jain saviours, particularly Rishabhadeva and Vardhamana in their former lives, arranged in long panels with labels. Some panels are filled by processions of elephants, soldiers, standard-bearers, dancers and musicians. One episode relates the story of Danendra, the serpent king, who offered his own kingdom to the relatives of Rishabhadeva so that they would not disturb the meditation of the saviour; the relatives are depicted within their walled cities. Another episode relates how Vardhamana overcame Sangama, a jealous god who assumed the form of a serpent; the hero stands before a tree, around which a snake is coiled. These narratives are twice interrupted by circular compositions that represent celestial audience chambers. They each show eight concentric rings containing miniature figures, trees and shrines, with a saviour enthroned in the middle.

The 9C **Chandraparabha Temple** stands immediately north of the Trailokyanatha. Its Pallava date is indicated by the rearing *yalis* on the wall pilasters, and the squat, square tower.

G. Uttiramerur

This town, 25km south of Kanchipuram, or 27km southwest of Chengalpattu, partly via NH45, is of interest for its two temples of the late Pallava period. These date from the reign of Dantivarman (798–817), and anticipate later Chola developments.

The **Sundaravarda Perumal Temple** was inspired by the Vaikuntha Perumal Temple at Kanchipuram, and consists of three sanctuaries arranged vertically, accommodating standing, seated and reclining forms of Vishnu. Other aspects of this divinity are housed in subsidiary shrines that project from three sides at each level. The upper storeys are reached by steps from the attached columned hall. The moulded basement of the outer walls of the Temple have *yalis* and *makaras* at the corners. The balustrades flanking the steps to subsidiary shrines are carved with panels, such as Lakshmi (south). The walls are plain, except for flat pilasters and shallow niches. The brick-and-plaster parapet that rises above the eaves has pronounced roof forms over the projecting shrines. The multi-storey tower is capped with a hemispherical roof. Its plaster ornamentation is recent.

· Only the lower parts of the nearby **Kailasanatha Temple** belong to the Pallava period; the attached hall and multi-storey tower are 11C additions. The hall columns display decorated shafts and fluted capitals.

H. Tiruttani

This small town, 86km northwest of Madras, 45km directly north of Kanchipuram, is renowned for the **Subrahmanya Temple**, built on top of a nearby hill. A path leads west from the centre of Tiruttani past a square tank with a central pavilion and a series of rest-houses, before climbing a long stepped path to the Temple. This is laid out on a sequence of ascending terraces. The doorways in the middle of the east side, which provide access to two concentric roofed enclosures, are cloaked in gilded brass sheets embossed with peacock motifs. The flagpole and altar between the two doorways are also clad in metal. The main sanctuary is a primitive structure dating from Pallava times, with icons of Subrahmanya on its outer walls. A gorgeously attired image of the god serves as the principal object of veneration within. The same divinity, riding a peacock and accompanied by consorts, is worshipped in two subshrines. A line of small stone statues of soldiers holding swords, representing Subrahmanya's votive army, is seen in the outer enclosure.

Of greater artistic interest is the modest **Virattaneshvara Temple**, located about 1.5km northeast of the centre of Tiruttani, on the other side of a rivulet. This 9C structure consists of a small east-facing apsidal-ended *linga* shrine. The similarly shaped vaulted roof has an arched frontal projection filled with the figures of a Somaskanda group. The sanctuary is entered through an antechamber and later porch. The niches on the outer walls house splendid examples of late Pallava sculptures: Vinayaka and Dakshinamurti (south), Vishnu (west) and Brahma and Durga (north). Loose icons of Shiva, Ganesha, Surya and the Matrikas are placed within the hall.

The road continues to Tirupati, 65km north.

I. Pulicat

This somewhat remote settlement gives its name to a shallow salt-water lagoon, about 60km long and up to 20km in breadth, beside the Bay of Bengal, on the border between Tamil Nadu and Andhra Pradesh. **Pulicat Lake** lies on the route of migratory birds, and harbours a host of flamingos, pelicans, kingfishers, cormorants, darters, egrets, herons, storks, spoonbills, ibis and ducks; there is an abundance of fish. The lagoon is separated from the ocean by a spit of land on which is situated the town of Pulicat, the ancient Palakkadu, 40km north of Madras.

> An important port for the Vijayanagara Governors of Chandragiri [35C] in the 15C–16C, Pulicat was well-known to European traders, especially for its finely woven and colourfully printed cotton textiles. In 1609 the Dutch built a fort here called Castel Geldria, which rapidly became the principal headquarters of Dutch commerce on the Coromandel Coast. This was occupied by the British in 1781–85 and again in 1795, before finally capitulating in 1824.

Of the original Dutch **Fort** at Pulicat, only the perimeter moat can now be made out. The **Dutch Cemetery**, to the west, is of greater interest. This is entered through an arched gate that bears the date 1656. The gateposts are carved with unusual life-size skeletal figures; one carries an hourglass on his head, the other a skull on a column. The tombstones, which range in date from 1658 to 1776, are elaborately carved with royal coats of arms; one example shows a relief representation of the original Fort. The mausoleum of one Dutch Governor is conceived as a small square structure with triple arches on four sides. The barrel vault which rises over has arched ends filled with plaster renditions of cherubs and coats of arms.

A dilapidated **Church** and a sundial adjoin the Cemetery.

38 · Vellore

Although Vellore may be visited as a day trip from Madras, an overnight stay is recommended, in order to have sufficient time to see the fort and temple within the city [A] and the relics of the Nawabs at nearby **Arcot** [B].

Hindu monuments of religious and artistic significance within easy reach of Vellore include those at **Vrinchipuram** [C], **Tiruvannamalai** [E] and **Chengam** [F]. An excursion to Tiruvannamalai may also include the Jain shrine at **Tirumalai** [D].

■ **Transport**. Vellore lies 140km west of Madras on NH4 and NH46, both highways continuing on to Bangalore [14]. The road connection with Madras and Kanchipuram [37F], 70km east, is preferred to the somewhat awkward rail link. Local buses reach all the sites mentioned here.

■ **Accommodation**. the *Hotel River View* (☎ 25568), 1km north of Vellore (STD code 0416) the city, is the best place to stay in Vellore; others include the *Mohan Mansion* (☎ 27083), *Nagha International Lodge* (☎ 26731) and *Mayura Lodge* (☎ 25488). It is also possible to stay at the new and comfortable *Hotel Trishul* (☎ 22219) at **Tiruvannamalai** (STD code 04175).

■ **Tourist Information**. None.

A. Vellore
This historical city, with its celebrated Fort, is best known today as the headquarters of the **Christian Medical College**, founded in 1900; its hospital and academic campus are prominent landmarks in the city.

> The Fort, northwest of the commercial heart of Vellore, a short distance from the Palar River, is traditionally associated with Chinna Bomma, the viceroy of the Aravidu kings of Chandragiri [35C] in the last decades of the 16C. He asserted his autonomy for a time, but was eventually crushed by Venkatapatideva in 1604, after which Vellore served as the second capital of the Vijayanagara emperors. The Fort was captured in 1676 by the Marathas, who held it until they were ousted in 1708 by Daud Khan, the general of the Mughal army. Soon after, Vellore became the headquarters of Murtaza Ali, the brother-in-law of the claimant to the Arcot throne. Vellore remained under the sway of Arcot until 1780, when a British garrison gained control in an attempt to resist the forces of Haidar Ali. After the fall of Srirangapattana [15C] in 1799, Tipu Sultan's family was detained here. The Fort remained in British hands until Independence, in spite of a mutiny in 1806.

Vellore's **Fort** is one of the outstanding examples of military architecture in Tamil Nadu. Its irregular quadrangular interior, almost 500m across, is defined by two lines of sloping walls, the outer skin being lower than the inner one. The walls are reinforced with round bastions topped by prominent curved battlements, with spaces between for musket fire. Finely finished box-like guardrooms project from the bastions and points between them. The walls are shielded by a broad moat bridged by a causeway on the east, the only entrance to the Fort.

The **Jalakanteshvara Temple** is one of the masterpieces of late 16C Vijayanagara architecture. Because it was abandoned for many years, the building was never subjected to disfiguring alterations or extensions; it was only reconsecrated as a place of worship in 1981. The Temple is contained within a square compound defined by high walls, some blocks of which are enlivened with shallow carvings of fish, entered on the south through an imposing *gopura*. The two lower granite storeys of this gateway are adorned with mouldings and ornate pilasters, some standing in pots, others framing niches, now empty. Above rise the seven diminishing storeys of the recently renovated brick-and-plaster pyramidal tower. The openings in the middle of each side are flanked by guardian figures. The arched ends of the vaulted roof are decorated with monster masks.

The **Kalyana Mandapa**, for which the monument is famous, is built into the southwest corner of the first enclosure of the Temple. The outer piers of the hall

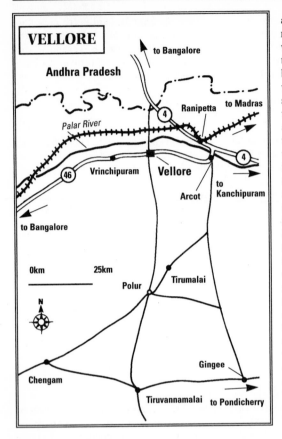

VELLORE

Andhra Pradesh

Palar River

to Bangalore

Ranipetta   to Madras

Vrinchipuram   **Vellore**

Arcot   to Kanchipuram

to Bangalore

0km   25km

N

Polur   Tirumalai

Gingee

Chengam

Tiruvannamalai   to Pondicherry

are fashioned as rearing *yalis*, some with elephant trunks, and richly bridled horses, all with riders; accessory themes include warriors, hunters and other beasts. The vitality of these vigorous compositions and the virtuosity of the carving, almost in the round, are unsurpassed in Southern Indian art. Panels of dancers separated by dwarfs adorn the low plinth on which the hall is raised. All the columns have blocks covered with miniature figures. The corner supports and those lining the central aisle are distinguished by attached colonettes of slender proportions. The ceiling over the central aisle is conceived as a pendant lotus, with parrots hanging upside-down from the petals. The flower is surrounded by a ring of dancing figures and rows of miniature deities. The dais on the elevated floor at the rear has a shallow tortoise base. A colonnade runs along the perimeter wall of the outer enclosure, expanded into columned halls at the corners. Numerous loose carvings are displayed here.

The inner *gopura* of the Jalakanteshvara Temple, imitating at a reduced scale that in the outer walls, gives access to the inner enclosure. The main shrine is a modest structure with undecorated walls. It is entered through the south porch of the columned hall to the east, requiring an almost complete circumambulation of the main unit. The hall gives access to a Nataraja sanctuary to the north and to the principal *linga* shrine to the west. The latter has a doorway flanked by large guardian figures, and is surrounded on three sides by a passageway. The plaster towers over the two shrines have been restored. A flag column and Nandi are placed outside a pierced stone window in the east wall of the hall. The peripheral colonnades wrap around shrines consecrated to Subrahmanya (west) and the goddess (northwest corner). A set of Shaiva saints is displayed in the south colonnade.

Several 19C British-style buildings are grouped around the tree-lined parade ground in the middle of the Fort. The finest is the **Court House**, at the south end. Facing east onto the square is the **Church of St John**, dating from 1846. Its modest but well-proportioned Neo-Classical portico is approached by a balustraded staircase. The **Archaeological Museum** next door (closed Fridays) occupies another historical building. The lower galleries are stocked with carvings and architectural pieces brought from various sites in the vicinity. They include a set of Dikpalas from Malpadi, and a large Lakshmi Narayana assembled from broken pieces. The upper level has an instructive photographic display of Indian maritime trade, as well as a selection of excavated prehistoric stone tools and pottery.

The ***Dargah* of Tipu Sultan's Family** lies 1.5km northeast of Vellore Fort, next to the road leading to Arcot. The tombs of Bakshi Begum, the wife of Haidar Ali and mother of Tipu, dated 1806, and of Badshah Begum, Tipu's wife, dated 1835, are conceived as octagonal arcaded chambers topped with ornamental parapets and domes raised on petalled necks. The graves of other family members are simpler structures.

B. Arcot

This town, 27km east of Vellore, on the south bank of the Palar River, is associated with a line of rulers known by their title as Nawabs.

> The Nawabs were descended from Daud Khan, the Mughal governor who occupied Arcot after the fall of Gingee [39E] in 1698. During the course of the 18C, both the French and the British came into conflict with the Nawabs for supremacy of this part of Tamil Nadu. In 1751 the East India Company sent Robert Clive to Arcot, to divert the enemy from the siege of Tiruchirapalli [41A]. The capture and subsequent defence of Arcot is an outstanding event in the military history of the period. Clive was forced to surrender to the French under Lally in 1758, but the town was recaptured by the British in 1760, only to be lost to Tipu Sultan in 1783. It was finally secured by the Government of Madras in 1799.

Perhaps because of the fierceness of these various struggles, Arcot preserves few relics of its past. The **Delhi Gate** is the only remaining portion of the brick walls that once surrounded the town. Of greater interest are the monuments near the river. The **Tomb of Sadatullah Khan**, who died in 1732, is surrounded by a colonnade topped with angled eaves and a parapet with domical finials. The same parapet and finials are repeated above the walls supporting the three-quarter spherical dome on a petalled neck. The **Jami Mosque**, in the northeast corner of the same compound, is topped with an ornate parapet running between slender octagonal minarets with domical tops. Other smaller tombs are located within the town.

Ranipetta, 4km north of Arcot on the opposite bank of the Palar River, is the railway station for Arcot. The settlement here marks the site that functioned as the cavalry station of the European quarter. The old **English Cemetery** has many tombs, dating from 1791 onwards. **St Mary's Church** of 1815 is a simple Neo-Classical structure typical of Cantonment religious architecture.

C. Vrinchipuram

This small town, 14km west of Vellore, on the south bank of the Palar River, is worth visiting because of the **Marghabandhu Temple**. This foundation is linked with the Nayakas of Gingee [39F], who were responsible for much of its renovation in the 17C. The Temple is a grandiose monument, out of all proportion to the earthern lanes and thatched houses that surround it. It is entered on the east through a large *gopura* of standard design; its seven-storey tower has been entirely refurbished. This gives access to the outer enclosure of the Temple. A hall with 36 columns, containing a flag column protruding above the roof, partly conceals the three-storeyed *gopura* leading to the inner enclosure. A well with a brick-and-plaster lion built over the steps is seen to the left; to the right is a columned hall with a raised platform at the rear.

Twin marriage halls with fine sculptures are fitted into the northwest and southwest corners of the outer enclosure. They appear to be modelled on the example at Vellore. The Vrinchipuram halls are smaller and lower, but repeat the same arrangement of *yali* and horse columns with riders on the periphery, and pilastered columns at the corners and along the central aisles. The northwest hall has additional figures of the Nayaka patron and wife projecting from the pair of columns in front of the raised dais at the rear. The apsidal-ended *linga* shrine at the core of the inner enclosure of the Temple, possibly dating back to the 12C, is contained within later colonnades. It is approached through a hall with lateral steps on the north and south; a window in the middle of the east wall is aligned with the sanctuary. A Natesha shrine is placed against the north wall of the enclosure.

D. Tirumalai

This small hamlet lies 18km northeast of Polur on the Tiruvannamalai road, 48km south of Vellore. The 16C Jain complex, built next to a granite outcrop, is of interest for the fragmentary paintings. The **Lower Temple** enshrines a large carved image of seated Mahavira; a tree of life is painted on the wall behind the saviour. Steps ascend to the **Upper Temple**, inside which brass images are displayed. The rock above has carvings of different Jinas, including Bahubali and Parshvanatha. **Brick Chambers** at two levels are built into the rocky overhang. The walls and granite ceilings at the upper level are plastered and painted. Floral designs cover most of the surfaces, but there are also unusual circular diagrams. These cosmographs show Jinas in the middle, surrounded by segments filled with different peoples.

E. Tiruvannamalai

This pilgrimage town is located 82km south of Vellore, but can also be reached from Pondicherry [39A], 103km east. The fort at Gingee, 37km east, can be visited on the way to Pondicherry.

Tiruvannamalai is celebrated for the Arunachaleshvara Temple, one of the grandest in Tamil Nadu. The festival that takes place here in November–December is accompanied by a popular cattle fair. On the night of the tenth day of celebrations, a huge bonfire is lit on the summit of the rocky hill that rises steeply west of the town. This fire burns for many days and is visible from a great distance. Devotees prostrate themselves at the sight of the flames, considered to be the manifestation of Shiva's fiery *linga* that is enshrined in the Temple below.

Tiruvannamalai is dotted with small shrines dedicated to different deities, including Durga and Subrahmanya. Its tanks are associated with the directional guardian divinities such as Agni and Indra. Float festivals take place here regularly. A popular rite is the auspicious circumambulation of the mountain. The route is marked by regularly spaced shrines and wells. **Sri Ramanasram**, the spiritual retreat founded by the celebrated guru Ramana Maharishi, who died in 1950, is pleasantly located in a shady compound 1km southwest of the town. Its international reputation is confirmed by the many foreign visitors who flock there.

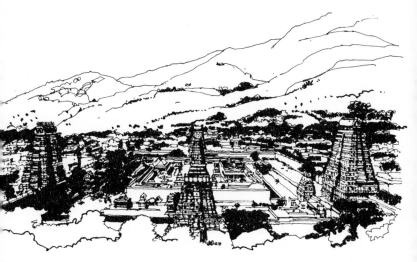

Arunachaleshvara Temple, Tiruvannamalai

The innermost streets of Tiruvannamalai echo the rectangular configuration of the **Arunachaleshvara Temple**, whose high walls define three concentric enclosures, the east portions of which extend to form a sequence of three spacious courts. The *gopuras* positioned on the four sides are aligned with each other in both directions, to create a layout of remarkable clarity. The Temple is usually approached from the east, through colonnades with wide central passageways accommodating a market of lively shops. One colonnade is roofed with corbelled timbers; another has modern painted compositions on its stone ceiling.

Of the four *gopuras* in the middle of the outermost circuit of walls, that on the east is the largest, rising no less than 66m high. It is assigned to the renovation undertaken by the Nayakas of Thanjavur [40A] in the first half of the 17C. The ornamentation of the lower granite elements of the gateways is elaborate, with decorated basements, pilasters and eaves. Finely carved figures are inserted into the wall niches: for example, on the outer (east) face, Shiva as Bhikshatanamurti (north) and the same god dancing within the skin of the elephant (south). The ten diminishing brick-and-plaster towers create a soaring pyramidal mass, capped by a vaulted roof with arched ends. Shallow projections lining the passageway walls are divided into panels framing dancing female figures, with *yalis* at either side; dwarfs serve as brackets above. The jambs have maidens clutching creepers. Carved panels on the lintels show the mock battle of Kama and Rati, Shiva seated with consorts, and elephants worshipping the *linga*. A painted ceiling composition depicts royal elephants.

The outermost court of the Arunachaleshvara Temple is reached after passing through the east *gopura*. The north side of the enclosure is occupied by an immense columned hall, dating from the 17C. The outer row of 34 piers has blocks carved with different deities. A *linga* chamber at one end is set at a lower level. A large stepped tank surrounded by colonnades is located on the south side of the enclosure. The small east-facing Subrahmanya shrine stands near the edge of the water. The intricate treatment of its walls and columns is typical of the late 16C style. A large seated Nandi and swing pavilion are placed in the middle of the compound. Four smaller *gopuras* with less decorated walls, partly dating back to the 14C, lead into the second enclosure. Here, there is another stepped tank, as well as a large columned hall, with an open colonnade facing south. Traces of paintings on the ceiling include a scene showing the marriage of Shiva and Parvati.

Access to the third innermost enclosure of the Temple is provided by a single *gopura* on the east. The lower portions of the gateway are modest and unadorned, suggesting a 11C date. The shrine to Shiva standing inside the enclosure, on an axis with this *gopura*, is surrounded on three sides by plain walls covered with inscriptions. This is entered through a columned porch on the east, partly containing an earlier lamp column, altar and Nandi. Small shrines, with exquisitely decorated walls and columns consecrated to Subrahmanya and Ganesha, are positioned at either side.

The *linga* sanctuary is surrounded on four sides by a spacious corridor, an addition of the 19C. The aisle approaching the sanctuary is adorned with hanging glass lamps; the doorway is decorated with an embossed arch frame. The sanctuary, a renovated Chola structure, displays later carvings of Dakshinamurti (south), Shiva appearing out of the *linga* (west) and Brahma (north) in its outer walls. Stone *lingas* and a complete set of brass Nayanmars are displayed in the surrounding colonnades. The associated Devi shrine occupies the northwest corner of the same enclosure. Two columned halls precede the principal sanctuary. The central; aisle of the inner hall is surrounded by an array of different goddesses, the almost three-dimensional figures dating from the 18C. A small *linga* shrine in the northeast corner of the enclosure dates from Chola times

F. Chengam

This small town, 34km west of Tiruvannamalai, is worth visiting for the unassuming, but artistic, **Venugopala Parthasarathi Temple**. This consists of a simple east-facing shrine preceded by an open hall, the inner space of which is defined by columns with *yalis* and cut-out colonnettes. The ceiling over the central space is covered with *Ramayana* paintings laid out in narrow registers, each incident identified by captions in Tamil and Telugu. Several episodes depict local versions of the story, such as the scene of Hanuman dragging Ravana's queen by the hair. Rows of geese surround the central carved lotus. The painted compositions are characterised by precise line work and lively postures.

39 · Pondicherry

This city, now officially renamed **Puduchcheri**, is the capital of the Union Territory named after it, which incorporates the former French settlements of Southern India that were handed over to the Indian Government in 1954. (These include Yanon [30G], Karaikal [40P] and Mahé [48E].) Though Pondicherry does not form part of Tamil Nadu, it makes a logical point from which to reach a number of historical sites in the state which surrounds it.

At least one day should be reserved for the sights of the city [A] and those of nearby **Ariyankuppam** [B], **Auroville** [C] and **Villianur** [D].

A full-day excursion to the fort at **Gingee** [F] can be combined with a stop at

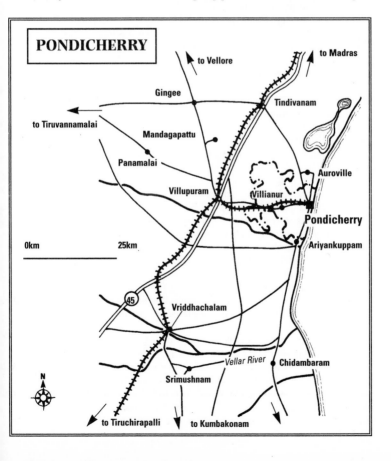

the cave-temple at **Mandagapattu** [E] or the hill shrine at **Panamalai** [G], both dating from the Pallava period. From Gingee it is possible to continue on to Tiruvannamalai [38E] and Vellore [38A].

Another full-day trip from Pondicherry may be devoted to the celebrated Nataraja temple at **Chidambaram** [H] and you can then continue on to Kumbakonam [40G]. The temples at **Srimushnam** [I] and **Vriddhachalam** [J] are accessible from Chidambaram.

■ **Transport**. Regular bus services link Pondicherry with Madras, 160km north, but the train link is unsatisfactory. Frequent local buses from Pondicherry reach all the destinations described here; Vriddhachalam is the only site with a reliable train connection.

■ **Accommodation**. The *Hotel Mass* (☎ 27221) and *Hotel Ram International* (☎ 27230) are the best in Pondicherry (STD code 04145) , but only the *Park Guest House* (☎ 36695), run by the Aurobindo *Ashram*, overlooks the ocean. Other *Ashram* accommodations are available at Auroville. An attractive alternative is to be based at the villa-styled *Hotel Pondicherry Ashok* (☎ 85460), 12km north of Pondicherry on the coastal road. Visitors wishing to explore **Gingee** (STD 04144) at some length may stay at the *Hotel Shivasand* (☎ 22218). The *Hotel Saradharama* (☎ 22966) offers adequate accommodation in **Chidambaram** (STD code 04144).

■ **Tourist Information**. The office of the Pondicherry Tourism Development Corporation is situated on Goubert Salai, overlooking the ocean (☎ 39497).

A. Pondicherry

The old part of Pondicherry facing the Bay of Bengal retains much of its French personality.

In 1672 the French secured land for a trading post beside the Bay of Bengal from Ali Adil Shah II, the ruler of Bijapur [23A]. The settlement established by François Martin, laid out over two years, served as the headquarters for the expansion of French influence in Southern India. Pondicherry was occupied by the Dutch in 1693–97, and changed hands between the British and the French no less than nine times in the course of the 18C. Under Joseph Francois Dupleix, Governor in 1741–54, Pondicherry regained its former importance. However, in 1761 the British captured the city and demolished many of its finest buildings. Pondicherry was finally restored to the French in 1817. In 1940 it declared for the Free French.

Pondicherry is known internationally as the headquarters of the **Sri Aurobindo** *Ashram*. This was founded in 1926 by Sri Aurobindo, one of India's greatest philosopher-poets, and has developed since then into a popular and affluent organization. After Aurobindo's death in 1950, the running of the *Ashram* was entrusted to Mirra Alfassa, his chief disciple, known as the Mother, who died at the age of 93 in 1973. The *Ashram* is located on Rue de la Marine, where the *samadhi* that entombs the mortal remains of Aurobindo and the Mother is on display.

AUROVILLE, MADRAS

N

SARDAR VALLABHAI PATEL SALAI (NORTH BLVD.)

THIYAGA RAJA ST

P COIL ST

M A COIL ST

I D COIL ST

K A COIL ST

P. COIL ST

L THOLLANDAL ST

B DERICHEMONT ST

Institut Français

SRI AUROBINDO ST

SUPAYA CHETTAR ST

DUPUY ST

Sri Aurobindo Ashram

C KOIL ST

CANTEEN ST

A MADAM ST

F MARTIN ST

RUE NEHRU

MISSION ST

RANGA PILLAI ST

Raj Nivas

VELLAJA ST

House of Ananda Rangapillai

NIDARAJAPAYER ST

ANNA SALAI (WEST BLVD)

SS PILAI ST

BHARATI ST

ST THERESA ST

Church of our Lady of the Immaculate Conception

CAPT XAVIER ST

GINGEE SALAI

V SIMONEL ST

GOVERNMENT PARK

Gandhi Memorial

SINNA PAPPARA ST

LAPPORTH ST

MONTHORSIER ST

C MUDHALIAR ST

MAHATMA GANDH ROAD

Museum

GOUBERT SALAI (BEACH RD)

CHIDAMBARAM, KUMBAKONAM

Church of Our Lady of the Angels

LAL BAHADUR SASTRI ST

RUE SUFFREN ST

ROMAIN ROLAND ST

i

Church of the Sacred Heart of Jesus

Ecole Française

BAY OF BENGAL

SUBBAIYAH SALAI (SOUTH BLVD)

Railway Station

PONDICHERRY

0   400 yards
0   400 metres

The **Plan** of old Pondicherry, with its distinctive grid pattern of roads, was laid out in 1756–77 by Jean Law. The most important streets run perpendicular to the Bay of Bengal. Goubert Salai, the broad Marina running beside the ocean, is lined with handsome whitewashed buildings with colonnaded balconies. Similarly styled mansions, many with lush gardens surrounded by high walls, can be glimpsed in the streets behind.

Several villas have been converted into research institutions, such as the **Ecole Française d'Extreme Orient** and the **Institut Français**, both with fine libraries. A typical example of Pondicherry domestic architecture is the **House of Ananda Rangapillai**, the diarist and protegé of Dupleix on Ranga Pillai Street (permission required to visit). Its reception rooms open off a central court with colonnades at two levels. The House is noteworthy for its carved woodwork. Midway along Goubert Salai is the **Gandhi Memorial**, with a statue of the Mahatma surrounded by an arc of eight lofty granite columns more than 11m high, allegedly brought from Gingee. The 27m high **Lighthouse** of 1836 stands nearby. The shady **Government Park** lies on an axis with the Memorial. Its tree-lined paths fan out from a central pavilion with pedimented façades, crowned by an urn. The north side of the Park is occupied by **Raj Nivas**, built on the site of Dupleix's residence.

The former Government Library, opposite Raj Nivas, is now the **Pondicherry Museum** (closed Mondays). The lower rooms contain stone and metal sculptures from the Pallava and Chola periods, as well as arts, crafts, arms and even snail shells. Among the most important exhibits are the artefacts recovered from excavations at Arikamedu [B]. They include fragments of 1C–2C Roman amphorae, gems, lamps and glass moulds. Local pottery from this site is represented by grey and red wares, usually with simple incised designs, and burial urns. The coins and fragments of Chinese celadon pottery found at Arikamedu date from the 11C–12C. The upper rooms of the Museum are stocked with furniture, paintings and other articles taken from various mansions in Pondicherry.

The French presence at Pondicherry is still evident in the many Catholic places of worship that dot the city. The **Church of Our Lady of the Angels**, on Rue Romain Rolland, south of Government Park, dates from 1855. Its façade, flanked by two unadorned square towers, faces east towards the ocean. The interior is roofed by a barrel vault, with a great dome rising over the crossing. The oil painting of Our Lady in the altar was presented by Napoleon III. The Tomb of the Marquis de Bussy, one of Dupleix's most enterprising followers, dated 1785, is seen in the cemetery next door. A statue of Jeanne d'Arc stands in the middle of the small square opposite.

The **Church of Our Lady of the Immaculate Conception**, on Cathedral Street, was begun in 1770 by the Jesuits, but was not completed until 1791. The imposing façade presents paired Doric columns below and Ionic above, the latter flanked by curving volutes. A statue of Our Lady occupies a round-headed niche in the central pedimented bay. The interior has plain barrel vaults, with a central dome pierced with eight circular openings. An octagonal lantern rises above.

The **Church of the Sacred Heart of Jesus**, on South Boulevard, is built in a contrasting Neo-Gothic manner, with towers flanking a central gable and stained-glass windows on the sides. The **Church of the Assumption** of 1851 is found at **Nellitoppu**, on the western outskirts of the city. An image of Our Lady is placed in a niche over the main entrance; on the left tower, a figure of St George is shown slaying a *yali*-like monster. The vaulted interior is notable for its elegant gilded altarpieces, the finest in Pondicherry. That at the west end shows a Crucifix within a canopy animated with flying angels.

B. Ariyankuppam

This insignificant village, 4km south of Pondicherry, is of interest for the **Church of Our Lady of Good Health**, founded in 1690 and subsequently rebuilt several times. The interior has rounded arches carrying a vault over the central aisle. A free-standing Crucifix is displayed upon the altar; brightly painted wooden images are set on shelves in the side walls.

The archaeological site of **Arikamedu** is located 1km east, on the south bank of a lagoon formed by the Ariyankuppam River. Excavations revealed traces of a port that flourished in the 1C–2C, trading mainly with the Mediterranean. The architectural remains, which included vestiges of brick structures, possibly warehouses, and a courtyard with two small tanks, are no longer visible. Roman artefacts were discovered here, many of which can be seen in the Pondicherry Museum.

C. Auroville

The Mother conceived the utopian settlement of Auroville, 8km north of Pondicherry. Founded in 1968, this has grown steadily over the years into a sizeable and cosmopolitan community, with comfortable villas set in spacious grounds on the fringe of the ocean. The names of the residences, Shanti (peace), Grace, Verité, Horizon, Transition, Gratitude, etc., express the spiritual aspirations of Auroville's population. Other than religious pursuits, the community has revived traditional industries: its workshops produce fine woven textiles, marble-dyed silks, handmade papers, perfumes and incense sticks. An active press disseminates the writings of Aurobindo and the Mother.

The visionary **Plan** of Auroville, with lines of buildings spiralling outwards in continuous motion, symbolises the universality of its faith. The nucleus of this scheme is marked by an open-air circular amphitheatre, the **Bharat Nivas**, intended for cultural performances, surrounded by meditation rooms and beautifully maintained gardens laid out in petal formation. They converge on the recently completed **Matrimandir** (check timings for visits), a remarkable spherical structure created from panels hung on a concrete frame. Its staircases ascend to an inner sealed chamber with white marble floor and walls. Daylight entering from a hole in the roof is directed to a large crystal globe which glows mysteriously, providing a focus for meditation.

D. Villianur

This small town, 11km west of Pondicherry, is of interest for the **Tirukameshvara Temple.** The Temple is entered from the east through a simple portico facing onto the main street. An open colonnade leads to an inner *gopura*, restored in 1887 with funds provided by a French official. This gives access to the east half of the inner zone, mostly occupied by a columned hall, with a central space surrounded by carvings of horses with riders and other figures. The central ceiling panel has a lotus surrounded by deities. The west half of the inner zone contains the principal *linga* sanctuary and subsidiary Devi and Murugan shrines, dating back to the 12C Chola era, which are entirely encased in later colonnades. North of this inner enclosure is a large square tank with a pavilion in the middle. The large *gopura* on the south has finely worked niches filled with sculptures. The seven-storeyed tower has been much renovated.

The **Church of Our Lady of Lourdes** at Villianur was erected in 1876 in imitation of the Basilica in France. The statue of Notre Dame was donated by the French Government a year later. The Church boasts its own tank, a unique feature. Large crowds gather here for ritual bathing during the festival honouring the Madonna, held in June.

E. Mandagapattu

The 7C **Cave Temple** at this site is located 60km northwest of Pondicherry, 2km east of the road leading to Gingee, 20km north of Villupuram. Mandagapattu is one of the earliest Pallava shrines, comparable with examples at Mamallapuram [37A] and Tiruchirapalli [41A]. Although an inscription of Mahendravarman I (580–630) mentions the worship of Brahma, Shiva and Vishnu, no icons of these gods have been found here. The façade present a simple line of massive part-octagonal columns leading into a hall. Guardian figures with clubs are seen at either end.

F. Gingee

This fortified site, the most spectacular in Tamil Nadu, lies 68km northwest of Pondicherry via Tindivanam; alternatively, it may be reached from Tiruvannamalai [38E], 37km west. The Gingee site lies about 1.5km west of the town of the same name, and is easily accessible by road.

> Gingee rose to prominence under Vijayanagara [20B–C] in the 15C–16C, as a strategic outpost guarding the northern reaches of the Tamil country. The Gingee Governors steadily asserted their autonomy, openly proclaiming their independence during the civil war of 1614, in which they took up arms against Venkatapatideva of Chandragiri [35C]. Gingee was threatened by the Adil Shahi forces of Bijapur [23A], and succumbed to them in 1648. The invaders renamed Gingee as Badshahbad, and occupied it for almost 30 years. In 1677 the Maratha chief Shivaji successfully besieged the fort, followed in 1698 by the Mughal general Zulficar Khan. But the site proved malarial, and in 1716 the Mughal forces, now virtually independent of Delhi, shifted their headquarters to Arcot [38B]. In the middle of the 18C Gingee was taken by a detachment of French soldiers, who held it until the capture of Pondicherry by the British. Gingee was garrisoned by Arcot troops and a few British soldiers in 1780, during Haidar Ali's invasion of Tamil Nadu. The site was abandoned by the beginning of the 19C.

Gingee consists of a trio of formidable mountain **Citadels**: Krishnagiri (north), Rajagiri (east) and Chandrayandurg (south), each defended by lines of thick granite walls built into the steep sides of the rocky hills. Substantial **Ramparts** with round bastions and a broad moat connecting the Citadels create a vast triangular zone, more than 1.5km from north to south. Intermediate walls divide this area into Inner and Outer Enclosures.

The tour of Gingee described here begins at the **East Gate** of the Inner Enclosure. This is shielded by outworks containing a passageway with no less than four changes of direction before the actual doorway is reached. An arched portal, standing freely inside, provides a ceremonial entrance to an ensemble of courtly structures, only partly revealed by the excavators. This is dominated by the towered **Kalyana Mahal**, a courtly feature consisting of a square pond, now devoid of water, surrounded by an arcade and overlooked on the north by a six-storeyed tower. This has arched openings on each side, and a staircase block in the middle. The rooftop pavilion is capped with a pyramidal roof displaying tiers of eave-like mouldings. The remains of earthenware pipes embedded in the walls suggest a sophisticated hydraulic system.

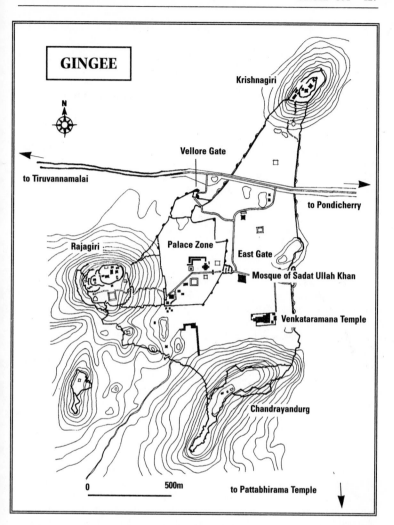

Triple lines of arcaded chambers, probably **Stables** for horses and their grooms, stretch north from the Kalyana Mahal. They define a large open **Parade Ground**. An excavated structure with a central chamber surrounded by a colonnade, at the west end of the Parade Ground, may have been a **Royal Residence**. In front (east) is a green-stone slab supported on legs, with a large block imitating a cloth bolster. This could have served as a formal seat for the Gingee Nayakas to oversee the processions of troops and animals.

A large **Tank** south of the Parade Ground, partly cut into the rock, is surrounded by colonnades. Several large **Granaries** with curving brick vaults stand in the vicinity. One example has ornate plaster decoration on the sides and ends of the vault; another example, further southwest, ingeniously combines three vaulted chambers and a connecting corridor within a quadrangle of walls. The path proceeding southwest from the Kalyana Mahal passes through a gate before ascending **Rajagiri**, the highest of the mountain Citadels, rising more than 165m above the plain. Though the summit is reached only after a strenuous climb, visitors are rewarded with splendid panoramas. At the top stand two small **Shrines**, several **Granaries** and the ruined **Flagstaff Tower**. The last structure may have once resembled the tower of the Kalyana Mahal. It is necessary to descend by the same route to the East Gate of the Inner Enclosure before continuing the tour.

Immediately in front (east) of the Gate stands the **Mosque of Sadat Ullah Khan I** (1703–10), erected by one of the Arcot rulers. The façade of the prayer chamber has seven arches with lobed profiles, surmounted by an arcaded parapet flanked by octagonal finials with domical tops. A small courtyard with a central pond in front is raised on arcades.

About 500m southeast stands the abandoned and dilapidated **Venkataramana Temple.** This 16C monument is entered through a prominent *gopura* on the east; the seven-storeyed tower is still intact. *Ramayana* scenes and Vaishnava divinities are carved on the side walls of the passageway. The outer enclosure of the Temple is occupied by columned halls of different designs. A second *gopura* on the east leads into the inner enclosure. Here stands a trio of east-facing shrines, the two side ones dedicated to Vishnu's consorts. The treatment of their outer walls is sombre. A fourth shrine projects outwards from the middle of the west enclosure wall. Pavilions with quartets of slender columns capped by brick towers stand in the fields outside the Temple.

Another feature worth seeing in the Outer Enclosure at Gingee is the **Vellore Gate**, easily reached from the main road that runs through the middle of the site. This, too, makes use of extensive curving outworks to shield the entrance. A line of steps ascends to **Krishnagiri** from a point where the Ramparts on the east side of the Outer Enclosure are cut by the main road. Several structures are clustered on the summit of this Citadel. They include an an open **Audience Hall**, with a curious fluted domed and projecting balconies, two vaulted **Granaries**, an **Oil Well** and the modest **Ranganatha** and **Krishna shrines**.

The last building to be described at Gingee is the **Pattabhirama Temple**, 2km southwest of the town, hidden from the main road and from the fortified site. Even more ruined than the Venkataramana Temple, this example is also laid out with a trio of east-facing shrines dedicated to the god and his two consorts. A short distance in front (east) of the *gopura* stands a lofty pavilion raised on a decorated basement. The steps in the middle of each side are flanked by balustrades decorated with pairs of elephants, *yalis*, geese and double-headed birds holding diminutive elephants in their beaks. The 12 slender columns with 16-sided shafts support curving stone eaves and a group of five brick towers.

Another noteworthy monument in the Gingee area is found at **Singavaram**, 3km north. This site is known for its 7C **Cave Temple**, cut into the east face of a large boulder perched above the village, reached by a long flight of steps. Structural additions from later periods, including a gateway, are built up to the Cave Temple. Guardian figures are sculpted either side of the colonnade that frames the hall. The shrine within has its rear wall almost entirely taken up with a 5m long image of Ranganatha. A stalk rising from the navel of the reclining god blossoms into a lotus upon which Brahma is seated. Bhudevi appears at the feet of the god, while Garuda and other attendants are seen to the sides. Immediately north of the Cave Temple is a deep niche with Durga standing on the buffalo head.

G. Panamalai

This small village, 75km west of Pondicherry on the road from Villupuram to Vettavalam, is of interest for the **Talagirishvara Temple** that stands on top of a nearby hill. This important 8C Pallava structure is built entirely out of local reddish granite. The walls of the square sanctuary project outwards on four sides to accommodate an entrance chamber and three subshrines. The regularly spaced pilasters have rearing lions at the bases. The pyramidal superstructure with vaulted roofs rises over the projecting shrines and entrance chamber; it is capped by a hemispherical roof. A multi-faceted *linga* on a circular pedestal stands before a relief Somaskanda panel in the central shrine. Similar, but smaller, *lingas* are placed in the subshrines. The traces of paintings here include a mural fragment in the north subshrine, depicting Shiva dancing attended by Parvati. The hall adjoining the sanctuary to the east is a later addition.

H. Chidambaram

This town, 67km south of Pondicherry, is celebrated for the great **Nataraja Temple**, in which Shiva is worshipped in his form as Lord of the Dance. The Temple is believed to mark the site of the legendary dance contest won by Shiva in a bid to impress his consort Parvati, and legend places it as the source of the original *linga*. Founded in the Chola era, it remains one of the major pilgrimage destinations in Tamil Nadu. The management of the shrines within the complex is under the control of local Dikshita brahmins.

The Nataraja Temple occupies an area of about 22ha in the middle of Chidambaram. It is contained within a quadrangle of enclosure walls surrounded by broad streets used for chariot festivals at various times throughout the year. When not in use, these ceremonial cars are parked in the streets, where they can be inspected for their intricately worked wooden carvings. The outermost set of enclosure walls, added in the 17C, has entrances with simple porticos in the middle of each side. Passageways flanked by low walls lead from each entrance to a towered *gopura* in the second set of walls.

The four **Gopuras** that frame the Temple are the finest of the Chola period, demonstrating the monumental style achieved in the 12C. The gates conform to a standard scheme. The lower granite walls are divided into two storeys, each with moulded basements, pilastered niches and overhanging eaves. The upper storey is heightened, and displays additional pilasters standing in pots and false windows with geometric designs. The architectural elements are adorned with delicately incised foliage and scrollwork. Sculpted icons inserted into the wall niches at both levels depict the full range of Shaiva mythology. They include Shiva as the ascetic with a trident and the same god dancing on the demon (east *Gopura*), Bhikshatanamurti, Durga and Sarasvati (north *Gopura*), Dakshina-murti and the Navagrahas (south *Gopura*) and Subrahmanya (west *Gopura*). Sages, guardians and attendants appear on all the *Gopuras*.

The jambs lining the lofty passageways inside the gates are divided into

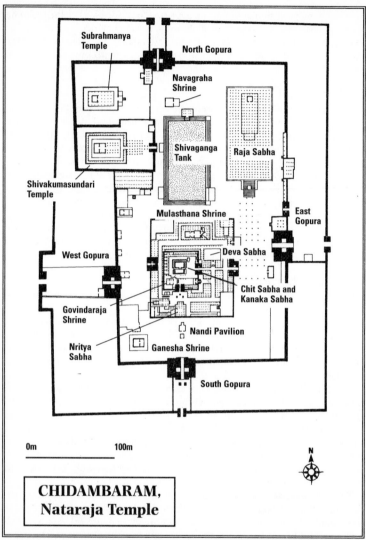

Subrahmanya
Temple

North Gopura

Navagraha
Shrine

Raja Sabha

Shivaganga
Tank

Shivakumasundari
Temple

Mulasthana Shrine

East
Gopura

West Gopura

Deva Sabha

Chit Sabha and
Kanaka Sabha

Govindaraja
Shrine

Nandi Pavilion

Nritya
Sabha

Ganesha Shrine

South Gopura

0m   100m

N

**CHIDAMBARAM,
Nataraja Temple**

panels carved with maidens in different dance movements; identification labels
accompany each of the 108 postures (east and west *Gopuras*). The wall niches
house sculptures of deities and donors. A delicately modelled portrait of
Krishnadevaraya of Vijayanagara (north *Gopura*) dates from the visit of this
emperor to the Temple in 1516. The brick-and-plaster towers above have been
much altered in later times. They are divided into seven diminishing storeys,
each covered with plaster sculptures. The shallow projections in the middle of
the long sides have openings at each level. The towers are capped by vaulted
roofs with arched ends and pot finials.

A spacious paved court is reached after passing through the *Gopuras*. The main Temple, contained within its own quadrangle of walls, occupies much of the south half of the enclosure. It is entered on the east or west through lesser *gopuras*. The space inside is almost entirely filled with colonnades and subshrines, many dating from the 19C. The **Nritya Sabha**, in the south corridor, is an ornate structure assigned to the late Chola period. This 13C hall is elevated on a double basement adorned with rows of dancers, dwarfs and *yalis*. The wheels with prancing horses are partly concealed by abutting colonnades of a later era. The columns of the Nritya Sabha are intricately carved with miniature temple façades; the ceiling is panelled with fully modelled lotuses. A wall niche housing a Bhikshatanamurti image is framed by fluted pilasters. Among the other features of interest here is the Devi shrine in the north corridor.

Two gates on the east, the one with a tower being recent, and on the south provide access to the innermost enclosure. In the middle stand the south-facing **Chit Sabha** and attached **Kanaka Sabha**, the two hut-like chambers that constitute the ritual focus of the Temple. They are unique in the religious architecture of Tamil Nadu, since they reproduce the forms of simple thatched structures. Raised on a common masonry platform, the two chambers are built entirely of wood, with timber columns, panelled walls and curving roofs cloaked in sheets of gilded copper. Though dating back to Chola times, the Sabhas have been continually renewed through the centuries. Two forms of Shiva are enshrined here: the bronze icon of Nataraja and the space (*akasha*) *linga*, fashioned of crystal. The east-facing Govindaraja shrine which stands next door houses a reclining image of Vishnu.

The **Raja Sabha**, a vast columned hall founded in the 12C, occupies the northeast corner of the outer enclosure. It seems to have served a royal ceremonial purpose and is linked with the Chola kings, who are known to have resided at Chidambaram. Large elephants with attendants are sculpted on the east and west sides of the high basement. The broad steps and porch on the south are additions of the 17C; the curving brick vaults belong to the 18C Maratha period. The dais at the north end of the central aisle is for displaying processional images at festival time; the two principal festivals celebrated are Ani Tirumanjanam in June–July, and Markashi Tiruvathirai in December–January. The large rectangular **Shivaganga Tank** dominates the north part of the enclosure. Two east-facing shrines, each standing within an independent walled compound, are located in the northwest corner of the enclosure.

The **Shivakamasundari Shrine** houses the goddess associated with Nataraja. Its entrance gate, with curving balustrades flanking the steps, is assigned to the Chola period, as is the surrounding colonnade, which is elevated on a basement enlivened with carvings of dancers and musicians. The columned halls preceding the sanctuary are later additions, as is obvious from the paintings that cover the ceiling of the outer hall. Those on the side aisles are among most important examples of Nayaka pictorial art. The 17C compositions are arranged in narrow registers. One set of panels (north aisle) relates the story of Shiva as Bhikshatanamurti. The god appears here as the naked beggar holding a parasol, accompanied by a beautiful, scantily clad woman, identified as Mohini. The following scene shows the sages being seduced by Mohini, while their wives fall under the spell of Bhikshatanamurti. In a later episode, the sages tend a sacrificial fire, out of which demons are produced, only to be repelled by Shiva.

The panels illustrating the life of Manikkavachakar are mostly devoted to the childhood of the saint and his exploits as a youth in the service of the Pandya king. A vivid episode illustrates Shiva's revenge on the king for punishing Manikkavachakar: disguised as a trader, Shiva delivers a pack of jackals transformed into horses to the king's stables; the jackals pounce on the king's horses; the saint stands on the bank of a river with a stone on his back; Shiva then makes the river overflow its banks, with people swimming frantically through the water. In the narrative of Cheraman Perumal (south aisle), another of the Nayanmars, the hero is shown riding an elephant accompanied by soldiers, on the way to Chidambaram to worship Nataraja. A further panel (north aisle) illustrates the story of Upamanyu. Modern paintings covering the ceiling over the central space of the hall illustrate the story of Kamasundari. The scenes are identified by helpful Tamil and English labels.

The **Subrahmanya Shrine**, in the compound immediately to the north, dates from the Chola era, as is clear from the treatment of the outer walls and the hall columns, with superimposed façades on the shafts. The later brick vaults are covered with 19C paintings, including views of the principal temples in Tamil Nadu associated with Murugan, to whom the Shrine is dedicated.

I. Srimushnam

This little-visited town, 40km west of Chidambaram, has a pair of religious monuments dating from different periods, unusually arranged back to back. The east-facing **Nityeshvara Temple** is a Chola foundation dating from the 10C, recently restored. It stands in a rectangular compound, entered through a gateway overlooking a large tank with a central pavilion. The small square sanctuary has finely executed figures set in niches headed with *makaras*: Dakshinamurti flanked by sages (south), Shiva appearing out of the *linga* (west), Brahma (north). The adjoining hall is a later addition.

The west-facing **Bhuvaraha Temple** is an elaborate 17C monument spnsored by the Gingee Nayakas. The complex is entered through *gopuras* on the north and west, the latter being more imposing, with a seven-storeyed tower, recently renewed. A lofty columned hall, with spacious cross aisles, altars and a Garuda shrine, leads to a 16-columned pavilion, originally a free-standing structure. Its ornate sculptural treatment marks this as one of the masterpieces of Nayaka art. Its peripheral supports are raised on a basement carved with friezes of musicians and dancers, as well as miniature divinities standing in niches. The shafts here have *yalis* and horses with riders projecting outwards, with groups of smaller figures beneath. The four central columns are embellished with portrait sculptures of the Nayaka rulers (not identified). The portly figures, carved almost in three dimensions, wear finely detailed jewelled costumes, crowns and daggers. The ceiling above has elaborate lotus medallions surrounded by hanging parrots and bands of figures, geese and scrollwork.

A doorway leads to the inner enclosure of the Bhuvaraha Temple. At the west end is the main shrine, in which Vishnu is venerated in his boar incarnation. The ornate treatment of the outer walls is typical of the Chola manner as revived by the Nayakas. The shrine is topped with a brick tower capped by a square-domical roof.

J. Vriddhachalam

This town lies 80km southwest of Pondicherry, but can also be reached directly from Chidambaram, 55km east. The **Vriddhagirishvara Temple**, after which the town takes its name, is a Chola foundation much extended in later times. The outer enclosure is framed by a quartet of imposing *gopuras*, the finest being that on the north. These 17C structures have deep niches framed by bold pilasters set into the double wall series. The passageways exhibit shallow jambs divided into small panels filled with female dancers. The pyramidal towers each have six diminishing storeys. Two additional *gopuras* on the east give access to the inner enclosures. The area between the outermost and intermediate *gopuras* on this side is partly occupied by a large open hall built up against the south side of an enclosed structure, now used as the Temple offices.

The hall occupying the space inside the intermediate gate has slender colonettes on the outer columns and sculpted *yalis* lining the central aisle. The portrait sculptures carved on the corner piers of the central bay resemble those at Srimushnam, suggesting that they also portray the Gingee rulers. A Nataraja shrine is located at the north end of this hall. The focal *linga* shrine, at the heart of the innermost enclosure, is contained within later colonnades.

40 · Thanjavur

The home to successive Chola, Nayaka and Maratha rulers, Thanjavur served for more than 1000 years as the capital of the densely populated heartland of Tamil Nadu, known traditionally as the Cholamandalam. The city stands at the head of the Kaveri River Delta, a richly irrigated zone traversed by water channels, dotted with towns and villages.

Thanjavur lies between Pondicherry [39] and Tiruchirapalli [41], the itineraries of which may be combined with that described here. Kumbakonam, 37km east, makes an alternative base from which to visit historical localities in the Delta area.

One full day is recommended for the temple, palace and museum at **Thanjavur** [A], with side trips to the shrines at **Tiruvaiyur** [B] and **Kilaiyur** [C].

A full-day journey to Kumbakonam may be combined with stops at **Pullamangai** [D], **Swamimalai** [E] and **Darasuram** [F], which lies on the way. The profusion of monuments at **Kumbakonam** suggests at least a morning for the city itself [G].

From Kumbakonam, visitors have the choice of alternative routes. The road leading northeast will take in the temples at **Tribhuvanam** [H], **Tirumangalakkudi** [I] and **Gangaikondacholapuram** [J], with the possibility of proceeding on to Chidambaram [39H] and Pondicherry. The road running south from Kumbakonam leads to the temple cities of **Mannargudi** [K] and **Tiruvarur** [L].

The Bay of Bengal seaboard east of Kumbakonam, best known to Europeans as the Coromandel (Cholamandalam) Coast, is lined with Hindu, Christian and Muslim places of worship, as well as sites of French and Danish settlements. **Nagapattinam** [M], **Velanganni** [N], **Nagore** [O], **Karaikal** [P], **Tarangambadi** [Q] and **Poompuhar** [R] may all be covered in a full-day outing.

THANJAVUR

0km   30km

to Pondicherry

N

Gangaikondacholapuram

Poompuhar

Tiruvvidaimarndur

to Tiruchirapalli

Tirumangalakkudi

Swamilamalai

Tarangambadi

Kilaiyur

Kaveri River

Tiruvaiyur

Tribhuvanam

Karaikal

Kumbakonam

Tiruvalanjuli

Darasuram

Pulumangai

Nagore

Thanjavur

Tiruvarur

to Tiruchirapalli

Mannargudi

Nagapattinam

Velanganni

to Pudukkottai

to Kodikkarai

■ **Transport**. Thanjavur lies on the main railway line from Madras [36] to Tiruchirapalli, the latter 55km west, the nearest city with an airport. Buses connect Thanjavur with all the important centres in this part of Tamil Nadu. Pondicherry, for example, lies 131km northwest. Frequent local transport reaches all the destinations described here.

■ **Accommodation**. The *Hotel Parisutham* (☎ 21466), *Oriental Towers* (☎ 21467) and *Hotel Tamil Nadu* (☎ 21024) are the best in Thanjavur (STD code 04362). For visitors who prefer to be located at **Kumbakonam** (STD code 0435), the *Hotel Raya's* (☎ 21362) and *Hotel Athitya* (☎ 21794) can be recommended. *Sterling Swamimalai* offers charming alternative lodging in a traditional rural setting midway between Swamimalai and Kumbakonam. **Nagapattinam** (STD code 04365) has a *Hotel Tamil Nadu*, as has **Poompuhar**.

■ **Tourist Information**. The TTTD office is situated opposite the post office in Jawan Bhavan (☎ 23017). There is also an office at the *Hotel Tamil Nadu* on Ghandiji Road (☎ 21421).

A. Thanjavur

This city, known as Tanjore in British times, attained prominence under the Cholas, who used it as one of their principal capitals in the 10C–12C.

Thanjavur seems to have been the preferred residence of Rajaraja I (985–1012), the greatest of the Chola monarchs. The city continued to dominate the Delta in later times. Under Vijayanagara [20B–C], it was the seat of a local line of Governors, known as Nayakas. The first of these figures, Shevappa Nayaka (1549–72), gradually asserted his autonomy. By the end of the 16C his successors were ruling as independent kings. Raghunatha (1614–34) and Vijayaraghava (1634–73), the most powerful Nayakas, were challenged by their rivals at Gingee [39F] and Madurai [44A], and their territories were raided by the Adil Shahis of Bijapur [23A]. In 1674 the Nayaka throne was captured by Ekoji (Venkaji), the brother of Shivaji, the celebrated Maratha chief. Thanjavur thereupon became the capital of an independent line of Marathas, whose rulers resisted attacks by the Mughals and their representatives, the Nawabs of Arcot [38B]. By the end of the 18C the British had taken command of the Thanjavur area, but the Marathas lived on as a declining royal family. Serfoji II (1798–1832) received an English education and achieved renown as a patron of culture.

The circular configuration of Thanjavur as developed under the Nayakas is revealed by the moat that partly encircles the **Old City**; however, the walls were torn down by the British at the end of the 18C. The great **Brihadishvara Temple** stands within a quadrangular **Fort**, southwest of the Old City, where stone walls with European-style brick battlements overlook a broad moat, partly rock-cut. The Brihadishvara Temple, the grandest architectural achievement of the Chola era, was erected in about 1010 by Rajaraja I, who personally donated the gilded pot finial at the summit of the tower.

The Temple stands in the middle of a spacious rectangular court, entered through two gateways on the east. These impressive structures are dominated by vaulted roofs adorned with later plaster sculptures. Outsized guardian figures protect the east doorway to the inner gate. Smaller carvings on the basement illustrate Shaiva legends, such as the marriage of Shiva and Parvati, and Shiva rescuing Markandeya. The 16 columned pavilion in front (east) of the main Temple shelters a huge monolithic Nandi, dating from the late 16C. The pavilion has slender columns with carvings of donors on the shafts. The adjacent brass-clad flagpole rises on a miniature pavilion carried by elephants with upraised trunks, and *ganas*.

The Temple itself consists of a square *linga* sanctuary adjoining an antechamber and a long columned hall on the east. The double-storeyed pilastered walls are raised on a high basement adorned with *yalis* and *makaras* (top moulding), and are covered with inscriptions relating the origins, construction and endowments of the monument (bottom mouldings). A seated dwarf supports the spout emerging from the sanctuary basement (north). Openings flanked by guardians, some with clubs, mark the middle of the sanctuary walls on three sides. The niche projections at either side are occupied by fully modelled figures, mostly of Shiva. The finest are Bhikshatanamurti (south wall, east end), Natesha (south wall, west end), Harihara (west wall, south end) and

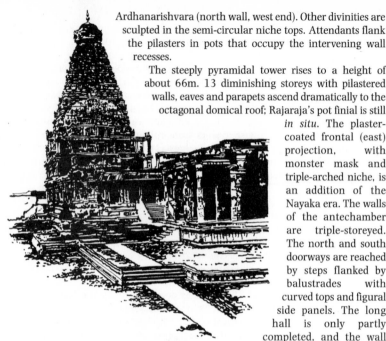

Ardhanarishvara (north wall, west end). Other divinities are sculpted in the semi-circular niche tops. Attendants flank the pilasters in pots that occupy the intervening wall recesses.

The steeply pyramidal tower rises to a height of about 66m. 13 diminishing storeys with pilastered walls, eaves and parapets ascend dramatically to the octagonal domical roof; Rajaraja's pot finial is still *in situ*. The plaster-coated frontal (east) projection, with monster mask and triple-arched niche, is an addition of the Nayaka era. The walls of the antechamber are triple-storeyed. The north and south doorways are reached by steps flanked by balustrades with curved tops and figural side panels. The long hall is only partly completed, and the wall sculptures are mostly unfinished. The east doorway is

Bridhadishvara Temple, Thanjavur

flanked by guardian figures. The porch in front, with columns showing cut-out colonettes and rearing animals overhung by deeply curving eaves, is a Nayaka extension, as are the columns inside the hall.

The sanctuary interior of the Brihadishvara Temple is dominated by a colossal *linga*, almost 4m high, elevated on a circular pedestal; worship here has been revived recently. The surrounding passageway on two levels is divided into chambers (access restricted to visitors). The sculptures in the lower passageway include a large dancing Shiva (north wall). Paintings in two layers adorn the walls and ceiling, but are only partly visible. Among the Chola fragments are delicately toned scenes of Shiva seated in the company of dancers and musicians, a royal visit to the temple at Chidambaram [39H] (west wall) and Shiva riding in a chariot drawn by Brahma (north wall). No less than 81 miniature dancers in different postures are sculpted on the basement of the upper passageway.

Subsidiary buildings dating from the Chola era stand freely in the Temple enclosure. The south-facing **Chandeshvara Shrine** imitates details of the main Temple at a smaller scale. The tower is crowned with an octagonal roof. Additions of the Nayaka and Maratha periods include the intricately worked **Subrahmanya Shrine**, assigned to the period of Raghunatha Nayaka. The outer walls have delicately fashioned pilasters, some standing in pots. Icons of Subrahmanya are set into the niches on three sides of the sanctuary; Ganapati (south) and Durga (north) appear on the hall walls. Delicately pierced stone

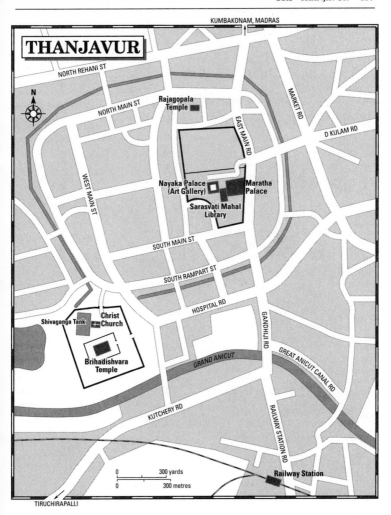

windows with geometric designs light the antechamber within. The three-storeyed tower is topped with a hexagonal roof.

The Subrahmanga Shrine is entered on the east by a porch with side steps. The long hall that extends east is a Maratha extension, as is evident from the 19C paintings on the inner walls that portray various royal figures. Another Maratha addition to the Brihadeshvara Temple is the hall in front of the **Brihadnayaki Shrine**. This is approached through a porch on the south, with piers displaying colonettes and yalis. The 19C paintings on the ceiling inside illustrate Shaiva legends; the scenes are identified by Tamil captions. The nearby south-facing **Natesha Shrine** dates from the 17C, as do the colonnades that line the enclosure walls. A small museum is located on the south side.

The large, square **Shivaganga Tank** is contained within the ramparts that extend west of the Brihadishvara Temple. The water is overlooked on the east by **Christ Church**, whose restrained Neo-Classical façade bears the date 1779. This simple building has triple vaulted aisles culminating in an apse roofed with a half-dome. The relief tablet by John Flaxman, set into the west wall, shows the death of the famous missionary, Reverend Schwartz, in 1798. It was donated by Serfoji II. The wooden pulpit was used by Schwartz.

The freshly restored **Nayaka Palace** stands surrounded by walls in the middle of the Old City. The royal complex, approached from the main street through two arched gates, was founded by Shevappa Nayaka, but was enlarged and altered many times. The central square court is entered on the north through a domed entrance chamber. Opposite, on the south side of the court, is a two-storeyed structure divided into large corridors and halls, with pointed arches supporting shallow domes and vaults. A square chamber with a steep pyramidal tower rises from the middle of the roof. Its diminishing eaves have Neo-Classical balustrades and fluted domical finials, evidently 18C–19C modifications.

The audience hall faces east onto the court. Its massive circular piers support broad lobed arches and a pointed vault with ribbed and fluted surfaces. A large plaster composition, depicting the coronation of Rama, adorns the walls at the rear of the chamber. The tableau looks down on a large green slab, about 5m square, set into the floor, the site of the royal throne. Animal brackets carry the eaves that overhang the outer arcade, while domes and vaults crowned by prominent lotus finials protrude above the roof. A seven-storeyed tower with arcades on all sides stands freely outside the north-west corner of the complex.

The **Art Gallery**, also referred to as the Rajaraja Museum (closed public holidays), occupies part of the Nayaka Palace. Its stone and metal sculptures have been assembled from many sites in the Kaveri Delta. Granite sculptures are exhibited in the domed entrance hall and the colonnades that surround the court. Among the 10C items are a damaged, delicately modelled Ardhanarishvara, a standing Shiva with an elaborate headdress, from Sendalai, and Shiva as Dakshinamurti seated beneath a tree. A seated Buddha from Pattisvaram testifies to the existence of Buddhism in this area. A set of 12C figures from Darasuram shows Shiva as Bhikshatanamurti, with begging bowl, fly-whisk and dog, attended by the wives of the sages. Another panel from Darasuram depicts Shiva dancing triumphantly within the skin of the elephant demon that he has just slain. The vitality of the twisted posture of the god is remarkable.

Bronzes are shown in the audience hall of the Nayaka Palace. Depictions of Shiva predominate in early Chola art, the finest being a set of 11C images from Tiruvengadu. As the archer (bow and arrow missing), the god is delicately posed with a slight tilt in his posture. Shiva stands with Parvati, sometimes gently taking the hand of the goddess, or seated with her and the child-like figure of Skanda. The masterpiece of the collection shows Shiva, with snakes in his hair, leaning slightly to the side, one arm outstretched. The refined posture and modelling of the god and his consort are unparalleled in Chola art.

Other fine pieces include an eight-armed Bhairava and Shiva as naked Bhikshatanamurti, accompanied by a jumping dog. Splendid images of Nataraja from Tiruvelvikudi and Jambavanodai show the god with one foot upraised, hair and tassels flying outwards, surrounded by a halo of flames. An unusual

Nataraja from Kiranur shows the god without flying hair. Among the standing images of Parvati are fine examples from Tiruvelvikudi and Kilaiyur. The figures of saints include Sundarar from Kilaiyur and Kannappa from Tiruvengadu. A seated Parvati and a Kali with her hair standing on end are both assigned to the Vijayanagara era. The portrait of Vijayaraghava, almost 1m high, shows the Nayaka ruler in the act of devotion.

The **Sarasvati Mahal Library** is accommodated in the adjacent apartments of the Nayaka Palace. A statue of Serfoji II stands in the entrance lobby. A small Museum (closed Wednesdays) shows a selection of the Library's large holdings. The exhibits include palm-leaf and paper manuscripts and albums, many from the Maratha period. Three pages from a *Ramayana* manuscript, with minutely detailed coloured scenes arranged in narrow strips, are of unusual interest. There are also European maps, engravings and prints from Serfoji's personal collection.

The **Maratha Palace**, east of the Library, is now much dilapidated. The audience hall, which faces west onto a spacious court, has slender timber columns carrying plaster-coated arches. These are filled with brightly painted gods, European-styled angels and courtly figures surrounded by stylised foliation. The attached **Royal Museum**, occupying part of the private quarters of the Maratha Palace, has a small collection of royal memorabilia. The **Tamil University Museum** (closed weekends), in the south wing of the Maratha Palace, is reached by a separate entrance from the main street. This is home to a diverse assemblage of pottery from prehistoric burial sites, coins, metalwork, weapons, palanquins, brass lamps and musical instruments.

Among the other religious monuments in Thanjavur is the **Rajagopala Temple**, which stands in a narrow street north of the Palace. Unlike the Brihadishvara temple, this is a Nayaka foundation. A flight of steps from the *gopura* on the east ascends to the upper Temple, preceded by corridors roofed with brick vaults. The 17C sanctuary has pilastered walls with a five-storeyed tower capped by a hemispherical roof. The 19C paintings that cover the walls of the attached hall depict Vaishnava topics.

Among the urban features of interest is **Rani's Clock Tower** near the market. This was erected in 1833 in an inventive Indo-Saracenic style, with funds provided by a Maratha Gheen.

4km southwest of the town is the sprawling campus of the **Tamil University**, dotted with outlandish revivalist buildings.

B. Tiruvaiyaru

This town, 13km north of Thanjavur, lies on the south bank of the Kaveri River. Tiruvaiyaru is famous for its music festival, which is held each January to commemorate the birth anniversary of Tyagaraja, the celebrated musician and saint (1767–1847) and who composed and practised in the **Panchanandishvara Temple**. This monument dates back to Chola times, but was much extended under the Nayakas and Marathas. It is entered on the east through a sequence of four *gopuras*. A large columned hall, partly open on three sides, faces south into the outermost enclosure. The space between the third and fourth east gopuras is filled by a grandiose hall with spacious aisles, flanked by *yali* piers; the animals are tripled at the crossing. The innermost enclosure is occupied by a small east-facing *linga* sanctuary that dates back to Chola times. At the rear (west) is a shrine dedicated to five *lingas*. A second shrine to Shiva, immediately south, is preceded by an ornate hall with finely worked piers displaying cut-out colonettes. The peripheral colonnade is mainly Chola, but the paintings of Shiva's exploits on the rear walls are modern.

C. Kilaiyur

This small village, 20km north of Tiruvaiyaru, is worth visiting for the finely finished twin **Agastishvara** and **Cholishvara Temples**. These structures were erected in the 9C by local chiefs who were contemporaries of the early Cholas. The two west-facing Temples have pilastered walls rising on basements with elegantly modelled friezes of petals and *yalis*. The central niches frame images of Shiva (south), Skanda (east) and Brahma (north), standing in the Agastishvara Temple, seated in the Cholishvara Temple. The niches are headed by semi-circular pediments filled with miniature figures. The Temples have two-storeyed towers with sculpted Nandis placed beneath the capping roofs, square in the Agastishvara Temple, hemispherical in the Cholishvara Temple.

D. Pullamangai

This insignificant hamlet, just off the main road midway between Thanjavur and Kumbakonam, is renowned for the 10C **Brahmapurishvara Temple**, a well-finished example of early Chola architecture. The outer walls of the sanctuary and attached hall have wide projections at the corners and in the middle of each side. Angled miniature figures are positioned beside the brackets over the pilasters. The narrower projections in the intervening recesses have shorter pairs of pilasters. These carry independent eaves and sequences of mouldings culminating in arched frames. The refined compositions in the central projections on three sides of the sanctuary show Dakshinamurti attended by sages, obscured by a modern cell (south), Shiva appearing out of the *linga*, witnessed by Brahma and Vishnu (west), and Brahma with sages (north). Seated Ganapati with a host of lively dwarfs (south), and Durga with devotees (north) are seen on the hall walls. The three-storeyed tower with later plasterwork is capped with a square roof. The Temple is entered through a Maratha-period *gopura* and arcaded hall.

E. Swamimalai

The celebrated Swaminatha Temple in this village stands 3km north of the main road, 29km east of Thanjavur, 8km west of Kumbakonam. In the settlement of **Tiruvalanjuli** at the turning stands the **Kapardishvara Temple**, which has several unusual features. Its Chola-period *linga* shrine is approached from the east through a sequence of four *gopuras*, most without towers. In the middle of the second enclosure stands the 17C Sveta Vinayaka shrine. This small, exquisite structure consists of a simple chamber with perforated stone screens on the east and a porch on the south, embellished with balustrades, wheels and leaping horses. The shrine is dedicated to a white relief icon of Ganesha. A later hall, with circular columns covered by architectural façades, is built up to the shrine on the east. A Nandi stands freely to the west, facing towards the *gopura* that leads into the third enclosure.

The northeast corner of this compound is occupied by a Chola-period hall. The double-bayed opening on the west is framed by unusual bulbous pilasters. The *linga* shrine in the fourth enclosure is topped by a small tower with a hemispherical roof; inscriptions cover its outer walls. It is surrounded by 17C colonnades roofed with brick vaults. A doorway in the south wall of the third enclosure leads to the Devi shrine, which has a separate enclosure. Ceiling paintings here depict the course of the Karevi river, flowing past Srirangam island [41B] to the Bay of Bengal.

Swamimalai, 2km north of Tiruvalanjuli, is known for the **Swaminatha Temple**, which occupies the summit of the hill above the small town. The complex is entered from the south through a *gopura* with a vividly painted tower. Double flights of steps ascend to the upper level. The finely detailed sanctuary, housing an image of Murugan, and its preceding hall have been entirely remodelled recently. Views from the terrace survey the surrounding fields and canals. Metal casting is a major industry in Swamimalai, and the town has many workshops with brass icons for sale.

F. Darasuram

This small settlement, beside the main road 34km east of Thanjavur, just 3km from Kumbakonam, is renowned for the **Airavateshvara Temple**, the finest of the late Chola era. Assigned to the reign of Rajaraja II (1146–72), this is now an archaeological monument. The complex is entered on the east through two *gopuras*. The outer detached gate, conceived on a grand scale, is incomplete and dilapidated. In front of the inner gate are a Nandi within a pavilion and two small, finely decorated altars. The inner gate is topped by a vaulted roof with plaster sculptures, and leads into a rectangular court surrounded by a colonnade with corner halls. That at the northeast corner is converted into a small museum, displaying sculptures and photographs.

The main unit of the Airavateshvara Temple consists of a sanctuary, antechamber and two halls, one enclosed, the other partly open, with a porch extension on the south. The outer walls of the sanctuary and enclosed hall are elevated on a basement. The bottom register is enlivened with *yalis* and dancing dwarfs. The top register has a row of miniature panels framing stories of Shaiva saints, among which are the legend of Chandesha, who cut off his father's leg when the latter kicked the *linga* that he was worshipping (south), and the deliverance of a child from the jaws of a crocodile by the intervention of Sundarar (north). The elongated spout that emerges from the north basement of the sanctuary is supported on a standing dwarf and rearing *yali*. Full-height pilasters divide the walls into projections; secondary pilasters frame niches or stand in pots in the recesses.

The carved black basalt panels in the central niches depict Shiva as Dakshinamurti (south, partly hidden), Shiva appearing out of the *linga* (west) and Brahma (north), all with attendant devotees and divinities. Similar panels on the walls of the antechamber show Ganesha (south) and Durga (north). The wall paintings are assigned to the 17C, as are the plaster restoration of the figures and the plaster decoration of the overhanging eaves and extended parapet. Three diminishing storeys with similar parapets constitute the pyramidal tower, which is capped with a hemispherical roof.

Steps on the north and south, flanked by curved balustrades, provide access to the antechamber of the Temple. The walls here, and those of the adjoining hall, have pilastered niches filled with icons. These show different aspects of Shiva, including an unusual dancing three-headed Bhairava (south). A small shrine built up to the wall nearby houses a unique form of Shiva, as a mythical beast subduing Narasimha.

The porch extension of the outer hall is approached from the south by two flights of steps, with balustrades fashioned as large striding elephants. Prancing horses pulling wheels are carved in high relief on the basement, suggesting that the Temple was conceived as a chariot. A seated Brahma, the driver of the chariot, appears on the central niche on the south. The peripheral columns have seated *yalis* at the base; other supports are decorated with medallions of scroll-work containing dancers and musicians or superimposed reliefs of temple façades. A detailed account of the story of Subrahmanya is depicted on several panels. Lotus medallions and groups of musicians are carved on the panels of the coffered ceilings. Pairs of guardian figures flank the inner doorways.

The **Daivanayaki Amman Temple**, immediately north of the Airavate-shvara Temple, is contained within its own walled compound. The sanctuary and antechamber are raised on a basement adorned with friezes of dwarfs and *yalis*; the pilasters on the sanctuary walls have rearing *yalis* at the base. The niches occupied by goddesses are interspersed with pierced stone windows, one with looped serpents. The tower over the sanctuary is elaborate, with later painted plasterwork. The roof is unusually cruciform in shape; its arched ends are adorned with flame motifs and monster masks.

An unusual image of Lajja Gauri is venerated in the small **Amman Shrine**, about 1km northeast of the Temples just described. This lotus-headed goddess is shown in a squatting posture, displaying her sex. This piece was brought from Karnataka as a trophy by the invading Cholas in the 12C.

G. Kumbakonam

The cultural capital of the Delta region, this city, on the south bank of the Kaveri River is second only to Thanjavur in historical significance. An idea of the popu-lation and wealth of Kumbakonam over many centuries may be had from the numerous temples and shrines dedicated to different cults, and the elaborate *mathas* and other religious institutions which still thrive here. Kumbakonam was an important centre under the Cholas in the 9C–12C. It was the residence of Govinda Dikshita, the powerful Minister of Raghunatha and other Nayakas of Thanjavur.

The **Mahamakam Tank** serves as the ritual core of Kumbakonam, the site of a great festival held here every 12 years, most recently in 1992. The waters of all the sacred rivers of India are believed to unite in the trapezoidal Tank. This is surrounded by steps and 16 small pavilions, erected by Govinda Dikshita for the Nayakas to perform ritual ceremonies. The pavilion near the northwest corner of the Tank has a raised dais in the middle. The carvings on the beams and ceiling inside show the Nayaka seated in a balance, being weighed against trea-sure, witnessed by warriors and courtiers. As in the other pavilions, the attached shrine has a small brick tower capped with a hemispherical roof. The Tank is overlooked on the east by the **Abhimukheshvara Temple**. Of greater interest

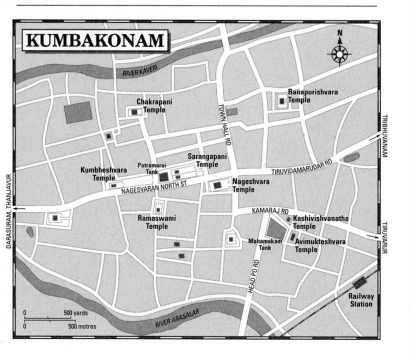

is the **Kashivshvanatha Temple**, on the north side of the Tank, where a set of nine river goddesses is accommodated in a subshrine in the hall. The central goddess, who personifies the Kaveri River, gazes south through a sequence of doorways to the Tank.

A short distance from the northwest corner of the Mahamakam Tank stands the **Nageshvara Temple**. Founded in 886, this is the earliest religious structure at Kumbakonam. The complex is entered from the east through a sequence of three *gopuras* of diminishing size. A large columned hall occupies the north side of the second enclosure. This is elevated on a carved basement, embellished with wheels and prancing horses in the typical Chola manner. Outsized stone elephants flank the balustraded steps on the south. 17C plasterwork embellishes the perforated windows set into the walls; a modern Nataraja shrine is built over the dais at the end of the hall. The pavilion opposite has an unusual wooden roof with metal cladding. A small *gopura* leads into the third and innermost enclosure, partly filled by a colonnade with crudely fashioned columns.

The early Chola Temple stands at the west end of the court. This is raised on a moulded basement enlivened with lotus petals and miniature legendary scenes. The niches accommodate images of sages and Dakshinamurti (south) Ardhanarishvara (west) and Brahma and Durga (north), the last now forming the focus for a modern pavilion. The figures are unsurpassed for their graceful postures, delicate modelling and sweetly detached expressions. A multi-storeyed tower crowned with a hemispherical roof, much renovated, rises above.

A street running west leads to the **Sarangapani Temple**, the largest Vaishnava monument in Kumbakonam. This vast complex is entered from the east through a lofty *gopura* topped with a steeply pyramidal tower, some 45m high. Dancing figures in panels, re-used from an earlier structure, embellish the basement. The ten-storeyed tower is densely packed with plaster sculptures; the openings in the middle of each stage are flanked by guardians. On the north side of the first enclosure is a detached hall, open on three sides, with a dais for processional images at the rear. The second *gopura* gives access to an extensive columned hall with two intersecting aisles.

The third *gopura*, in line with the previous two, leads to the innermost enclosure. Here stands the original Temple, an ornate structure founded in the late Chola era. The middle of its east wall is marked by three carved screens of different designs, through which the doorway to the sanctuary may be glimpsed. A long stone tray set into the basement is carried on squatting figures and timber-like blocks. Two outsized guardian figures are placed in front. The basement on the north and south sides of the Temple displays wheels with leaping horses and striding elephants. The walls above have deeply set niches interspersed with single pilasters standing in pots, all finely finished. The carved panels in the niches, including several Narasimha icons, are 17C insertions.

Access to the principal scantuary of the Temple is through doorways reached by steps on the north and south sides of the sanctuary, used alternatively at different seasons. The 12 columns inside the hall have shafts covered with superimposed façades. The ceiling above shows a lotus surrounded by rings of geese, interlocking dancers and acrobats. A large image of reclining Vishnu is venerated within the sanctuary. The Lakshmi shrine, in the southwest corner of the enclosure, belongs partly to the Chola era, as is evident from the treatment of the basement as seen from outside. The west *gopura* in the outer walls leads to a large rectangular tank with a pavilion in the middle.

Other religious monuments face onto the north–south Bazaar Street, where the **Kumbheshvara Temple**, after which the city is named, stands. The Kumbheshvara myth explains the creation of the world from the waters of the cosmic pot, or *kumbha*, broken by Shiva's arrow. Most parts of the Temple date from the 17C–18C. The complex is approached from the east through a long colonnade crowded with stalls; the wooden chariots parked in the street outside are partly concealed by shops. The colonnade leads to the lofty east *gopura*, the first of three.

The outermost enclosure of the Temple is partly occupied by a tank with a central octagonal pavilion and a walled garden; an unfinished *gopura* is seen on the south. The second enclosure has a grandiose columned hall with a flagpole and a large Nandi in the middle. The ceiling over the crossing where two broad aisles meet shows signs of the zodiac. The third, innermost enclosure is occupied by three east-facing shrines standing close by each other. The *linga* shrine in the middle is the devotional focus of the Temple; this emblem is fashioned out of earth, in accordance with the creation myth, and is for this reason never washed with water. The Somaskanda shrine stands to the south, the Devi shrine to the north, the latter with an elaborate colonnade in front (east). The supports here are fashioned as attendant women and leaping animals in high relief.

The north-facing **Ramaswami Temple**, marking the south end of the Bazaar Street, was founded by Govinda Dikshita in 1620. A wooden chariot covered with *Ramayana* panels is parked just outside its towered entrance, with bronze workshops nearby. The brightly painted *gopura* of the Temple leads immediately to a spacious hall with magnificent sculptures, the finest of the Thanjavur Nayaka period. The central aisle is flanked by paired guardian figures (north end), Rama and Sita, donor figures, attendant maidens, and Rati and Kama (south end). Leaping horses and *yalis* mark the peripheral supports.

A second *gopura* leads to the inner enclosure where the main Temple stands, its sanctuary enshrining fully modelled images of Rama, Sita, Lakshmana and Hanuman. The outer walls have shallow niches but no original sculptures. The five-storeyed tower is capped with a hemispherical roof. The colonnade surrounding the open court in which the Temple stands is of interest for the brightly coloured paintings of *Ramayana* scenes, renewed as recently as 1992, all with Tamil labels.

Near to the northern extremity of the Bazaar Street, onto which the Ranga-swami Temple faces, stands the **Chakrapani Temple**, the last religious monu-ment at Kumbakonam to be described. Two *gopuras* provide access to the Temple from the east. The Temple is raised high on a solid basement, reached by steps from the north and south, used alternatively. Here are displayed brass portraits of Serfoji II of Thanjavur and his consort. The Chola-style sanctuary houses a small brass image of Vishnu standing in a six-pointed star, or *chakra*, hence the name Chakrapani. Lakshmi is venerated in a detached shrine to the north.

Other historical features at Kumbakonam are to be seen on the banks of the Kaveri River, which are here lined with Maratha-period pavilions and *ghats*. The **Government College** on the opposite bank, formerly the summer resort of Sefoji, has a picturesque clock tower. Founded in 1854 as the first English college in the Madras Presidency, its most famous student was the mathematician Ramanujan.

H. Tribhuvanam

The road that runs northeast from Kumbakonam beside the Kaveri River arrives after 8km at Tribhuvanam (also spelt Thirubhuvanam). This village is domi-nated by an important monument of the late Chola period, a royal commission of Kulottunga III (1178–1218). The **Kampahareshvara Temple** has a sequence of two enclosures, each with an impressive *gopura* on the east; the outer enclosure has an additional *gopura* on the south. Many of the stone sculp-tures in the walls of these gateways are intact. The upper brick storeys form squatly proportioned towers.

The main Temple, in the middle of the inner enclosure, comprises a *linga* sanc-tuary and attached hall, separated by a transept from two additional halls. The walls of the main unit are elevated on a high basement carved with friezes of well-formed *yalis*; the miniature panels above show *Ramayana* scenes. Single pilasters standing in pots alternate with pilastered niches containing icons. The finest are Shiva appearing out of the *linga* (west) and Durga standing on the buffalo head (north). The paintings on the intervening walls are Maratha addi-tions. The steeply pyramidal five-storeyed tower repeats at diminishing scale the features of the walls beneath; the crowning roof is hemispherical. The wall niches of the halls are mostly empty, but the semi-circular pediments are filled with reliefs. The stone windows have geometric designs. Warrior figures and large *yalis* enliven the balustrades flanking the steps on the north and south, which lead to the transept. The basement of the porch projecting south from the outer hall is adorned with dancing figures and attendant maidens. The supports have attached colonettes or superimposed architectural façades.

A small Chandeshvara shrine with a hemispherical roof stands north of the main Temple. The Devi shrine nearby has goddess figures on the outer walls and a rectangular vaulted roof. The Sharabheshvara shrine, at the northeast corner, is dedicated to a composite aspect of Shiva. Vividly painted ceiling panels show the exploits of this deity.

2km beyond Tribhuvanam is the town of **Tiruvidaimarudur**, known for its grandiose **Mahalinga Perumal Temple**. This large-scale complex consists mostly of columned halls and spacious corridors dating from the 17C–18C. A large rectangular tank with a central pavilion is located just outside the *gopura* that serves as the main entrance to the Temple on the east. This gives access to a columned structure containing a Ganesha shrine, flagpole and large Nandi. Two more *gopuras* have to be passed through before the innermost *linga* shrine is reached. Together with its attached hall, this stands in a small compound surrounded on four sides by a colonnaded corridor. The shrine itself dates from the Chola era, as is evident from the icons carved on its outer walls: Dakshina-murti (south), Shiva appearing out of the *linga* (west) and Brahma (north). Metal images of the Nayanmars are displayed in the corridor to the north. The Murugan shrine, in the southwest corner of the innermost enclosure, is also assigned to the Chola period. The Devi shrine on the south side of the second enclosure, provided with its own compound walls and *gopura*, may also be an early foundation. It is, however, preceded by later structures.

I. Tirumangalakuddi

This village lies beyond the north bank of the Kaveri River, 15km northeast of Kumbakonam. The **Pramanatheshvara Temple** is of interest primarily for its 18C paintings, which cover the ceiling of the corridor that leads to the Nataraja shrine within the inner enclosure. One bay is dedicated to local legends. The bottom register has scenes of a hunter arriving at a *linga* sanctuary, a woman crossing the Kaveri River, a hunter in a grove with two deer, and the hunter killing a tiger. In the middle register three demons meet a guardian inside a pavilion, and a family with two children worship a *linga*. The top register shows deities with female devotees, and a family worshipping Shiva and Parvati. The adjacent panel depicts shrines along the Kaveri River. Other paintings are seen on the ceiling in the hall attached to the core *linga* shrine. They include the story of the life of one of the Naynmars.

The **Surya Narayana Temple**, 500m northeast, is unique. It consists of a Chola-period sanctuary dedicated to Surya, surrounded by eight small shrines, recently renovated, for planetary deities.

J. Gangaikondacholapuram

The great **Brihadishvara Temple** at this site lies 20km north of Tirumangalakuddi, a total of 35km from Kumbakonam. Together with the monument of the same name at Thanjavur, 72km distant, this is the grandest structure erected by the Cholas. Gangaikondacholapuram was established as a capital by Rajendra I (1012–44) after his successful military expedition to

Northern India, where he claimed to have crossed the Ganga River. Other than the Brihadishvara Temple, the only remains of Rajendra's time are the foundations of brick structures with stone column blocks, believed to be the remains of a palace, excavated in the fields on the outskirts of the village of **Maligaimedu**, 2km southwest of the Temple.

The Brihadishvara Temple stands in the middle of a rectangular enclosure with an imposing gate on the east, now dilapidated. Most visitors enter from a doorway on the north. The Temple is obviously modelled on the Thanjavur monument, and is even dedicated to Shiva under the same name. The sanctuary has double pilastered walls elevated on a moulded basement, with lions and scrollwork beneath and *yalis* and *makaras* above. The pilastered projections house fully modelled sculptures. The lower panels show (in clockwise sequence) Ganapati, Ardhanarishvara, Dakshinamurti (replacement), Harihara and Nataraja (south); Shiva receiving Ganga in his hair, Shiva appearing out of the *linga*, Vishnu with Lakshmi and Bhudevi, Subrahmanya and Shiva with Parvati (west); Shiva killing the demon, Durga, Brahma with consorts, Bhairava and Shiva (north). Miniature figures sculpted on blocks cover the walls between.

The six-storeyed tower, rising almost 60m above the walls, has a slightly concave profile. The parapet roof forms are emphasised, but the dome-like capping roof is smaller than that at Thanjavur. The plaster sculptures on the tower, including the chamber built up to the east side, are 17C additions. The transept between the sanctuary and the columned halls is entered by doorways flanked by guardian figures on the north and south, approached by flights of steps. The niches on the walls west of the steps house panels of Shiva as Bhikshatanamurti (south) and Shiva bestowing a wreath on the kneeling saint Chandesha, sometimes identified as the royal patron (north), the latter considered one of the masterpieces of Chola art. The niches on the walls east of the steps show Lakshmi (south) and Sarasvati (north). A massive *linga*, raised on a circular pedestal, is enshrined within the sanctuary. The hall to the east was never finished; parts date from the 17C. The doorway at the east end is sheltered by a porch reached by double flights of steps. Several fine bronzes are displayed inside, including Shiva with Uma, Subrahmanya and Devi. A stone altar carved with a lotus top has the Navargahas carved on the sides.

The subsidiary shrines dedicated to Kailasanatha, both north and south of the main Temple, were erected by Rajendra's queens. These almost identical buildings have small towers capped by hemispherical roofs. A small structure at the southwest corner houses a Ganesha image. A large Nandi, fashioned from stone blocks covered with plaster, is positioned east of the main Temple. A plaster-coated lion is built over the entrance to a flight of steps that descends to a circular well to the north.

The small **State Museum** (closed Fridays) next to the Temple displays items found in the excavations at Maligaimedu, such as coins, coloured-glass bangles, terracotta tiles, pots, fragments of Chinese celadon and sculpted stone fragments.

K. Mannargudi

This town, 34km southeast of Thanjavur, and about the same distance south of Kumbakonam, is renowned for the **Rajagopala Temple**, which houses the protective divinity of the Thanjavur Nayakas. An open hall with donor portraits on the column bases, and a free-standing column topped with a diminutive pavilion stand in the middle of the square east of the main gate. A wooden chariot covered with carvings is parked nearby. The innermost shrine of the Temple is approached through a sequence of four *gopuras*. The outermost gate, the largest of the series, has double pilastered walls with empty niches. The 11-storeyed tower has been remodelled. Grandiose colonnades, with spacious aisles flanked by horses and *yalis*, some with elephant trunks, occupy much of the second and third enclosures.

L. Tiruvarur

The **Tyagaraja Temple** at Tiruvarur, one of the most important in the Delta region, lies 27km east of Mannargudi, a total of 53km east of Thanjavur. The monument enshrines the Somaskanda form of Shiva who, together with Nataraja at Chidambaram, was especially honoured by the Cholas. Tamil saints such as Appar and Sambandar glorified Tyagaraja in their devotional hymns. The Temple overlooks the immense Kamalaya Tank on the west side of the town. Outside the main entrance to the complex on the east is a small shrine with wheels carved in high relief on the basement of the porch. The figure beneath one of these wheels refers to a legend in which a prince was crushed to death but restored to life by Shiva.

The outer enclosure of the Tyagaraja Temple is entered through four *gopuras*, those on the east and west being massive 12C structures. They display high basements with rearing *yalis* in panels and double pilastered walls with sculptures of different deities set into niches. The squat pyramidal towers are topped with vaulted roofs, all much renovated. The north and south *gopuras* date from the 17C. The rows of detached plain columns immediately inside the east *gopura* are roofed with thatch during the festival held here in April–May.

The hall north of these columns has its ceiling almost entirely covered with paintings assigned to the 17C. The animated compositions, on brilliant red backgrounds, illustrate legends from Shaiva mythology. One set of panels (east aisle) is devoted to the story of the saint Muchukunda. The hero is portrayed riding majestically in procession on an elephant; he is received with great pomp by Indra at the entrance to his heavenly city, where celestial nymphs wave lamps and offer garlands. Other scenes show the seven identical images of Tyagaraja created by Indra to confuse Muchukunda, which are then conveyed to earth in palanquins. Monkeys swing through the coconut trees behind the palace, while fireworks with blazing sparks scatter over the spectators, who carry parasols and standards.

A second *gopura* on the east leads to the second enclosure of the Temple, where many Chola-period sanctuaries still stand. The hall immediately in front (east) of the gate has columns displaying lion bases. The Achaleshvara shrine, in the southeast corner, has a west-facing sanctuary with pilastered walls framing sculptures of Dakshinamurti (south), Shiva appearing out of the *linga* (east) and Brahma (north). The pyramidal tower is crowned with a decorated hemispherical roof. The attached hall is a later addition.

Several structures display brick vaults typical of the Maratha period, such as the two-storeyed octagonal pavilion roofed with a dome. A *gopura* on the east, the third in line, gives access to the innermost enclosure. Here stand the twin east-facing Vanmikanatha and Tyagaraja shrines, both dating back to the 11C, which have pyramidal towers capped with hemispherical roofs. The Tyagaraja

shrine displays *yalis* on the basement and wall niches, with the usual arrangement of Dakshinamurti (south), Vishnu (west) and Brahma (north) carvings
capped by semi-circular pediments. A later colonnade links the two shrines.
Another feature of interest within the complex is the Kalambal shrine, in the
northwest corner of the outer enclosure.

M. Nagapattinam

This city overlooks the Bay of Bengal 24km east of Tiruvarur, a total of 79km
east of Thanjavur by road or train.

> Nagapattinam was once a busy emporium of textiles and spices, benefitting
> from seaborne links with Southeast Asia and China. It was an important
> centre of Buddhism in Chola times, and many fine 13C Buddhist images
> have been discovered here, including those in the Government Museum,
> Madras [36D]. Nothing, however, is to be seen of the multi-storeyed brick
> tower erected for the Chinese Buddhist community, noted in the 19C. In the
> early 16C Nagapattinam became one of the first Portuguese settlements on
> the Coromandel Coast, but it was not until the Dutch took over in 1657 that
> the port was extensively developed. The city remained in Dutch hands until
> 1781, when it was occupied by the British; it thereafter declined in impor-
> tance.

Among the few vestiges of European occupation is the **Church of St Peter**,
with its Dutch-styled façade, near the railway station. Dutch tombs dating from
1664 can be seen in the **Karikop Cemetery**. Among the shrines in worship in
Nagapattinam are the **Kayarohana** and **Tyagaraja Temples**, both Chola foundations that have been much altered in later times.

N. Velanganni

This small village on the Bay of Bengal, 12km south of Nagapattinam, became
known in the 16C as the place where the Virgin miraculously appeared to two
local boys, and later to Portuguese sailors in distress. The first Catholic shrine
was established at Velanganni under the sponsorship of the Portuguese community of Nagapattinam. With the decline of this port towards the end of the 18C,
Velanganni emerged as an independent parish under the Franciscan order. The
Basilica that stands here is the most famous Christian shrine in Tamil Nadu,
attracting huge crowds of pilgrims throughout the year.

The current **Basilica of Our Lady of Health** is a modern structure, renovated and extended on several occasions, most recently in 1974. The Church,
which faces east toward the Bay of Bengal, is Neo-Gothic in style. Its brightly
whitewashed east façade is flanked by octagonal towers with tapering spires; the
crossing within is marked by a lofty octagonal drum with circular windows,
capped by a small spire. The interior is decorated with an inlaid stone floor and
stained-glass windows. The celebrated image of the crowned Virgin holding the
Christ child is seen on the main altar. The Virgin is dressed in a blue robe and
stands on the crescent moon. The altar is surrounded by blue-and-white Dutch
tiles. A second Church at the rear (west), also with twin towers, is divided into
two levels.

The **Museum of Offerings**, in front (east) of the Church, is stocked with gold and silver items, models of houses and trains, *ex voto* objects, testimonials and other curiosities offered by grateful devotees. A **Holy Path**, lined with the Stations of the Cross, leads west from the Basilica to Our Lady's Tank. This commemorates the spot where the Virgin first appeared.

The **Polint Calimere Wildlife Sanctuary** at **Kodikkarai**, 45km south of Velanganni, consists of 17sq km of tidal swamps, which form an ideal habitat for flamingos and other waterbirds.

O. Nagore

This small town, 8km north of Nagapattinam, is known for its famous ***Dargah***, entombing the remains of Hazrat Sayyid Shahul Hamid Qadir Wali. Born in Northern India in 1491, this saint attained fame in Tamil Nadu by curing the son of Shevappa Nayaka. The Thanjavur ruler responded by granting the land at Nagore to the saint, who lived here until his death in 1570. The *Dargah* was endowed by the Maratha rulers of Thanjavur, as well as by prominent members of the Muslim communities of Nagapattinam and other towns in the Delta region. It currently attracts crowds of devout Muslims from all over Southern India and even from Southeast Asia, especially during the Kandiri Festival, one of the greatest Muslim celebrations of Southern India, celebrated on the anniversary of the saint's death.

The *Dargah* is a low, arcaded building, with a domed chamber in the middle of the north side accommodating the saint's grave. The doors to the chamber are embellished with sheets of embossed silver. Minarets at the four corners rise above the roof line. These tapering square structures are divided into seven stages, with round-headed openings in the middle of each side. Low domes crown the minarets. In front (west) stands an isolated fifth minaret, erected in 1753, with funds provided by the Maratha ruler of Thanjavur. Its nine stages are topped with a small dome and corner domical finials, attaining a height of 43m.

P. Karaikal

Part of the Union Territory of Pondicherry, this town is situated a short distance inland from the Bay of Bengal, 12km north of Nagore. Karaikal was one of the lesser holdings of the French on the Coromandel Coast, but still preserves something of its European character, with regularly laid-out streets and 19C residences. **Government House**, a mansion with original colonnades and wooden shutters, stands at the north end of the main street. The **Church of Our Lady of the Angels** nearby was erected in 1828 in a distinctive Neo-Gothic manner. The tower that soars over the east porch is crowned with an octagonal lantern, an addition of 1891.

The main street, proceeding north through Karaikal, passes by the gate to the **Ammaiyar Temple**. A plaster sculpture over the entrance shows the emaciated female saint to whom the shrine is consecrated. This figure is celebrated in Tamil devotional poetry and is consiered one of the Nayanmars.

Q. Tarangambadi

This quiet town, 15km north of Karaikal, or 63km east of Kumbakonam via Mayuram, was once the headquarters of the Danish East India Company.

In 1620 the Company purchased a small piece of land on the Coromandel Coast from Raghunatha Nayaka; four years later Tranquebar, as this territory came to be known, was transferred to King Christian IV. Until 1807, when it was taken by the British, this settlement was the principal headquarters for Danish commercial activities in Southern India. By the time it was restored to Denmark in 1814–45, Tranquebar had dwindled into insignificance.

Tarangambadi preserves its European character due to the 17C–18C houses, churches and fort that still stand here. The settlement is entered from the west through the brick archway of the **Town Gate**. The Danish coat of arms and the date 1792 are displayed in the pediment. The road which leads from the Gate to the sea is lined with houses, many with porticos and round-headed windows. Here stands the **New Jerusalem Church** of the Evangelical Lutherans. Its main entrance is framed by a decorated triangular gable framing a crown, the royal emblem and the date 1718. The interior has four equal transepts roofed by pointed tiled roofs. The Church is associated with Bartolomeus Ziegenbalg, the first Lutheran missionary in Southern India and the translator of the New Testament into Tamil, which he had printed on a newly introduced press. He died in 1719; his grave is set into the floor in front of the altar. The cemetery outside contains other interesting tombs. The **Church of Zion** nearby, founded in 1701 but subsequently remodelled, was the main place of worship for Europeans. A bell tower, topped by a shallow dome and a miniature obelisk, rises over the entrance. The long nave is roofed with a pointed brick vault.

A large open square is laid out beside the Bay of Bengal. The north side is occupied by the **Governor's Bungalow**, a dilapidated building with an imposing colonnaded verandah. Opposite, on the south side of the square and directly overlooking the ocean, is **Dansborg**. This fort was begun in 1620 by Ovo Gedde, the first Danish Governor, and was subsequently strengthened on several occasions. It consists of a quadrilateral compound bounded by broad ramparts, entered on the north through a pedimented arched gate. The east side of the fort is occupied by a long low building with sloping walls and small windows. A central upper chamber has a small tower. The vaulted rooms of the lower storey serve as a small Museum (closed Fridays), housing a collection of maps, documents, weapons and other artefacts pertaining to Danish history.

R. Poompuhar

This popular spot, 12km north of Tarangambadi, is situated at the mouth of the Kaveri River, the waters of which are little more than a trickle as they enter the ocean. Poompuhar is identified with Kaveripompattinam, an ancient emporium with trade links with Rome, that later flourished under the Cholas. Excavations have revealed brick remains from the 11C–12C.

Recently developed as a recreational centre, Poompuhar benefits from a good beach and tourist facilities. The seven-storeyed **Art Gallery**, built in a somewhat bizarre temple-like style, houses a set of modern stone reliefs illustrating the Tamil classic, *Silappadikaram*, Story of the Anklet. Set in Poompuhar, it tells the tale of Kannagi, the exemplary Tamil wife, and Kovalan, her princely husband.

41 · Tiruchirapalli

Still known as Trichy, an abbreviation of its British period name of Trichinopoly, this historical city in the heartland of Tamil Nadu stands on the south bank of the Kaveri River, overlooked by a great rock rising 83m above the water. Tiruchirapalli is now an important industrial centre, second only in Tamil Nadu to Madras [36], yet historical features are still to be seen. Allow a half day for the shrines and churches on and around the great rock [A].

A tour of the two grandiose religious monuments on **Srirangam Island**, immediately north of Tiruchirapalli, will occupy a full day [B], especially if the Chola temple at **Srinivasanallur** [C] is included. From here it is possible to continue on to Salem [42].

A day trip south of Tiruchirapalli can take in the temples at **Kodumbalur** [D], **Sittanavasal** [E] and **Narttamalai** [F], all from the early Chola era.

Additional time will be required to visit the Tondaiman capital of **Pudukkottai** [G] and the temple sponsored by these rulers at **Avudayarkoil** [H]. Instead of returning to Tiruchirapalli, there is the option of travelling from Pudukkottai to Madurai [42].

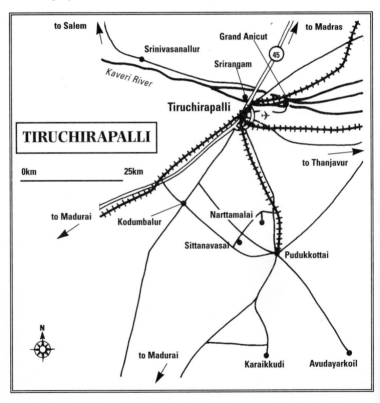

Though Thanjavur may easily be reached as a day trip from Tiruchirapalli, the many sights in and around this city recommend an overnight stop. It is here treated as a separate itinerary [40].

■ **Transport**. Tiruchirapalli is linked to Madras by both plane and express train. NH45 provides direct road connections with Madras, 404km northeast, and Madurai, 142km southeast. Lesser routes lead from Tiruchirapalli to Salem, 133km northwest, and Thanjavur, 55km east. All the localities described here are accessible by local bus. Trains also run to Pudukottai, Thanjavur and Kumbakonam [40G].

■ **Accommodation**. Many new hotels are situated in the Cantonment area of Tiruchirapalli (STD code 0431). The *Sangam Hotel* (☎ 464700), *Jenney's Residency* (☎ 461301) and *Femina Hotel* (☎ 461551) are the best, with the *Hotel Tamil Nadu* (☎ 460383) and *Hotel Arun* (☎ 41421) providing more modest alternatives. The *Sri Lakshmi Lodge* (☎ 2821) offers acceptable accommodation for those wishing to stay in **Pudukkottai** (STD code 0874).

■ **Tourist Information**. The TTDC maintains an office at 1 Williams Road, in the Cantonment area (☎ 401136).

A. Tiruchirapalli

Tiruchirapalli was an important centre under the Cholas, judging from the hydraulic projects that were undertaken in the area during the 11C–12C. The **Grand Anicut**, 14km downstream (east) of the city, is a long earthen dam traversing the Kaveri River, with side channels to divert water for irrigation.

Tiruchirapalli served as a second capital for the Nayakas of Madurai, and was the scene of bitter fighting between these rulers and the Mughals in the late 17C. The city was later occupied by the Nawabs of Arcot [38B]. Much missionary work took place here in the 18C–19C, during which period a major military Cantonment, 3km south of the Old City, was laid out by the British; its broad curving streets, with a few dilapidated bungalows set in spacious gardens, can still be seen. The British also undertook repairs to the Grand Anicut and the construction of new dams and channels.

The tour of Tiruchirapalli described here begins at the great **Rock** that forms the focus of the **Old City**. In Nayaka times the Rock was surrounded by a ring of high walls, but these were demolished by the British at the end of the 18C. Their circuit can still be traced by a street that encircles the base of the Rock. Two early sanctuaries are excavated into the Rock. The **Lower Cave Temple**, at the base of the south face, is assigned to the Pandyas in the 8C. It consists of a hall with massive, unadorned columns. The side shrines house images of Shiva and Vishnu. Other deities are carved on the rear wall: Ganesha (left), Subrahmanya, Brahma, Surya and Durga (right).

The ascent of the Rock begins nearby, with a covered staircase flanked by columned halls, one with carvings of donor figures and divinities. The first feature of interest to be seen is the **Upper Cave Temple**, associated with the Pallava ruler Mahendravarman I (580–630). Its hall, which is entered from the side, has columns with medallions on the shafts. The doorway to the small shrine (right) is flanked by guardian figures. The panel opposite (left) depicts Shiva receiving the goddess Ganga in his hair. The steps continue upwards until they pass by the **Rock Temple**, which occupies a bluff on the west flank of the Rock. This complex is contained within bare high walls, giving the appearance of a fortress. It is entered on the east through a towered gate which leads to a columned hall (access restricted to visitors). Here can be seen the tower of a Devi shrine located at the lower level. The west-facing *linga* shrine, reached only after passing through the hall, is a Chola-period structure, but the colonnade that surrounds it is later. The ascent of the Rock ends at a small **Ganesha Temple**. The columns in the open hall that precedes the sanctuary have donor figures, deities and horses. Fine views may be had from here across the city to Srirangam Island.

The Rock is surrounded by crowded streets and shops, with a large **Tank** on the west. A short distance north of the Tank is **Christ Church**, associated with the Reverend Frederick Christian Schwartz, who founded it in 1766 on land donated by the Nawab of Arcot. The modest Neo-Classical building has a small square tower at one corner. Plain Doric columns line the central aisle within. The polygonal stanctuary at the end has its walls covered with inscribed granite slabs. The grave of Schwartz, who died here in 1766, lies nearby.

A portion of the 18C city walls, including an arched **Gate** and a quadrangular bastion, is seen near the southwest corner of the Tank, on West Boulevard Road, the main north–south road running through the Old City. The imposing **Cathedral of Our Lady of Lourdes**, a Neo-Gothic church consecrated in 1841, stands on the opposite side of the road. Its east façade has a rose window, surmounted by a lofty tower with octagonal and square turrets and a tapering spire, completed in 1895. The nave is roofed with pointed cross vaults. **St Joseph's College**, a large Jesuit institution founded in 1840, stands next door.

The ***Dargah* of Natar Shah**, containing the tomb of a popular saint who lived in the city in the 17C, is located about 500m south of the Rock. The building is recognised by the large dome framed by corner pinnacles. The *Dargah* was endowed by the last Nayaka queen, Minakshi (1731–36). It is also the burial place of Wallajah Muhammad Ali (1749–95) of Arcot.

The tour of Tiruchirapalli continues with a visit to the Cantonment area. The **Church of St John** of 1816 has a handsome pedimented portico, partly hidden by a modern porch. The outer walls are lined with shuttered doors that are opened for ventilation during worship. The Doric columns inside carry a flat wooden roof. The altar and furniture are all finely worked. A small brass tablet set into the floor marks the grave of Bishop Heber. The adjacent cemetery is crowded with tombs, some with obelisks. The small **Government Museum** (closed Fridays) in the vicinity has a small collection of stone sculptures and bronzes, including a fine 12C image of Manikkavachakar, as well as painted album pages. There are also models of the Rock and of the Ranganatha complex at Srirangam.

B. Srirangam

This 30km long island is formed by two branches of the Kaveri River. Here stand two great religious monuments: the Ranganatha Temple, dedicated to Vishnu reclining on the cosmic serpent, and the Jambukeshvara Temple, consecrated to

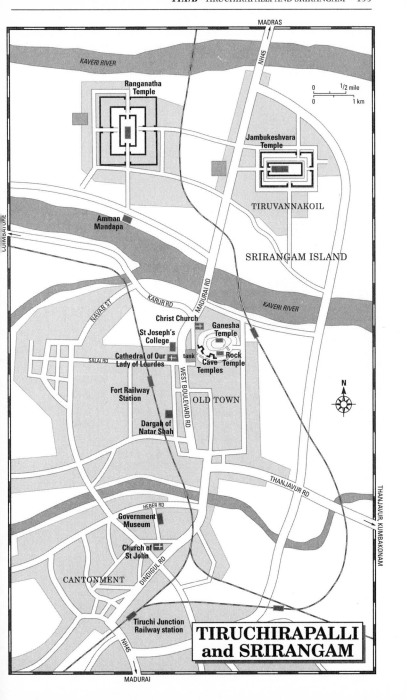

the water (*ap*) *linga* of Shiva. Lesser shrines and numerous tanks dot the island.

The **Ranganatha Temple**, 4km north of the Rock at Tiruchirapalli, is one of the largest sacred complexes in Tamil Nadu, its outermost walls defining a rectangle 950m by 816m.

The Temple was founded in the Chola period, and benefitted from the sponsorship of the Pandyas and Hoysalas in the 12C–13C before being thoroughly sacked by the Delhi troops in 1323. After the expulsion of the invaders from Southern India in 1371, the Temple was repaired and expanded under the emperors and commanders of Vijayanagara [20B–C]. The most vigorous period of growth was during the 16C–17C Nayaka period. Building works continue today: the great tower over the outermost south *gopura* was completed only in 1987.

The Ranganatha Temple is remarkable for the geometric clarity of its **Plan**. It is laid out in a series of seven concentric rectangular enclosures defined by high walls containing an overall area of 63ha. The *gopuras* in the middle of each side are aligned along roads that proceed axially inwards towards the central shrine. The outer three enclosures are occupied by houses accommodating the town's population. The broad thoroughfares separating these outer enclosures are used for chariot festivals in December–January. Devotees mostly approach the monument from the south, along Big Bazaar Street, which leads directly to the south-facing shrine of Ranganatha.

Sheshagiri Mandapa, Ranganatha Temple, Srirangam

The outermost south *gopura* of the Temple dates from the 17C, being an unfinished project of Tirumala Nayaka of Madurai (1623–60). Its lower granite storeys present a vast mass divided into a high basement, and two pilastered storeys with sequences of niches set into the wall projections. The recent brick-and-cement pyramidal tower, with 13 diminishing storeys, rises to a height of 77.5m, making it one of the tallest in the state. The road proceeding north passes through *gopuras* of diminishing size. The gate in the second enclosure has paint-

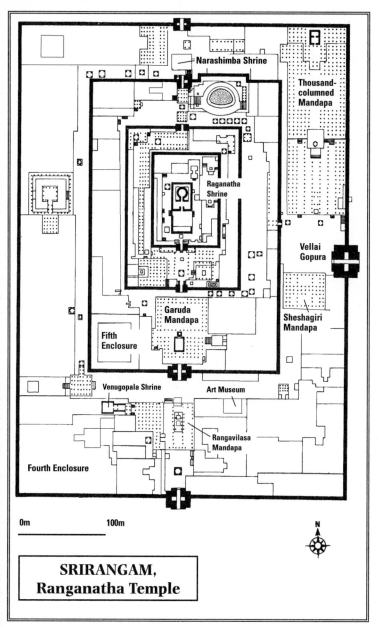

Narashimba Shrine

Thousand-
columned
Mandapa

Raganatha
Shrine

Vellai
Gopura

Garuda
Mandapa

Sheshagiri
Mandapa

Fifth
Enclosure

Venugopala Shrine

Art Museum

Rangavilasa
Mandapa

Fourth Enclosure

0m   100m

N

**SRIRANGAM,
Ranganatha Temple**

ings of religious processions on the passageway ceiling; the *gopura* in the third
enclosure displays Vijayanagara emblems, with a boar, sun and moon incised on
the jambs.

The *gopura* in the fourth enclosure marks the entrance to the sacred precinct. A court is reached immediately on entering, with shops at either side and the **Rangavilasa Mandapa** at its north end. This late 17C hall has three spacious aisles defined by piers with attached colonettes, alternating with *yali* piers at the south end. The small pavilion in the middle has ceiling paintings illustrating the Vasanta festival, with a mock battle between Kama and Rati, as well as episodes from the *Ramayana*.

To the west stands the small east-facing **Venugopala Shrine**, an exquisitely finished structure of the early 17C, entered on the east through a small porch with double flights of steps. The Shrine is elevated on a boldly modelled basement, the walls above showing deeply recessed niches filled with figures, among the finest in Nayaka art. Gracefully posed maidens holding musical instruments, mirrors and a parrot flank icons of Krishna playing the flute in the middle of the sanctuary walls; Tumburu and Narada are seen on the outer walls of the antechamber. The pyramidal tower above is crowned with a hemispherial roof. (A terrace nearby provides a rooftop panorama of the complex, including the gilded tower of the focal sanctuary.)

The **Art Museum** (no closed days), immediately east of the Rangavilasa Mandapa, has a small but remarkable collection of Nayaka ivory figurines and caskets, as well as copper-plate grants, bronze statuettes, arms and textiles. The **Sheshagiri Mandapa** is reached by passing around to the east side of the fourth enclosure. This hall is famous for the carvings on its eight outermost piers, which show riders on richly bridled horses leaping upwards on their hind legs; smaller warriors beneath slay panthers and *yalis*. The animation and virtuosity of the almost three-dimensional animals and figures are unsurpassed. Together with the sculptures at Vellore [38A], these are the most notable examples of Vijayanagara art in the late 16C.

Immediately east of the Sheshagiri Mandapa is the **Vellai *Gopura***, one of the finest of the series. Its well-proportioned nine-storeyed tower has prominent projections in the middle of the long sides; the lowest storey has stone columns set into the window openings. The Vijayanagara emblem is seen on one of the lintels in the passageway. The **Thousand-Columned Mandapa**, north of the Sheshagiri Mandapa, occupies the northeast corner of the enclosure. Ten rows of columns on rising floor levels lead to a small sanctuary at the north end. Wheels and prancing horses are sculpted on the basement of a porch contained with the hall.

The tour of the Ranganatha Temple continues by returning to the *gopura* on the south side of the fifth enclosure. This gives access to the 17C **Garuda Mandapa**, a spacious hall with a shrine at the south end containing a huge image of the kneeling eagle-headed mount of Vishnu. Pillars with attached colonettes and clusters of corbelled brackets define seven aisles running north–south. The central aisle, north of the Garuda shrine, has additional sculptures of donors, probably portraits of the later Nayakas of Madurai. The figures stand in attitudes of worship, dressed in finely detailed costumes and crowns, bearing daggers and knives. Among other features of interest in this enclosure are the three circular brick granaries on the west and the elliptical pond on the north.

A single *gopura* on the south leads into the sixth and seventh enclosures (access restricted to visitors) that constitute the core of the Ranganatha complex. Here stands the small part-circular Ranganatha shrine that houses a reclining image of Vishnu. Its tower is capped by a gilded hemispherical roof, with a frontal (south) arched frame containing a standing figure of the same god. The walls of the corridor surrounding the sanctuary are covered with paintings dating from the early 18C. They illustrate legends pertaining to Ranganatha, as well as scenes from the life of Krishna. At the end of one composition is a portrait of Vijayaranga Chokkanatha of Madurai (1706–32) and his queens, adoring the temple divinity.

Other places of interest associated with the Ranganatha Temple stand outside the complex. A large square tank to the west is used for float ceremonies at festival time in February. The **Amman Mandapa** on the bank of the Kaveri River, 1km south of the complex, leads to a popular bathing *ghat*. This structure was originally built by one of the Madurai queens.

2km east of the Ranganatha complex is the village of **Tiruvannakoil** and the **Jambukeshvara Temple**, the second great religious monument on Srirangam Island. This impressive complex is entered through a sequence of five *gopuras* on the west. These follow a standard pattern, diminishing in height and area from outside to inside. The largest *gopura*, a vast unfinished project, is seen in the middle of the outermost east enclosure wall. The first *gopura* on the west leads to a large open columned hall, facing south towards a square tank with a central pavilion. The sacred precinct is reached after passing through the second and third *gopuras*. Here stands an impressive hall with wide corridors; the spacious central crossing is defined by complex piers, with clusters of heavy brackets carrying the lofty ceiling. The hall is probably no earlier than the 19C.

Two more *gopuras* give access to the two sanctuaries that constitute the ritual heart of the monument (access restricted to visitors). Their modest scale and simple features contrast with the grandiose architecture of the outer enclosures. A small unadorned chamber has a *linga* at a lower level, over which water pours perpetually from a hidden spring. The adjacent open chamber contains a *jambu* tree with spreading branches. Subsidiary Natesha shrines are placed at the northwest corners of the two innermost enclosures. The east-facing **Akhilandeshvari Shrine** stands in the north part of the complex, in a separate compound surrounded by colonnaded corridors. A flagpole, altar, seated Nandi and Ganesha shrine are arranged in a row outside the two *gopuras* that lead to the goddess shrine.

C. Srinivasanallur

The Chola temple at this small village, 45km northwest of Tiruchirapalli, stands on the road running upstream along the north bank of the Kaveri River after crossing Srirangam Island. (The road continues to Namakkal [42D], 37km northwest, on NH7.)

The **Koranganatha Temple**, erected in about 927, is a typical examples of the early Chola style. The basement that runs around the building has friezes of fully rounded *yalis* and *makaras*. The pilasters on the south wall frame a niche carving of Dakshinamurti discoursing with sages, with Bhikshatanamurti to one side. No original carvings survive in the west and north niches, but attendants are seen on the flanking walls. The figures are remarkable for the elegant postures, many turned at a slight angle to the wall plane, and the delicate modelling. The niche pediments are carved with foliated *makaras* and miniature figures. The brick-and-plaster pyramidal tower, perhaps once containing an upper sanctuary, is capped by a square roof. Foliate decoration is incised on the jambs of the east doorway.

D. Kodumbalur

This small settlement, 36km southwest of Tiruchirapalli, is notable for the **Muvarkoil**, a small complex dating from the early Chola era. Only two out of the three 9C shrines still stand. These small west-facing structures have moulded basements adorned with boldy sculpted *yalis*. The pilastered wall niches house icons of Shiva in the middle of three sides, with the god as Bhikshatana appearing on the north. Sculptures are inserted into the upper storeys of the tower. The icon of Shiva dancing (south shrine, east face) is exceptional for the angular posture of the figure and the delicately incised details of the staring eyes and raised eyebrows. The two-storeyed towers are capped with square, heavy roof forms topped by pot finials. A platform with moulded stone sides extends in front of the three shrines.

The modest **Muchukundeshvara Temple**, another early Chola foundation, is located about 500m to the east.

E. Sittanavasal

The Jain **Cave Temple**, cut into the west flank of a long granite outcrop overlooking a spacious landscape, lies about 24km southeast of Kodumbalur or 15km directly northwest of Pudukkottai. This 9C monument, approached by a flight of steps, presents an austere portico, with two columns with rolled brackets. This leads to a small hall with carvings of the Parshvanatha (right) and Mahavira (left) in the side walls; three more Jinas are cut into the rear wall of the small shrine chamber. The interior is of particular interest for its delicately toned paintings. Dancing maidens and a royal figure with female attendants are painted on the columns. The hall ceiling is covered with a large composition, showing a lotus pond with elegantly drawn stalks, leaves and flowers in deep green and red. The pond is populated by youths bearing flowers, elephants, fish and ducks. The ceiling inside the sanctuary has a textile-like design with interlaced knotted patterns.

A natural **Cavern**, beneath a rocky overhang on top of the hill a short distance away, has polished beds used by Jain monks. A 1C–2C BC inscription may also be seen.

A prehistoric **Megalithic Site** is visible from the road 500m east of the Cave-Temple. This consists of a number of stone circles with cists, some up to 4.5m in diameter, also and dolmens.

F. Narttamalai

The structures at this rocky location, 40km south of Tiruchirapalli, are built on a terrace with a commanding view across the landscape. (The site can also be reached directly from Sittanavasal, about 16km away, via a back road.) Named after the founder of the Chola dynasty, the 9C **Vijayalaya Cholishvara Temple** at Narttamalai is actually the work a subordinate chief. The solidly proportioned building consists of a west-facing circular sanctuary contained within a square of outer walls, attached to a small hall. The pilastered walls are surmounted by eaves and a parapet, over which rises the two-storeyed tower. Guardian figures are placed either side of the doorway on the west, while Nandis appear beneath the hemispherical roof. The vestiges of wall paintings inside the hall include a large Bhairava figure. The Temple is surrounded by six subsidiary shrines that face towards the central shrine.

Two rock-cut shrines, 16m apart, are cut into the face of the nearby granite outcrop. The walls of the **Vishnu Cave Temple** are lined with identical images of the god sculpted in high relief, five on either side of the sanctuary doorway and one at either end. The sanctuary is devoid of any icon. The moulded plinth of a structural hall is seen outside. The adjacent **Shiva Cave Temple** has a *linga* sanctuary and a 7C inscription.

Loose carvings from ths site have mostly been removed to the Government Museum at Pudukkottai, 18km south.

G. Pudukkottai

This small city, 58km south of Tiruchirapalli, was once the capital of the Tondaimans, minor rulers who emerged at the end of the 17C under the Nayakas of Madurai. From 1753 these figures assisted British troops in their campaigns again Haidar Ali and the French. Thereafter, Pudukkottai was recognised as a princely state.

Nothing is now left of the Old Palace of the Tondaimans, but the New Palace, now the **Collector's Office**, stands about 1km west of the commercial heart of the city. This handsome stone building was built for Rajgopala Bahadur in 1929. It is entered through a porch with ornate arches on polished granite columns; the Tondaiman coat of arms is displayed in the pediments. A dome rises above the two-storeyed arcades of the main block. An inner rectangular court is surrounded by loggias at two levels. Another Tondaiman civic monument is the **District Headquarters**, on the south side of the city. This large red brick complex has twin towers with domical tops on either side of the entrance on the east. Among the places of worship in the city is the **Catholic Church**, a Neo-Gothic building with a gabled façade framed by tall steeples.

Tirugorakarna, the old part of Pudukkottai, is located 3km northwest of the city centre. Here stands the **Gokarneshvara Temple**, a 7C foundation much extended by the Tondaimans. The Temple is approached from the south through a long ceremonial corridor, the ceiling of which is covered with *Ramayana* paintings dating from the 18C. The panels over the east aisle show the gods seeking the help of Vishnu, the opening scene of the *Ramayana*. The sequence ends with Rama and Lakshmana leaving for the forest. The panels above the central aisle are devoted to the marriages of Dasharatha's four sons. The narrative continues over the west aisle, where the episode of Hanuman setting fire to Lanka shows an aerial view of the Ravana's city. The enclosure between the two *gopuras* at the north end of the corridor is occupied with a columned hall with sculpted *yalis* and riders on horses, as well as figures of Karna and Kama with Rati. The innermost enclosure accommodates the small Bakulavaneshvara and Brihadambal sanctuaries, the latter enshrining the protective goddess of the Tondaimans.

A small doorway at the northwest corner leads to the summit of the granite shelf on which the Temple is built. Here can be seen a small **Rock-cut Chamber**, assigned to the Pallava era. This is entered through a verandah with four squat columns. Ganesha (south) and Shiva receiving Ganga in his hair (north) are carved on the side walls. A set of Matrikas is carved out of the rock face to the southwest.

The **Government Museum** is situated near the entrance to the Temple. The archaeology section displays sculptures found at nearby sites such as Kodumbalur, as well as a set of 9C images from Narttamalai, depicting the Matrikas and Shiva as Dakshinamurti. The earliest bronzes date from the 10C. Images from the Chola and later periods illustrate a range of divinities. Copies of the Sittanavasal paintings are also on display.

From Pudukkottai it is possible to continue on to Madurai, 100km southwest, or Karaikkudi [44K], 43km south.

H. Avudaiyarkoil

The small town of Avudaiyarkoil, 47km southeast of Pudukkottai, is associated with the saint Manikkavachakar, who spent the larger part of his life here. The **Atmanatha Temple** is an artistically interesting complex, dating from the 17C–18C Tondaiman period. Its outermost *gopura* is approached through a large hall, with a broad passageway flanked by piers raised on a high platform. The supports display carvings of Tondaiman royal figures and their ministers; those at the end show almost three-dimensional images of Shiva in his fierce aspects, and armed guardians. A small shrine on the west is preceded by a square hall lined with donors and *yalis*.

The first *gopura* of the Atmanatha Temple series has a double sequence of basement mouldings; the pilastered walls are devoid of niches. The hall located between this and the second *gopura* has *yalis* projecting outwards from the peripheral columns. The central part of the hall is surrounded by *yalis*, warriors and donors, one of whom is identified as the Tondaiman minister. A later brick shrine, consecrated to Manikkavachakar, is situated to the west. The passageway around the central chamber has its walls entirely covered with murals illustrating the life of the saint. These are no earlier than the turn of the present century, as is evident from the episodes set in Pudukkottai's busy streets. Another hall with carved pillars stands in the second enclosure. The figures here include Manikkavachakar and Patanjali in the company of royal donors, warriors and maidens.

The focal shrine in the middle of the third enclosure is of interest, since it contains no image; here, devotees venerate an empty pedestal. This practice is said to be in accordance with Manikkavachakar's monistic philosophy. The shrine is an ornate structure, its outer walls enlivened with delicately fashioned pilasters. Perforated stone windows are inserted into the outer walls of the attached hall, which can only be entered through doorways at the two north corners. The surrounding columns display carvings of donors, sages, including the saint himself, and aspects of Shiva and Devi. The Ambal shrine, in the northwest corner, is also empty.

42 · Salem

Pleasantly surrounded by the Shevaroy and Nagaramalai Hills, this industrial city in the uplands of Tamil Nadu is an important textile and steel manufacturing centre. Though there is little of historical interest to be discovered in Salem, the city makes a convenient base from which to explore the pleasant hill resort at **Yercaud** [A], the picturesque mountain fort of **Sankaridrug** [B] and the artistic temples at **Tiruchengodu** [C], **Namakkal** [D] and **Punjai** [E].

■ **Transport**. Salem lies 328km southwest of Madras [36], partly by way of NH45, to which it is also linked by train. Situated on NH7, Salem enjoys direct connections with Bangalore [14], 205km north, and Madurai [44], 227km south. Tiruchirapalli [41] is 140km southeast, and Coimbatore [43] 158km west via NH47, the latter also joined by rail. Local buses reach all of the sites described here.

■ **Accommodation**. The *National* (☎ 54100) and *Hema International* are acceptable hotels in Salem (STD code 0427), but the *Hotel Pandiya*, just outside **Namakkal**, is another possibility. A stay at **Yercaud** (STD code 04281) is recommended as a pleasant alternative, the *Hotel Shevaroys* (☎ 2288) being the finest there.

■ **Tourist Information**. The TTDC maintains an office on Rajaram Nagar (☎ 66449).

A. Yercaud

This agreeable resort, nestling in the Shevaroy Hills at an altitude of almost 1500m, is renowned for its schools and coffee estates. The spot, 23km northeast of Salem, was settled by the British in the early 19C, and coffee was introduced in the 1820s. The whitewashed, red-tiled houses of the town stand south of **Yerikadu**, the Forest Lake which gives its name to the resort. The bazaar square is overlooked by the well-maintained **Holy Trinity Church**, a modest gabled building with Neo-Gothic windows. The cemetery at the rear has many of its graves intact. The **Club**, below the Church, is where planters still meet.

B. Sankaridrug

This picturesque hill **Fort** lies 35km southwest of Salem via NH7 or rail. The upper part of the east face of the rock on which the Fort is built rises about 500m above the plain. It is crescent-shaped in contour, giving the appearance of a conch shell, or *shanka*, hence the name Sankaridrug.

The Fort came under the command of the Nayakas of Madurai in the 17C, but was added to the kingdom of the Wodeyars of Mysore [15A] by the conquest of Chikka Deva Raja in 1689. After being taken from Tipu Sultan by the British in 1792, Sankaridrug served as the headquarters of an British battalion. It was abandoned in 1828.

The ascent of Sankaridrug is most easily made from the east, the path being shielded by a sequence of ten **Gates**. The first Gate is set in a circuit of walls that extends around the foot of the rock. Beyond the third Gate stands the small **Varadaraja Perumal Temple**. A steep flight of steps climbs to the fourth Gate, strongly built in stone. The fifth Gate is defended by bastions, one square the other round. The ramparts here are assigned to Tipu Sultan. On the left they run to a cave associated with a Muslim saint, on the south spur of the hill. Another flight of steps leads to the next three Gates, situated about halfway up the hill. These are the work of Lakshmi Kanta Raja, the Governor of the Fort under the Wodeyars.

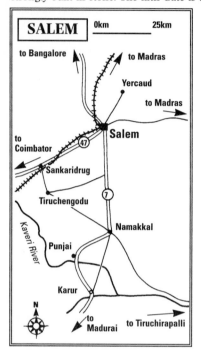

A **Magazine** with a barrel-vaulted roof stands between the seventh and eighth Gates, the latter partly demolished. The ninth Gate, erected in 1799, commands the point where the path reaches the brow of the hill. Steps from here give access to the topmost Gate, set in a ring of walls running around the summit. The few structures that survive here include a small Vishnu shrine and a modest mosque on the verge of a precipice. The highest point is marked by a platform for a flag staff, near to which stand rectangular flat-roofed granaries and a store with three compartments.

C. Tiruchengodu

This small town is situated 11km south of Sankaridrug or 50km directly south-west of Salem. Two temples, one in the middle of the town and the other at the summit of a bare granite hill that rises to the west, are Chola foundations, much patronised by the Nayaka and Wodeyar Governors of Sankaridrug in the 17C–18C. The lower **Kailasanatha Temple** is entered on the east through a 25m high *gopura*, which faces towards a 16m high fluted stone column and a large colonnade crowded with shops. Chariots with excellent wooden carvings are parked in the street nearby. The entrance *gopura* has finely worked basement mouldings and pilastered niches. The brightly painted, multi-storeyed tower is crowded with figures. This leads to the main Temple, approached through a spacious hall, with outer supports fashioned as leaping *yalis* with riders. Paintings cover the ceiling over the central space. The small *linga* shrine beyond is unremarkable, as are the twin subshrines immediately north. Of greater interest are the 63 Nayanmars and *naga* stones housed in a colonnade on the south side of the enclosure. A plaster covered Nandi in the northeast corner conceals steps descending to a small well.

A winding path of 1200 steps, passing by halls, subsidiary shrines and a large Nandi, ascends to the upper **Ardhanarishvara Temple**, perched near the summit of the hill more than 250m above Tiruchengodu. One portion of the steps is treated as a hallowed site for taking oaths. The steps arrive at a terrace with fine views of the town beneath. The *gopura* here is a large ornate structure, with signs of the zodiac carved on the passageway ceiling; the doors preserve their wooden panels. This serves as the main gate on the north side of the square Temple compound. Visitors arriving by car, however, will enter through a modern *gopura* on the west.

The twin shrines of this Temple, dedicated to Ardhanarishvara and Subrahmanya, stand in a walled zone surrounded by halls with elaborate carvings. Leaping *yalis* with riders mark the outer supports, while those lining the central aisles on both the east and west sides of the inner unit have fully carved figures of donors and attendant ladies, as well as paired images of Manmatha and Rati, Virabhadra and Kali. Even an Englishman, hat in hand, is seen here. He represents the British Collector of Salem, who undertook repairs to the Temple in 1823. The ceilings are exceptional for their depictions of mock battles between Manmatha and Rati, and the ornate central lotuses surrounded by parrots. The west-facing Ardhanarishvara sanctuary houses a unique cult object: a treated tree trunk dressed in *lungi* and sari. The adjacent Subrahmanya sanctuary faces in the opposite direction. The Nageshvara subshrine, in the west part of the complex, is intricately carved with royal figures and European guards, as well as divinities.

D. Namakkal

This town, 50km south of Salem on NH7, or 35km southeast of Tiruchengodu, nestles at the base of a massive granite rock, with remnants of a Fort on top. The principal monument at Namakkal is the **Narasimha Temple**, a largely 18C complex built up to the west flank of the hill, into which is excavated a much earlier Cave Temple. The complex is entered through a towerless *gopura*, beyond which stands an open hall sheltering an altar and flagpole. A second *gopura*, also missing its superstructure, leads to the inner compound, where a Garuda shrine is seen. Here stands the main Temple, entirely walled in, entered by steps on the north and south. The two halls within lead to the 8C **Cave Temple**, which enshrines an impressive image of Narasimha seated with Surya and Chandra. The side walls have additional icons of Varaha and Trivikrama (right) and Narasimha killing Hiranyakashipu and Vishnu seated on the serpent (left). The large scale and vigorous postures of these figures are typical of Pandya art.

The **Fort** on top of the 65m high hill is attributed to Ramachandra Nayaka, the Governor under the Wodeyars in the 18C. It was taken by the British in 1768, but was lost the following year to Haidar Ali; after 1792 it was garrisoned by the East India Company's troops. The summit is most easily accessible from the southwest, on which side narrow steps have been cut into the rock. The remains of the first line of **Fortifications** are seen on the lower south slope. The stone ramparts are topped by a brick parapet with projecting guardrooms. A masonry platform that runs around the walls gives access to loop holes set into them. A ruined treasury and a magazine stand inside the small walled area at the top.

E. Punjai

This small town, known also as Vellur, on the north bank of the Kaveri River, is located 22km southwest of Namakkal, just off NH7. The **Naltunai Ishvara Temple** here has outstanding examples of early Chola sculpture. The 10C structure presents the standard arrangement of sanctuary, antechamber and columned hall. Miniature panels illustrating narrative scenes are carved on the basement. The niches in the pilastered walls accommodate delicately modelled icons of Ganesha, Agastya and Dakshinamurti flanked by sages (south), Shiva appearing out of the *linga* (west), and Brahma and Durga (north). Guardian figures flank the east doorway. Most of the upper part of the building is a later replacement.

43 · Coimbatore

Coimbatore derives much of its economic importance from its location immediately east of Palghat, the broadest pass in the Western Ghats between Tamil Nadu and Kerala. While the city itself [A] offers only a few features of interest, it serves as the gateway to the Nilgiri Hills, the highest in Southern India, a great attraction for many visitors.

Coonoor [B] and **Udhagamandalam** [C], the latter more familiar as Ootacamund or simply Ooty, are the most popular of the stations founded by the British. A stay at either is recommended.

Unlike other parts of Tamil Nadu, the Coimbatore area has few religious monuments. That at **Avanashi** [D] is one of the largest. It is reached in a half-day trip, with the possibility of continuing on to Salem [42].

For wildlife enthusiasts there are the National Park at **Annamalai** [E] and the Wildlife Sanctuary at **Parambikulam** [F].

■ **Transport**. Coimbatore is well served, with air services from Madras [36] and Madurai [44], as well as from Bombay [1], Bangalore [14] and Thiruvananthapuram [46]. The city lies on the main rail line from Madras to Kochi [47] in Kerala, with connections to Tiruchirapalli [41]. NH47 links Coimbatore with Salem, 158km east, and Kochi, 184km west. The road running north to Udhagamandalam, 98km northwest, continues 154km further north to Mysore [15] in Karnataka.

The journey by narrow-gauge train from Mettupalayam, 53km north of Coimbatore, to Udhagamandalam via Coonoor, is delightful. The train negotiates 16 tunnels and 250 bridges, climbing through tea plantations and lush forests before reaching the grassy high plains of the Nilgiri Hills. Buses are available to most destinations in the vicinity, but a car is essential to reach Annamalai and Parambikulam.

■ **Accommodation**. The *Hotel City Tower* (☎ 230681) and *Surya International Hotel* (☎ 217751) are the best in Coimbatore (STD code 0422). A larger range of accommodation is available at **Udhagamandalam** (STD code 0423), the most comfortable being the *Savoy Hotel* (☎ 44142), *Fernhill Palace* (☎ 43910), *Southern Star Palace* (☎ 43601) and *Lake View* (☎ 43904). The luxurious *Taj Garden Retreat* (☎ 20021) at **Coonoor** (STD code 04624) is an attractive alternative.

■ **Tourist Information**. A TTDC office is maintained at the railway station, and there is one on Commercial Road in Udhagamandalam (☎ 43977).

A. Coimbatore

Coimbatore's forested mountain setting has not prevented the city from developing into a major industrial centre. Since the 1930s hydro-electric power from the nearby **Pykara Falls** has boosted cotton manufacturing; textile mills are scattered all over the city. Coimbatore is also of importance for agricultural development, and serves as the home of the **Agricultural College and Research Institute**.

The **Botanical Gardens**, on the western edge of Coimbatore, were established at the turn of the century. Extending over some 300ha, they incorporate formal plantations of roses and a recently developed section with flowering trees. The nearby **Museum of the Agricultural College** (closed Sundays) displays seeds, fibres, minerals, rocks, implements and tools.

The only historical monument of note in the Coimbatore area is at **Perur**, 6km west of the city centre. The **Patteshvara Temple**, dating back to the 14C, was much developed by the Nayakas of Madurai before being extensively renovated in the 19C. A 11m high stone lamp pole stands immediately inside the entrance *gopura*. Carvings of Indian soldiers holding muskets are seen on the pillars of the outer hall. The stone Nandi placed on an axis with the main shrine is associated with the saint Sundarar, who is supposed to have visited the Temple. Almost three-dimensional figures adorn the columns in the hall leading to the main shrine. Among the deities are Shiva dancing on the dwarf and the same god holding out the skin of the elephant demon that he has just slain.

B. Coonoor

At 1858m above sea level, this is the second largest hill station in the Nilgiri Hills, after Udhagamandalam. Coonoor lies at the head of a deep ravine on the east side of the Dodabetta range, 85km northwest of Coimbatore. The climate is noticeably warmer and less wet than that at Udhagamandalam, 13km northwest.

Sim's Park, the major attraction of Coonoor, was founded in the middle of the 19C. The Park, which spreads across a ravine, is laid out as a botanical garden, with a large variety of trees and plants, including huge tree-ferns, giant rhododendrons and more than 300 varieties of roses. The **Pasteur Institute** (open Saturdays), opposite the main gate, established in 1907, researches into rabies and manufactures polio vaccines. The **Silkwork Rearing Station** is situated next door. The nearby **All Souls Church** was consecrated in 1872. This bold basalt building has steep gables and a corner tower topped with a gallery and steeple.

Numerous excursions are possible from Conoor. **Lamb's Rock**, 6km away, offers panoramas of the the coffee and tea plantations covering the lower slopes of the Nilgiri Hills, with the plains of Coimbatore beyond. Catherine's Falls can be viewed at **Dolphin's Nose**, 10km distant. The ruins of a fort used by Tipu Sultan at **Droog**, 13km away, require a walk of 3km from the nearest road.

Wellington, 3km above Coonoor, was established in 1852 as a military cantonment. It still serves as the headquarters of the 250-year-old Madras Regiment.

C. Udhagamandalam

This celebrated hill station, with its numerous relics of the British period, is still affectionately known as Ooty or Ootacamund. It is situated 2240m above sea level, at which elevation the Nilgiri Hills form a high plateau, with grassy rolling slopes planted with eucalyptus and imported conifers. Heavy rain and mist are characteristic of the winter season. This landscape is the original habitat of the **Todas**, an indigenous tribal people who tend herds of shaggy buffalo. The Todas live in barrel-vaulted thatched houses and worship in similarly constructed conical-shaped temples, which function like dairies. Many Todas have now converted to Christianity.

In 1799 the East India Company annexed the Nilgiri Hills, together with their Toda population, from the territory of Tipu Sultan. It was not until 1818 that the Udhagamandalam site was identified by two young assistants of John Sullivan, the Collector of Coimbatore. Within a few years a bridle path was completed to the new station, and by 1823 Sullivan had completed his Stone House on land purchased from the Todas. This encouraged the settlement of Europeans, who were attracted by the cool climate and the availability of English fruits, vegetables and trees that were planted here. In 1861 Udhagamandalam, which had by this time been Anglicised as Ootacamund, began to function as the summer capital of the Madras Presidency. The Governors and their retinues flocked to the resort, followed by other Europeans and even princely personalities. The active life of the station included a lively programme of sporting events. Tea was introduced by a French botanist, M. Perrotett; coffee was a later import. The popularity of the resort has continued to increase, and it is now the largest hill station in Tamil Nadu.

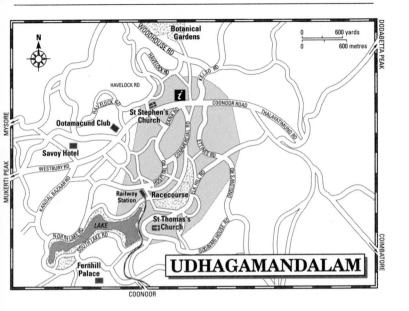

The main town lies between the Lake and the Botanical Gardens, two of Udhagamandalam's chief attractions. The 2.5km long **Lake** covers an area of more than 25ha, with the famous narrow-gauge 'toy' railway line running along one bank; rowing boats are available for hire. **St Thomas's Church** of 1870, on the east side of the Lake, is a modest structure with a low steep roof. The adjoining **Cemetery** has a large pillar surmounted a cross, marking the grave of William Patrick Adam, a Governor of Madras, who died in 1881. **Fernhill Palace**, just south of the Lake, was built in 1842 as a holiday retreat for the Mysore ruler. It is now a hotel.

Two main bazaar streets proceed in parallel formation from the railway station until they unite in Commercial Road. To the south is the **Race Course**, the site of the most active equestrian club in Tamil Nadu, dating back to 1894. The bazaar terminates at **Charing Cross**, a major intersection marked by a cast-iron fountain. A short distance further along stands Sullivan's **Stone House**, now the residence of the principal of the Government Art College which has its campus opposite.

A road running perpendicular to Commercial Road leads to St Stephen's Church. On the way it passes the red-brick **Nilgiri Library** of 1885, designed by Robert Fellowes Chisholm. Its lofty reading room is lit by five arched windows, with a tall Neo-Gothic window at the end. The nearby **District and Sessions Court** is contained in a red-brick range, with a steeply pitched corrugated-iron roof and a slender clock tower capped with a spire. It was erected in 1873 as a private school.

St Stephen's Church, one of Udhagamandalam's most important landmarks, was consecrated in 1831 by the Bishop of Calcutta and was named in honour of Stephen Lushington, the then Governor of Madras. The building has a long narrow nave flanked by windows, separated by buttresses that protrude as steeples above the battlemented parapet. A quartet of similar steeples crowns the massive square tower. The Church is entered through an arcaded porch. The timbers used in its roof are reputed to have been pillaged from Tipu Sultan's palace at Srirangapattana [15C]. The cemetery which climbs up the hill behind is filled with graves, many of children.

A short distance beyond St Stephen's Church stands the exclusive **Ootacamund Club**. A drive lined with conifers leads to the main building, erected in 1830 by Sir William Rumbold as his private residence. Among his guests were Lord William Bentinck, who suppressed the practice of *suttee*, and Thomas Babington Macaulay, who wrote the Indian Penal Code, both of whom stayed here in 1834. The Club was convened in 1843, and maintains its British traditions. The walls are hung with hunting trophies, and there are portraits of British and Indian worthies. The game of snooker is said to have been invented in the billiards room; the rules, dated 1881, are posted on the wall. The Ooty Hunt, which still rides to hounds in pursuit of jackals, is the Club's other major claim to fame. A short distance beyond stands the **Savoy Hotel**, originally intended as a school for the Church Mission Society.

Among the other sights of interest are the **Botanical Gardens**, 2km northeast of the station, established in 1848. Over 20ha are planted, with more than 1000 varieties of plants, shrubs and trees, including orchids, ferns, alpines and medicinal plants among beautiful lawns, lily ponds and glass houses. The annual Flower Show is a popular event in May. The half-timbered gateway to **Raj Bhavan**, formerly Government House, is superbly sited on Dodabetta Ridge at the top of the Gardens. The mansion, which stands in its own well-maintained grounds, was built in an Italianate style in 1880 for the Duke of Buckingham, when he was Governor of Madras. A typical Toda village, or *mund*, with thatched wooden houses is seen to the east of the Gardens.

Udhagamandalam spreads over a number of hills, many now built up. **Dodabetta**, Big Mountain, which rises to 2637m, east of the town, is still comparatively bare. The valleys of the Nilgiri Hills contain a large number of lakes and reservoirs, one of the closest is Marlimund Lake, 5km distant. **Kalhatti Falls**, which drop some 40m, are 12km north. **Mukerti Peak** is a spectacular lookout on the west edge of the Nilgiris, gazing down into Kerala from a perpendicular rock face some 2000m deep. The Peak forms part of the **Nilgiri Tahr Sanctuary**, noted for its wild buffalo.

D. Avanashi

This town, 40km northeast of Coimbatore, takes its name from the **Avanishvara Temple.** Dating back to the 13C, this monument was substantially renovated in the 18C under the patronage of the Wodeyars of Mysore. The *gopuras* through which the complex is entered were entirely rebuilt in 1756. A colossal Nandi is located on an axis with the main sanctuary. The nearby carvings of two alligators, each shown vomiting up a child, refer to the legend of the saint Sundarar, who interceded with Shiva for the life of a child who had been swallowed by an alligator. A shrine to the saint is included within the complex.

E. Annamalai

This **National Park** covers some 960sq km of forest in the Western Ghats, 60km south of Coimbatore via Pollachi. There is a large range of wildlife, including langur, elephant, tiger, panther, sloth and wild boar, as well as many birds.

F. Parambikulam

This **Wildlife Sanctuary**, 35km further south of Pollachi, is notable for its tropical rainforest, sheltered by the Neeliampathi Hills on the west. The reserve, which is rich in birdlife, is noteworthy for its teak forest, under management since 1845; some trees are reputed to be more than 400 years old. The Sanctuary contains three dams, the waters of which are home to a variety of endangered species, such as crocodiles, otters and turtles.

44 · Madurai

This city [A] is celebrated for its great temple, perhaps the largest in Southern India and certainly one of the most vibrant. This complex is testimony to the wealth and patronage of the Madurai Nayakas in the 16C–17C, who were responsible for building the palace at Madurai, as well as the religious monuments at nearby **Tirupparankunram** [B] and **Alagarkoil** [C]. Two days should be reserved for these sights.

A trip northwest of Madurai may take in the fort at **Dindigul** [D] and the hill temple at **Palani** [E], but additional time will be required to reach the hill station at **Kodaikanal** [F], a recommended overnight excursion.

The twin temples at **Srivilliputtur** [G], south of Madurai, may be visited on the way to Tirunelveli [45].

A journey to the Setupati palace at **Ramanthapuram** [H], the port of **Kilakkarai** [I] and the sacred island of **Rameswaram** [J], southeast of Madurai, will demand another overnight stay.

A tour of the mansions of **Karaikkudi and Devakottai** [K] makes an unusual day trip from Madurai, with the option of continuing on to Pudukkottai [41G] and Tiruchirapalli [41A].

■ **Transport**. Madurai is connected by plane and rail to Madras [36]; by road it lies 461km southwest of the state capital on NH45. Madurai is about midway between Tiruchirapalli, 142km north on NH45, and Tirunelveli, 154km south on NH7, the itineraries for which may be combined with that described here. Rail connections are available with both two cities, as well as with Dindigul, Palani, Ramanathapuram and Rameswaram. A convenient and picturesque train runs between Madurai and Kolam [46H] in Kerala. As elsewhere in Tamil Nadu, bus services are frequent.

■ **Accommodation**. The finest hotels at Madurai (STD code 0452) are located outside the city. The *Taj Garden Retreat* (☎ 601020) occupies an old planter's cottage 6km southwest of the centre; the *Pandyan Hotel* (☎ 542471) and *Hotel Madurai Ashok* (☎ 42531) are 2km north. More modest, yet adequate, lodgings within the city are provided by the *Hotel Aarathy* (☎ 541571), *Hotel*

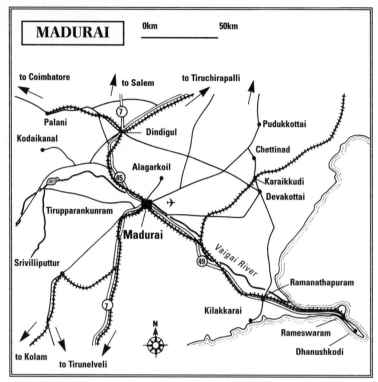

| MADURAI | 0km | 50km |

to Coimbatore

to Salem

to Tiruchirapalli

Palani

Kodaikanal

Dindigul

Pudukkottai

Chettinad

Alagarkoil

Karaikkudi

Devakottai

Tirupparankunram

Madurai

Vaigai River

Srivilliputtur

Ramanathapuram

Kilakkarai

Rameswaram

Dhanushkodi

to Kolam

to Tirunelveli

Supreme (☎ 543151) and *Hotel Times* (☎ 546351). For overnight stays at **Kodaikanal** (STD code 04542), the *Carlton* (☎ 40056), *Hotel Kodai International* (☎ 40649) and *Valley View Hotel* (☎ 40635) may be considered. Accommodation is still limited at **Rameswaram** (STD code 04573), the *Hotel Tamil Nadu* (☎ 21277) being the best available. The *Hotel Malar* (☎ 2321) at **Karaikkudi** (STD code 04565) will be useful to visitors wishing to explore the Chettinad region.

■ **Tourist Information**. The TTTDC has an office on West Veli Street (☎ 34757) and one at the railway station (☎ 33888). Information centres are also maintained at **Kodaikanal**, at the Rest House Complex near the bus stand, and at **Rameswaram**, at 14 East Car Street (☎ 21371).

A. Madurai

This city, on the south bank of the Vaigai River, served as the capital of the Pandyas, the most important rulers in the southern part of Tamil Nadu during the 7C–13C.

No vestiges of the Pandya period survive, because of the destruction caused by the Delhi forces under Malik Kafur, who conquered the Madurai kingdom in 1323. The city thereupon became the centre of Muslim rule in

Southern India. The sultans of Madurai did not last beyond 1378, when the city was absorbed into the empire of Vijayanagara [20B–C]. Because of the great distance from the capital in Karnataka, the Vijayanagara Governors, known as Nayakas, enjoyed considerable freedom, gradually asserting their independence. By the second half of the 16C the Madurai Nayakas were effectively autonomous, ruling over the previous territories of the Pandyas. Of the many powerful kings of this dynasty, Tirumala (1623–60) is famous for his ambitious building programmes; his portraits are found in many temples throughout the region. The Madurai Nayakas came into conflict with their counterparts in Thanjavur [40A] and Gingee [39F], but managed to resist the Mughal and Maratha invasions that extinguished these other lines. The last Nayakas were taken up with battles against the Nawabs of Arcot [38B]. In 1763 the city came under the control of the British, and was garrisoned for some years afterwards.

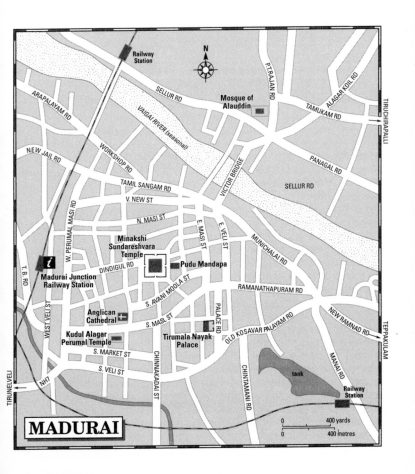

The centre of Madurai is dominated by the **Minakshi Sundareshvara Temple**, founded by the Pandyas, but entirely rebuilt in later times. Almost all the Madurai Nayakas, their wives and ministers made donations to the monument; as a result, the Temple is an amalgam of different structures, most of which date from the 17C–18C. This is even true of the twin shrines to Sundareshvara, a form of Shiva, and the goddess Minakshi, the guardian deity of Madurai and protector of its ruling house, which were completely rebuilt during this period. The Temple calendar is replete with ceremonies and celebrations, the most important being the 12-day festival in April-May, which commemorates the coronation of Minakshi and her marriage to Shiva. The climax of this event is the great Chariot festival, which takes place in the broad streets that run parallel to the outer walls of the complex.

The Temple is contained by high walls that create an almost square enclosure, some 254m by 238m, entered in the middle of each side by *Gopuras* that soar above the houses of the city. The gates are exceptional for their towers with elongated proportions and curved profiles, which achieve a dramatic sweep upwards; that on the south is the tallest, attaining a height of 55m. The lower granite portions of the *Gopuras* have moulded basements and double sequences of pilastered storeys. The carvings here are confined to miniature animals and figures at the base of the walls and pilasters. The brick towers above have openings in the middle of the long sides to light the hollow chambers at each level. The openings immediately above the eaves sheltering the entrance passageways have pairs of free-standing stone colonettes. The upper storeys are crowded with plaster figures of divinities, celestial beings, guardians and animal mounts. Fierce monster masks with protruding eyes and horns mark the arched ends of the vaulted roofs. All these elements are painted in vibrant colours.

Visitors generally enter the Temple through the **Ashta Shakti Mandapa**, or Hall of the Eight Goddesses, projecting outwards from the enclosure wall south of the east *gopura*. This porch was erected by two of Tirumala's queens. Eight goddesses and two male donor figures are carved on the columns; modern paintings cover the curved brick vault above. A doorway flanked by sculptures of Ganesha and Subrahmanya leads into the **Minakshi Nayaka Mandapa**, a spacious columned hall used for shops and stores. This was built in 1707 by Shanmugan Minakshi, the minister of Vijayaranga Chokkanatha II (1706–32). Its piers have lion brackets carrying suspended beams. At the far end (west) of this hall is a doorway surrounded by a brass frame covered with oil lamps. The towered gateway here is on an axis with the Minakshi shrine further west.

The corridor beyond the gateway is flanked by superb carvings of dancing men, attendant women and Shiva as Bhikshatanamurti. It leads to the courtyard of the **Potramarai Kulam**, or Golden Lily Tank. This rectangular stepped tank has a brass lamp column in the middle and colonnades on four sides. The sculptures in the middle of the north side depict early Pandya kings. The walls of the colonnade on the north and east are decorated with dilapidated murals, representing the 64 legendary deeds that Shiva performed in and around Madurai. The ceilings are painted with large medallions. One composition, illustrating the marriage of Shiva and Minakshi, covers the ceiling of a small pavilion that projects over the water on the west side of the tank. The hall here is known as the **Pancha Pandava Mandapa**, after the heros of the *Mahabharata* epic sculpted in full relief on the columns lining the central north-

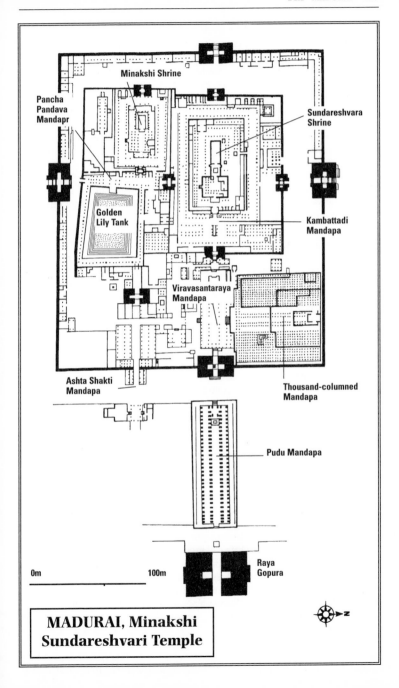

Minakshi Shrine

Pancha
Pandava
Mandapr

Sundareshvara
Shrine

Golden
Lily Tank

Kambattadi
Mandapa

Viravasantaraya
Mandapa

Ashta Shakti
Mandapa

Thousand-columned
Mandapa

Pudu Mandapa

Raya
Gopura

0m   100m

**MADURAI, Minakshi
Sundareshvari Temple**

south aisle. The carvings date from the late 17C. This hall precedes the **Minakshi Shrine**, which stands in its own compound, together with subsidiary sanctuaries (access restricted to visitors). The bedchamber in the northeast corner is where the image of Sundareshvara is brought each night, having been transported in a palanquin from the god's own sanctuary.

A small *gopura* at the north end of the Pancha Pandava Mandapa marks the entry into the colonnaded enclosure that surrounds the **Sundareshvara Shrine** on four sides. The fish emblems on the column shafts are emblems of Minakshi. A large Ganapati image is positioned opposite the *gopura* just noted. Entry to the main Shrine, which also stands in its own compound, is through a small gate on the east flanked by guardian figures (access restricted to visitors). Immediately in front (east) is the **Kambattadi Mandapa**, an imposing hall with a seated Nandi within a pavilion, and an altar and gilded flagpole in the middle. These features are surrounded by eight piers carved with outsized images of Natesha, Virabhadra, Kali and other Shaiva deities.

A *gopura* on the east side leads to the **Viravasantaraya Mandapa**, a project of Vijayaranga Chokkanatha. This immense corridor, more than 75m long, is lined with piers leading to the outermost east *gopura* of the complex. The Viravasantaraya Mandapa is usually filled with merchants and pilgrims. To the south is the wooden-roofed Kalyana Mandapa, where the ritual marriage of Minakshi and Sundareshvara is celebrated at festival time.

To the north is the extensive Thousand-columned Hall, actually with 985 supports, now the **Temple Art Museum** (no closed days). The frontal (south) porch has animals and figures fashioned almost in three dimensions. They include a mounted warrior, dancing bearded man and gypsy woman. The corner supports are concealed by clusters of cut-out colonettes. A corridor lined with rearing *yalis*, female musicians and attendants, leads to an impressive bronze image of dancing Shiva, raised on the dais at the north end of the Hall. Stone carvings, bronzes, ivory figurines and metal ritual objects form part of the Museum display. Instructive copies of the murals surrounding the Potramarai Kulam are also exhibited.

The **Pudu Mandapa**, completed in 1635 by Tirumala Nayaka, stands outside the Minkashi Temple, on an axis with the east *gopura*. This grandiose structure now accommodates the tailors of Madurai, all busy with their sewing machines. The peripheral columns at either end of the Pudu Mandapa have riders on magnificent animals rearing outwards. Large fully modelled icons of Kali (south) and Natesha (north) mark the ends of the front (west) corridor. Here, too, can be seen a composition illustrating the marriage of Minakshi with Sundareshvara, attended by Vishnu, the bride's brother. The side aisles have lofty ceilings carried on brackets fashioned as seated *yalis*.

The interior of the Pudu Mandapa opens up into a large space. The columns are carved with robust royal figures, portraying all of the Nayaka kings up to Tirumala. Each ruler is accompanied by his family members and ministers. A small pavilion, with slender polished black stone columns and a wooden roof, stands at the west end of the hall. The lowest storeys of Tirumala's unfinished **Raya Gopura** are seen on the other side of the street, west of the Pudu Mandapa. This gate is more than twice the dimensions of the other *Gopuras* of the Temple. The door jambs, more than 15m high, have finely carved scrollwork. A short distance southwest of the Temple stands the **Anglican Cathedral**, consecrated in 1881. This somewhat austere Neo-Gothic building, designed by Chisholm, well known for his work in Madras, has an unplastered masonry tower devoid of any steeple. The **Kazimar Mosque**, regarded as the Jami of the city, is located nearby. This 14C structure consists of a simple colonnaded prayer chamber and antechamber preceded by a porch, now obscured by a recent extension on the east.

The **Kudal Alagar Perumal Temple**, the principal sanctuary of Vishnu at Madurai, is located near the bus stand, 1km southwest of the Minakshi Sundareshvara Temple. This monument represents the 17C Nayaka style at its finest. It is entered through a *gopura* on the east, which gives access to a lofty corridor. Its north–south aisle has *yalis* carved on the central quartet of piers. The main shrine is approached through two halls. The outer example has a porch with staircases on the north and south flanked by animal balustrades, and a small Garuda shrine on the east. The Vishnu shrine consists of three superimposed sanctuaries of diminishing size housing seated, standing and reclining images of the god (bottom to top). (This unusual scheme is obviously modelled on that of the Vaikuntha Perumal at Kanchipuram [37F].) The outer walls are raised on an elaborate basement, with varying sequences of mouldings. The slender pilasters with differently shaped shafts have miniature *yalis* at their bases. The high-relief temple towers cap single pilasters standing in pots. Pierced stone screens with graceful designs, inlcuding one with figures in entwining stalks (south), light the passageway within. The steeply pyramidal tower which rises above is topped by a hemispherical roof. A shrine to Lakshmi stands in its own compound to the south of the Temple.

The **Nayaka Palace**, particularly associated with Tirumala, though used by most of Madurai's rulers, stands 1km southeast of the Minakshi Sundareshvara Temple. Only portions of what must have been an extensive royal complex survive; even so, they are impressive for the monumental scale of the interior spaces and the exuberance of the plaster ornamentation, much of

Nayaka Palace, Madurai

it restored in the 19C. A doorway on the east leads to a rectangular **Court**, surrounded by colonnades with massive circular shafts, more than 12m high. The animal brackets above the peripheral supports are sheltered by curving eaves. The interior colonnades present prespectives of broad arches with pointed and lobed profiles.

The Throne Hall, at the west end of the Court, is roofed with pyramidal domes and shallow vaults, some raised on clerestory walls with small windows to admit light. An enlarged octagonal dome rises some 21m over the central chamber. A doorway in the northwest corner gives access to the Dance Hall. This double-height space has side arcades, from which spring transverse arches carrying the pointed vault. The lobes of the arches are richly encrusted with plaster animals and birds in scrollwork and flame-like tufts. Stone sculptures from various sites in the vicinity are assembled here; they belong to the collection of the State Department of Archaeology. A second colonnaded court with a domed chamber at one end once adjoined the Dance Hall, but has now collapsed.

The other important Nayaka feature in Madurai is the **Teppakulam**, at the eastern fringe of the city, near the Vaigai River. This great tank was initiated by Tirumala in 1636, as a setting for festivals in which sacred images were floated in illuminated barges. These rites continue to this day, each January–February. The square reservoir has steps, flanked by animal and bird balustrades, leading down to the water in the middle of each side. A pavilion with a pyramidal tower occupies an island in the middle. Similar but smaller pavilions dot the four corners of the island.

Monuments associated with the Madurai sultans are located north of the Vaigai River. The 14C **Tomb of Sultan Alauddin and Sultan Shamsuddin** stands in a small compound. The building consists of a domed chamber surrounded by a colonnade, originally open but later filled in, topped with curving eaves and a battlemented parapet. The adjacent **Mosque of Alauddin** is notable for the tapering octagonal minarets on either side of the flat-roofed prayer hall. The nearby octagonal domed **Tomb of Bara Mastan Sada**, a local Sufi saint, is a later 16C structure.

B. Tirupparankunram

This small town, 6km southwest of Madurai, is known for its sacred granite hill, which rises 345m above sea level. The core of the **Murugan Temple**, at the south end of the main street of Tirupparankunram, is a Pandya-period Cave Temple dated 773, cut into the side of the hill. This is reached only after passing through an ascending sequence of columned halls linked by multiple flights of steps, all 17C–18C additions. The complex is approached from the north through an outer hall, the peripheral columns of which are adorned with riders on horses and *yalis* with elephant snouts, all brightly painted. The central space within is lined with further animals; the ceiling shows a painting of Subrahmanya. A large *gopura* on the south, with an impressive pyramidal tower rising over the hall roof, marks the entrance into a great inner hall (access restricted to visitors). Flights of steps climb to an upper hall accommodating large sculptures of Nandi and the peacock, the latter associated with Subrahmanya. A doorway on the west leads a large outdoor tank. Further steps on the south ascend to a smaller hall at the highest level, built up to the original

Cave Temple. Nayaka patronage is evident in the portraits of Tirumala and other courtly donors, carved on the column shafts.

The **Cave Temple** itself consists of a central shrine, with carvings of Durga flanked by Ganapati (right) and Subrahmanya (left), and lateral shrines housing a Shiva *linga* (right) and Vishnu image (left). Subrahmanya, known popularly as Murugan, has been singled out for particular veneration, since it is to this deity that the whole complex is dedicated. A subsidiary shrine to Shanmuga, a six-headed form of Subrahmanya, is located east of the principal sanctuary. The great event in this Temple is the 14-day festival in March–April, which celebrates the victory of Subrahmanya over the demon Suran, his coronation and subsequent marriage to Devayanai.

The ***Dargah* of Sikandar Shah**, a popular pilgrimage spot for both Muslims and Hindus, marks the summit of the hill. The shrine contains the tomb of the last Madurai sultan, who took refuge here and lost his life in 1378, defending the city against the Vijayanagara army. In later times, Sikandar Shah came to be revered as a pious saint. The path to the *Dargah* begins southwest of the town. Halfway up are a number of graves, believed to be those of Sikandar Shah's soldiers slain in battle. The saint himself is buried in a simple grave, under a large rock which juts out of the ground. The small domed chamber built over the rock was added in the 17C–18C. The flat-roofed halls in front are 15C structures.

C. Alagarkoil

This imposing Vaishnava complex, 12km north of Madurai, is built up to the base of a forested hill. The **Alagar Perumal Temple** is dedicated to a form of Vishnu known as Kallalagar. This deity is considered the brother of Minakshi, and is an important participant in the marriage festival that takes place at Madurai in April–May each year. The Alagarkoil complex is approached from the south through dilapidated compounds. A columned hall beside the road is of interest for the elegant carvings of donor figures, including a gracefully posed Nayaka queen. The outer enclosure of the Temple has a large unfinished *gopura* in the middle of the south walls, now picturesequely overgrown; it recalls the similarly uncompleted project of Tirumala at Madurai. Visitors generally enter through a nearby break in the walls, from where they make their way to the principal *gopura* on the east. This gate has double sets of walls with bold projections, miniature *yalis* appearing at the base of the pilasters, exactly as in the *gopuras* at Madurai, with which this example is contemporary. The steeply pyramidal tower has seven storeys.

The enclosure within is of interest for the hall, which has almost three-dimensional figures and animals projecting inwards from the piers lining the central space. They show incarnations of Vishnu, such as Trivikrama, Narasimha and Krishna, as well as Garuda, Hanuman and *yalis*; donors appear on the two columns at the east end. Another large *gopura* provides access to the innermost enclosure (access restricted to visitors). A hall with piers decorated with lions and lotus brackets stands immediately in front (west). Here, too, is a small, part-circular shrine that houses an image of Garuda gazing inwards to the main sanctuary. This stands within its own rectangle of walls, entered through a single doorway on the east.

The focal shrine is a small 12C circular structure, a rare example of Pandya architecture. The walls are raised on a frieze of boldly modelled *yalis*. The wall pilasters alternate with perforated stone windows, overhung by simple curved eaves. The hemispherical roof which rises above has been renovated and gilded. A colonnade on three sides has its rear walls covered with murals, showing Vaishnava shrines at other sites. The Lakshmi shrine, on the south side of the innermost enclosure, is a later structure.

Visitors are encouraged to visit the **Vasanta Mandapa**, on the south side of the outer enclosure of the Temple. This small, square structure has an internal pavilion sheltering a dais used for ceremonies at the time of the spring festival. 18C paintings cover the ceiling and the upper parts of the walls. *Ramayana* scenes are arranged in narrow strips, with Tamil labels on black bands. On the ceiling of the central pavilion they proceed clockwise, from the sacrifice of Dasharatha and the birth of Rama and his three brothers, to the exploits of the youthful Rama and the departure of the wedding parties. The large panel in the middle shows Vishnu with Lakshmi and Bhudevi.

D. Dindigul

This city, 64km north of Madurai on NH45, is renowned for its great **Rock Fort**, which rises some 90m above the surrounding plain.

> The Rock Fort was developed in the 17C as an outpost of the Madurai Nayakas, guarding the only pass between their capital and Coimbatore [43A]. In the 18C the Rock was much contested by the Marathas and the Wodeyars, being successively occupied by Haidar Ali and the British. The Fort was improved by Saiyad Sahib, a relative of Tipu Sultan and Governor of Dindigul in 1784–90. It was further strengthened by the British after they captured it permanently in 1792.

Dindigul's bare Rock presents a bare and forbidding wedge of granite, 400m long by 300m wide. Stone **Walls** with openings for cannon run around the crest. A flight of some 600 shallow steps, hewn into the stone at the thin edge of the Rock, ascends to a single **Gate** defended by a robust barbican and a long passageway with a turn. A Persian inscription is incised on the lintel. West of the Gate are several structures, possibly **Prisons**, with barrel vaults sunk below the level of the ground. Two **Magazines** with steeply pitched roofs, probably of British construction, are located above. A larger building nearby may have served as officers' quarters. A small, abandoned **Goddess Temple** crowns the summit of the Rock.

The **Cemetery**, which has many British tombs dating from the early decades of the 19C, is located opposite the end of the Rock, facing the steps.

E. Palani

This pilgrimage site, 57km west of Dindigul, is perhaps the most famous of all the mountain abodes of the god Subrahmanya; it is the site of a mass pilgrimage every January–February. The town is charmingly situated on the edge of the great **Vyapuri Tank**, with distant views of the bold cliffs of the Palani range. On the east side of this prospect is Shivagiri, a hill which rises steeply 148m above the plain. A flight of 659 steps, on which devotees have cut their names and footprints, winds past lesser shrines and subsidiary structures until it arrives at the summit, marked by the **Subrahmanya Temple.** The complex is dedicated to Subrahmanya as Dandayudhapani, Bearer of the Staff. Curiously, the image worshipped here is neither of stone or metal, but is composed of nine different kinds of poisons blended together into a substance resembling wax. The Temple marks the spot where Murugan retired in anger after having been tricked by his brother, Ganapati, of the fruit symbolising Shiva's approval.

The east-facing Dandayudhapani sanctuary is surrounded by colonnades on three sides. The squat tower rising above is encrusted with plaster sculptures and topped by a hemispherical roof. The goddess shrine, immediately south, is capped by a similarly squat tower.

It is possible to travel from Palani via the National Park at Annamalai [43E] to Coimbatore, 108km northwest.

F. Kodaikanal

This popular hill resort is easily reached by bus from Madurai, 120km southwest, but the nearest railhead, on the Madurai–Dindigul line, is 80km distant (buses available). Kodaikanal occupies a natural wooded basin in the Palani Hills, 2133m above sea level. Steep escarpments give dramatic panoramas to the north and southwest.

The site was first popularised by members of the American Mission of Madurai, who chose this spot in 1845 as a retreat from the plains. The station grew steadily, and by the end of the 19C there were more than 2000 inhabitants, mostly members of the Mission and British civil servants. A prominent figure at this time was Sir Vere Henry Levinge, who was responsible for building the dam that creates Kodaikanal Lake. The difficult ascent from the plain was eased in 1916 with the completion of the motorable road.

Kodaikanal Lake, covering 24ha in a star formation, is surrounded by wooded slopes; boating is popular, and fishing is permitted. The **Boat Club** and the **Levinge Memorial** overlook the water. **Bryant Park**, on the east side of the Lake, is noted for its flowers, hybrids and grafts. The annual horicultural show is held here in May. The International School and other educational institutions are located near the small **Bazaar**, north of the Lake. At the end of the main street of the Bazaar is **Union Church**, previously the American Church, with a severe stone tower rising over the main entrance. Here begins **Coaker's Walk**, which offers glorious views of the 2440m high volcano-like peak of Perumal, 11km distant. The end of the Walk is marked by the **Church of St Peter** of 1884, notable for its stained glass, and the small **Telescope House**.

The so-called **Biscuit-Tin Church** stands on a wooded hill south of the Lake. A granite **Obelisk** nearby marks the site of the first American Mission Church. British and American graves lie overgrown in the adjacent **Cemetery**. A popular walk from here leads to **Bear Shola**, 1.5km northwest of the Lake.

The **Shenbaganur Museum** (no closed days), 1.5km northeast of the Lake, is maintained by the Sacred Heart College, a theological seminary founded in 1895. This houses a small but interesting collection of local flora and fauna. Its archaeological artefacts include pottery fragments with varying designs, brought from burial sites in the vicinity. These prehistoric sites are marked by box-shaped constructions created by upright slabs in rectangular or circular formation. **Chettiar Park**, 500m beyond the Museum, is much visited because of the nearby **Kurunji Andavar Temple**.

Other features of interest at Kodaikanal are located further away. 3km west of the Lake is the **Solar Astro-Physical Observatory**, established in 1898 at an altitude of 2347m. **Pillar Rocks**, 7km southwest of the Lake, is a striking viewpoint, with three granite formations over 120m high. The lookout has a beautifully planted flower garden.

G. Srivilliputtur

This temple town, 74km southwest of Madurai, is celebrated for its twin **Vatapatrashayi** and **Andal Temples,** the latter dedicated to the female saint who attained renown for her devotional compositions in honour of Vishnu. It is, however, the Vatapatrashayi Temple, consecrated to Vishnu, that dominates the town, thanks to its 63m high *gopura* on the east. Reputedly the tallest in Southern India, its 11-stage tower represents the climax of the *gopura* form as developed by the Madurai Nayakas in the 17C. This example also serves as the official emblem for the state of Tamil Nadu.

The two-storeyed hall in front (east) of the main shrine within the inner enclosure of the Vatapatrashayi Temple is notable for its timber vault roofing the upper level. Carvings of different deities are seen on the angled struts. A smaller hall with sculpted *yali* piers leads to the rectangular shrine, in which Vishnu is venerated in his reclining form as Ranganatha. This small structure is capped by a vaulted roof with arched ends. A subsidiary shrine in the southwest corner of the outer enclosure enshrines an unusual bronze image of triple-faced Vishnu and a seated image of Narasimha in yoga posture.

The Andal Temple is also entered from the east, through a lesser *gopura* which stands at the end of a long colonnade. Its broad central aisle is flanked by piers with leaping *yalis* inclining inwards; the enlarged heads of the beasts have fierce expressions and detailed manes. The *gopura* gives access to the two concentric enclosures, packed with corridors and colonnades. The main Temple is entered through a porch with side entrances, the corner piers concealed by clusters of colonettes. This leads to a hall, in the middle of which stands a small swing pavilion, its columns and canopy encased in brass. Portraits of Tirumala Nayaka and his brother on the columns are also sheathed in metal. The shrine accommodates an image of Ranganatha flanked by images of Andal and Garuda.

H. Ramanathapuram

Previously called Ramnad, this town lies 117km southeast of Madurai on NH49.

Ramnathapuram rose to prominence at the end of the 17C as the headquarters of the Setupatis, local rulers who began their careers under the Madurai Nayakas, deriving prestige and income from control of the isthmus leading to Rameswaram Island. In the course of the 18C the Setupatis were involved with the struggles against the British and the Nawabs of Arcot [38B], but succumbed to the East India Company's forces in 1772. Ramanathapuram surrendered in 1792, thereby bringing the Setupati line to an end.

The **Setupati Palace**, in the west part of the town, was first established by Kilavan (1674–1710), though little of his period survives. The complex is surrounded by a high stone wall, with the main entrance on the east. This gate is an ornate structure with turrets and a small dome.

The **Ramalinga Vilasa**, on the north side of the complex, is the most interesting feature at Ramanathapuram. The principal east façade presents arcades at two levels, capped with a long vault; domical towers are seen at either side. Paintings almost entirely cloak the interior walls of the audience hall, antechamber and private apartments, the last arranged on two levels at the rear (west) of the building. The clear line work and vivid tones of red, ochre and blue are typical of the 18C pictorial style; labels in Tamil and Telugu identify the scenes. Episodes from the *Ramayana*, *Mahabharata* and *Bhagavata Purana* are arranged in horizontal bands. The depictions of *linga* and goddess shrines refer to different holy spots within the Setupati kingdom. Royal topics also contribute to the overall decor: the murals in the audience hall show formal receptions with seated Setupati kings, one of whom is specified as Muttu Vijaya Raghunatha Tevan (1710–28). The battle scenes include lines of animated soldiers brandishing weapons, even a British officer firing a cannon.

The walls and arches in the sleeping chambers are adorned with representations of the royal figure: standing with his women, who hold mirrors, fans and standards; listening to an exposition of sacred texts; sitting in a European chair, holding the holy sceptre of the family goddess Rajarajeshvari; reclining on a cushion in full military attire, holding a long sword; being entertained by female dancers and singers; receiving gifts from Portuguese Jesuits; thrusting his bow up as part of a hunting expedition, while kissing his favourite consort. One item of curiosity within the audience room is a square stone pedestal on which the Setupatis were once crowned. The small north-facing **Rajarajeshvari Shrine** stands within its own compound immediately south of the Ramalinga Vilasa.

Christ Church was built in 1799 as a Catholic place of worship by Manuel Martinez, a Portuguese military officer, who was buried here in 1810. It is now used for Protestant services. Its gabled façade has unusual corner pinnacles. The windows are fitted with stained glass.

I. Kilakkarai

This port on the Gulf of Mannar lies 16km southwest of Ramanathapuram. Because the coastline is steadily emerging from the sea, the land is dotted with maritime fossils, to a height of 5m. Kilakkarai is famous as a centre for pearl diving and fishing for conch shells. The lucrative commerce in these products has long attracted foreign visitors, but it was not until 1759 that the Dutch gained a concession from the Setupatis of Ramanathapuram to set up a trading post. The remains of the **Factory** that they established can still be seen. A **Catholic Church** stands nearby.

The town has a large Muslim population, many of whom are traders. Pearls and conches may still be purchased here, the latter fashioned into bangles, rings, lamps and other items. The most important place of prayer is the **Jami Mosque**, which incorporates the tombs of Sitakathi Markayar and Sathakkathulla Appa, two renowned holy figures.

J. Rameswaram

This sacred island, almost 50km long and little more than 12km wide, forms a sandy spit that protrudes from the mainland towards the coast of Sri Lanka. That Rameswaram was connected to the mainland in past times is indicated by the submerged blocks of a causeway that can still be seen from the modern bridge that now provides the road and rail link with Ramanathapuram, 55km west.

Rameswaram is identified with several important episodes in the *Ramayana* legend. The **Ramanatha Temple**, in the middle of the island, marks the spot where Rama worshipped Shiva after returning from Lanka. Having killed Ravana, Rama wished to purify himself by making offerings to the *linga*. This emblem is the chief object of worship within the innermost sanctuary. Devotees generally bathe in the sea at nearby Agni Tirtha before entering the Temple, where they hasten to be sprayed with water from 22 wells, known as *tirthas*, within the complex. Only then, dripping wet, do they pay homage to the twin *linga* shrines and goddess shrine that form the ritual core of the Temple.

The Ramanatha Temple dates back to the Pandya period, but was greatly extended in the 17C–18C under the Setupatis. It is contained within a vast rectangle of walls, with *gopuras* in the middle of three sides. The gates on the north and south remain unfinished, and the stonework is much eroded by the salt air; that on the west is topped with a pyramidal tower. The main entrance from the east is through two doors in the outer walls, one aligned with the Ramalingeshvara shrine, the other with the Parvati shrine, both within the third, innermost enclosure. Both entrances are preceded by columned halls that project outward from the walls. They lead to a spacious corridor which surrounds the second enclosure on four sides. The corridor is exceptional for its great length, 220m on the north and south, with receding perspectives of piers. The supports, raised on a continuous plinth, are adorned with scrollwork and lotus designs touched up with plaster; pendant lotus brackets rest on crouching *yalis*. Portraits of the Setupatis and their ministers adorn the central piers in the east corridor. Painted medallions adorn the ceilings throughout.

The west corridor is interrupted by another one, that runs from the west *gopura* to the second enclosure wall. The piers here are carved with royal figures, warriors, maidens and rearing animals. Subsidiary shrines, dating from the 12C, can be seen near the intersection of the two corridors. These small structures have simply moulded basements, pilastered walls and towers crowned with hemispherical roofs. A large square tank is located nearby.

The entrance to the second enclosure from the east is through the largest *gopura* of the series. This leads via a second door into the third, innermost enclosure, which is divided into three compounds. That on the east contains a Nandi pavilion and a square bathing pond. The north compound is where the Ramalinga and Vishvanatha linga shrines are located. The former is preceded by a hall with columns carved with effigies of the Ramanthapuram rulers and their ministers. The Parvati shrine stands in a separate compound to the south. Its hall has donor portaits and attendant maidens sculpted on the column shafts.

Gandhamadana Hill, crowned by a small shrine containing the footprint of Rama, lies 3km northwest of the Ramanatha Temple. **Dhanushkodi**, at the extreme tip of the island, 18km distant, is where Vibhashana, Ravana's brother, surrendered to Rama. Though this bathing spot was washed away in the cyclonic storm of 1964, the small **Kodandarama Temple** here survives intact.

K. Karaikkudi and Devakottai

These two towns form the heart of Chettinad, a region associated with the Chettiar merchant communities. **Devakottai**, the larger centre, is located some 95km northeast of Madurai or 70km north of Ramanathapuram. This somewhat arid territory is dotted with small settlements, marked with grand houses laid out in regular streets. These residences are notable for their intricately carved woodwork, the finest to be seen anywhere in Tamil Nadu. Many of the houses date from the late 19C and early 20C, at which time the Chettiars had become prosperous as merchants and financiers in Madras, Burma and Malaya. Much of the wood with which these houses were built was in fact imported from Southeast Asia. Curiously, these houses are rarely lived in for any length of time; today, as in the past, they are used intermittently for family reunions and celebrations. This situation, however, does not prevent some of the houses from being beautifully maintained.

The typical Chettinad **Mansion**, as seen in Karaikkudi and Devakottai, as well as in the surrounding villages, is fronted with a European-style masonry façade with arcaded storeys and corner towers. Most examples are entered through columned verandahs, with the supports standing on stone bases, and brackets ornately carved with pendant lotuses. The doorways are elaborate, with intricately worked jambs and lintels, often with panels above filled with images of Ganesha or Lakshmi with elephants. Angled struts cut into the semblance of horses with riders, *yalis*, birds and *makaras* support overhangs with pendant brass lotus buds. The interiors have sequences of interior courts surrounded by colonnades and smaller rooms that lead to kitchens and service areas at the rear.

One of the most imposing mansions is the **Palace** at **Chettinad**, a modest village 11km north of Karaikkudi, which gives its name to the region. The home of the descendants of the most prominent family in the region, this mansion conforms to the scheme just described. However, it has an additional two-storeyed reception hall immediately inside the front door. This imposing room is paved in marble and lit by clerestory windows, as well as by European glass chandeliers suspended from the timber vault.

45 · Tirunelveli

The lush landscape of the Tambraparni River Valley provides a delightful setting for a host of historical sites.

An hour or two should suffice to visit the great religious monument in Tirunelveli, the largest city in this zone and a convenient base for sightseeing [A].

A full day will be required to reach the temples at **Krishnapuram** [B], **Alvar Tirunagari** [D] and **Tiruchendur** [E], with a diversion to the interesting Iron Age site at **Adichannalur** [C], all on the road running east from Tirunveli.

Additional time will have to set aside to explore the Christian and Muslim places of worship at the small settlements of **Manapadu** [F] and **Kayalpattinam** [G] on the Gulf of Mannar. **Tuticorin** [H], the biggest port on this coast, is of lesser interest.

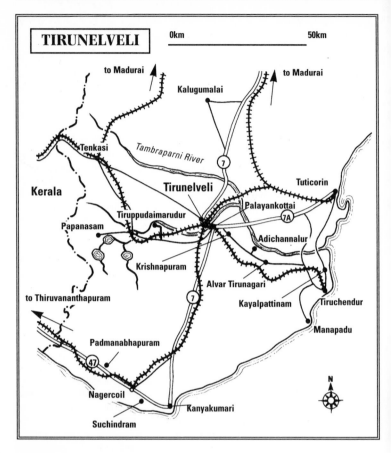

A journey from Tirunelveli north towards Madurai [44] can take in the rock-cut monument at **Kalugumalai** [I].

The waterfalls near **Tenkasi** [J] and at **Papanasam** [L] are located west of Tirunelveli. A stop is recommended at **Tiruppudaimarudur** [K] to inspect a set of remarkable murals. Allow a full day for these sights.

Kanyakumari [M], at the southern tip of Tamil Nadu, attracts many visitors. An overnight stay permits ocean views of a simultaneous sunset and sunrise. It will also facilitate an excursion to the temple at **Suchindram** [N] and the palace at **Padmanabhapuram** [O], on the way to Thiruvananthapuram [46].

■ **Transport**. Tirunelveli lies 154km south of Madurai, to which it is linked by NH7 and rail. The nearest airport is also at Madurai. NH7 proceeds south from Tiruneveli to Kanyakumari and from there to Thiruvananthapuram, 84km northwest via NH47. Road and rail from Tirunelveli to Tenkasi continue to Kollam [46H], a total of 154km west. Trains also run to Tiruchendur and Tutucorin. Bus services are available to all the destinations described here.

■ **Accommodation**. The *Sri Janakiram Hotel* (☎ 24451) and *Aryaas Hotel* (☎ 339001) are the best in Tirunelveli (STD code 0462). The *Hotel Tamil Nadu* (☎ 71257) provides the only accommodation with sea views at **Kanyakumari** (STD code 04653). Another *Hotel Tamil Nadu* (☎ 4268) is located at **Tiruchendur** (STD code 04639).

■ **Tourist Information**. The TTDC has a counter at the railway station (☎ 26235).

A. Tirunelveli

This city, on the bank of the Tambraparni River, was much developed by the Madurai Nayakas in the 16C–17C.

By the beginning of the 18C, Tirunelveli was under the control of a line of local chiefs, who were much engaged in struggles with the rulers of the adjacent Travancore kingdom. The Tirunelveli chiefs eventually succumbed to the Nawabs of Arcot [38B]. The city was ceded to the British in 1797.

Tirunelveli preserves a large and important religious monument, the **Nellaiyappa Temple**, which dates back to Pandya times in the 13C. However, the twin Shiva and Devi shrines of the complex were entirely remodelled and extended in the 17C–18C. The Nellaiyappa Temple is approached from the east along the crowded main street. An open stone colonnade and a pavilion with a wooden vault with carved bracket figures stand immediately in front of the east *gopura*. The long rectangular pyramidal tower that rises above is visible throughout the city. An altar, brass-clad lamppost and gigantic Nandi surrounded by six massive piers are arranged in a line immediately inside. Spacious corridors proceed around the first enclosure; major *gopuras* mark the middle of four sides. Immediately west of the Nandi is a porch with frontal piers carved with fully modelled figures of Virabhadra, Karna and Arjuna, overhung by deeply curved eaves. A *gopura* with finely carved wooden doors leads to the second enclosure (access restricted to visitors).

The *linga* shrine beyond is entered through a raised porch with side steps flanked by elephant balustrades. Columns here have clusters of slender colonettes, with up to 48 cutout elements at the corners. A great bell also hangs here. Guardian figures with clubs flank the entrance to the hall that precedes the shrine. Shiva is not the only god worshipped here; a large image of reclining Vishnu is placed in the corridor immediately north. To the northeast is a second *linga* shrine, set beneath the level of the floor, with a small tower, possibly dating back to the Pandya era. A small Devi shrine occupies the south side of the same enclosure. An unusual square structure near the northwest corner has wooden screens and a metal-clad pyramidal roof; carvings adorn the timber struts and brackets. A Somaskanda shrine at the southwest corner is partly obscured by a modern plaster rendition of Kailasa, Shiva's mountain home.

The colonnade that proceeds around the first enclosure of the Nellaiyappa Temple has already been noted. On the west this passes by a long hall with *yali* piers, in which an icon of Subrahmanya is venerated. Donor sculptures portraying the Tirunelveli chiefs are seen in the south colonnade. The *gopura* on this side leads directly to the adjacent **Ambal Temple**. A corridor set at a slight angle has piers sculpted with almost three-dimensional representations of Rama and Lakshmana in the company of Sugriva and Hanuman, flanked by *yalis* with enlarged heads. The corridor leads past a square tank surrounded by colonnades. A lamppost, altar and Nandi pavilion are aligned with the doorway of the goddess sanctuary. Turning east, towards the entrance *gopura*, it is necessary to pass through a long hall, with *yali* piers lining the central aisle. As in the Nellaiyappa Temple, the east *gopura* is fronted by a wooden vaulted entrance structure with carved brackets.

Christian evangelists were active in Tirunelveli from the end of the 18C. The headquarters of the Church Missionary Society in Tamil Nadu is at **Palayankottai**, 3km east of the city, also the site of a demolished fort. **Trinity Church**, the Society's principal place of worship, was erected in 1826. Its handsome Neo-Classical tower is surmounted by a tall spire that attains an overall height of 35m. The Jesuit Mission also maintains a presence in Palayankottai; their **Church of St Francis Xavier** was completed in 1863.

B. Krishnapuram

The **Venkatachala Temple** in this small village, 13km east of Palayankottai, is renowned for its remarkable 17C–18C carvings. The monument is entered on the east through a *gopura* of standard design, with carved wooden doors. The gate is preceded by an open columned hall with a raised dais at one end. The **Virappa Nayaka Mandapa**, immediately to the right inside the first enclosure, is named after one of the Madurai kings. Its front six piers have smoothly rounded figures modelled in almost three dimensions: (left to right) female dancer, tribal man, Karna, Arjuna, tribal woman and female dancer; mounted warriors appear on the sides of two piers. A long colonnade proceeds west towards the doorway into the second enclosure. The hall beyond has a central aisle flanked by *yalis* alternating with vigorously posed figures: attendants, Virabhadra, Rati and dancing ascetic (north row); Virabhadra, Manmatha and Bhima (south row); guardian figures with clubs (west). The principal sanctuary at the end (west) houses Vishnu with consorts. Twin Lakshmi shrines occupy the two west corners of the first enclosure.

C. Adichanallur

This **Iron Age Site**, 14km east of Krishnapuram on the south bank of the Tambarapani River, just off the road leading to Tiruchendur, is worth visiting for the prehistoric burials that have been unearthed here. **Sepulchral Urns** of thick red earthenware, up to 1m in diameter, are found all over the site, especially on a long piece of high ground overlooking the river, where about 40ha have been fenced off for protection. The Urns are accommodated in separate hollow cavities, with bands of uncut rock in between. When excavated, these chambers revealed the bones and skulls of the dead, as well as an abundance of other items. More than 1000 iron weapons, implements and ornaments were collected, including swords, spears, arrows, axes, adzes, hammers, chisels, rings, bangles and lamps; a few gold items were also discovered. Most of these artefacts have been removed to the Government Museum, Madras [36D].

D. Alvar Tirunagari

This small town, 31km east of Tirunelveli, marks the birthplace of Nammalvar in about the 9C. Nammalvar holds a high position among the Vaishnava saints, and it was in his honour that the extensive **Adinatha Temple** was founded in the 13C. Most of the buildings incorporated into this extensive monument are, however, no earlier than the 16C–17C. The principal *gopura* on the east is approached through a long colonnade built outside the walls. Another similar colonnade occupies the space between the first and second *gopuras*. The two columned halls that abut the colonnade on the north show *yalis* and energetic figures on the columns. A similarly adorned hall on the north has an elaborate porch with slender colonettes grouped around the column shafts; heros and female dancers embellish the internal supports.

The second enclosure of the Adinatha Temple, entered through lesser *gopuras* on the east and north, is filled with colonnades, halls and subshrines. The hall leading to the focal Vishnu sanctuary incorporates a small Garuda shrine, brass-clad flagpole and altar. Another shrine, on the north side, is consecrated to Nammalvar. The columns on its east porch are sculpted with lively heroes and dancing women. A small open court at a higher level to one side has a tamarind tree growing freely in the middle, under which Nammalavar is believed to have meditated. The two small shrines in the west part of the enclosure are dedicated to Lakshmi and Bhudevi.

E. Tiruchendur

This seaside town, 51km east of Tirunelveli, is a popular place of pigrimage, due to the **Subrahmanya Temple**, built on a small rocky promontory extending into the Gulf of Mannar. References to the Temple go back to the 9C, but the corrosive effects of the sea air are such that the monument was substantially renewed at the turn of the 20C; the shrine was reconsecrated in 1941.

The Temple is entered on the west through the lofty Mela *Gopura*. Its nine-storeyed tower, which reaches a height of 45m, is a prominent landmark visible from the ocean. The pyramidal tower is covered with plaster figures, some showing the life of the saint Manikkavachakar. The bell fixed into the topmost storey was presented by a British official. The other entrance to the Temple is from the south, through the Shanmuga Vilasa, an imposing modern structure with four corridors meeting at a central hall some 15m square. Together with the Mela Gopura, this structure gives access to the outer rectangular enclosure, partly occupied by a colonnade that runs along the perimeter walls on four sides. Additional doorways are provided on the north, but there is no access from the seaside on the east.

The Vasanta *Mandapa*, on the west side of the corridor, displays portraits of the saintly personalities who assisted in the reconstruction of the monument. A small subshrine, dedicated to Vishnu, is incorporated into the north corridor. The ritual core of the Temple consists of a pair of shrines, each with a pyramidal tower capped by a hemispherical roof. The Subrahmanya sanctuary, which faces east towards a lesser *gopura* in the second set of walls, has a stone image of the god placed next to a small monolithic *linga*. The south-facing Shanmuga sanctuary accomodates metal icons of six-headed Subrahmanya and consorts.

Rock-cut shrines and natural caves with carvings of Subrahmanya dot the shoreline nearby. A sanctuary with an image of Dattatreya is seen 200m north of the Temple. Two square wells, one inside the other, filled with different tasting waters, are found about the same distance south.

F. Manapadu

This predominantly Roman Catholic village lies on the arid shore of the Gulf of Mannar, 18km south of Tiruchendur. Manapadu was one of the first places to be visited by St Francis Xavier in 1542, when he initiated missionary activity on the Fishery Coast. A **Grotto** on the seaward face of a cliff is pointed out as the spot where the saint lived and prayed. Close to the sea is the **Church of the Holy Cross**, founded in 1581. This possesses what is believed to be a fragment of the True Cross of Jerusalem. The public display of this relic each September attracts thousands of pilgrims.

G. Kayalpattinam

This small port on the Gulf of Mannar, 11km north of Tiruchendur near the mouth of the Tambraparni River, is inhabited almost exclusively by Muslims. Local accounts claim that the inhabitants of Kayalpattinam are descended from immigrants who came from Arabia in Pandya times. This suggestion is supported by the obviously foreign dress and customs of the local population, as well as the religious monuments that date back to the 14C.

The **Al-Kabir Mosque** of 1337, in the middle of the town, has a large prayer hall divided by columns into long aisles, with an arched *mihrab* projecting away from the west wall. A central space in the middle, defined by 12 piers, is roofed with a large dome, an addition of the 18C. The **Al-Saghir Mosque** opposite is simpler and plainer. Several graves in the adjoining tomb chamber, known as the Shrine of the Seven Martyrs, bear 15C dates.

The nearby **Qadiriya Madrasa** of 1871 is of greater architectural merit. Its colonnaded court is surrounded by chambers for students. The remarkable circular prayer hall of the **Mahlara Mosque** forms part of the complex. Four external buttresses rise as tapering octagonal minarets, crowned with domical tops. The pointed dome that roofs the chamber within is more than 12m in diameter.

The **Mosque of Rettaikulampalli**, at the north end of the town, displays 18C piers lining the central aisle. Other mosques, such as **Marakkayarpalli** and **Appapalli**, have diminutive rectangular tombs roofed with pyramidal vaults that enshrine the graves of 17C–18C saints.

H. Tuticorin

This port, 51km east of Tiruneveli via NH7A, or 30km north of Tiruchendur, is the busiest in Tamil Nadu after Madras, its chief exports being cotton and rice. Until recently Tuticorin was also the chief arrival point for overnight passenger ferries to Sri Lanka. It was celebrated in past centuries as the centre of the local pearl fishing industry and marketing.

> Tuticorin was settled originally by the Portuguese in 1540, but it was captured in 1658 by the Dutch, and remained mostly in their possession until it was ceded to the British in 1824.

The two small temples in Tuticorin are of little architectural merit; the Christian places of worship are more interesting. In spite of its name, the **English**

Church was founded in 1750 by the Dutch East India Company. The monogram VOC appears on the ornately plastered gable over the entrance. The monuments in the adjacent cemetery include a lofty obelisk with corner urns and an inscription of 1824. The **Roman Catholic Church** dedicated to Our Lady of the Snows, at the south end of the beach, dates from the 17C.

I. Kalugumalai

The monolithic temple at Kalugumalai, Hill of the Vulture, about 50km north of Tirunelveli, partly via NH7, is a rare example 8C Pandya architecture. The **Vattuvan Kovil** is hewn out of a massive outcrop of granite, facing east through a cleft towards the village beneath. Begun in the 8C, the temple was never completed beyond its pyramidal tower, capped with an octagonal domical roof. The tower is adorned with friezes of dwarfs beneath the eaves and fully modelled Nandis at the corners. Gracefully posed seated images of Dakshinamurti (south), Narasimha (west), Brahma (north) and Shiva with Uma (east) are seen in the middle of each side. The arch-shaped motifs are embellished with delicately incised foliage and jewelled garlands. The attached hall remains an unshaped block of granite.

Rows of standing Jinas are carved on the flank of the main rock; Ambika between a lion and a dancer is seen to one side. A crowned king kneels in front of a Tirthankara shown larger than human size. Another Tirthankara is seated on a lion throne, surrounded by attendants.

J. Tenkasi

Nestling at the base of the Western Ghats, 52km northwest of Tirunelveli, Tenkasi was the home of the later Pandya chiefs in the 15C–16C. It later came under the sway of the Madurai Nayakas. The town is dominated by the **Vishvanatha Temple**, entered on the east through an immense *gopura*, the tower of which has only recently been completed. The carvings on the jambs are finely finished; the columns in the side chambers show Shiva with the wives of the sages, Rama with Lakshmana, and Kali. The columned structure outside the *gopura* serves as a market. The first enclosure within the *gopura* is occupied by a large hall. The piers lining the central aisle have 2m high figures of Shiva dancing, Rati and Bhikshatanamurti (north row); Kali, Krishna, Manmatha and Virabhadra (south row). These remarkable, almost three-dimensional sculptures are dated to the end of the 17C. At the west end of the hall is a second smaller *gopura* that leads to the second enclosure.

The principal *linga* shrine, a Pandya structure, has its outer walls adorned with pilastered niches that frame images of Dakshinamurti (south), Shiva (west) and Brahma (north). The colonnades surrounding the shrine on four sides incorporate sets of Nayanmars on the south, sanctuaries of Vinayaka and Subrahmanya at the two west corners, a small cistern on the north, and a jackfruit tree at the northeast corner. A shrine to Subrahmanya, standing freely south of the outer enclosure, has ornate basement mouldings, pilastered walls and overhanging eaves. The 12-columned pavilion in front is animated by leaping *yalis* at the corners, a pair of guardians on the west and legendary heros elsewhere. The Devi shrine stands in its own compound further south.

The resort of **Kuttalam** lies 5km south of Tenkasi. Though no more than 150m above sea level, the site possesses the climate and flora of a much higher elevation; it was developed as a sanatorium in British days for these reasons. The sacred waterfall here takes its name from the nearby **Kuttalanatha Temple**.

K. Tiruppudaimarudur

This small village, 25km west of Tirunelveli, is home to the **Narumbunatha Temple**, picturesquely sited on the south bank of the Tambraparni River. The monument is notable for the remarkably well-preserved paintings and wooden sculptures in the upper storeys of the second east *gopura*. Successive chambers within the hollow brick tower are reached by steep wooden steps. The intricately carved timber columns with ornate brackets carry ceilings with lotus panels. The plaster walls are covered with murals with animated black line work and bright colours; the red and green backgrounds do not quite meet the linework, leaving a curious white band around the figures.

A large variety of legends and narratives is illustrated here. Rama on Hanuman and Rama battling Ravana appear on either side of the west window in the first chamber. The story of Arjuna fighting Shiva as the hunter is seen nearby, as is the legend of Sambandar converting the Pandya king. Narasimha and Nataraja appear in the second chamber. Other compositions show battle scenes, receptions with parades of horses and elephants, and even a ship with warriors. The columns have carvings of dancing Virabhadra and *yalis* on the shafts. Yet more wooden sculptures are seen in the third chamber. The paintings at this level show the *avataras* of Vishnu, a large composition of Vishnu reclining on the serpent, and Rama seated in the company of Hanuman. Krishna, Bhairava and a set of *linga* shrines with sages are represented in the murals of the fourth, topmost chamber.

A covered space links the second and third *gopuras* of the Narumbanatha Temple. The interior of the third enclosure is filled with halls and colonnades, dominated by twin shrines dedicated to Shiva and Devi. The doorways in the west sides of the enclosure walls lead down to the river bank, where there is a delightful assortment of shrines and bathing *ghats*.

L. Papanasam

The natural beauty of this spot, 47km west of Tirunelveli, is enhanced by the **Waterfall** by which the Tambraparni River descends into the plains. The water drops about 100m over an almost sheer wall of rock, guarded on both sides by forested hills. The cascade is imbued with great sanctity, since the water here is believed to wash away all human sin. The unassuming **Temple of Papavinaseshvara**, about 1km beneath the Waterfall, has broad flights of steps leading down to the water. The nearby cotton mills, in operation since the late 19C, are worked by water power.

M. Kanyakumari

Previously known as Cape Cormorin, this rocky promontory at the southern tip of the Indian peninsula, 83km south of Tirunelveli, marks the point where the waters of the Bay of Bengal and the Arabian Sea mingle with the Indian Ocean. Kanyakumari takes its name from Kumari, the goddess who protects India's shores. Pilgrims come to bathe in a rocky ocean pool near the **Temple of**

Kumari. This is entered from the east through a small porch which leads to three concentric enclosures, with the goddess sanctuary at the core (access resticted to visitors). The sanctuary dates from about the 18C, but has been much remodelled since then.

The **Gandhi Memorial**, west of the Temple, is where the Mahatma's ashes were exhibited before being immersed in the ocean. Its painted concrete tower, capped with a ribbed circular element, derives from Orissan architecture. The **Vivekananda Memorial**, on a rocky islet 250m southeast of the promontory, is accessible by regular ferry services. This revivalist structure, supposedly incorporating all the different styles of Indian architecture, dates from 1970. It commemorates the Bengali religious leader and philosopher, who lived here from 1892 as a simple monk and devotee of the goddess, swimming out to the rock and sitting there in deep meditation. In later years he founded the Ramakrishna Mission in Madras.

N. Suchindram

This village, 13km west of Kanyakumari, is dominated by the **Sthanumalaya Temple**, attractively sited on the south side of a large square tank. The east entrance to the complex is preceded by a colonnade, the central columns of which are sculpted with sages and rearing *yalis*. The passageway of the *gopura* beyond is flanked by demonic figures and smaller panels of Natesha and Trivikrama. The upper storeys are covered with plaster figures, with paintings depicting events from the *Ramayana* epic and local legends inside. The interior of the Temple is dominated by two focal shrines, one accommodating the Sthanumalaya *linga* (north), representing the triad of Shiva, Brahma and Vishnu, the other housing an image of Vishnu (south). These small unadorned structures date back to the 13C, but the remainder of the monument is assigned to the 17C–18C, when the region was contested by the Madurai Nayakas and the Travancore rulers.

Devotees approaching the *linga* shrine, aligned with the *gopura* already noted, pass by a small pavilion with a dais in the middle. The corner columns have fully modelled images of Manmatha and Rati (east) and Karna and Arjuna (west). A flagpole and a large seated Nandi in plaster-covered brick are located to the west. A small pavilion, sheltering a standing image of Garuda, stands immediately south, on an axis with the Vishnu shrine. Its columns have almost three-dimensional portraits of Nayaka donors and their queens. To the west is a columned hall with sculpted piers defining two aisles leading to the main shrines. The ceiling is painted with floral designs. The friezes on the supporting beams show episodes from the *Ramayana* and Krishna legends.

A spacious corridor runs around four sides of the perimeter walls of the Temple. Large brackets and crouching lions support the flat ceiling. A small west-facing *linga* shrine, near the southwest corner of the colonnade, is elevated on a granite boulder covered with Tamil inscriptions. The Murugan shrine, next to the north arm of the corridor, is preceded on the east by the Alankara Mandapa, which features ornate carvings on the central aisle. The clusters of colonettes framing carvings of royal figures include a portrait of Martanda Varma of Tiruvananthapuram. The Chitra Sabha, in the northeast corner, has sculptures of heroes in the company of Venugopala and Bhikshatanamurti. The aisle leads to a small Natesha shrine.

O. Padmanabhapuram

The Palace at Padmanabhapuram, 35km northwest of Kanyakumari, once served as the headquarters of the rulers of the kingdom of Tiruvitankur, better known as Travancore.

The Pumukham, Padmanabhapuram Palace

In the 16C–17C the site was known as Kalkulam, but Martanda Varma (1729–58) renamed it Padmanabhapuram, City of the Lotus Born, in reference to the aspect of Vishnu, the guardian deity of the Travancore family. Martanda Varma was responsible for remodelling the Palace, and much of the present structure dates from his era. After 1750, when the capital was shifted to Tiruvananthapuram, 52km northeast, Padmanabhapuram was reduced to a minor residence. It survives as the principal example of Kerala royal architecture, even though it is now located in Tamil Nadu.

The **Padmanabhapuram Palace** (closed Mondays) is laid out in sequence of four walled compounds, creating a transition from public to private zones, connected by simple doorways. The complex consists of individual structures linked by a maze of corridors, colonnades, verandahs and courts. The principal entrance, on the west, is through an outer court reserved for public ceremonies. The **Padipura**, the main gate, displays an ornamented gabled roof. The **Pumukham**, inside the second court, serves as an audience hall on the upper level of a two-storeyed building with circular wooden columns and angled timber screens. To the north is a dance hall, known as the **Navaratri Mandapa** after the festival formerly celebrated here. The polished blackened plaster floor reflects the sculpted female attendants on the granite piers. The central aisle leads to a small shrine dedicated to Sarasvati. Detached carvings are displayed in the surrounding colonnades, including several 12C stone images, and wooden figures from a temple chariot.

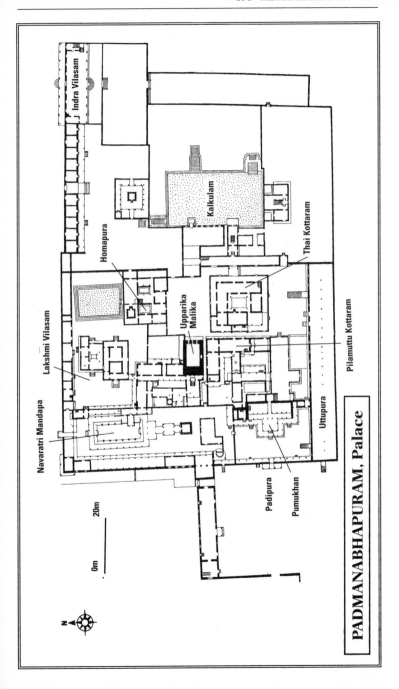

PADMANABHAPURAM, Palace

The third court marks the beginning of the private zone of the Palace. Here stands the **Upparika Malika** of 1749, a masonry tower that soars above the sloping tiled roofs of the adjacent buildings. Its four chambers, arranged one above the other, connected by steep steps, served as a treasury, royal sleeping chamber, royal meditation chamber and shrine room, with an empty bed for Padmanabha. The 18C wooden cots intended for the king and the god have decorated head panels incorporating the arms of the Dutch East India Company. Wooden balconies with angled screens project outwards from the upper levels; shutters permitted the ruler to discreetly survey the activities of the court below. The walls of the shrine room at the top of the Upparika Malika are covered with brightly toned murals. These splendid examples of Kerala pictorial art are devoted to mythological topics. Padmanabha appears on the end walls, the god reclining on the coils of the cosmic serpent with rearing multi-headed hoods. The north wall is covered with compositions of a *linga* with eyes being worshipped by women (left); Ganesha above and Natesha with sages beneath; Shashta above and seated Krishna below; and Vishnu with consorts (right). The south wall shows Lakshmi with Krishna playing the flute (left); Rama and Sita above, and Durga beneath; Vishnu on Garuda; Shiva and Parvati , and Vishnu beneath; and the *linga* with eyes (right).

Residences of other members of the royal family are situated nearby. The **Lakshmi Vilasam** and **Pilamuttu Kottaram** are for courtly women. The queen mother's apartment, the **Thai Kottaram**, is one of the oldest buildings in the complex. Its chambers are distributed a small internal court with a shallow pond in the middle. The upper level has wooden screens overhung by a pyramidal tiled roof. Nearby stand the **Homapura**, a building for ritual use, with its own stepped tank, and the **Uttupura**, which has two long dining halls, one above the other, used for feeding priests on special occasions; each hall has a central row of columns,.

The fourth court of the Palace occupies the east part of the complex. Additional dining rooms and apartments are disposed around the **Kalkulam**, a reservoir reached by a flight of steps. The **Indra Vilasam**, incorporating a residence and audience hall, is partly built in a Neo-Classical stlye. It faces a garden, now sadly neglected. The offices at the north end of this compound are accessible from the street that runs outside the Palace walls.

NH47 continues to Thiruvananthapuram, 50km to the west.

Kerala

The smallest state in Southern India, but also the one with the highest population density, Kerala is notable for its distinctive cultural and art traditions.

Tourists arriving at **Thiruvananthapuram** [46] in southern Kerala can visit the 18C temple and palace associated with the former kings of Travancore. **Kochi** [47], further north, was the headquarters of the Zamorins, the rulers of central Kerala when the first Europeans arrived in the 16C. The cosmopolitan nature of Kochi's mercantile population is evident from the synagogue and churches that dot the city.

17C–18C temples adorned with wood carvings and vivid murals are seen at **Ettumanur** [47G], **Kaviyur** [47K], **Thrissur** [47W] and other towns within easy reach of Kochi.

Churches of the same period are mostly clustered around **Kottayam** [47I], from which journeys may be made to the pilgrimage shrine at **Sabarimalai** [47O], as well as to the **Periyar Wildlife Sanctuary** [47P], the most developed in Southern India.

The highway running parallel to the coast leads from Kochi to **Kozhikode** [48], of interest for its tiled-roofed mosques. Excursions from this city can take in the European forts at **Thalassery** [48F] and **Kannur** [48G], both overlooking the Arabian Sea.

The route from Kozhikode continues to **Mysore** [15] or to **Mangalore** [17], both in Karnataka.

46 · Thiruvananthapuram

The current name of Thiruvananthapuram revives the indigenous spelling for Trivandrum, by which name this city is still familiar. Once the headquarters of the rulers of Travancore and now the capital of Kerala, Thiruvananthapuram is a delightful city that retains much of its traditional charm, in spite of recent rapid development. A half-day tour is recommended [A], even for visitors who choose to stay beside the ocean at nearby Kovalam.

The temples at **Nemam** [B], **Tiruvallam** [C], **Vizhinjam** [D] and **Kazhakuttam** [E] can be reached as short side trips. An excursion to **Anjengo** [F], **Varkala** [G] and **Kollam** [H] may be completed in a single day, with the possibility of continuing on to Alappuzha [47B] and Kochi [47A] by road or boat. Additional time will be required to reach the hill station at **Ponmudi** [I].

■ **Transport**. Thiruvananthapuram has an international airport, with flights arriving from the UK, as well as from the Gulf, the Maldives and Sri Lanka. Air connections link the city with Delhi, Bombay [1], Panaji [11], Bangalore [14] and Madras [36]. Trains connect Thiruvananthapuram with Kollam, Alappuzha and Kochi, the last 223km north, as well as Tirunelveli [45], Madurai [44] and Kanyakumari [45L] in Tamil Nadu. Thiruvananthapuram lies on NH47, the major route running the entire length of the state along the Arabian Sea coast. Bus services reach all the sites described here, including the beach resort at Kovalam, 16km south of the capital.

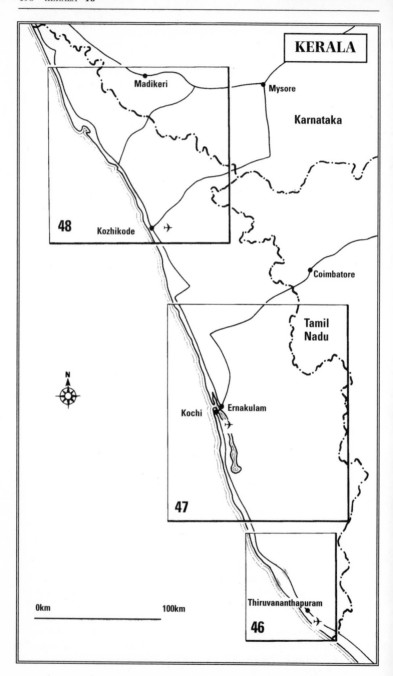

KERALA

Karnataka

Madikeri

Mysore

48

Kozhikode

Coimbatore

Tamil
Nadu

N

Kochi   Ernakulam

47

0km   100km

Thiruvananthapuram

46

River travel. A more characteristic form of travel is by small craft on the internal network of rivers, channels and lagoons known as the backwaters. Services begin at Kollam for Alappuzha [47B], a journey requiring a full day.

■ **Accommodation**. The finest hotels in Thiruvananthapuram (STD code 0471) are the *Hotel Continental Luciya* (☎ 463443), *Hotel Fort Manor* (☎ 462222), *South Park* (☎ 65666) and *Mascot Hotel* (☎ 438990), but there is no shortage of more modest lodgings. Attractive seaside accommodation at **Kovalam** (STD code 04723) is available in all price ranges; among the best are the *Ashoka Beach Resort* (☎ 480101) and *Hotel Samudra* (☎ 480089), both with private beaches, also the *Varma's Beach Resort* (☎ 480478), *Hotel Neptune* (☎ 480662) and *Hotel Sea Rock* (☎ 480422). Several quieter places with secluded bathing are located 5 km S of Kovalam: the luxurious *Surya Samudra Beach Resort* (☎ 480413) and *Somatheeram Ayurvedic Beach Resort* (☎ 480600) are recommended. **Varkala** (STD code 04724) offers alternative oceanside lodgings, the *Taj Residency* (☎ 403000) being the finest.

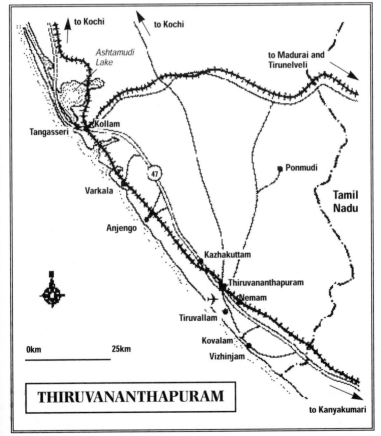

■ **Tourist Information**. The Kerala Tourist Development Corporation (KTDC) runs a reception centre (☎ 437033) in front of the Chaithram Hotel, near the railway station and long-distance bus depot. The Government of India Tourist Information office is at the airport (☎ 451498).

A. Thiruvananthapuram

Thiruvananthapuram spreads agreeably over wooded hills a short distance inland from the Arabian Sea.

> In 1750, Martanda Varma (1729–58) shifted the capital of the Travancore kingdom to Tiruvananthanpuram from Padmanabhapuram [450], 52km southwest. Under this ruler and his successor, Rama Varma (1758–98), Travancore attained its greatest influence, extending from Kanyakumari to the south almost as far as Kochi to the north. The kingdom survived into the British period as a princely state, merging with the Indian Union in 1956.

The original royal zone to the south of Thiruvananthapuram is marked by the **Padmanasbhaswamy Temple**, the principal religious monument of the city. Although records for this shrine go back to the 10C, it was totally rebuilt at the orders of Martanda Varma. The deity worshipped here, Vishnu reclining on Ananta, gives its name to the capital: Sacred Ananta's City. The cult of this form of Vishnu was central to the Travancore kings, and the monument is still managed by a descendant of the royal family. This figure is still obliged to lead the procession during the Arat Festival in March–April, when the image of Padmanabha is carried to Shanmuga beach, to be ritually bathed in the ocean.

The Padmanabhaswamy Temple is laid out as a vast square, with entrances in the middle of each side. The **Gates** on three sides have tiled gabled roofs in the typical Kerala manner. The east Gate, the largest, is modelled on Tamil-styled *gopuras*. Its lower two granite storeys have slender wall projections flanked by pilasters. The four diminishing brick storeys of its squatly proportioned tower are capped with a long barrel vault; gilded pot finials line the ridge. The *gopura* is approached through a long colonnade, near to which there is a large tank. The hall immediately inside (access restricted to visitors) has columns with portrait sculptures, one supposedly depicting the architect. The corridors to the north and south form part of a free-standing **Colonnade**, which runs around four sides of the inner enclosure. Its piers are enlivened with female devotees bearing lamps. Small halls, each with 16 columns, terminate each arm of the colonnade. The hall in front (east) of the entrance to the inner enclosure has lofty piers with high relief carvings of Shiva dancing, Bhairava, Krishna and the Pandava heroes.

A greater array of sculpted gods and goddesses appears in the **Kalasekhara Hall** to the south, where each figure is framed by a miniature pavilion with cut-out colonettes. The inner enclosure of the Temple is contained within a double line of masonry walls and timber screens. The **Main Shrine** within accommodates a large icon of the reclining form of Vishnu. The head, navel and feet of Padmanabha, created in brightly painted plasterwork, are viewed through a row of three doorways. The outer walls have pilastered projections covered with murals representing different aspects of Vishnu and his consorts. Tiers of wooden gables covered with copper sheets rise above. A large wooden hall in

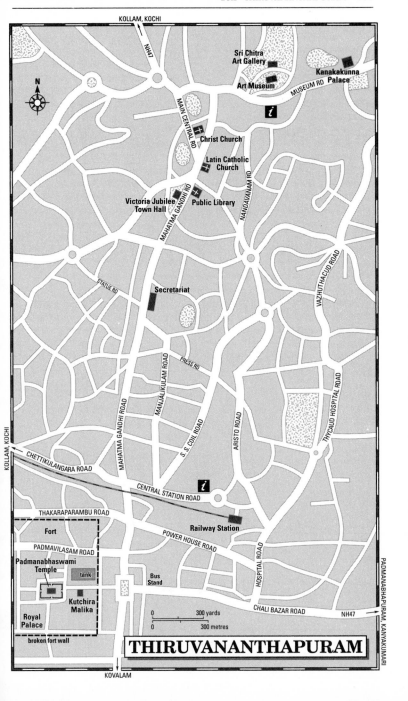

KOLLAM, KOCHI

NH47

N

Sri Chitra
Art Gallery

Art Museum

Kanakakunna
Palace

MUSEUM RD

i

MAIN CENTRAL RD

Christ Church

Latin Catholic
Church

Victoria Jubilee
Town Hall

MAHATMA GANDHI RD

Public Library

NANDAVANAM RD

STATUE RD

Secretariat

VAZHUTHACUD ROAD

MANJALIKULAM ROAD

PRESS RD

MAHATMA GANDHI ROAD

S. S. COIL ROAD

ARISTO ROAD

THYCAUD HOSPITAL ROAD

KOLLAM, KOCHI

CHETTIKULANGARA ROAD

CENTRAL STATION ROAD

i

THAKARAPARAMBU ROAD

Fort

PADMAVILASAM ROAD

Padmanabhaswami
Temple

tank

Royal
Palace

Kutchira
Malika

broken fort wall

Railway Station

POWER HOUSE ROAD

Bus
Stand

HOSPITAL ROAD

CHALI BAZAR ROAD

NH47

PADMANABHAPURAM, KANYAKUMARI

0   300 yards
0   300 metres

THIRUVANANTHAPURAM

KOVALAM

front shelters devotees; its ceiling has square lotus panels with miniature celestials and *nagas* serving as brackets. The **Krishna Shrine**, near the northwest corner of the colonnade in the outer enclosure, stands in a small compound. It, too, has a gabled wooden roof.

Several features of interest are seen near the approach road leading to the east Gate of the Padmanabhaswamy Temple. The **Kutchira Malika** is a traditional wooden residence with a polished floor and sloping tiled roofs. The **Mettanmani** nearby is a curious tower with a mechanical clock. Various structures that once formed part of the 18C **Royal Palace** are located southwest of the Temple. The combination of European Neo-Classical features with indigenous tiled roofs is characteristic. Portions of the laterite walls of the **Fort** laid out by Martand Varma can still be seen to the west.

Mahatma Gandhi Road, the principal route running north through the middle of the city, passes by the **Secretariat** of 1939 and the **Victoria Jubilee Town Hall**. The **Public Library** opposite, founded in 1829, is the oldest such institution in Southern India. The Palayam Junction is marked by the formidable Neo-Gothic bulk of the city's main **Latin Catholic Church**. Nearby **Christ Church**, also built in the Neo-Gothic manner, was erected in 1859 by Anglican missionaries. The building has generous side windows and a two-stage tower over the arcaded porch. At the northern extremity of Mahatma Gandhi Road is the attractively planted **Public Park**, in which stand the city's main cultural institutions.

The **Art Museum** (closed Mondays), originally the Napier Museum, is a unusual building of considerable charm, designed by Robert Fellowes Chisholm in 1872. It successfully fuses wooden balconies, timber screens and tiered tiled roofs with ornate gables typical of the Kerala manner, with Neo-Gothic elements such as polychrome brickwork, arcaded ranges and slender pinnacled towers. The collection (closed Mondays) of metal, stone and wooden sculptures comes from various sites in the vicinity. The Chera period bronzes from the 9C are the earliest metal images from this part of Kerala; the smoothly modelled standing Vishnu with inlaid gold eyes is particularly fine. The small, detailed icons from the 17C–18C include images of Narasimha, Virabhadra and Vishnu on Garuda. The seated figure of Shasta, the head surrounded by a halo of hair, is perhaps the most interesting of these later metal images. Brass lamps fashioned as miniature female figures are also on display. An impressive set of wooden bracket figures comes from the 17C temple at Kulathapuzha. They include a remarkable image of Durga standing on the buffalo, one leg pressing down on the animal's head. The lower part of a chariot covered with carvings, and a small wooden pavilion are also on display.

The adjacent **Sri Chitra Art Gallery** (closed Mondays) houses a collection of Indian paintings, including a representative sample of Mughal and Rajput miniatures. There are many notable examples of Kerala's most famous artist, Ravi Varma, and a collection of early 20C Bengal paintings. The artists, who mainly worked in oils, attempted to fuse indigenous themes with European techniques and styles. The **Museum of Natural History** and the **Children's Museum** stand next door. The sprawling **Botanical Gardens**, with their wealth of exotic plant life, and the **Zoo** and **Aquarium** are attractively set in wooded hilly parkland to the north.

The **Kanakakunna Palace**, east of the Botanical Gardens, is one of many royal residences dating from the early 20C scattered around the city. Its sprawling arcades survey the landscaped grounds.

B. Nemam

This village, 7km southeast of Thiruvananathapuram, just off NH47, is of interest for the 11C **Niramankara Temple**, best known today for its Vishnu image, which is enshrined in a subsidiary structure of recent origin. This magnificent icon, one of the finest in Kerala, is a fully sculptured four-armed figure dressed in elaborate costume and jewellery. The Temple itself, usually dated to the 14C, is now ruined and abandoned, but is worth examining, since it reveals the interior arrangement of a typical Kerala-style structure. A small, square *linga* sanctuary at the core of the Temple displays pilastered walls topped with an octagonal-domed roof. The surrounding eight columns once supported timbers for the conical roof. The sanctuary and columns are contained in a circle of outer walls, complete with moulded basement, wall pilasters, some organised into niches with ornate pediments, and continuous eaves.

C. Tiruvallam

This small settlement, 8km south of Thiruvananthapuram, on the road to Kovalam, is of interest for the triple-shrined **Parashurameshvara Temple**. The complex is entered on the north through a traditional structure with sloping tiled roofs. Three small north-facing sanctuaries of different shapes stand in the middle of the inner compound: a part-circular Brahma shrine on an axis with the entrance, a small square Vishnu shrine, and a circular Shiva shrine encasing a square sanctuary, the last with a conical metal-clad roof. The Brahma shrine, the basement and walls of which are assigned to the 13C, has clearly articulated pilasters interspersed with blind niches headed by curving pediments that frame miniature divinities. The circular brick-and-plaster tower above is topped with a hemispherical roof. The other shrines, including a rectangular west-facing Matsya sanctuary, are additions of the 16C–17C.

D. Vizhinjam

This seaside village, 2km south of Kovalam, was a former Dutch and British factory, of which nothing can now be seen. There are two **Mosques** on the beach: the Moienuddin Palli, a traditional structure with twin minarets, and a large new prayer hall in an international Islamic style.

Some of the earliest architectural remains in Kerala, dating back to the 9C–10C, are located here. The **Shiva Shrine** is a small square sanctuary, with a short tower capped by a square dome-like tower in plaster-covered brick. The adjacent **Bhagavati Shrine** is rectangular in layout, but lacks its original brick superstructure. The sculptures placed here include an icon of Kaumari. A modest rock-cut temple a short distance east, though unfinished, has graceful reliefs of Shiva as the hunter, holding the bow, and of dancing Shiva with Parvati.

E. Kazhakuttam

The **Mahadeva Templ**e at this town, 10km north of Thiruvananthapuram on NH47, is an important early foundation, going back to the 9C. The outer enclosure is entered through a main gate on the east, which has characteristic sloping roofs. Here stand a number of subsidiary shrines with different-shaped roofs, dedicated to Ganapati, Krishna, Vishnu and Shasta, the last with an apsidal-ended plan. The focal sanctuary at the core of the inner enclosure is a square sanctuary, with a passageway running around the innermost *linga* chamber. The outer walls have well-articulated pilastered projections, with doors in the middle of three sides flanked by niches framing window-like panels. The pilasters carry rounded eaves with carved animals on top, and a line of ornamental roof forms with barrel-vaulted elements in the middle. Angled timber struts fashioned as deities and attendants are placed between the roof elements. The second storey repeats this scheme at a reduced scale. Both storeys are partly concealed by sloping tiled roofs, the upper roof forming a pyramid with dormer windows in the middle of each side. A later pavilion with a pyramidal roof is built up against the east entrance to the shrine.

F. Anjengo

This small port, 30km north of Thiruvananthapuram, just off NH47, was occupied by the Portuguese in the 16C. The modest **Church** that they built still survives. The English arrived in 1684, establishing their own factory and warehouse. These have vanished, leaving only the crumbling laterite **Fort** which protected the trading post. The **English Cemetery** preserves a number of 18C tombs, the earliest dated 1704.

G. Varkala

This attractive coastal town, 45km north of Thiruvananthapuram on NH47, already noted for its seaside accommodation, is also a health resort supplied with curative mineral springs. The **Janardana Temple**, built on a rocky eminence overlooking the ocean, has records going back to the 13C. The European bell inside the main gate is said to have been presented by a Dutch sea captain in the 17C. The shrine is approached through a columned hall with supports sculpted in the Tamil manner, with three-dimensional figures of Nataraja, Bhikshatanamurti, Manmatha and Rati.

The *Matha* at **Sivagiri**, 3km east, is a well-known religious institution founded by Narayana Guru (1855–1928). This socio-religious reformer is revered in Kerala for his dictum, 'One Caste, One Religion, One God for Man'.

H. Kollam

Formerly called Quilon, this lively commercial and industrial city, 72km north of Thiruvananthapuram, occupies a narrow strip of land between the Arabian Sea and Ashtamudi Lake, the southern point of Kerala's inland lagoon and the beginning of the backwaters. Kollam is intimately connected with Kerala's history, giving its name to the era by which the Malayali calendar begins, traditionally fixed at 825.

Kollam has been known through the centuries as one of Kerala's premier ports. Annals of the Tang dynasty note the visit of Chinese merchants in the 7C–8C. Marco Polo passed by in 1293, referring to the port as Koilum. The Portuguese established a factory and fort here in 1503. They were evicted in 1653 by the Dutch, who maintained a post here until 1741, when Kollam was captured by the Thiruvananthapuram army. The city thereafter served as the second capital of the Travancore kingdom. British forces were stationed here from 1795 onward.

The oldest building to be preserved within the city is the 15C **Ganapati Temple** in Tamarakulam (opposite Old Tobacco Godown). This has a square sanctuary with a high basement and boldly articulated walls, capped by a brick-and-plaster dome-like roof. Unlike most other temples in Kerala, there is no sloping tiled roof. Such a roof does occur, however, on the open pavilion that stands in front (west). This is raised on a stone basement with animal balustrades flanking the access steps. The **Rameshvara Temple** nearby, though almost completely rebuilt, has a moulded basement dating from the 14C.

Kollam is arguably the oldest Catholic diocese in Southern India: Friar Jordanus was consecrated bishop by John XXII in 1328, though he probably died before assuming his episcopal functions. The **Cathedral**, no earlier than the 18C, has a Baroque-styled façade divided into three stages by pilastered elements capped with vase-like pinnacles. The central bays are flanked by double side volutes. Another interesting Christian monument is the **Syrian Church**, supposedly founded in 1519, but much rebuilt in later times. This small structure has an unpretentious gabled front. Unusual 18C murals cover the rear wall of the inner sanctuary: Mar Aproth and Mar Sapor in the central panels, with the Madonna, St John, St Peter and St Thomas at the sides. St George slaying the dragon appears on the left wall.

The **Valiakada Arikade**, Kollam's largest and most important mosque, was totally renovated in 1962. Concrete balconies and corner minarets conceal the traditional prayer hall, which is roofed with sloping tiles. The **Janakappurampalli Mosque**, near the beach, is older in origin and bigger, but has also been rebuilt.

The **Travellers Bungalow**, on the bank of Ashtamudi Lake, north of the city, once the home of the British Resident, is worth visiting for its period charm. It has an fascinating collection of military prints and Chinese porcelain.

Tangasseri, 3km northwest of Kollam, was a trading post connected with the Portuguese and Dutch, both of whom were involved with the construction of **Fort Thomas.** The compact square enclosure has sloping laterite walls with rounded corner bastions. The East India Company installed a factory at Tangasseri in 1683, trading successfully until 1782, when it was challenged by the forces of Haidar Ali of Srirangapattana [15C]. Two European **Cemeteries** are located nearby.

I. Ponmudi

This small hill station lies 65km north of Thiruvananthapuram, at about 1000m elevation. It is surrounded by rubber and tea estates which spread over the forested ranges of the Western Ghats. There has been little modern development, giving the station a calm and peaceful air.

47 · Kochi

Still widely known by its former name of Cochin, the port of Kochi represents the historical and commercial hub of Central Kerala. This densely populated region is home to peoples of different religions, which explains the profusion of temples, churches, mosques and even synagogues.

Most visitors will begin this itinerary with a tour of **Kochi** itself [A], for which at least a half day should be set aside. An attractive excursion by the backwaters to **Alappuzha** [B] will require a full day.

Travelling by road south from Kochi, it is possible to pass through many towns with historical monuments: **Tripunithura** [C], **Udayamperur** [D], **Vaikom** [E], **Kaduthuruthi** [F], **Ettumanur** [G], **Palai** [H], **Kottayam** [I], **Tiruvalla** [J], **Kaviyur** [K], **Chengannur** [L], **Mavelikkara** [M] and **Kayankulam** [N] have been singled out here. Allow two days and more to visit a selection of these spots.

The pilgrimage to **Sabarimalai** [O], southeast of Kochi, attracts great crowds of visitors, especially in January. Many devotees spend one night making the journey there and back on foot.

From this remote mountain shrine it is possible to continue on to the Periyar Wildlife Sanctuary, near **Kumily** [P]. An overnight stop permits glimpses of the animals at dusk and dawn. A stay is also recommended at the tranquil hill station of **Munnar** [Q].

Historical sites north of Kochi can be visited on the route to **Thrissur** [W], a well-known temple centre. They include the churches and temples at **Anganmaly** [R], **Kaladi** [S], **Kodungallur** [T], **Triprayar** [U] and **Peruvanam** [V]. The art academy at **Cheruthuruthi** [X] and the celebrated pilgrimage shrine at **Guruvayur** [Y] lie beyond Thrissur.

■ **Transport**. Kochi benefits from direct air connections with Delhi, Bombay [1], Panaji [11], Bangalore [14] and Madras [36]. Ernakulam, the city on the mainlaind, is easily reached by train and bus from Thiruvananthapuram [46], 223km south, and Kozhikode [48], 219km north, also from Coimbatore [43], 173km northwest. The road to Madurai [44], 255km east, passes by Kumily. Local buses with frequent services reach all the sites described here.

Boat trips on the backwaters of Central Kerala offer incomparable scenery as well as glimpses of everyday life. The best place to begin is Alappuzha, from where it is possible to reach Kottayam and Kollam [46H]. Kochi harbour bustles with ferries plying from Ernakulam to Willingdom and Bolgatty Islands, as well as to Kochi Fort.

■ **Accommodation**. The *Taj Malabar Hotel* (☎ 666811) and *Casino Hotel* (☎ 668221) on Willingdon Island, and the somewhat rundown *Bolgatty Palace Hotel* (☎ 355003) on Bolgatty Island offer views of the Kochi harbour. (The STD code for Kochi is 048.) The best places to stay on the mainland are the *Taj Residency* (☎ 371471), *Hotel Abad Plaza* (☎ 361636) and *Avenue Regent Hotel* (☎ 372660). Cheaper alternatives include the *Sealord Hotel* (☎ 352682), *Grand Hotel* (☎ 353211) and *Bharat Tourist Home* (☎ 353501), the last conveniently near to the ferry landing. Visitors may chose to stay in more peaceful surroundings at **Kumarakom** (STD code 048192), beside Vembanad Lake, 58km south of Kochi by road, but with direct boat connection from the airport. Two deluxe hotels have opened here, the *Taj Garden Retreat* (☎ 668377), a converted planter's bungalow, and the *Coconut Lagoon Resort* (☎ 668001).

Overnight accommodation at **Periyar** (STD code 04869) can be had at the *Spice Village* (☎ 22315), on the main road at **Kumily**, or at the more pleasantly situated *Lake Palace* (☎ 22023), within the Sanctuary itself. The *Government House* (☎ 30385) and *East End* (☎ 30451) are the best hotels at

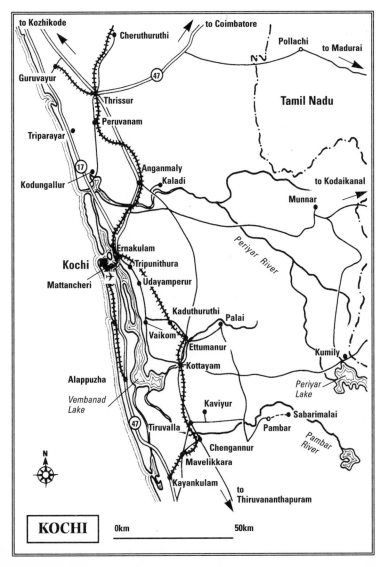

to Kozhikode
to Coimbatore
Cheruthuruthi
Pollachi
to Madurai
Guruvayur
47
Thrissur
Tamil Nadu
Peruvanam
Triparayar
17
Anganmaly
Kodungallur
Kaladi
to Kodaikanal
Munnar
Periyar River
Ernakulam
Kochi
Tripunithura
Mattancheri
Udayamperur
Kaduthuruthi
Palai
Vaikom
Ettumanur
Kumily
Kottayam
Alappuzha
Periyar Lake
Vembanad Lake
Kaviyur
Sabarimalai
47
Tiruvalla
Pambar
Pambar River
Chengannur
N
Mavelikkara
Kayankulam
to Thiruvananthapuram

KOCHI   0km   50km

Munnar. Convenient stop-overs are also possible in other centres: for instance, the *Alleppey Prince Hotel* (☎ 243752) at **Allappuzha** (STD code 0477) and the *Elite International* (☎ 21033) at **Thrissur** (STD code 0487).

■ **Tourist Information**. The Government of India Tourist Office is located next to the Taj Malabar Hotel on Willingdon Island (☎ 668352). The KTDC Reception Centre is on Shanmugam Road in **Ernakulam** (☎ 353234). A counter is also maintained at the airport.

■ **Travel agents and tour companies**. Among the companies offering services for hotel bookings and travel arrangements are *Aries*, Hotel Avenue Regent, Mahatma Gandhi Road (☎ 353662), *Great India Tour Co*, Pithmu Smarana, Srikandath Road (☎ 369246) and *Harrison Malayalam*, Willingdon Island (☎ 36007).

A. Kochi

Situated on a magnificent inland waterway, Kochi enjoys a unique situation, which helps to explain its commercial significance today as in the past. The area known as the Fort and the nearby quarter of Mattancheri occupy the tip of a long peninsula that runs between the Arabian Sea and an extensive lagoon.

The outlet to the sea, a natural meeting place for ocean vessels and river craft, dates in fact only from 1341, when there was a drastic change in the course of the Periyar River. Prior to this date, Kochi was only of minor importance. In 1405 the king of Central Kerala decided to move his capital here, after which Kochi supplanted Kozhikode as the most active port on the Malabar coast. An interesting aspect of commercial life in Kochi was the contribution of Jewish merchants with international trade connections.

Pressure from the Samutiri (Zamorin) rulers of Kozhikode encouraged the Kochi rulers to welcome the Portuguese. Vasco da Gama landed in 1500 in search of pepper, returning two years later. Albuquerque spent time here in 1503, obtaining permission to construct a fortified factory. He brought with him friars who founded a chapel and began missionary activities. These efforts were boosted by the Jesuits, who arrived in 1524, and who set up a printing press here in 1577, the first in Southern India.

The Portuguese domination of economic and political affairs at Kochi continued until 1663, when they were ousted by the Dutch, much to the benefit of local Jews, who had been persecuted by the Portuguese. The Dutch remained here throughout the 18C, continuing to trade here even after Haidar Ali of Srirangapattana [15C] captured the port in 1773. With the fall of Holland to Napoleon in 1795, the British seized the Indian Dutch possessions and Kochi passed into British hands, where it remained until Independence.

Kochi has affirmed its position in the 20C as one of the premier ports of Southern India. Its harbour, much developed in the 1930s, enjoys a reputation for ship repair. Ernakulam is a busy city with a large range of engineering industries.

The tour described here begins appropriately at **Fort Kochi**, reached most conveniently by ferry from Ernakulam or Willingdon Island. The town retains

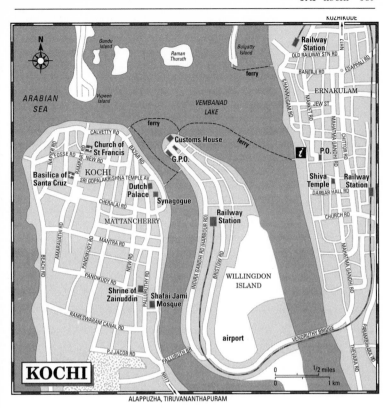

KOCHI

ALAPPUZHA, TIRUVANANTHAPURAM

much of its traditional character, with many old warehouses stocked with grains and spices and several traditional mansions facing onto crowded streets. There is, however, no sign of the original ramparts of the Fort.

The **Church of St Francis** is located at the north end of the town, within sight of the Chinese fishing nets by the water's edge. Reputed to be the earliest European Christian place of worship in Southern India, the Church occupies the site of the 1503 wooden chapel, which was entirely rebuilt in masonry in 1506–16. Vasco da Gama was buried here in 1524, and his body was conveyed to Portugal 12 years later. The Dutch renovated the Church, using it for Protestant services; the sombre façade with triple volutes dates mostly from this era. The building was further remodelled by the British in 1887. The interior is of little merit, other than the tombs set into the walls and floor. The earliest is of Simao de Miranda, dating from 1524 (left wall of nave). The nearby **Dutch Cemetery** contains British as well as Dutch graves, now in a very dilapidated condition.

A short distance south is the **Basilica of Santa Cruz**. This Catholic place of worship dates back to Portuguese times, but the original building of 1557 was demolished by the British in 1795, at which time it was being used as a warehouse. The present Church, which dates from 1904, has a handsome Neo-Classical façade. The finest features of the interior are the carved wooden pulpit and stucco altar. The adjacent house of the Catholic bishop accommodates the small **Padroado Museum** (permission required to visit) of Kochi's ecclesiastical history.

The **Dutch Palace** in **Mattancheri** (closed Mondays) lies 2km southeast of the Church of St Francis. Built by the Portuguese in 1557 for Kerala Varma, the ruler of Kochi, in exchange for trading rights, the Palace was totally remodelled by the Dutch in 1663, hence its name. The exterior is European in character, with raked masonry walls and round-headed windows and doors; the sloping tiled roof and wooden balconies are, however, indigenous features. The Palace is entered by a flight of steps through a portico on the south, which gives access to a suite of public rooms on the upper level. These look down onto an inner court, inside which stands a small shrine dedicated to Bhagavati, the protective goddess of the Kochi royal family. The rooms serve as a setting for a display of regal memorabilia, including ceremonial robes, headdresses, weapons, palanquins and furniture. The Palace is best known for its murals, which constitute one of the most important (and accessible) series of wall paintings in Kerala. Their crowded and animated compositions and vivid colour schemes, with varying orange, red, green and deep blue tones, suggest several phases spanning the 17C–19C.

The king's bedchamber, left of the entrance, occupies the southwest corner of the Palace. The walls are covered with scenes from the *Ramayana*, which relate its story in some detail (labels provided). The epic begins (east wall) with the fire sacrifice of Rishyashringa, the devotions of Dasharatha, and the birth of Rama and his three brothers (left panel). The story is interrupted with two depictions of Krishna (central panel) before continuing with Vishvamitra meeting Dasharatha, Rama killing Tataka, the sacrifice of Vishvamitra, Rama liberating Ahalya, Rama breaking Shiva's bow, the marriage of Rama and Sita, and Rama tying the string of Parashurama's bow (right panel). The narrative continues (south wall) with Dasharatha appointing Rama as his heir, Rama leaving for the forest, the meeting of Bharata and Rama, and Lakshmana disfiguring Suparnaka (left panel); Rama and Sita in the forest, Rama killing the golden deer, the abduction of Sita by Ravana, and Jatayu's attempt to stop Ravana (right panel). Further scenes (west wall) show the meeting of Rama with Sugriva, Rama shooting the arrow through the seven palm trees, the fight of Vali and Sugriva (left panel); Rama giving the ring to Hanuman, Hanuman leaping through the air with the mountain of sacred herbs, Hanuman entering Lanka, Ravana attempting to woo Sita, Rama performing penance, the building of the stone bridge, and battles between Ravana and Sugriva, Rama and Kumbakarna, and Rama and Ravana, and the fire ordeal of Sita (central panel); and Rama returning to Ayodhya, the reception at the palace, received by attendants holding lamps (right panel).

Another important series of paintings in the Dutch Palace is found in the upper staircase room right of the entrance. Among the compositions are Lakshmi seated on the lotus, sleeping Vishnu, Shiva seated with Parvati, the coronation of Rama, and Shiva as *kirata*, the hunter. The adjacent chamber has a single panel depicting Vishnu seated on the serpent.

Narrow steps descend to a series of rooms at the lower (ground) level. The paintings here are quite different in style. The first chamber has unfinished paintings with faint but delicate ochre line work, showing the marriage of Shiva and Parvati in the company of courtly maidens. The second chamber has large panels, the figures of which are enhanced by deep shading, indicating a 19C date. Here appear Shiva with Parvati, Shiva and Mohini, Krishna lifting Govardhana Hill, and the same deity in reclining position, attended by women.

Immediately south of the Palace is the small **Krishna Temple** (access restricted to visitors). The central circular sanctuary, roofed with a smooth cone of copper tiles, stands in a rectangular compound entered from the west.

The **Synagogue** (closed Saturdays), the finest Jewish place of prayer in Southern India, stands at the end of a small lane a short distance east of the Palace. After their expusion from Kodungallur in 1568, the Jewish community moved to Kochi, where they founded a Synagogue. This was destroyed by the Portuguese in 1662, but was restored in 1664. The present building is mostly the result of the reconstruction by Ezekial Rahabi in 1761, reflecting the community's new-found wealth under the Dutch.

Though the Jewish community is now reduced to some 50 members, the Synagogue is well maintained. It presents an unadorned masonry exterior with simple window openings, capped by a tiled roof. The corner tower, an addition of 1767, has clocks on four sides with different scripts: Malayalam on the north (facing towards the Palace), Hebrew, Roman and Arabic. The interior is enlivened with a floor entirely covered in blue-and-white tiles from Canton, showing willow patterns and other motifs. Wooden benches line the walls; the central prayer stand has a gleaming brass balustrade. The tabernacle, set into the rear wall, is framed by carved wooden panels with Corinthian colonettes at the sides. The three scrolls of the Torah are kept in gilded and embossed metal containers. Ornate glass chandeliers hang from the ceiling. The cemetery nearby contains many tombstones with Hebrew script. Among the documents kept in the Synagogue is a copper-plate record from Kodungallur, recording a grant by Bhaskara Ravi Varman (962–1020), indicating the antiquity of Kerala's Jewish community.

The old Muslim quarter of Kochi is located a short distance south of the Dutch Palace and the Synagogue. The **Shafai Jami Mosque**, known locally as Chembattapalli, is built in traditional style with double sloping roof tiers covered in terracotta tiles (below) and copper sheets (above), both supported on a timber framework. The entrance chamber has coffered wooden ceiling and carved wooden panels with Arabic inscriptions over the doorways. That above the north door mentions the date 1420, but this probably only refers to the masonry walls of the prayer hall itself; the timber portions date from the 16C–17C. The hall is of interest for the unusual wooden pulpit, and the *mihrab* in the masonry wall topped with a painted lobed arch. A ladder in the entrance chamber provides access to the upper level, surrounded by angled screens set between curved backets angling outwards.

Among the other Muslim religious buildings in this part of Kochi is the **Shrine of Shaykh Zainuddin**, with its tiled gable roof sheltering a triangular panel filled with Arabic script.

Most visitors to Kochi enjoy the ferry rides across the splendid natural harbour, starting from the Sea Lord Jetty at Ernakulam. One historical feature stands on **Vypeen Island**, immediately north of the Chinese nets. **Our Lady of Hope** dates from 1605, and is built on the site of a church founded in 1560. This was the principal Catholic church in the Dutch era. Its Portuguese origins are seen in the gabled façade and Baroque-styled doorway. The screen within was removed from the Church of St Francis.

Palm-fringed **Bolgatty Island**, to the north, enjoys an idyllic location and serene atmosphere. The **Palace Hotel** incorporates a palatial bungalow built in 1744 by the Dutch; it served as the home of the British Resident at Kochi after 1799. The original building retains much of its period charm, with verandahs and deep overhanging roofs. The **Customs House**, on **Willingdon Island** opposite, surveys the impressive panorama of Kochi's busy port. The **Church of St Peter and St Paul** at **Vanduthuruthi** on Willingdon Island, just south of the bridge to Ernakulam, has a Baroque façade. The altarpiece within is finely worked.

Ernakulam, on the east edge of the harbour, does not benefit from the historical prestige of Kochi and Mattancheri. Even so, there are a few buildings of interest, including the **Shiva Temple** (access restricted to visitors), in the middle of the city. This is entered on the east through a gabled porch, in front of which stands a brass-clad lamp column. The **Parikshith Thamburam Museum** nearby (closed Mondays) occupies a Darbar Hall with typical Kerala woodwork. Here are displayed sculptures, coins and 19C oil paintings by Ravi Varma and other Kerala artists, which were formerly in the royal collection.

B. Alappuzha

Formerly called Alleppey, this port lies between Kochi, 56km north, and Kollam, 84km south, connected to both by NH47 as well as by inland waterways. Alappuzha dates only from the period of the Travancore rulers, who annexed this part of Kerala in the middle of the 18C. After 1762 the port was vigorously developed by the Travancore prime minister, Kesava Pillai, who constructed warehouses and invited merchants to settle here from other parts of the country. His programme of shipbuilding encouraged trade between Alappuzha and Bombay and Calcutta.

Alapphuzha derives its wealth from tea, rubber, pepper and other highland products, which are shipped via a network of rivers and canals to Vembanad Lake. The city occupies a narrow strip of land between the Lake and the ocean, crisscrossed by canals that connect the two bodies of water. Numerous bridges cross these canals, lending a distinctive character to the city. Alappuzha remains one of the world's chief suppliers of coir mats and matting.

Other than the bulky **Lighthouse** of 1862, the beams of which are visible for 25km out to sea, there are few buildings of merit. The city is of greater interest for the colourful water carnival, culminating in the famous snakeboat race, with up to 100 oarsmen in each boat, which takes place on Independence Day each August.

The Baroque-styled **Catholic Church** at **Tamboli**, 4km north of Alapphuzha, has a remarkable 17C interior. The altar on the right side of the nave has a painted wooden crucifix set against painted panels depicting the Virgin Mary, Mary Magdalen and St John in the company of soldiers. The finely worked altar opposite is intricately carved and gilded. The Virgin holding the Infant Christ, which forms the focus of the principal altar, is said to have been imported from Europe.

C. Tripunithura

This town, 8km south of Ernakulam, served for a time as a residence of the Kochi rulers and their nobles, as can be seen from the may mansions which dot the city. One of these, in the middle of Tripunithura, has been opened to the public: the **Hill Palace Museum** (closed Mondays) displays regalia and arms, as well as paintings and sculptures from the royal collection. The nearby **Purnathrayisha Temple** was rebuilt in a traditional style after a fire in 1920. The west gate, which survived the fire, has a finely sculpted wooden ceiling. The circular sanctuary within has its curving masonry walls entirely cloaked in brass sheets embossed with images of different deities. The **Church of St Mary** on the main road, a Jacobite Syrian structure, has a charming Baroque-styled façade with an octagonal bell tower.

D. Udayamperur

This small settlement, 6km south of Tripunithura, is celebrated for its **Roman Catholic Church** of 1510. This was the venue of the Synod of Diamper, held by Archbishop Alexis de Menenzes in 1599, which attempted to bring the entire Syrian church under Roman obedience while preserving its unique Syriac history. The building itself is a modest structure, with a sombre façade flanked by curved volutes. The mortal remains of a local ruler who embraced Christianity are preserved here. The granite cross which stands in front may date back to pre-European times.

E. Vaikom

The sprawling town of Vaikom, 14km south of Udayamperur, a total of 38km south of Ernakulam, figures prominently in the recent history of Kerala. This was the scene of the famous *sathyagraha* movement of 1925, in which Mahatma Gandhi participated, which led to the opening of temple roads to all castes.

The **Vaikkathappan Temple** (access restricted to visitors) is contained in a vast rectangular compound with gates in the middle of four sides; only that on the east is roofed with sloping tiles. Brass-clad lamp columns flank the path leading to the east entrance to the second enclosure. This is marked by a monumental hall, with granite piers showing attached colonettes and crouching *yali* brackets in the typical Tamil manner. The peripheral supports are sculpted with rearing *yalis* and fierce guardians. The enclosure walls have an outer line of timber screens, with brass lamps and wooden *yali* brackets carrying a tiled roof; dormer windows mark the corners. The inner line of stone contains the colonnade that runs around the inner enclosure. The *linga* shrine that stands freely in the middle is an elliptical masonry structure, the only example of this shape in Kerala. A spout emerging from the north side is supported on a demonic guardian brandishing a club.

The walls display pilastered niches into which wooden windows have been inserted. The projecting timber brackets carry a conical roof sheathed in copper, capped with a gilded pot finial. The paintings that cover the walls probably date back to the 17C; they have been reworked recently. Among the major compositions are Shiva dancing in the company of the gods, Vishnu riding on Garuda, Bhairava, and Rama battling with Ravana. Guardian figures holding clubs and trampling on serpents are repeated several times. The small, square hall, sheltering a seated Nandi image immediately in front (east), has carved stone columns. These support a carved wooden ceiling, above which rises a metal-clad pyramial roof.

A smaller, but similarly artistic, monument is located at nearby **Udayanapuram**, 2km north of Vaikom. The **Peruntirukkoil** (access restricted to visitors) consists of a circular *linga* sanctuary, the outer walls of which have wooden screens set in pilastered niches. Carved guardian figures flank the doorway on the east. The paintings show divinities, including Parvati with infant Ganesha, and Garuda supporting Vishnu's consorts on outstretched wings. The wooden struts beneath the roof overhang are fashioned as heroes and hunters, in illustration of the story of Arjuna's fight with Shiva disguised as the hunter.

F. Kaduthuruthi

This long-established Christian centre, 14km south of Vaikom, is known for its Syrian Catholic churches. The oldest is the **Church of St Mary**, rebuilt in 1599 immediately after the Synod of Diamper. Its three-storeyed façade is built in the Baroque manner, recently repainted in pale blue, pink and yellow. Pairs of Corinthian colonettes flank the central bays, with a superimposed round-headed doorway, a window with a triangular pediment, and a niche housing a statue of the Virgin. Relief figures enliven the façade: fish-tailed humans bearing boats on their heads, with peacocks above, are seen on the second stage; angels appear on the third stage in the company of the Virgin, with standing monsters in the quarter-circle volutes at either side. Mary surmounted by the Holy Trinity fills a medallion beneath the cross that tops the whole composition. Further reliefs on the rear wall show hunting scenes, including an armed male, accompanied by a dog, shooting a stag.

Epitaphs with Persian crosses are fixed into the walls inside the Church. Here can be seen a circular granite font probably dating from the 15C–16C, its sides embellished with scrollwork and miniature figures. The glory of the interior is, however, the brilliantly gilded wooden altar, one of the most elaborate in Kerala, probably no earlier than the 18C. Fully sculpted saints occupy Neo-Classical niches arranged around a sunburst medallion of the Holy Ghost, topped with a small spire. The Virgin with Christ and God the Father are painted on the topmost panel. Luxuriant volutes filled with musicians are surrounded by carved angels bearing garlands, those at either side dressed in Portuguese costume. Modern paintings adorn the barrel-vaulted ceiling. An important antiquity associated with this Church is the 10m high monolithic cross that stands in the yard outside. This was erected in 1599 on an elaborate stone platform adorned with miniature figures of the Virgin Mary and Infant Jesus, as well as hunters, fighters and dancers.

Rivalling the Church of St Mary in artistic merit is the **Forane Church of the Holy Ghost** at **Muttuchira**, 1.5km south of Kadathuruthi, which also has a stone cross standing in front. The five-bayed façade has unadorned volutes framing the upper stages; windows with grilles are placed in the upper levels. The exuberantly carved and gilded altar focuses on a central sunburst with an expressive three-dimensional Crucifix above. The composition is topped with a scene of the Coronation of Mary, surrounded by volutes filled with angels. The smaller, but equally ornate, side altars contain brightly painted figures of the Virgin, the Pietà, and the Christ child. The Church is overlooked on one side by a five-stage octagonal tower, whose tile-coated gabled roof is topped with a large cross.

G. Ettumanur

The **Mahadeva Temple** at Ettumanur stands on the main road 19km south of Kadathuruthi, a total of 60km south of Ernakulam. This grandly conceived shrine dates back to the 12C, but was entirely remodelled in 1542. The monument is entered from the west through a traditional-style gate with wooden columns, supporting a sloping tiled roof in two tiers, with a carving of Yoga Narasimha in the central gable. The vividly toned murals on the inner walls show Padmanabha, the form of Vishnu reclining on the serpent (right), and multi-armed Nataraja surounded by admiring celestials (left). A path leads past a brass-clad lamppost to the porch that gives access to the inner enclosure (access restricted to visitors). A porch sheltering a stone altar and a metal lamp is contained within wooden screens overhung by a low roof. Similar screens running around the stone walls of the innner enclosure have dormer windows at the corners.

The circular *linga* shrine of the Mahadeva Temple has a conical roof sheathed in copper tiles. The walls consist of intricately carved wooden panels and screens framed by friezes of warriors, musicians, sages and animals. The panels show brightly painted deities in the company of miniature attendants: Vishnu and consorts, Rama and Sita, Ganesha and consort, Krishna, Nataraja and Surya. The angled struts beneath the roof overhang are sculpted in three dimensions as female dancers and characters from the story of Arjuna, and Shiva as the hunter. Small stone guardians are placed on either side of the four doorways leading to the shrine; the access steps are flanked by carved balustrades. Immediately in front (west) of the shrine stands an open square hall topped with a simple pyramidal roof, also covered in metal tiles. The stone columns support wooden brackets and beams; the ceiling has 25 lotus panels surrounded by miniature deities. Two Nandis, one of stone, the other of brass, are placed here.

H. Palai

This small town, 16km east of Ettumanur, is the headquarters of an important bishop of the Syrian Catholic church. Close to the new cathedral stands its predecessor of 1502, the **Cathedral of St Thomas**, one of the grandest churches in Kerala. The building preserves its traditional character, with sloping tiled roofs and a central squat tower topped by a pyramidal roof. These features are concealed by the monumental five-bayed façade. The three stages of the central bay are framed by pairs of Corinthinan colonettes and topped with a volute and cross. The bays are enlivened with relief figures of angels, two flanking a statue of St Thomas set in a niche in the third stage. Other saintly personalities occupy niches in the second stage of the intermediate bays. Two sets of fanned volutes provide the transition to the end bays.

The interior is dominated by the magnificent set of gilded altars set into the rear wall. The central altar is placed within a recessed bay roofed by a coffered barrel vault with painted woodwork. It shows the Apostle and five other saintly figures occupying two tiers of triple Baroque-styled niches. The Coronation of the Virgin is painted on the topmost panel, surrounded by a sunburst ending in fanciful volutes. A fully carved angel in Portuguese costume, holding a garland, is seen at each side. The side altars, dedicated to the Virgin (right) and a king holding an orb and sceptre (left), are smaller but no less ornate. They are accompanied by painted angels and pediments with sunburst motifs. Another feature of merit is a carved wooden pulpit with a curving floral festoon at its base. A small pavilion with a pyramidal tiled roof standing is used by musicians.

Other than the Cathedral and several lesser churches in Palai, there are two important **Shiva Temples**, one in the middle of the town, the other on the bank of the nearby Meenachil River. The latter, recently consecrated, is built with an unusual curving masonry tower, probably inspired by Northern Indian models. Worshippers can view the deity within from doorways on four sides.

I. Kottayam

This city lies 11km south of Ettumanur, a total of 72km south of Ernakulam, on the Minachil River, a navigable waterway connected with Vembanad Lake. Practically all the hill produce of central Kerala passes through Kottayam, from where it is shipped to Alappuzha and Kochi, still partly by boat. The economic importance of the city is matched by its religious significance as one of the main headquarters of both the Orthodox Syrian and Latin Catholic communities.

Puthenangadi, one of Kottayam's northern suburbs, preserves many Syrian churches. The **Valliyapalli**, the oldest, was founded in 1550, but dates from 1588 in its present form. It stands on top of a small hill overlooking the river. An interesting pre-European arched block, set into the gate leading into the churchyard, is adorned with carvings of a bird and a cross with leaves at either side. The church is a plain structure with a square tower at one corner, entered from a side arcade. A gleaming altar stands in front of the oil paintings on the rear wall. A stone relief of a cross surrounded by early styled script is seen above a side altar on the right. (This closely resembles the Pahlavi inscription in the church on St Thomas Mount in Madras [36I].)

Cheriapalli is another Syrian church at Puthenangadi. Its handsome Baroque façade, complete with fan volutes, is partly concealed behind a modern entrance porch. The entrance on the west is bridged by an arched block sculpted with figures and peacocks flanking a cross. The interior of the church is of interest for the painted panels, narrating the life of the Virgin, on the walls behind the main altar. Figures and floral motifs adorn the wooden barrel vault above.

Remnants of the old **Palaces** of the Chenganassery rulers are seen in **Thazhathangadi**, another quarter of Kottayam. These kings had one of their capitals at Kottayam before they were overrun by Travancore in the middle of the 18C. The nearby **Mosque** is a traditional structure, with sloping tiled tiers roofing the double-storeyed prayer hall. It is entered on the east through a porch, with a decorated gable displaying carved colonettes and struts.

J. Tiruvalla

This town, 27km south of Kottayam, makes a worthwhile stop because of the **Vallabha Temple**, one of the largest religious complexes in central Kerala. Inscriptions on the monument go back to the 13C, but most of the carving is no earlier than the 17C. The Temple is approached from the east by a long and wide flight of steps, which leads by way of a large open construction into a spacious outer enclosure. Here stands a remarkable building with triple tiers of diminishing gables; its porches project outwards on four sides of the lowest level. Rising through the roof of this structure is a 16m high column of black granite, supporting a gilded image of kneeling Garuda. Vishnu's eagle mount gazes reverently west towards the gate leading into the inner enclosure (access restricted to visitors). This consists of an imposing structure, with tiers of tiled roofs and ornate gables showing carved wooden struts. Carvings cloak the ceiling of the screened entrance chambers. The circular Vishnu shrine, standing in the middle of the enclosure, has a conical roof cloaked in copper tiles. The walls are raised on a masonry basement.

The balustrades flanking the steps leading to the east door show images of Shiva as Dakshinamurti and Yogeshvara, suggesting that they may not have been intended for this sanctuary. A standing *yaksha* bears a stone spout that emerges from the north side of the shrine. The walls have regularly spaced pilasters; guardians are painted on the inner circuit of walls, just inside the door. The square hall that stands freely in front (east) of the sanctuary is distinguished by its pyramidal roof. The ceiling inside preserves a panel of Vishnu surrounded by 24 petals, each containing a different emanation of the god. The supporting beams are exquisitely sculpted with *Ramayana* and other narrative friezes.

Tiruvalla is the headquarters of the Mar Thomites, a reformed, Protestant-influenced offshoot of the Syrian church, in communion with Anglicans. **St John's Cathedral**, a modern work by the British architect Laurie Baker, who lives in Kerala, is based on indigenous temple forms, as is evident from the drum-shaped shrine with a conical roof.

K. Kaviyur

This small town, 7km east of Tiruvalla, is worth visiting to see the **Mahadeva Temple**, which is renowned for the quality of its carved woodwork, among the finest in Kerala. The main entrance to the Temple is from the east, through a modest gate with double-tiered tiled roofs. A sacred tree with *naga* stones set around its base is seen on the right. The path towards the inner enclosure is marked by a brass-clad lamppost with miniature deities at its base. The gate consists of two successive porches roofed by an ornate gable on the east, whose rear panel shows a *linga* flanked by guardians, with elephants beneath. The porches have wooden ceilings divided into square bays, surrounded by intricately sculpted miniature figures set at an angle. They show Rama and other *Ramayana* characters, holding bows and arrows, supported on elephant torsos. Diminutive figures, depicting *Ramayana* scenes and other epic topics, are arranged in continuous rows. Small figures seated beneath snake hoods are arranged below.

The inner enclosure of the Mahadeva Temple is surrounded by colonnades, the peripheral walls of which consist of the usual lines of wooden screens and masonry. The circular *linga* shrine within, approached by four dooways, is roofed with a smooth copper-clad roof topped by a gilded pot finial. The roof shelters wooden panels and screens, which create the outer circular wall of the shrine and are almost entirely covered with delicate, but vigorous, carvings. The screens are divided into square perforations, with the central and side panels occupied by miniature divinities.

Other topics appear on the intermediate uprights: they include pairs of fierce guardians on either side of the doorways, full sets of Vishnu's *avataras* and the Dikapalas, and a scene of Shiva with ascetics. Among the accessory themes is the story of the rescue of Gajendra, showing the elephant trapped in the lotus pond (beneath), the appearance of Vishnu, and the elephant paying homage to the god (top) (southwest quadrant). Large icons of Nataraja (left) and Trivikrama (right) are painted on the recessed walls on either side of the east door. Equally fine carvings are seen in the ceiling of the square hall that stands in front (east). Here, Yogeshvara Shiva is surrounded by the Dikpalas in a nine-panelled composition. The brackets and friezes in the entrance porch recall similar themes.

1.5km north of Kaviyur is a small **Cave Temple**, set into the west face of a granite hill. This is the best-preserved monument of the Chera period, dated to the 8C–9C. The Temple consists of a small chamber with a monolithic *linga*, preceded by a columned verandah. The fully rounded figures carved on the walls show a chieftain with folded arms, possibly the donor of the monument, a bearded sage, Ganesha, and a guardian leaning on a large club.

L. Chengannur

This sprawling town, 10km south of Tiruvalla, is dotted with temples and churches. The small **Narasimha Temple** at **Chathankulangana**, in the west part of Chengannur, is renowned for its exquisite woodwork, dating from the 17C–18C. The outer gate to the complex is a colonnaded structure with double tiers of sloping tiled roofs. It faces the main street on the north. The entrance porch to the second enclosure is, however, from the east. A lamp post stands in front, with a large tank beyond. The porch leads to the second enclosure (entry prohibited to women), inside which stands the square sanctuary, which is roofed with a pyramid of copper sheets and topped by a gilded pot finial.

The west-facing masonry chamber, housing an image of Narasimha, is completely surrounded by wooden screens with geometric designs. Friezes of animals are seen beneath, and the small panels at the sides are filled with figures: among others, Krishna up the tree, hiding the clothes of the *gopis* (north wall, left), monkeys building the stone bridge to Lanka (east wall, right), Padmanabha accompanied by sages and Vishnu's *avataras* (east wall, left), and Vishnu rescuing Gajendra (west wall, right). The intermediate uprights are treated sculpturally; they show figures holding clubs guarding the doorways in the middle of four sides, and demonic Narasimha, seated Yoga Narasimha (west wall), Krishna killing the horse demon, Krishna (north wall), Krishna killing the bull, Ganesha (east wall), and a maiden with a mirror (south wall). Friezes run along the beams on top of the screens. Among the topics depicted here are the forest episodes from the *Ramayana* (north wall) and the churning of the ocean (south wall). The small square pavilion in front, also with a pyramidal roof, is devoid of carvings.

There is one Christian place of worship of artistic importance in Chengannur. The **Church of St Thomas** consists of a long nave roofed with double tiers of sloping tiles. The main entrance is concealed within a porch with an ornate frontal gable. The door panels are elaborately carved with leafy designs and a composition showing the visit of the Three Magi. The rear portion of the nave is marked by a square tower capped with a pyramidal roof. A sculpted relief of a hunting scene, dating from the 15C–16C, is set into the walls. Another relic of the same era is the stone baptismal font within the Church; its base is enlivened with a frieze of petals and flowers. A monolithic cross on a high stepped plinth stands in the yard outside.

The route from Chengannur continues to Tiruvananthapuram, 118km south.

M. Mavelikkara

This town, 14km south of Tiruvalla, was the site of battles between the Travancore and Kayankulam rulers in the early 18C. Remains of the square laterite **Fort**, with bastions on each side, dating from this time, can still be seen. A curiosity of Mavelikkara is the statue of **Buddha** which was found in 1936 in the fields outside the town and was subsequently set up as an object of worship by local people, who installed it in a modern shrine. Dating probably from the 9C–10C, the image demonstrates that Buddhism was once prevalent in Kerala. The seated Master is shown in the lotus posture, his eyes closed in meditation.

The **Mahadeva Temple** at **Kandiyur**, 2km north of Mavelikkara, is of interest for its unusual stone carvings. The *linga* shrine, mostly a 16C–17C structure, stands in a colonnaded compound with entrances on four sides, that on the east marked by an elaborate gable-roofed structure. Carvings adorn the basement. The walls of the shrine, raised on a high plinth, are divided into bays by pilasters and niches. The outer surfaces are enlivened with small panels showing mythological scenes, sculpted in a manner resembling woodwork. Double tiers of sloping copper tiles rise above. The steps leading to the east doorway have ornate balustrades carved with dancing scenes. The open hall in front (east) has 16 columns supporting a pyramidal roof.

N. Kayankulam

This town lies on NH47, 48km south of Alappuzha or 28km south of Tiruvalla. Kayankulam served as the capital of a local line of rulers, who fought against Travancore until they were vanquished in 1746. The principal attraction is the **Krishnapuram Palace**, 2km south of Kayankulam. This is attributed to Ramayya Dalawa, the governor of northern Travancore under Rama Varma (1758–98). Together with Padmanabhapuram [450], the Krishnapuram Palace is the best-preserved example of Travancore royal architecture.

The Palace (closed Mondays) stands in a rectangular compound, entered through a small gate on the east. This leads to a garden overlooked by a pillared verandah. The main building is a traditional structure with a roof of sloping tiled tiers, ending in gables with carved wooden rafters. The balconies, with inclined slats on curving brackets, project outward. The interior consists of rooms disposed either side of a central corridor. This ends in a balconied chamber that overlooks a square pond on the west side of the Palace. The small interior courts have floor recesses for collecting rainwater. One chamber, left of the corridor, has a large vividly coloured mural on the rear (east) wall. This shows Vishnu riding on Garuda, in the company of gods and attendant women; a small panel of Balakrishna is seen beneath. The steps nearby descend to a room with side seating at a lower level, from which it is possible to enter the pond. Copies of *Ramayana* murals are displayed in one of the balconied rooms on the upper level. They depict Rama, the death of an ogress, Rama with Lakshmana, and Hanuman with monkey warriors.

NH47 continues to Kollam [46H], 36km south.

O. Sabarimalai

This remote site, 120km southeast of Ernakulam or 182km north of Tiruvananthapuram, both routes by way of Kottayam, can be approached only by foot through dense forest. The most convenient starting point for the journey is the parking area at Pamba, from where there is 5km climb up a well-maintained stepped path.

Sabarimalai is famous throughout Southern India for the **Ayyappa Temple**, which stands at over 900m elevation in the rugged terrain of the Western Ghats. Ayyappa, known also as Shasta, is a child deity believed to be the offspring of Shiva and Vishnu disguised as the goddess Mohini. He is looked upon as the guardian of mountainous tracts, and is famous for his ability to grant boons.

> In spite of the arduous journey, the concourse of pilgrims is steadily on the increase. The shrine attracts devotees from all over Southern India. In order to prepare themselves before embarking upon pilgrimage, the Ayyappas, as these devotees call themselves, observe rigorous fasting and penance for 41 days during the Mandalam Festival in November–December; they dress only in black or blue, and leave their hair uncut. In this regime they are under the direction of an older, more experienced guru. Only boys and men may visit Ayyappa's shrine, though female children and old women are also permitted. The sanctuary is open for about four months, during April, one day in May–June, and late August–early September; the final ceremonies of Mandalam take place on 14 January, after which the shrine is closed.

The Ayyappa Temple is a modest structure, out of all proportion to the crowds that congregate here. The final 18 steps of the path in front of the entrance are held to be especially sacred, and are clad in metal. The Temple dates only from the 1940s, being built after a fire destroyed the original building. The innermost sanctuary is a small square building with a pyramidal tiled roof, within which the seated image of the god is housed.

P. Kumily

This small settlement, 180km southeast of Ernakulam, on the border between Kerala and Tamil Nadu, serves as the gateway to the **Periyar Wildlife Sanctuary**. This is the oldest natural park in the state, created in 1934 by the Travancore government. This vast reserve of some 780 sq km varies in altitude from 900m to 1800m. The terrain ranges from open grasslands to dense tropical forest. An artificial lake, formed by damming the Periyar River, covers some 26 sq km; it provides an enchanting setting for the abundant wildlife of the Sanctuary. The best season to visit is December–May.

The Sanctuary is well known for its large herds of elephants, but bison, wild boar and spotted and sambar deer are also common. Tigers and leopards are only rarely sighted. Smaller animals include black langurs, lion-tailed monkeys and flying squirrels. There are plenty of darters, cormorants, egrets, herons and white-necked storks, which perch on the dead trees in the lake; owls and horn-bills may be spotted in the forests. Viewing is facilitated by specially constructed platforms; however, the noisy, crowded launch trips on the lake are not recommended.

The road from Kumily continues to Madurai [44A], 145km northeast. It is also possible to travel through the Western Ghats directly to Munnar, 117km north.

Q. Munnar

The route from Ernakulam, 224km west, passes through a variety of landscapes before arriving at this delightful hill station at an altitude of 1524m. This resort owes its birth and growth to planters, who were responsible for the tea, coffee and cardamom estates in the vicinity. Recreational life for residents in the rambling town that forms the centre of Munnar focuses on the **High Range Club**, which proudly preserves its original traditions. The Men's Bar is decorated with hunting trophies such as bison heads and elephant tusks. The **Protestant Church** of 1911 and its adjacent cemetery occupy a hill above. Fine panoramas of the surrounding Annamalai hills may be had from **Lockhart Gap**, 20km southeast on the route to Kumily. Expeditions can be arranged to **Anaimudi**, at 2694m the highest peak in Southern India, 12km north of Munnar.

For wildlife enthusiasts there is the nearby **Eravikulam National Park**, which shelters Nilgiri tahr, the only wild goat in Southern India, as well as herds of sambar, gaur or bison, and langur monkeys, within its 98 sq km. The best season to visit is October–April. Trout fishing in local streams is possible, but permission is required.

The road from Munnar also continues to Kodaikanal in Tamil Nadu [44F], 92km east.

R. Angamaly

This town, 32km north of Ernakulam on NH47, has a large Christian population, as is evinced by the many places of worship dating from the 17C–18C. **St George's Church** has a simple Baroque façade, the upper stage having three openings surmounted by triangular pediments. There is a single round-headed doorway beneath. The stone cross to one side is elevated on a finely detailed stone base. **St Mary's Church** is of interest for the murals on the side walls of the nave. The scenes include the Last Judgement (left) and a vivid illustration of hell, crowded with tortured figures (right). A composition showing Christ commanding St Thomas to visit India is located near the side altar.

Another Christian monument of artistic interest is to be seen at **Kanjoor**, 3km east of Angamaly. **St Mary's Church** is a traditional structure, with a central tower rising above a gabled roof. The Baroque-styled façade is partly hidden by an early 20C porch; the outer walls are covered with curious paintings illustrating the defeat of Tipu Sultan. The west façade is an ornate composition divided into bays by pairs of ornate columns. The topmost pedimented stage contains a niche occupied by a statue of St Mary. The carved wooden doors set within a broad arch serve as the principal entrance to the Church. Murals adorn the side walls of the chancel.

S. Kaladi

This historic village, 11km east of Angamaly on the north bank of the Periyar River, was the birthplace of Shankaracharya, the great Hindu philosopher and teacher (788–820). The site has been revived for worship. and is now a popular place of pilgrimage. The two **Shrines** next to the river, erected in 1910, have identical polygon-shaped pyramidal towers. One is dedicated to Shankaracharya as Dakshinamurti, the teaching form of Shiva; the other to Saradamba, the protective goddess of the sage.

A more recent building is the **International Temple**, which enshrines a life-size marble statue of the philosopher, and has a splendid library. Beside the road nearby stands the recently completed 45m tall **Keerthi Sthamba Mandapam**. This nine-stage octagonal tower commemorates Shankaracharya's life and work in words, symbols and pictures.

T. Kodungallur

Formerly called Cranganore, this small town, just off NH17, 51km north of Ernakulam, faces the lagoon near the mouth of the Periyar River and can be reached by boat directly from Kochi.

Archaeologists have identified Kodungallur as Muziris, cited by Pliny the Elder in the 1C as the premier port on the Kerala coast, celebrated for its exports of spices to Alexandria and Oman. Roman coins found in the area support this identification. The site was also of local importance, acting as the headquarters of the Cheras in the early centuries of the present era. Emigrating Jews, Christians and Muslims alike claim Kodungallur as the place of their first settlement in Kerala.

Kodungallur figures repeatedly in the wars between the Kochi and Kozhikode rulers. In spite of the silting up of its port, the town attracted the attention of European traders. The Portuguese sacked the town in 1504; 30 years later, they built a watchtower on the river bank to control pepper exports. The Dutch captured Kodungallur in 1662 and held it until Tipu Sultan's forces arrived in 1790. By the time it passed into the hands of the British a few years later, the Periyar River had silted up and international trade had come to an end.

According to local legend, St Thomas is believed to have landed on the island of Malankara, near the village of **Pallipuram**, 5km south of Kodungallur. The **Church of St Thomas** here is supposed to have been founded by the Apostle after he landed here in AD 52. As it stands today, the building is no earlier than the 17C. It houses a relic set in an ornate metal casket, believed to be a bone of St Thomas, transferred here from Mylapore [36G].

A fabled account is also given for the **Cheraman Mosque**, believed to have been erected in 630 by Malik Bin Dinar, an Arab missionary and teacher. Except for its granite plinth, however, the present structure does not predate the 18C; it has recently been renovated. The masonry walls with round-headed openings define a small prayer hall and antechamber roofed with flat timbers. The arched *mihrab* is semi-circular in plan.

The **Mahadeva Temple** at **Thiruvanchikulam**, the finest religious monument in Kodungallur, stands a short distance east of the Cheraman Mosque. The complex is entered on the east through a gate roofed with triple sloping tiers. The central gable has carvings of guardian figures, with Lakshmi and elephants beneath. This leads past a multi-stage metal lamp on a tortoise base and a brass-clad lamp column, to the porch that marks the entrance to the second enclosure (access restricted to visitors). Carved figures of Rama and Lakshmana, together with Hanuman and Sugriva, appear in the frontal gable. The interior of the porch has a stone altar surrounded by wooden screens. Brahma and the Dikpalas appear in the panels of the wooden ceiling above.

Immediately inside the enclosure stands the open hall, sheltering a stone Nandi. The stone columns have bulbous fluted capitals; maidens bearing lamps adorn the corner supports. The columns support the angled beams of the pyramidal roof, their projecting ends sheathed in embossed metal caps. The ceiling within repeats the Brahma and Dikpala theme of the porch; *naga* figures and celestials are seen beneath. The main *linga* shrine is a square masonry structure with pilastered wall projections, repeated at a diminishing scale on the upper level before being roofed with angled tiles. Stone guardian figures guard the doorway on the east. The paintings on the Saptamatrika shrine, to the south, include a *Mahabharata* battle scene.

The **Krishna Temple** at **Thirukkalasekharapuram**, only a short distance from Thiruvanchikulam, is of particular architectural interest, since it is one of the few religious monuments in Kerala with many of its original 10C–11C features intact. In spite of its name, the deity enshrined within the central sanctuary is a four-armed Vishnu. Two sets of passageways surround the sanctuary on four sides. The outer walls, raised on a high but plain plinth, have clearly articulated pilastered projections alternating with niches. These frame sculptures of two-armed figures, possibly Dakshinamurti, Arjuna and guardians. The niches are headed with elaborate pediments of eaves and miniature towers.

The roof rises in two tiers of sloping tiles, the upper one forming a pyramid. The square hall, which adjoins the sanctuary on the east, is also roofed with tiles. The main unit stands in the middle of a colonnaded compound. The subshrines in the outer enclosure are dedicated to different deities. The Govardhana shrine has delicate carvings of dancers and musicians on the sides of the balustrades flanking the access steps. The plinth exhibits a frieze of well-formed *yalis*.

Other than the monuments at Thiruvanchikulam and Thirukkalasekhara-puram just noted, the most popular shrine at Kodungallur is the **Kurumba Devi Temple**. This is consecrated to Bhagavati, the potent eight-armed goddess who presides over smallpox and cholera. The festival held here in February attracts large crowds of worshippers. The present Temple, a modern construction of traditional design, has several unusual features. A small chamber adjoining the sanctuary on the west houses a set of Saptamatrikas. Another chamber on the east, lacking any openings and possibly built around a prehistoric megalith, can only be reached by means of an underground passage. A unique 4m high stone figure of a guardian holding a mace, dated to the 17C, stands within the Temple compound.

U. Triprayar

The **Rama Temple** at this small village, 20km north of Kodungallur, just off NH17, is enchantingly situated on the Triprayar River. A portico shelters the landing stage used by devotees arriving by boat. The complex is contained within a square enclosure surrounded by a colonnade (access restricted to visitors). At the core stands a circular sanctuary with doorways on four sides and a copper-tiled conical roof. The outer walls are raised on a moulded basement with an inscription belonging to the 11C. The paintings covering the walls are assigned to the 18C. They have escaped retouching, and are among the finest murals on any temple in Kerala. Executed in glowing yellow and ochre tones, they illustrate Vishnu with consorts, *Ramayana* battle episodes, the story of Narasimha and other *Vaishnava* topics. Intricately carved wooden figures on elephant brackets are angled beneath the roof overhang. They show Rama with Lakshmana and Ravana, Ravana on the chariot, Narasimha, celestial maidens and sages. The pyramidal roofed hall in front has a wooden ceiling divided into panels occupied by Brahma and the Dikpalas.

V. Peruvanam

This village, 10km east of Triprayar, 9km south of Thrissur, is renowned for the **Mahadeva Temple**, one of the most imposing monuments in Kerala. The Temple is contained within a quadrangular enclosure defined by a double skin of timber screens and masonry walls. The two entrances (access restricted to visitors) in the long columned hall flanking the walls on the west are marked by small stone altars outside. The south entrance is aligned with the Madattilappan shrine; that on the north with the Irattayyappa shrine. These west-facing shrines, both dedicated to Shiva, are built in contrasting styles.

The Madattilappan shrine is a square masonry structure that rises in multiple storeys, each with well-defined pilastered projections capped by bold arch-like motifs. The lowest level is solid; worshippers have to climb a steep flight of steps to reach the porch and the *linga* sanctuary, surrounded by a double passageway housed at the second level. Both this level and that above are partly concealed by angled tiled roofs carried on wooden struts carved as various divinities. The struts in the middle of three sides show seated Uma Maheshvara (south), triple-headed Shiva (east) and Vishnu (north). The elevation is crowned by a fourth storey crowned by an octagonal roof with small gables on each side, achieving a total height of 21.5m.

The adjacent Irattayyappa shrine is a circular structure containing a square sanctuary with two *lingas*. The roof rises in a smooth metal-sheathed cone capped by a pot finial. The walls have pilastered projections and paintings, now much faded. The struts are fashioned as heroes and hunters, in illustration of the story of Arjuna fighting Shiva disguised as the hunter, as well as other figures such as Garuda. Stone guardians flank the doorway on the west. The square pavilion in front is roofed with a pyramid of metal tiles. Rows of miniature figures and animals adorn the wooden beams inside. A stone structure identified as a treasury stands between the two shrines. An inscription on its base records the renovation of the Temple by the Kochi ruler in 1758.

W. Thrissur

This city, formerly called Trichur, 69km north of Ernakulam on NH47, became a second capital for the Kochi kingdom during the 16C, when the Portuguese presence was dominant. Thrissur was occupied by the Zamorin of Kozhikode in 1750–60, and then by Haidar Ali and Tipu Sultan of Srirangapattana in 1776–90. However, the city was reclaimed by the Kochi rulers, who resided here intermittently during the 19C.

Vadakkunnatha Temple, Thrissur

Thrissur is built around a low hill crowned by the famous **Vadakkunnatha Temple**. The Puram Festival, held here in April–May, is a spectacular event attracting huge crowds, with processions of richly caparisoned elephants and magnificent fireworks. The Temple, one of the largest in Kerala, dates back to the 9C, but was substantially remodelled in the 16C–17C. The complex is contained within a vast quadrangle of walls, entered through imposing gates in the middle of each side. They follow a standard scheme, with double or triple tiers of sloping tiled roofs showing prominent frontal projections. The path from the main gate on the west passes by stone altars and metal lamps. On the left stands the *kuttambalam*, a hall used for theatrical and dance performances, a magnificent timber structure with angled screens and an imposing tiled roof.

The interior has an independent pavilion with 16 stone columns, some with intricately carved shafts. They carry a carved wooden ceiling divided into nine squares, with Shiva appearing out of the *linga* occupying the central square; miniature figural brackets are seen beneath. Three entrances on the west pass through timber screens and stone walls flanked by colonnades, defining the inner enclosure (access restricted to visitors). The entrances are aligned with the three west-facing shrines that stand freely inside. Paintings adorn the walls left of the north entrance.

The square Vadakkunnatha shrine (north) consists of a square *linga* sanctuary contained within a circle of masonry walls. These are raised on a moulded basement, with a spout protruding on the north, supported by a kneeling figure. Stone guardian figures flank the west doorway. The pilastered walls are overhung by the low conical roof, carried on projecting beams and sheathed with copper shingles. The hall in front is capped with the usual pyramidal roof. Immediately south stands a rectangular masonry sanctuary, dedicated to Ganesha.

The circular Shankara Narayana shrine, smaller but more finely finished than the Vadakkunnatha shrine, stands in the middle of the enclosure. The paintings here, among the few 18C examples to be preserved in the Temple, include large compositions of Nataraja and Padmanabha, as well as Nataraja, Dakshinamurti and Ganesha. The intricately carved wooden struts depict various divinities on elephant brackets; they include Garuda with pointed wings. The conical roof rises in two stages. The Rama shrine (south) is a square masonry structure, whose pilastered walls are adorned with murals. Carved struts are placed beneath double tiers of sloping roofs, with dormer windows in the upper tier. A small east-facing sanctuary is contained within an extension on the north side of the enclosure. The paintings here show Krishna playing the flute, and other mythological topics.

A fine collection of archaeological items and art objects is displayed in the museum complex, in the east part of the city. The **Archaeological Museum** (closed Mondays) displays excavated artefacts from various sites, including pottery from megalithic sites near Guruvayur. 1C–2C Roman pottery and 14C–15C Persian and Chinese ceramic fragments discovered at Kodungallur testify to Kerala's long-standing overseas trade contacts. A selection of stone sculptures, hero stones and bronze figurines, some going back to the 12C, is also on display, as are instructive models of temples and copies of mural paintings in the Dutch Palace at Mattancheri.

The **State Museum**, next door, presents a large range of costumes, weapons, brass utensils and stone epigraphs. The finest items are in the adjacent **Art Museum**; these include a superb pair of 17C bronze guardians with encrusted costumes and headdresses, and a contemporary image of Devi standing within an ornate frame. Hanging bronze lamps are assembled in the upstairs gallery. Some are fashioned as miniature shrines, with temple-like towers; others have pairs of divinities set in ornate frames. Large metal vessels, ivories and paintings on glass are also on display.

Thrissur is the headquarters of a small community of Nestorian Christians. The **Church of St Mary**, much rebuilt in the 19C, has a Baroque façade hidden by a modern entrance structure. The interior has an extraordinary wooden pulpit, supported on a stalk issuing from the mouth of a black lion. The symbolism of this motif remains obscure. More impressive is the Catholic **Church of Our Lady of Dolours**, built in an exuberant Neo-Gothic manner with corner belfries topped with ornate octagonal steeples. A similarly decorated dome rises over the crossing of the transepts. The vast interior is reputedly the largest of any church in Southern India. The main altar is flanked by fine altars on each side.

NH47 makes a turn at Thrissur, continuing to Coimbatore [43A] via Palghat, 109km northeast. The road running north from Thrissur meets up with NH17 and proceeds to Kozhikode, 125km north.

X. Cheruthuruthi

This small town, 30km north of Thrissur, is famous for the **Kalamandalam** (closed weekends), an academy of performing arts founded at the beginning of the 20C by the celebrated Malayali poet, Vallathol. This school has done much to stimulate the revival of indigenous forms of dance and drama. The Kalamandalam offers courses in Mohini Attam and Ottam Thullal, as well as Kathakali. Visitors can watch training sessions and performances.

Y. Guruvayur

Together with Sabarimalai, this is the most popular pilgrimage spot in Kerala. Guruvayur lies 29km north of Thrissur, a total of 100km north of Ernakulam, a short distance off NH17. The deity worshipped in the **Krishna Temple** is conceived as an infant engaged in childish pranks, taking unconcealed delight in sweets and the good things of life. The importance of the monument dates from the 16C–17C, as indicated by the many grants made to it by local rulers, including the Zamorins of Kozhikode. Tipu Sultan plundered Guruvayur in 1789, but the main image was buried for safety.

The Krishna Temple is approached along a wide street lined with shops. A 36m high flagpost, encased in gilded brass, stands in front of the main gate on the east side of the complex. The stone columns of its porch are carved with heads of elephants and bulls. The rear walls are covered with murals depicting Arjuna's adventures from the *Mahabharata*. The roof above has two sloping tiers. The focal sanctuary within the inner enclosure (access restricted to visitors), although much altered by recent renovation, is a small square structure with a double pyramidal roof sheathed in copper. The cult divinity enshrined here is a standing figure of Krishna holding a conch, discus, mace and lotus. This image is bathed in the large tank north of the complex during ten days of ceremonies in February–March. The Ekadashi festival attracts large crowds in November–December.

Punnathoor Kotta, 4km east of Guruvayur, is an old mansion with an exquisitely carved doorway. The elephants associated with the Krishna Temple are kept in a compound here.

The region immediately east of Guruvayur is known for its prehistoric remains, which date back at least 2000 years. Sites near **Chovannur** and **Porkalam** villages, both within 10km of Guruvayur, preserve megalithic monuments such as stone burial pits covered with *kudaikals* (hood-stones), and *topikals* (hat-stones) raised on four pieces of stone, as well as dolmens and menhirs. Pottery fragments discovered by excavators are displayed in the Archaeological Museum at Thrissur.

48 · Kozhikode

Northern Kerala narrows to a coastal strip lined with glorious beaches and dotted with historical towns and forts. This is flanked for much of its length by a wooded plateau that rises almost 1000m above sea level, the home to extensive tea, coffee, pepper and areca nut estates. The Muslim presence is noticeable, and there are many mosques to be seen, the finest being in **Kozhikode** [A]. Allow a

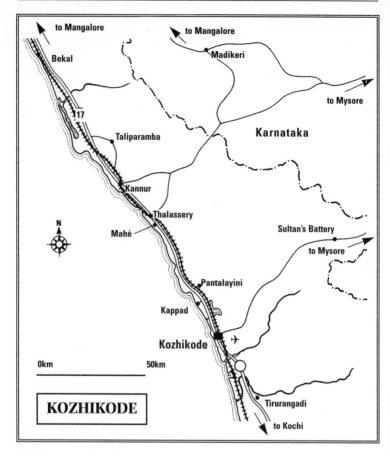

KOZHIKODE

half day to see the sights of this city, the traditional capital of the Zamorins.
The journey inland through the forests of the Western Ghats, passing by
Sultan's Battery [B], may be extended as far as Madikeri [16] or Mysore [15] in
Karnataka.

Most visitors will chose to explore the coastal scenery of the region. An excursion south is easily made to **Tirurangadi** [C], to visit the mosque and shrine there.

A full-day trip north will take in the mosques of **Pantalayini** [D], the French
and British vestiges at **Mahé** [E] and **Thalassery** [F], and the fort, mosques and
churches of **Kannur** [G]. Additional time will be required to reach the temples
at **Taliparamba** [H].

From the citadel at **Bekal** [I], near the northern tip of the state, it is possible
to continue on to Mangalore [17].

■ **Transport**. Kozhikode is connected by air with Bombay [1], Bangalore [14]
and Madras [36]. NH17, beside which the railway runs for much of its
journey up the coast, links Kozhikode with Kochi, 219km south, and

Mangalore, 239km north. Stops are available at all the places described here. Mysore is 211km distant, the bus connection passing through Sultan's Battery.

■ **Accommodation**. The best hotels in Kozhikode (STD code 0495) are the *Kalpaka Tourist Home* (☎ 76171), *Malabar Mansion* (☎ 76071) and *Sea Queen* (☎ 366604).

■ **Tourist Information**. The KTDC Centre is located at the *Malabar Mansion Hotel*.

A. Kozhikode

This port, formerly called Calicut, was the traditional capital of northern Kerala under the Samutiri rulers, better known to Europeans as the Zamorins.

The wealth of the Kozikhode region has always attracted foreigners. The Chinese were the first to establish commercial contacts with the city, bringing gold, silver, copper, silks and exchanging them for peppper, cinammon, ginger and woven cotton. By the time the North African traveller Ibn Battuta was in Kozhikode, in 1342–47, the Muslims were the dominant commercial class, many having emigrated from Arabia and the Middle East. They enjoyed the protection of the Zamorins, whose army they equipped with imported arms and horses.

The arrival of the Portuguese threatened Arab commercial supremacy. Vasco da Gama made his first landfall near Kozhikode on 20 May 1498, after rounding the Cape of Good Hope, but he was not welcomed. Only after attacking the Zamorins in 1513 were the Portuguese permitted to build a fortified trading post at the mouth of the Kallai River. Unable to defend their settlement, the Portuguese left in 1525. Other Europeans followed: the English erected a factory here in 1667, followed by the French in 1703 and the Danes in 1752. In 1766, Kozhikode was occupied by Haidar Ali of Srirangapattana [15C]. The city was ceded to the British in 1792 and thereafter became the headquarters of the Malabar District.

The bustling commercial character of Kozhikode is still much in evidence. Other than tea, coffee and spices, timber is the primary industry. Kozhikode is also a centre for the export of cotton goods, including the light textiles called calicos after the former name of the city. Warehouses line the narrow crowded streets that run down to the port, which lacks any natural harbour. Today, as in the past, large boats have to anchor off shore, and goods are transferred to smaller craft. The 33.5m high **Lighthouse** was erected in 1847.

The centre of Kozhikode is marked by **Mananchira**, a large tank with a park on the north side. Several Christian places of worship are located nearby. The **Catholic Church**, dating from the 18C, has an altar with the Crucifixion and an image of the Virgin Mary. The **Basel Mission Church**, established in the middle of the 19C, is now run by the Church of South India. Its sombre façade is dominated by a lofty square tower, crowned with a pointed steeple in the German style.

The **Tali Temple**, the largest and most important temple in the city, is situated 1.5km east of Mananchira. The complex is approached from the east through a gate roofed with sloping tiled roofs. The path passes between subshrines dedicated to Krishna (north) and Narasimha (south), both with their own walled compounds. An altar and brass-clad lamp post stand in front (east) of the columned hall, which serves as the entrance to the inner enclosure (access restricted to visitors). The carved and painted wooden ceiling over the central passageway shows Brahma surrounded by Dikpalas. The inner enclosure is defined by the double lines of wooden screens and stone walls.

The main shrine is an imposing structure, consisting of a square *linga* sanctuary and attached antechamber. Both have pilastered walls, with clearly articulated niches raised on a high basement. Animals are carved on the eaves and parapet elements above, with angled wooden struts positioned beneath the overhanging roof. The walls of the sanctuary rise in a second stage, capped with a pyramidal tiled roof. The antechamber walls display unusual stone sculptures of divinities: Sarasvati, Vishnu, Shiva, Bhagavati, and Rama with Hanuman. The square hall which stands in front (east) has supporting stone columns concealed by wooden screens, with corner brackets fashioned as long *yalis* eating foliage. The ceiling within is carved with rows of miniature figures and animals.

Mithqalpalli, Kozhikode

Kozhikode's mosques are of particular architectural merit, since they preserve their traditional multi-tiered tiled roofs. The finest examples are seen in the Mappila quarter near the port, on the other side of the railway line. **Mithqalpalli**, the largest of the series, takes its name from its founder, Nakhuda Mithqali, a local trader during the time of Ibn Battuta. Only the stepped plinth is assigned to the 14C; the remainder was reconstructed after the building was burned down by the Portuguese in 1510. The prayer hall is divided into bays by timber columns, approached through a later antechamber and ablutions area. Both hall and antechamber are contained in a double line of plastered masonry walls marked by alternating openings and niches, both with round-headed arches. The narrow space between these walls is occupied by the *mihrab* in the middle of the west wall. Steps ascend to an upper level, until recently used as a school. The building is capped with an imposing roof rising in three broad stages, each carried on angled beams and rafters concealed by wooden screens. The roofs terminate in decorated gables on the east side only. Three brass pot finials line the roof ridge.

The **Jami Mosque** is one of two such places of worship standing on either side of a large tank known as **Kuttichira**, a short distance south. Though the foundation date of the Jami Mosque is uncertain, an inscription inside mentions a restoration of 1481. The building is raised on a stepped plinth and is contained by masonry walls. The prayer hall and antechamber both have steps ascending to the upper level. The entrance porch, in the middle of the east side, is a multi-storeyed structure with angled roofs and a prominent gable filled with colonettes and rafters. The wooden beams that carry the decorated coffered ceiling within the porch have a frieze of foliation and a long Arabic inscription, which mentions another renovation in the late 17C. The central panels of the ceiling are filled with carved lotus medallions. The 1481 epigraph is cut into a wooden lintel inserted into the walls of the antechamber.

Mucchandipalli is another important Mosque. The original prayer hall can easily be made out, together with additions on the east. Two inscriptions, one a bilingual record in Arabic and Malayalam, the other mentioning renovations, appear to belong to the 14C–15C. The building stands on a 1.5m high plinth. The semi-circular *mihrab* in the rear walls is an arched niche. Similar arches mark the openings in the outer walls, but these are cut out of stone slabs. The decorated wooden beams carry a coffered ceiling resembling that in the Jami Mosque. The double-tiered roof has an elaborate frontal gable, but the timber screens beneath the upper tier have been replaced by plaster walls.

Two smaller Mosques nearby, **Allahrapalli** and **Idrispalli**, are similar to those already described. Both display double tiers of sloping roofs and decorated frontal gables with carved struts. They contrast with the **Tomb of Sayyid Abdullah**, in front (east) of the Idrispalli Mosque. This is the burial place of a saint who died here in 1771. The building, however, may be earlier. It consists of a square domed chamber with plain outer walls, the corners topped by small finials.

The **Pazhassiraja Museum** (closed Mondays) at East Hill, 5km east of Kozhikode's centre, has a collection of local arts and crafts, metal and wood sculptures, coins and other antiquities. The display includes models of different prehistoric monuments found in the area. The **Art Gallery** next door has an excellent collection of paintings by Keralan artists, especially Ravi Varma, as well as wood and ivory carvings. A separate section, the **Krishna Menon Museum**, houses personal memorabilia of V.K. Krishna Menon, a locally born political leader who rose to become a prominent minister under Jawaharlal Nehru.

B. Sultan's Battery

In about 1780 Tipu Sultan erected a small **Fort** at this site, 67km east of Kozhikode, strategically located in the Western Ghats on the main route leading from Mysore down to the Arabian Sea. The British captured the Fort in 1805, reducing it to ruins. Only traces of overgrown laterite walls remain.

6km southwest, on the western slopes of **Edakkal Hill**, is a natural cleft with enigmatic **Relief Carvings** of figures and symbols. The date and meaning of these signs remain unknown. They appear to be earlier than nearby inscriptions, which date from the 12C–13C.

C. Tirurangadi

This town, 36km south of Kozhikode on NH17, occupies the south bank of the Kadalundi River.

Tirurangadi was active against the Portuguese, and also successfully resisted an attempt by the Zamorins of Kozhikode to capture it in the 1740s. A fierce engagement between the British and the forces of Haidar Ali took place here in 1780, followed ten years later by a decisive victory over Tipu Sultan's troops. The town returned to prominence in August 1921, when it was one of the centres of the Mappila rebellion, a violent revolt against British authority in northern Kerala.

Two monuments are of interest here. The **Jami Mosque**, built on a wooded hill overlooking the river, preserves its traditional structure. It consists of two super-imposed masonry walls with tiled overhangs, upon which rises a wooden struc-ture with timber slate carrying a sloping tiled roof with a frontal gable. Four pot-like finials mark the roof ridge. The **Shrine of Sayyid Alawi** at **Mambram**, directly opposite, on the north bank of the Kadalundi River, marks the resting place of an influential teacher. The Shrine is a rectangular building with a dome raised on a circular drum concealed within a conical roof at one end. The tombs in the ground-floor hall beneath the dome include that of Sayyid Alawi, who died in 1843, his uncle, and other relatives. The adjacent hall is used for sermons and public readings.

D. Pantalyini

This small town, 25km north of Kozhikode, just off NH17, is a place of histor-ical significance linked with the Zamorins, who maintained a residence here. The town has a **Jami Mosque** that enjoys a reputation similar to that of the mosque at Kodungallur [47T], supposedly erected by the 7C Arab missionary Malik bin Dinar. However, the present building is entirely remodelled and shows no evidence of its early history.

A local curiosity is to be seen on a rock near the seashore, 3km west of the town. This is believed to be the outline of a footprint, said to be that of Adam as he landed in India on his way to Sri Lanka, where there is a similar footprint at the summit of the mountain known as Adam's Peak.

8km south, at **Kappad**, is a modern memorial pillar that marks Vasco da Gama's first landing place in Southern India.

E. Mahé

This former French enclave, no larger than 7.5sq km, now part of the Union Territory of Pondicherry [39A], lies 62km north of Kozhikode on NH17.

Originally known as Mayyali, the small port of Mahé took its name from Mahé de La Bourdonnais, who occupied it for the French East India Company in 1721. It thereupon became their principal trading post on the Malabar coast. Mahé suffered from the vicissitudes of Franco-British rivalry, being occupied by the British in 1761–65 and 1779–85, then again in 1793–1817, during the Napoleonic wars.

Mahé overlooks a wide estuary of a coastal river that affords shelter to ocean-going vessels. This water-seaside location and the European character of some of the buildings, including the former **French Residency**, lend the town a certain charm. A reminder of the French presence is the cast-iron **Monument**, erected in 1889, with an inscription recording that in 1789 the French Republic granted the people of Mahé full rights of French citizenship. The whitewashed façade of the **Church of St Therese d'Avila** presents a simplified Baroque manner.

F. Thalassery

In about 1683, the East India Company began operations at this attractive coastal town, previously known as Tellicherry, 6km south of Mahé, trading primarily in pepper and cardamom. The **Fort,** begun in 1708, is built of massive laterite walls laid out in the form of a square. A lighthouse on the ramparts looks out towards the surf breaking on the reefs. An overgrown cemetery on the landward side is all that remains of the English presence. Traditional warehouses and residences, many belonging to Mappila traders, cluster around the Fort. Some were used by Portuguese refugees during the invasion of Haidar Ali. Here, too, stands the **Odothilpalli**, a traditional-styled mosque, founded in the 17C–18C. Its traditional copper-clad roof rises in two sloping tiers, separated by screens with timber slats. A small octagonal turret sits on the frontal gable of the upper tier. Three gilded pot finials are arranged along the ridge behind.

The **Jami Mosque** in the town has recently been rebuilt in a Neo-Mughal style. Its imposing arched portal is flanked by domed pavilions. Among the Christian buildings in the town are **St Joseph's Church**. Its Baroque façade, flanked by squat towers with corner pilasters, dates from the 19C, but the monolithic cross that stands in the yard at the rear is earlier. The **Church of St Peter** is a modern structure, with domed pavilions raised on corner towers.

G. Kannur

Formerly called Cannanore, this historical port, 22km north of Thalassery, 92km north from Kozhikode on NH17, was the seat of the Ali Rajas. These rulers, the only Muslim royal house in Kerala, were noted by Ibn Battuta as being among the most powerful on the Malabar coast.

One of the Ali Rajas that gave the Portuguese permission to build Fort St Angelo in 1505. The Dutch captured the Fort in 1663, but sold it back to the Ali Rajas in 1772, by which time these rulers had formed an alliance with Tipu Sultan, offering strong resistance to the British. But the Fort was eventually captured in 1783, after which it housed the largest British garrison in Malabar District.

Fort St Angelo occupies a delightful site on a rocky promontory jutting out into the ocean, northwest of the town. It is a massive triangular structure of laterite, with strong flanking bastions surrounded by water on two sides, and a dry ditch on the landward side. The ramparts are in a fairly good state of preservation, though parts have collapsed and fallen into the sea. A few obsolete guns are still to be seen lying around. Dungeons, once used as a jail, and the magazine still stand. A small lighthouse has been erected inside the Fort. The remains of the

British military **Cantonment** are located nearby. The **Church of St John** of 1811 is a simple tiled-roofed structure, with steep gables and frontal verandahs. The **Jami Mosque** in the old town, south of the Fort, is of interest for its double-storeyed prayer hall roofed with sloping tiles. It is flanked by a pair of octagonal minarets with internal staircases, both recent additions.

The **Palace** of the Ali Rajas is a charming ensemble of modest whitewashed buildings with characteristic tiled roofs. The interiors are traditional, with wooden floors and ceilings and shuttered windows. The complex includes a small mosque.

From Kannur it is possible to proceed directly to Mysore, 191km northeast.

H. Taliparamba

This town, 22km north of Kannur, is celebrated for its two temples, which are among the finest in northern Kerala. Both monuments date back to the 9C, though they were substantially renovated in the 16C–17C. The **Rajarajeshvara Temple** is entered on the east through a dilapidated unfinished gate. A Nandi pavilion and an intricately carved stone altar mark the path to the main entrance. This is reached only after passing through the wooden screen that surrounds the outer walls of the inner enclosure. The entrance has a sloping tiled roof with ornamented gables. The carved wooden ceiling over the passageway shows the Navagrahas with Surya in the middle, with rows of elephants and playful dwarfs beneath. An unusual wooden female figure, 1.5m high, is placed to the right of the passageway.

The main *linga* shrine inside the enclosure is a large square structure, with a double passageway surrounding the central chamber. The outer walls, rhythmically divided into pilastered bays, rise in two stages, each marked by sloping tiled roofs, the upper roof forming a pyramid. Finely sculpted angled wooden struts are placed beneath the roof overhang. Those at the corners are fashioned as enlarged *yalis* on elephants at the corners. Deities appear at the lower level: Dakshinamurti (south), Narasimha (west) and Parameshvara (north). The warriors at the upper level form part of the story of Arjuna's battle with Shiva disguised as the hunter. Similar struts are seen in the square pavilion that stands in front (east) of the sanctuary. The internal four columns of this structure are of turned wood.

The **Krishna Temple** at **Trichambaram**, 1.5km south of the centre of Taliparamba, is attractively sited in a small grove. Steps lead past a small pond, in which stands a small Shiva shrine. A gable roofed entrance porch on the east gives access to the enclosure (access restricted to visitors), where there is a square double-storeyed sanctuary, repeating the same roof scheme of the Rajarajeshvara Temple. The walls, however, are more deeply articulated, with secondary niches marking the projections and wooden window screens inserted into the recesses. Traces of paintings can be seen. Friezes of *yalis* and *makaras* surmount the curved eaves. Angled wooden struts, with *yalis* at the corners, appear at both levels, together with maidens and couples below, and divinities above. Similar *yalis* appear at the corners of the pavilion that stands in front (east). The ceiling inside is carried on beams with intricately worked friezes of the Krishna story.

I. Bekal

This town, 77km north of Kannur on NH17, includes the largest and best-preserved coastal Fort in Northern Kerala.

Bekal was founded by Shivappa Nayaka of Nagar [19F] in the middle of the 17C, and remained one of the principal strongholds of the Nayakas until it was taken by Haidar Ali in 1763. Bekal passed into the hands of the British in 1792, together with the other dominions of Tipu Sultan.

Bekal **Fort** consists of an irregular quadrangle built up to the sands of the Arabian Sea. The laterite ramparts with sloping walls and round bastions are well preserved, as are the battlements, which have wide embrasures for gun emplacements. Only a few isolated structures stand within the open ground inside the Fort. They include a rectangular building with a rounded vault, possibly a powder magazine.

NH17 continues to Mangalore, 60km north.

Andaman Islands

The Union Territory of the Andaman and Nicobar Islands consists of a string of more than 300 richly forested islands. These form a broken archipelago that stretches 755km from north to south in the middle of the Bay of Bengal, some 1200km east of the coast of Southern India.

Visitors are lured to the Andamans by the beauty of the tropical habitat, with its profusion of exotic flora and fauna. There is also an abundance of beaches, with exquisitely clear waters and colourful coral reefs. These natural wonders can be explored most conveniently from **Wandoor** [49B], a short distance from **Port Blair** [49A], the principal port of entry, which preserves isolated relics of its career as a penal colony under the British.

49 · Port Blair

Port Blair, the capital of the Union Territory of the Andaman and Nicobar Islands, retains only isolated remains of the British occupation. Even so, a half day may be set aside for the sights of the town and nearby Ross Island [A].

Boat rides from **Wandoor** offer opportunities for snorkelling and scuba diving, as well as trips around the lagoons of the National Marine Park [B].

■ **Transport**. Air connections from Madras [36] and Calcutta to Port Blair (STD code 03192) are preferred to lengthy boat trips from either city, occasionally also from Visakhapatnam [31]. Buses and taxis are available at Port Blair, as are ferries and private boats to the various islands.

■ **Accommodation**. The finest places to stay in Port Blair (STD code 03192) are the *Bay Island Hotel* (☎ 20888), designed by Charles Correa, *Sinclair Bay View* (☎ 20937) and the *Tourist Home Complex* (☎ 20076) at **Megapode Nest**. The *Andaman Beach Resort* (☎ 21463) and *Hornbill Nest Yatri Niwas* (☎ 20018) overlook delightful **Corbyn's Cove**, 4km south of the town. A new resort on **Havelock Island**, 54km northeast of Port Blair, is accessible only by boat. The *Dolphin Yatri Niwas Complex* (☎ 20694) is the best place to stay.

■ **Tourist Information**. The Government of India has its tourist bureau in the Super Shoppe complex. The Andaman and Nicobar Islands tourist office is situated next to the Secretariat. Foreigners are issued permits on arrival. Visitors are restricted in their movements around the Islands.

Indigenous Peoples. Traders have been attracted to the Andamans for centuries by the valuable shells and rich reserves of timber. Records of Chinese and Arab travellers who passed by the Islands in the 7C–9C portray the native tribal populations as fierce and cannibilistic, an opinion borne out by Marco Polo in the 13C. These notorious accounts were popularised by Malay pirates, who held sway over the surrounding seas and who wished to discourage intruders. When European missionaries and colonisers arrived in the 18C–19C, they discovered a people who lived a virtual Stone Age existence, practising hunting and gathering, and using bows and arrows.

Though now reduced to less than 10 per cent of the overall population of the Islands, these populations preserve their mixed negroid and Mongoloid ethnic composition. Most now live in Tribal Reserve Areas, inaccessible to outsiders.

A. Port Blair

In 1788 the British Lieutenant Alistair Blair chose South Andaman harbour, subsequently named after him, as the site for a penal colony. But even though a few convicts were sent there in 1794, the scheme was abandoned.

In 1858 Port Blair became a prison settlement, the first inmates being activists involved in the Mutiny of 1857. They were made to clear land and build their own prison. Many lost their lives or died from attacks by Andamanese tribes, who objected to forest clearance. Nevertheless, the colony expanded, the number of convicts growing to 3000 in 1864. The British considered closing the prison in 1919, but then found it useful for confining a new generation of freedom fighters. The Islands were occupied by the Japanese in the Second World War, but the British forces moved back in 1945, finally abolishing the penal settlement. After Partition, refugees from Bangladesh and Burma were given land in Port Blair. Together with the descendants of ex-prisoners who chose to stay, they greatly outnumber the indigenous population.

The chief historical feature in Port Blair is the **Cellular Jail** (closed Sundays), which overlooks the sea from a hill northeast of the town centre. Built in 1886–1906, its tiny cells for individual inmates were arranged in wings radiating outwards from a central tower; only three still stand. Conditions were grim, the cells being dirty and ill-ventilated, and many prisoners died here. Hunger strikes and executions were common. The main entrance, flanked by castellated round towers, has been restored.

Other sights in Port Blair are mostly restricted to museums. The **Marine Museum** (closed Sundays), south of the Cellular Jail, has displays of corals and shells, as well as more than 350 species of marine life, including tropical fish, sea crocodiles, barracudas and dolphins. The small but informative **Anthropological Museum** (closed Sundays), in the Haddo area west of the town centre, illustrates the life of the Islanders. Tools, implements and handicrafts are supplemented by photographs and models. The **Forest Museum** (closed Sundays) shows local types of timbers, such as red padauk and satinwood.

Chatham Mill (closed Sundays), situated on the promontory that marks the northern extremity of Port Blair, 5km distant from the town centre, is the oldest and largest timber-processing plant on the Islands.

Ross Island, 2km east of Port Blair, is reached by regular ferries. The island was chosen by the British for their headquarters, and it was here that Reverend Corbyn established his home for converted Andamanese. Deserted since 1945, the jungle has engulfed the administrative and residential buildings. The disintegrating remains of Government House and are seen near the water; the overgrown church is situated on the top of the hill.

ANDAMAN ISLANDS

0km   50km

N

Port Blair
Wandoor

Viper Island, a short distance from Haddo Warf at Port Blair, was where convicts were interned before the Cellular Jail was finished. Gallows and whipping posts are gruesome reminders of the punishments inflicted on the unfortunate prisoners.

B. Wandoor

The **Mahatma Gandhi National Marine Park** is most easily accessible from Wandoor, a small seaside settlement 28km southwest of Port Blair. The diverse scenery of the Park encompasses some 15 islands with mangrove creeks, tropical rainforest and reefs with different types of colourful coral. Boats from Wandoor visit **Jolly Buoy** and **Redskin Islands**.

Glossary

The listing is restricted to Indian names and terms.

Abdul Razzq, 15C Persian traveller
Abdul Wahad Khan, 17C Adil Shahi commander
Abdullah, 17C Qutb Shahi ruler
Achaleshvara, name of Shiva
acharya, saint
Achyutadevaraya, 16C Tuluva ruler
Adi Keshava, name of Vishnu
Adil Shahi, 16C–17C dynasty of Karnataka ruling from Bijapur [23A]
Adinatha, first of the 24 Tirthankaras
Adinatha, name of Vishnu worshipped at Alvar Tirunagari [45D]
Adivaraha, Varaha
Afaqi, newcomers to the Deccan
Afzal Khan, 17C Mughal commander
Agastishvara, name of Shiva
Agastya, legendary sage
Aghoreshvara, fierce form of Shiva
Agni, god of fire, one of the Dikpalas
Ahalya, woman liberated by Rama in the *Ramayana*
Ahilyabai, 18C Holkar queen
Ahmad, 15C Bahmani ruler
Ahmad, 15C–16C Nizam Shahi ruler
Airavateshvara, name of Shiva
Akbar, 16C Mughal emperor
Akhilandeshvari, name of Devi
Alagar Perumal, name of Vishnu worshipped at Alagarkoil [44C]
alam, Shia standard
Alara, hero of the *Samkhapala Jataka*
Ali, 16C and 17C Adil Shahi rulers
Ali, 17C Baridi ruler
Ali Raja, 14C–18C dynasty of northern Kerala, ruling from Kannur [48G]
Alauddin, 14C Madurai ruler
Alauddin, 16C Imad Shahi ruler
Alvar, Vaishnava saint
Amareshvara, name of Shiva worshipped at Amaravati [29K]
Ambal, Devi
Ambaranatha, name of Shiva worshipped at Amarnath [2J]
Ambedkar, Dr Babasaheb, 20C social reformer
Ambika, Jain mother goddess
Ammaiyar, female Shaiva saint at Karaikal [40F]
Amman, Ammanavara, goddess
Amriteshvara, name of Shiva
Ananta, serpent mount of Vishnu
Anantashayana, Vishnu reclining on the serpent Ananta

Ananteshvara, name of Vishnu
Andal, poetess, worshipper of Vishnu
Andhaka, demon killed by Shiva
Angre, 17C–19C naval commanders of the Marathas, based at Alibag [2G]
anicut, irrigation dam
Anjaneya, name of Hanuman
ankusha, elephant goad
Appar, one of the Nayanmars
Aravidu, 16C–17C dynasty of Andhra Pradesh and Tamil Nadu, ruling from
   Penukonda [33D] and Chandragiri [35C]
Ardhanarishvara, Shiva and Parvati joined
Arjuna, hero of the *Mahabharata*
Arunachaleshvara, fiery *linga* worshipped at Tiruvannamalai [38E]
Asaf Jahi, 18C–20C dynasty of Andhra Pradesh and Maharashtra, ruling from
   Hyderabad [26A]
Ashoka, 3C BC Maurya ruler
ashram, religious and spiritual centre
ashurkhana, congregational hall of Shia Muslims used at Muharram
Atmanatha, invisible form of Shiva worshipped at Avudayarkoil [41H]
Aurangzeb, 17C–18C Mughal emperor
Aurobindo Ghosh, 20C teacher at Pondicherry [39A]
Avalokiteshvara, Bodhisattva
Avanishvara, name of Shiva
avataras, incarnations of Vishnu
Ayyappa, son of Shiva and Mohini worshipped at Sabarimalai [47O]
Azam Shah, 17C Mughal noble

Baba Musafir, 17C Sufi saint at Aurangabad [5A]
Babulnath, name of Krishna worshipped in Bombay [1G]
badgir, wind tower
bagh, garden
Bahadur Shah, 16C ruler of Gujarat
Bahmani, 14C–15C dynasty of Karnataka, Maharashtra and Andhra Pradesh
   ruling from Gulbarga [24A] and Bidar [25A]
Bahubali, son of the first Tirthankara
bala hisar, *bala kila*, citadel
Baladeva, name of Shiva worshipped at Parel [1H]
Balaji Bajirao, 18C Peshwa ruler
Balaji Vishvanath, 18C Peshwa ruler
Balakrishna, infant Krishna
Ballala, 13C Hoysala ruler
Banashankari, name of goddess
Banganga, Rama's magic bow
baradari, pavilion
Barid, 16C dynasty of Karnataka, ruling from Bidar [25A]
basti, Jain temple
bauri, reservoir
bazaar, market street
Bedar, 17C–19C rulers of Shorapur [24G]

Begum Rabia Durani, wife of Aurangzeb buried at Aurangabad [5B]
Bhagavata Purana, story of Krishna
Bhagavati, fierce aspect of Devi
Bhairava, Bhairaveshvara, fearful aspect of Shiva
Bhairavi, fierce aspect of Devi
Bhaktavatsaleshvara, name of Shiva
bhakti, devotion to a Hindu deity
Bharata, brother of Rama in the *Ramayana*
Bharata, brother of Bahubali
Bharata Mata, goddess personifying the Indian nation, worshipped at Daulatabad [5C]
Bhavani, form of Durga worshipped at Tuljapur [9C]
Bhave, Vinoba, 20C social reformer
Bhikshatanamurti, Shiva as the naked ascetic
Bhima, mighty Pandava hero
Bhimalingeshvara, Bhimeshvara, name of Shiva
Bhoganandishvara, name of Shiva worshipped at Nandi [14F]
Bhonsale, 18C–19C dynasty of northern Maharashtra, ruling from Nagpur [10A]
Bhringi, attendant of Shiva
Bhu, Bhudevi, consort of Vishnu
bhuta, spirit
Bhutanatha, name of Shiva
Bhuvaneshvari, name of Parvati
Bhuvaraha, Varaha rescuing Bhu
bidri, inlaid metalwork produced at Bidar [25A]
Bimbisara, 6C ruler of Northern India, contemporary of Buddha
bodhi, tree of enlightenment
Bodhisattva, Buddhist saviour
Brahma, creator god
Brahmalingeshvara, name of Shiva
Brahmapurushivara, name of Shiva
Brihadambal, name of Devi
Brihadishvara, name of Shiva
Brihadnayaki, name of Parvati
Buddha, founder of Buddhism in the 6C–5C BC, later worshipped as a divinity
Bukka, 14C Sangama ruler
Burhan, 16C Nizam Shahi ruler, 16C Imad Shahi ruler

Chakrapani, name of Vishnu
Chakreshvara, name of Shiva
chaitya, vaulted Buddhist hall, horseshoe-shaped arch
Chalukya, see Early Chalukya, Eastern Chalukya and Late Chalukya
Champeyya, serpent hero of a *Jataka* story
Chamunda, terrifying form of Devi
Chamundaraya, 10C Ganga commander
Chamundeshvari, goddess worshipped on Chamundi Hill [15B]
Chand Bibi, 16C–17C Nizam Shahi queen
Chandra, moon god

Chandesha, Chandeshvara, devotee of Shiva
Chandragupta, royal devotee of Bahubali
Chandralamba, name of Devi
Chandramauleshvara, name of Shiva
Chandranatha, Chandranatheshvara, Chandraprabha, one of the Tirthankaras
Chandrashekhara, name of Shiva
Chandreshwar, name of Shiva worshipped on Chandranatha Hill [13G]
Changla Vateshvara, name of Shiva
char kaman, four arches
char minar, four minarets
chaturmukha, four-faced
Chenchu, tribal people of the Eastern Ghats
Chennakeshava, name of Vishnu
Cheraman Perumal, one of the Nayanmars
cheruvu, lake
Chhaddanta, elephant hero of a *Jataka* story
Chhatrapti, title of Maratha rulers, name of the 18C–19C Maratha dynasty, ruling from Satara [7G]
chhatri, cenotaph
Chikka Deva Raja, 17C Wodeyar ruler
Chinna Bomma, 16C Aravidu governor
Chintala, tamarind tree
Chishti, Sufi order
Chola, 9C–13C dynasty of Tamil Nadu, ruling from Thanjavur [40A] and Gangaikondacholapuram [40J]
Cholishvara, name of Shiva

dad mahal, hall of justice
daitya, demon
Dakhni, Muslim nobles of the Deccan, local form of Persian
Dakshinamurti, Shiva as the teacher
Dandayudhapani, name of Subrahmanya worshipped at Palani [44E]
Dantidurga, 8C Rashtrakuta ruler
darbar, formal audience
dargah, Muslim tomb
darshana, auspicious gaze
darush shifa, hospital
darwaza, gate
Dasara, royal festival
Dasharatha, father of Rama in the *Ramayana*
Dashavatara, ten incarnations of Vishnu
Dattatreya, emanation of Vishnu
Daud Khan, 17C–18C Mughal commander
Devaraya, 15C Sangama ruler
Devadatta, cousin of Buddha
Devayanai, wife of Subrahmanya
Devi, consort of Shiva
Dharmaraja, eldest of the Pandava brothers

Digambara, Jain sect
Dikpala, guardians of the eight directions
Dilawar Khan, 17C Nizam Shahi commander
Diwan, prime minister
diwan-i am, public audience hall
Doddashankanna, 16C Ikkeri [19C] Nayaka ruler
Doddeshvara, name of Shiva
Draupadi, common wife of the Pandava brothers
Durga, powerful goddess created by the gods to kill Mahishasura
Dvarkadishvara, name of Krishna

Early Chalukya, 6C–8C dynasty of Karnataka, Maharashtra and Andhra
Pradesh, ruling from Badami [22A]
Eastern Chalukya, 9C–10C dynasty of Andhra Pradesh
Ekadashi, Hindu festival
Ekambaranath, Ekambareshvara, name of Shiva worshipped at Kanchipuram
[37F]
Ekanatheshvara, name of Shiva
Ekakeshvara, name of Shiva
Eknath Maharaj, 16C Hindu teacher
Ekoji, 17C Thanjavur Maratha ruler

Fathullah, 15C–16C Imad Shahi ruler
Faruqi, 14C–16C dynasty of Khandesh in northern Maharashtra, ruling from
Thalner [4F] and Burhanpur in Madhya Pradesh
Firuz Shah, 14C Tughluq ruler

gadigge, memorial shrine
gagan mahal, sky[-reaching] pavilion
Gajendra, elephant rescued by Vishnu
Galaganatha, name of Shiva
gana, dwarf attendants of Shiva
Ganapati, Ganesha, lord of the ganas, popular elephant-headed deity, son of
Shiva
Ganapatideva, 13C Kakatiya ruler
gandabherunda, two-headed eagle, royal emblem
Ganga, 9C–11C dynasty of Karnataka, ruling from Talkad [15E]
Ganga, goddess of the Ganges river
Gangadhareshvara, name of Shiva when bearing the weight of Ganga's
descent to earth
Garuda, eagle mount of Vishnu
Gautama, family name of Buddha
Gesu Daraz, 14C–15C Sufi teacher at Gulbarga [24A]
ghat, bathing place
Ghrishneshvara, *jyotirlinga* worshipped at Ellora [5E]
giri, hill
Gokarneshvara, name of Shiva
Golingeshvara, name of Shiva
Gommateshvara, name of Bahubali

Gond, rulers of the Nagpur [10] region

Gondeshvara, name of Shiva worshipped at Sinnar [4D]

gopi, milkmaid companion of Krishna

Gopinatha, name of Krishna

gopura, towered temple gateway

Govardhana, mountain lifted by Krishna to shield the herds from Indra's storm

Govinda Dikshita, 17C Thanjavur Nayaka prime minister

Govindaraja, name of Krishna

Gowda, 16C–17C dynasty of southern Karnataka, ruling from Bangalore [14A]

gudi, temple

gumbad, *gumbaz*, dome, domed tomb

guru, teacher

Haidar Ali, 18C commander, usurper of the Wodeyar throne

Hamid Qadir Wali, 15C–16C Muslim saint at Nagore [40O]

hammam, steam bath

Hanuman, monkey hero in the *Ramayana*

Harihara, **Harihareshvara**, Shiva and Vishnu joined

Harishena, 5C Vakataka ruler

Hariti, consort of Panchika

Harsha, 7C ruler of Northern India

Hayat Baksh Begum, 17C Qutb Shahi queen

Hazara Rama, thousand Ramas

Hazrat, title of Muslim saint

Hidimbeshvara, name of Shiva

Hiranyakashipu, demon killed by Narasimha

Holkar, 18C–19C Maratha dynasty of Madhya Pradesh, ruling from Indore

Hoysala, 11C–14C dynasty of southern Karnataka, ruling from Halebid [18B]

Hoysaleshvara, name of Shiva worshipped at Halebid [18B]

Hussain, 16C Nizam Shahi ruler

Ibn Battuta, 14C Arab traveller

Ibrahim, 16C Qutb Shahi ruler

Ibrahim, 16C–17C Adil Shahi ruler

idgah, outdoor mosque

Ikshvaku, 2C–4C dynasty of Andhra Pradesh, ruling from Nagarjunakonda [27H]

Imad Shahi, 16C dynasty of Berar in northern Maharashtra, ruling from Achalpur [10E]

Indra, lord of the heavens, one of the Dikpalas

Irattayyappa, Ayyappa

Iravataneshvara, name of Shiva

Ishvara, Shiva

Jagadishvar, name of Shiva worshipped at Raigad [7C]

Jalakanteshvara, name of Shiva worshipped at Vellore [38A]

Jambukeshvara, name of Shiva worshipped at Tiruvannakoil [41B]

Jambulinga, name of Shiva

Jami mosque, Friday congregational mosque
Janardana, name of Vishnu
Jataka, folk tale, narrative of one of the former lives of Buddha
Jatayu, vulture who attacked Ravana in the *Ramayana*
Jeejeebhoy, Jamsetjee, 19C Parsi businessman and philanthropist
Jehangir, 17C Mughal ruler
Jijibai, mother of Shivaji
Jina, Tirthankara
Jnanaprasumbha, name of Parvati
Jvarahareshvara, name of Shiva
Jyeshtha, Shakti
jyotirlinga, luminous *linga* of light worshipped at Bhimashankar [3G], Trimbak [4C], Ellora [5E], Srisailam [32C] and Rameswaram [44J]

Kadamba, 11C–13C dynasty of Goa and western Karnataka
Kailasa, mountain home of Shiva
Kailasanatha, name of Shiva
Kakatiya, 12C–14C dynasty of Andhra Pradesh, ruling from Warangal [28A]
Kala, name of Yama
Kala Rama, name of Rama worshipped at Nasik [4A]
Kalachuri, 5C–6C dynasty of western Maharashtra
Kalahastishvara, name of Shiva worshipped at Sri Kalahasti [35F]
Kalambal, Devi
kalamkari, printing and dyeing textile technique
Kali, goddess of death
kali, mosque, black mosque
Kalidasa, 5C Sanskrit poet and dramatist
Kaliya, serpent demon subdued by Krishna
Kalleshvara, name of Shiva
kalyana mandapa, marriage hall
Kama, god of love
Kamakshi, name of Parvarti worshipped at Kanchipuram [37F]
Kameshvara, name of Shiva
Kampahareshvara, name of Shiva
Kanhoji, 17C and 19C Angre rulers
Kannagi, heroine of a Tamil story
Kannappa, Shaiva saint at Sri Kalahasti [35F]
Kapaleshvara, name of Shiva
Kapardishvara, name of Shiva
Kapoteshvara, name of Shiva
Karna, hero of the *Mahabharata*
Karttikeya, warrior son of Shiva, also known as Kumara
Kashivishvanatha, Kashivishveshvara, name of Shiva worshipped at Kashi (Varanasi)
Kaumari, consort of Kumara
Kayarohana, name of Shiva
Kedareshvara, name of Shiva
Kempe, 17C Gowda ruler
Keshava, name of Krishna

Khaja Burhanuddin, 14C Sufi saint at Khuldabad [5D]
Khaja Seyed Zinuddin, 14C Sufi saint at Khuldabad [5D]
Khan Jahan Bahadur, 17C Mughal governor
Khandoba, form of Shiva worshipped at Jejuri [3K]
khazana, treasury
Khilji, 14C dynasty of North Indiaern, ruling from Delhi
kila, fort
Kilavan, 17C–18C Setupati ruler
kirata, forest hunter, disguise of Shiva when fighting Arjuna
Kodandarama, Rama with the bow
koil, temple
Koran, holy book of Muslims
Koranganatha, name of Shiva
kota, fort
kovil, temple
Krishna, incarnation of Vishnu, also cult deity of Hinduism
Krishna, 8C Rashtrakuta ruler
Krishna Menon, 20C political leader
Krishnadevaraya, 16C Tuluva ruler
Krishnaraja, 19C–20C Wodeyar rulers
Kshatrapa, 2C–4C dynasty of western Maharashtra and Gujarat
Kubera, chief of the *yakshas*, one of the Dikpalas
Kudal Alagar, name of Vishnu worshipped at Madurai [44A]
Kufic, early Arabic script
kulam, pond
Kulottunga, 12C–13C Chola ruler
Kumari, name of Durga worshipped at Kanyakumari [45M]
Kumbhakarna, brother of Ravana in the *Ramayana*
Kumbha Mela, river festival at Nasik [4A]
Kumbheshvara, name of Shiva worshipped at Kumbakonam [40G]
kund, well or pond
Kurmanatha, tortoise *avatara* of Vishnu worshipped at Srikurman [31G]
Kumara, name of Subrahmanya
Kumari, name of Durga worshipped at Kanyakumari [45M]
kuttambalam, performance hall in Kerala temples

Ladle Sahib, 14C Sufi saint at Aland [24C]
Lajja Gauri, lotus-headed squatting goddess displaying her sex
Lakshmana, brother of Rama
Lakshmi, goddess of prosperity, consort of Vishnu
Lakulisha, yogic aspect of Shiva
Lanka, island home of Ravana
Lankeshvara, name of Shiva worshipped at Ellora [5E]
Late Chalukya, 10C–12C dynasty of northern Karnataka, ruling from Basava-kalyan [25D]
lena, cave
linga, phallic emblem representing Shiva
Lingayat, Shaiva sect

Lokeshvara, Bodhisattva
lungi, men's cloth

Madha, Madhavaraya, name of Vishnu
Madhava, 12C Vaishnava philosopher
Madhukeshvara, name of Shiva
madrasa, Muslim theological college
Madu Qadiri, 17C Adil Shahi governor
maha chaitya, great *stupa*
Mahabaleshvara, name of Shiva worshipped at Mahabaleshwar [7A]
Mahabharata, epic story of the Pandavas and Kauravas
Mahadeva, name of Shiva
Mahajanaka, royal hero of a *Jataka* story
Mahakali, name of Kali
Mahakapi, monkey hero of a *Jataka* story
Mahakuteshvara, name of Shiva
mahal, pavilion
Mahalakshmi, title of Lakshmi
Mahalasa, female aspect of Vishnu worshipped at Mardol [11H]
Mahalinga, name of Shiva
Mahalrao, 18C Holkar ruler
Mahamakam, bathing festival at Kumbakonam [40G]
Mahanandishvara, name of Shiva
Mahanavami, festival at Vijayanagara [20C]
maharaja, great king
Mahatma Gandhi, 20C social reformer
Mahavira, last of the 24 Tirthankaras
Mahayana, Great Vehicle, later school of Buddhism
Mahboob Ali Khan Bahadur, 19C–20C Asaf Jahi ruler
Mahendravarman, 7C and 8C Pallava rulers
Maheshvara, name of Shiva
Mahishamardini, Mahishasuramardini, Durga
Mahishasura, buffalo demon killed by Durga
Mahmud Gawan, 15C Bahmani prime minister
Mahosadha, hero of a *Jataka* story
Maitreya, future Bodhisattva
makara, aquatic monster
Makhtum Faikh Ali Paru, 15C Muslim saint at Mahim [1H]
Malik Ambar, 16C–17C Nizam Shahi prime minister
Malik bin Dinar, 7C Arab missionary
Malik Kafur, 14C Tughluq commander
Malik Raja, 14C Faruqi ruler
Malik Rihan, 17C Adil Shahi governor
Malika Jahan, 16C Adil Shahi queen
Malleshvara, name of Shiva
Mallikarjuna, name of Shiva worshipped at Srisailam [32C]
Mamalla, 7C Pallava ruler
Mandala, sacred diagram

Manmatha, Kama
mandapa, columned hall
mandir, temple, hall
Mandhatu, royal hero of a *Jataka* story
Mangesha, name of Shiva worshipped at Mangeshi [11G]
Manikanteshvara, name of Shiva
Manikkavachakar, Shaiva saint at Avudaiyarkoil [41H]
Manjunatha, name of Shiva worshipped at Mangalore [17A]
Manjushri, Bodhisattva
Manmatha, god of love
Mappila, Muslim trading community of northern Kerala
maqbara, Muslim tomb
Mara, temptor of Buddha
Maratha, 17C–18C dynasty of Maharashtra, ruling from Rajgad [3M] and Satara [7G]
Maratha, 17C–19C dynasty of Tamil Nadu, ruling from Thanjavur [40A]
Marghabandhu, name of Shiva worshipped at Vrinchipuram [38C]
Markandeya, devotee rescued by Shiva from Yama
Martanda Varma, 18C Travancore ruler
Marubhuta, previous birth of Parshvanatha
Matangeshvara, name of Shiva
matha, Hindu monastery
Matiposaka, youthful hero of a *Jataka* story
Matrikas, the mothers
Matrimandir, hall of the Mother
Maurya, 4C–2C BC dynasty of Northern India
Maya, mother of Buddha
mihrab, prayer niche in a mosque
mimbar, stepped pulpit in a mosque
Minakshi, goddess worshipped at Madurai [44A]
minar, minaret, tower for calling the faithful to prayer in a mosque
Mir Akbar Ali Khan Sikandar, 18C Asaf Jahi ruler
Mir Osman Ali Khan, 20C Asaf Jahi ruler
Miran Mubarak, 15C Faruqi ruler
Mohini, female form of Vishnu
Moro Pingle, 17C Maratha commander
Muchalinda, serpent who protected Buddha
Muchukunda, Shaiva saint
Muchukundeshvara, name of Shiva
Mughal, 16C–18C dynasty of Northern India, ruling for a time from Aurangabad [5A]
Muhammad, Prophet of Islam
Muhammad, 17C Adil Shahi ruler
Muhammad, 17C Qutb Shahi ruler
Muhammad Ali, 18C Wallajah ruler
Muhammad Mayshakha, 14C saint at Holkonda [24B]
Muhammad Quli, 16C–17C Qutb Shahi ruler
Muhammad Shah, 14C Tughluq ruler
Muhammad Shah, 18C Mughal ruler

Muharram, Shia festival commemorating the martyrdom of Imam Hysayn
Mukambika, name of goddess worshipped at Kollur [17J]
Mukteshvara, name of Shiva
Mukunanayanar, Shaiva saint
Mumbadevi, name of the goddess worshipped at Bombay [1E]
mundu, men's cloth
Murugan, name of Subrahmanya
Murtaza, 16C Nizam Shahi ruler
muslin, fine cotton cloth
Muttu Vijaya Raghunatha Tevan, 18C Setupati ruler

naga, cobra
Nagakumara, royal hero of a Jain legend
Naganatha, Nagesha, Nageshvara, name of Shiva
Nammalvar, Vaishnava saint at Alvar Tirunagari [45D]
Nameshvara, name of Shiva
Nana Phadnavis, 18C Maratha prime minister
Nanda, cousin of Buddha
Nandi, bull mount of Shiva
Nandikeshvara, name of *bhuta* in the form of a bull
Nandivarman, 8C Pallava ruler
Nanjundeshvara, name of Shiva worshipped at Nanjangud [15F]
Naoriji, Dadabhai, 19C–20C member of the British Parliament
Narada, celestial musician
Narashankara, name of Shiva
Narasimha, Man-lion incarnation of Vishnu
Narasimha, 13C Hoysala ruler
Narasimha, 15C Saluva ruler
Narayana, name of Vishnu
Narayana Guru, 19C–20C religious reformer
Narumbunatha, name of Shiva
Nataraja, Natesha, Shiva as lord of the dance
Navagrahas, nine planetary deities
Navalinga, nine *lingas*
Navaratri, Dasara
Nawab, title of 18C dynasty of southern Andhra Pradesh, ruling from Cuddapah [34A]
Nawab, title of Wallajah rulers
Nayaka, 16C commanders under the Tuluva rulers; 16C–17C dynasties of Karnataka, ruling from Keladi [19B], Ikkeri [19C] and Chitradurga [20K], and of Tamil Nadu, ruling from Gingee [39F], Thanjavur [40A] and Madurai [44A]
Nayanmar, Shaiva saint
Nehru, Jawaharlal, first prime minister of Independent India
Nellaiyappa, name of Shiva worshipped at Tirunelveli [45A]
Neminatha, one of the Tirthankaras
Nilakanteshvara, name of Shiva
Nirmankara, name of Shiva
nirvana, enlightenment

Nityeshvara, name of Shiva
Nizam, title of Asaf Jahi rulers
Nizam Ali Khan, 18C Asaf Jahi ruler
Nizamul Mulk, 18C Mughal governor, first Asaf Jahi ruler
Nizam Shahi, 16C dynasty of Maharashtra, ruling from Ahmadnagar [6A]
Nolamba, 9C–11C dynasty of Karnataka and Andhra Pradesh, ruling from Hemavati [33H]
nritya sabha, dance hall

Olakkanatha, name of Shiva
Omkareshvara, name of Shiva

Padmanabha, reclining form of Vishnu worshipped at Thiruvananthapuram [46A]
Padmapani, name of Avalokiteshvara
Padmavati, name of Lakshmi
Pahari school, paintings from the Himalayan valleys
Paigarh, 19C–20C nobles under the Asaf Jahis
Pallava, 4C–9C dynasty of Tamil Nadu, ruling from Kanchipuram [37F]
palli, old mosque or church in Kerala
Pampa, goddess worshipped at Hampi [20B]
pancha, five
panchaganga, five rivers
panchalinga, five *lingas*
Panchalingeshvara, Shiva as five *lingas*
Panchanandishvara, name of Shiva
Panchatantra, folk tales with animal and bird heroes
panchayatana, group of five temples
Panchika, chief *yaksha*
Pandava, five brothers of the *Mahabharata*
Pandya, 7C–13C dynasty of Tamil Nadu, ruling from Madurai [44A]
Papanatha, name of Shiva
Papavinaseshvara, name of Shiva worshipped at Papanasam [45L]
Parameshvara, name of Shiva
Parashurama, Rama with the axe *avatara* of Vishnu
Parashurameshvara, name of Shiva
Parinirvana, death of Buddha
Parshvanatha, second last of the 24 Tirthankaras
Parsi, follower of the Zoroastrian religion
Parthasarathi, name of Krishna worshipped at Triplicane [36F]
Parvati, consort of Shiva
pata, painted cloth scroll
Pataleshvara, name of Shiva
Patanjali, mythical philosopher
Pattabhirama, Rama crowned
Patteshvara, name of Shiva
Perumal, name of Vishnu
Peshwa, 18C Prime Minister of the Marathas, ruling from Pune [3A]
Pramanatheshvara, name of Shiva

Prataparudra, 13C–14C Kakatiya ruler
Pratapsinh, 19C Maratha ruler of Satara [7G]
puja, rite of worship
pujari, Brahmin priest
Pulakeshin, 6C and 7C Early Chalukya rulers
Pundalika, devotee of Vitthoba
Purna, convert of Buddha
Purundevi Tayar, consort of Varadaraja

Qasim Barid, 15C–16C Baridi ruler
Quli Qutb al-Mulk, 16C Qutb Shahi ruler
Qutb Shahi, 16C–17C dynasty of Andhra Pradesh, ruling from Golconda [27E] and Hyderabad [27A]
Qutbuddin Mubarak, 14C Khalji ruler

Radha, consort of Krishna
Raghoji, 19C Angre ruler
Raghuji, 18C Bhonsale ruler
Raghunatha, name of Rama
Raghunatha, 17C Thanjavur Nayaka ruler
Raghurajeshvari, name of Parvati
raja, king
Raja, 17C Wodeyar ruler
Rajagopala, name of Krishna
Rajamalla, 10C Ganga ruler
Rajaraja, 10C–11C Chola ruler
Rajarajeshvara, name of Shiva
Rajarajeshvari, name of Durga
Rajaram, 18C Maratha ruler
Rajasimha, 8C Pallava ruler
Rajendra, 11C Chola ruler
Rama, incarnation of Vishnu and hero of the *Ramayana*
Rama Varma, 18C Travancore ruler
Ramakrishna, mission established by Vivekananda
Ramalingeshvara, Ramanatha, name of Shiva who worshipped Rama at Rameswaram [44J]
Ramana Maharishi, 20C teacher at Tiruvannamalai [38E]
Ramanuja, 11C–12C Vaishnava philsopher
Ramaraya, 16C Tuluva commander
Ramaswami, Rama
Ramayana, epic story of Rama
Rameshvara, name of Shiva worshipped at Rameswaram [44J]
Ranganatha, reclining form of Vishnu
Ranganayaka, name of Vishnu
rangin mahal, coloured pavilion
Rashtrakuta, 8C–10C dynasty of Maharashtra, Karnataka and Andhra Pradesh
Raste, 18C Maratha family at Wai [7F]
ratha, chariot, temple model

Rati, consort of Kama
rauza, Muslim funerary complex
Ravana, demon king of Sri Lanka, opponent of Rama in the *Ramayana*
Ravi Varma, 20C painter
raya, king
Readymoney, nickname of Courasji Jehangir, 19C Parsi businessman and philanthropist
Recherla Rudra, 13C Kakatiya commander
Reddi, 15C–16C dynasty of eastern Andhra Pradesh, ruling from Kondavidu [29M]
Rishabhadeva, one of the Tirthankaras
Rishyashringa, deer-headed sage in the *Ramayana*
Rudradeva, 12C Kakatiya ruler
Rudramadeva, 13C Kakatiya queen
Rukmini, wife of Krishna
Rumi Khan, 16C Nizam Shahi commander

sabha, hall
Sadashiva, 16C Tuluva ruler
Sadashiva, 16C Nayaka ruler from Keladi [19B]
Sadat Ullah Khan, 18C ruler of Arcot [38B]
sagar, lake, tank
sahasra linga, *linga* on which a thousand miniature *lingas* are represented
Sai Baba, 19C–20C teachers at Shirdi [6C] and Puttaparthi [33E]
Salabat Khan, 16C Nizam Shahi prime minister
Salar Jung, 20C Asaf Jahi prime minister
Saluva, 15C–16C dynasty, ruling from Vijayanagara [20B–C]
Sama, hero of a *Jataka* story
samadhi, Hindu memorial or tomb
Sambandar, Shaiva saint
Sambhaji, 17C Maratha ruler
Samkhapala, serpent hero of a *Jataka* story
Samutiri, 16C–17C dynasty of north Kerala, ruling from Kozhikode [47A]
Sangama, 14C–15C dynasty of Karnataka, Andhra Pradesh and Tamil Nadu, ruling from Vijayanagara [20B–C]
Sangameshvara, name of Shiva
Saptakoteshvara, name of Shiva worshipped at Naroa [12F]
Saptamatrikas, seven Matrikas
sarai, resting place
Sarangapani, name of Vishnu worshipped at Kumbakonam [40G]
Sarasvati, river goddess, also consort of Brahma
sarovar, lake, pond
Sassoon, 19C–20C Jewish business family
Satavahana, 2C BC–3C AD dynasty of Maharashtra, northern Karnataka and northern Andhra Pradesh, ruling from Paithan [5L]
Serfoji, 19C Thanjavur Maratha ruler
Setupati, 17C–18C dynasty of Tamil Nadu, ruling from Ramanathapuram [44H]
Shachi, consort of Indra

Shah Abdul Faid, 15C Muslim saint at Bidar [25B]
shah, royal title
Shah Jhan, 17C Mughal ruler
Shahji, 17C Maratha commander under the Adil Shahis, father of Shivaji
Shahu, 18C Maratha ruler
Shaiva, belonging to the cult of Shiva
Shaka, 1C–2C dynasty of Western India
Shakti, female divinity associated with Shiva
Shakyamuni, title of Buddha
Shankara, name of Shiva
Shankara, Shankaracharya, 8C–9C Shaiva philosopher
Shanmuga, name of Subrahmanya
Shantadurga, name of Durga worshipped at Quelem [12K]
Shantinatha, Shantishvara, Tirthankara
Sharabheshvara, composite animal form of Shiva
Shasta, name of Ayyappa
shaykh, title of a saint
Shesha, serpent mount of Vishnu
Sheshashayi, name of Vishnu
Shevappa, 16C Thanjavur Nayaka ruler
Shia, unorthodox Muslim creed
Shilaharas, 11C–12C dynasty of western Maharashtra, ruling from Kolhapur [8A]
shilakhana, armoury
Shinde, 18C–19C Maratha dynasty of Madhya Pradesh, ruling from Gwalior
Shitab Khan, 15C–16C Bahmani governor
Shiva, principal cult deity of Hinduism
Shiva Purana, collection of stories about Shiva
Shivaganga, tank of Shiva
Shivaji, 17C Maratha ruler crowned at Raigad [77C]
Shivaji, 19C Maratha ruler of Kolhapur [8A]
Shivakamsundari, Shiva's consort worshipped at Chidambaram [39H]
Shivappa, 17C Nayaka ruler based at Nagar [19F]
Shivaratri, Shaiva festival in February-March
Shivarajeshvar, name of Shiva identified with Shivaji, worshipped at Sindhudurg [8D]
Shravanakumara, youthful hero of a *Ramayana* story
Shri, Shridevi, name of Lakshmi
Shrirama, Rama
Siddha, Siddhara, saint
Siddhartha, personal name of Buddha
Siddheshvara, name of Shiva
Sidi, 17C–18C Abyssinian admirals based at Janjira [2I]
Sikandar Shah, 14C Madurai ruler
Simhala, princely hero of a *Jataka* story
Sirajuddin Junaydi, 14C saint at Gulbarga [24A]
Siriyala, one of the Nayanmars
Sirul Khan, 18C Sidi ruler
Sita, wife of Rama

Skanda, name of Subrahmanya
Somanatha, 13C Hoysala general
Somanatheshvara, name of Shiva
Somaskanda, Shiva with Parvati and Skanda
Someshvara, name of Shiva
Srinivasa, name of Venkateshvara
Sthanumalaya, Shiva and Vishnu worshipped at Suchindram [45N]
stupa, hemispherical funerary mound symbolic of Buddha's teachings
Subrahmanya, son of Shiva and Parvati
Sufi, mystical Islamic philosophy
Sugriva, rightful monkey king in the *Ramayana*
Sundarar, Shaiva saint
Sundaravarda, name of Vishnu
Sundareshvara, name of Shiva worshipped at Madurai [44A]
Sunni, orthodox Muslim creed
Suparnaka, demoness in the *Ramayana*
Surya, sun god
Sutasoma, lioness heroine of a *Jataka* story
svastika, auspicious cross-shaped emblem
swami, lord
Swaminatha, name of Murugan

Tagore, Abanindranath, 20C painter
Tajuddin Firuz, 14C–15C Bahmani ruler
takht mahal, throne chamber
Talagirishvara, name of Shiva
talao, lake, pond
Tata, 19C–20C Parsi business family
Tataka, demoness killed by Rama in the *Ramayana*
Tara, consort of Avalokiteshvara
teppakulam, great tank
Tilak, Lokmanya, 19C–20C social reformer
Timmaraja, 17C Wodeyar ruler
Tipu Sultan, 18C commander based at Srirangapattana [15C]
Tirthankara, Jain saviour
Tirukameshvara, name of Shiva
Tirumala, 17C Madurai Nayaka ruler
Tiruvengalanatha, name of Venkateshvara
Toda, tribal people of the Nilgiri Hills
Tondaiman, 17C–18C dynasty of southern Tamil Nadu, ruling from Pudukkottai [41G]
Trailokyanatha, name of Rama
Travancore, 17C–19C dynasty, ruling from Thiruvananthapuram [46A]
Trikuteshvara, Shiva as triple *lingas*
Trimbakeshvar, *jyotirlinga* worshipped at Trimbak [4C]
Trimurti, trio of Brahma, Vishnu and Shiva
Tripurantaka, Shiva as destroyer of the demon of the triple cities
Trivikrama, incarnation of Vishnu pacing out the universe in three steps

Tughluq, 14C–15C dynasty of Northern India, ruling from Delhi and Daulatabad [5C]

Tuluva, 16C dynasty of Karnataka, Andhra Pradesh and Tamil Nadu, ruling from Vijayanagara [20B–C]

Tumburu, celestial musician

Tyagaraja, name of Shiva worshipped at Tiruvarur [40L], 18C musician who lived at Tiruvaiyaru [40B]

Ucchalingamma, name of Devi

Uma, name of Parvati

Umamaheshvara, Shiva and Parvati

Upamanyu, one of the Nayanmars

Urs, festival commemorating the death of a Muslim saint

Vadakkunnatha, name of Shiva worshipped at Thrissur [47V]

Vaidyeshvara, Vaidyanatheshvara, name of Shiva

Vaikkathappan, name of Shiva worshipped at Vaikom [47E]

Vaikuntha, heavenly abode of Vishnu

Vaishnava, belonging to the cult of Vishnu

Vakataka, 4C–5C dynasty of Maharashtra, ruling from Nandavardhan near Ramtek [10B]

Vali, wicked monkey king in the *Ramayana*

Vallabha, name of Vishnu worshipped at Tiruvalla [47J]

Valmikinatha, name of Shiva

Vamana, dwarf incarnation of Vishnu

Varadaraja, name of Vishnu worshipped at Kanchipuram [37F]

Varaha, boar incarnation of Vishnu

Varaha Deva, 5C feudatory of the Vakatakas

Vardhamana, one of the Tirthankaras

Varuna, god of the ocean, one of the Dikpalas

Vasanta, spring festival

Vatapatrashayi, name of Vishnu

Vayu, god of air, one of the Dikpalas

Vedagirishvara, name of Shiva

Vedanta, philosophy derived from the Vedas

Vedas, ancient scriptures of Hinduism

Venkatachala, name of Vishnu

Venkatadri Nayadu, 18C Asaf Jahi governor

Venkatadri Nayaka, 17C Aravidu governor

Venkatapatideva, 16C–17C Aravidu ruler

Venkatappa, 17C Ikkeri [19C] Nayaka ruler

Venkataramana, Venkateshvara, name of Vishnu worshipped at Tirumala [34B]

Venugopala, Krishna playing the flute

Vessantara, princely hero of a *Jataka* story

Vidhurapandita, royal hero of a *Jataka* story

Vidyaranya, pontiff of Sringeri [19H]

Vidyashankara, Shankara

vihara, Buddhist monastery
Vinayaka, name of Ganapati
Vijayaditya, 8C Early Chalukya ruler
Vijayaraghava, 17C Thanjavur Nayaka ruler
Vijayaranga Chokkanatha, 18C Madurai Nayaka ruler
Vikramaditya, 8C Early Chalukya ruler
vilasa, vilasam, palace, hall
Virabhadra, fierce form of Shiva
Virattaneshvara, name of Shiva
Virupaksha, name of Shiva worshipped at Hampi [20B]
Vishnu, principal cult deity of Hinduism
Vishnukundin, 5C–6C dynasty of eastern Andhra Pradesh
Vishnupad, footprint of Vishnu
Vishnuvardhana, 12C Hoysala ruler
Vishvakarma, mythical architect of the gods
Vishvamitra, teacher of Rama in the *Ramayana*
Vishvanatha, Vishveshvara, name of Shiva
Vishvarupa, form of Vishnu with multiple heads and arms
Vitthala, Vitthoba, name of Vishnu worshipped at Pandharpur [9G]
Vivekananda, 20C teacher and philosopher
Vriddhagirishvara, name of Shiva worshipped at Vriddhachalam [39J]

wada, palace, mansion
Wadiya, 19C–20C Parsi business family
Walkeshwar, name of Shiva worshipped at Bombay [1G]
Wallajah, 18C dynasty of northern Tamil Nadu, ruling from Arcot [38B]
Wodeyar, 17C–19C dynasty of southern Karnataka, ruling from Mysore [15A]

Yadava, 11C–14C dynasty of Maharashtra, ruling from Devagiri [5C]
yagna, fire sacrifice
yaksha, earth spirit, guardian
yali, leonine beast
Yama, god of death
Yamuna, goddess of the Jumna river
Yellamma, guardian folk goddess
yoga, mental and physical discipline
Yogeshvara, Shiva as a *yogi*
Yogeshvari, name of Durga
yogi, practitioner of *yoga*
yoni, female sexual emblem
Yusuf Adil Khan, 16C Adil Shahi ruler

Zamorin, *see* Samutiri
zenana, women's quarters
Zulficar Khan, 17C–18C Mughal commander

Index

The numbers and letters which follow each index entry refer to the chapters in the guide. The relevant chapter names, numbers and letters are listed at the top of each page.

If Kerala is God's own country, the Taj is his holiday home.

Beautiful, beguiling Kerala, where countless experiences await you. Ideally you would start at Taj Malabar in Cochin. After soaking in the area's rich sprinkling of Dutch palaces, Jewish synagogues, Chinese nets, and the finest antique market in India, you could travel to Elephant Country – Thekkady. Base yourself at the Taj Garden Retreat, Thekkady, and explore the region's wild side. Next, we suggest you stop over at the Taj's Kumarakom retreat and take *vallum*-rides down dreamy, tree-lined lagoons. Scenic Varkala is just a few hours south. Here, as in Kumarakom, you can rejuvenate yourself with infusions of herbal oil and traditional massage. And you can even pay a visit to the 2000-year-old Janardhan Temple nearby. Happily, Kerala has so much to offer: her famed cuisine, her bewitching beauty, her beckoning past. Truly, no one brings you this magical, mystical place quite the way the Taj does. Come to Kerala. And see it with the Taj.

TAJ MALABAR, COCHIN	198 KMS	6 HRS
TAJ GARDEN RETREAT, THEKKADY	128 KMS	4 HRS
TAJ GARDEN RETREAT, KUMARAKOM	140 KMS	3 HRS
TAJ GARDEN RETREAT, VARKALA	54 KMS	1 HR
TRIVANDRUM		

THE TAJ GROUP *of* HOTELS

THE TAJ GROUP. INDIA'S *first.* **SOUTH ASIA'S** *finest.*

CENTRAL RESERVATIONS FAX IN MUMBAI FOR ALL TAJ HOTELS : (91-22) 283 7272.

OR CALL **UTELL** OR YOUR TRAVEL PLANNER